This volume examines the phenomenon of interpersonal expectations – how the expectations of one person affect the behavior of another in an interactive setting – from theoretical, applied, and basic research perspectives. Since Robert Rosenthal, author of *Pygmalion in the Classroom*, first began the systematic study of interpersonal and experimenter expectancy effects some 35 years ago, scores of published studies of interpersonal expectations have appeared. Peter Blanck's book brings together these efforts for the first time in a comprehensive review of the field, assessing the future directions for and implications of the research.

The volume is divided into three parts that review real-world applications, such as the courtroom, the classroom, and the operating room; the mediation of interpersonal expectations through verbal and nonverbal behavior; and the emerging methodological and statistical techniques for understanding the implications of interpersonal expectations. In each part, critical commentary and analysis by leading scholars in the field are presented.

Studies in Emotion and Social Interaction

Paul Ekman
University of California, San Francisco

Klaus R. Scherer
Université de Genève

General Editors

Interpersonal expectations

Studies in Emotion and Social Interaction

This series is jointly published by the Cambridge University Press and the Editions de la Maison des Sciences de l'Homme, as part of the joint publishing agreement established in 1977 between the Fondation de la Maison des Sciences de l'Homme and the Syndics of the Cambridge University Press.

Cette collection est publiée co-édition par Cambridge University Press et les Editions de la Maison des Sciences de l'Homme. Elle s'intègre dans le programme de co-édition établi en 1977 par la Fondation de la Maison des Sciences de l'Homme et les Syndics de Cambridge University Press.

For a list of other books in the series, see page following the Index.

Interpersonal expectations

Theory, research, and applications

Edited by

Peter David Blanck

Professor, University of Iowa College of Law, and Senior Fellow, the Annenberg Foundation Washington Program

CAMBRIDGE
UNIVERSITY PRESS

& Editions de la Maison des Sciences de l'Homme

Paris

Published by the Press Syndicate of the University of Cambridge
The Pitt Building, Trumpington Street, Cambridge CB2 1RP
40 West 20th Street, New York, NY 10011-4211, USA
10 Stamford Road,Oakleigh, Melbourne 3166, Australia
and
Editions de la Maison des Sciences de l'Homme
54 Boulevard Raspail, 75270 Paris, Cedex 06

First published 1993

Printed in the United States of America

Library of Congress Cataloging-in-Publication Data
Interpersonal expectations : theory, research, and applications /
edited by Peter David Blanck.
   p.   cm. – (Studies in emotion and social interaction)
Includes index.
ISBN 0-521-41783-X (hard). – ISBN 0-521-42832-7 (pbk.)
1. Expectation (Psychology)   2. Interpersonal relations.
I. Blanck, Peter David, 1957– .   II. Series.
BF323.E8I68   1993   92-36925
158'.2 – dc20   CIP

A catalog record for this book is available from the British Library.

ISBN 0-521-41783-X hardback
ISBN 0-521-42832-7 paperback
ISBN 2-7351-0492-3 hardback France only
ISBN 2-7351-0493-1 paperback France only

for
Robert Rosenthal
friend, colleague, mentor, teacher; in
each, enabler of our own best self-fulfilling
prophecies.

Contents

Contents

Preface

The systematic study of interpersonal expectations took root in 1956, when Robert Rosenthal set forth a hypothesis in his doctoral dissertation regarding a phenomenon he labeled *unconscious experimenter bias*. Rosenthal realized that prior discussions of experimenter bias had dealt with only the theoretical impact such biases may have on the designs of research questions and on the interpretation of results (Rosenthal, 1956, pp. 69–70; referenced in chapter 1, this volume). He wrote: "It is almost as though the E[xperimenters] were considered another [separate] instrument in his [*sic*] actual conduct of the research. . . . [I]t behooves us to check his calibration" (p. 70).

Now some 37 years later, this volume seeks to examine the "calibration" of interpersonal expectations in basic and applied research and in theory. Rosenthal's then-controversial research on the unintended interpersonal expectancy biases of psychological researchers was first presented formally at the meeting of the American Psychological Association in 1959. Since that time, published studies of interpersonal expectations, though increasing in number and scope, have heretofore not been brought together systematically in a single volume.

This volume provides innovative and critical reviews of the study of interpersonal expectations in three basic areas: (1) real-world applications of research on interpersonal expectations, (2) exploration of the mediation of interpersonal expectations through verbal and nonverbal behavior, and (3) discussion of emerging statistical and methodological techniques for understanding and studying interpersonal expectations.

In chapter 1, Robert Rosenthal provides a rich overview of the development of theory, research, and application of the study of interpersonal expectations. Rosenthal describes the historical development of research on interpersonal expectations. He also discusses the substantive and methodological antecedents and consequences of the study of the subject.

In chapter 2, Donald Campbell provides additional insight into the historical development of the study of interpersonal expectations. Campbell clarifies the importance of the topic and then provides a previously unpublished 1959 symposium paper on experimenter bias that set the stage for the study of interpersonal expectations.

This book is next divided into three parts. Each part is preceded by an introduction, which places the chapters into the larger context, and is followed with a commentary.

Part I

Part I contains a discussion of research on interpersonal expectations in several applied contexts. In chapter 3, John Darley and Kathryn Oleson introduce the part, providing a discussion of the relevance of the study of interpersonal expectations in various contexts. They examine the psychological components of interpersonal expectations and the possible mechanisms (verbal and nonverbal) for the transference of expectancy effects, and set forth a general social interaction sequence that may be useful for understanding interpersonal expectations.

In chapter 4, I review the relevance of interpersonal expectations in the courtroom, provide a model for the study of interpersonal expectations, and report the results of the preliminary empirical tests of the model. I then describe the central importance of understanding in this area to our system of justice.

In chapter 5, Marylee Taylor explores interpersonal expectancies and the perpetuation of racial inequity. Several important questions are addressed, including the following: Is there evidence that the psychological mediators linking the job applicant's or student's race to the interviewer's or teacher's behavior are interpersonal expectations? What are the remedies for expectations that may aggravate racial inequality in education and employment?

In chapter 6, Elisha Babad explores the role of interpersonal expectations in the classroom. The chapter illuminates the central issues in teacher expectancy research and examines the development of the field since Rosenthal and Jacobson's seminal work *Pygmalion in the Classroom*.

In chapter 7, Dov Eden outlines the importance of interpersonal expectations in organizations. The chapter presents a review of research on interpersonal expectancy effects in nonschool organizations and some ideas for practical applications designed to improve organizational effectiveness.

In chapter 8, Howard Friedman deals with the role of interpersonal expectations and the maintenance of health. Friedman addresses whether people's expectations about their health, derived from others, have a meaningful effect on their psychobiological functioning. The concept of the *self-healing personality* and the link between health outcomes and interpersonal expectations are examined.

In chapter 9, Miron Zuckerman, Holley Hodgins, and Kunitate Miyake describe the variables related to interpersonal impressions that act as precursors to interpersonal expectations. The central question explored is whether physical and vocal attractiveness may act as a self-fulfilling prophecy in everyday life.

In his commentary in chapter 10, Harris Cooper argues that no single hypothesis better captures the spirit of social psychology than does the concept of interpersonal expectations. Cooper considers the reasons why the interpersonal expectations hypothesis has generated an enormous amount of research in the various applied settings set forth in Part I. Finally, he contends that the expectancy hypothesis is more than a hypothesis; rather, it is a "social fact."

Part II

Part II deals with research on the mediation of interpersonal expectations through nonverbal behavior. In chapter 11, Ross Buck introduces the part, discussing the mediation of interpersonal expectations by nonverbal behavior. Buck explores the "covert" communication process and argues that it is in fact a biologically based process involving the spontaneous communication of motivational and emotional states.

In chapter 12, Dane Archer, Robin Akert, and Mark Costanzo present the design alternatives that confront researchers interested in the ways that nonverbal behavior mediates interpersonal expectations. For each design alternative, the chapter attempts to show the theoretical and methodological consequences.

In chapter 13, Bella DePaulo discusses the central importance of nonverbal behavior as a mediator of interpersonal expectations. DePaulo explores whether people can behave at will in nonverbally "warm" ways that reap positive outcomes as a consequence.

In chapter 14, Judy Hall and Nancy Briton document the expectations for male and female nonverbal behavior styles, showing that there is a good correspondence between gender-style expectations and actual gender differences in behavior. They then discuss possible causal connections between gender expectations and male and female differences in nonverbal communication. Finally, Hall and Briton examine the role of gender in determining the magnitude of expectancy effects in randomized experiments.

In chapter 15, Robin DiMatteo is concerned with the important relationship between physician rapport, nonverbal communication, and the mediation of interpersonal expectations. DiMatteo analyzes the importance of expectations in the physician–patient relationship and their implications for patient adherence to medical treatment recommendations.

Klaus Scherer provides commentary in chapter 16 that highlights the relation between interpersonal expectations, social influence, and emotion transfer. Scherer argues for the need to set forth an integrative theory of interpersonal expectations that considers cultural, applied, interdisciplinary, and other factors.

Part III

Part III consists of chapters that underscore recent innovations in the study and analysis of interpersonal expectations. The chapters in this part explore a number of methodological implications. Chapter 17, by Dane Archer, opens the part with a provocative analysis of "insoluble problems versus investigable questions" in the development of new procedures, methods, and statistical tools to study interpersonal expectations.

In chapter 18, Monica Harris outlines a model and method of study for the development of a taxonomy of the mediation of interpersonal expectations. The result is a first step toward understanding the processes underlying expectancy effects, as well as methodological guidance for how to choose mediating behaviors to study in expectancy research.

In chapter 19, Frank Bernieri offers an overview of the importance of various statistical and methodological decisions in the study of interpersonal expectations. Several issues regarding the optimal application of ANOVA techniques as they pertain to research on interpersonal expectations are discussed.

In chapter 20, Donald Rubin analyzes recent meta-analytic techniques that have been employed in the analysis of interpersonal expectation research. Rubin then proposes the *effect size surface* perspective as a superior means for statistical literature synthesis.

In chapter 21, Ralph Rosnow reviews the importance of the concept of the volunteer subject to the study of interpersonal expectations. Rosnow focuses on the characteristics of subjects who volunteer for research participation and the effects associated with their perception of the experimenter's expectations.

In chapter 22, Mary Amanda Dew deals with applications, methodological issues, and dilemmas in the study of interpersonal expectations. Dew takes up the issue of experimenter expectancy effects in the context of applied mental health research that uses primarily nonlaboratory and field research methods.

Marylee Taylor's commentary in chapter 23 considers *moderating* and *mediating* forces in the study of interpersonal expectations. Taylor suggests ways in which the study of such intervening forces help in the analysis of the notion of *expectancy confirmation*, providing parallels for her arguments from other lines of social psychological research. Taylor points out how similar variables under study may serve as either moderating or mediating functions in the transmission of interpersonal expectancy effects.

Taken together, the chapters and commentary in this volume offer a view of the issues facing scholars concerned with understanding the theory, applications, and research on interpersonal expectations. The authors report on the current state of the field and suggest important directions for future research.

The volume is addressed primarily to behavioral and social scientists, health and organizational psychologists, and methodologists. I believe, however, that physicians, lawyers, anthropologists, sociologists, and statisticians may be equally interested. The text may also prove useful for graduate and advanced undergraduate classes in many of the previously mentioned disciplines.

This volume is a collaborative effort. I am grateful to the contributors for the time and energy they put into its development. I gratefully acknowledge support from the University of Iowa, College of Law Foundation during the preparation of this book and from the Annenberg Foundation Washington Program.

Paul Ekman's editorial guidance greatly strengthened the text. I also appreciate the help of my editor at Cambridge University Press, Julia Hough.

Finally, I thank Wendy and my children, Jason and Daniel, for their positive expectations in support of this effort.

Contributors

Robin Akert
Adlai E. Stevenson College
University of California, Santa Cruz

Dane Archer
Adlai E. Stevenson College
University of California, Santa Cruz

Elisha Babad
School of Education
Hebrew University of Jerusalem

Frank J. Bernieri
Department of Psychology
Oregon State University

Peter David Blanck
College of Law
University of Iowa and
The Annenberg Foundation
Washington Program

Nancy J. Briton
Department of Psychology
Northeastern University

Ross Buck
Department of Communication
University of Connecticut, Storrs

Donald T. Campbell
Social Relations
Lehigh University

Harris Cooper
Department of Psychology
University of Missouri

Mark Costanzo
Adlai E. Stevenson College
University of California, Santa Cruz

John M. Darley
Department of Psychology
Princeton University

Bella M. DePaulo
Department of Psychology
University of Virginia

Mary Amanda Dew
Western Psychiatric Institute and
Clinic
University of Pittsburgh

M. Robin DiMatteo
Department of Psychology
University of California, Riverside

Dov Eden
Department of Work Relations
Tel Aviv University

Howard S. Friedman
Department of Psychology
University of California, Riverside

Judith A. Hall
Department of Psychology
Northeastern University

Monica J. Harris
Department of Psychology
University of Kentucky

Holley S. Hodgins
Department of Psychology
University of Rochester

Kunitate Miyake
Department of Psychology
University of Rochester

Kathryn C. Oleson
Department of Psychology
Princeton University

Robert Rosenthal
Department of Psychology
Harvard University

Ralph L. Rosnow
Department of Psychology
Temple University

Donald B. Rubin
Department of Statistics
Harvard University

Klaus R. Scherer
Department of Psychology
University of Geneva

Marylee C. Taylor
Department of Sociology
Pennsylvania State University

Miron Zuckerman
Department of Psychology
University of Rochester

Introduction

1. Interpersonal expectations: Some antecedents and some consequences

ROBERT ROSENTHAL

It is a classic conception of progress that it is spiral in form. This volume, artfully conceived and orchestrated by Peter Blanck, lends support to that geometric conception. The spiral underlying this volume begins with the classic context-setting paper by Donald Campbell. That paper was presented at the first symposium on the social psychology of the psychological experiment, a 1959 symposium that dealt, in part, with the unintended effects of experimenters' expectations on the results of their experiments. It is now 1993, and this volume gives the current position of the moving spiral.

It is a heartening and enlightening experience to see more than 30 years of science go flashing by, beginning with Don Campbell's Janus-like classic that looks back to Francis Bacon's idols while it looks forward to the next generation of researchers. Campbell's classic, miraculously unpublished until this volume, seemed almost to have saved itself for this occasion. And some of the scholar-scientists of that next generation are also represented in this volume. All are young by my criteria, although ranging in career age from senior scholars of international renown to younger scholars in their first academic positions. But even the youngest scholars are already beginning to acquire that international renown.

One purpose of this introductory chapter is to review the history of some experiments designed to test the hypothesis of interpersonal expectancy effects. The earliest such experiments were designed to test this hypothesis in the context of the psychological experiment itself, with the experimenter serving as expecter and the research subject serving as expectee. What follows describes how this came about and then discusses some substantive and methodological consequences.

Experimenter expectancy effects and an unnecessary statistical analysis

As a graduate student at UCLA in the mid-1950s I was much taken with the work of two giants of personality theory, Freud and Murray. I was taken with Freud, as were so many others, for the richness and depth of his theory. I was taken with Murray, as were not enough others, for similar reasons but also because of Murray's brilliant way of inventing whatever tool was needed to further his inquiry. Thus, the Thematic Apperception Test (TAT) was invented simply as a tool to further his research, though it has become recognized as a major contribution in its own right. My dissertation was to depend on the work of both of these great theorists.

Sigmund Freud's projection

As a graduate student in clinical psychology I was (and still am) very much interested in projective techniques. Murray's TAT, Shneidman's Make a Picture Story Test, and, of course, the Rorschach were exciting methods for understanding people better. Shneidman, a brilliant researcher and clinician, was my first clinical supervisor during my Veterans Administration clinical internship. Bruno Klopfer, one of the all-time Rorschach greats, was the chair of my doctoral committee. It was natural, therefore, for me to be concerned with the defense mechanism of projection for the part it might play in the production of responses to projective stimuli.

Harry Murray's party game

Freud's defense mechanism of projection, the ascription to others of one's own states or traits (Freud, 1953; Rosenthal, 1956), is only one of the mechanisms that has been isolated as contributing to the process of producing responses to projective stimuli. Another mechanism is complementary apperceptive projection, that is, finding in another the reasons for one's own states or traits. It was this mechanism that Harry Murray investigated in his classic paper on "The Effect of Fear Upon Estimates of the Maliciousness of Other Personalities" (Murray, 1933). At his 11-year-old daughter's house party, Murray arranged a game called "Murder" that frightened delightfully the five party-going subjects. After the game, Murray found that the children perceived photographs as being more malicious than they did before the game. Murray's wonderfully direct and deceptively simple procedure of assessing projective processes by assessing changes in perceptions of photographs was the basic measuring device I adopted for my dissertation.

"An attempt at the experimental induction of the defense mechanism of projection"

With the foregoing as its almost unbearable title, my dissertation employed a total of 108 subjects: 36 college men, 36 college women, and 36 hospitalized patients with paranoid symptomatology. Each of these three groups was further divided into three subgroups receiving success, failure, or neutral experience on a task structured as, and simulating, a standardized test of intelligence. Before the subjects' experimental conditions were imposed, they were asked to rate the degree of success or failure of persons pictured in photographs. Immediately after the experimental manipulation, the subjects were asked to rate an equivalent set of photos on their degree of success or failure. The dependent variable was the magnitude of the difference scores between pre- and postratings of the photographs. It was hypothesized that the success condition would lead to the subsequent perception of other people as more successful, whereas the failure condition would lead to the subsequent perception of other people as having failed more, as measured by the pre- and postrating difference scores.

In an attack of studently compulsivity, an attack that greatly influenced my scholarly future, I did a statistical analysis that was extraneous to the main purpose of the dissertation. In this analysis I compared the mean *pre*-treatment ratings of the three experimental conditions. These means were: success = −1.52, neutral = −0.86, and failure = −1.02. The pre-treatment rating mean of the success condition was significantly lower than the mean of either of the other two conditions. It must be emphasized that these three treatment groups had not yet undergone their treatment; they were only destined to become the subjects of the three conditions. If the success group started out lower than the other groups, then, even if there were no differences among the three conditions in their post-treatment photo ratings, the success group would show the greatest gain, a result favoring one of my hypotheses, namely, that projection of the good could occur just as well as projection of the bad. Without my awareness, the cards had been stacked in favor of obtaining results supporting one of my hypotheses.

It should be noted that the success and failure groups' instructions had been identical during the pre-treatment rating phase of the experiment. (Instructions to the neutral group differed only in that no mention was made of the experimental task, since none was administered to this group.)

The problem, apparently, was that I knew for each subject which experimental treatment he or she would subsequently be administered. As I noted in 1956 with some dismay: "The implication is that in some subtle manner, perhaps by tone, or manner, or gestures, or general atmosphere, the experimenter, although formally testing the success and failure groups in an identical way, influenced the success subjects to make lower initial ratings and thus increase the experimenter's probability of verifying his hypothesis" (Rosenthal, 1956, p. 44). As a further check on the suspicion that success subjects had been treated differently, the conservatism extremeness of pre-treatment ratings of photos was analyzed. (The mean extremeness-of-rating scores were as follows: success = 3.92, neutral = 4.41, and failure = 4.42.) The success group rated photos significantly less extremely than did the other treatment groups. Whatever it was I did differently to those subjects whom I knew were destined for the success condition, it seemed to affect not only their mean level of rating but their style of rating as well.

The search for company

When I discussed these strange goings-on with some faculty members, they seemed not overly surprised. A not very reassuring response was "Oh, yes, we lose a few PhD dissertations now and then because of problems like that." There followed a frantic search of the literature for references to this phenomenon, which I then called *unconscious experimenter bias*. As far back as Ebbinghaus (1885), psychologists had been referring to something like this phenomenon, including such notables as Oskar Pfungst (1911), of Clever Hans fame, Ivan Pavlov (1929), and Saul Rosenzweig (1933). Unfortunately, none of these investigators (or even later ones) had explicitly designed and conducted an experiment to test the hypothesis of unconscious experimenter bias; that remained to be done.

There is something I want to add about the paper by Rosenzweig (1933), which appeared the same year as Harry Murray's paper (cited earlier) and, incidentally, the same year that I appeared. In my own several reviews of the literature (e.g., 1956, 1966), I had completely missed the Rosenzweig paper. I believe it was my good friend, my long-time collaborator, and my scholarly tutor, Ralph Rosnow, who called my attention to Rosenzweig's extraordinarily insightful and prophetic paper. Not only did Rosenzweig anticipate the problem of unconscious experimenter bias, he also anticipated virtually the entire area now referred to as the *social psychology of the psychological experiment*. The Rosenzweig paper makes good reading even today, some 60 years later. There is a superb appreciation of the Rosenzweig paper in Ralph Rosnow's brilliant book about the methodology of social inquiry: *Paradigms in Transition* (Rosnow, 1981).

The production of company

If it was my unconscious experimenter bias that had led to the puzzling and disconcerting results of my dissertation, then presumably we could produce the phenomenon in our own laboratory, and with several experimenters rather than just one. Producing the phenomenon in this way would yield not only the scientific benefit of demonstrating an interesting and important concept, it would also yield the considerable personal benefit of showing that I was not alone in having unintentionally affected the results of my research by virtue of my bias or expectancy.

There followed a series of studies employing human subjects in which we found that when experimenters were led to expect certain research findings, they were more likely to obtain those findings. These studies were met with incredulity by many investigators who worked with human subjects. However, investigators who worked with animal subjects often nodded knowingly and told me that was the kind of phenomenon that encouraged them to work with animal subjects. In due course, then, we began to work with animal subjects and found that when experimenters were led to believe that they were working with maze-bright rats, the rats learned faster than did the rats randomly assigned to experimenters who had been led to believe that their rats were dull. That result surprised many psychologists who worked with animal subjects, but it would not have surprised Pavlov, Pfungst, or Bertrand Russell, who in 1927 had said: "Animals studied by Americans rush about frantically, with an incredible display of hustle and pep, and at last achieve the desired result by chance. Animals observed by Germans sit still and think, and at last evolve the solution out of their inner consciousness" (pp. 29–30).

Our experiments on the effects of investigators' expectancies on the behavior of their research subjects should be distinguished from the much older tradition of examining the effects of investigators' expectations, theories, or predilections on their observations or interpretations of nature. Examples of such effects have been summarized elsewhere (Rosenthal, 1966; see especially chapters 1 and 2 on observer effects and interpreter effects), and there is continuing lively interest in these topics (Gorman, 1986; Mahoney, 1989; Mitroff, 1974; Rudwick, 1986; Tweney, 1989).

Teacher expectation effects and an essential principal

If rats became brighter when expected to, then it should not be far-fetched to think that children could become brighter when expected to by their teachers. Indeed, Kenneth Clark (1963) had for years been saying that teachers' expectations could be very important determinants of intellectual performance. Clark's ideas and our research should have sent us right into the schools to study teacher expectations, but that's not what happened.

What did happen was that after we had completed about a dozen studies of experimenter expectancy effects (we no longer used the term *unconscious experimenter bias*), I summarized our results in a paper for the *American Scientist* (Rosenthal, 1963). (As an aside, I should note that although this research had begun in 1958, and although there had been more than a dozen papers, none of them had been able to find their way into an American Psychological Association [APA] publication. I recall an especially "good news–bad news" type of day when a particular piece of work was simultaneously rejected by an APA journal and awarded the American Association for the Advancement of Science Socio-Psychological Prize for 1960. During these years of nonpublication, there were three "psychological sponsors" who provided enormous intellectual stimulation and personal encouragement: Donald T. Campbell, Harold B. Pepinsky, and Henry W. Riecken; I owe them all a great deal.)

I concluded this 1963 paper by wondering whether the same interpersonal expectancy effects found in psychological experimenters might not also be found in physicians, psychotherapists, employers, and teachers (subsequent research showed that indeed it could be found in all these practitioners). "When the master teacher tells his apprentice that a pupil appears to be a slow learner, is this prophecy then self-fulfilled?" was the closing line of this paper (Rosenthal, 1963, p. 280).

Among the reprint requests for this paper was one from Lenore F. Jacobson, the principal of an elementary school in South San Francisco, California. I sent her a stack of unpublished papers and thought no more about it. On November 18, 1963, Lenore wrote me a letter telling of her interest in the problem of teacher expectations. She ended her letter with the following line: "If you ever 'graduate' to classroom children, please let me know whether I can be of assistance" (Jacobson, 1963).

On November 27, 1963, I accepted Lenore's offer of assistance and asked whether she would consider collaborating on a project to investigate teacher expectancy effects. A tentative experimental design was suggested in this letter as well.

On December 3, 1963, Lenore replied, mainly to discuss concerns over the ethical and organizational implications of creating false expectations for superior performance in teachers. If this problem could be solved, her school would be ideal, she felt, with children from primarily lower-class backgrounds. Lenore also suggested gently that I was "a bit naive" to think one could just *tell* teachers to expect some of their pupils to be "diamonds in the rough." We would have to administer some new test to the children, a test the teachers would not know.

Phone calls and letters followed, and in January 1964 a trip to South San Francisco to settle on a final design and to meet with the school district's administrators to obtain their approval. This approval was forthcoming because of the leadership of the school superintendent, Dr. Paul Nielsen. Approval for this research had already been obtained from Robert L. Hall, Program Director for Sociology and Social Psychology for the National Science Foundation, which had been supporting much of the early work on experimenter expectancy effects.

The Pygmalion experiment (Rosenthal & Jacobson, 1966, 1968)

All of the children in Lenore's school were administered a nonverbal test of intelligence, which was disguised as a test that would predict intellectual "blooming." The test was labeled the *Harvard Test of Inflected Acquisition.* There were 18 classrooms in the school, 3 at each of the six grade levels. Within each grade level, the three classrooms were composed of children with above-average, average, and below-average ability, respectively. Within each of the 18 classrooms, approximately 20%

of the children were chosen at random to form the experimental group. Each teacher was given the names of the children from his or her class who were in the experimental condition. The teacher was told that these children's scores on the Test of Inflected Acquisition indicated that they would show surprising gains in intellectual competence during the next 8 months of school. The only difference between the experimental group and the control group of children, then, was in the mind of the teacher.

At the end of the school year, 8 months later, all the children were retested with the same test of intelligence. Considering the school as a whole, the children from whom the teachers had been led to expect greater intellectual gain showed a significantly greater gain than did the children in the control group. The magnitude of this experimental effect was .30 standard deviation units, equivalent to a point biserial r of .15 (Cohen, 1988).

Some substantive consequences: Processes of social influence

Among the most interesting and important implications of the research on interpersonal expectancy effects are those for the study of subtle processes of unintended social influence. The early work in this area has been summarized in detail elsewhere (e.g., Rosenthal, 1966, 1969). When we look more particularly at the mediation of teacher expectancy effects, we find early summaries by Brophy and Good (1974), workers whose contributions to this area have been enormous, and by Rosenthal (1974). More recent summaries of this domain are by Brophy (1985) and by Harris and Rosenthal (1985). There is space here only to illustrate the types of research results that have been accumulating. A preliminary four-factor theory of the communication of expectancy effects suggests that teachers (and perhaps clinicians, supervisors, and employers) who have been led to expect superior performance from some of their pupils (clients, trainees, or employees) tend to treat these "special" persons differently than they treat the remaining less special persons in the following four ways (Rosenthal, 1971, 1973, 1974):

1. *Climate.* Teachers appear to create a warmer socioemotional climate for their special students. This warmth appears to be at least partially communicated by nonverbal cues.
2. *Feedback.* Teachers appear to give their special students more differentiated feedback, both verbal and nonverbal, as to how these students have been performing.

3. *Input.* Teachers appear to teach more material and more difficult material to their special students.
4. *Output.* Teachers appear to give their special students greater opportunities for responding. These opportunities are offered both verbally and nonverbally (e.g., giving a student more time in which to answer a teacher's question).

A recent simplification of the four-factor theory of the mediation of teacher expectation effects has been proposed (Rosenthal, 1989). This simplification, called the *affect/effort theory*, states that a change in the level of expectations held by a teacher for the intellectual performance of a student is translated into (1) a change in the affect shown by the teacher toward that student and, relatively independently, (2) a change in the degree of effort exerted by the teacher in teaching that student. Specifically, the more favorable the change in the level of expectation held by the teacher for a particular student, the more positive the affect shown toward that student and the greater the effort expended on behalf of that student. The increase in positive affect is presumed to be a reflection of increased liking for the student for any of several plausible reasons (Jussim, 1986). The increase in teaching effort is presumed to be a reflection of an increased belief on the part of the teacher that the student is capable of learning, so that the effort is worth it (Rosenthal & Jacobson, 1968; Swann & Snyder, 1980).

Some of the aspects of affect/effort theory currently under investigation with Nalini Ambady have very exciting implications. For example, we have been able to predict student ratings of a college instructor's effectiveness over the course of an entire semester from an examination of a 30-second slice of teaching behavior in which we have access only to the silent videotape or to the tone of voice (not the content) in which the instructors are communicating with their students. These predictive correlations, often in the range of .6 to .7, have been replicated in high school settings and fit very well with the results of many other studies of "thin slices" of nonverbal behavior summarized meta-analytically (Ambady & Rosenthal, 1992, 1993).

Similarly, work with Sarah Hechtman has shown the potential for affect/effort theory to help explain the traditional sex differences in cognitive functioning. We have found that teachers teaching verbal material to males and quantitative material to females (the so-called sex-inappropriate materials) showed greater hostility to their students in the nonverbal channels (video-only) than did teachers teaching the so-called sex-appropriate materials to these same students. These bias effects were smaller for female than for male teachers, and they were smaller for more androgynous than for more sex-typed teachers (Hechtman & Rosenthal, 1991).

Some methodological consequences
for a better understanding of replication

Unfriendly reactions to the research on interpersonal expectancy effects and claims of failures to replicate the effects led me to examine closely and, no doubt, defensively the concept of replication in behavioral research (Rosenthal, 1966, 1990).

There is a long tradition in psychology of our urging one another to replicate each other's research. But, although we have been very good at calling for replication, we have not been very good at deciding when a replication has been successful. The issue we now address is: When shall a study be deemed successfully replicated?

Successful replication is ordinarily taken to mean that a null hypothesis that has been rejected at Time 1 is rejected again, and with the same direction of outcome, on the basis of a new study at Time 2. We have a failure to replicate when one study was significant and the other was not. Let us examine more closely a specific example of such a failure to replicate.

Pseudo-failures to replicate

The saga of Smith and Jones. Smith has published the results of an experiment in which a certain treatment procedure was predicted to improve performance. She reported results significant at $p < .05$ in the predicted direction. Jones publishes a rebuttal to Smith, claiming a failure to replicate. In situations of that sort, it is often the case that, although Smith's results were more significant than Jones's, the studies were in quite good agreement as to their estimated sizes of effect, as defined either by Cohen's d [$(\text{mean}_1 - \text{mean}_2)/\sigma$] or by r, the correlation between group membership and performance score (Cohen, 1988; Rosenthal, 1991). Thus, studies labeled as *failures to replicate* often turn out to provide strong evidence for the replicability of the claimed effect.

On the odds against replicating significant results. A related error often found in the behavioral and social sciences is the implicit assumption that if an effect is real, we should therefore expect it to be found significant again upon replication. Nothing could be further from the truth.

Suppose that there is in nature a real effect with a true magnitude of $d = .50$ [i.e., $(\text{mean}_1 - \text{mean}_2)/\sigma = .50 \ \sigma$ units] or, equivalently, $r = .24$ (a difference in success rate of 62% versus 38%). Then suppose that an investigator studies this effect with an N of 64 subjects or so, giving the researcher a level of statistical power of .50, a very common level of power for behavioral researchers of the last 30 years (Cohen, 1962; Sedlmeier & Gigerenzer, 1989). Even though a d of .50 or an r of .24 can reflect a very important effect, there is only one chance in four that both the original investigator and a replicator will get results significant at the .05 level. If there were two replications of the original study, there would be only one chance in eight that all three studies would be significant, even though we know that the effect in nature is real and important.

Contrasting views of replication

The traditional, not very useful, view of replication has two primary characteristics:

1. It focuses on significance level as the relevant summary statistic of a study, and
2. it evaluates whether replication has been successful in a dichotomous fashion. For example, replications are successful if both or neither $p < .05$ and they are unsuccessful if one $p < .05$ and the other $p > .05$. Psychologists' reliance on a dichotomous decision procedure accompanied by an untenable discontinuity of credibility in results varying in p levels has been well documented (Nelson, Rosenthal, & Rosnow, 1986; Rosenthal & Gaito, 1963, 1964).

The newer, more useful views of replication success have two primary characteristics:

1. A focus on effect size as the more important summary statistic of a study, with a relatively minor interest in the statistical significance level, and
2. An evaluation of whether replication has been successful is made in a continuous fashion. For example, two studies are not said to be successful or unsuccessful replicates of each other; rather, the degree of failure to replicate is specified.

Some metrics of the success of replication

Differences between effect sizes. Once we adopt a view of the success of replication as a function of the similarity of effect sizes obtained, we can become more precise in our assessments of the success of replication. Replication success can be indexed by the difference between the effect sizes obtained in the original study and in the replication. For example, we could employ the differences in Cohen's d's or the effect size r's obtained, or we could employ Cohen's q, which is the difference between r's that have been first transformed to Fisher's Z's. Fisher's Z metric is distributed nearly normally and can thus be used in setting confidence intervals and testing hypotheses about r's, whereas r's distribution is skewed, and the more so as the population value of r moves further from zero. Cohen's q is especially useful for testing the significance of difference between two obtained effect size r's (Rosenthal, 1991; Rosenthal & Rubin, 1982; Snedecor & Cochran, 1989). When there are more than two effect size r's to be evaluated for their variability (i.e., heterogeneity), we can simply compute the standard deviation (S) among the r's or their Fisher Z equivalents. If a test of significance of heterogeneity of these Fisher Z's is desired, a simple χ^2 test of heterogeneity is readily available (Hedges, 1982; Rosenthal & Rubin, 1982).

Meta-analytic metrics. As the number of replications for a given research question grows, a full assessment of the success of the replicational effort requires the application of meta-analytic procedures. An informative summary of the meta-analysis might be the stem-and-leaf display of the effect sizes found in the meta-analysis (Tukey, 1977). A more compact summary of the effect sizes might be Tukey's (1977) box plot, which gives the highest and lowest obtained effect sizes, along with those found at the 25th, 50th, and 75th percentiles. For single index values of the consistency of the effect sizes, one could employ (1) the range of effect sizes found between the 75th (Q_3) and 25th (Q_1) percentiles, (2) some standard fraction of that range (e.g., one-half or three-quarters), (3) S, the standard deviation of the effect sizes, or (4) SE, the standard error of the effect sizes.

As a slightly more complex index of the stability, replicability, or clarity of the average effect size found in the set of replicates, one could employ the mean effect size divided either by its standard error ($\sqrt{k}$, where k is the total number of replicates) or simply by S. The latter index of mean effect size divided by its standard deviation (S) is the reciprocal of the coefficient of variation or a kind of coefficient of robust-ness.

The coefficient of robustness of replication. Although the standard error of the mean effect size, along with confidence intervals placed around the mean effect size, are of great value (Rosenthal & Rubin, 1978), it will sometimes be useful to employ a robustness coefficient that does not increase simply as a function of the increasing number of replications. Thus, if we want to compare two research areas for their robustness, adjusting for the difference in number of replications in each research area, we may prefer the robustness coefficient defined as the reciprocal of the coefficient of variation.

The utility of this coefficient is based on two ideas – first, that repli-cation success, clarity, or robustness depends on the homogeneity of the obtained effect size, and second, that it depends also on the clarity of the directionality of the result. Thus, a set of replications grows in robustness as the variance of the effect sizes decreases and as the distance of the mean effect size from zero increases. Incidentally, the mean may be weighted, unweighted, or trimmed (Tukey, 1977). In-deed, it need not be the mean at all but any measure of location or central tendency (e.g., the median).

What should be reported?

Effect sizes and significance tests. If we are to take seriously our newer view of the meaning of the success of replications, what should be reported by authors of papers seen to be replications of earlier studies? Clearly, reporting the results of tests of significance will not be sufficient. The effect size of the replication and of the original study must be reported. It is not crucial which particular effect size is em-ployed, but the same effect size should be reported for the replication and the original study. Complete discussions of various effect sizes and when they are useful are available from Cohen (1988) and elsewhere (e.g., Rosenthal, 1991, in press). If the original study and its replication are reported in different effect size units, these can usually be translated to one another (Cohen, 1988; Rosenthal, 1991; Rosenthal & Rosnow, 1991; Rosenthal & Rubin, 1989).

Power. Especially if the results of either the original study or its replication were not significant, the statistical power at which the test of significance was made (assuming, for example, a population effect size equivalent to the effect size actually obtained) should be reported (Cohen, 1988). In addition to reporting the statistical power for each study separately, it would be valuable to report the overall probability that both studies would have yielded significant results given, for example, the effect size estimated from the results of the original and the replication study combined.

The equally likely effect size. A marvelous suggestion has been made by Donald Rubin that would go a long way toward helping us solve our problem of the relative risks of Type II versus Type I errors. He has suggested that whenever we conclude that there is "no effect," we report both the effect size and the confidence interval around the effect size that ranges from the effect size of zero to the equally likely effect size greater than the one we obtained. For example, suppose that a replicator, Jones, did not reject the null hypothesis but obtained an effect size of $d = .50$. If Jones had been required to report that his d of .50 was just as close to a d of 1.00 as it was to a d of 0, Jones would have been less likely to draw his wrong conclusion that he had failed to replicate the work of Smith, who had found a very similar effect size.

Replication and meta-analytic procedures

Any discussion of replication and of the evaluation of the success of a particular replication cannot avoid some consideration of meta-analytic procedures and a meta-analytic *Weltanschauung*.

Some obvious benefits

Some beneficial consequences of a meta-analytic view of data and of data analysis are fairly obvious. Our summaries are likely to be more complete, more explicit, more quantitative, and more powerful in the sense of decreasing Type II errors. There are also some less obvious benefits.

Less obvious benefits

Moderator variables. These are more easily spotted and evaluated in a quantitative research summary. This aids theory development and increases empirical richness.

Cumulation problems. Meta-analytic procedures address, in part, the chronic complaint that the social sciences cumulate poorly compared to the physical sciences. It should be noted that recent historical and sociological investigations have suggested that the physical sciences may not be much better off than the social sciences when it comes to successful replication (Collins, 1985; Hedges, 1987; Pool, 1988). For example, Collins (1985) has described the failures to replicate the construction of TEA lasers despite the availability of detailed instructions for replication. Apparently TEA lasers could be replicated dependably only when the replication instructions were accompanied by a scientist who had actually built a laser.

Decreased overemphasis on single studies. One not so obvious benefit that will accrue to the social sciences is the gradual decrease in the overemphasis on the results of a single study. There are good sociological grounds for our monomaniacal preoccupation with the results of a single study. Those grounds have to do with the reward system of science, where recognition, promotion, reputation, and the like depend on the results of the single study, also known as the *smallest unit of academic currency*. The study is "good," "valuable," and, above all, "publishable" when $p \leq .05$. Our disciplines would be further ahead if we adopted a more cumulative view of science in which the impact of a study were evaluated less on the basis of p levels, and more on the basis of its own effect size and on the revised effect size and combined probability that resulted from the addition of the new study to any earlier studies investigating the same or a similar relationship.

Decreased "differentiation drive," renomination, and concept capture. Related to the problem of overemphasis on single studies is the problem of *differentiation drive*, a motivational state (and trait) frequently found among scientists. This is the drive to be different; to be more first, to be more right, to be more unique than others. Priority strife is one reflection of the differentiation drive. Another reflection is the occurrence of *renomination*, the mechanism by which a well-known process is given a new name in hopes of effecting *concept capture*. Concept capture is the mechanism by which ownership of a concept is claimed by virtue of renaming it. Differentiation drive keeps us from viewing the world meta-analytically, i.e., in a more Bayesian way; it keeps us from seeing the similarity of our work to the work of others.

B. F. Skinner has spoken eloquently, if indirectly, on this matter: "In my own thinking, I try to avoid the kind of fraudulent significance which comes with grandiose terms or profound 'principles.' But some psychologists seem to need to feel that every experiment they do demands a sweeping reorganization of psychology as a whole. It's not worth publishing unless it has some such significance. But research has its own values, and you don't need to cook up spurious reasons why it's important" (Skinner, 1983, p. 39).

"The new intimacy." This new intimacy is between the reviewer and the data. We cannot do a meta-analysis by reading abstracts and discussion sections. We are forced to look at the numbers and, very often, compute the correct ones ourselves. Meta-analysis requires us to cumulate *data,* not *conclusions.* "Reading" a paper is quite a different matter when we need to compute an effect size and a fairly precise significance level – often from a results section that never heard of effect sizes or precise significance levels (or the *Publication Manual* of the APA).

The demise of the dichotomous significance testing decision. Far more than is good for us, social and behavioral scientists operate under a dichotomous null hypothesis decision procedure in which the evidence is interpreted as anti-null if $p \leq .05$ and pro-null if $p > .05$. If our dissertation p is $< .05$, it means joy, a PhD, and a tenure-track position at a major university. If our p is $> .05$ it means ruin, despair, and our advisor's suddenly thinking of a new control condition that should be run. That attitude really must go. God loves the .06 nearly as much as the .05. Indeed, I have it on good authority that she views the strength of evidence for or against the null as a fairly continuous function of the magnitude of p. As a matter of fact, two .06 results are much stronger evidence against the null than one .05 result; and 10 p's of .10 are stronger evidence against the null than 5 p's of .05.

The overthrow of the omnibus test. It is common to find specific questions addressed by F tests with $df > 1$ in the numerator or by χ^2 tests with $df > 1$. For example, suppose that the specific question is whether an increased incentive level improves the productivity of work groups. We employ four levels of incentive, so that our omnibus F test would have 3 df in the numerator or our omnibus χ^2 would be on at least 3 df. Common as these tests are, they reflect poorly on our teaching of data-analytic procedures. The diffuse hypothesis tested by these omnibus tests usually tells us nothing of importance about our research questions. The rule of thumb is unambiguous: Whenever we have tested a fixed effect with $df > 1$ for χ^2 or for the numerator of F, we have tested a question in which we are almost surely not interested.

The situation is even worse when there are several dependent variables as well as multiple df for the independent variable. The paradigm case here is canonical correlation, and special cases are multivariate analysis of variance (MANOVA), multivariate analysis of covariance (MANCOVA), multiple discriminant function, multiple path analysis, and complex multiple partial correlation. Although all of these procedures have useful exploratory data-analytic applications, they are commonly used to test null hypotheses that are scientifically almost always of doubtful value. The effect size estimates they yield (e.g., the canonical correlation) are also almost always of doubtful value.

Meta-analytic questions are basically contrast questions. F tests with $df > 1$ in the numerator or χ^2s with $df > 1$ are useless in meta-analytic work. That leads to an additional scientific benefit:

The increased recognition of contrast analysis. Meta-analytic questions require precise formulation of questions, and contrasts are procedures for obtaining answers to such questions, often in an analysis of variance or table analysis context. Although most textbooks of statistics describe the logic and the machinery of contrast analyses, contrasts are still employed too rarely. That is a pity given the precision of thought and theory they encourage and (especially relevant to these times of publication pressure) given the boost in power conferred by the resulting increase in .05 asterisks (Rosenthal & Rosnow, 1985).

A probable increase in the accurate understanding of interaction effects. Probably the most misinterpreted empirical results in psychology are the results of interaction effects. A recent survey of 191 research articles involving interactions found only 2 articles that showed the authors interpreting interactions in an unequivocally correct manner (i.e., by examining the residuals that define the interaction) (Rosenthal & Rosnow, 1991; Rosnow & Rosenthal, 1989). The rest of the articles simply compared means of conditions with other means, a procedure that does not investigate interaction effects but rather the sum of main effects and interaction effects.

Most standard textbooks of statistics for social scientists provide accurate mathematical definitions of interaction effects, but then interpret not the residuals that define those interactions but the means of cells that are the sums of all main effects and all interactions.

Since many meta-analytic questions are by nature questions of inter-action (e.g., that opposite-sex dyads conduct standard transactions more slowly than same-sex dyads), we can hope that increased use of meta-analytic procedures will bring with it increased sophistication about the meaning of interaction.

Meta-analytic procedures are applicable beyond meta-analyses. Many of the techniques of contrast analyses among effect sizes, for example, can be used within a single study (Rosenthal & Rosnow, 1985). Computing a single effect size from correlated dependent variables or comparing treatment effects on two or more dependent variables serve as illustrations (Rosenthal & Rubin, 1986).

The decrease in the splendid detachment of the full professor. Meta-analytic work requires careful reading of research and moderate data-analytic skills. We cannot send an undergraduate research assistant to the library with a stack of 5×8 cards to bring us back the "results." With narrative reviews, that seems often to have been done. With meta-analysis the reviewer must get involved with the actual data, and that is all to the good.

Back to the spiral

Donald Campbell's prelude and the book that lies ahead represent an integration of much that has been learned about interpersonal expectations and about some of the substantive and methodological implications of that research. Although I have spent some 35 years studying the issues raised here, I have never had so clear a vision of this domain as I have acquired from reading the contributions to this book. Not only are the individual chapters outstanding, but the introductions to each of the three parts and the commentaries on these parts are extraordinarily insightful, original, and integrative.

Not that I'm surprised by the enormous erudition, insight, originality, and wisdom flowing from the quills, pens, typewriters, and word processors of this collection of my heroes, tutors, and friends. Yes, and all of them are all of these and have been so for many years. Could I have expected otherwise?

Note

This introduction is based in part on the Donald T. Campbell Address presented at the Annual Meeting of the American Psychological Association, New Orleans, August 14, 1989, on a chapter entitled "From Unconscious Experimenter Bias to Teacher Expectancy Effects" in Jerome B. Dusek (Ed.) (1985), *Teacher expectancies* (Hillsdale, NJ: Erlbaum), and on a chapter entitled "On Being One's Own Case Study: Experimenter Effects in Behavioral Research – Thirty Years Later" in W. R. Shadish (Ed.) (1992), *The social psychology of science* (New York: Guilford). Although much of the work reported has been supported over the years by the National Science Foundation and more recently by the Spencer Foundation, the views expressed are solely the responsibility of the author. I thank Donald T. Campbell, Harold B. Pepinsky, and Henry W. Riecken for their support during the "critical period" and beyond, and I thank Bill Cochran, Jack Cohen, Bill Estes, Paul Holland, Fred Mosteller, Ralph Rosnow, and Don Rubin for all they taught me about science, methodology, and the analysis of data.

References

Ambady, N., & Rosenthal, R. (1992). Thin slices of expressive behavior as predictors of interpersonal consequences: A meta-analysis. *Psychological Bulletin, 111,* 256–274.

Ambady, N., & Rosenthal, R. (1993). Half a minute: Predicting teacher effectiveness from their slices of nonverbal behavior and physical attractiveness. *Journal of Personality and Social Psychology,* in press.

Brophy, J. E. (1985). Teacher–student interaction. In J. B. Dusek (Ed.), *Teacher expectancies.* Hillsdale, NJ: Erlbaum.

Brophy, J. E., & Good, T. L. (1974). *Teacher–student relationships.* New York: Holt, Rinehart and Winston.

Clark., K. B. (1963). Educational stimulation of racially disadvantaged children. In A. H. Passow (Ed.), *Education in depressed areas.* New York: Bureau of Publications, Teachers College, Columbia University.

Cohen, J. (1962). The statistical power of abnormal–social psychological research: A review. *Journal of Abnormal and Social Psychology, 65,* 145–153.

Cohen, J. (1988). *Statistical power analysis for the behavioral sciences* (2nd ed.). Hillsdale, NJ: Erlbaum.

Collins, H. M. (1985). *Changing order: Replication and induction in scientific practice.* Beverly Hills, CA: Sage.

Ebbinghaus, H. (1885). *Memory* (trans. 1913). New York: Teachers College, Columbia University.

Freud, S. (1953). *Collected papers. Vol. 4.* London: Hogarth.

Gorman, M. E. (1986). How the possibility of error affects falsification on a task that models scientific problem solving. *British Journal of Psychology, 77,* 85–96.

Gruenberg, B. C. (1929). *The story of evolution.* Princeton, NJ: Van Nostrand.

Harris, M. J., & Rosenthal, R. (1985). The mediation of interpersonal expectancy effects: 31 meta-analyses. *Psychological Bulletin, 97,* 363–386.

Harris, M. J., & Rosenthal, R. (1988). Human performance research: An overview. Background paper commissioned by the National Research Council. Washington, DC: National Academy Press.

Hechtman, S., & Rosenthal, R. (1991). Teacher sex and nonverbal behavior in the teaching of sexually stereotyped materials. *Journal of Applied Social Psychology, 21*, 446–459.

Hedges, L. V. (1982). Estimation of effect size from a series of independent experiments. *Psychological Bulletin, 92*, 490–499.

Hedges, L. V. (1987). How hard is hard science, how soft is soft science? *American Psychologist, 42*, 443–455.

Honorton, C. (1985). Meta-analysis of psi ganzfeld research: A response to Hyman. *Journal of Parapsychology, 49*, 51–91.

Hyman, R. (1985). The ganzfeld psi experiment: A critical appraisal. *Journal of Parapsychology, 49*, 3–49.

Hyman, R., & Honorton, C. (1986). A joint communiqué: The psi ganzfeld controversy. *Journal of Parapsychology, 50*, 351–364.

Jussim, L. (1986). Self-fulfilling prophecies: A theoretical and integrative review. *Psychological Review, 93*, 429–445.

Mahoney, M. J. (1989). Participatory epistemology and psychology of science. In B. Gholson, W. R. Shadish, Jr., R. A. Neimeyer, & A. C. Houts (Eds.), *Psychology of science: Contributions to metascience* (pp. 138–164). Cambridge: Cambridge University Press.

Merton, R. K. (1948). The self-fulfilling prophecy. *Antioch Review, 8*, 193–210.

Mitroff, I. I. (1974). *The subjective side of science*. Amsterdam: Elsevier.

Murray, H. A. (1933). The effect of fear upon estimates of the maliciousness of other personalities. *Journal of Social Psychology, 4*, 310–329.

Nelson, N., Rosenthal, R., & Rosnow, R. L. (1986). Interpretation of significance levels and effect sizes by psychological researchers. *American Psychologist, 41*, 1299–1301.

Pavlov, I. (See Gruenberg, 1929).

Pfungst, O. (1911/1965). *Clever Hans* (C. L. Rahn, trans). New York: Holt, Rinehart and Winston, 1965.

Pool, R. (1988). Similar experiments, dissimilar results. *Science, 242*, 192–193.

Rosenthal, R. (1956). *An attempt at the experimental induction of the defense mechanism of projection*. Doctoral dissertation, UCLA.

Rosenthal, R. (1963). On the social psychology of the psychological experiment: The experimenter's hypothesis as unintended determinant of experimental results. *American Scientist, 51*, 268–283.

Rosenthal, R. (1966). *Experimenter effects in behavioral research*. New York: Appleton-Century-Crofts.

Rosenthal, R. (1969). Interpersonal expectations. In R. Rosenthal & R. L. Rosnow (Eds.), *Artifact in behavioral research* (pp. 181–277). New York: Academic Press.

Rosenthal, R. (1971). The silent language of classrooms and laboratories. *Proceedings of the Parapsychological Association*, No. 8, 95–116.

Rosenthal, R. (1973). The mediation of Pygmalion effects: A four factor "theory." *Papua New Guinea Journal of Education, 9*, 1–12.

Rosenthal, R. (1974). *On the social psychology of the self-fulfilling prophecy: Further evidence for Pygmalion effects and their mediating mechanisms* (Module 53, pp. 1–28). New York: MSS Modular Publications.

Rosenthal, R. (1976). *Experimenter effects in behavioral research* (enlarged ed.). New York: Irvington.

Rosenthal, R. (1985). Nonverbal cues in the mediation of interpersonal expectancy effects. In A. W. Siegman & S. Feldstein (Eds.), *Multichannel integration of nonverbal behavior* (pp. 105–128). Hillsdale, NJ: Erlbaum.

Rosenthal, R. (1986). Meta-analytic procedures and the nature of replication: The ganzfeld debate. *Journal of Parapsychology, 50,* 315–336.

Rosenthal, R. (1989). Experimenter expectancy, covert communication, and meta-analytic methods. Donald T. Campbell Award presentation, American Psychological Association meeting, August 14, 1989. (ERIC Document TM014556.)

Rosenthal, R. (1990). Replication in behavioral research. *Journal of Social Behavior and Personality, 5,* 1–30.

Rosenthal, R. (1991). *Meta-analytic procedures for social research* (rev. ed.). Newbury Park, CA: Sage.

Rosenthal, R. (in press). Parametric measures of effect size. In H. Cooper & L. Hedges (Eds.), *Handbook of research synthesis.* New York: Russell Sage.

Rosenthal, R., & Gaito, J. (1963). The interpretation of levels of significance by psychological researchers. *Journal of Psychology, 55,* 33–38.

Rosenthal, R., & Gaito, J. (1964). Further evidence for the cliff effect in the interpretation of levels of significance. *Psychological Reports, 15,* 570.

Rosenthal, R., & Jacobson, L. (1966). Teachers' expectancies: Determinants of pupils' IQ gains. *Psychological Reports, 19,* 115–118.

Rosenthal, R., & Jacobson, L. (1968). *Pygmalion in the classroom.* New York: Holt, Rinehart and Winston.

Rosenthal, R., & Jacobson, L. (1992). *Pygmalion in the classroom* (enlarged ed.). New York: Irvington.

Rosenthal, R., & Rosnow, R. L. (1985). *Contrast analysis: Focused comparisons in the analysis of variance.* New York: Cambridge University Press.

Rosenthal, R., & Rosnow, R. L. (1991). *Essentials of behavioral research: Methods and data analysis* (2nd ed.). New York: McGraw-Hill.

Rosenthal, R., & Rubin, D. B. (1978). Interpersonal expectancy effects: The first 345 studies. *The Behavioral and Brain Sciences, 3,* 377–386.

Rosenthal, R., & Rubin, D. B. (1982). Comparing effect sizes of independent studies. *Psychological Bulletin, 92,* 500–504.

Rosenthal, R., & Rubin, D. B. (1986). Meta-analytic procedures for combining studies with multiple effect sizes. *Psychological Bulletin, 99,* 400–406.

Rosenthal, R., & Rubin, D. B. (1989). Effect size estimation for one-sample multiple-choice-type data: Design, analysis, and meta-analysis. *Psychological Bulletin, 106,* 332–337.

Rosenzweig, S. (1933). The experimental situation as a psychological problem. *Psychological Review, 40,* 337–354.

Rosnow, R. L. (1981). *Paradigms in transition.* New York: Oxford University Press.

Rosnow, R. L., & Rosenthal, R. (1989). Definition and interpretation of interaction effects. *Psychological Bulletin, 105,* 143–146.

Rudwick, M. J. S. (1986). The group construction of scientific knowledge: Gentlemen-specialists and the Devonian controversy. In E. Ullmann-Margalit (Ed.), *The kaleidoscope of science* (pp. 193–217). Dordrecht, The Netherlands: Reidel.

Russell, B. (1927). *Philosophy.* New York: Norton.

Sedlmeier, P., & Gigerenzer, G. (1989). Do studies of statistical power have an effect on the power of studies? *Psychological Bulletin, 105,* 309–316.

Skinner, B. F. (1983, August). On the value of research. *APA Monitor,* p. 39.

Snedecor, G. W., & Cochran, W. G. (1989). *Statistical methods* (8th ed.). Ames: Iowa State University Press.

Swann, W. B., Jr., & Snyder, M. (1980). On translating beliefs into action:

Theories of ability and their application in an instructional setting. *Journal of Personality and Social Psychology, 38,* 879–888.

Swets, J. A., & Bjork, R. A. (1990). Enhancing human performance: An evaluation of "new age" techniques considered by the U.S. Army. *Psychological Science, 1,* 85–96.

Tukey, J. W. (1977). *Exploratory data analysis.* Reading, MA: Addison-Wesley.

Tweney, R. D. (1989). A framework for the cognitive psychology of science. In B. Gholson, W. R. Shadish, Jr., R. A. Neimeyer, & A. C. Houts (Eds.), *Psychology of science: Contributions to metascience* (pp. 342–366). Cambridge: Cambridge University Press.

2. Systematic errors to be expected of the social scientist on the basis of a general psychology of cognitive bias

DONALD T. CAMPBELL

Preamble: Interpersonal expectation has turned out to be a crucial aspect of the new social psychology of science. Indeed, Robert Rosenthal's first studies of powerful effects of interpersonal expectations are in his extensive program of experiments on the social psychology of experimentation.

Belatedly, we are attempting to consolidate a new field, the *psychology of science* (e.g., Gholson, Shadish, Neimeyer, & Houts, 1989) and, more particularly, the *social psychology of science* (e.g., Shadish, 1992). This field should include not only speculative extrapolations of social cognitive principles to the activities of scientists, not only analogue experiments in which undergraduates in lab sessions work on tasks designed to capture aspects of scientific decision making, not only empirical studies using history of science exemplars as the data base, but also, were it possible, meta-experiments – *experiments with the very process of science itself.* Rosenthal is not only the pioneer in this area (e.g., Rosenthal, 1976, summarizing experiments going back to 1958), he also has done the great majority of all such experiments. He is *Mr. Experimental Social Psychologist of Science* himself. This book (or, given Rosenthal's relative youth, the next one dedicated to his achievements) should have had a chapter on "Interpersonal Expectations of Experimenters and Research Participants (a.k.a. 'Subjects') as Sources of Bias in Laboratory Experimentation." The present chapter is not that but is intended to celebrate the achievement.

The social psychology of science joins the sociology of science and the new externalist history of science in placing great emphasis on social contexts and the life world of scientists. And the older historians of science loved stories of heroic overcoming of obstacles, of initially rejected outsiders becoming central figures in the scientific establishment. These ingredients are being formalized in the new social psychology of science, as in relating the results of the experimental study of minority influence to historical episodes in scientific theory change (e.g., Rosenwein, 1992). There is also an experimental literature relevant to interpersonal expectations on bias in the refereeing of journal articles: bias due to the prestige of the institution of the author, as well as due to the threat to the reviewer's ideology of the reported results (e.g., Cicchetti, 1991). Case studies are relevant to these issues. I offer a very condensed one in the next few paragraphs.

In 1956 and 1957 most new UCLA PhDs in psychology wanted jobs in Southern California for climate, surfing, and cultural ambiance. Bob Rosenthal, an Angeleno from age 16, was like the rest in this. His PhD was in clinical psychology, which greatly increased the options available to achieve a Southern California career. But his stubborn desire to be a university professor so overcame these preferences that he accepted a job at the University of North Dakota. Most of the able intellectuals there were sulking in their tents, feeling like exiles to Siberia in terms of both weather and university prestige. They were avoiding students and shortchanging their teaching, withdrawing to desperate scholarly efforts to earn their exit credentials. Retaining the stereotyped interpersonal expectations they came there with, they despised their students as ignorant country clods unworthy of their attention.

Not so Bob. He treated the students as precious, worthy of his full attention. He worked hard to be an inspiring teacher. Soon he had most of the bright and committed students taking his courses and volunteering to be his unpaid research assistants. And they turned out to be very able students, the brightest from the whole state of North Dakota who could not afford to go out of state to more elite universities. (The phenomenon of experimental bias has been well cross-validated by others [Rosenthal, 1976], but if the effects are not as strong as Rosenthal achieved at North Dakota, it is because on other campuses one fails to replicate the degree of enthusiastic commitment to one's professor's projects that he achieved in those years.)

His 20 major studies of his Dakota years involved 300 apprentice experimenters, 1,800 subjects, and 15 person-years of analysis and write-up. The striking findings were replicated again and again with increasing experimental precautions. Yet the results were so threatening to the established experimental psychologists, and North Dakota's prestige was so low, that the resulting articles were regularly rejected by the major journals and he had to publish them in unrefereed journals such as *Psychological Reports, Perceptual and Motor Skills,* and other low-prestige outlets. (The first exception to this was in 1963.) The peer review by funding agencies was almost equally negative. All but the last of his 20 North Dakota studies were done without any external research support, but they produced a cumulative product that would have given pride to a Big 10 or Ivy League social psychologist funded (for those years) at $75,000 per year. It was not until 1961 that he received a research grant from the National Science Foundation or the National Institutes of Mental Health. (A thorough case study should try for access to all of those anonymous peer reviews.)

The threat to the scientific enterprise was wrongly perceived. Unlike the popular consensus in contemporary sociology of science, Rosenthal has used evidence of bias to improve the validity of experimental social psychology, not to deny the possibility of such validity (see Campbell, 1992, for extended citation and discussion). Finally, the defensive walls of the old scientific consensus were broken down. On the same day in 1961, and for the same manuscript, he received both his usual rejection notice from a refereed journal and the announcement that he had won the American Association for the Advancement of Science's annual award for the best study in social psychology. He became both famous and ambivalently respected, and moved from a North Dakota appointment to one at Harvard. The outsider had become a key mainstreamer.

While still at North Dakota, Bob recruited me for a social psychology of science symposium at the American Psychological Association meetings in Cincinnati in 1959. The paper I prepared for that session is published here for the first time. Had Bob been able to get the whole session published, I would have been proud to have had my paper included. But lacking that, I failed to submit it anywhere. It was not along the lines of my major work. It was speculative and theoretical, presenting no new data. Moreover, it was in a new genre with no established journals. Not for many years, after the consolidation of the effects of the publication of Thomas Kuhn's revolutionary *Structure of Scientific Revolutions* (which first appeared 3 years later, in 1962), did a market for such essays appear.

My essay provides theses as to the biasing effects of interpersonal expectations in science and serves to honor Bob Rosenthal's great contributions to this area, even though there are no citations of Rosenthal's work, unnecessary because his own presentation followed mine at the symposium. From one point of view, my essay would have been slightly more useful if up-to-date confirmations of the principles had been added. But it is more valuable to leave it in its 1959, pre-Kuhnian form, as historical evidence of the climate of ideas at the time, a climate that produced both it and, at least in part, Kuhn's *Structure*.

This [1959] symposium is devoted to psychological research on psychological research. It points to specific bias effects in the two-person social interaction of data collection. It should lead to a critical reevaluation of past research and to the introduction of new controls in the design of future experiments.

We thus will have before us today an example from an empirical science of scientific methodology. It is the purpose of this as the introductory paper to focus attention on this more general perspective. To dramatize the perspective, this dogmatic allegation can be made: *The methodological precepts guiding the concrete decisions of data collection are themselves the products of science, inductively justified and demanded. Analytical philosophy of science has not provided principles of scientific method, nor does it intend to.* Although few philosophers of science would disagree with this statement, it may contradict the prevalent attitude of dependence upon philosophy of science engendered in many of our courses introducing graduate research in psychology.

The dominant position in the philosophy of science today joins Hume in regarding any effort to justify an inductive scientific achievement in some logical or analytical way as impossible. Furthermore, this holds not only for specific inductions, but also for general principles of efficacious inductive procedure. The following quotations from the two philosophers of science working closest to psychology reiterate this point and in the process call attention to the potential psychology of science, which is our topic today. First, some quotations from Feigl (1956, pp. 22–26):

> There are no philosophical postulates of science [p. 22]. . . . The mere fact that some of the allegedly indubitable first principles have been called into doubt, indicates that they cannot be indispensable presuppositions of science [p. 24]. . . . Assumptions about the uniformity of nature are neither necessary nor effective for the justification of inductive probability. . . . This has, of course, been known ever since Hume's incisive critique of causality and induction. If we attempt to transform induction into deduction, we require premises whose validity cannot be anything but inductive. And if we try to demonstrate the (certain or even only the probable) success of inductive inference on the basis of its success to date, then we assume the very principle we propose to prove [p. 25]. . . . I fail to see the philosophical importance of any attempt in this direction. If it were the success of human adaptive learning and theorizing behavior that is to be accounted for, I would be the first to admit that this is a genuinely meaningful question – but surely a question of science, not of philosophy.

This question can indeed be answered. And the answer is clearly along the lines of the biology and psychology of knowledge. It is the same sort of question that can be raised on a more lowly level in regard to the learning and generalizing behavior of that pet of our psychologists, the white rat. Given the rat's equipment of learning capabilities, how complicated a maze will he be able to master, in how many trials, under what conditions of previous training, etc? While it is a long way from the orientation of rats in a maze to the intellectual adaptions (if I may be forgiven the irrelevant comparison) of the Newtons, Maxwells, and Einsteins in their theoretical constructions of the physical universe, the nature of the problem is the same.

Bergmann, discussing in another context the difference between the philosopher's and the scientist's tasks, has said, "The logical analysis of science is one thing, the psychology of discovery is another thing. The former is a philosophical enterprise; the latter, if we only knew more about it, would be a branch of the science of psychology" (1957, p. 51).

In these quotations the psychology of science or the empirical science of science is introduced only as background to the philosopher's delineation of philosophy's task and is thus left in an amorphous and abstract state. To make concrete the possibility of such a discipline, let us examine the methodological advances in experimental procedure over the past five decades. These have in large part been the result of inductive achievements. The discovery of practice effects in repeated measurements early called for the introduction of the control group. The discovery of an interaction between measurement and susceptibility to change called for the elimination of the pretest, and in Solomon's (1949) first presentation of his extended control group design, he reported an empirical study showing such effects. The discovery of surgical shock necessitated the introduction of the sham operation control group in ablation studies. The discovery of suggestibility in patients undergoing experimental treatments necessitated the introduction of the placebo experiment, and the possibility of similar suggestibility on the part of experimenters led to the double-blind experiment. Similarly, the discovery of halo effects, response sets, and other unwanted method factors necessitates the multitrait-multimethod test-validation matrix (Campbell & Fiske, 1959). Methodology at this practical level is an inductive achievement. Where the processes of a human observer or human subject are involved, this inductive achievement belongs to the field of psychology. The psychology of science thus delineated takes its place beside the sociology of knowledge and the history of science as a part of the science of science. It is relevant not only to the methodology of psychology, but also to the methodology of all of the sciences. In the specifics of experimental control just cited, it is particularly applicable to the science of man. A psychology of theory building and belief in theories would apply to all.

The problems and facts of a psychology of science would obviously have some parallels with learning, perceiving, and other knowledge processes. With the parallels come opportunities for analogies. If the analogies be regarded only as sources of hypotheses to be verified in the new field of application, they may be welcomed rather than shunned. With this caution in mind, one can tentatively place the psychology of science with a more general psychology of knowledge processes. In this fashion, for example, Piaget (1950) is willing to classify competing points of view in physics, in biology, and in the social sciences in terms of a conceptual scheme of development originally devised for the cognitions of children. Along different theoretical lines (Campbell, 1959, 1960), I have explored analogies between the processes of science, on the one hand, and both trial-and-error learning (1959) and the visual-perceptual achievement of distal objects on the other (1958a). It is in a similar vein that I suggest today that we examine psychology's inventory of cognitive biases to get leads as to the systematic error tendencies that we might expect of our science and of ourselves in the process of coming to know the complexities of our problem area.

When we look for an inventory of cognitive biases, one of the earliest we encounter is Francis Bacon's of 1620, in his lists of "idols" or "false images." For our immediate purpose, it is of particular interest that he generated his list from observations of his contemporary scientists and philosophers, thus performing as a psychologist of science. Let me quote briefly from his "idols."

First, he presents his general statement of the problem:

> For the mind, darkened by its covering the body, is far from being a flat, equal, and clear mirror that receives and reflects the rays without mixture, but is rather . . . an uneven mirror which imparts its own properties to different objects . . . and distorts and disfigures them. (*Advancement of learning*, Book V, Chapter IV, Paragraph 7; *Novum Organum*, Aphorisms, Book I, XLI, changed to make *mirrors* singular.)

He then goes on to specify the particular distortions to which the mind is prone. The first group of these are the "Idols of the Tribe," which he sees as "imposed upon the mind by the general nature of mankind."

1. "The human understanding, from its peculiar nature, easily supposes a greater degree of order and equality in things than it really finds."

2. (a) "When any proposition has been laid down, the human under-standing forces everything else to add fresh support and confirmation." (Aphorisms, XLVI)
   (b) "It is the peculiar and perpetual error of the human understanding to be more moved and excited by affirmatives than negatives." (XLVI)
3. "The human understanding is most excited by that which strikes and enters the mind at once and suddenly." (XLVII)
4. "The human understanding resembles not a dry light, but admits a tincture of the will and passions, which generate their own system accordingly, for man always believes more readily that which he prefers." (XLIX)
5. "Whatever strikes the senses preponderates over everything, however superior, that does not strike them." (L)
6. "The human understanding is, by its own nature, prone to abstraction, and supposes that which is fluctuating to be fixed . . . for forms are a mere fiction of the human mind, unless you will call the laws of action by that name." (LI)

A second group of biases he calls the "Idols of the Cave," in reference to Plato's parable, and refers to the biases coming from individual idiosyncrasies and preoccupations, "for everybody has his own individual den or cavern which intercepts and corrupts the light of nature, either from his own peculiar and singular disposition, or from his education . . . habit and accident" (XLII).

A third group of phantoms he calls "Idols of the Market." These are "formed by the reciprocal intercourse and society of man with man, . . . from the commerce and association of men with each other; for men converse by means of language but words are formed at the will of the generality, and there arises from a bad and unapt formation of words a wonderful obstruction to the mind" (XLIII). "For men imagine that their reason governs words, whilst in fact words react upon the understanding" (LIX). The fallacies which he sees imposed by words are of two kinds:

1. "The names of things that have no existence." (LX)
2. "The names of actual objects which are confused, badly defined, and hastily and irregularly abstracted from things." (LX)

In Bacon's fourth class are the "Idols of the Theater." These come from adherence "to the dogmas of peculiar systems of philosophy" and are so called because Bacon regards "all the systems of philosophy hitherto received or imagined, as so many plays brought out and performed, creating fictitious and theatrical worlds" (XLIV).

A recent effort of mine to summarize the unwieldy literature on constant errors, biases, illusions, and so on (Campbell, 1958b) showed research confirmation for most of Bacon's points. Their relevance to the errors to be expected in the development of a new science is argued here.

Let's begin with Bacon's first principle: "The human understanding . . . easily supposes a greater degree of order and equality in things than it really finds." Under this principle can be assembled the ubiquitous evidence of a bias toward cognitive structures or response tendencies that fail of perfect matching of the environment in the direction of too great simplicity or symmetry, too little "information," too few parameters. Such errors predominate strongly over errors of overcomplication, even though there are many more possibilities for the latter (Campbell, 1958b, pp. 342–344; Campbell & Gruen, 1958).

Two evolutionary considerations anticipate this error. First, structural limitations will have this effect. The evolutionary sequence is from simple mechanisms that are responsive and adaptive to the most frequent aspects of a very few environmental parameters. Environmental pressures lead to increasing complexity and subtlety of fit between behavior and environment, but at all stages, structural and behavioral complexity is finite and lags behind full environmental complexity, leading to systematic "mistakes" in ecologically atypical environments, mistakes that are the counterpart of an oversimplified cognitive structure.

A second source comes from considerations of economy in problem-solving strategy. The cost of the lost behavioral output in an error of overcomplication is greater than for an error of oversimplification, and a strategy of testing simple hypotheses first could be expected to be an adaptive one, leading, nonetheless, to a predictable directionality to the average error, rather than an unbiased distribution of errors around the correct answer. Somewhat related is a law of least effort, built into vertebrates in the form of finding the simpler of two otherwise equivalent response patterns or cognitions the more rewarding.

At the level of the psychology of science, several predictions can be drawn:

1. The scientific formulations of any given period will in general turn out to be more simple than those accepted as true at a later date.

2. Of two inadequate theories of comparable inefficiency in explaining the data, the simpler will have the more fanatical adherence of its originator.
3. Of two adequate theories, the simpler will be more accepted as true by the scientific community as a whole.

Of these predictions, probably only the first will strike you as exceptionable, and that because of those instances in science in which a highly complex and qualified theory has been replaced by a simpler one based upon a novel perspective. What seems to be the case is that within any one system of conceptualization, increases in scientific knowledge have increased the complexity of the theory, but that whole conceptual systems have occasionally been discarded for elegant novel simplifications, which themselves then represent a first step in a new series of increasing complexity of conceptualization.

Bacon's second Idol of the Tribe is even more strongly confirmed in our experience. It reads: "When any proposition has been once laid down, the human understanding forces everything else to add fresh support and confirmation. It is the peculiar and perceptual error of the human understanding to be more moved and excited by affirmatives than negatives." We may take as substantiating this principle all of those studies in which set has reduced the threshold for expected events and increased the threshold for nonexpected ones. The Galloway experiment (Galloway, 1946; Wyatt & Campbell, 1951) elegantly shows this by demonstrating the liability to accurate perception of premature guesses as to the content of a slide gradually being brought into focus. The principle is continuous with the tendency to repeat responses even though they have not been reinforced, and just because they are familiar, as found in the law of exercise, in Spence's (1956) interpretation of $_sH_R$[1] in his learning theory, and in the development of norms on the part of solitary observers in Sherif's (1936) autokinetic experiments. The specific interpretation of the effect favored by Bacon, that is, the tendency to be more excited by affirmatives than by negatives, has received confirmation in many studies of problem solving (e.g., Hovland, 1952) and in a study of guessing and intermittent reinforcement presented by Shelly (1959) at these current meetings.

In the psychology of science the principle is similarly ubiquitous. As informal comments on the liability of premature theories, note the following, first from Tolman (1932):

> And once set up, a system probably does as much harm as it does good. It serves as a sort of sacred grating behind which each novice is

commanded to kneel in order that he may never see the real world, save through its interstices.

Krech and Crutchfield (1948) comment in a similar vein:

> This principle also helps us to understand the tenacity with which people hold on to "disproved" scientific theories or economic and political dogmas. No matter how much evidence one can bring to bear that a scientific theory does not fit the known facts, scientists are reluctant to give it up until one can give them another integration in place of the old. In the absence of some other way of organizing facts, people will frequently hold onto the old, for no other reason than that.

From the discussive writing of scientists, such comments could be duplicated in great number.

More factual verification comes from the level of methodology. The classic experiment of Stanton and Baker (1942) showed interviews to be biased by the interviewers' expectations. In more recent experimentation on the interview recording process, Smith and Hyman (1950) have demonstrated a similar effect. Field research on interviewer bias shows the same findings (e.g., Wyatt & Campbell, 1950). The effect also necessitates the placebo experiment, in its double-blind form as far as the scientist's expectations are concerned. As an effect upon respondents rather than experimenters, it becomes the commitment effect, demonstrated by Crespi (1948) and Hovland, Lumsdaine, and Sheffield (1949). This effect reduces responsiveness to persuasive efforts and makes desirable the abandonment of the pretest in studies in which truly random assignment to treatments can be achieved (Campbell, 1957). Kennedy (1939) and Kennedy and Uphoff (1939) (1939b) have demonstrated the bias in recording errors in extrasensory perception experiments, in which the preponderant error is to record the presented stimulus and the guess as the same when in fact they are different, rather than to record them as different when in fact they are the same.

Bacon's third Idol of the Tribe states that "The human understanding is most excited by that which strikes and enters the mind at once and suddenly." If we expand this by including the conditions of stimulus strikingness, we can use it as an introduction to adaptation-level (Helson, 1959) or contrast biases. Whenever human judges are used as a measuring device, their calibration is subject to systematic unconscious alterations, so that the central tendency of the stimulus context to which they are adapted comes to appear as neutral or intermediate, whereas the stimuli that deviate most from this adaptation level appear most striking. If in the course of judgments the central tendency of the presented stimuli shifts, this produces a shift in judgment standards of which the judge is unaware. Such effects have been found for every type of stimulus attribute for which they have been examined, including water temperature, weight, beauty, pleasantness, loudness, pitch (Campbell, Hunt, & Lewis, 1957, 1958; Jones, 1957). Of these studies, the last group are clearly appropriate to the psychology of science, inasmuch as they deal with an arena in which human observers have not yet been replaced by more stable instruments. In every research setting in social and clinical psychology in which raters are employed to record behavior or to code protocols, such effects will be present, and the research must be designed so as to prevent their being confounded with the crucial experimental comparisons. The following anecdote serves to illustrate the principle's relevance for sciences such as anthropology: In the last several years, considerable numbers of Russian experts from American universities have been sent on visits to the USSR. In part, they have had different itineraries, some going first to Leningrad and the others first to Moscow, and so on. In comparing notes later, they found themselves in disagreement as to which Russian city (e.g., Leningrad or Moscow) was the more drab and which the more lively. These differences in opinion have turned out to be correlated with the differences in itinerary: Whichever city one visited first seemed the more drab. Against the adaptation level based upon experience with familiar U.S. cities, the first Russian city seemed drab and cold indeed. But the stay in Russia modified the adaptation level, changed the implicit standard of reference so that the second city was judged against a more lenient standard. (I am indebted to Deming Brown and Raymond Mack for this information.)

I also find in this principle of stimulus relativism an explanation for the personality psychologist's and social psychologist's stubborn interest in individual differences to the neglect of motives and processes that all persons have in common. Individual differences from the norm are continually striking, whereas the norm itself adapts out and becomes a part of the unnoticed background. I would be willing to judge this a chronic bias tendency in our science, one that we can see recurring on the part of each of our graduate students even when we have partially overcome it ourselves.

Bacon's fourth idol introduces motivational distortion: "The human understanding resembles not a dry light, but admits a tincture of the will and passions which generate their own system accordingly, for man always believes more readily that which he prefers." We have just gone through a 20-year period in which social-personality research has been dominated by efforts verifying this proposition. Questionnaire research has amply confirmed the correlation of beliefs and preferences (e.g., Smith, 1947). The tremendous literature on autistic perception (Murphy, 1947) and motivated perceptual selectivity (Bruner, 1951; Postman, 1951, 1953) has overwhelmingly documented the point. This research background provided by social scientists reflexively justifies a considerable skepticism of the work of fallible, human, and highly motivated social scientists in motive-laden problem areas. Although I share this skepticism on occasion, the emphasis is often so one-sided as to overlook the necessity of motivation in the achievement of objective knowledge.

The statement that scientific behavior is often functional, goal-directed, and motivated, rather than a random and disinterested search for truth, should not be confused with the problem of the accuracy of the models of the environment or recipes for behavior that are achieved. Let us simplify this distinction by looking at the rat in the maze: Is his problem-solving activity value-free? No, it is not. He is moved by the most ultimate of values. Hunger, thirst, or the need to avoid cats or shocks has set the problem for him. Is the knowledge of the maze that he achieves biased on this account? Does he delude himself as to the nature of reality? Do autisms and wishful thinking lead him to illusory predicates for behavior? Usually not. Usually, he displays an admirable objectivity, and soon achieves a stable model of the maze that serves him without need of further modification. His knowledge of the maze is selective, is functional, but is not for that reason biased or errorful.

In the social sciences, there are many areas of inquiry that the normally motivated tribe members would never undertake. Some maladjustment or social background divergence from the norm may be essential to provide the motivation to undertake the inquiry. And in addition, as Park (1928) and Veblen (1919) have pointed out, the status of being culturally uprooted provides special advantages of perspective that the undisturbed ingroup member lacks. We should expect, therefore, to find anxious persons studying anxiety, to find rigid persons studying rigidity, minority group members studying prejudice, normless sociologists studying social norms, rebellious sons studying authority systems, and so forth. This interaction of the variety of motivation patterns and the topics of inquiry should advance rather than hinder science where reality testing is done. But the psychological fact of an omnipresent tendency toward motivational bias fully justifies those many aspects of experimental procedure, objective scoring, instrumentation, and the like that guard against self-deception. In addition, recognizing that for many of the important problems in the domain of the social sciences no reality testing is possible should make us cautious about using the name of science for our pronouncements in these areas.

A ubiquitous bias, which we might approximately place with Bacon's Idols of the Marketplace, can be called *conformity-induced pseudo-confirmation*. Tremendously important in the establishment of both common-sense and scientific knowledge is consensual validation, the confirmation of observations by other persons. Just as one eye's view confirms that of the other, so one person's report validates another's. But the gain is more than just validation. If the images of the two eyes are in predominant agreement, so that triangulation on the same object is confirmed, then the slight discrepancies present due to parallax add a depth dimension not available to either eye alone. So also in social knowing, if observers duplicate each other's reports enough to confirm that they are talking about the same thing, then the discrepancies in their reports attributable to their separate points of vantage can make possible through triangulation a depth of interpretation that none of the solitary views would provide.

There are two aspects to this process: On the one hand, each person must describe the world as uniquely seen from his own particular point of vantage. On the other hand, each must take seriously the reports of others as to what they see. In many settings, these two essentials can run counter to each other. Insofar as systematic biases have been observed, they are overwhelmingly as an excess of the second aspect, that is, a tendency to contaminate one's reports in the direction of agreement with what others are reporting and thus to fail to report what is uniquely available from one's own perspective. In addition, the agreement achieved represents pseudo-confirmation. The tremendous literature on conformity and suggestion shows how strong and persuasive this effect is. It could scarcely fail to operate among teams of scientists. It is no doubt one of the human bias tendencies that make possible the existence of "schools" of thought in the underdeveloped areas of science.

It is true of these biases in general (with the exception of adaptation level or stimulus relativism) that they are most pronounced when the situation is ambiguous and ill-defined, and where reality testing and feedback are lacking. The literature is rife with ground glass screens, near-threshold exposures, withholding knowledge of results, and so on. It is also true that the biases operate more strongly under conditions of frustration and overmotivation (e.g., Postman & Bruner, 1948). As seen in the light of these considerations, the problems of bias are more acute in the social sciences than in the physical sciences. We can more readily trust Archimedes when he says that a lever has moved a stone than Demosthenes when he says that a speech has moved an audience. The social sciences have, therefore, a greater need for an "anxious" experimental methodology full of elaborate precautions against possible biases. Our methodology is in fact much more rigorous than that of the successful sciences at comparable levels of development. This is as it should be. But we are also generating in each generation of training and experience in social science a number of disillusioned persons who come to deny the fruitfulness of the scientific approach in the model of the physical sciences. Efforts to make a scientific contribution in the social sciences can generate some such ambivalence in all of us. An analysis of our situation in terms of a final bias, *causal misperception* or *continguity-conditioned hostility,* may give us insight into one of the sources of this disillusionment.

The role of experimentation and scientific method in science is an essentially negative one of rejecting inadequate hypotheses. The sources of the hypotheses being tested are various and are formally irrelevant to the question of validity. The number of possible wrong theories is infinitely large. The number of theories consistent with any extended body of research findings is relatively small. Inevitably the process of experimentation will be rejective of the great majority of the theories that are tested. Each instance of confrontation of theory with experimental data is a perceptual or conditioning experience for the experimenter. Each rejection of theory will produce a frustration-induced hostility or a causal perception of blaming (Heider, 1944; Michotte, 1946). In any one instance, the conditioned hostility might be associated with the theory under test as one of the concomitants. However, primitive emotional conditioning or causal perception is primarily a matter of pure contiguity, and the process of experimenting is equally available to be perceived as to blame, or as the conditioned stimulus for the conditioned hostility reaction. Two other conditions may make it the more likely target. First, the researcher is apt to use different theories in the course of different investigations, and the apparatus of science may turn out to be the only common component in a number of such experiences. In addition, the experimental process may be the more striking stimulus event. The theoretical belief may have been present for a long and indefinite time, whereas the experimental process constitutes a defined, discrete stimulus event immediately prior to the painful outcome, and thus is ideally placed both to be perceived as the source of causation and to be the conditioned stimulus for the hostile reaction. From introspective evidence of encountering negative results from my own experiments, I feel that we social scientists are human or animal enough so that this contiguity is a very real factor in our attitudes toward the scientific process.

Note

1. $_sH_R$ is habit strength, one of several theoretical parameters S_1 (stimulus) and R (response); others include D (drive) and K (learned incentive).

Preamble references

Campbell, D. T. (in press). The social psychology of scientific validity: An epistemological perspective and a personalized history. To appear in W. R. Shadish (Ed.), *Social psychology of science*. New York: Guilford Press.

Cicchetti, D. V. (1991). The reliability of peer review for manuscript and grant submissions: A cross-disciplinary investigation. *Behavioral and Brain Sciences, 14,* 119–186.

Gholson, B., Shadish, W. R., Neimeyer, R. A., & Houts, A. C. (Eds). (1989). *Psychology of science: Contributions to metascience*. New York: Cambridge University Press.

Kuhn, T. S. (1962). *The structure of scientific revolutions*. Chicago: University of Chicago Press.

Rosenthal, R. (with G. Persinger, L. Vikan-Kline, & R. Mulry). (1963). The role of the research assistant in the mediation of experimenter bias. *Journal of Personality, 31,* 313–335.

Rosenthal, R. (1976). *The experimenter effects in behavioral research* (enlarged ed.). New York: Irvington.

Rosenwein, R. (in press). Social influence in science: Agreement and dissent in achieving scientific consensus. To appear in W. R. Shadish, *Social Psychology of Science*. New York: Guilford Press.

Shadish, W. R. (in press.). *Social psychology of science*. New York: Guilford Press.

1959 references

Bacon, F. (1620). *Novum organum.* (Trans. in J. Devey, *The physical and metaphysical works of Lord Bacon.* London: Henry G. Bohn, 1853.)

Bergmann, G. (1957). *Philosophy of science.* Madison: University of Wisconsin Press.

Bruner, J. S. (1951). Personality dynamics and the process of perceiving. In R. S. Blake & G. V. Ramsey (Eds.), *Perception: An approach to personality.* New York: Ronald.

Campbell, D. T. (1957). Factors relevant to the validity of experiments in social settings. *Psychological Bulletin, 54*(4), 297–312.

Campbell, D. T. (1958a). Common fate, similarity, and other indices of the status of aggregates of persons as social entities. *Behavioral Science, 3*(1), 14–25.

Campbell, D. T. (1958b). Systematic error on the part of human links in communication systems. *Information and Control, 1*(4), 334–369.

Campbell, D. T. (1959). Methodological suggestions from a comparative psychology of knowledge processes. *Inquiry, 2,* 159–182.

Campbell, D. T. (1960). Blind variation and selective survival as a general strategy in knowledge processes. In M. C. Yovits & S. H. Cameron (Eds.), *Self-organizing systems* (pp. 205–231). Oxford: Pergamon Press. (Revised and extended as: Blind variation and selective retention in creative thought as in other knowledge processes. *Psychological Review, 67*[6], 380–400, 1960.)

Campbell, D. T., & Fiske, D. W. (1959). Convergent and discriminant validation by the multitrait-multimethod matrix. *Psychological Bulletin, 56*(2), 81–105.

Campbell, D. T., & Gruen, W. (1958). Progression from simple to complex as a molar law of learning. *Journal of General Psychology, 59,* 237–244.

Campbell, D. T., Hunt, W. A., & Lewis, N. A. (1957). The effects of assimilation and contrast in judgments of clinical materials. *American Journal of Psychology, 70*(3), 347–360.

Campbell, D. T., Hunt, W. A., & Lewis, N. A. (1958). The relative susceptibility of two rating scales to disturbances resulting from shifts in stimulus context. *Journal of Applied Psychology, 42*(4), 213–217.

Campbell, D. T., Lewis, N. A., & Hunt, W. A. (1958). Context effects with judgmental language that is absolute, extensive, and extra-experimentally anchored. *Journal of Experimental Psychology, 55*(3), 220–228.

Crespi, L. P. (1948). The interview effect in polling. *Public Opinion Quarterly, 12,* 99–111.

Feigl, H. (1956). Some major issues and developments in the philosophy of science of logical empiricism. In H. Feigl & M. Scriven (Eds.), *The foundations of science and the concepts of psychology and psychoanalysis,* Vol. 1 of Minnesota Studies in the Philosophy of Science (pp. 3–37). Minneapolis: University of Minnesota Press.

Galloway, D. W. (1946). An experimental investigation of structural lag in perception. *American Psychologist, 1,* 450. (Abstract)

Heider, F. (1944). Social perception and phenomenal causality. *Psychological Review, 51,* 358–374.

Helson, H. (1959). Adaptation level theory. In S. Koch (Ed.), *Psychology: A study of a science,* Vol. 1, *Sensory, perceptual, and physiological formulations.* New York: McGraw-Hill.

Hovland, C. I. (1952). A "communication analysis" of concept learning. *Psychological Review, 59,* 461–472.

Hovland, C. I., Lumsdaine, A. A., & Sheffield, F. D. (1949). *Experiments on mass communication.* Princeton, NJ: Princeton University Press.

Jones, N. F. (1957). Context effects in judgment as a function of experience. *Journal of Clinical Psychology, 13,* 379–382.

Kennedy, J. L. (1939). A methodological review of extra-sensory perception. *Psychological Bulletin, 36,* 59–103.

Kennedy, J. L., & Uphoff, H. F. (1939). Experiments on the nature of extra-sensory perception. III. The recording error criticisms of extra-chance scores. *Journal of Parapsychology, 3,* 226–245.

Krantz, D. L. (1959). Stimulus and response relationship in absolute judgment. Unpublished M.A. thesis, Northwestern University, August 1959. (Published as Krantz, D. L., & Campbell, D. T., Separating perceptual and linguistic effects of context shifts upon absolute judgments. *Journal of Experimental Psychology, 62*[1], 35–42, 1961.)

Krech, D., & Crutchfield, R. S. (1948). *Theory and problems of social psychology.* New York: McGraw Hill.

Michotte, A. E. (1946). *La perception de la causalité,* Vol. VI, *Etudes Psychology.* Louvain: Inst. sup. de Philosophe. (Translated as *The perception of causality,* London: Methuen, 1963.)

Murphy, G. (1947). *Personality.* New York: Harper.

Park, R. E. (1928). Human migration and the marginal man. *American Journal of Sociology, 33,* 881–893.

Piaget, J. (1950). *Introduction a l'epistemologie genetique.* I. *La pensee mathematique.* II. *La pensee physique.* III. *La pensee biologique, la pensee psychologique, et la pensee sociologique.* Paris: Presses Universitaires de France.

Postman, L. (1951). Toward a general theory of cognition. In J. A. Rohrer & M. Sherif, *Social psychology at the crossroads.* New York: Harper.

Postman, L. (1953). The experimental analysis of motivational factors in perception. In J. S. Brown, et al., *Current theory and research in motivation.* Lincoln: University of Nebraska Press.

Postman, L., & Bruner, J. S. (1948). Perception under stress. *Psychological Review, 55,* 314–323.

Shelly, M. W. (1959). Further studies of factors affecting the probability of changing responses on successive trials. *American Psychologist, 14,* 405 (abstract).

Smith, G. H. (1947). Beliefs in statements labeled fact and rumor. *Journal of Abnormal and Social Psychology, 42,* 80–90.

Smith, H. L., & Hyman, H. (1950). The biasing effect of interviewer expectations on survey results. *Public Opinion Quarterly, 14,* 491–501.

Solomon, R. W. (1949). An extension of control group design. *Psychological Bulletin, 46,* 137–150.

Spence, K. W. (1956). *Behavior theory and conditioning.* New Haven: Yale University Press.

Stanton, F., & Baker, K. H. (1942). Interviewer bias and the recall of incompletely learned materials. *Sociometry, 5,* 123–134.

Veblen, T. (1919). The intellectual pre-eminence of Jews in modern Europe. *Political Science Quarterly, 34,* 33–42.

Wyatt, D. F., & Campbell, D. T. (1950). A study of interviewer bias as related to interviewers' expectations and own opinions. *International Journal of Opinion and Attitude Research, 4*(1), 77–83.

Wyatt, D. F., & Campbell, D. T. (1951). On the liability of stereotype or hypothesis. *Journal of Abnormal and Social Psychology, 46*(4), 496–500.

PART I

Research on interpersonal expectations

3. Introduction to research on interpersonal expectations

JOHN M. DARLEY AND KATHRYN C. OLESON

More than any other individual, Robert Rosenthal has put the concept of the *self-fulfilling prophecy* on the research agenda of the psychological community. Following his lead, other psychologists have moved the self-fulfilling prophecy from the psychological agenda to the national social policy agenda, drawing attention to the manifold implications that the existence of self-fulfilling prophecies has for interactional processes in legal, educational, organizational, and other social settings.

Putting an issue on such diverse agendas is no mean feat, and it is worth tracing how Rosenthal accomplished this. This answer is a sobering one; it required not only an incisive grasp of an important concept, but an incredibly large commitment of disciplined experimental energy over a period of years.[1]

Nor can one argue that Rosenthal chose the maximally ingratiating and tactful way to introduce the construct of self-fulfilling prophecies to the psychological research community. In the 1960s, word swept the research community that an individual from the Dakotas, and then from Harvard, was demonstrating *experimenter bias* effects that fundamentally called into question the interpretations of the results of many experiments. We suspect that the general reaction of the research community was similar to the reactions of the corners of the community that the first author observed: initial resistance, later annoyed acceptance of the implications for the design of research, and still later the realization that an extremely general human phenomenon had been illuminated.[2]

Recall the sequence of events and discoveries that led to the recognition of the self-fulfilling prophecy effect. The first set of studies demonstrated the phenomenon of experimenter bias, the tendency for experimenters in behavioral research to obtain the results they expect solely because they expect those results. Rosenthal's 1966 book on *Experimen-*

ter Effects in Behavioral Research gives us the best overview of those studies. Looking backward from the 1990s, one can see the compelling and calm case being presented for the modifications of experimental design and procedure that are now standard in psychological experimentation: the tendency to keep the persons running the experiment blind to subjects' experimental conditions if possible and minimizing experimenters' contact with subjects (through the use of tape recordings, etc.). Rosenthal also cautioned us to use expectancy-control groups when they are required, to use more than one experimenter to run subjects, and, if possible, to use experimenters who are carefully trained but are not personally overinvested in the outcome of the research.[3]

That the implications of the underlying dynamics of the expectancy-confirmation effect went well beyond the domain of experimenter-induced bias was called to our attention by the publication of Rosenthal and Jacobson's *Pygmalion in the Classroom* in 1968. This study has a flamboyance that strikes us as atypical of Rosenthal's previous research strategy for the experimenter bias work. Instead of building up a tightly connected mosaic of studies that gave a richly detailed picture of the processes, Rosenthal and Jacobson reported a single study in which they attempted to show that teacher expectancies in real classroom settings, working over the course of the school year, could affect such central and politically charged dispositions as the intelligence of school children. In terms of the familiar sports metaphor, this experiment was the research equivalent of the *long bomb*, the football play that attempts to score a quick touchdown rather than building the slow accumulation of gains.

As will be remembered, there was considerable debate about whether the ball had, in fact, gotten across the goal line. A number of critics questioned whether the data from that study actually warranted many of the conclusions that were drawn from it (Barber & Silver, 1968; Elashoff & Snow, 1971; Jensen, 1969; Thorndike, 1968). But Rosenthal (1968, 1969a, 1969b) vigorously defended his study and later defended the general existence of the self-fulfilling prophecy effect by reviewing the quickly developing base of experimental studies, done by his associates and others, that demonstrated the effect in a variety of more tightly controlled settings.

In conducting this defense, Rosenthal characteristically drew on another interest of his, which involved the proper procedures for statistically combining the results of independent studies. *Meta-analytic procedures*, as these procedures came to be called, were first used to assess the evidence for the existence, generality, and magnitude of self-fulfilling prophecy effects (see Rosenthal & Rubin, 1978). Rosenthal and Rubin's famous review of 345 studies on interpersonal expectancy effects drew critical responses from some commentators, yet few could deny the existence and the significant impact of these effects. Later, and more scientifically interestingly, as the analytic possibilities of meta-analyses became better understood, they were used to assess the support for various postulated mechanisms of transmission of expectancy effects (see Harris & Rosenthal, 1985, 1986).[4]

This suggests that the concern for demonstrating conclusions about expectancy effects became the stimulus for the development of a generally useful analytic technique, meta-analysis. We now have a well-formulated set of procedures for meta-analysis and, perhaps more important, a sense of how, in the hands of inventive and disciplined researchers, meta-analysis can be made to cast an admittedly somewhat cold, but illuminating, light on the results of original research. Meta-analysis has become the "weapon of choice" in many empirical reviews.[5]

Self-fulfilling prophecy research

What has happened to self-fulfilling prophecy research since Rosenthal's earlier work? Following the publication of Rosenthal and Jacobson's (1968) *Pygmalion in the Classroom,* researchers interested in the self-fulfilling prophecy turned their attention in three directions: (1) analyzing the psychological components of the effect, (2) examining the possible mechanisms for the transference of the expectancy from the perceiver to the target, and (3) constructing some sort of process account that embedded the effect within it. We will examine each of these three areas in order and then close by summarizing our perceptions of the present state of the field and by considering areas of future experimentation.

Constructing the psychological processes underlying the effect

One way of describing the impact of Rosenthal and Jacobson's study is that it cued psychologists in to the social importance of a phenomenon that they had previously regarded as having largely methodological implications, and largely labor-intensive and unpleasant methodological implications at that. The psychological community, its interest engaged, responded in a predictable way. It carried out an exquisitely thoughtful and nuanced analysis of the possible psychological processes underlying the effect. Seeing a possible psychologically fascinating and socially important outcome, it concerned itself with explicating the processes that led to that outcome.

At first, our attention became focused on Merton's statement: "The self-fulfilling prophecy is, in the beginning, a *false* definition of the situation evoking a new behavior which makes the originally false conception come *true*. The specious validity of the self-fulfilling prophecy perpetuates a reign of error. For the prophet will cite the actual course of events as proof that he was right from the very beginning" (1948, p. 195). Quite soon, the richly enigmatic possibilities contained in the phrase "became true" were recognized. True to whom, and in what sense true? These questions led to distinctions that have proved useful in differentiating a set of four closely related effects (Darley & Fazio, 1980).

From the development of attribution theory (Jones & Davis, 1965), we were coming to understand that a perceiver observes the actions of others but interprets those actions in the light of possible underlying dispositions revealed. Expectancies, in a way called to our attention by Bruner (1951), guided those interpretations. If a perceiver expects a target to "be" altruistic, mendacious, clumsy, or graceful, then the expectancies may color the perceiver's judgments of actions by the target that are not actually altruistic, mendacious, clumsy, or graceful. This is generally referred to as a *perceptual confirmation* effect. It includes the tendency to see ambiguous behaviors of the target as expectancy-confirming, to discount or attributionally dismiss behaviors that do not fit the expectancy, to see behaviors that do fit the expectancy as highly typical of the actor (Darley & Gross, 1983) and the memory processes associated with these perceptual errors (see Sherman, Judd, & Park, 1989).

A second effect, the effect at the heart of self-fulfilling prophecy, is *behavioral confirmation*. For behavioral confirmation to occur, the expectancies actually lead to new behavior that confirms the expectancy. It is not merely that the perceiver is dismissing contradictory behavior or seeing ambiguous behavior as confirming; the target is acting in line with the initial expectancy. A couple of links in the theoretical chain are missing here; it is necessary to specify how the perceptions held by one individual cause alterations of the behavior patterns of another individual. Logically, it must be some alteration in behavior on the part of the perceiver that provokes the answering alteration in behavior on the part of the target. However, to go back one step earlier in the process, it is likely that for the perceiver to behave in such a way, the perceiver be mistaken about the source of the target's behavior, locating the behavioral source in the dispositions of the target.

This first link in the chain – the mistaken source of the target's behavior – can now be specified; it has been demonstrated in an impressive and counterintuitive set of studies by Jones and his colleagues (Jones, 1979) and others conducting research on *correspondence bias*, a perceptual error of such general import that Ross (1977) referred to it as the "fundamental attribution error." In other words, the perceiver sees the target as having a hostile disposition, rather than reacting in a way that is driven by the situation. Seeing a hostile person, the perceiver acts in the future toward that person in ways consistent with that expectation and provokes hostile responses from the target, thus "ful filling" the prophecy. Research on correspondence bias indicates that people do have this general tendency: Perceivers exaggerate the degree to which actors' behaviors are generated by their dispositions rather than by situational demands.

Gilbert, Jones, and their colleagues (Gilbert & Jones, 1986; Gilbert, Jones, & Pelham, 1987; Gilbert, Pelham, & Krull, 1988) realized that this misattribution of behavior process went even further and was even more counterintuitive than we had originally realized. Recall how we described the behavioral confirmation process: "logically, it must be some alteration in behavior on the part of the perceiver that provokes the answering alteration in behavior on the part of the target." But what this means is that the perceiver must be making what would seem to be a particularly egregious form of the fundamental attribution error. He or she must not notice, or give insufficient weight to, the role of *his or her own actions* in provoking the responding actions of the targets. It is as if a puppeteer genuinely believed that the puppet was alive!

Remarkably, people do make this error. In one memorable experiment on the *perceiver-induced constraint* bias (Gilbert & Jones, 1986), perceivers who directed a target to answer a set of questions with either a set of liberal or conservative answers saw the target as having the liberal or conservative disposition corresponding to the answers that the target gave, even when the perceivers know that those answers were scripted and, obviously, that the kind of answer given was dictated by the perceiver's own actions.

Return now to the question of the existence of behavioral confirmation effects. Do people sometimes behave toward others in ways that elicit expectancy-confirming behaviors from those other people? The evidence is now undeniable that they do. An elegant study by Snyder, Tanke, and Berscheid (1977) found that when male subjects spoke over an intercom system to a female subject who they thought was very attractive, they treated her as if she were more attractive (by acting more friendly, open, and sociable) and she responded as if she indeed were attractive (i.e., she acted more friendly, likable, and sociable), as assessed by judges' ratings of the men's and women's responses. Word, Zanna, and Cooper (1974) found similar results with black and white job candidates. Black candidates were interviewed in a less immediate manner (the interviewer sat farther away from them, made more speech errors, and took less time to give the interview) than white candidates. In response, the black candidates tended to receive lower performance ratings. Snyder and Swann (1978), using a similar conceptual design, found that subjects who had initially been labeled hostile were treated in a more hostile manner and later behaved in more hostile ways in a different setting.[6] These studies (and many others; see Snyder, 1991, for an extensive review) provide converging evidence that targets' behavior changes in response to the other person's expectancy.

A third possible effect, one that is often included under the heading of behavioral confirmation, is that the target does not merely change his or her behavior in that specific context, but rather in all future interactions with that perceiver. An implicit social contract has developed between the two individuals in which each agrees to take on certain roles with one another (Goffman, 1959). The expectancy has developed into a definite role for the target person; therefore, the target person has been permanently changed in future interactions with the other.

A final possible effect of the self-fulfilling prophecy chain, and a socially frightening one, is that of personality change on the part of the target. The psychological processes underlying that change are as follows: Targets may conclude that the behavior they performed "under the influence" of the perceiving individual reflects their underlying personalities. Again, research suggests that this can happen; an elegant study by Fazio, Effrein, and Falender (1981) suggests that if individuals are asked questions designed to elicit specific responses, they will not only respond in that given manner, but will describe themselves on personality scales as persons who possess the trait that underlies the behavior. Their initial responses also carry over to behaviors in a different setting. Recent research by Tice (1987) also found that similarly situationally elicited behavior can lead individuals to see their personalities differently and to act differently in later situations. The "reign of error" seems far-reaching, indeed, for not only do perceivers believe that their expectancies were true, at least sometimes the targets also believe them and come to alter their perceptions of their own personalities.

Transmission mechanisms

Return now to a question that we raised earlier: How is the perceiver's expectancy transferred from the perceiver to the target? What are the mechanisms involved? In the early 1970s, Rosenthal (1973, 1974) proposed four possible groups of factors mediating the teacher-expectancy effect; these mediating variables can also be applied more generally to expectancy effects. First, there is the climate that teachers create for high-expectancy students. Teachers may be warmer and more socially supportive of these students. Teachers also may give feedback more in tune with the high-expectancy students' behavior, being more receptive to correct and incorrect responses. A third factor is that teachers may teach high-expectancy students more information and harder information. Finally, teachers may increase high-expectancy students' output by giving them more opportunities to respond.

Harris and Rosenthal (1985) summarized the evidence for the four mediating variables by meta-analyzing 31 behavior categories to determine by which behaviors the expectations were transmitted. Overall, they found strong support for the four-factor theory.[7] These meta-analyses also found strong support for the importance of nonverbal communication in the transference of the expectancy. Rosenthal had long been interested in *nonverbal communication mechanisms,* those spontaneous and often nonvoluntary signals, such as smiles, frowns, eye blinks, and voice tone shifts, by means of which we convey clues about our internal states to others (Rosenthal, 1979, 1985; Rosenthal, Hall, DiMatteo, Rogers, & Archer, 1979). Thus, he had been alerted to the existence of these nonverbal channels of communication as possible mediators of expectancy confirmation effects. Eye contact, smiles, nods, and cues that provoke feelings of social distance all proved to be significant mediators of the self-fulfilling prophecy effect.

Drawing on his earlier four-factor theory of expectancy mediation and his research on nonverbal communication, Rosenthal (1989) has recently proposed his affect-effort theory of self-fulfilling prophecies. He maintains that the mechanisms for the transference of the expectancy from the perceiver to the target can be mapped onto the dimensions of *affect* and *effort*. Affect, he argues, is transmitted primarily through nonverbal means, whereas effort is communicated primarily through verbal means. In a classroom setting, teachers convey their high expectancies through warm responses to students and by putting more time and energy into teaching them.

When searching for other possible mediating factors, we were struck by the potential importance of *bystanders* to the interaction. Does the occurrence of the self-fulfilling prophecy require, or is it amplified by, bystanders to the perceiver–target interaction? Putting the question generally, is it the case that my expectancies, as perceiver, are simply transmitted to the target, or are processes required that bring in the other participants in the interaction? It is worth considering what these processes might be. Two general classes strike us as possible.

The target perceives differential treatment. Recall the Rosenthal and Jacobson study. In each class, some students were singled out as those who would "bloom" during the year. Therefore, others were implicitly identified as "regulars." Did the teacher treat those two classes of children differently, and did the students perceive these differences? More specifically, did the "late bloomers" realize that the teachers were treating them differently, and then infer conclusions about themselves and teacher expectations from that treatment? Rosenthal's four-factor approach suggests this comparative component. He discusses expectancy transmission in classrooms where students are able to compare, for instance, the feedback given to them, as opposed to the teacher's "pet," or to see that some students are receiving more materials than they are.

Bystanders perceive and act on differences. Bystanders may also be aware of the differential treatment. Consider that even quite young students are capable of drawing the appropriate inferences from a teacher's differential treatment of children (Lord, Umezaki, & Darley, 1990). This would seem most important when the expectancy being conveyed is a negative one. If a teacher treats a child as stupid in a classroom, the other children are going to catch on, see that child as stupid, and probably treat him or her as stupid. This seems likely to amplify the impact of the processes that arise directly from the teacher's expectations. The stereotyped child, assigned to the lowest reading group by the teacher, finds that he or she is also not taken seriously as an intellect by the other children. It is hard not to think that this joint message, with its apparently independent sources of converging inter-pretation, will not be seen as more convincing by the target.

As we read the evidence, expectancy amplification processes taking place via bystanders are not *required* for the occurrence of the self-fulfilling prophecy. Some of the original experimental demonstrations of the effect, exactly because they were concerned with demonstrating it in its purest form, did not have bystanders present and yet found the effect (Snyder et al., 1977; Word, Zanna, & Cooper, 1974). Interesting recent work conducted by Dov Eden in organizational settings (dis-cussed in this volume) further suggests that social comparison is not necessary for the self-fulfilling prophecy to occur. By raising a man-ager's expectations about an entire group, the whole group shows increases in productivity. The increases did not seem to depend on group members' awareness of differential treatment. However, it strikes us that the possible contributing role of various expectancy amplifica-tion processes has not been systematically examined and should be addressed in future research.

Interaction process theories and limits on the self-fulfilling prophecy effect

During the early to mid-1980s, a number of psychologists pointed out that the existence of self-fulfilling prophecy effects implies a process organization of social interaction, and that this process takes place in all interactions, whether they result in self-fulfilling prophecies or not. It is therefore useful to postulate a general social interaction sequence that can accommodate self-fulfilling prophecy effects. Darley and Fazio (1980) postulated one such sequence, in which each actor, perceiver or target, interpreted the meaning of the latter's action in the light of his or her own expectancies and understandings of the situation and then re-sponded accordingly. Perhaps because of its generality, this conceptual-ization of the interaction process has received some acceptance.[8]

If encasing the self-fulfilling prophecy effect in a general social inter-action sequence went some way toward dispelling the apparent magic of its occurrence, some mystery remained. The original formulations of the effect made it seem ubiquitous. Therefore, a second generation of studies was conducted that suggested qualifications on the general effect. Noting that the classic demonstration of the effect was done with the target unaware of the existence of the expectancy about him, Hilton and Darley (1985) made the target aware of the expectancy. They demonstrated that in at least some instances the target was then able to block the occurrence of the expectancy confirmation in the perceiver.

Zuckerman, Hodgins, and Miyake (this volume) also consider the effect of awareness; in particular, they propose that one's awareness of stereotypes and their possible impact may play a key role in the occurrence (or lack of occurrence) of the self-fulfilling prophecy. For instance, if a target is aware that he or she possesses a specific attribute (e.g., "I am quite physically attractive") and is also aware that that attribute affects others' responses (e.g., "They think that I am physically attractive, so they are acting as if I am extraverted"), then the target will discount accordingly, causing the self-fulfilling prophecy not to occur. Zuckerman et al. suggest that by understanding the varying levels of awareness that people have about their personal attributes and about the impact of these attributes on interpersonal perception, we will be able to predict more accurately when the self-fulfilling prophecy will occur. One implication is that teacher expectancies may be especially influential because children probably have little awareness of their personal attributes (e.g., low socioeconomic status) and the role that these attributes may play in shaping a teacher's expectations (e.g., a child has low intelligence).

Yet, awareness is not the only qualifier. In an impressively conceived and interrelated set of experiments, Swann (1983, 1987; Swann & Ely, 1984) has demonstrated that, in the "war" of perceiver expectancy versus target dispositional characteristic, the target's disposition often "wins." That is, when a perceiver is given an expectation about another person, and that expectation contradicts a disposition that the target confidently holds about himself or herself, then as the length of the interaction increases, the perceiver increasingly comes to perceive the target as possessing the "true" disposition, rather than the one suggested by the original expectancy.

Recent research on the limits on the self-fulfilling prophecy suggests that what we need now is a taxonomy of situations that will tell us in which situations the perceiver's or the target's expectancy will dominate. We can make some suggestions for the beginnings of such a taxonomy. First, drawing on some recent insights of Jones (1991), it seems that some trait expectancies seem "unidimensionally corrigible" and others less so. For instance, the trait expectation of stupidity–intelligence seems "upwardly corrigible," in that if an individual thought to be stupid solves even one difficult problem with imaginative accuracy, then we would be inclined to see her as intelligent.[9] On the other hand, the trait expectation of dishonest–honest seems "downwardly corrigible," meaning that if we were to see a person who had acted honestly many times now act dishonestly, we would be inclined to say that the person was "fundamentally" dishonest. We might conclude that he had acted honestly all of the other times because, since we had observed those times, it was clear to him that the actions were observable, and thus he was acting honestly because of the situation. Other traits, such as introversion–extraversion, are more symmetrically confirmable or disconfirmable (see Birnbaum, 1972, 1973; Reeder & Brewer, 1979, for relevant discussions on asymmetry and symmetry).

Second, as suggested by the recent work of Hilton and Darley (1985), the degree to which the target is aware of the expectancy, and the degree to which he or she is motivated to overcome it, are likely to play a role in its disconfirmation. The second variable is an interesting one because it is apt to work in a complex interactive way. If the target is likely to gain a great deal by overcoming the expectancy of the perceiver, then he is likely to expend a good deal of strategic thought and effort on doing so; on the other hand, the perceiver is likely to be equally aware of what is to be gained by overcoming her expectancies, and equally discounting of any attempts to do so.

A third crucial element of our taxonomy, demonstrated most clearly by Swann's research, is what might be called the *triumph of personality over expectancy*. In one study (Swann & Ely, 1984), persons who described themselves as possessing a trait, and to whom possessing that trait was a fairly central aspect of their personality, were more likely to be perceived as possessing that trait, regardless of the initial impression of the perceiver. Given time, the personality of the target overcame the expectancy of the perceiver.

Fourth, as Darley and Fazio (1980) note, it is necessary to look at the relative power possessed by the perceiver and the target, particularly the power possessed by the perceiver in terms of terminating the interaction. If the perceiver is a personnel director interviewing many candidates for a single job, he may have both the power and the inclination to terminate the interaction quickly, to the disadvantage of the person about whom he has the negative expectancy. The extreme of this is the Broadway casting call, in which each individual is given 3 or 4 minutes to perform; it is unlikely that most people will be able to overcome the expectancies created by their first impressions in this limited period of time.[10] In order to make the best use of their limited opportunities, individuals who possess less power may develop various strategies to impress or appease the other. For instance, Jones and his colleagues (1984) suggest that for stigmatized individuals, this may lead them to develop various strategies (withdrawal, role acceptance), which may be adaptive in many ways but which may also hinder their chances of disconfirming negative expectancies.

The current state of the field: Functional theories of social interaction processes

When reflecting on the present state of the field of expectancy effects, we see that the focus of research and theorizing has changed a great deal in recent years. In 1984, Mark Snyder comprehensively reviewed the body of research on behavioral confirmation. Yet, since that time, several new accounts of the social interactional sequence have appeared that complicate the simplicity of the expectancy-confirmation process. These accounts share one characteristic: They suggest that the general social interaction process is a goal-driven or functional one (Hilton & Darley, 1991; Hilton, Darley, & Fleming, 1989; Jones, 1986, 1991; Snyder, 1991). In doing so, they reinstate the insight contained in the chapter by Jones and Thibaut (1958): that social perception is rarely a process that is carried out in the abstract, in which the perceiver seeks to arrive at an "accurate" characterization of the target individual. Rather, two individuals are in interaction, each with his or her own goals and purposes, each seeking to gain certain treatments from the other, each seeking to create certain impressions in the other.

As this suggests, one cannot specify whether an expectancy held by a perceiver about a target will be confirmed in their interaction unless one is very clear about the dynamics indicated by functional considerations on their interaction. Sometimes these functional considerations involve the long-term goals of the interactants; for a competitive perceiver, the expectancy that another is skilled in some field of human endeavor, or knowledgeable in some field of human thought and creativity, is a spur to probing exploration of that expected skill or knowledge; to an individual cast in the role of leader of a problem-solving collective, it may trigger a role assignment of the target that is at least initially consistent with expectations.

Swann and Snyder (1980), in a study that has attracted less attention than it should, demonstrated that the same expectancy information about a target (whether the target possessed high or low ability) triggered either increased or decreased tutoring efforts involving that individual, depending on whether the teacher thought that the individual's ability was produced by external factors (e.g., the teacher's instruction) or by intrinsic potential. Those teachers who believed that the individual's ability was influenced by external factors tutored the "high-ability" students more, which in turn led these students to perform better than those labeled "low ability." On the other hand, instructors who thought that one's ability was due to intrinsic factors tutored the "low-ability" students more, which led them to outperform those labeled "high ability." Therefore, behavioral confirmation occurred only when the instructors believed that ability was affected by factors external to the pupil (e.g., when the instructors believed that their goal was to bring out the good students' potential). When the instructors believed that ability was intrinsic, behavioral disconfirmation occurred.

Work by Darley, Fleming, Hilton, and Swann (1988) further suggests that perceivers' interaction goals have a major impact on the strategies they adopt in an interaction. In their study, all subjects had an expectancy about another person. For half of the subjects, this expectancy was relevant to the upcoming interaction. Subjects for whom it was relevant to know if the expectancy was true tended to ask more expectancy-relevant questions during the interaction, and correspondingly, then, to learn if the expectancy was true or false.

Recent work by Snyder and colleagues (Copeland & Snyder, 1990; Snyder & Haugen, 1990) has also found that inducing various interaction goals leads to varying degrees of behavioral confirmation. For instance, Snyder and Haugen (1990) found that when they induced perceivers to see the interaction as a time to develop a sense of what the other person was like (an acquiring knowledge goal), targets about whom an expectancy was given tended to respond more in ways that confirmed the expectancy than targets about whom no expectancy was given. On the other hand, when Snyder and Haugen induced perceivers to see the interaction as a time to find ways to have a comfortable conversation by being sensitive to the other person's characteristics (regulating social interaction goal), they found no behavioral confirmation differences between the expectancy and no-expectancy groups. Copeland and Snyder (1990) found similar results when inducing some subjects to have a knowledge-oriented goal (as opposed to a goal of getting along well): When the perceiver was interested in seeking knowledge, behavioral confirmation differences occurred between the expectancy and no-expectancy groups. No confirmation differences occurred between the "get along well" conditions. In both studies, different interaction goals led to varying degrees of behavioral confirmation.

Concluding comments

This then is our view of what has been done with the concept of the self-fulfilling prophecy in experimental social psychology: We now have a set of elegantly crafted experiments that demonstrate the component processes in the prophecy and show the causal ordering of those processes. In the process of elucidating the self-fulfilling prophecy, social psychologists have been led to conceptualize the general nature of the social interaction process within which the self-fulfilling prophecy process is contained. Further, and as the following chapters will show, the self-fulfilling prophecy has been discovered at work in other fields of psychology, and dramatic demonstrations of its relevance have been made in educational, organizational, legal, and mental health settings, just to name a few, that Babad, Eden, Blanck, and Friedman discuss in this volume. Thus Rosenthal's work has led to the construction of some of the major theoretical advances in social psychology in the past two decades and most recently has returned us to the functional, goal-oriented perspective of Dewey (1896) and James (1890). This is a considerable contribution.

In fact, a recent article (Jussim, 1991) may make clear the magnitude of the shift in thinking that began with the research that originated in Rosenthal's concept of the self-fulfilling prophecy. In that article, Jussim argues that psychologists are now so convinced of the validity of the social construction notion that they give no credence to the operation of realities at all. He argues, that, for instance, we have so overstated the social constructionist possibilities that exist in classrooms that we give no role to the real IQ and abilities of the children in schools. It strikes us that Jussim greatly overstates the case, citing as he does the arguments of psychologists who were trying to make people see that there existed the possibilities of significant intrusions of social constructionist processes into processes otherwise governed by factual constraints. However, it is interesting, and no minor tribute to Rosenthal, that an idea, that of the self-fulfilling prophecy, first treated by the psychological community as heretical, could so quickly become accepted that in 1990 an author would be able to claim that it so dominated people's thinking that we needed to restore a place for factual constraints in shaping social perceptions.

Surely the task for future researchers is to conceptualize the workings of social constructionist principles in interaction with what we might call the *social-perceptual facts*. As this is done, it is likely that we will see that some facts, some events, like a baseball hit into the center field bleachers, are rocklike in their factual character, whereas others, such as a high score on an exam, are less so. Putting this in a currently fashionable language, some *readings* of a *text* are plausible and arguable, but others are merely ridiculous. The social perceptual process is an inferential one, but this does not mean that all inferences are possible (McArthur & Baron, 1983). The task that social psychology must next address is to discover the concrete ways that individual expectations, cultural factors, and perceptual facts contribute to the interpretations made by social interactants. As the recent theoretical work has made clear, this must be done within a perspective that recognizes the goal-driven character of social interaction, and therefore the malleable character of social perception.

Notes

This material is based upon work supported by a National Science Foundation Graduate Fellowship to Kathryn C. Oleson. Work relevant to this article was carried out when John M. Darley was a fellow at the Center for Advanced Study in the Behavioral Sciences and furthered while he was a visiting fellow at the Institute of Governmental Studies at the University of California at Berkeley. He is grateful for the financial support provided by the National Science Foundation (BNS 8011494), the John D. and Catherine T. McArthur Foundation, the John Simon Guggenheim Foundation, and Princeton University. Any opinions, findings, conclusions, or recommendations expressed in this chapter are those of the authors and do not necessarily reflect the views of the National Science Foundation.

1. Those of us who have followed Rosenthal's career have recognized that he has, in abundance, this unusual combination of the ability to recognize an important idea and the energetic willingness to expend the time, energy, and effort to establish the importance of that idea in the minds and life spaces of others.
2. We think that it was Professor William McGuire who commented that one individual's artifact was another person's effect – and perhaps life work. Rosenthal made us realize that his effect was our artifact, and we altered our designs to eliminate those artifactual possibilities. Later he led us to realize that it was all of our effect, and one to be proud of.
3. It peeves social psychologists that the experimenter bias demonstrations, and the revised methodology that are necessary to avoid experimenter bias, have not completely penetrated other fields of experimental research. Rosenthal and Rubin's (1978) meta-analysis suggested that animal learning

studies were more susceptible to experimenter expectancy effects than person perception studies, yet person perception researchers seem more concerned with avoiding experimenter bias.

4. With characteristic energy and intelligence, Rosenthal himself contributed to the development of the statistical underpinnings of meta-analytic techniques. When he began applying meta-analytic techniques to the study of interpersonal expectancy effects, the "science" of meta-analysis was rather fragmentary and underdeveloped. After his contributions and the contributions of others, it has become a coherent, well-justified set of procedures.

5. The account that we have unfolded assigns a central and causal role to Rosenthal's desires to defend the existence of experimenter bias effects and to demonstrate the robust existence of self-fulfilling prophecy effects, to his development of meta-analytic procedures. We do not doubt that one could take the line that another of Rosenthal's research interests, for instance his interest in nonverbal communication, could be assigned a similar central role in driving Rosenthal's research career, and the interest in self-fulfilling prophecies could be made derivative on that. His career interests have been so tightly knit that it is difficult to separate them.

6. Trope and Bassok (1982) suggest that perceivers will not always behave in ways that will elicit expectancy-confirming responses. They may prefer more diagnostic methods if they are aware of the various alternatives and are not constrained in the methods they can choose.

7. The feedback factor, although having a statistically significant effect, did not prove to have an effect of large practical importance. Harris and Rosenthal suggested that more research be conducted. Rosenthal's (1989) recent work places less emphasis on the feedback factor.

8. Brophy (1983) suggests that the process sequence proposed by Darley and Fazio (1980) seems to work well for relatively simple expectations but does not capture all the complexities of teacher expectancy effects. When considering specific domains, additional factors may need to be considered. Monica Harris's chapter in this volume suggests many important differences between expectancy domains.

9. We would still have the problem of accounting for all of her observed poor performances. As Weiner (1974) points out, we might do so by attributing poor motivation to her.

10. But, of course, sometimes persons are able to do so. Of such stories are legends created. Actors, being aware of the expectancy-confirmation phenomenon, are likely to aim the first milliseconds of their performance at countering the expectancies that their appearances create. The duel between perceiver and target continues.

References

Barber, T. X., & Silver, M. J. (1968). Fact, fiction, and the experimenter bias effect. *Psychological Bulletin Monograph Supplement, 70*, 1–29.

Birnbaum, M. H. (1972). Morality judgments: Tests of an averaging model. *Journal of Experimental Psychology, 93*, 35–42.

Birnbaum, M. H. (1973). Morality judgments: Tests of an averaging model with differential weights. *Journal of Experimental Psychology, 99*, 395–399.

Brophy, J. E. (1983). Research on the self-fulfilling prophecy and teacher expectations. *Journal of Educational Psychology, 75*, 631–661.

Bruner, J. S. (1951). Personality dynamics and the process of perceiving. In R. R. Blake and G. V. Ramsey (Eds.), *Perception – An approach to personality* (pp. 121–147). New York: Ronald Press.

Copeland, J. T., & Snyder, M. (1990). Unpublished research on the functions of the perceiver in peer counseling interactions. University of Minnesota.

Darley, J. M., & Fazio, R. H. (1980). Expectancy confirmation processes arising in the social interaction sequence. *American Psychologist, 35,* 867–881.

Darley, J. M., Fleming, J. H., Hilton, J. L., & Swann, W. B. (1988). Dispelling negative expectancies: The impact of interaction goals and target characteristics on the expectancy confirmation process. *Journal of Experimental Social Psychology, 24,* 19–36.

Darley, J. M., & Gross, P. H. (1983). A hypothesis-confirming bias in labeling effects. *Journal of Personality and Social Psychology, 44,* 20–33.

Dewey, J. (1896). The reflex arc concept in psychology. *Psychological Review, 3,* 357–370.

Elashoff, J. D., & Snow, R. E. (Eds.) (1971). *Pygmalion reconsidered.* Worthington, OH: Charles A. Jones.

Fazio, R. H., Effrein, E. A., & Falender, V. J. (1981). Self-perceptions following social interactions. *Journal of Personality and Social Psychology, 41,* 232–242.

Gilbert, D. T., & Jones, E. E. (1986). Perceiver-induced constraint: Interpretations of self-generated reality. *Journal of Personality and Social Psychology, 50,* 269–280.

Gilbert, D. T., Jones, E. E., & Pelham, B. W. (1987). What the active perceiver overlooks. *Journal of Personality and Social Psychology, 52,* 861–870.

Gilbert, D. T., Pelham, B. W., & Krull, D. S. (1988). On cognitive busyness: When person perceivers meet persons perceived. *Journal of Personality and Social Psychology, 54,* 733–740.

Goffman, E. (1959). *The presentation of self in everyday life.* New York: Anchor Books.

Harris, M. J., & Rosenthal, R. (1985). The mediation of interpersonal expectancy effects: 31 meta-analyses. *Psychological Bulletin, 97,* 363–386.

Harris, M. J., & Rosenthal, R. (1986). Four factors in the mediation of teacher expectancy effects. In R. S. Feldman (Ed.), *The social psychology of education: Current research and theory* (pp. 91–114). New York: Cambridge University Press.

Hilton, J. L., & Darley, J. M. (1985). Constructing other persons: A limit on the effect. *Journal of Experimental Social Psychology, 21,* 1–18.

Hilton, J. L., & Darley, J. M. (1991). The effects of interaction goals on person perception. In M. P. Zanna (Ed.), *Advances in Experimental Social Psychology* (Vol. 24, pp. 235–267). New York: Academic Press.

Hilton, J. L., Darley, J. M., & Fleming, J. H. (1989). Self-fulfilling prophecies and self-defeating behavior. In R. Curtis (Ed.)., *Self-defeating behaviors: Experimental research and practical applications* (pp. 41–65). New York: Plenum.

James, W. (1890). *Principles of psychology* (Vols. 1 and 2). New York: Holt.

Jensen, A. R. (1969). How can we boost IQ and scholastic achievement? *Harvard Educational Review, 39,* 1–123.

Jones, E. E. (1979). The rocky road from acts to dispositions. *American Psychologist, 34,* 107–117.

Jones, E. E. (1986). Interpreting interpersonal behavior: The effects of expectancies. *Science, 234,* 41–46.

Jones, E. E. (1991). *Interpersonal perception.* New York: Freeman.

Jones, E. E., & Davis, K. E. (1965). From acts to dispositions: The attribution process in person perception. In L. Berkowitz (Ed.), *Advances in experimental social psychology* (Vol. 2, pp. 219–266). New York: Academic Press.

Jones, E. E., Farina, A., Hastorf, A. H., Markus, H., Miller, D. T., & Scott, R. (1984). *Social stigma: The psychology of marked relationships.* New York: Freeman.

Jones, E. E., & Thibaut, J. (1958). Interaction goals as bases of inference in interpersonal perception. In R. Taguiri & L. Petrullo (Eds.), *Person perception and interpersonal behavior* (pp. 151–179). Stanford, CA: Stanford University Press.

Jussim, L. (1991). Social perception and social reality: A reflection-construction model. *Psychological Review, 98,* 54–73.

Lord, C., Umezaki, K., & Darley, J. M. (1990). Developmental differences in decoding the meanings of the appraisal actions of teachers. *Child Development, 61,* 191–200.

McArthur, L. Z., & Baron, R. M. (1983). Toward an ecological theory of social perception. *Psychological Review, 90,* 215–238.

Merton, R. K. (1948). The self-fulfilling prophecy. *Antioch Review, 8,* 193–210.

Reeder, G. D., & Brewer, M. B. (1979). A schematic model of dispositional attribution in interpersonal perception. *Psychological Review, 89,* 61–79.

Rosenthal, R. (1966). *Experimenter effects in behavioral research.* New York: Appleton-Century-Crofts.

Rosenthal, R. (1968). Experimenter expectancy and the reassuring nature of the null hypothesis detection procedure. *Psychological Bulletin Monograph Supplement, 70,* 30–47.

Rosenthal, R. (1969a). Unintended effects of the clinician in clinical interaction: A taxonomy and a review of clinician expectancy effects. *Australian Journal of Psychology, 21,* 1–20.

Rosenthal, R. (1969b). Interpersonal expectations: Effects of the experimenter's hypothesis. In R. Rosenthal & R. L. Rosnow (Eds.), *Artifact in behavioral research* (pp. 181–277). New York: Academic Press.

Rosenthal, R. (1973). The mediation of Pygmalion effects: A four factor "theory." *Papau New Guinea Journal of Education, 9,* 1–12.

Rosenthal, R. (1974). *On the social psychology of the self-fulfilling prophecy: Further evidence for Pygmalion effects and their mediating mechanisms* (Module 53). New York: MSS Modular Publications.

Rosenthal, R. (Ed.) (1979). *Skill in nonverbal communication.* Cambridge, MA: Oelgeschlager, Gunn, & Hain.

Rosenthal, R. (1985). Nonverbal cues in the mediation of interpersonal expectancy effects. In A. W. Siegman & S. Feldstein (Eds.), *Multichannel integrations of nonverbal behavior* (pp. 105–128). Hillsdale, NJ: Erlbaum.

Rosenthal, R. (1989). *Experimenter expectancy, covert communication, and meta-analytic methods.* Invited address at the annual meeting of the American Psychological Association, New Orleans, LA.

Rosenthal, R., Hall, J. A., DiMatteo, M. R., Rogers, P. L., & Archer, D. (1979). *Sensitivity to nonverbal communication: The PONS test.* Baltimore: Johns Hopkins University Press.

Rosenthal, R., & Jacobson, L. (1968). *Pygmalion in the classroom: Teacher expectations and pupils' intellectual development.* New York: Holt, Rinehart, & Winston.

Rosenthal, R., & Rubin, D. B. (1978). Interpersonal expectancy effects: The first 345 studies. *The Behavioral and Brain Sciences, 3,* 377–386.

Ross, L. (1977). The intuitive psychologist and his shortcomings: Distortions in the attribution process. In L. Berkowitz (Ed.), *Advances in experimental social psychology* (Vol. 10, pp. 174–221). New York: Academic Press.

Sherman, S. J., Judd, C. M., & Park, B. (1989). Social cognition. In M. R. Rosenzweig & L. W. Porter (Eds.), *Annual review of psychology* (Vol. 40, pp. 281–326). Palo Alto, CA: Annual Reviews.

Snyder, M. (1984). When belief creates reality. In L. Berkowitz (Ed.), *Advances in experimental social psychology* (Vol. 18, pp. 247–305). New York: Academic Press.

Snyder, M. (1991). Motivational foundations of behavioral confirmation. In M. P. Zanna (Ed.), *Advances in experimental social psychology* (Vol. 25, pp. 67–114). New York: Academic Press.

Snyder, M., & Haugen, J. A. (1990, August). *Why does behavioral confirmation occur? A functional perspective.* Paper presented at the annual meetings of the American Psychological Association, Boston, MA.

Snyder, M., & Swann, W. B. (1978). Behavioral confirmation in social interaction: From social perception to social reality. *Journal of Experimental Social Psychology, 14,* 148–162.

Snyder, M., Tanke, E. D., & Berscheid, E. (1977). Social perception and interpersonal behavior: On the self-fulfilling nature of social stereotypes. *Journal of Personality and Social Psychology, 35,* 656–666.

Swann, W. B., Jr. (1983). Self-verification: Bringing social reality into harmony with the self. In J. Suls & A. G. Greenwald (Eds.), *Social psychological perspectives on the self* (Vol. 2, pp. 33–66). Hillsdale, NJ: Erlbaum.

Swann, W. B., Jr. (1987). Identity negotiation: Where two roads meet. *Journal of Personality and Social Psychology, 53,* 1038–1051.

Swann, W. B., & Ely, R. J. (1984). A battle of wills: Self-verification versus behavioral confirmation. *Journal of Personality and Social Psychology, 46,* 1287–1302.

Swann, W. B., & Snyder, M. (1980). On translating beliefs into action: Theories of ability and their application in an instructional setting. *Journal of Personality and Social Psychology, 38,* 879–888.

Thorndike, R. L. (1968). Review of *Pygmalion in the classroom. American Educational Research Journal, 5,* 708–711.

Tice, D. M. (1987). *Similarity of others and dispositional versus situational attributions.* Unpublished doctoral dissertation, Princeton University.

Trope, Y., & Bassok, M. (1982). Confirmatory and diagnosing strategies in social information gathering. *Journal of Personality and Social Psychology, 43,* 22–34.

Weiner, B. (1974). *Achievement motivation and attribution theory.* New York: General Learning Press.

Word, C. O., Zanna, M. P., & Cooper, J. (1974). The nonverbal mediation of the self-fulfilling prophecies in interracial interaction. *Journal of Experimental Social Psychology, 10,* 109–120.

4. Interpersonal expectations in the courtroom: Studying judges' and juries' behavior

PETER DAVID BLANCK

Introduction

In a criminal trial, due process mandates that the trial judge does not show actual bias toward the defendant. Trial judges are not only required to be fair and impartial, they must also "satisfy the appearance of justice" (Blanck, 1991a; Blanck, Rosenthal, & Cordell, 1985; Blanck, Rosenthal, Hart, & Bernieri, 1990). Thus, the trial judge's appearance and behavior in a criminal jury trial must never indicate to the jury that the judge believes the defendant is guilty. The appearance of judicial bias alone is grounds for reversal even if the trial judge is, in fact, completely impartial (Blanck et al., 1985).

The courts, legal scholars, practitioners, and social scientists recognize that trial judges' verbal and nonverbal behavior may have important effects on trial processes and outcomes (Blanck, 1991a; Kalven & Zeisel, 1966; Ryan, Ashman, Sales, & Shane-DuBow, 1980). Courts caution repeatedly that juries may accord great weight and deference to even the most subtle behaviors of the trial judge. One judge concludes that "[juries] can be easily influenced by the slightest suggestion from the court, whether it be a nod of the head, a smile, a frown, or a spoken word" (*State v. Wheat*, 1930). Despite the danger of improperly influencing the jury, trial judges in a criminal jury trial, like all human beings, develop certain beliefs and expectations about the defendant's guilt or innocence.

This chapter describes an empirically based framework and a theoretical model for exploring judges' and juries' expectations and behavior in actual trials. The research model and program tests the long-standing observation that sometimes subtle and perhaps unintentional nonverbal behavior of judges, as well as other extralegal variables, might alone predict trial processes and trial outcomes. To explore these ideas, part I

64

of this chapter sets forth a research model that employs various legal, extralegal, and behavioral variables (e.g., the nonverbal behavior of the judge) to describe and document trial judges' and juries' behavior. The preliminary findings of the model, presented in part II, suggest that extremely prejudicial behavior by judges might sometimes deny defendants their constitutionally protected right to a fair and impartial trial. Finally, part III discusses future uses of our findings.

The intention in modeling judges' and juries' behavior here is not to suggest that there is a bright-line standard for detecting, quantifying, or measuring the legally permissible limits of judges' behavior – for example, for separating a judge's expectations or verbal and nonverbal behaviors that are legally appropriate from those that may unduly influence a jury. Nor is it my intention to suggest that trial judges display great stone faces, showing no emotion or reaction to the events in the courtroom. Rather, the immediate goal of this chapter is to highlight a model of study and an empirical method to aid in the description of the behavior of judges and juries (Blanck, 1991b, 1992a). Indeed, appellate courts, in a more legally formal manner, attempt this by describing the effect and propriety of judges' behavior during the trial (Blanck, 1991a). In this regard, appellate courts attempt to balance a number of factors on a "sliding scale" to assess the propriety of judges' behavior. These factors include (1) the relevance of the behavior; (2) the emphatic or overbearing nature of the verbal or nonverbal behavior; (3) the efficiency of any instruction used to cure the error; and (4) the prejudicial effect of the behavior in light of the entire trial (see Harris's discussion of the four-factor theory of nonverbal mediation of expectancy effects in this volume).

As the tendency to videotape and televise actual trials to better document and analyze courtroom behavior grows, the empirical framework presented in part I may become increasingly useful to courts and practitioners in systematically assessing the propriety of the behavior of judges and of other trial participants (Blanck, 1987). In part, this is because it is now apparent that verbal and nonverbal behaviors of judges and trial participants, not previously recorded by the written court transcript or trial record, can be preserved and summarized by videotape or by on-line behavioral analyses. Thus, it will be possible for courts and counsel to describe these behaviors more accurately for appellate review (see Grisso, Baldwin, Blanck, Borus-Rotheram, Schooler, & Thompson, 1991).

Legal practitioners may likewise employ the basic framework and model described here to aid in a more systematic and economical assessment of judges' "global" and "micro" behavioral or communicative styles and of juries' reactions to those styles (Blanck et al., 1990). Further, increased sensitivity to a particular judge's behavioral style may help practitioners in the selection and preparation of expert witnesses, at least in terms of maximizing their communicative strengths to judges and juries.

Judges, as a community of professionals, are also interested in the issues presented by the empirical model of courtroom behavior described in this chapter. Judicial training programs across the country teach judges the importance of communication behavior and style in the courtroom (Blanck et al., 1985). Hopefully, the research framework and model will provide a standard to help judges evaluate the qualities of their behavior and generally to guide future empirical studies of behavior in the courtroom.

Legal scholars are similarly interested in the impact of judges' communicative behavior on courtroom fairness. The American Bar Association's (ABA) 1990 amendments to the Code of Judicial Conduct include a new canon that emphasizes the need for the appearance of fairness and justice in the courtroom.[1] The commentary to the canon states:

> A judge must perform judicial duties impartially and fairly. A judge who manifests bias on any basis in the proceeding impairs the fairness of the proceeding and brings the judiciary into disrepute. Facial expressions and body language, in addition to oral communication, can give to parties or lawyers in the proceeding, jurors, the media and others an appearance of judicial bias. A judge must be alert to avoid behavior that may be perceived as prejudicial.

The program of research to be described should facilitate the systematic assessment of this canon.

Finally, for social scientists, the theoretical model and its preliminary results may help to reveal the richness and complexity of the field study of judges' and juries' expectations and behavior. The program of study described herein suggests that empirical research can tell judges, lawyers, and social scientists a good deal by replacing unsubstantiated myths about courtroom behavior with empirically validated facts (Blanck & Turner, 1987; Konecni & Ebbesen, 1979). Still, as part III of this chapter illustrates, a more cumulative model of judges' and juries' behavior is warranted, and any single social science study, no matter how well conceived and conducted, yields only a limited degree of external or real-world validity (Bernieri, this volume; Rosnow & Rosenthal, 1989; Rubin, this volume). I present our research efforts next as a step toward developing this body of research.

I. The study of judges' and juries' behavior

This program of empirical study explores how trial judges sometimes intentionally or unintentionally convey their expectations, beliefs, or biases to juries and the subsequent impact of this on trial processes and outcomes. A trial judge's beliefs or expectations of a defendant's guilt or innocence may be manifested either verbally (by the spoken word) or nonverbally (by facial gestures, body movements, or tone of voice) and can be reflected in a judge's comments on evidence, responses to witnesses' testimony, or rulings on objections (Blanck et al., 1985; see generally part II of this volume). Some of the principal ways in which judges can impermissibly influence the criminal trial process include (1) disparaging remarks toward the defendant; (2) bias in rulings or comments; (3) consideration of matters not in evidence; (4) forming expectations of the trial's outcome before the defense has presented its case; (5) inappropriate statements of opinion to the jury during the trial; and (6) failing to control the misconduct of counsel.

In exploring the contention that a judge's expectations and behavior somehow impermissibly influence the trial process or outcome, the research relies on three main sources that I developed previously (Blanck, 1987). Briefly, the first source is the vast case law that requires judges to be fair and impartial and to satisfy the appearance of justice. The second source is a survey of judges' and practitioners' views on the importance of verbal and nonverbal communication in the courtroom. The third source is the findings of empirical studies in analogous contexts to validate the development of the research model set forth herein (e.g., Babad, this volume – organizational context; Eden, this volume – educational context). The research model is thus based, in part, on social psychological research in other contexts on how nonverbal behavior might convey an individual's beliefs for social outcomes (Blanck, 1987; see generally part I, this volume). From these sources, it is possible to design an interdisciplinary methodology that explores or models judges' behavior (Blanck, 1993).

A. A model for the study of judges' and juries' behavior

The program of study employs a theoretical framework or working model to determine the effects of judges' expectations and behavior on jury verdicts and on other trial process variables (Rosenthal, 1981). The model identifies several types of variables that need to be studied to achieve a systematic understanding of judges' behavior and its potential influence on juries' decision-making processes.

The basic elements of the model are as follows:

A: the background variables of the trial participants, such as the defendant's criminal history;
B: the judge's attitudes and beliefs about trial processes prior to the trial outcome;
C: the verbal and nonverbal global and micro behaviors that communicate the judge's attitudes and beliefs to the trial participants, and in particular to the jury;
D: the outcome of the trial in terms of the jury's decision;
E: the extent to which the judge and jury agree as to the trial outcome; and
F: the relative magnitude of the sentence imposed by the judge.

The model is illustrated in Figure 4.1, and the six variables are discussed in turn.

A: Background variables. Background variables refer to the stable attributes of the trial participants, such as gender, race, social status, intellectual ability, and other personal history factors. The model describes, for example, the relationship and impact of the background variables on trial outcome, the A–D relationship. Elsewhere, studies show that the background variables of defendants influence significantly judges' and jurors' views of defendants' guilt or innocence (Blanck et al., 1985). The model also enables a description of the relationship between defendants' criminal histories and judges' subsequent style of verbal and nonverbal behavior in relating to their juries, the A–C relationship.

We are particularly interested in the extent to which information about defendants' criminal histories might predict, or be predicted by, the other variables in the model. This is because frequently the defendants' prior criminal history is known to the judge but not to the jury unless the defendant takes the stand to testify, thus making, for example, an A–C relationship even more striking (McElhaney, 1990). In fact, the most important decision for a criminal defendant is whether to take the stand and testify on his or her own behalf, and the most

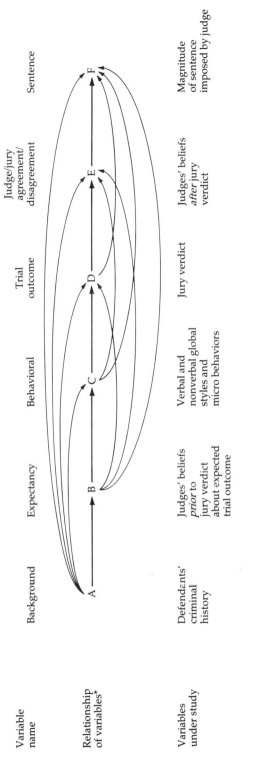

Variable name	Background	Expectancy	Behavioral	Trial outcome	Judge/jury agreement/ disagreement	Sentence
Relationship of variables*	A	B	C	D	E	F
Variables under study	Defendants' criminal history	Judges' beliefs *prior* to jury verdict about expected trial outcome	Verbal and nonverbal global styles and micro behaviors	Jury verdict	Judges' beliefs *after* jury verdict	Magnitude of sentence imposed by judge

*The simple relationships are between any two variables in the model. Cumulative relationships (e.g., A–B–C predicting D) involve more than two variables.

Figure 4.1. Model for the study of judges' and juries' behavior.

important factor in making that decision is whether the judge will let the prosecutor cross-examine a defendant with prior convictions.

B: Attitudinal or expectancy variables. A judge's attitudes, beliefs, or expectations about the trial outcome can influence the decision-making process of the jurors or the actual trial outcome. An *expectation* in this context is the particular belief that a judge has about the trial process or outcome. When judges expect or predict a certain trial outcome, they intentionally or unintentionally behave in a way that indicates what they think the outcome should be. In doing so, they set into motion behaviors and trial processes that may increase the likelihood of the occurrence of a certain trial outcome. This predictive behavior has been called a *self-fulfilling prophecy* or an *interpersonal expectancy* effect (see, e.g., Darley & Oleson, this volume; Jones, 1990). The model predicts that trial judges' expectations for a trial outcome may prophesy, become related to, or in some cases improperly influence the trial outcome. The model explores, therefore, judges' expectations for trial outcomes and the strength of those expectations.

C: Verbal and nonverbal communicative behaviors. Verbal and nonverbal behaviors communicate judges' beliefs and expectations to the trial participants. In order to maximize the real-world generalization of the findings, portions of actual trials were videotaped to assess judges' verbal and nonverbal behaviors. Briefly, independent groups of raters are employed to assess the videotapes' communicative content on different emotional dimensions (e.g., warm, hostile, professional). Raters assess several modified versions of the videotapes to isolate the specific verbal and nonverbal *channels* and global behaviors of communication. The altered versions of the tapes include (1) normal video- and audiotapes; (2) audio-only tapes (normal speech); (3) visual-only cues (facial expressions and body movements); and (4) tone-of-voice-only tapes (by a filtered audio recording that allows rhythm, pitch, and tone, but not verbal content, to be conveyed).

Our subsequent studies also examine trial judges' micro nonverbal behaviors (Blanck, 1993). Micro nonverbal behaviors are seven discretely coded actions regularly employed in the study of nonverbal behavior, including (1) amount of eye contact with the jury; (2) number of smiles; (3) number of head nods; (4) number of significant hand movements; (5) number of forward leans toward and away from the jury; (6) number of significant changes in body position (fewer shifts designated as *postural attention*); and (7) number of self-touching behaviors, such as chin rubbing (Blanck et al., 1990).

The initial study in this series analyzed the behavior of five California state court judges who were videotaped while delivering final, or *pattern*, instructions to jurors in 34 criminal trials. The sampling of pattern jury instructions in these cases enabled a control for the effects of the verbal content of the instructions. In this way, videotaped trials enabled the separation and fine-grained comparison of both the verbal (content of speech) and nonverbal (face and body movements and tone of voice) behaviors of the trial judges (Levi, 1990).

As mentioned previously, both the courts and practitioners recognize the particular importance of judges' nonverbal behavior in influencing trial outcomes. A judge's facial expressions or tone of voice alone can influence jury verdicts, sometimes in impermissible ways. For example, in the often cited case of *State v. Barron*, a Missouri appellate court reversed a burglary conviction on the grounds of nonverbal prejudicial error by the judge. When listening to the defendant's brother testify that the defendant was at home watching television when the alleged burglary occurred, the trial judge placed his hands to the sides of his head, shook his head negatively, and leaned back, swiveling his chair 180 degrees.

More recently, in analogous situations, social scientists demonstrated that teachers', doctors', and psychotherapists' nonverbal behaviors significantly influence the course of social interaction (see generally parts I and II, this volume). The earliest such studies showing that nonverbal cues are systematically involved in the transmission of expectancy effects concerned college students asking other student experimenters to judge whether a person in a photograph had been experiencing success or failure in life (Rosenthal, 1981). Although all the experimenters read the same pattern verbal instructions, students responded in accordance with the expectations that were induced randomly in the minds of the experimenters. In other words, the students found the person in the photograph to be more successful if the experimenters were led to believe that the person was more successful. Because all experimenters read pattern instructions, the results suggested that only the nonverbal component of the interaction led experimenters to make the predictions. To examine this hypothesis here, the research model explores how trial judges' verbal and nonverbal behaviors alone may communicate their beliefs or expectations to their juries (Blanck & Rosenthal, 1992).

D: Outcome variables. Outcome variables refer to the behavior of the expectee (the juror) after interaction with the expecter (the judge). The model measures trial outcome variables in terms of the jury's finding of guilt or innocence. This form of archival data is collected easily because trial outcomes are available as public records.

E: Judge–jury agreement/disagreement variables. These refer to the judges' attitudes about the trial process after the jury reaches its verdict. In our model, this variable also refers to the magnitude of the agreement or disagreement between judge and jury in terms of their views of the trial outcome. The E variable is similar conceptually to the classic study in *The American Jury* that explored the sources and explanations of judge–jury disagreement (Kalven & Zeisel, 1966). Relationships involving the E variable are reported here in preliminary form, and additional analyses are presently being conducted to explore the variable (Blanck, 1993). As described in more detail in part III of this chapter, the inclusion of the E variable in the model is an attempt to develop the insight of *The American Jury* research into a more comprehensive model of judges' and juries' behavior.

F: Sentence-imposed variable. This variable forms the final link in our model and is assessed in terms of its magnitude relative to the maximum possible sentence under the change. At this point in the research process, the suggestions to be made with regard to the F variable are based on hypothesized predictions. Empirical data on the F variable are just now becoming available for analytical purposes (Blanck, 1993).

Nevertheless, a number of empirical studies on sentencing patterns and behavior have been conducted (for a review, see Wrightsman, 1991). What is most apparent from this research is that trial judges have great discretion in the sentencing process. In fact, the discretion of the judge provides an important function in the sentencing process since it allows the judge to consider individual and community perceptions of the crime, the background of the criminal, and the circumstances of the particular case. It is precisely these sorts of background and trial process variables that the model of judges' and juries' behavior can assess. Thus, the model will enable the systematic and comprehensive assessment of the impact of judges', defendants', and/or victims' background (A) and behavioral (C) variables on the sentencing process (Diamond, 1981; Wrightsman, 1991).

Along these lines, Ebbesen and Konecni (1981) observed more than

400 sentencing hearings in San Diego courts over a 2-year period to study empirically the factors that influence judges' sentencing decisions. Using an approach similar to that of the model presented here, they sought to isolate the factors that accounted for the systematic variation among judges' sentences. Four factors accounted for the vast majority of variation in sentencing, which may be also employed in subsequent tests of our model: (1) the type of crime, (2) the defendant's criminal history, (3) the status of the defendant between arrest and conviction (e.g., released on bail or held in jail), and (4) the probation officer's sentence recommendation.

Of these four factors, the judges followed the recommended sentence of the probation officer in 84% of the cases studied. Ebbesen and Konecni concluded that the probation officer's recommendation is, in fact, likely based on the other three variables studied, that is, based on a knowledge of the defendant's criminal history (the A variable in our model) and on perceptions of the seriousness of the crime (Wrightsman, 1991). In future tests of the model, the sentencing recommendation of the probation officer may be incorporated as an additional post-verdict variable.

To summarize, the theoretical model is designed to further the general understanding of judges' and jurors' behavior, and of how judges' expectations and behavior may predict and sometimes influence jury verdicts. More important, the model provides researchers with a framework to study empirically "chains" of variables that together may predict more accurately certain aspects of trial processes and outcome.

II. Preliminary results of the study

This part presents preliminary results from our ongoing studies of judges' and juries' behavior. Section A summarizes our findings with regard to trial judges' communicative behaviors and styles. Section B presents some preliminary and exploratory results derived from our tests of the model of judges' and juries' behavior.

A. Global and micro dimensions of judges' behavior

Before examining the simple relationships between any two variables in the model (e.g., the A–D chain) and cumulative relationships of the model (e.g., A–B–C–E predicting D), it is useful to describe briefly the findings regarding what we have named the *global* and *micro* dimensions of trial judges' verbal and nonverbal behavior in relating to their juries (Blanck et al., 1990). The term *global dimension* describes the general demeanor or model of judges' communicative and interpersonal behavior that is often conveyed independently of verbal content (Blanck, Rosenthal, & Vannicelli, 1986; Blanck, Rosenthal, Vannicelli, & Lee, 1986). Although a particular global behavior or style may reflect a judge's general orientation for relating to others during the trial, judges show different global behaviors at different times, depending on the circumstances of the trial process. For example, when responding to improper attorney behavior, a judge might show more directive or controlling behavior. Conversely, when dealing with a child witness, a judge might show more caring and patient behavior.

Our earlier studies provide a description of trial judges' global behavior. Principal components analyses yielded four basic global dimensions of behavior, namely, *judicial, directive, confident,* and *warm* (Blanck et al., 1990). These four global dimensions can be subdivided further into those that appear more legally or procedurally oriented, as reflected by the judicial and directive dimensions, and those that appear more emotionally based, as reflected by the confident and warm global dimensions.

Based on our quantitative results and qualitative interviews with judges and practitioners, the following tentative conclusions about the appearance of judges' four global dimensions may be drawn:

1. A judge high on the judicial dimension is rated as more professional, wise, competent, and honest. The judicial dimension is thus focused, perhaps in the broadest sense, on the appearance of judicial propriety and fairness (Redish & Marshall, 1986).
2. A judge high on the directive dimension is rated as more dogmatic and dominant. The directive dimension typifies the qualities of the trial judge as a courtroom leader and as an administrator (Flanders, 1984; Resnik, 1982).
3. A judge high on the confident dimension is rated as less anxious and less hostile. This dimension may reflect the extent to which the judge appears emotionally comfortable, self-assured, respectful, and patient with others during the trial.
4. A judge high on the warm dimension is rated as warmer, more open-minded, and more emphatic. This dimension may reflect the extent to which the judge appears to be supportive of, and courteous to, the trial participants.

Together, the four global dimensions of behavior provide one of the first empirically based descriptions of actual judges' behavior. More important, the global dimensions of behavior are useful for predicting trial processes and outcomes in the theoretical model because they reflect practical, interpretable, and externally valid dimensions of judges' communicative style that are consistent with prior case-oriented and clinically derived descriptions of judges' behavior (Blanck, 1993). In fact, the National Conference of State Trial Judges (1989) describes the essential qualities of a good judge as including graciousness, moral courage, a reputation for fairness, mercy, patience, the ability to communicate, decisiveness, innovation, open-mindedness, brevity, dignity, honesty, and integrity.

The program of empirical study also explored what we have called the *micro* behaviors of trial judges (e.g., eye contact with the jury, head nods, or hand movements). In our studies, two raters independently code the tapes for the micro behaviors. The median rater reliability for these variables is .71, suggesting that the two raters are very consistent in their rating of the judges' micro behaviors.

The judges' micro behaviors assessed in the model have been employed regularly in studies of courtroom nonverbal behavior (Hemsley & Doob, 1978; Pryor & Leone, 1981). Like our findings for the global dimensions, these findings provide a practical description of two basic constellations of judges' micro behaviors. A first component of *engaged* micro behaviors emerged, with judges high on this component displaying more eye contact, more postural attention, and less self-touching. A second component of *emotional* micro behaviors emerged, with judges high on this component displaying more smiles, head nods, hand movements, and forward leans. The two micro constellations are conceptually similar to the judicial and warm global dimensions of judges' behavior.

Analysis of the predictive relationship between the global and micro constellations illustrates the potentially important methodological contribution of the model. The results of this analysis suggest that the micro nonverbal behaviors of the trial judge may serve as important predictors of the four global dimensions of judges' behavior (Blanck et al., 1990). This is an interesting finding given the large body of research demonstrating the important effects of eye contact on social influence in the courtroom. Furthermore, the results show that more engaged micro behaviors, such as eye contact and head nods by the judge directed to the jury, predict judges' judicial and directive global behaviors, whereas more relaxed micro behaviors, such as less postural attention, predict the judges' warm global behaviors. Together, these results provide preliminary evidence that judges' micro behaviors alone can be used to predict significantly, and with practical benefit, the four global dimensions of judges' behavior.

The finding that micro behaviors of judges predict those same judges' global behaviors suggests methodologically effective and economical shortcuts to researchers and practitioners interested in studying and assessing judges' behaviors and attitudes during the live trial process. This is true even where our study involved a relatively small sample of judges, all of whom knew that they were being videotaped and assessed by a naive group of raters. Moreover, the findings are particularly encouraging given the brief period during which the judges' behaviors were rated.

Even moderate relationships between the quantifiable micro behaviors and the impressionistic global behaviors could be of value to social scientists, legal researchers, and practitioners. In part, this is because of the serious logistical and ethical problems associated with studying and videotaping actual trials to assess judges' behavior (Blanck, 1987). Moreover, researchers could use the easily codable and unobtrusively collected micro behaviors as an index of a judge's global behaviors and style. In this way, the model may also eventually prove to be useful when employed by training or educational programs for judges devoted to the fine-grained analysis of courtroom behavior.

B. Testing the model

The model generates 15 *simple* relationships (the correlation between any two variables) and several other *cumulative* relationships (two or more variables predicting a third variable using multiple regression analyses) that will be explored. From a practical point of view, the cumulative relationships in the model, that is, several individual variables employed to predict a single criterion variable, facilitate a more realistic and comprehensive test of the model.

Simple relationships in the model.

BACKGROUND–EXPECTANCY (A–B) RELATIONSHIPS. This relationship describes how a judge's expectations for the trial outcome may be predicted solely from the background variables of the trial participants.

The results suggest that judges' beliefs about trial outcomes are related to defendants' criminal histories in predictable ways. For example, judges usually expect a guilty verdict when defendants have serious criminal histories and expect innocent verdicts when defendants have less serious criminal histories (Blanck et al., 1985).

BACKGROUND–BEHAVIOR (A–C) RELATIONSHIP. This relationship describes how a defendant's criminal history may be related to a judge's expression of global and micro behaviors during the trial. Preliminary results suggest that information about a defendant's criminal history (A), information that the jury is ordinarily not allowed to learn unless the defendant takes the stand to testify, relates to the judge's behavior (C variable) when instructing the jury (Blanck et al., 1985). Specifically, in the overt verbal channels, judges' behavior seems to be rated as *more* judicial, directive, and warm when delivering instructions for defendants with more serious criminal histories. The nonverbal channels, however, tell a different story: Judges tend to be relatively *less* judicial, directive, and warm when delivering instructions for defendants with more serious criminal histories. These results suggest that judges may sometimes "leak" or reveal to juries their underlying beliefs about defendants through nonverbal channels alone.

BACKGROUND–OUTCOME (A–D) RELATIONSHIP. The background variable of defendants' criminal histories also tends to be related predictably to the trial outcome. For example, defendants with more serious criminal histories are more likely to be found guilty (Blanck et al., 1985). Granted, defendants with criminal histories may be more likely to be guilty. Nonetheless, viewed in combination with the nonverbal tendency for judges to reveal the criminal history (the A–C results), this finding indicates that a defendant's criminal history, a legally irrelevant factor unless the defendant takes the stand to testify, might influence juries more than was previously assumed.

BACKGROUND–JUDGE/JURY AGREEMENT (A–E) RELATIONSHIP. This relationship describes how a defendant's criminal history might be related to the judge's views about the trial outcome. Preliminary tests of this relationship suggest a slight trend for judges' disagreement with their juries' verdicts to be stronger when defendants have more serious criminal histories (Blanck, 1991a). We hypothesize further that in cases where the judge knows the defendant's prior criminal history and the jury does not, the judge will view a jury verdict of innocence to be overly lenient. This suggestion, to be discussed, is consistent with

Kalven and Zeisel's conclusion in *The American Jury* that in cases of judge–jury disagreement, juries tended to be viewed as more lenient than judges.

BACKGROUND–SENTENCE (A–F) RELATIONSHIP. This relationship describes how a defendant's criminal history is related to the sentence imposed by the judge. Expectedly, we hypothesize that the magnitude of the sentence imposed by the judge will reflect the relevant prior criminal history of the defendant. This suggestion is consistent with the findings, described earlier, of Ebbesen and Konecni that defendants' criminal histories and perceptions of the seriousness of the crime predict judges' sentences.

Additionally, an interesting subset of cases to study further will be those in which the defendant does not take the stand to testify. For this subset of cases, we might expect that generally defendants receive relatively lighter sentences. This finding should be particularly apparent in cases where the judge initially expects (B variable) an innocent verdict.

EXPECTANCY–BEHAVIOR (B–C) RELATIONSHIP. This relationship describes how judges' expectations for trial outcomes relate to their global and micro behavioral styles. The preliminary findings support the suggestion that judges may reveal their beliefs to juries through nonverbal channels alone. That is, in the purely nonverbal channels, judges expecting a guilty verdict tend to be somewhat less judicial and warm in relating to their juries (Blanck et al., 1985).

These results imply, but do not prove, that judges' verbal and nonverbal channels in some extreme cases may convey messages concerning the defendant's guilt or innocence to their juries. Intentionally or unintentionally, judges' beliefs may influence their communication styles when relating to their juries, although on the written trial transcript or in response to a pencil-and-paper questionnaire, the judges may appear (or actually believe themselves to be) impartial.

EXPECTANCY–OUTCOME (B–D) RELATIONSHIP. This relationship describes how judges' expectations for trial outcomes relate to the actual trial outcomes. Taken alone, the B–D findings for our sample of 34 trials suggest that a judge's belief about a trial outcome (as assessed by questionnaires) does not predict accurately the actual trial outcome (Blanck et al., 1985). The implications of this finding for conclusions drawn in *The American Jury* research, which relied solely on the questionnaire data of judges, are discussed in part III of this chapter.

Nevertheless, the preliminary findings suggest that judges who send expectancy effects to juries should be held accountable, because biasing messages (at least as assessed by our methods) might not be an inevitable product of courtroom dynamics (Blanck, 1993). As will be suggested, empirical testing of the cumulative impact of the model (e.g., A–B–C–E predicting the D chain) is necessary to understand this relationship more completely.

EXPECTANCY–JUDGE/JURY AGREEMENT (B–E) RELATIONSHIP. This relationship describes how judges' expectations prior to the trial outcome predict those same judges' agreement or disagreement with their juries' verdicts. Consistent with our previous discussion, the initial findings seem to suggest that those judges who expect a guilty verdict prior to the trial outcome are more likely to agree with a verdict of guilt than with a verdict of innocence (Blanck, 1991a). In other words, judges who are convinced early in the trial that the defendant is guilty may likely reflect or confirm this attitude in the subsequent magnitude of their agreement with the jury's verdict.

The strength of the B–E relationship may also be moderated by the severity of the defendant's criminal history, by the magnitude of the judge's expectations, and by whether or not the defendant testified. This suggestion would parallel Kalven and Zeisel's view in *The American Jury* that in cases where the judge has some knowledge of the defendant's criminal history that the jury does not have, the judge and jury may in fact be trying two different cases. In other words, had the jury known what the judge knew, it would likely have agreed with the judge.

EXPECTANCY–SENTENCE (B–F) RELATIONSHIP. We hypothesize that this relationship will show that the sentence imposed by the judge reflects the judge's expectations about the defendant's guilt or innocence formed during the trial. It will be most interesting to explore the types of cases or circumstances in which judges deviate from their preconceived notions or biases formed during the trial in sentencing the defendant. We might predict, as Ebbesen and Konecni found, that judges' perceptions and attitudes about a particular crime or defendant help predict those same judges' sentencing behaviors and patterns.

BEHAVIOR–OUTCOME (C–D) RELATIONSHIP. This relationship describes how judges' behaviors alone may predict the verdicts returned by their juries. The findings suggest a trend for judges' global behavior to be less judicial and directive and for their micro behavior to be significantly more engaged when the verdict returned is guilty (Blanck, 1991a). Thus, certain communicative channels and/or styles of judges' behavior may predict with greater accuracy their juries' verdicts. Subsequent fine-grained analyses of behavior are needed to understand how the C–D relationship varies with the type of verbal or nonverbal behavior under study.

Perhaps one encouraging general conclusion to be drawn from the examination of the C–D relationship is that in most cases where judges' expectations for trial outcomes are conveyed to juries either verbally or nonverbally, jurors still tend to make their own independent assessments of the evidence. We are examining this suggestion further in marginal or "close" cases. We expect, as obvious as it might sound, that the strength of the evidence will generally be an important predictor of trial outcomes (Blanck, 1993). Alternatively, in close versus clear cases, the judges' beliefs and behavior, the defendants' background variables, or other extralegal factors will play an increasingly important role in predicting trial outcomes and the ultimate sentence imposed by the judge (Kalven & Zeisel, 1966).

BEHAVIOR–JUDGE/JURY AGREEMENT (C–E) RELATIONSHIP. This relationship describes how a judge's global and micro behaviors at trial may predict (or be predicted by) that judge's views about the trial outcome. Preliminary tests of this relationship suggest a trend for judges' engaged micro behaviors to be related to their views about the trial outcome, particularly when controlling for other variables in the model (Blanck, 1991a). Although further analysis is required, this potential relationship supports the earlier suggestion that judges' behavior alone may reflect their views about the perceived correctness of the jury's ultimate conclusion.

BEHAVIOR–SENTENCE (C–F) RELATIONSHIP. This relationship describes how a judge's behavior is related to the sentence imposed by the judge. To the best of my knowledge, this relationship has not been tested empirically, nor is there an empirical framework for assessing it. For this relationship, we might predict that judges' global and micro behaviors at trial, reflecting relatively less warm or more directive and engaged attitudes, may predict the imposition of more severe sentences. Again, this relationship may provide a promising avenue for future study, given the relative logistical ease with which micro behaviors can be assessed.

OUTCOME–JUDGE/JURY AGREEMENT (D–E) RELATIONSHIP. The initial data exploring this relationship show that trial outcome is predicted by a knowledge of the magnitude of judges' agreement/disagreement with their juries' verdicts (Blanck, 1991a). Not surprisingly, judges are more likely to agree with guilty verdicts and to disagree with not-guilty verdicts. On its face, this result supports Kalven and Zeisel's general conclusion that judges tend to view juries' results as more lenient than their own. Further research is being conducted to isolate this result, given that in our research (unlike *The American Jury* study) the judges completed the questionnaires both before and after they knew the jury's verdict (Blanck, 1993).

OUTCOME–SENTENCE (D–F) RELATIONSHIP. This relationship describes how jury verdicts (e.g., guilty verdicts) relate to the sentence imposed by the judge. As suggested previously, this simple relationship is likely affected by other variables in the model (e.g., defendants' criminal histories) in meaningful ways. Interestingly, analysis of this simple relationship also may reveal judges' individual disparities in the sentencing process or in their adherence to legislatively mandated sentencing guidelines (Blanck, 1993).

JUDGE/JURY AGREEMENT–SENTENCE (E–F) RELATIONSHIP. This relationship expresses the extent to which judges' views about the trial outcome may predict the sentence they impose. We expect that the magnitude of the judge–jury agreement or disagreement will be particularly important in assessing this relationship. In other words, judges may impose relatively less severe sentences when they disagree with the jury's finding of guilt or vice versa. Consistent with the findings of *The American Jury* described in the next part of this chapter, judges' sentencing behavior may also be influenced by evidentiary factors or by other facts known only by the judge (e.g., in some cases, the defendant's criminal history).

Cumulative relationships in the model. The basic purpose of the model is to increase the general understanding of how judges' behavior may influence jury verdicts and trial processes. The model is most powerful or most predictive when it examines the chains of variables taken together. One such primary chain is highlighted next.

In exploring the cumulative chains in the model, we employ multiple regression statistical analyses (Cohen & Cohen, 1983). From a practical point of view, the regression analyses enable a more detailed assessment of the relationship between a set of variables in the model with one other variable in the model (Blanck, 1991b, 1992a). Typically, the analyses will employ several of the variables in the model as predictors of either trial outcome (D) or sentence imposed (F).

A primary chain that we have pilot-tested is the extent to which trial outcomes (D) are predicted by the set of variables including (A) the defendants' criminal histories, (B) judges' expectations for the trial outcome, (C) the engaged micro behaviors of the judge at trial, and (E) the magnitude of judge–jury agreement/disagreement as to the verdict.

Initial results for this test of the model suggest that judges' expectations for the trial outcome (B), judges' engaged micro behavior at trial (C), and the magnitude of judge–jury agreement or disagreement (E) together predict trial outcomes better than any single variable in the model alone (Blanck, 1991a).

We are conducting further analyses to explore the direction and magnitude of the A–B–C–E predicting D chain (Blanck, 1993). The following scenario, however, may be hypothesized: In cases where the evidence is close, a guilty jury verdict is likely to result when (1) the defendant has a more serious criminal history; (2) the judge (early in the trial) expects a guilty verdict; (3) the judge's micro behaviors at trial are more engaged (or serious); and (4) the judge, at some point in the trial, comes to agree strongly with the jury's ultimate determination of guilt. This is one descriptive example of how analyses of the cumulative chains of variables in the model may explore the long-standing observation that legal and extralegal factors influence judges' and juries' behavior. As the next part suggests, the uses and tests of the model in the study of actual courtroom behavior are not confined to these relationships.

III. *The American Jury* revisited

The discussion thus far highlights the ongoing effort to explore and refine a model of judges' and juries' behavior. The inclusion of the E variable, judge–jury agreement/disagreement, represents an attempt to provide additional insight into the ground-breaking work presented in *The American Jury*.

The American Jury provided knowledge about the operation of judges and juries in actual criminal jury trials. This task was accomplished through the analysis of an extensive survey (questionnaire) of judges' views of the trial process. The basic purpose of the survey was to answer the question "When do trial by judge and trial by jury lead to divergent results?" The data base for *The American Jury* research consisted of information on some 3,500 trials. The main focus of this research is an analysis of the frequency of agreement and disagreement between judge and jury by comparing the actual decision of the jury with the survey response from the judge stating how he or she would have decided the case had it been tried before the judge without a jury. In extensive analyses, *The American Jury* research seeks to understand the possible reasons for judge–jury agreement/disagreement.

Unfortunately, despite the great visibility of *The American Jury* research, there has been little attempt to replicate and refine that study using both survey methods and the observation of actual trials. Such study is clearly warranted given the dramatic changes that have occurred with regard to the function, composition, and role of the jury over the last several decades. Thus, one long-term purpose of our model of judges' and juries' behavior is to replicate (albeit on a much smaller scale), and to provide a framework for replication by others, the findings of *The American Jury* research. For example, analyses of our E variable are presently being conducted to explore whether, as evidenced in *The American Jury*, the judges' reports of their verdicts would have been the same as their juries roughly 75% of the time.

The high level of agreement found in *The American Jury* study occurred even in very complex cases, leading several legal commentators to speculate that judges may unintentionally communicate their expectations for trial outcomes to their juries through nonverbal channels (Elwork, Sales, & Suggs, 1981; Greenbaum, 1975). Nonetheless, to date, this suggestion has not been tested empirically.

The Kalven and Zeisel result is important to replicate, given the debate over exactly what is an optimal degree of agreement between judge and jury. That is, although judge–jury agreement 100% of the time might be undesirable because it could indicate that the jury was a "rubber stamp" of the judge, agreement only 50% of the time could indicate a deviation in the jury's mandate to follow the law or the judge's instructions (Wrightsman, 1991).

The degree of judge–jury agreement/disagreement should not obscure the suggestion that, in most cases, juries base their decisions on the strength of the evidence presented in the particular case (Blanck et al., 1991, 1993; Visher, 1987). Alternatively, in close or marginal cases, other extralegal factors, such as those identified by the model, will increasingly impact on the jury's decision-making process. In fact, the main focus of *The American Jury* research is on describing (1) the impact of extralegal information in the 25% of the cases in which there was

judge–jury disagreement and (2) how such information accounts for
their finding that, in the vast majority of the cases where disagreement
occurred, the jury was more lenient than the judge.

The program of empirical study set forth and tested by our model
builds on the work of *The American Jury* research by exploring actual
trial behavior, using videotape and survey data, from the perspective
of the judge, the defendant, counsel, and the jury. In forthcoming
analyses of the model, we explore the relationship between other background (A) variables of the trial participants (e.g., competency of counsel), as rated by different trial participants, with trial outcome (D variable) and with judge–jury agreement/disagreement (E variable) (Blanck,
1993).

In subsequent analyses, we will also explore the complexity of the
facts and evidence, as perceived by different trial participants, and its
relationship to other variables in the model. In addition, we will closely
analyze data on what Kalven and Zeisel have called the importance of
jury sentiments or intuitive feelings in close cases. Kalven and Zeisel
suggest that jury sentiments about the defendant (e.g., empathy with
the defendant) or about the law (e.g., fairness of the law) may provide
additional insight into the reasons for judge–jury disagreement in close
cases. These analyses may begin to provide a more comprehensive
view, from several vantage points, of what empirical research can tell
us about judges' and juries' decision-making processes. The model
provides a framework for several other avenues of future study. In
terms of the developing theoretical contribution of the model, it will be
important to test the model, and to replicate *The American Jury* research,
in the civil jury context (Blanck, 1992b). Comparison of judges' behavior
in bench and jury trials is also warranted (Blanck, 1993).

Additionally, we have begun research on tests of the model of judges'
and juries' behavior in different legal cultures and systems. In particular, we plan to explore trial participants' conceptions of the judges' role
and the appearance of justice in the German and French (Continental)
systems of justice. The comparative and cross-cultural research will
build on the American studies by exploring how procedural and cultural norms impact trial processes and the participants' ultimate perceptions of fairness (Lind, Thibaut, & Walker, 1976; Reitz, 1991).

It is worth noting again that there are many things that our empirical
research and model may not be able to tell us about judges' and juries'
behavior, given the constraints of our sample size or our inability to
assign defendants randomly to bench or jury trials (Blanck, Bellack,

Rosnow, Rotheram–Borus & Schooler, 1992). Such issues raise questions about the generalizability of studies of actual courtroom behavior. With regard to our research, such questions may be raised about the extent to which the results would hold true across the population of trial judges or over different types of trials. The primary answer to these questions lies in replicating and refining with further field and social science experimental research the results of any single study of actual courtroom behavior (Rosenthal & Blanck, 1993).

Conclusion

In attempting to contribute to the study of judges' and juries' behavior in the live courtroom setting, we have worked with judges in a collaborative manner. Through this collaborative venture, we may begin to understand collectively the potential impact of judges' behavior on the people embroiled in the trial process. It is my hope that questions such as how people – the judges, jurors, counsel, parties, and the press – react to the operation of the legal system, and how they manifest their expectations, beliefs, attitudes, and biases about that system, can be addressed more systematically through empirically based models such as the one presented here.

Note

1. Canon 3(B)(5) states: "A judge shall perform judicial duties without bias or prejudice. A judge shall not, in the performance of judicial duties, by words or conduct manifest bias or prejudice based upon race, sex, religion, national origin, disability, age, sexual orientation or socioeconomic status, and shall not permit staff, court officials and others subject to the judge's direction and control to do so" (ABA Model Code of Judicial Conduct, Standing Committee on Ethics and Professional Responsibility, August 1990, pp. 9–10).

References

Blanck, P. D. (1987). The process of field research in the courtroom: A descriptive analysis. *Law and Human Behavior, 11*(4), 337–351.

Blanck, P. D. (1991a). What empirical research tells us: Studying judges' and juries' behavior. *American University Law Review, 40*(2), 775–804.

Blanck, P. D. (1991b). The emerging work force: Empirical study of the Americans with Disabilities Act. *Journal of Corporate Law, 16*(4), 693–803.

Blanck, P. D. (1992a). Empirical study of the employment provisions of the Americans with Disabilities Act: Methods, preliminary findings and implications. *New Mexico Law Review, 22*(3), 119–241.

86   Peter David Blanck

Blanck, P. D. (1992b). *The appearance of justice in criminal and civil trials.* Presentation at the Annenberg Symposium on Jury Communication, Washington, DC.
Blanck, P. D. (1993). Calibrating the scales of justice: Studying judges' behavior in jury and bench trials. *Indiana Law Journal, 68*(4).
Blanck, P. D., Bellack, A. S., Rosnow, R. L., Rotheram–Borus, M. J., & Schooler, N. R. (1992). Scientific rewards and conflicts of ethical choices in human subjects research. *American Psychologist, 47,* 959–65.
Blanck, P. D., & Rosenthal, R. (1992). Nonverbal behavior in the courtroom. In R. Feldman (Ed.), *Application of Nonverbal Behavioral Theories and Research* (pp. 89–115). Hillsdale, NJ: Erlbaum.
Blanck, P. D., Rosenthal, R., & Cordell, L. H. (1985). The appearance of justice: Judges' verbal and nonverbal behavior in criminal jury trials. *Stanford Law Review, 38,* 89–136, 157–158.
Blanck, P. D., Rosenthal, R., Hart, A. J., & Bernieri, F. (1990). The measure of the judge: An empirically-based framework for exploring trial judges' behavior. *Iowa Law Review, 75*(3), 653–684.
Blanck, P. D., Rosenthal, R., & Vannicelli, M. (1986). Taking to and about patients: The therapist's tone of voice. In P. D. Blanck, R. Buck, & R. Rosenthal (Eds.), *Nonverbal communication in the clinical context* (pp. 99–143). University Park, PA: Penn State Press.
Blanck, P. D., & Rosenthal, R., Vannicelli, M., & Lee, D. T. (1986). Therapist's tone of voice: Descriptive, psychometric, interactional, and competence analyses. *Journal of Social and Clinical Psychology, 4,* 154–175.
Blanck, P. D., & Turner, A. N. (1987). Gestalt research: Clinical field research approaches to studying organizations. In J. Lorsch (Ed.), *The handbook of organizational behavior* (pp. 109–123). New York: Prentice-Hall.
Cohen, J., & Cohen, P. (1983). *Applied multiple regression/correlational analyses for the behavioral sciences* (2nd ed.). Hillsdale, NJ: Erlbaum.
Diamond, S. (1981). Exploring sources of sentencing disparity. In B. D. Sales (Ed.), *The trial process* (pp. 387, 402). New York: Plenum Press.
Ebbesen, E. B., & Konecni, V. J. (1981). The process of sentencing adult felons: A causal analysis of judicial decisions. In B. D. Sales (Ed.), *The trial process* (pp. 431–58). New York: Plenum Press.
Elwork, A., Sales, B. A., & Suggs, B. (1981). The trial: A research review. In B. D. Sales (Ed.), *The trial process* (pp. 1–30). New York: Plenum Press.
Flanders, J. (1984). Blind umpires – A response to Professor Resnik. *Hastings Law Journal, 35,* 505–522.
Greenbaum, A. (1975). Judges' nonverbal behavior in jury trials: A threat to judicial impartiality. *Virginia Law Review, 61,* 1266.
Grisso, T., Baldwin, E., Blanck, P. D., Borus-Rotheram, M. J., Schooler, N., & Thompson T. (1991). The advancement of scientific integrity. *American Psychologist, 46,* 758–766.
Hemsley, G. D., & Doob, A. N. (1978). The effect of looking behavior on perceptions of a communicator's credibility. *Journal of Applied Social Psychology, 8,* 136.
Jones, E. (1990). *Interpersonal Perception* (pp. 237–259). New York: Freeman.
Kalven, H., & Zeisel, H. (1966). *The American jury.* Boston: Little, Brown.
Konecni, V. J., & Ebbesen, E. B. (1979). External validity of research in legal psychology. *Law and Human Behavior, 3,* 39–42.
Levi, J. (1990). The study of language in the judicial process. In J. Levi & A.

Walker (Eds.), *Language in the judicial process* (pp. 75–125). New York: Plenum Press.

Lind, E., Thibaut, J., & Walker, L. (1976). A cross-cultural comparison of the effect of adversary and inquisitorial processes on bias in legal decisionmaking. *Virginia Law Review, 62,* 271–282.

McElhaney, J. (1990). The rub. *American Bar Association Journal,* 80–83.

National Conference of State Trial Judges. (1989). *The judge's book* (pp. 31–38). Chicago: American Bar Association.

Pryor, B., & Leone, C. (1981). Behavioral stereotypes of deceptive communication. *Trial, 17,* 14–19.

Redish, M. H., & Marshall, L. L. (1986). Adjudicatory independence and the values of procedural due process. *The Yale Law Journal, 95,* 455–505.

Reitz, J. (1991). Why we probably cannot adopt the German advantage. *Iowa Law Review, 75,* 987–1009.

Resnik, J. (1982). Managerial judges. *Harvard Law Review, 96,* 376, 380, 445.

Rosenthal, R. (1981). Pfungst's horse and Pygmalion's PONS: Some models for the study of interpersonal expectancy effects. In *The Clever Hans Phenomenon* (pp. 182–210). New York: Academy.

Rosenthal, R. & Blanck, P. D. (1993). Science and ethics in conducting, analyzing and reporting social science research: Implications for social scientists, juries, judges and lawyers. *Indiana Law Journal, 68*(4).

Rosnow, R. L., & Rosenthal, R. (1989). Statistical procedures and the justification of knowledge in psychological science. *American Psychologist, 44,* 1276, 1280.

Ryan, J. P., Ashman, A., Sales, B. D., & Shane-DuBow, S. (1980). *American trial judges: Their work styles and performance.* New York: Free Press.

Saks, M. J., & Blanck, P. D. (1992). Improving on justice: The unrecognized benefits of sampling and aggregation in the trial of mass torts. *Stanford Law Review, 44,* 815–51.

State v. Wheat, 131 Kan. 562, 569, 292 P. 793 797 (1930).

State v. Barron, 465 S.W. 2d 523, 527–78 (Mo. Ct. App. 1971).

Visher, C. (1987). Juror decision making: The importance of evidence. *Law and Human Behavior, 11,* 1–18.

Wrightsman, L. (1991). *Psychology and the legal system* (2nd ed.) (pp. 236–238, 372–382). Pacific Grove, CA: Brooks/Cole.

5. Expectancies and the perpetuation of racial inequity

MARYLEE C. TAYLOR

Introduction

Twenty-five years ago, scientists and the public were introduced to experimental demonstrations of expectancy effects in science, education, and medicine (Beecher,1966; Rosenthal, 1966; Rosenthal & Jacobson, 1968). At the same time, the pervasiveness and complexity of racial inequity in the United States were becoming increasingly evident. Recent decades have brought fuller recognition that barriers to racial change are produced by intrapersonal, interpersonal, and institutional dynamics, often linked in intricate positive feedback systems. This chapter examines the role of intrapersonal, interpersonal, and institutionalized expectations in these feedback systems, considering a set of topics related to *racial inequity in education:*

1. white opposition to busing,
2. long-term effects of segregated schooling on blacks, and
3. white teachers' treatment of black students;

and a second set of topics related to *racial inequity in employment:*

4. interaction of black employees with white supervisor and co-workers,
5. white reactions to race-targeted interventions, and
6. psychological effects of affirmative action on its black beneficiaries.

These six topics were selected for their importance and because a research literature exists on each. The reader will soon realize, however, that only a small proportion of the research reviewed here examines expectation effects explicitly. Translating findings and ideas from other social psychological frameworks into the language of expectancy effects is part of the work of this chapter.

Interpersonal, intrapersonal, and institutionalized expectations

The multifarious roles of expectations in positive feedback systems that perpetuate racial inequity can best be understood if distinctions and relationships among interpersonal, intrapersonal, and institutionalized expectations are appreciated. A highly useful discussion of interpersonal and intrapersonal expectations was provided by Darley and Fazio (1980). These analysts note that *interpersonal* behavioral sequences, in which the perceiver's behavior evokes confirming behavior from the target, is the essence of the self-fulfilling prophecy effect described by Merton (1948).[1] However, their outline and a congruent sketch by Jones (1986) also describe two forms of *intrapersonal* expectation dynamic, one that falls short of Merton's criterion and one that goes beyond it.

Falling short refers to the possibility that the expectation sequence never reaches the interpersonal stage, remaining an intrapersonal process within perceivers, who may process information or take action so as to confirm their expectations.[2] Darley and Fazio (1980) note that even expectation sequences truncated before becoming interpersonal can be very consequential for targets, especially where the perceiver has power over the target's fate. For example, an employer may simply refuse even to interview an applicant for whom low expectations are held. Or a supervisor, operating on biased perceptions, may lower a job evaluation, however competent the target's performance – a pattern Miller and Turnbull (1986) would call *behavioral disconfirmation/perceptual confirmation*.

Going beyond means that a given expectancy sequence leaves its imprint on the target, encouraging other confirming behavior in the future; the interpersonal expectancy sequence is thus echoed in an intrapersonal expectancy pattern within the target. The precise form of this continuing influence is suggested by Darley and Fazio to depend on the targets' attributions for their confirming behavior. Attributions to the situation, for example, encourage confirming behavior in similar situations; dispositional attributions to the self create more generalized tendencies for continuing confirmation (Darley & Fazio, 1980). Experimental demonstration of such lasting effects has been provided by Snyder and Swann (1978a) and by Fazio, Effrein, and Falender (1981).

Interpersonal expectations and intrapersonal expectations that fall short and go beyond the interpersonal will receive much attention in the pages that follow, but our consideration must be broader still: We cannot begin to comprehend the full role of expectations in perpetuating and magnifying racial inequity without considering also their institutionalization. Laboratory experiments deliberately disembed expectations from their normal context, and much has been learned through this strategy. But in the real social world, race-linked expectations feed into organized social policies and practices, that is, they become *institutionalized*. Equally important, expectations are often derived from institutional arrangements. Thus emerge positive feedback cycles in which intrapersonal, interpersonal, and institutional influences play off each other.

Crucial to a consideration of institutionalized expectations is the acknowledgment that imbalance in the power of racial majority and minority groups has important implications. Just as intrapersonal expectation processes are particularly consequential when the perceiver has power over the target, so it is the dominant racial group that can exponentially increase the leverage of its expectations by embodying them in institutional practice.

An exemplar – the Word, Zanna, and Cooper study of interracial interviewing

The ingenious two-stage study of Word, Zanna, and Cooper (1974) is often taken as an exemplar of research demonstrating the operation of expectancy effects in maintaining racial segregation and inequity. By examining both the questions actually addressed by Word et al. and the adjunctive issues raised by their findings, we can see the manner in which interpersonal, intrapersonal, and institutionalized expectation dynamics may be interlaced.

Word et al. observed the behavior of white interviewers as they conducted sessions with black and white "job applicants," actually experimental confederates trained to exhibit standard behavior. Having found that the white interviewers evidenced more *low immediacy* behaviors when the applicant was black (the interviewers made frequent speech errors, maintained greater interaction distance, and terminated interviews early), the researchers conducted a second round of interviews, this time employing white subjects in all roles. However, some of the white interviewers had been trained to interact with low immediacy, as had been typical for interviewers of black subjects in the first phase of the research, whereas the remaining interviewers were trained to behave in ways that characterized the earlier white–white interviews. The impact of this differing interviewer behavior was revealed in blind raters' judgments that job applicants showed inferior performance when their interviewers manifested the low immediacy behaviors typically directed to black applicants.

Word et al. showed interviewers' behavior to be a function of the expectations presumably generated in their minds by the race of the job applicants;[3] the research then demonstrated that applicants' behavior responds to such variations in interviewer behavior. In the world outside the lab, it is reasonable to suppose that the kind of *interpersonal* expectation sequence Word et al. demonstrated would often be accompanied by *intrapersonal* expectancy sequences within both perceivers and targets – perceptual confirmation that falls short of interactional confirmation, perhaps in the form of biased evaluations by interviewers; and on the part of minority applicants, pessimism or lowered self-esteem that will have ramifications far beyond the original interview. Also, and most important, whether perceptual or behavioral, confirmation of white employers' low expectations for black job applicants is often taken as evidence against the desirability of affirmative action hiring, thereby influencing *institutional* practice. The segregated workforce thus encouraged breeds the stereotypes presumably at the root of white interviewers' expectations, and the positive feedback loop is complete.

Expectations and the linkage of individual psychology with social structure

Cataloging the roles of expectations in psychological–institutional feedback systems is a uniquely social psychological task in the sense envisioned by C. Wright Mills (1959). As paraphrased in Taylor and Johnson's (1986) discussion of strategies for linking individual psychology and social structure Mills saw that

> [s]ocial psychology in its grandest aspirations must strive for an appreciation and understanding of the intersection of biography and history," that is, the intersection of "human behavior . . . located in the character of individuals and relationships with particular others" and "the temporally dynamic organization of many such lives and situations into institutions. (p. 181)

Stereotypes and attributions have been identified as critical means for linking individual and macrosocial levels of analysis (Pettigrew, 1981, p. 304). Expectations should certainly be added to that list.

Race inequity in education

White opposition to busing

> Stereotypic expectancies white Americans hold for blacks derive in sub-
> stantial measure from societal patterns of discrimination and inequality.
> By encouraging such negative policy opinions as opposition to busing,
> these expectancies then feed back to retard institutional changes that
> would increase racial equality. This impact of stereotypic expectancies is
> magnified by virtue of the linkage between school and housing segrega-
> tion, itself reflecting the operation of self-fulfilling prophecies.

The 1954 *Brown* decision was followed by a series of judicial acknowl-
edgments that simply declaring formal school segregation unconstitu-
tional would not suffice to change patterns of segregated education,
particularly in urban centers. Entrenched housing segregation and a
history of school siting decisions geared to capitalize on housing patterns meant that segregated schools would remain a fact of life in U.S.
metropolitan areas unless active, corrective measures were taken (Orfield, 1978).

Race-conscious school assignment plans, often requiring the provi-
sion of transportation, have been the most common intervention to
achieve desegregated schools. The past two decades of experience have
shown that the probability of *successful* desegregation is increased by
the presence of certain conditions, among them support from teachers
and the community at large (Epstein, 1985; Orfield, 1978). In fact, the
courts have often taken formal account of community sentiment in their
decisions (see, e.g., *Dowell v. Board of Education of the Oklahoma City
Public Schools*). In short, public opinion about busing has implications
for the extent and character of desegregated schooling.

White support for busing has crept up slowly over the years (Jaynes
& Williams, 1989). In the national probability sample of white respondents to the 1990 General Social Survey (GSS), 31% of those giving a
substantive answer say they support busing (Taylor, 1991b). In some
respects, opinion on busing is a maverick among racial cognition measures: The uniform distribution of busing opposition across socioeconomic status levels has been noted in earlier research (Schuman, Steeh,
& Bobo, 1985), and in the 1990 GSS data, opinion on busing was
essentially uncorrelated with level of education, though related to age
and region, older whites and Southerners being more likely to oppose
busing (Taylor, 1991b).

Whites' opinions about busing have been examined in relation to other racial cognitions, as well as in relation to demographic factors; in fact, opinion on busing has been at the center of much debate among students of racial attitudes (see, e.g., Bobo, 1983; McConahay, 1982). Among the social psychological variables showing the strongest association with opposition to busing in the 1990 GSS responses are attribution of black poverty to individual and not structural factors; the belief that reverse discrimination exists; and aversion to interracial contact. The 1990 GSS data show that opinion on busing is also significantly, though modestly, related to racial *stereotyping* – beliefs that whites and blacks differ on such dimensions as intelligence, laziness, and the propensity to use violence (Taylor, 1991a, 1991b).[4]

Racial stereotypes are often, and quite reasonably, construed as expectancies, probabilistic beliefs about the likely characteristics of individuals in the stereotyped group. What has been learned about the genesis of stereotypic expectancies, such as those white Americans commonly hold about blacks?

Sociologists' considerations of stereotypes often emphasize such factors as self-interest and the need to justify historical exploitation. Psychologists offer other perspectives; for example, Ashmore and DelBoca (1981) compare sociocultural, psychoanalytic, and cognitive perspectives on stereotyping. The relevant literature is much too extensive for a comprehensive summary here, but two perspectives on stereotyping will be sketched. From cognitive social psychology has come an emphasis on the *illusory correlation*, perceivers' tendency to associate distinctive characteristics or behaviors, such as deviant misdeeds, with distinctive peoples, such as racial minorities (Hamilton, 1981). As Hamilton describes it, racial segregation means that blacks will be rare and thus distinctive in the experience of impressionable white children, making conditions ripe for the generation of illusory correlations. Avoidance is a common consequence of the negative perceptions whites develop about blacks, increasing blacks' distinctiveness in white experience and their vulnerability as targets for more illusory correlational thinking (Hamilton, 1981). To round things off, Hamilton describes how existing stereotypes are reinforced through biased information processing that encourages illusory correlations, that is, through intrapersonal expectancy confirmation. Recent experimental research shows that illusory correlations created through the presentation of distinctive stimuli generalize to personality domains about which no information at all has been presented (Acorn, Hamilton, & Sherman, 1988). Although cognitive processing is the motor that drives the sequence Hamilton describes, the fuel is a social structural reality – the segregated pattern of American social life.

More explicit attention is given to the dependence of stereotyping on societal patterns in Bobo and Kluegel's (1991) analysis of 1990 GSS data. The researchers report that whites' stereotypes of African-Americans, Hispanic-Americans, and Asian-Americans mirror the material and social statuses of those groups, emphasizing that stereotyping must be viewed as an *outcome* of sociological conditions, produced in large part by whites' need to explain the disadvantaged position of minorities. In the end, these writers concur with Rothbart's concise conclusion: "If we wish to change our stereotypes of female and black inferiority, we would do well to change *first* their inferior social and economic status" (Rothbart, 1981, p. 171).

Though differing in emphasis, both Hamilton's (1981) analysis and that of Bobo and Kluegel (1991) describe stereotypic expectations as links between individual psychology and societal realities, in this case, as in many, serving to retard social change: Existing patterns of social segregation and inequality encourage stereotypic expectancies that then, along with a profusion of other detrimental effects, lead whites to oppose busing. Such opposition retards the desegregated schooling of the next generation, slowing the movement toward racial equity that potentially could end this problematic cycle.

But there are broader ramifications of the process just described, owing to the link between *school* and *housing* desegregation, in which another form of self-fulfilling prophecy plays a role. Among families with children, housing choices are heavily influenced by the characteristics of schools in the area. Analysts have long described whites' spiraling avoidance of neighborhoods they fear will become predominantly black or neighborhoods where racial turnover in schools is feared. This, of course, is a classic self-fulfilling prophecy dynamic: Common fears about the behavior of others create the feared situation, much like runs on banks.[5] Pearce, Crain, Farley, and Taeuber (1987) have shown that housing desegregation is more likely to develop and persist in areas where school desegregation plans are in operation, presumably because the assurance of a stable racial mix defuses fears and thus deactivates the self-fulfilling prophecy dynamic.

Long-term effects of segregated schooling on blacks

Where school segregation remains unremedied, intra- and interpersonal expectation effects are implicated in producing deleterious effects over black students' lifetimes and beyond. Employers hold lowered expectations for blacks with a record of segregated schooling. Segregated schooling appears to lower blacks' expectations of positive outcomes in education and employment and to discourage future participation in desegregated settings; translated into poor performance or avoidance, these expectations become self-fulfilling. Especially if they are transmitted to the next generation, such social psychological products of segregated schooling feed back to reproduce societal segregation.

Implementation of school desegregation in some areas of the United States notwithstanding, segregated primary and secondary education remains a reality for large numbers of black students (Jaynes & Williams, 1989). Litigation about school desegregation continues, making evidence about the effects of segregation a matter of pragmatic significance as well as scholarly interest.

Early studies of the impact of school segregation typically compared the educational achievement, psychological characteristics, and inter-group attitudes of schoolchildren in segregated and desegregated schools. A most important development has been the recent research attention to long-term effects of segregated education on the life course of black Americans.

One means by which segregated schooling becomes a lifelong liability for blacks is that employers often respond to a segregated educational history as a cue that lowers their expectations for prospective black employees. Evidence from responses by a national sample of 1,101 nonminority employers to an experimental vignette are instructive (Braddock, Crain, McPartland, & Dawkins, 1986). The employers were asked to identify the job they would assign a hypothetical applicant described in terms of a number of crossed factors, including race, sex, level of education, and, for the high-school educated, whether the school was inner city or well-reputed suburban. For hypothetical black women applicants, inner-city high school education increased the likelihood of being placed in a job with a high proportion of black workers. For hypothetical black men applicants, inner-city high school education brought assignment to a lower-status job, a pattern not seen in the white applicant condition.

Such influence of segregated schooling on prospective white employers' perceptions and expectations is a serious liability for black Americans. Also critically important are effects of segregated schooling on expectations generated in black students themselves. Hartford, Connecticut, is one of the rare locations where desegregation was experimentally manipulated: During the 1970s, inner-city black students were randomly selected either to be enrolled in predominantly white suburban schools or to stay in their predominantly black inner-city high schools. Subsequent research on participants in the Hartford experiment revealed that black female students from desegregated schools were less likely than the control group to drop out of high school because of pregnancy, and black male students randomly chosen for desegregated schooling were less likely to become delinquent and drop out (Crain, Hawes, Miller, & Peichert, 1992). In both cases, plausible mediators are intrapersonal expectations – confidence that the individuals' efforts had the promise of yielding such outcomes as advanced education or occupational success.

More generally, a large body of evidence now documents the *perpetuation of segregation* phenomenon (Braddock, 1985). Blacks who are segregated at one level of education are likely to avoid desegregated education thereafter. In the South, where traditionally black colleges are available, black students from segregated secondary schools are disproportionately likely to attend traditionally black institutions of higher education. Northern black students with segregated elementary and secondary experience are less likely to attend college at all, presumably because they do not have the option of entering black institutions of higher learning (Braddock & McPartland, 1982). Blacks who have attended segregated schools more often hold segregated jobs traditional for blacks, jobs that have lower status and pay (Braddock, Crain, & McPartland, 1984). Furthermore, segregated schooling for blacks is negatively associated with a preference for interracial housing and with actual desegregated housing experience in adulthood (Orfield, 1980).

One explanation for the perpetuation of desegregation phenomenon is external resources: Black adults from segregated schools are, for example, less likely to have knowledge of desegregated jobs or the social networks useful in gaining them (Crain & Weisman, 1972).

A second explanation, however, is social psychological: Segregated schooling appears to reduce the confidence that a fair opportunity exists and that the outcomes of interracial interaction will be positive (Braddock, 1985; Crain & Weisman, 1972). Research using samples of black students on a predominantly white university campus supports the notion that such social psychological factors are important mediators of the perpetuation of segregation pattern. Black college students from largely black high schools, especially males, are more likely than blacks from racially mixed high schools to say they would be uncomfortable working under a white supervisor. Similarly, these black college students from segregated high schools are less likely to find the predominantly white university environment hospitable; they are more likely to perceive discrimination on campus; they are less likely to want or to have positive interracial contacts (Taylor, 1987). Importantly, researchers have concluded that for black students, unlike whites, the perceived interracial climate has a large impact on achievement (Crain & Weisman, 1972). The tendency for black students from segregated high schools to see the predominantly white university as inhospitable is congruent with the trend Braddock and McPartland (1989) report for segregated schooling to depress black adults' ratings of their white co-workers and supervisors. In neither case are the patterns strong enough to be definitive, but they do suggest an important direction for further research.

In short, a history of segregated schooling may create pessimistic expectations about the outcomes of potential interracial transactions in future settings.[6] Insofar as these prophecies are associated with poor performance (Crain & Weisman, 1972) and with the avoidance of desegregated environments (Braddock & McPartland, 1983), they are self-fulfilling.

The patterns just described are effects of *personal prophecies* (Jussim, 1990a, p. 2), that is, intrapersonal expectations. But just as Eccles, Jacobs, and Harold (1990) documented parent-to-child transmission of gender-linked expectations of competence, it is likely that intergenerational perpetuation of segregation is encouraged by parents' transmission to their children of their own segregation-bred negative expectancies for interracial transactions.[7] In one sample, a correlation of .6 was found between black college students' attitudes toward whites and the attitudes these students reported their parents to have (Taylor, 1987). Such evidence has been used in school desegregation litigation to argue that social psychological dynamics as well as resource deficits create *second-generation liabilities* for the children of black Americans who had been subject to official, de jure school segregation.

In sum, segregated schools can be described as an institutional embodiment of the negative orientation held by white Americans toward blacks, an orientation that presumably encompasses threat, hostility, aversion, *and* stereotypic expectations. This institutional pattern promotes a panoply of damaging inter- and intrapersonal expectations. A history of attendance at predominantly black schools serves as a cue for white employers, producing low expectations for prospective black workers and often leading employers to truncate interaction. In black students, segregated schooling discourages confidence in the payoff of education, resulting in higher rates of dropping out, teen pregnancy, and delinquency. Segregated schooling reduces black adults' confidence in the prospects for successful interracial transactions and the inclination to try them. And it may lead black parents to transmit skepticism and avoidance to their children. Behavioral responses to these intra- and interpersonal expectations complete the feedback loop: Social segregation is reproduced, thereby promoting low expectations about black Americans, pessimism among blacks, and continued organizational exclusion.

White teachers' treatment of black students

> Teacher–student relationships are fertile ground for the operation of interpersonal expectation effects, and with potentially devastating consequences. There is indirect and some direct evidence that white teachers may hold lowered expectations for black pupils, and research on interracial interaction among adults documents subtle forms of behavioral discrimination through which such social cognitions can find expression. Pupil race may also have more complicated effects on teacher behavior, interacting with ability expectations. Also, teacher expectations for their pupils as a group can be reflected in decisions about classroom structure and procedures. Here again, a positive feedback system may be at work: White teachers' expectations for black pupils necessarily reflect the teachers' own education and societal experience; and to the extent that teacher expectations impede the development of black pupils, they serve to perpetuate the societal inequality that was their genesis.

Where formal school desegregation has been accomplished, black pupils often obtain white teachers as well as white classmates. The best-controlled studies suggest that on average, school desegregation brings nontrivial achievement gains of about one grade level by the end of elementary school for black students whose desegregated experience began early (Crain & Mahard, 1983). However, these gains have not been as large or consistent as many reformers had hoped, and white teachers have been suspect as impediments to black children's learning.[8]

It is plausible that many white teachers convey negative expectancies to their black pupils, producing *Golem effects* (Babad, Inbar, & Rosenthal, 1982). Sensitive measures reveal that substantial stereotyping of blacks by white Americans persists, even among college-educated whites, and low intelligence is one critical dimension of the stereotype. In the national probability sample responding to the 1990 GSS, approximately 44% of college-educated whites rated blacks as a group lower on intelligence than whites as a group (Bobo & Kluegel, 1991). Teachers come from this college-educated population. Why should they be different?

The most direct and comprehensive evidence about pupil race effects on teacher expectancies is provided by the meta-analysis of Baron, Tom, and Cooper (1985). For combined results of experimental studies performed between 1969 and 1981, teacher expectations – perceptions about student performance, achievement, or ability – show a significant effect in favor of white students. The combined effect size suggests that "the average white student was given higher expectations by the teacher than about 58% of the black students" (p. 258). The experiments represented in the Baron et al. meta-analysis are, needless to say, subject to the external validity concerns that haunt most experimental work. But the congruence of these conclusions with broader evidence about the attitudes and perceptions of white Americans enhances their credibility.

Negative racial expectancies may, of course, be held without finding behavioral expression. However, research on white American adults suggests that behavioral discrimination is common. Helping studies and other research using nonreactive measures indicate that many white Americans do manifest subtle behavioral discrimination, especially when the situation is ambiguous enough that the appearance of out-and-out racism can be avoided (Crosby, Bromley, & Saxe, 1980; Dovidio, Mann, & Gaertner, 1989). Again, we might ask how white American teachers could be expected to escape this pattern.[9]

An especially insidious combination of behaviors was noted among Weitz's (1972) white subjects as they anticipated the arrival of a black co-worker: Those whites who professed the most pro-black attitudes showed particularly negative subtle behavior, such as coolness in tone of voice. This pattern, if present in classrooms, would place black pupils in the kind of "double bind" that is harder to handle than consistent negative messages (Bateson, Jackson, Haley, & Weakland, 1956). In a series of studies, Babad and his collaborators (see chapter 6 in this volume) found evidence that teachers respond to low-achieving students with this kind of mix – compensatory, positive, controllable behaviors, accompanied by negative "leakage" in behavioral dimensions less subject to control. It is not implausible that a similar incongruous mix may often be directed at black children by white teachers.

For all such suggestive considerations, direct evidence that substantial numbers of white teachers systematically differentiate between black and white pupils is sparse. Researchers have noted negative teacher treatment of black pupils in natural classroom settings (e.g., Leacock,

1969), but the often unassessed correlates of pupil race make such observations difficult to interpret.[10] Better-controlled lab studies finding no effects of pupil race on outcomes like teacher evaluations (e.g., Long & Henderson, 1974) have faced questions about verisimilitude; other studies claiming pupil race effects took teacher evaluations rather than behaviors as the outcome of interest (e.g., Harvey & Slater, 1975).

Intriguing and alarming results were produced in one lab study that did focus on teaching behaviors (Rubovits & Maehr, 1973). Interaction effects were observed between pupil race and a Pygmalion-type expectancy manipulation: The gifted label proved to be an advantage for white students but a *disadvantage* for black students. These results underline the problem with simply equating pupil race effects and expectancies. If such an equation held, pupil race effects would mirror main effects of expectancy manipulations. Instead, in this case, teachers were suggested to have worked to *dis*confirm positive expectancies for black students, as if trying to suppress the achievement of high-potential blacks. Although this suggestion is consonant with Shore's (1969) finding that teachers lower the personality and adjustment ratings of pupils who disconfirm negative expectancies, no published replication of the Rubovits and Maehr race-by-expectancy interaction has been located. In fact, Taylor (1979) found a pupil-race-by-expectancy interaction effect in the opposite direction: White teachers-in-training emitted more positive affect when they believed they were teaching high-ability black and low-ability white pupils. Thus, the Rubovits and Maehr conclusion should be treated as a provocative hypothesis.

What about the form of expectation effect that Darley and Fazio (1980) describe as falling short of behavioral confirmation but nonetheless highly consequential – perceptual bias on the part of teachers, slanted evaluation of pupils as a means of making reality conform to prophecy? From his investigation of sixth-grade math classes, Jussim (1989) finds evidence of "modest" evaluational bias in favor of high-expectancy students. Researchers have yet to obtain a sound evidential base for assessing perceptual bias in teachers' evaluations of black students.

If research evidence is sparse regarding teachers' differential treatment of individual black and white students, what about differential teacher treatment of black and white student *groups?* Talking about expectancy effects, Brophy (1983) concludes: "Differential teacher treatment of intact groups and classes may well be a much more widespread and powerful mediator of self-fulfilling prophecy effects on student achievement than differential teacher treatment of individual students within the same group or class" (p. 643). Evidence of the potency of such group-based teacher expectations effects is provided in Epstein's (1985) research on 5,284 fifth-graders and 886 teachers in 94 schools: Teachers holding a negative view of school desegregation were most likely to adopt tracking and within-class ability grouping, effectively resegregating their classrooms, and the achievement of black students in their classes suffered measurably. Congruent with this finding, school-level differences in outcomes for disadvantaged students have been associated with administrators' and teachers' expectations (Jaynes & Williams, 1989).[11]

To recap, white teachers have been suspected of holding race-linked expectations for their pupils, expectations that may work at the intra-personal level to bias evaluations of student work and that, through behavioral expression, may evoke interpersonal confirmation. Implicit when not explicit is the concern that any such self-fulfilling prophecy dynamics may go beyond the interpersonal level to leave black pupils with lasting doubts about their educational potential. Studies of resegre-gative ability grouping and school-level variation in effectiveness under-line the worrisome potential for the impact of negative expectations to be magnified through institutionalization. We must await more individ-ual- and institutional-level research before drawing firm conclusions about the prevalence of debilitating expectations held by white teachers of black pupils. However, existing evidence is suggestive enough of problematic patterns to spur a call for more conclusive research.

Before leaving the topic of teacher–student interaction, a word is in order about a prominent theme in recent literature – the accuracy of teachers' expectancies. Some analysts have argued that if teacher expec-tations are largely a response to pupil performance, self-fulfilling proph-ecies play a limited role (Brophy, 1983; Jussim, 1989, 1990b). Babad, in this volume, disagrees, insisting that *self-maintaining expectations* belong under the self-fulfilling prophecy umbrella because of their potential to "fixate" and "exaggerate" existing variation in pupil achievement.

The precise nature of any differences in the teacher treatment di-rected toward various groups of students, and the impact of these differences, are crucial to this debate. If behavioral expressions of teach-ers' low expectations are functional strategies for promoting the learn-ing of low-achieving students, these expectations are a boon where accurate and a problem only if inaccurate. On the other hand, if low expectations lead teachers to behave in ways that retard the learning of students with achievement problems, accurate expectancies are at least as problematic as accurate ones. Rosenthal's (1973) *four-factor theory* of teacher expectancy mediation identifies climate, input, output, and feedback as behavioral dimensions mediating self-fulfilling prophecy effects in the classroom. A subsequent meta-analysis suggested climate and input to be the most prominent factors (Harris & Rosenthal, 1985). Reducing the rate of input to pupils with learning problems is arguably an appropriate teaching strategy. On the other hand, it is difficult to see how a chilly climate can be similarly functional, especially if it is an element in the incongruous positive and negative behavioral mix described earlier.

Reflecting on a different body of data, Epstein (1985) notes that many programs developed for "disadvantaged" learners have systematically minimized opportunities for students' control of "their own learning, behavior, or interaction," a pedagogical approach research shows to have negative consequences, if any (p. 40).

The accuracy argument has special import where teacher expectations cued by pupil race are involved. By definition, insofar as teacher behavior reveals effects of pupil race per se, considerable *in*accuracy is necessarily involved: Even for those subpopulations of black pupils who show the greatest educational deficits, there exists variability in academic potential and performance. But perhaps more important, for those acutely disadvantaged subpopulations in which race and a history of low achievement are strongly linked, there are particularly compelling reasons *not* to accept low teacher expectations as "mere" reflections of reality if there is any chance that they will interfere with effective teaching. Through a web of intrapersonal, interpersonal, and institutional dynamics, learning difficulties in many black students have been socially produced. For that reason, public schools bear extra responsibility to serve as an antidote to an otherwise bleak environmental press.

Though he stresses the accuracy of teacher expectations and the modesty of their impact, Jussim (1990b) acknowledges that repeated small effects can cumulate to nontrivial magnitudes. Accumulation of disadvantage, stemming from inequitable processes across all institutional spheres, is a hallmark of the black American experience (Pettigrew & Taylor, 1992). This pervasiveness of race-linked disadvantage makes any one facet all the more problematic and increases the urgency for teachers to counteract the dynamics of spiraling disadvantage, not participate in them.[12]

Race inequity in employment

Interaction of black employees with white supervisors and co-workers

> Negative interpersonal expectancies held by white interviewers may often put black job applicants at a disadvantage, and a history of negative interviews may generate low expectations among potential minority applicants, discouraging their continuing efforts. In the workplace, the supervisor's outlook can create interpersonal expectation effects that undermine the performance of minorities, whether the expectations be low or unrealistically high. Minorities seen as "token" affirmative action hires are particularly likely targets. Low expectations from supervisors can take a toll even if they "fall short" of creating interpersonal effects, insofar as they lead supervisors to withhold high-payoff assignments or assign low evaluations. These interpersonal and intrapersonal dynamics are encouraged by traditional institutional realities, and they serve to decrease the chances for structural changes that could break the cycle.

Having considered the orientation of white schoolteachers to their black pupils, we turn to the workplace interaction of black employees with white supervisors and co-workers. Social psychological dynamics impinging on affirmatively hired minority employees have been skillfully analyzed by Pettigrew and Martin (1987), who successively treat three aspects of employment: application; workplace interaction and performance; and supervisor evaluations. Self-fulfilling prophecy effects can interfere with minority employment success in each of these phases.

Application for employment. Pettigrew and Martin (1987) suggest that anticipated stressfulness of the application process, often reality based, can dissuade minorities from applying for employment openings in the first place. This claim is admittedly based on extrapolation from evidence about potential female job applicants, and at least one commentator believes that the generalization from gender to race is unjustified (Perman, 1987). But the Word et al. (1974) results described earlier in this chapter point to reasons many black adults may have learned to avoid interracial employment interviews.[13] In addition to apprehension about the stress of interracial interaction, potential black job applicants may assume that cognitive biases will lead white interviewers to evaluate them negatively, whatever their actual performance, making the effort a losing proposition in any case (Pettigrew & Martin, 1987).

The behavioral patterns observed in the white interviewers of Word et al. can be construed in several ways. Ickes (1984) discusses a white *avoidance disposition* relative to interracial interaction, and Stephan and Stephan (1985) present a model of *intergroup anxiety* experienced during interaction with outgroup members. But the white interviewer behavior pattern observed in Word et al. (1974) has most often been described as a manifestation of race-linked expectations. Similarly, antiblack evaluation biases on the part of white interviewers are interpretable as outcomes of ethnocentrism, by analogy to Frable's (1989) finding that gender identity predicted sex bias in evaluations of job applicants, but interviewers' cognitive biases can also be viewed as a form of intrapersonal self-fulfilling prophecy (Dipboye, 1982).

Whether or not white interviewer behavioral and evaluational biases are seen as products of expectancies, the hypothesized black avoidance of employment application would represent a self-fulfilling prophecy in its own right – apprehension producing a *certain* negative outcome, eliminating all chance of gaining the job.

Workplace interaction and performance. Turning to the situation of the black worker new to a job setting in which minorities are rare and perhaps also seen as affirmative action tokens, Pettigrew and Martin (1987) emphasize the important role of interpersonal expectations held by supervisors. Supervisors holding low expectations may actually evoke impaired performance from their black subordinates, or they may structure the situation so as to preclude superior performance by withholding challenging assignments, an analog of teachers reducing input in the classroom.

Still another possibility was suggested to Pettigrew and Martin by results of laboratory research on *solo* status (Taylor, Fiske, Close, Anderson, & Ruderman, 1975), namely, unrealistically high expectations for minorities, expectations that ultimately can only produce disappointment. The analysts suggest that when operating with such polarized low or high expectations, solos can't trust the feedback they receive and are deprived of appropriate similar others as bases for comparison.[14] Whether spotlighted solos face exaggerated low or high expectations, one mediator of impaired performance may be self-consciousness that is incompatible with full attention to the task at hand, or so implies Saenz and Lord's (1989) finding that turning the tables, asking minorities to evaluate co-workers, improved minorities' task performance.[15]

Adding to problems rooted in their minority and solo status, being viewed as a token affirmative action hire is one more impetus for low expectations from supervisors and co-workers. Whites' assumptions about their dissimilarity can lead to minorities' exclusion from informal work groups, exclusion that has negative professional as well as personal consequences (Pettigrew & Martin, 1987). Relevant here are Thomas's (1990) findings that same-race mentor–protégé relationships offered more psychosocial support to the managers under study than cross-race relationships, and that black managers were more likely than whites to report having a mentor other than their supervisor or a department member. The researcher concluded that mentorship from those structurally nearer was often unavailable to black managers.

Any doubts about the role of stereotypes in perpetuating racial inequity in employment must be quelled by Kirschenman and Neckerman's (1991) accounts of 1988–1989 interviews with Chicago-area employers about the local labor force. The employers' responses led the Chicago researchers to warn that attention to minority hiring is not enough. "Productivity is not an individual characteristic. Rather it is embedded in social relations. The qualities most likely to be proxied by race are not job skills but behavioral and attitudinal attributes – dependability, strong work ethic, and cooperativeness – that are closely tied to interactions among workers and between workers and employers. Our evidence suggests that more attention should be paid to social relations in the workplace. Antagonisms among workers and between workers and their employers are likely to diminish productivity. Thus employers' expectations may become self-fulfilling prophecies" (Kirschenman & Neckerman, 1991, p. 231).

Supervisor evaluations. Finally, stereotypic expectations can bias information seeking, labeling, and recall, leading to negative evaluations of minorities who are in fact performing well (Pettigrew & Martin, 1987). Where positive information must be acknowledged, minorities often fall victim to the *ultimate attribution error* (Pettigrew, 1979) – assignment of responsibility for positive behavior to transitory factors such as luck or unfair special advantage or to such situational factors as good equipment. In other words, by avoiding dispositional attributions of positive minority performance, supervisors can maintain their stereotypic expectations and continue to assign low evaluations.

Kraiger and Ford's (1985) meta-analysis of target race effects in performance evaluations underlines the need for concern about this form of intrapersonal expectations bias among white supervisors. Overall, a modest but nontrivial tendency for raters to favor same-race targets was found. Although actual race differences in performance may play some part in the observed effect, the analysts conclude that rater bias is implicated in some measure. Target effects were approximately equal in size (but opposite in direction) for black and white raters; however, given the preponderance of white supervisors in U.S. firms, such rater bias will in the aggregate work against black employees. Rating type, rating purpose, and rater training did not appear to moderate the target race effects, but two moderators were identified: (1) The effects were larger in field than in lab studies; (2) importantly, target race effects were *most* pronounced where blacks represented the *smallest* proportion of the workforce, arguably reflecting once again the impact of solo status (Taylor et al., 1975).[16]

Whether the focus is interviews, on-the-job relations with co-workers and supervisors, or performance evaluations, individual effects of minority status need not be large to be telling: As Blanchard (1989) notes, one implication of numerical minority status is that slights from the numerous dominant group members are concentrated on a small number of targets, potentially cumulating to become very serious problems.

Pettigrew and Martin (1987) conclude with some "micro-level" suggestions for diminishing problematic dynamics in work settings – for example, circulating information that documents the competence of individual minority hires, and training and rewarding supervisors to encourage their investment in successes for their minority subordinates. However, because so many of the dysfunctional dynamics outlined previously are predictable outcomes of fundamental institutional procedures and the imbalanced proportions they produce, the analysts warn that micro-level remedies represent an uphill battle at best. Congruent with the present chapter's focus on the interplay of intrapersonal, interpersonal, and institutional factors, Pettigrew and Martin conclude that fundamental change must come from macro-level adjustments – for example, reform of job recruitment procedures and increased accountability for full representation within firms. Unfortunately, the toll that processes outlined previously take on minority representation, performance, and ratings encourages many observers to see minority individuals' behavior as the problem, diverting attention from the institutional procedures in need of remedy. Here the positive feedback system runs in high gear.

White reactions to race-targeted interventions

Support for programs explicitly aimed to redress racial inequity is weakest among those who hold stereotypic expectancies about blacks. Nurtured if

not produced by existing inequity, such expectancies then retard its reduction. Also,workers whose employers practice affirmative action are
most likely to accept the assumptions on which this ameliorative program
is based; thus, opposing affirmative action for fear it will increase racial
polarization is a classic self-fulfilling prophecy dynamic, the negative
prediction actually encouraging the feared outcome.

White workers at affirmative workplaces are not, however, any less
vulnerable than other white workers to racial stereotyping. Cognitive
social psychology has offered many insights about why even positive
intergroup contact does not reliably diminish stereotypic expectancies:
biased information-seeking, perception, attribution, and recall play a role,
and at the interpersonal level, behavioral confirmation can be evoked;
even when contact brings a positive perception of the interactants themselves, memory bias and "subtyping" can limit generalization to the
group. Recent cognitive social psychology discussions insist that adequate
understanding of stereotypic expectancies will require attention not only
to motivation but also to normative and institutional factors supporting
stereotypes, a theme consonant with the emphasis of this chapter on the
reciprocal causal relations of psychological and social structural factors.

Recent evidence sheds light on two questions about white reaction to
race-targeted interventions: (1) What are the correlates of support for
and opposition to race-targeted programs? (2) What is the impact on
white workers of exposure to affirmative action in their workplace? As
we shall see, both questions can be considered in terms of interpersonal, intrapersonal, and institutionalized expectations.

White public opinion about race targeting. Prevalent themes in sociological social psychology and psychological social psychology seem to
make contradictory predictions about the relationship between racial
stereotyping and opposition to affirmative action (Taylor, 1991b; Taylor
& Pettigrew, 1992). Prominent in sociological social psychology is the
position that racial equity will be furthered if color-conscious policies
such as affirmative action are implemented (see, e.g., Kluegel, 1985).
Meanwhile, psychological social psychology *minimal group paradigm* research and related cognitive approaches have emphasized the negative
consequences of any ingroup–outgroup categorization. By implication,
color consciousness in any form risks worsening intergroup relations.

These competing perspectives were tested using data from the national probability sample of 1,150 white respondents answering the 1990
GSS, and support was found for the hypothesis prevalent in sociological social psychology (Taylor, 1991a, 1991b). Stereotyping of blacks was
positively correlated with three indicators of opposition to race-targeted
policies: denial that the government has a special obligation to help
blacks; opposition to such targeted programs as minority college schol-
arships and tax breaks to industries locating in minority neighborhoods;

and the belief that the government is spending too much on black Americans.

Apparently, support for race-targeted programs is not tied to the categorical thinking stereotypes represent, but it is most common among whites who *don't* stereotype blacks. The self-fulfilling prophecy element in this pattern is clearer when the relationship is described from the other direction: Opposition to race-targeted programs is linked to stereotypic thinking. As noted in the earlier discussion of stereotyping vis-à-vis white public opinion on busing, institutionally produced inequity is probably critical in the genesis and perpetuation of stereotypes among superordinate group members. The data reported here suggest that those stereotypic expectancies feed back to discourage support for the institutional intervention that could disrupt existing patterns by reducing racial inequities.

Attitudinal effects of workplace affirmative action on white employees. The crescendo of debate about affirmative action in this country has apparently encouraged those on all sides of the issue to assume that a trade-off is necessary, that out of self-interest or some less rational motivation, whites who work in firms practicing affirmative action will resent it and be provoked to develop more negative racial feelings and perspectives. Serious doubt is cast on this assumption by Taylor's (1991b) recent findings, based on analysis of the 1990 GSS.

Comparison of white GSS respondents reporting that their employers practice affirmative action with respondents from non-affirmative-action workplaces gives no sign of negative attitudinal reactions among whites experiencing affirmative action firsthand. Stereotyping of blacks, old-fashioned prejudice, and inclination for interracial contact do not differ for the two groups of white workers. Some attitudinal effects of affirmative action in the workplace do appear in the data – all positive. After demographic factors are controlled, whites from affirmative action firms are more likely to acknowledge that blacks face discrimination in jobs and housing; they are more likely to say that blacks have too little influence in American life and whites too much; they are more likely to believe that past discrimination obliges the government to give special help to blacks; and they are more likely to report themselves willing to take action against discrimination. Importantly, workforce race composition is not the critical factor: The pattern exists as described, and stronger if anything, when workforce race composition is controlled. Institution of affirmative action programs may often be accompanied by management-sponsored public relations programs that are successful at selling white workers on the rationale for affirmative action. A complementary explanation is the existence of the same fait accompli dynamic observed in white public responses to the decline of official segregation in housing (Pettigrew, 1975) – attitudes and beliefs accommodate to changing social realities.

The 1990 GSS findings relate to self-fulfilling prophecy dynamics at two levels. First, the assumption that affirmative action programs generate white resistance is central in many policy debates. Taylor's (1991b) results suggest that the strategy of avoiding affirmative action in order to promote "interracial harmony" is useless at best, counterproductive at worst. To the extent that this strategy is implemented, apprehension about aggravating racial tensions may dissuade decision makers from taking a route that would actually increase white support for programs to address racial inequity – the negative prediction thereby encouraging the feared outcome.

Second, at the individual level, it is noteworthy that affirmative action and the interracial contact it typically brings do not have across-the-board positive effects on white workers' attitudes. This *absence* of relationships demonstrates the resilience of stereotypic expectancies, their resistance to disconfirming information.

Why doesn't interracial contact work more efficiently and systematically to dispel stereotypes? A large body of relevant scholarship reveals that the question must be bisected: (1) Why is interracial contact so often unsuccessful at dispelling stereotypic views of the interactants themselves? (2) Why does intergroup contact producing improved relations among interactants not generalize reliably to their respective social categories?

One answer to the first question is that where racial stereotypes are relevant, a given behavior may actually be *seen* differently as a function of the actor's race. Sagar and Schofield (1980) reported that their white and black middle school subjects were more likely to interpret behavior as violent when the actor was black rather than white. Some research suggests such influences on perception to be greatest when the pertinent social category is highly salient (see, e.g., Wilder, 1981). Fiske and Neuberg (1990), on the other hand, conclude that category membership may exert a relatively stable effect; the factor having more *variable* impact may be the salience of individuating information.[17]

Information seeking, as well as processing and memory, may be biased by stereotypes (Hamilton, Sherman, & Ruvolo, 1990), and interaction can produce behavioral confirmation of expectancies (Snyder, 1981).[18]

The difficulty of meeting conditions under which contact is most likely to bring positive shifts in perception is underlined by Norvell and Worchel's (1981) finding that equal status in the microcosm is not sufficient: Historical inequalities impede the benefits of intergroup contact unless they are counteracted in the microcosm.

Another dynamic, attributional bias, may mitigate against changes in preconceptions. As noted earlier, Pettigrew (1979) has described the *ultimate attribution error*, the tendency for individuals to interpret outgroup members' negative behaviors dispositionally and their positive behaviors situationally, whereas ingroup members are favored by the mirror image attributional pattern. Support for this description was reported by Whitehead, Smith, and Eichhorn (1982), and Yarkin, Town, and Wallston's (1982) data are interpretable as partial support as well. Crocker, Hannah, and Weber (1983), and at about the same time Kulik (1983), presented evidence for a formulation that is very close to the ultimate attribution error idea, though framed differently. These analyses did not focus on intergroup relations, but rather on dispositional and situational attributions as a function of consistency with prior beliefs about the actor. The researchers found that situational pressures are ignored and dispositional attributions are chosen for consistent behavior, whereas behavior inconsistent with prior beliefs is attributed to the situation. If we add the assumption that beliefs held about ingroup members are likely to be predominantly positive and beliefs held about outgroup members predominantly negative, this formulation and its supporting evidence translate neatly into the ultimate attribution error notion. A useful summary representing attributional along with other cognitively based analyses is presented by Hewstone (1989).

But even where contact does dispel stereotypic expectancies about interactants, the experience seems often not to generalize to the larger outgroup. Memory biases may work to weaken the impact of experiences that disconfirm expectancies (Rothbart, 1981). Outgroup interactants who deviate from stereotypic assumptions may be distinguished from others, that is, *subtyped* (Weber & Crocker, 1983).[19] Crosby and Clayton (1990) suggest that intermittent confirmation may be particularly effective in maintaining stereotypes, implying that occasional disconfirmation can work against change.

An apparent dilemma relevant to the generalization of positive contact experience has been noted by a number of analysts (e.g., see

Rothbart & John, 1985; Wilder, 1984). On the one hand, if an outgroup-er's category membership is salient, the perceiver is less likely to move beyond categorical expectations about that interactant, that is, discon-firming information is less likely to be recognized as such. But reduced salience of the interactant's category membership discourages general-ization to the outgroup as a whole. Pettigrew and Martin (1987) note that Cook's (1984) research suggests a potential solution: Discourage category salience during the early stages of intergroup contact, and *then* call attention to category membership once the individual relationship is secure.[20]

Fiske and Neuberg's (1990) rich discussion of category-based and individuating processes in impression formation encompasses two ele-ments that are particularly important if the dominant, cognitive ap-proaches to stereotype maintenance and change are to be useful in understanding racial stereotyping. First, this analysis joins other recent calls for cognitive social psychology to attend seriously to the role of motivation (see, e.g., Devine,1989; Neuberg, 1989; Omoto & Borgida, 1987). Second, Fiske and Neuberg explicitly consider the important influence of "third parties" on a perceiver's motivation. They discuss the role of supervisors at the workplace, but their point surely general-izes to the influence of leaders at the macro as well as the micro level, and to normative support more broadly. Again, we are reminded that intra- and interpersonal expectation processes cannot be fully under-stood without reference to the institutional context in which they un-fold.

Psychological effects of affirmative action on its black beneficiaries

Social psychologists are addressing a question relevant to current public debates about affirmative action, viz. whether benefitting from affirmative hiring or promotion can evoke negative intrapersonal expectations among beneficiaries and set in motion a spiral of debilitation – first low self-confidence, then impaired job performance derived from the negative "personal prophecies." An often-explicit concern of researchers in this area is that any such depressed performance by minority beneficiaries of affirmative action may feed back to reinforce stereotypes held by the dominant group, decreasing the likelihood of shifts in organizational practice that would broaden minority inclusion by means other than affirmative action. Claims of documentation for this phenomenon have probably been exaggerated. In fact, a recent analysis of national survey data finds no evidence for any form of the beneficiary debilitation notion. However, in light of the relevance of this hypothesis for public policy, more definitive research should be pursued.

The earlier discussion of workplace relations suggested that token status can lower expectations held by dominant group members and interfere with minorities' working relationships. Does affirmative action also have direct negative psychological consequences for its beneficiaries, producing self-doubt or an *imposter syndrome* (Nacoste, 1989)? If so, does this negative intrapersonal expectation impair job commitment and ultimately job performance? These questions are the focus of a growing research literature, and some analysts have concluded that the answer is a conditional yes. Subjects in this research have been women, but it is frequently assumed that findings can be generalized to black Americans.

An early study by Chacko (1982) found that women managers who believed they had been hired because of their gender reported less job commitment than other women managers in their southwestern city, as well as less job satisfaction, more unhappiness with co-workers and supervisors, and greater role conflict. Examining *procedural stigma*, Nacoste and Lehman's (1987) role-play study led them to conclude that unless the employer in question had been found guilty of historical discrimination, preferential treatment lowered beneficiaries' expectations about forthcoming evaluations by others. Another moderating variable – perceived fairness of affirmative action – was the focus of Nacoste's 1989 study: Among subjects assigned a laboratory task on the basis of their sex, those who believed affirmative action to be unfair showed symptoms of the imposter syndrome, working more efficiently while devaluing their performance.

The self-confidence of beneficiaries has been central in research conducted by Heilman and her associates. The active ingredient affecting the intrapersonal expectations of beneficiaries is *external verification of competence*, asserted to be provided in merit selection and absent in preferential selection (Heilman, Lucas, & Kaplow, 1990). Women, who are assumed to approach leadership tasks with less confidence than men, were predicted and found to be more likely than men to respond to preferential selection with lowered self-evaluations and decreased interest (Heilman, Simon, & Repper, 1987). Congruent findings in a later study led the researchers to conclude that preferential selection can be harmful to beneficiaries unless it is accompanied by the assurance that "competence played a central [role] in the selection process" (Heilman et al., 1990, p. 215).

Preferential selection was found by Turner and Pratkanis (in press-a) to depress women's evaluations of specific aspects of their own performance and to encourage *self-handicapping* (Jones & Berglas, 1978) among those believing task success to be primarily a function of effort. The potential for individual-level feedback to counteract some negative effects of preferential treatment was documented by Turner, Pratkanis, and Hardaway (1991) and emphasized in a subsequent Turner and Pratkanis review (in press-b). Despite such qualifications, the cumulative message from the research outlined previously is that affirmative action carries serious risks of doing psychological damage to the intended beneficiaries unless special measures are taken to avert these dangers.

However, multiple limitations of the evidence on which these conclusions were based have been noted by Taylor (in press):

1. Affirmative action efforts often consist of such measures as broad-based advertising for entry-level jobs or posted announcements of promotion opportunities, *not* involving preferential selection in any form. Also, with rare exceptions, the law requires that any *preferential treatment* be of the *plus factor* type, that is, it must be embedded in a broader consideration of qualifications. In rare instances, the documented history of discrimination by an employer has convinced a court to impose race or sex quotas on that particular firm. However, as a rule, race or sex consciousness in hiring and promotion is legally permissible only when used along with other considerations and after qualification to do the job has been assured. If relevance to affirmative action is to be claimed or implied, research on psychological liabilities should not focus exclusively on the rare set-aside programs or even on plus factor preferential treatment, but should assess the impact of benefiting from the broad range of institutional adjustments that constitute affirmative action.
2. Preferential treatment based on *sex* was the focus of all the studies reviewed previously. Generalizability to race-based preferential treatment is sometimes claimed, but without actual evidence about the impact that affirmative action beneficiary status may have on racial minorities.
3. Laboratory studies have been the mainstay of research on the impact of beneficiary status. With few exceptions, subjects have been college students, not representatives of the workforce. Thus questions about the plausibility of experimental manipulations and the existence of demand characteristics must be asked.
4. Lab experiments equip us only to examine immediate effects of iso-

lated experiences as a beneficiary: Effects that are delayed, or that depend on prolonged "exposure" or context, would not be revealed in research of this kind.

Attempting to address these problems, Taylor (in press) analyzed self-reports from employed black repondents to the 1990 GSS, conducted by the University of Chicago's National Opinion Research Center. No significant or appreciable negative impact of employment at an affirmative action firm was found on ambition, appreciation for intrinsic features of jobs, job satisfaction, life satisfaction, sense of well-being, cynicism, or black ingroup esteem. Black workers did show two positive effects of employment at an affirmative action firm: greater ambition and belief in the helpfulness of people.

Given the small number of black respondents to the GSS and the difficulty of adequately controlling the influence of potential extraneous variables, Taylor's (in press) results should be considered only suggestive, a reminder that affirmative action is broader than preferential treatment; that gender and race are not interchangeable categories; that laboratory evidence must be complemented with field data; and that the impact of prolonged experience may differ from that of one-time exposure.

Though not convincingly demonstrated by existing data, any debilitating effects of affirmative action beneficiary status would be important to note; continuing research should certainly be encouraged. At the least, this research calls attention to the possibility for intended remedies to go awry. And where an intended remedy may boomerang so as to hamper the performance of minorities and lower expectations held by others, the result can be increased support for the very institutional shortcomings that created the need for remedy in the first place.

Concluding comments

Many aspects of the expectations framework exemplified in Rosenthal and Jacobson's (1968) *Pygmalion in the Classroom* study make it an apt model with which to examine individual- and institutional-level dynamics implicated in continuing racial inequity. One stands out: Psychology research on self-fulfilling prophecy effects turns the tables on conventional assumptions about the direction of causality. It is generally assumed that teachers' perceptions of their pupils are derived from the students' behavior. Expectancy research calls attention to the causal flow in the other direction. In American race relations, conventional wisdom similarly assumes particular causal sequences (e.g., interviewers don't recommend minority applicants because their interview performance showed them to be unworthy), whereas the expectations framework appropriately calls attention to the reverse causal flow. But the insight of the expectations framework is not simply substituted for the common causal assumption: It is added, transforming a recursive into a nonrecursive model. Indeed, though only incompletely acknowledged in theory or methodology (Taylor, 1988), this nonrecursivity is a central feature of racial stratification, a point powerfully illustrated by the identification of feedback loops, one after the other, in the preceding pages.

Like those of Word et al. (1974), many of the provocative and potentially important findings reviewed previously stand in need of replication and extension. Robert Rosenthal's influence has been evident in the emphasis on replication and quantitative synthesis of findings on interpersonal expectancy effects generally. Efforts to understand the range of individual- and institutional-level expectancy dynamics implicated in racial inequity, whether located in psychology, sociology, or related disciplines, can benefit from similar attention to the systematic cumulation of findings.

In this catalog of hypotheses and research evidence implicating expectation effects in patterns of racial inequity, positive feedback mechanisms that serve to maintain current social realities have been emphasized. If this emphasis has impressed the reader with the difficulty of effecting substantial racial change, such recognition is probably appropriate. However, the intent of this discussion is decidedly not to encourage fatalism. Quite the reverse. The social psychological insights reported here actually represent potentially invaluable guidelines for interventionist social policy.

The stereotyping literature can be read to make perceptual confirmation of expectations seem virtually inevitable, and descriptions of interpersonal expectancy effects sometimes suggest similarly bleak prognoses. However, potential levers for change in positive feedback cycles are identified as analysts learn more about the mediation and moderation of expectations effects. When Darley and Fazio (1980), Jones (1986), and Miller and Turnbull (1986) talk about the importance of motives held by perceivers and targets, or of targets' awareness of expectancies directed toward them, they offer strategies for breaking self-perpetuating patterns.

Similarly, examining the interplay of institutional factors and individual expectations as contributors to continuing racial inequity shines the spotlight on new classes of mediators and moderators, thereby exposing potential levers for change. Actions by state and local school officials, as well as by the courts, determine whether public schooling will continue to segregate black and white students, leaving psychological scars on both groups and opening the door to arguably more powerful group-based teacher expectations effects. Maneuvering among political leaders to define public understandings of affirmative action is relevant to the probability that protected groups will think worse of themselves for that protection. Hiring and promotion practices within organizations determine whether enough minorities enter so that the liabilities of solo status are avoided. Employing sociological as well as psychological analyses – fulfilling some of its grandest aspirations – social psychology can play an important role, identifying means to disrupt the pernicious micro/macro feedback cycles that retard racial progress.

Notes

1. A well-known experimental demonstration of this kind of expectancy effect was produced by Snyder, Tanke, and Berscheid (1977). Snyder and Swann (1978b) identified one mechanism by which confirming behavior can be elicited from the target – biased questions, reflecting perceivers' assumptions about the answers.
2. The distinction is parallel to the one Rosenthal (1966) makes between interactional and noninteractional experimenter effects.
3. In relation to the Word et al. study and other works cited in this chapter, it is appropriate to ask whether the psychological mediator linking job applicants' race to interviewers' behavior was in fact expectancy. Self-fulfilling prophecy research in the tradition of Rosenthal (1966), Rosenthal and Fode (1963), and Rosenthal and Jacobson (1968) initiated the critical causal sequence by direct manipulation of expectations. When experimenters were told that their rats were "maze bright," or teachers were alerted that some children were on the verge of "blooming," the manipulation was tailored to arouse expectations. Even in such nonexperimental self-fulfilling prophecy research as Seaver's (1973) study of the difference made by teachers' familiarity with their pupils' siblings, expectations are the most plausible active ingredient. However, if white interviewers adjust their behavior toward black applicants in dysfunctional ways, is there reason to infer low expectations rather than hostility? Or aversion? Or anxiety in the face of unfamiliar circumstances? It must be acknowledged that especially where the data are gross behavioral patterns, talk of underlying expectations must be based more on intuition than on evidence.
4. Stereotyping shows substantial correlations with a number of other policy-relevant opinions. Thus, this consideration of the link between stereotyping and busing actually represents a broader set of relationships.

5. Miller and Turnbull (1986) refer to this as a *coaction* pattern, apparently distinguished by the fact that all actors are equally both perceivers and targets.
6. The conclusion that lifelong effects of segregation are in part mediated by expectations is congruent with the fact that the social psychological outcome of segregation most clearly documented in research of the past two decades is locus of control, segregated children showing a weaker sense of fate control (St. John, 1975; Epps, 1978).
7. Interpersonal transmission of expectancies described to take place in education, social research, and medicine is typically an outgrowth of reciprocal, complementary role relations – between teachers and students, researchers and subjects, doctors and patients. Parent-to-child transmission of expectations about interracial outcomes presumably represents a different process.
8. Questions have been raised about the role of black teachers as well. As in many other research areas, however, studies focusing on blacks have been rare. For that reason, this discussion is necessarily confined to white teachers.
9. Similar questions are being asked in other countries as well, e.g., about white British teachers' treatment of West Indian pupils (Short, 1985).
10. There exists laboratory experimental evidence as well as observational accounts that expectations are cued by social class background, a factor strongly correlated with race (Darley & Gross, 1983).
11. Similar organizationwide expectancy effects in work settings are discussed by Eden in chapter 7 of this volume.
12. A program of interventions aimed at short-circuiting spirals of disadvantage is described by Cohen (1982). Among other strategies developed by *expectation states* theorists, teachers are trained to actively engender expectations of success in black students and to encourage equal participation by students in interracial work groups.
13. Other research similarly shows whites to maintain greater physical distance when interacting with blacks than with whites (Hendricks & Bootzin, 1976).
14. Crocker and McGraw (1984) remind us that the effects of solo status are not simply a matter of numbers in the microcosm, but of microcosm proportions in conjunction with status in the larger society. Solo men and solo women meet very different reactions.
15. Saenz and Lord (1989) talk of *token* status, but in the language used by Pettigrew and Martin (1987), they intend *solo* status.
16. For a review of evidence on "biased intergroup performance evaluations," see Hinkle and Schopler (1986).
17. One recent line of research emphasizes the impact of individuating information, even when it is not directly diagnostic (Hilton & Fein, 1989; Krueger & Rothbart, 1988; Locksley, Hepburn, & Ortiz, 1982).
18. But for evidence that perceptual disconfirmation can occur under ideal circumstances, see Desforges, Lord, Ramsey, Mason, Van Leeuwen, West, and Lepper (1991).
19. Interesting research on the subtyping of black Americans is being done by Devine and Baker (1991).
20. Jackman and Crane (1986) would say that this strategy is too optimistic, that positive interpersonal feelings toward racial minority individuals often coexist with regressive opinions on race-relevant social policy because the

latter reflect not psychological dynamics but a sense of group position and interest.

References

Acorn, D. A., Hamilton, D. L., & Sherman, S. J. (1988). Generalization of biased perceptions of groups based on illusory correlations. *Social Cognition, 6,* 345–372.

Ashmore, R. D., & DelBoca, F. K. (1981). Conceptual approaches to stereotypes and stereotyping. In D. L. Hamilton (Ed.), *Cognitive processes in stereotyping and intergroup behavior* (pp. 1–35). Hillsdale, NJ: Erlbaum.

Babad, E. Y., Inbar, J., & Rosenthal, R. (1982). Pygmalion, Galatea, and the Golem: Investigations of biased and unbiased teachers. *Journal of Educational Psychology, 74,* 459–474.

Baron, R. M., Tom, D. Y., & Cooper, H. M. (1985). Social class, race, and teacher expectations. In J. B. Dusek (Ed.), *Teacher expectancies* (pp. 251–269). Hillsdale, NJ: Erlbaum.

Bateson, G., Jackson, D., Haley, J., & Weakland, J. (1956). Towards a theory of schizophrenia. *Behavioral Science, 1,* 251–264.

Beecher, H. K. (1966). Pain: One mystery solved. *Science, 151,* 840–841.

Blanchard, F. A. (1989). Effective affirmative action programs. In F. A. Blanchard & F. J. Crosby (Eds.), *Affirmative action in perspective* (pp. 193–207). New York: Springer-Verlag.

Bobo, L. (1983). Whites' opposition to busing: Symbolic racism or realistic group conflict? *Journal of Personality and Social Psychology, 45,* 1196–1210.

Bobo, L., & Kluegel, J. R. (1991). *Modern American prejudice: Stereotypes, social distance, and perceptions of discrimination toward blacks, Hispanics, and Asians.* Paper presented at the American Sociological Association Meeting, Cincinnati, Ohio.

Braddock, J. H. (1985). School desegregation and black assimilation. *Journal of Social Issues, 41,* 9–22.

Braddock, J. H., Crain, R. L., & McPartland, J. M. (1984). A long term view of school desegregation: Some recent studies of graduates as adults. *Phi Delta Kappan, 66,* 259–264.

Braddock, J. H., Crain, R. L., McPartland, J. M., & Dawkins, R. L. (1986). Applicant race and job placement decisions: A national survey experiment. *International Journal of Sociology and Social Policy, 6,* 3–24.

Braddock, J. H., & McPartland, J. M. (1982). Assessing school desegregation effects: New directions in research. *Research in Sociology of Education and Socialization, 3,* 259–282.

Braddock, J. H., & McPartland, J. M. (1983). *More evidence on social-psychological processes that perpetuate minority segregation: The relationship of school desegregation and employment segregation.* Report No. 338. Baltimore: Johns Hopkins University, Center for Social Organization of Schools.

Braddock, J. H., & McPartland, J. M. (1989). Social-psychological processes that perpetuate racial segregation: The relationship between school and employment desegregation. *Journal of Black Studies, 19,* 267–289.

Brophy, J. E. (1983). Research on the self-fulfilling prophecy and teacher expectations. *Journal of Educational Psychology, 75,* 631–661.

Chacko, T. I. (1982). Women and equal employment opportunity: Some unintended effects. *Journal of Applied Psychology, 67,* 119–123.

Cohen, E. G. (1982). Expectation states and interracial interaction in school settings. *Annual Review of Sociology, 8*, 209–235.

Cook, S. W. (1984). Cooperative interaction in multiethnic contexts. In N. Miller & M. B. Brewer (Eds.), *Groups in contact: The psychology of desegregation* (pp. 155–185). New York: Academic Press.

Crain, R. L., Hawes, J. A., Miller, R. L., & Peichert, J. A. (1992). *Finding niches: Desegregated students sixteen years later.* New York: Institute for Urban and Minority Education, Teachers College of Columbia University.

Crain, R. L., & Mahard, R. E. (1983). The effect of research methodology on desegregation-achievement studies. *American Journal of Sociology, 88*, 839–854.

Crain, R. L., & Weisman, C. (1972). *Discrimination, personality, and achievement: A survey of northern blacks.* New York: Seminar Press.

Crocker, J., Hannah, D. B., & Weber, R. (1983). Person memory and causal attribution. *Journal of Personality and Social Psychology, 44*, 55–66.

Crocker, J., & McGraw, K. M. (1984). What's good for the goose is not good for the gander. *American Behavioral Scientist, 27*, 357–369.

Crosby, F., Bromley, S., & Saxe, L. (1980). Recent unobtrusive studies of black and white discrimination and prejudice: A literature review. *Psychological Review, 87*, 546–563.

Crosby, F., & Clayton, S. (1990). Affirmative action and the issue of expectancies. *Journal of Social Issues, 46*, 61–79.

Darley, J. M., & Fazio, R. H. (1980). Expectancy confirmation processes arising in the social interaction sequence. *American Psychologist, 35*, 867–881.

Darley, J. M., & Gross, P. H. (1983). A hypothesis-confirming bias in labeling effects. *Journal of Personality and Social Psychology, 44*, 20–33.

Desforges, D. M., Lord, C. G., Ramsey, S. L., Mason, J. A., Van Leeuwen, M. D., West, S. C., & Lepper, M. R. (1991). Effects of structured cooperative contact on changing negative attitudes toward stigmatized social groups. *Journal of Personality and Social Psychology, 60*, 531–544.

Devine, P. G. (1989). Stereotypes and prejudice: Their automatic and controlled components. *Journal of Personality and Social Psychology, 56*, 5–18.

Devine, P. G., & Baker, S. M. (1991). Measurement of racial stereotype subtyping. *Personality and Social Psychology Bulletin, 17*, 44–50.

Dipboye, R. L. (1982). Self-fulfilling prophecies in the selection-recruitment interview. *Academy of Management Review, 7*, 579–586.

Dovidio, J. F., Mann, J., and Gaertner, S. L. (1989). Resistance to affirmative action: The implications of aversive racism. In F. A. Blanchard & F. J. Crosby (Eds.), *Affirmative action in perspective* (pp. 83–102). New York: Springer-Verlag.

Eccles, J. S., Jacobs, J. E., & Harold, R. D. (1990). Gender role stereotypes, expectancy effects, and parents' socialization of gender differences. *Journal of Social Issues, 46*, 183–201.

Epps, E. G. (1978). Impact of school desegregation on the self-evaluation and achievement orientation of minority group children. *Law and Contemporary Problems, 42*, 57–76.

Epstein, J. L. (1985). After the bus arrives: Resegregation in desegregated schools. *Journal of Social Issues, 41*, 23–43.

Fazio, R. H., Effrein, E. A., & Falender, V. J. (1981). Self-perceptions following social interaction. *Journal of Personality and Social Behavior, 41*, 232–242.

Fiske, S. T., & Neuberg, S. L. (1990). A continuum of impression formation, from category-based to individuating processes: Influences of information and motivation on attention and interpretation. *Advances in Experimental Social Psychology, 23,* 1–74.

Frable, D. E. S. (1989). Sex typing and gender ideology: Two facets of the individual's gender psychology that go together. *Journal of Personality and Social Psychology, 56,* 95–108.

Hamilton, D. L. (1981). Illusory correlation as a basis for stereotyping. In D. L. Hamilton (Ed.), *Cognitive processes in stereotyping and intergroup behavior* (pp. 115–144). Hillsdale, NJ: Erlbaum.

Hamilton, D. L., Sherman, S. J., & Ruvolo, C. M. (1990). Stereotype-based expectancies: Effects on information processing and social behavior. *Journal of Social Issues, 46,* 35–59.

Harris, M., & Rosenthal, R. (1985). Mediation of interpersonal expectancy effects: 31 meta-analyses. *Psychological Bulletin, 97,* 363–386.

Harvey, D. G., & Slater, G. T. (1975). The relationship between child's SES and teacher expectations: A test of the middle-class bias hypothesis. *Social Forces, 54,* 140–159.

Heilman, M. S., Lucas, J. A., & Kaplow, S. R. (1990). Self-derogating consequences of sex-based preferential selection: The moderating role of initial self-confidence. *Organizational Behavior and Human Decision Processes, 46,* 202–216.

Heilman, M. S., Simon, M. C., & Repper, D. P. (1987). Intentionally favored, unintentionally harmed? Impact of sex-based preferential selection on self-perceptions and self-evaluations. *Journal of Applied Psychology, 72,* 62–68.

Hendricks, M., & Bootzin, R. (1976). Race and sex as stimuli for negative affect and physical avoidance. *The Journal of Social Psychology, 98,* 111–120.

Hewstone, M. (1989). Changing stereotypes with disconfirming information. In D. Bar-Tal, C. F. Graumann, A. W. Kruglanski, & W. Stroebe (Eds.), *Stereotyping and prejudice: Changing conceptions* (pp. 207–233). New York: Springer-Verlag.

Hilton, J. L., & Fein, S. (1989). The role of typical diagnosticity in stereotype-based judgments. *Journal of Personality and Social Psychology, 57,* 201–211.

Hinkle, S., & Schopler, J. (1986). Bias in the evaluation of in-group and out-group performance. In S. Worchel & W. G. Austin (Eds.), *Psychology of intergroup relations* (pp. 196–212). Chicago: Nelson-Hall.

Ickes, W. (1984). Compositions in black and white: Determinants of interaction in interracial dyads. *Journal of Personality and Social Psychology, 47,* 330–341.

Jackman, M. R., & Crane, M. (1986). "Some of my best friends are black . . .": Interracial friendship and whites' racial attitudes. *Public Opinion Quarterly, 50,* 459–486.

Jaynes, G. D., & Williams, R. M. (Eds.) (1989). *A common destiny: Blacks and American society.* Washington, DC: National Academy Press.

Jones, E. E. (1986). Interpreting interpersonal behavior: The effects of expectancies. *Science, 234,* 41–46.

Jones, E. E., & Berglas, S. (1978). Control of attributions about the self through self-handicapping strategies: The appeal of alcohol and the role of underachievement. *Personality and Social Psychology Bulletin, 4,* 200–206.

Jussim, L. (1989). Teacher expectations: Self-fulfilling prophecies, perceptual biases, and accuracy. *Journal of Personality and Social Psychology, 57,* 469–480.

Jussim, L. (1990a). Expectancies and social issues: Introduction. *Journal of Social Issues, 46,* 1–8.

Jussim, L. (1990b). Social reality and social problems: The role of expectancies. *Journal of Social Issues, 46,* 9–34.

Kirschenman, J., & Neckerman, K. M. (1991). "We'd love to hire them, but . . ." The meaning of race for employers. In C. Jencks & P. E. Peterson (Eds.), *The Urban Underclass* (pp. 203–232). Washington, DC: Brookings Institution.

Kluegel, J. R. (1985). If there isn't a problem, you don't need a solution. *American Behavioral Scientist, 28,* 761–784.

Kraiger, K., & Ford, J. K. (1985). A meta-analysis of rate race effects in performance ratings. *Journal of Applied Psychology, 70,* 56–65.

Krueger, J., & Rothbart, M. (1988). Use of categorical and individuating information in making inferences about personality. *Journal of Personality and Social Psychology, 55,* 187–195.

Kulik, J. A. (1983). Confirmatory attribution and the perpetuation of social beliefs. *Journal of Personality and Social Psychology, 44,* 1171–1181.

Leacock, E. (1969). *Teaching and learning in city schools.* New York: Basic Books.

Locksley, A., Hepburn, C., & Ortiz, V. (1982). Social stereotypes and judgments of individuals: An instance of the base-rate fallacy. *Journal of Experimental Social Psychology, 18,* 23–42.

Long, B. H., & Henderson, E. H. (1974). Certain determinants of academic expectancies among southern and non-southern teachers. *American Educational Research Journal, 11,* 137–147.

McConahay, J. B. (1982). Self-interest versus racial attitudes as correlates of anti-busing attitudes in Louisville: Is it the busing or the blacks? *The Journal of Politics, 44,* 692–720.

Merton, R. K. (1948). The self-fulfilling prophecy. *Antioch Review, 8,* 193–210.

Miller, D. T., & Turnbull, W. (1986). Expectancies and interpersonal processes. *Annual Review of Psychology, 37,* 233–256.

Mills, C. W. (1959). *The sociological imagination.* New York: Oxford University Press.

Nacoste, R. W. (1987). But do they care about fairness? The dynamics of preferential treatment and minority interest. *Basic and Applied Social Psychology, 8,* 177–191.

Nacoste, R. W (1989). Affirmative action and self-evaluation. In F. A. Blanchard & F. J. Crosby (Eds.), *Affirmative action in perspective* (pp. 103–109). New York: Springer-Verlag.

Nacoste, R. W., & Lehman, D. (1987). Procedural stigma. *Representative Research in Social Psychology, 17,* 25–38.

Neuberg, S. L. (1989). The goal of forming accurate impressions during social interactions: Attenuating the impact of negative expectancies. *Journal of Personality and Social Psychology, 56,* 374–386.

Norvell, N., & Worchel, S. (1981). A reexamination of the relation between equal status contact and intergroup attraction. *Journal of Personality and Social Psychology, 41,* 902–908.

Omoto, A. M., & Borgida, E. (1988). Guess who might be coming to dinner? Personal involvement and racial stereotyping. *Journal of Experimental Social Psychology, 24,* 571–593.

Orfield, G. (1978). *Must we bus?* Washington, DC: Brookings Institution.

Orfield, G. (1980). School segregation and residential segregation. In W. Stephan & J. Feagin (Eds.), *School desegregation: Past, present, and future* (pp. 227–247). New York: Plenum Press.

Pearce, D. M., Crain, R. L., Farley, R., & Taeuber, K. E. (1987). Lessons not lost: The effect of school desegregation on the reduction of residential segregation in large central cities. Unpublished manuscript.

Perman, L. (1987). Getting the population straight: Young workers, women workers, and black workers. *Journal of Social Issues, 47,* 95–98.

Pettigrew, T. F. (1975). Black and white attitudes toward race and housing. In T. F. Pettigrew (Ed.), *Racial discrimination in the United States* (pp. 92–126). New York: Harper and Row.

Pettigrew, T. F. (1979). The ultimate attribution error. Extending Allport's cognitive analysis of prejudice. *Personality and Social Psychology Bulletin, 5,* 461–476.

Pettigrew, T. F. (1981). Extending the stereotype concept. In D. L. Hamilton (Ed.), *Cognitive processes in stereotyping and intergroup behavior* (pp. 303–331). Hillsdale, NJ: Erlbaum.

Pettigrew, T. F., & Martin, J. (1987). Shaping the organizational context for black American inclusion. *Journal of Social Issues, 43,* 41–78.

Pettigrew, T. F., & Taylor, M. C. (1992). Discrimination. In E. F. Borgatta and M. L. Borgatta (Eds.), *Encyclopedia of sociology* (pp. 498–503). New York: Macmillan.

Rosenthal, R. (1966). *Experimenter effects in behavioral research.* New York: Appleton-Century-Crofts.

Rosenthal, R. (1973). On the social psychology of the self-fulfilling prophecy: Further evidence for Pygmalion effects and their mediating mechanisms. *MSS Modular Publications,* Module 53, 1–28.

Rosenthal, R., & Fode, K. L. (1963). The effect of experimenter bias on the performance of the albino rat. *Behavioral Science, 8,* 183–189.

Rosenthal, R., & Jacobson, L. (1968). *Pygmalion in the classroom.* New York: Holt, Rinehart and Winston.

Rothbart, M. (1981). Memory processes and social beliefs. In D. L. Hamilton (Ed.), *Cognitive processes in stereotyping and intergroup behavior* (pp. 146–181). Hillsdale, NJ: Erlbaum.

Rothbart, M., & John, O. P. (1985). Social categorization and behavioral episodes: A cognitive analysis of the effects of intergroup contact. *Journal of Social Issues, 41,* 81–104.

Rubovits, P. C., & Maehr, M. L. (1973). Pygmalion black and white. *Journal of Personality and Social Psychology, 25,* 210–219.

Saenz, D. S., & Lord, C. G. (1989). Reversing roles: A cognitive strategy for undoing memory deficits associated with token status. *Journal of Personality and Social Psychology, 56,* 698–708.

Sagar, H. A., & Schofield, J. W. (1980). Racial and behavioral cues in black and white children's perceptions of ambiguously aggressive acts. *Journal of Personality and Social Psychology, 39,* 590–598.

St. John, N. (1975). *School desegregation: Outcomes for children.* New York: Wiley.

Schuman, H., Steeh, C., & Bobo, L. (1985). *Racial attitudes in America: Trends and interpretations.* Cambridge, MA: Harvard University Press.

Seaver, W. (1973). Effects of naturally induced teacher expectancies. *Journal of Personality and Social Psychology, 28,* 333–342.

Shore, A. L. (1969). Confirmation of expectancy and changes in teachers' evaluations of student behavior. *Dissertation Abstracts, 30,* 1878–1879.

Short, G. (1985). Teacher expectation and West Indian underachievement. *Educational Research, 27,* 95–101.

Snyder, M. (1981). On the self-perpetuating nature of social stereotypes. In D. L. Hamilton (Ed.), *Cognitive processes in stereotyping and intergroup behavior* (pp. 183–212). Hillsdale, NJ: Erlbaum.

Snyder, M., & Swann, W. B. (1978a). Behavioral confirmation in social interaction: From social perception to social reality. *Journal of Experimental Social Psychology, 14,* 148–162.

Sndyer, M., & Swann, W. B. (1978b). Hypothesis-testing processes in social interaction. *Journal of Personality and Social Psychology, 36,* 1202–1212.

Snyder, M., Tanke, E. D., & Berscheid, E. (1977). Social perception and interpersonal behavior: On the self-fulfilling nature of social stereotypes. *Journal of Personality and Social Psychology, 35,* 656–666.

Stephan, W. G., & Stephan, C. W. (1985). Intergroup anxiety. *Journal of Social Issues, 41,* 157–175.

Taylor, M. C. (1979). Race, sex, and the expression of self-fulfilling prophecies in a laboratory teaching situation. *Journal of Personality and Social Psychology, 37,* 897–912.

Taylor, M. C. (1987). *Second generation effects of school segregation.* Paper presented at the Eastern Sociological Society Meeting, Boston, May 1–3.

Taylor, M. C. (1988). *Estimating race and sex inequity in wages: Substantive implications of methodological choices.* Paper presented at the Research Conference of the Association of Public Policy and Management, Seattle, October 27–29.

Taylor, M. C. (1991a). *Roots of white opposition to "special treatment" for black Americans.* Paper presented at the 71st Annual Convention of the Western Psychological Association, San Francisco, April 26–28.

Taylor, M. C. (1991b). *Two faces of color-blindness.* Paper presented at the American Sociological Association Meeting, Cincinnati, Ohio.

Taylor, M. C. (in press). The impact of affirmative action on beneficiaries: Evidence from the 1990 General Social Survey. In M. E. Turner & A. R. Pratkanis (Eds.), *Basic and Applied Social Psychology* [special issue].

Taylor, M. C., & Johnson, M. P. (1986). Strategies for linking individual psychology and social structure: Interdisciplinary and cross-disciplinary social psychology *British Journal of Social Psychology, 25,* 181–192.

Taylor, M. C., & Pettigrew, T. F. (1992). Prejudice. In E. F. Borgatta and M. L. Borgatta (Eds.), *Encyclopedia of sociology* (pp. 1536–1541). New York: Macmillan.

Taylor, S. E., Fiske, S. T., Close, M., Anderson, C., & Ruderman. (1975). *Solo status as a psychological variable: The power of being distinctive.* Unpublished paper, Harvard University.

Thomas, D. A. (1990). The impact of race on managers' experiences of developmental relationships (mentoring and sponsorship): An intraorganization study. *Journal of Organizational Behavior, 11,* 479–492.

Turner, M. E., & Pratkanis, A. R. (in press-a). Effects of preferential and meritorious selection on performance: An examination of intuitive and self-handicapping perspectives. *Personality and Social Psychology Bulletin.*

Turner, M. E., & Pratkanis, A. R. (in press-b). Recipient reactions to preferential selection: Towards the effective management of affirmative action programs. In M. E. Turner & A. R. Pratkanis (Eds.), *Basic and Applied Social Psychology* [special issue].

Turner, M. E., Pratkanis, A. R., & Hardaway, T. J. (1991). Sex differences in reactions to preferential selection: Towards a model of preferential selection as help. *Journal of Social Behavior and Personality, 6,* 797–814.

Weber, R., & Crocker, J. (1983). Cognitive processes in the revision of stereotypic beliefs. *Journal of Personality and Social Psychology, 45,* 961–977.

Weitz, S. (1972). Attitude, voice, and behavior: A repressed affect model of interracial interaction. *Journal of Personality and Social Psychology, 24,* 14–21.

Whitehead, G. I., Smith, S. H., & Eichhorn, J. A. (1982). The effect of subject's race and other's race on judgments of causality for success and failure. *Journal of Personality, 50,* 193–202.

Wilder, D. A. (1981). Perceiving persons as groups: Categorization and inter-group relations. In D. L. Hamilton (Ed.), *Cognitive processes in stereotyping and intergroup behavior* (pp. 213–257). Hillsdale, NJ: Erlbaum.

Wilder, D. A. (1984). Intergroup contact: The typical member and the exception to the rule. *Journal of Experimental Social Psychology, 20,* 177–194.

Word, C. O., Zanna, M. P., & Cooper, J. (1974). The nonverbal mediation of self-fulfilling prophecies in interracial interaction. *Journal of Experimental Social Psychology, 10,* 109–120.

Yarkin, K. L., Town, J. P., & Wallston, B. S. (1982). Blacks and women must try harder: Stimulus persons' race and sex attributions of causality. *Personality and Social Psychology Bulletin, 8,* 21–24.

6. Pygmalion – 25 years after interpersonal expectations in the classroom

ELISHA BABAD

I. Introduction

Some years ago, the Israeli humorist Ephraim Kishon wrote a successful comedy entitled *Ho, Julia,* in which he fantasized about the life of the middle-aged Romeo and Juliet, presuming they had survived their dramatic death scene and lived happily ever after. In the same vein, it might be possible to visit Pygmalion and Galatea one generation later, or to analyze the life and work of Robert Rosenthal, the man known among educators and behavioral scientists as "Mr. Pygmalion." Indeed, *Pygmalion in the Classroom* also survived deadly criticisms, and the field of teacher expectancies is an important area of educational psychology today. Rosenthal was directly involved in all stages of development of this field throughout the years – introducing self-fulfilling prophecy (SFP) effects to education through *Pygmalion;* specializing in methodology and meta-analysis during the periods of controversy over the existence of SFP effects; investigating interpersonal interaction processes when the study of behavioral mediation of expectancies gained momentum; and studying nonverbal communication when the study of expectancies moved in that direction. In all of these fields, Rosenthal became a leading expert and a scientific authority.

This chapter is intended to illuminate and discuss central issues in teacher expectancy research and to examine the development of this field since the publication of *Pygmalion in the Classroom* (Rosenthal & Jacobson, 1968). In the historical analysis (part II), I attempt to trace the underlying psychological reasons for the intense controversies over (teacher) expectancy effects, and to delineate not only the strong trends but also the areas that have remained relatively neglected in teacher expectancy research. Part III discusses the influence of teacher expectations on students' performance in real classrooms. Some educators question the practical significance of experimental demonstrations of SFP effects and of meta-analytic reports of effect sizes, maintaining that actual teachers' expectations are accurate and reflect real differences among students. Part IV reviews the research on the behavioral mediation of teacher expectancies, summarizing the mediation models and the major categories of mediating teacher behaviors. Special attention is given to teachers' nonverbal behavior, investigated through a context-minimal method. Teachers' growing tendency to intentionally compensate low-expectancy students in teaching-related behaviors complicates the picture, creating noticeable gaps between various categories of teacher behavior (e.g., learning-related versus affective behaviors, controllable versus noncontrollable behaviors). Part V discusses the relatively neglected area of students' perceptions of teachers' differential, expectancy-related behavior, pointing out the gaps between students' and teachers' perceptions. Part VI focuses on personality correlates of teacher expectancy effects. The applied significance of teacher expectancy research depends on the identification of teachers prone to manifest expectancy effects in their classrooms and on the isolation of personality attributes involved in the causation of expectancy effects. Applied interventions for reducing harmful effects of teacher expectancies are discussed in part VII. Unfortunately, this is the weakest link in teacher expectancy research. The major obstacles to effective application of research findings are discussed, along with a review of the most notable intervention programs.

The topic of expectations is treated differently by educational psychologists and cognitive social psychologists. Rosenthal's early experiments on SFP (especially the person-perception, photo-rating studies of the mid-1960s) clearly represented social psychology, and *Pygmalion* shifted the focus to the educational domain. Cognitive social psychologists have long been interested in SFP (see, e.g., Jones, 1977), and recent works have examined conceptual issues in the formation of expectancies, their influence on their holders and expression in their behavior, and the processes through which they might influence the self-concept and behavior of their targets (see, e.g., Darley & Fazio, 1980; Jones, 1986; Miller & Turnbull, 1986; Snyder, 1984). Educational psychologists are interested in the same issues, but their perspective is more practical than theoretical, focused on the classroom context and on teacher–student interaction. They are concerned about potential (particularly negative) influences of teacher expectancies on students and wonder whether teacher behavior can be changed. The two streams of literature are unfortunately quite disparate, with relatively little cross-referencing and little utilization of empirical findings of one group by the other – due mostly to differences in methodological ideology. (Jussim's 1986 review is one of the few attempts to integrate the educational and the cognitive social-psychological perspectives.) The present chapter is mostly educational in content, but I have tried to integrate a social-psychological conceptualization in the discussion whenever relevant.

A final introductory comment refers to the term *teacher expectancies*. From the controversy over *Pygmalion* and teachers' SFP effects, the research has widened over the years to include self-maintaining expectancies (SME) as well, that is, expectations that might be based on real differences among students rather than on bogus differences fabricated by experimenters. My approach is to include all differential teacher behavior under teacher expectancies, since differential behavior is always expectancy related, in whole or in part.

II. A brief history of teacher expectancy research

Pygmalion in the Classroom was a pivotal study that has had an enduring impact on the field of educational psychology. It caught the imagination of many researchers and evoked sharp controversies, providing impetus for research by supporters and antagonists alike. The explicit focus of the argument was whether the *Pygmalion* study indeed proved that experimentally manipulated teachers' beliefs about "late blooming" caused systematic changes in students' IQ. (A book consisting of various reanalyses of the *Pygmalion* results was published by Elashoff and Snow in 1971.) The implicit concern involved an implication that was not even investigated in *Pygmalion*, namely, that teachers might harm their low-achieving students through their negative expectations (the *Golem effect*; see Babad, Inbar, & Rosenthal, 1982a). The publication of Rist's (1970) observations on the negative treatment of low achievers, and Rubovitz and Maehr's (1973) findings on negative teacher behavior directed at black high-expectancy students (as well as other reports of a similar nature) added fuel to these concerns.

Pygmalion was "born" in 1968 into a cultural milieu characterized by exasperated excitement: There was overall unrest and anxiety due to the Vietnam War; a strong antiestablishment movement had left its mark on university campuses; the government was giving low priority to education; continuous struggles over busing and school desegregation were draining much energy; and Jensen (1969) reopened the heredity–environment controversy, using a rather deterministic approach and arguing that "compensatory education [of the disadvantaged] has failed." (See also Marylee Taylor, this volume.)

Rosenthal's earlier experimental SFP studies also evoked criticism (e.g., Barber & Silver, 1968), the underlying reason being, in my opinion (Babad, 1978), that they threatened the reliability of the psychological experiment – psychology's major claim to scientific credibility. *Pygmalion* provided a potential opening for "teacher bashing" (Rist, 1987), and educators were apprehensive that its results would be used to blame teachers for the educational failures of their disadvantaged students. Wineburg (1987), for example, argued that *Pygmalion* was being inappropriately used in legislation and court cases. School desegregation and the growing number of integrated, heterogeneous classrooms increased the probability of differential expectancy effects, increasing the chances that the highly publicized *Pygmalion* would be used to criticize teachers.

The development of expectancy research in the years following *Pygmalion* was thus characterized by the controversy over the *Pygmalion* study, its results, and its implications (see Elashoff & Snow, 1971; Jensen, 1969; Thorndike, 1968; and even Wineburg as recently as 1987!). Numerous expectancy and SFP studies were conducted in these years, some attempting to replicate and other to not replicate *Pygmalion*, and many researchers simply saw scientific potential in investigating this interesting phenomenon. The development of meta-analysis (see Rubin, this volume) made it possible to examine empirically the accumulated results of the various SFP studies, and over the years Rosenthal published several meta-analytic summaries proving the validity of the SFP phenomenon (see, e.g., Rosenthal & Rubin, 1978). Today there is no doubt that SFP effects exist, and teacher expectations – based on fabricated information as well as on real differences among students – can have systematic influences on (in descending order of effect magnitude) teachers' impressions of students, teachers' grades, students' performance on objective achievement tests, and even students' IQ (Smith, 1980). However, this phenomenon is probabilistic, and SFP effects do not take place in every classroom and for every teacher. (For a methodological discussion, see Rubin and Bernieri, this volume.)

The most extensive and durable line of expectancy research throughout the years has been the study of the behavioral mediation of expectancies – how teachers (and experimenters) transmit their differential expectations to students. Mediation research widened the scope of investigation from SFP to SME and from experimental studies to actual classroom studies, making it possible to examine directly teachers' behavior toward low-expectancy students. (It is, of course, unethical to implant negative expectations about randomly selected students, and therefore *Pygmalion* studies compare a positive-expectancy group to a neutral, no-expectancy control group but do not include a low-expectancy group.) The shift from controlled experiments with bogus information to field studies involving existing expectations based on real differences (see, e.g., Brophy & Good, 1970) gave the research a more applied nature but raised the need to distinguish between components of teacher behavior reflecting expectations alone compared to components caused by real differences among students.

Brophy (1983) summarized a list of 17 salient mediating behaviors from different studies, and Harris and Rosenthal (1985) meta-analyzed 31 mediating behaviors from 136 mediation studies. Rosenthal's (1973; Harris & Rosenthal, 1985) four-factor theory of mediation has been widely quoted. In recent years, mediation research has been shifting to the nonverbal domain, focusing on subtle and implicit nuances of teachers' expectancy-related behavior. (See also Harris, this volume.)

Bias research has been another enduring and relevant area of investigation. Bias studies examine the formation of expectancies on the basis of given information and commonly held stereotypes. Numerous studies were conducted over the years by educational and cognitive social psychologists, investigating either theoretical questions or specific biases caused by racial, ethnic, gender, or achievement labels.

Several areas of research discussed later in this chapter have remained relatively neglected compared to mediation and bias research:

1. Investigations of personality characteristics aimed at identifying teachers more likely to manifest expectancy effects in their classrooms have been scarce. Cooper (1979, 1985; Cooper & Good, 1983) proposed a theory and conducted empirical research on the moderating influence of teachers' sense of control, and Babad, Rosenthal, and their associates (e.g., Babad et al., 1982a) conducted a series of studies on susceptibility to biasing information as a personality correlate of teacher expectancy effects (part VI of this chapter).

2. Most expectancy studies focused on the formation of expectancies or the relations between expectations and differential teacher behavior (links A–B and B–C in Rosenthal's 10-arrow model; see Harris & Rosenthal, 1985; Rosenthal, 1985). Relatively few studies examined the influence of teacher expectancies on actual student achievement (or IQ, as

was the case in the original Pygmalion study), and studies examining affective outcomes (students' self-concept, sense of efficacy, motivation, morale, and school satisfaction) are almost nonexistent (part III of this chapter; see also Blanck, this volume, on outcomes in courtroom research).

3. Students' perceptions of teachers' expectancy-related behavior constitute a critical and necessary link in the mediation of expectancies, and yet almost all studies employed adult, trained observers to measure teacher behavior. Researchers may implicitly assume that students' experiences parallel observers' perceptions, but that is not borne out by existing evidence. Only a few studies (Babad, 1990a; Cooper & Good, 1983; Weinstein, 1985, 1989) examined students' perceptions of their teachers' expectancy-related behavior (part V of this chapter).

4. The weakest aspect after 25 years of teacher expectancy research is the scarcity of applied intervention based on the accumulated empirical evidence. Some intervention programs purport to change teacher expectations, but they are based on very global conceptions of expectancies rather than on specific research findings, and their effects have generally not been evaluated systematically. Investment of effort and resources in educational intervention can always be potentially fruitful to some ends, but it is a sad commentary that such a large and complex body of research on phenomena of high practical significance has generally not been applied in educational practice, and the gap between scientific knowledge and specific application about teacher expectancies is wide (part VII of this chapter).

III. Can teacher expectations influence student performance?

This central question may appear to be simple, but any attempt to answer it raises complex educational and empirical issues. In the original SFP and Pygmalion studies, the question was whether changes (or differences) in students' (subjects') performance could be attributed to teachers' (experimenters') expectations, to the exclusion of any other causal factor. From the accumulation of studies and meta-analyses, the empirical answer is positive: *Person A's expectations can potentially influence person B's performance.* But the more important educational question is whether teacher expectations *actually* have exclusive causal influence on students' performance in regular classrooms. And if they do, what is the magnitude of that influence? Do teacher expectations cause long-term and irreversible influences on student achievement? Do positive and negative expectations cause a similar process in their respective directions? etc.

Today it is possible to meta-analyze a multitude of studies and reach conclusions about the effect magnitude of a given construct across all studies. In that sense, meta-analyses of expectancy effects have given clear answers (see Harris & Rosenthal, 1985; Rosenthal, 1985; Rosenthal & Rubin, 1978; Rubin, this volume; Smith, 1980). But many practitioners are apprehensive, often believing that meta-analysis is a method used by sophisticated researchers to magically turn a host of weak and insignificant results into a strong, uniform finding. In addition, the concept of *effect magnitude* (in terms of correlations or proportion of variance accounted for) is incomprehensible to most educators, and even experienced statisticians often err in estimating effect sizes. Brophy (1983) concluded that the influence of teacher expectations on student performance amounts to a negligible magnitude of 5–10% of the performance variance, and many of his readers would accept that 5% or 10% is indeed negligible. Rosenthal and Rubin (1982) introduced the *Binomial Effect Size Display (BESD)* for simple demonstration of effect magnitudes in concrete terms, namely, the proportion of improving the survival rate of a new drug compared to an old drug. Viewed via the BESD, effect sizes of 5–10% (correlations of .22–.32) are substantial. For instance, 10% of variance accounted for is equivalent to a change in the survival rate from 34% to 66% (see also Bernieri, this volume).

All reviews of the teacher expectancy literature published over the years have emphasized the distinction between experimental Pygmalion studies, where positive expectancies are randomly manipulated, and field studies based on real (high *and* low) teachers' expectations in their classrooms. Experimental studies are methodologically clean and they allow causal conclusions about the effects of positive expectancies, but these situations are contrived and they cannot represent real classroom situations. Field studies are of higher ecological validity, but they mix expectancy effects (*teacher effects on students,* to use the term in Brophy, 1983), with the effects of the real differences among students (*student effects on teachers*). Babad et al. (1982a) integrated the two designs, manipulating bogus positive expectancies attributed to randomly selected students while concurrently identifying real high- and low-expectancy students. They found that biased teachers manifested both Pygmalion (SFP) and Golem (SME) effects. Harris and Rosenthal (1985) showed that mediation effects in experimental and field studies are quite similar to each other.

The literature on biases, stereotypes, and types of information that *can* influence the formation of expectancies is rich. Biased teacher expectations can be formed by various stereotypic labels (racial, ethnic, gender, etc.; Dusek & Joseph, 1985), as well as by ability labels (Babad, 1980, 1985; Babad, Ariav, Rosen, & Salomon, 1987). But again, the educational question is what actually influences classroom teachers and how *they* form their expectations about particular students. Brophy (1983, 1985) and others (e.g., Hall & Merkel, 1985) maintained that teachers usually possess accurate information about their students, and therefore their differential expectations are unbiased and represent real differences among students. They argued that fabricated information that has no reality base cannot bias teachers' expectations for long, due to the continuous flow of real information from ongoing classroom interaction. That argument is supported by evidence that fabricated expectancies have a reduced potential for creating SFP effects if implanted more than 2 or 3 weeks into the school year (Raudenbush, 1984).

This conception concerning the accuracy of teacher expectations is inaccurate. It makes a dichotomous assumption that perceptions are either accurate or inaccurate, and if accurate as claimed, it is assumed that teachers' behavioral transmissions reflect only these accurate expectations. Cognitive social psychologists (Darley & Fazio, 1980; Jussim, 1986; Miller & Turnbull, 1986; Salomon, 1981) argue that the process is far more complex, since behavioral components play a major role in the formation, maintenance, and confirmation of expectancies. Expecters behave (via fine and subtle nuances) in ways that cause expectees to respond in ways that would strengthen the expectations. Thus, even if expectations have an initial reality base, the circular process of self-confirmation is likely to deviate from reality and exaggerate existing differences. This is certainly true for racial or gender stereotypes, which constitute primary bases of teacher expectancies (Cooper & Tom, 1984; Dusek & Joseph, 1985). Despite their reality basis and their kernel of truth, stereotypes are consensually considered to be distorted overgeneralizations of reality.

Brophy (1983, 1985) presented most explicitly the position defending teachers' accuracy, and his position was supported by other writers, such as Meyer (1985) and Hall and Merkel (1985). Based on his distinction between teacher effects on students and student effects on teachers, Brophy argued that teachers' differential behavior reflects real differences among students; that teacher behavior is "accurate, reality-based, and open to corrective feedback"; and that the influence of expectancies (teacher effects) is negligible.

SFP studies provide a conceptual *ceiling effect* – demonstrating that even fabricated information can influence teacher behavior and student performance. Although exclusive SFP effects are less likely to occur in conventional classrooms, there is no justification for complacency. SMEs are potentially dangerous and harmful even if the initial expectations had been reality based in whole or in part. In addition, I doubt teachers' openness to corrective feedback. Expectations (like stereotypes) have two salient characteristics: (1) they polarize perceptions and sharpen differences, and (2) they are rigidly held, readily fixated and resistant to change. Dramatic rags-to-riches changes in the style of the Pygmalion and Galatea myth are not likely to occur due to teacher expectancies, but small and consistent cycles of self-fulfillment can take place, with the effect of sharpening existing differences, improving the performance of the high achievers, and decreasing that of the low achievers. Thus, expectancies both fixate and exaggerate existing differences. Dusek and Joseph (1985) provided an impressive example of the fixation of teacher expectancies to the performance of a previously taught *sibling*. Babad et al. (1987) demonstrated the perseverance of expectancy bias in the face of disconfirming information. I think that teachers are complacent and unaware of the extent to which their behavior is expectancy related. This is particularly true in the affective domain, as will be shown later. Nobody could justify teachers' transmissions of negative affect to low-expectancy students as appropriate behavior.

To conclude this discussion of the effects of expectancies, I call attention to Jussim's (1989) recent analysis of bias, accuracy, and SFP in prediction of teacher grades and objective achievement scores in mathematics – an area where accuracy should be maximal due to the clarity of the performance information. Jussim found that teacher expectations (perceptions) about students' ability significantly predicted objective achievement even when the critical reality factors (teacher grades and previous objective achievement) were partialed out, with clear evidence of SFP (stronger for teacher grades and weaker, yet significant and of substantial effect size, for objective achievement scores). Moreover, Jussim found that these expectations were biased, based most strongly on *other* perceptions of the teachers and almost unrelated to students' previous performance. It is true that previous achievement scores and teacher grades (i.e., indices of accuracy) had stronger power in predicting students' performance, but clear SFP effects were nevertheless traced even for a field like mathematics. (For a similar approach to the analysis of teacher expectancies, see Crano & Mellon, 1978.)

IV. Current knowledge on the mediation of expectations through teacher behavior

Early studies on the mediation of expectancies attempted to trace what experimenters transmit to their subjects to cause SFP effects. Friedman (1967) had difficulties identifying clear mediating behaviors, despite painstaking analyses of molecular behaviors, in one of the earliest studies using videotape recordings. Adair and Epstein (1968) found that SFP effects could be reproduced by audiotape recordings of biased experimenters.

Numerous educational studies of expectancy mediation have been published since *Pygmalion*. Harris and Rosenthal (1985) meta-analyzed 31 behaviors (each investigated in at least four studies) from 136 mediation studies. The studies varied greatly in design and methodology: Some employed experimental simulations with random assignment of students into expectancy groups (sometimes even "teachers" were randomly assigned, to the extreme of employing sixth graders as tutors), whereas others were conducted in real classrooms, with teachers nominating their actual high- and low-expectancy students. The mediating behaviors selected by the various investigators ranged from very wide categories such as "direct influence" to specific behaviors such as the number of smiles. Assessment of teacher behavior was usually made by adult, trained observers, either in classrooms or from video recordings.

In terms of Rosenthal's (1985; Harris & Rosenthal, 1985) 10-arrow model, the majority of studies investigated the B–C link (i.e., relations between teachers' expectations and their differential behavior), and a smaller number investigated the C–D link (i.e., relations between teachers' differential behavior and students' performance). Most of the meta-analyzed behaviors showed similar effects in B–C and C–D studies, although some behaviors (e.g., criticism, indirect influence) showed significant effects in B–C but not in C–D studies, and for other behaviors (e.g., speech rate, gestures, encouragement) significant C–D but near-zero B–C effects were found.

Brophy (1983) summarized 17 mediation behaviors enacted differentially by teachers toward high- and low-expectancy students. Harris and Rosenthal (1985) concluded that 16 of the 31 meta-analyzed behaviors play a meaningful role in the mediation of teacher expectancies. Despite differences in phrasing, the two lists are quite similar to each other. To reduce the various behaviors to several clusters, Rosenthal (1973) introduced a four-factor theory of mediation. This model was quoted by numerous writers, and Harris and Rosenthal (1985) summarized their various meta-analyses for these four factors. (See also Harris, this volume.) The four factors are:

1. *Climate* – teachers' affective behaviors (e.g., warmth, support, smiling) and the socioemotional climate they create for high- and low-expectancy students.
2. *Feedback* – teachers' reward and punishment, praise and criticism (contingent or noncontingent upon students' performance).
3. *Input* – amount and quality of teaching behaviors directed at particular students.
4. *Output* – the degree to which teachers provide opportunities for the student to respond (e.g., calling on students, eye contact).

In meta-analyses, the climate and input factors yielded the strongest effect sizes (around $r = .35$), output behaviors yielded meaningful but weaker effects (around $r = .20$), and the effect size for the feedback factor was rather small ($r = .07$). This led Rosenthal (1989) to reformulate his theory of mediation, which now consists of two factors only: affect and effort.

The meta-analytic finding on the feedback factor illuminates an interesting issue. When teachers are asked informally to name behaviors that are enacted differentially by teachers as a function of expectancies, they intuitively mention praise and criticism first. The feedback factor was salient in the early mediation studies (e.g., Brophy & Good, 1970), and it continues to be quoted as a central mediation mechanism in theoretical explanations (e.g., Jussim, 1986). And yet feedback emerged in meta-analyses as the weakest factor of mediation, and teachers seem to dispense their praise and criticism equitably. In my opinion, this reflects to some extent the applied impact of *Pygmalion* and subsequent expectancy research on the field. Being aware of potential expectancy effects, teachers try to control their behavior, to be more equitable, and to refrain from dispensing their praise and criticism differentially. The feedback factor is both the most salient intuitively and the most amenable to self-control.

Teachers' behavior reflects the salient ideological concern about disadvantaged students. In recent years, more and more teachers have *intentionally compensated disadvantaged students* in their heterogeneous classrooms, investing extra energy in them and teaching them more. Such compensation leaves teachers satisfied that they are dealing with the issue of differences among students. And indeed, the profile of differential teacher behavior has been changing in recent years, with greater investment of effort and more vigilance in teaching low achievers compared to high achievers (see Weinstein, 1985, 1989, and Babad, 1990a). However, the existing evidence shows that this compensation is limited to explicit and easily controllable behaviors in the teaching domain, whereas affective behaviors and more subtle behaviors show substantial expectancy effects. (One example consists of extremely small differences in continued eye contact with high- compared to low-expectancy students following an insufficient or wrong answer.) Since affective behaviors are implicit, teachers who compensate disadvantaged students in overt teaching behaviors are often quite complacent, unaware of their negative affective transmissions to these students.

In recent years, Babad, Bernieri, and Rosenthal (1987, 1989a, 1989b, 1991; Babad & Taylor, in press) have developed a context-minimal method for examining isolated components of teachers' verbal and nonverbal behavior. The context was minimized through (1) extremely brief exposure (10-second video clips); (2) separation of channels (teacher's face, body, voice, speech content, etc.); and (3) showing only the teacher, not the students. Teachers were videotaped while *talking about* and *talking to* high- and low-expectancy students, and judges viewed 10-second clips of separate channels and combination of channels, randomized over the various conditions (of which the judges were, of course, not aware). In some studies the judges rated the teachers' behaviors directly; in other studies they made guesses about the unseen students from the teachers' faces, bodies, and speech, rating their academic success and the extent to which they were liked by the teachers.

Brief exposure to teachers' faces and/or bodies provided sufficient information to make clear detection of their expectancies. When the videotaped teachers were less cautious (talking about an absent student), their speech and verbal content gave away their expectations. When they were more cautious (talking to the student), they seemed to control their speech, but expectancies were detected from their facial expressions and body movements, and they were rated as transmitting more positive affect to high- compared to low-expectancy students. In line with the conception of compensation, the teachers showed a higher level of activity toward the low-expectancy students together with the more negative affect. We also found evidence of *leakage* in some instances (Babad et al., 1989a, 1989b). When people try to conceal their negative affect and transmit instead false-positive affect, their deceit is successful in more controllable channels (e.g., speech content) and not as successful in less controllable channels (e.g., the face and then the body), resulting in differences in judged affect among channels within the person. (See the discussion of leakage by Zuckerman and Blanck in this volume.) In our studies, teachers were not able to conceal their negative affect in the less controllable channels.

The context-minimal studies, and particularly the leakage analyses, illuminated an issue that has not been addressed in previous mediation research, namely, the incompatibility among channels or between messages. When active and more vigilant teaching is accompanied by negative affect, that might change considerably the way teaching would be experienced by low-expectancy students. The intended compensation and extra investment may thus boomerang in its meaning for their receivers. It seems that teachers believe that they can fully control their behavioral transmissions and deceive their students at will. For example, in the investigation of the teacher's pet phenomenon (Tal & Babad, 1989, 1990) the majority of the investigated teachers reported that they could conceal from their students their special attraction to their pets – a belief that was *not* borne out by the empirical findings. I think that despite the myths that "children see everything" and "nobody could deceive me," teachers believe that children are malleable and that they can deceive their students whenever they wish. The empirical findings of the context-minimal studies showed that negative affect toward low-expectancy students was detected by all groups of judges, including 10- and 13-year-old children who served as judges. Since teachers put on their best and most appropriate behavior when being videotaped, these findings may well underestimate what actually takes place in daily classroom interaction.

Students' affective reactions to teachers' differential behavior were not investigated in mediation studies. The teacher's pet studies (Tal & Babad, 1989, 1990) showed that inequitable and favoristic division of a teacher's affect evokes strong reactions, reducing students' morale, satisfaction, and wish to continue studying with that teacher. As mentioned earlier, nobody could argue that transmission of negative affect to low-expectancy students is appropriate, accurate, or justified by the students' real characteristics. It could be argued that such behavior is "only human" and cannot be brought under complete control, but such an argument must be put to an empirical test. I believe that well-designed training can increase self-control over affective behaviors, much as actors can learn to display fine nuances of verbal and nonverbal behavior at will. Teachers who believe that they should honestly express *all* their feelings in the classroom are more likely to show negative affect to low-expectancy students, much as teachers who put on a show of false love to students they really dislike are likely to leak negative affect.

V. Students' perceptions of teachers' expectancy-related differential behavior

All theoretical models of expectancy mediation (e.g., Brophy, 1983; Cooper, 1985; Darley & Fazio, 1980; Jussim, 1986) include a link in which students perceive the teacher's behavior that transmits her expectations. Weinstein (1989) noted that the emerging social-cognitive perspective in expectancy research highlights teachers' and students' perceptions and cognitions about each other's actions. And yet students' perceptions have been largely neglected, and trained adults have been employed as observers of teacher behavior in mediation studies. It must then be assumed that what students perceive and experience in the classroom is identical to the reports of these judges. This assumption was not confirmed in an empirical examination (Cooper & Good, 1983), and Babad (1990b) showed that a teacher behavior that has a uniform meaning in conventional mediation studies – calling on students – is interpreted differently by students, depending on *whom* the teacher calls on.

Numerous reasons justify the use of adult observers in the study of expectancy mediation. Children are not necessarily capable of describing objectively and reliably the behavior of their own teachers, and using children as "scientific observers" in a foreign classroom seems almost ludicrous. But since it cannot be assumed that students' perceptions and judges' observations are identical, it becomes important to investigate how students perceive and interpret teacher behavior, as well as to identify areas of agreement and disagreement between students and adult judges.

The method of questioning is crucial in the investigation of students' perceptions, and some measurement methods used with adult observers are not appropriate for young students. Weinstein (1985, 1989) and Babad (1990a) discovered independently that the most effective way was to ask students about the behavior of their teacher toward hypothetical high- and low-expectancy students, whereas other methods (e.g., self-report comparing oneself to other students, or abstract questions about how the teacher divides a particular behavior in the classroom) were ineffective. When we employed children as judges of the behavior of unfamiliar teachers using the context-minimal method (Babad et al., 1991), we found that conventional ratings of teacher behavior (e.g., warm, flexible, task-oriented, condescending) were not effective with the young judges, but that they could readily guess (detect) from brief clips depicting teacher behavior the unseen student's academic excellence and the teacher's liking for that student.

Weinstein (1985, 1989) and her associates, Cooper and Good (1983), and Babad (1990a) found that children are highly sensitive to their teachers' differential behavior. In the Weinstein studies, first graders showed as much sensitivity as older children, and students' sensitivity was not distinguished by their gender or ability level. Low achievers were systematically perceived in these studies as receiving fewer chances but greater teacher concern and vigilance, more negative feedback and direction, and more work- and rule-oriented treatment. Teacher interactions with high achievers were reported to reflect high expectations, academic demand, special privileges, more opportunity, and greater choice.

Cooper and Good (1983) found compatibility between students' and teachers' reports for five of nine investigated behaviors. The main disagreement was found for teachers' praise, where students reported that high achievers received more praise than low achievers, whereas the teachers reported the opposite. Comparisons with empirical observations of the same behaviors in the classroom showed that the observations were more consonant with teachers' reports than with students' reports. I found no other study comparing these three sources. This is unfortunate, since Cooper and Good focused heavily on feedback behaviors, which were subsequently reported by Harris and Rosenthal (1985) to be of weak magnitude in mediation of expectancies.

Babad (1990a) compared students' and teachers' perceptions of the teachers' differential behavior. Students and teachers agreed that low achievers receive more learning support and less pressure than high achievers. However, students reported that high achievers received more emotional support, whereas the teachers reported giving more emotional support to low achievers. These findings again showed compensation of low-expectancy students in the teaching domain, accompanied by concurrent transmission of negative affect.

In the two most recent context-minimal studies (Babad et al., 1991; Babad and Taylor, in press), we compared perceptions of students (aged 10, 13, and 16 years) and experienced teachers. The important finding was that all groups of judges clearly detected expectancy differences from these extremely brief clips. Detection of expectancy (i.e., perceiving the high-expectancy student as a better learner and as better liked by the teacher than the low-expectancy student) was facilitated by teachers' facial expressions and body language.

In these studies, a nonsignificant but systematic trend showed differences between the perceptions of the young judges and the experienced teachers. Whereas ratings of face and body showed uniform perceptions of teacher differentiality, the teacher's voice (audio) sometimes confused the younger judges, and in those instances they judged the low-expectancy student to be a better learner and better liked, or as receiving more warmth and flexibility from the teacher. This was found only for the young judges' ratings of audio clips, and it was reversed from their judgments of video (face and body) clips. The experienced teachers showed no such reversal between channels, detecting the same high–low expectancy differences consistently from the voice, as well as from the face and body clips. The same pattern was repeated in the New Zealand study (Babad & Taylor, in press), where the verbal content was totally incomprehensible to all judges. Again, the teachers' voices somewhat misled the younger (but not the adult) judges, reversing the direction of the high–low expectancy difference.

VI. Personality correlates of teacher expectancy effects

Compared to the multitude of mediation studies, the investigation of moderator variables and personality correlates of expectancy effects has remained relatively neglected. SFP and expectancy effects represent a probabilistic phenomenon, and discovering lawfulness in attributes of people more likely to show expectancy effects not only enriches theoretical knowledge, but permits identification of appropriate candidates for potential intervention.

A few methodological comments precede the more substantial discussion. First, different designs were used in the existing studies (correlational designs, extreme group designs with the expectancy and personality variables serving as either dependent or independent variables, etc.), but almost invariably, personality attributes were measured via self-report questionnaires. I am apprehensive about self-report questionnaires and what they allegedly measure, suspecting that respondents falsify their self-presentation consciously or unconsciously. Whenever possible, I prefer to use behavioral or performance measures of personality. In my own research, the Dogmatism Scale never distinguished between biased and unbiased teachers, although performance indices and behavioral observations clearly indicated that dogmatism is a major correlate of SFP and expectancy effects. Second, the following discussion focuses on teachers' personality only. Some recent publications have analyzed adult expectees' attributes in experimental SFP situations (e.g., Cooper & Hazelrigg, 1988; Harris, 1989; Harris & Rosenthal, 1986), but no research has been published on personality attributes of students likely to be influenced by teacher expectations.

Conceptually, two types of personality constructs are hypothesized to be involved in SFP effects – one involving the susceptibility of the expecter to biasing information (so that expectations can be formed), the other reflecting the expecter's influence on the behavior of the target (*suggestibility* and *communicability*, the terms used in Finn, 1972). The teacher's (experimenter's) personality structure, need system, and cognitive style must be such that biasing information about the student (subject) would be internalized, and a clear stereotypic expectation would be formed on the basis of that information. That person's cognitive style must be sufficiently rigid to ensure that the expectation would be resistant to disconfirming information, that is, that the person would hold on to unchangeable views. The dogmatic (Rokeach, 1960) or authoritarian (Adorno, Frenkel-Brunswick, Levinson, & Sanford, 1950) personality syndrome best fits the preceding description, including its dynamic (authoritarian submission, anti-intraception, etc.) and cognitive aspects (rigidity, intolerance of ambiguity, resistance to disconfirming information). The second construct involves the expression of the expectancy in the interaction between the expecter and the expectee. Expectations must be transmitted, received, interpreted, and eventually acted upon. Cooper and Hazelrigg (1988) described two communicability components, one being the expressivity of the expecter, and the other the degree to which the expecter is attractive and evokes the wish to conform to her or his wishes.

As mentioned, almost all studies on personality correlates of SFP have involved experimental situations, mostly Rosenthal's photo rating task. An experimental SFP situation differs from a classroom in several ways: (1) it is a short, one-time interaction between strangers; (2) the expectancy information constitutes all (or almost all) the knowledge available about the subject; and (3) the experimenter's behavior is not expected to have a long-term influence on the subject.

Demographic variables (including age, gender, professional experience, locale, socioeconomic status, and ethnic background) were not found to show a systematic correspondence with SFP proneness. As to personality variables, the clearest pattern emerging from the experimental studies consisted of several constructs loosely connected with the dogmatic syndrome, with stronger bias and SFP effects recorded for more dogmatic experimenters. These variables included need for social approval (Perlmutter, 1972), social desirability (Blake & Heslin, 1971), repression-sensitization (Dana & Dana, 1969), locus of control (Clarke, Michie, Andreasen, Viney, & Rosenthal, 1976), level of differentiation (Brattesani, Weinstein, & Marshall, 1984), and cognitive complexity and intolerance of ambiguity (Tom & Cooper, 1983; Tom, Cooper, & McGraw, 1984).

In their recent meta-analysis of personality correlates of experimental SFP effects, Cooper and Hazelrigg (1988) found a significant effect of moderate magnitude for the need for social influence (which included dogmatism-related components such as the need for social approval, influenceability, dominance, etc.) and close to significant, smaller effects for expressiveness and likability. In addition, they concluded that the personality of the experimenter played a greater role than the personality of the expectee in causing SFP effects. In a different experimental situation – peer counseling – Harris and Rosenthal (1986) reported that counselors who were more successful in biasing their clients' behavior in the direction of their expectancy scored higher on dogmatism. In a recent replication, Harris (1989) confirmed the importance of cognitive rigidity in determining expectancy effects.

As mentioned, studies of personality correlates of teacher expectancy effects have been scarce. Brophy and Good (1974; see also Brophy, 1983, 1985) described a hypothetical typology of teachers that, to the best of my knowledge, has never been empirically tested. They claimed that (1) the majority of teachers are *reactive*, that is, open to feedback and holding no rigid expectations, therefore not particularly amenable to SFP; (2) some teachers are *proactive* – experienced and realistic teachers who hold positive expectancies that cause low-achieving students to advance (similar to the concept of *Pygmalion managers* in Eden, 1990; see also chapter 7 in this volume); and (3) only a small minority of teachers are *overreactive*, holding rigid expectations that are harmful to low achievers.

Cooper and his associates (Cooper, 1979, 1985; Cooper & Good, 1983;

Cooper & Tom, 1984) conducted a series of studies on the moderating influence of teachers' sense of control over students' performance. According to Cooper's conceptualization, differences in teachers' sense of control over high and low achievers lead to differential behavior (such as limiting the initiations of low achievers in the classroom) aimed at maximizing their control. But sense of control is also a dimension of individual differences among teachers, and the hypothesis that this dimension would predict expectancy-related behavior was borne out in these studies. Cooper and Good (1983) also showed that teachers' attributions about success and failure of high and low achievers varied as a function of their sense of control.

Babad, Rosenthal, and their associates conducted over the last dozen years a series of studies on susceptibility to stereotypically biasing information, using a performance measure of personality to assess teachers' susceptibility. The measurement was based on the Goodenough-Harris Draw-A-Person test (Harris, 1963). The subjects (teachers and education students) learned the scoring system and were subsequently asked (under the guise of a reliability exercise) to score drawings allegedly made by two children, one of high status and one of low status on demographic, ethnic, and socioeconomic status variables. The drawings were actually reproduced from the test manual, and the difference between the scores attributed to the two drawings represented the scorer's level of susceptibility to biasing information. Over a series of administrations to different samples, we found that about one-sixth of the subjects were unbiased (i.e., uninfluenced by the biasing information in scoring the drawings), about one-half were mildly biased, one-fourth were highly biased, and 3–5% of the respondents showed a pattern of *reversed bias*, attributing a higher score to the drawing allegedly made by the low-status child. All studies described in the following paragraphs consist of comparisons between extreme groups of highly biased and unbiased respondents.

The Dogmatism Scale did not distinguish between biased and unbiased subjects. However, susceptibility to biasing information was found to be related to the extremity of held attitudes in both the political (Babad, 1979) and educational domains (Babad, 1985); to the tendency to show halo effects in making judgments about students when dividing them into high- and low-expectancy groups (Babad, Inbar, & Rosenthal, 1982b); and to several other cognitive variables characterizing dogmatism, such as the number of dogmatic statements written in open-ended accounts of educational events (Babad & Inbar, 1981).

Investigation of classroom behavior (measured by classroom observations and confirmed by judgments of the teachers' immediate supervisors) showed that biased teachers differed substantially from unbiased teachers in overall teaching style (Babad & Inbar, 1981). A central study in this series (Babad, Inbar, & Rosenthal, 1982a; see also Rosenthal & Babad, 1985) was designed to include teacher nominations of high- and low-expectancy students (typical of field studies), as well as a Pygmalion manipulation of bogus information (typical of experimental studies), and the dependent variables included both teachers' differential behavior and students' performance for these teachers. We found SFP effects – especially Golem effects – for biased but not for unbiased teachers.

In the studies utilizing the context-minimal method, we found the hypothesized differences between biased and unbiased teachers (Babad et al., 1989a). Furthermore, nonverbal leakage of negative affect was found for biased but not for unbiased teachers (Babad et al., 1989b). However, the differences between biased and unbiased teachers in the context-minimal studies were smaller than the differences found in the previous studies. Expectancy-related differential behavior was found in the context-minimal studies for unbiased teachers as well.

Finally, in an unpublished study, I measured susceptibility to biasing information of all entering freshmen in an Israeli teacher training college, and examined longitudinally all information accumulated in the students' files throughout their training. Differences between biased and unbiased teachers-in-training were found in intellectual abilities, academic performance in the college, fieldwork evaluations, and drop-out rates. These findings indicated that the biased group was lower in intellectual and professional level than the unbiased group. If the characterization and behavior of biased teachers will hold up in future research of other investigators, the emerging application question will be whether expectancy-related behavior of biased teachers can be changed by an appropriate intervention.

VII. Applied interventions for reducing harmful effects of teacher expectations

The weakest aspect of teacher expectancy research is the relative absence of applied intervention. The progress in theoretical–empirical research has not been accompanied by parallel development of efforts to apply the findings in the field. This is not to say that expectancy research did not have an impact on the field, nor does it mean that no intervention projects have been conducted. Expectancy research had a strong impact on the field, as indicated by growing trends toward compensation, equalization of praise and criticism, and common knowledge about *Pygmalion*. Intervention projects have been conducted; Kerman and Martin (1980; see also Penman, 1982) reported that their Teacher Expectations and Student Achievement (TESA) program had been undertaken by at least 600 groups of teachers. But such projects were based on a very global conception of expectancies, did not reflect the developing research, and did not apply specific findings accumulated over the years.

Numerous obstacles prevent effective application of expectancy research. The gap between research and applied intervention in psychology is very wide, particularly in social psychology. Theoretical knowledge on attitudes, bias, stereotyping, and prejudice is far ahead of applied knowledge about psychological change in these areas. In education, researchers and intervention specialists are two distinct and separate professional groups. Usually researchers are not involved in intervention and practitioners do not conduct research, nor are they updated often on current research. Most applied projects are not designed in ways that would allow one to ascribe causal influence to identifiable variables. Interventions tend to be global and sweeping and to include numerous aspects and methods, and empirical evaluations are carried out only when demanded by funding agencies. Finally, the successes reported in numerous educational projects may well reflect Hawthorne effects, and successful implementation is not assured even if pilot projects were successful.

Perhaps the most critical obstacle to effective application of expectancy research is the fact that individual differences among teachers have not been considered at all in the existing interventions. Since teachers differ in proneness to SFP effects, and since the likelihood of finding expectancy effects varies among classrooms, intervention efforts should concentrate on teachers who most need the treatment and should be tailored to fit these teachers' personality style. Actually, the existing interventions have been administered mostly to enthusiastic volunteers, the group least in need of change (see Rosnow, this volume).

Next, I discuss three types of interventions:

1. sets of recommendations;
2. controlled experimental studies;
3. large in-service training projects.

Several authors have added to their reviews of teacher expectancy research sets of recommendations, advising teachers how to deal with differences and with their differential expectations. Some sets (e.g., Brophy, 1983; Cooper & Tom, 1984) focused on reducing expectancy effects through changes in teacher behavior toward low-expectancy students. Other sets (e.g., Heger, 1984) purported to deal with expectancies, but they actually included global recommendations for changes in school climate. Frankly, sets of recommendations are not very likely to have a real impact in changing teacher behavior. Cooper and Tom (1984) commented that it is easier to make recommendations than to carry them out in the field. They stated that efforts to retrain teachers to avoid expectancy effects through teacher–student interaction rules proved largely unsuccessful because teachers "react" more than they "act," and their reactive conduct does not follow their intended plans.

A second group of works consists of controlled studies focusing on particular aspects of expectancy. In such studies, intervention is limited to an isolated variable, so that subsequent change can validly be ascribed to that intervention. Examples of such studies include Smith and Luginbuhl's (1976) investigation of the effects of an explicit warning given to college students serving as teachers about the influence of expectations on teacher behavior; Dweck's (1975) study on attributional retraining given to students to prevent learned helplessness through encouragement to replace "lack of ability" by "lack of effort" attributions for failure; Good and Brophy's (1974) investigation of changes in teachers' and students' behavior following empirical feedback given to teachers from classroom observations; and Babad's (1990a) study on feedback data given to teachers on gaps between their own and their students' perceptions of their differential classroom behavior. All four studies showed positive effects of the investigated interventions, although they did not escape criticism: The first study involved a contrived, unreal classroom situation; Eccles and Wigfield (1985) questioned the wide-range applicability of attributional retraining, especially if failure is experienced repeatedly; Good and Brophy (1974) found changes in quantitative but not qualitative aspects of teacher behavior; and Babad's (1990a) study is too recent, but potential criticism could touch on the fact that the change in teacher behavior was described quite differently by the students and the teachers.

I believe that controlled studies focusing on isolated, well-defined aspects constitute a necessary link between research and intervention. Despite reservations about their generalizability, studies of this type allow relatively valid inferences about the effects of specific intervention components. Sweeping programs may yield more impressive outcomes, but their implementation potential is limited, because it is not possible to isolate specific components for future implementation.

The third group consists of broad in-service intervention programs. Examples include the TESA in-service training package (Kerman, 1979; Kerman & Martin, 1980; see also Penman, 1982, and Proctor, 1984), the STILE program (Terry, 1980; see also Banuazizi, 1981); and Weinstein's (1988) researcher–teacher collaborative program. These programs integrated various components and change strategies, including theoretical and research input about teacher expectations; small group discussions; specific behavioral training to improve teacher–student interaction; training in observation; and feedback from classroom observation.

As mentioned, some of the projects were very broad and loosely connected with teacher expectancies. For example, the Connecticut project (Proctor, 1984) was a large school effectiveness improvement program, of which TESA was but one component. Similarly, Weinstein (1988) objected to the approach of addressing single pieces of the problem, advocating a more global approach to improve motivational climate. Weinstein's model included eight factors in the organization and processes of school life.

In the reports about these projects, the participating teachers and the designers and administrators of the programs express excitement and enthusiasm. It is well known that many educational projects are successful in the experimental stage (with its characteristic commitment and investment) but that their effectiveness is diminished in subsequent implementation.

Relatively little evaluation data are available on these programs, and the existing reports are faulty and open to criticism. The few program evaluations that I was able to find (Banuazizi, 1981; Penman, 1982; Proctor, 1984; Soule, 1988) showed positive outcomes, but serious faults in design and measurement were evident: (1) The designs included numerous variables, and no plans were made to isolate effects attributable to specific intervention components. (2) The participating teachers were volunteers. (3) Participants' proneness to expectancy effects was not assessed prior to the intervention. (4) Control groups were either nonexistent or faulty (e.g., teachers volunteering to be in the control group). (5) None of the projects included a placebo control to distinguish Hawthorne effects from effects attributable to the specific intervention. (See also part III of this volume.)

In the behavioral domain directly relevant to teacher expectancies, TESA and STILE put strong emphasis on equalizing the distribution of praise and criticism. In recent meta-analyses, this factor was found to have the weakest magnitude in mediation of expectancies. Specific findings (Penman, 1982; Proctor, 1984; Terry, 1980) showed changes mostly in quantitative aspects of teacher behavior (asking questions, criticizing, etc.) but relatively no changes in the qualitative and affective aspects of teacher–student interaction.

Two objectives characterize the conception of the existing interventions: (1) to change expectations or, more accurately, to improve teachers' expectations for low achievers; (2) to equalize teacher behavior by reducing negative behavior to low-expectancy students. The first factor is somewhat similar to Eden's conception of *Pygmalion management* (Eden, 1984, 1990; see also Eden, this volume). If teachers could be made to hold high expectations for weak students, that could cause positive changes in these students' performance. But negative expectancies would not be eliminated altogether, since attributes and behavior of certain students do realistically create negative expectations. I am afraid that heavy-handed attempts to improve negative expectations may lead to self-deception and phoniness. (Many students enjoy imitating teachers' phony cheerfulness and friendliness.) The negative affect does not disappear; it is simply suppressed and not dealt with. The second factor, behavioral training, has been and will be a critical component in every intervention program. But as mentioned, existing training (e.g., TESA and STILE) is concentrated on the wrong set of behaviors, enhancing compensation (with its resultant complacency and self-righteousness) but not necessarily reducing potentially harmful effects of negative teacher expectations in the affective domain.

This analysis leads to the conclusion that the existing intervention model must be expanded. Through group methods of self-inquiry (Babad, Birnbaum, & Benne, 1983), teachers can become aware of their own stereotypes, prejudices, and biases. Since negative affect and negative expectations are natural and will always exist in heterogeneous classrooms, teachers should become aware of their negative feelings rather than deny them. At the same time, they should be given directed training to control their relevant verbal and nonverbal behaviors, especially in the affective domain. To reduce leakage of negative affect, teachers would be trained to minimize the expression of false affect and to maintain a relatively uniform emotional distance from all students. Videotaped feedback (from simulated situations or actual classroom interaction) would be used to illuminate subtle aspects of nonverbal behavior (facial expressions, body language, tone of voice, etc.) – serving as data for behavioral practice and subsequently for empirical assessment of teachers' progress.

The behavioral training suggested here is indeed difficult, but I am more apprehensive about resistance to self-inquiry (Babad et al., 1983). Many teachers might prefer to express phony high expectations than to face their negative affect, especially since they are not aware of their leakage. This might be particularly true for dogmatic teachers – those indicated by our research to be more likely to manifest expectancy effects in their classrooms.

If funds are limited, it would be crucial to administer such interventions to susceptible teachers only. If training is administered to teachers at large, the intervention should be designed to fit prone teachers' personality, and special attention should be given to examine the effects of the intervention in their classrooms.

In the long run, compact intervention programs should be developed for wide implementation. I think that preventive expectancy training should be included in the curriculum of teacher training, and practicing teachers could obtain (with the assistance of colleagues or school psychologists) periodic behavioral data from their students' perceptions *and* classroom observations, and use these data to change and improve their classroom conduct.

References

Adair, J., & Epstein, J. (1968). Verbal clues to the mediation of experimenter bias. *Psychological Reports, 22,* 1045–1053.

Adorno, T., Frenkel-Brunswick, E., Levinson, D., & Sanford, R. (1950). *The authoritarian personality.* New York: Harper & Row.

Babad, E. (1978). On the biases of psychologists. *The Behavioral and Brain Sciences, 3,* 387–388.

Babad, E. (1979). Personality correlates of susceptibility to biasing information. *Journal of Personality and Social Psychology, 37,* 195–202.

Babad, E. (1980). Expectancy bias in scoring as a function of ability and ethnic labels. *Psychological Reports, 46,* 625–626.

Babad, E. (1985). Some correlates of teachers' expectancy bias. *American Educational Research Journal, 22,* 175–183.

Babad, E. (1990a). Measuring and changing teachers' differential behavior as perceived by students and teachers. *Journal of Educational Psychology, 82,* 683–690.

Babad, E. (1990b). Calling on students: How a teacher's behavior can acquire disparate meanings in students' minds. *Journal of Classroom Interaction, 25,* 1–4.

Babad, E., Ariav, A., Rosen, I., & Salomon, G. (1987). Perseverance of bias as a function of debriefing conditions and subjects' confidence. *Social Behaviour, 2,* 185–193.

Babad, E., Bernieri, F., & Rosenthal, R. (1987). Nonverbal and verbal behavior of preschool, remedial, and elementary school teachers. *American Educational Research Journal, 24*, 405–415.

Babad, E., Bernieri, F., & Rosenthal, R. (1989a). Nonverbal communication and leakage in the behavior of biased and unbiased teachers. *Journal of Personality and Social Psychology, 56*, 89–94.

Babad, E., Bernieri, F., & Rosenthal, R. (1989b). When less information is more informative: Diagnosing teacher expectations from brief samples of behaviour. *British Journal of Educational Psychology, 59*, 281–295.

Babad, E., Bernieri, F., & Rosenthal, R. (1991). Students as judges of teachers' verbal and nonverbal behavior. *American Educational Research Journal, 28*, 211–234.

Babad, E., Birnbaum, M., & Benne, K. (1983). *The social self*. Beverly Hills, CA: Sage.

Babad, E., & Inbar, J. (1981). Performance and personality correlates of teachers' susceptibility to biasing information. *Journal of Personality and Social Psychology, 40*, 553–561.

Babad, E., Inbar, J., & Rosenthal, R. (1982a). Pygmalion, Galatea, and the Golem: Investigations of biased and unbiased teachers. *Journal of Educational Psychology, 74*, 459–474.

Babad, E., Inbar, J., & Rosenthal, R. (1982b). Teachers' judgment of students' potential as a function of teachers' susceptibility to biasing information. *Journal of Personality and Social Psychology, 42*, 541–547.

Babad, E., & Taylor, P. (In press). The transparency of teacher expectancies across language and cultural boundaries: Detection from nonverbal cues. *Journal of Educational Research*.

Banuazizi, A. (1981). *An evaluation of the first year's activities of the national demonstration Title II project (basic skills improvement program) in selected elementary grades of Cambridge public schools*. Cambridge, MA: City School Committee.

Barber, T., & Silver, M. (1968). Fact, fiction, and the experimenter bias effect. *Psychological Bulletin Monograph Supplement, 70* (No. 6, part 2), 1–29.

Baron, R., Tom, D., & Cooper, H. (1985). Social class, race, and teacher expectations. In J. B. Dusek (Ed.), *Teacher expectancies* (pp. 251–269). Hillsdale NJ: Erlbaum.

Berliner, D. (1976). Impediments to the study of teacher effectiveness. *Journal of Teacher Education, 27*, 5–13.

Blake, B., & Heslin, R. (1971). Evaluation apprehension and subject bias in experiments. *Journal of Experimental Research in Personality, 5*, 57–63.

Brattesani, K., Weinstein, R., & Marshall, H. (1984). Student perceptions of differential teacher treatment as moderators of teacher expectancy effects. *Journal of Educational Psychology, 76*, 236–247.

Brophy, J. (1983). Research on the self-fulfilling prophecy and teacher expectations. *Journal of Educational Psychology, 75*, 631–661.

Brophy, J. (1985). Teacher–student interaction. In J. Dusek (Ed.), *Teacher expectancies* (pp. 303–328). Hillsdale, NJ: Erlbaum.

Brophy, J., & Good, T., (1970). Teachers' communication of differential expectations for children's classroom performance: Some behavioral data. *Journal of Educational Psychology, 61*, 365–374.

Brophy, J., & Good, T. (1974). *Teacher–student relationships: Causes and consequences*. New York: Holt, Rinehart and Winston.

Clarke, A., Michie, P., Andreasen, A., Viney, L., & Rosenthal, R. (1976).

Expectancy effects in a psychological experiment. *Physiological Psychology, 4,* 137–144.

Cooper, H. (1979). Pygmalion grows up: A model for teacher expectation communication and performance influence. *Review of Educational Research, 49,* 389–410.

Cooper, H. (1985). Models for teacher expectation communication. In J. Dusek (Ed.), *Teacher expectancies* (pp. 135–158). Hillsdale, NJ: Erlbaum.

Cooper, H., & Good, T. (1983). *Pygmalion grows up.* New York: Longman.

Cooper, H., & Hazelrigg, P. (1988). Personality moderators of interpersonal expectancy effects: An integrative research review. *Journal of Personality and Social Psychology, 55,* 937–949.

Cooper, H., & Tom, D. (1984). Teacher expectation research: A review with implications for classroom instruction. *Elementary School Journal, 85,* 77–89.

Crano, W., & Mellon, P. (1978). Causal influence of teachers' expectations on children's academic performance: A cross-lagged panel analysis. *Journal of Educational Psychology, 70,* 39–49.

Dana, J., & Dana, R. (1969). Experimenter bias and the WAIS. *Perceptual and Motor Skills, 28,* 634.

Darley, J., & Fazio, R. (1980). Expectancy confirmation processes arising in the social interaction sequence. *American Psychologist, 35,* 867–881.

Dusek, J., & Joseph, G. (1985). The bases of teacher expectancies. In J. B. Dusek (Ed.), *Teacher expectancies* (pp. 229–250). Hillsdale, NJ: Erlbaum.

Dweck, C. (1975). The role of expectations and attributions in the alleviation of learned helplessness. *Journal of Personality and Social Psychology, 31,* 674–685.

Eccles, J., & Wigfield, A. (1985). Teacher expectations and student motivation. In J. B. Dusek (Ed.), *Teacher expectancies* (pp. 185–228). Hillsdale, NJ: Erlbaum.

Elashoff, J., & Snow, R. (1971). *Pygmalion reconsidered.* Belmont, CA: Wadsworth.

Eden, D. (1984). Self-fulfilling prophecy as a management tool: Harnessing Pygmalion. *Academy of Management Review, 9,* 64–73.

Eden, D. (1990). *Pygmalion in management.* Lexington, MA: Lexington Books.

Finn, J. (1972). Expectations and educational environment. *Review of Educational Research, 42,* 389–409.

Friedman, N. (1967). *The social nature of psychological research.* New York: Basic Books.

Good, T., & Brophy, J. (1974). Changing teacher and student behavior: An empirical examination. *Journal of Educational Psychology, 66,* 390–405.

Hall, V., & Merkel, S. (1985). Teacher expectancy effects and educational psychology. In J. B. Dusek (Ed.), *Teacher expectancies* (pp. 67–92). Hillsdale, NJ: Erlbaum.

Harris, D. (1963). *Goodenough-Harris Drawing Test Manual.* New York: Harcourt, Brace & World.

Harris, M. (1989). Personality moderators of interpersonal expectancy effects: Replication of Harris and Rosenthal (1986). *Journal of Research in Personality, 23,* 381–397.

Harris, M., & Rosenthal, R. (1985). Mediation of interpersonal expectancy effects: 31 meta-analyses. *Psychological Bulletin, 97,* 363–386.

Harris, M., & Rosenthal, R. (1986) Counselor and client personality as determinants of counselor expectancy effects. *Journal of Personality and Social Psychology, 50,* 362–369.

Heger, H. (1984). Supporting excellence through teacher expectations. *College Student Journal, 18*, 327–334.

Jensen, A. (1969). How much can we boost IQ and scholastic achievement? *Harvard Educational Review, 39*, 1–123.

Jones, E. (1986). Interpreting interpersonal behavior: The effects of expectancies. *Science, 234*, 41–46.

Jones, R. (1977) *Self-fulfilling prophecies.* Hillsdale, NJ: Erlbaum.

Jussim, L. (1986). Self-fulfilling prophecies: A theoretical and integrative review. *Psychological Review, 93*, 429–445.

Jussim, L. (1989). Teacher expectations: Self-fulfilling prophecies, perceptual biases, and accuracy. *Journal of Personality and Social Psychology, 57*, 469–480.

Kerman, S. (1979). Teacher expectations and student achievement. *Phi Delta Kappan, 60*, 716–718.

Kerman, S., & Martin, M. (1980). *Teacher expectations and the student achievement (Teacher handbook).* Los Angeles: County Superintendent of Schools.

Meyer, W. (1985). Summary, integration, and prospective. In J. B. Dusek (Ed.), *Teacher expectancies* (pp. 353–370). Hillsdale, NJ: Erlbaum.

Miller, D., & Turnbull, W. (1986). Expectancies and interpersonal processes. *Annual Review of Psychology, 37*, 233–256.

Penman, P. (1982). The *efficacy of TESA training in changing teacher behavior and attitudes towards low achievers.* Unpublished doctoral dissertation, Arizona State University.

Perlmutter, L. (1972). Experimenter–subject needs for social approval and task interactiveness as factors in experimenter expectancy effects. *Dissertations Abstracts International, 32*, 6692–6693.

Proctor, C. (1984). Teacher expectations: A model for school improvement. *Elementary School Journal, 84*, 469–481.

Raudenbush, S. (1984). Magnitude of teacher expectancy effects on pupil IQ as a function of the credibility of expectancy induction: A synthesis of findings from 18 experiments. *Journal of Educational Psychology, 76*, 85–97.

Rist, R. (1970). Student social class and teacher expectations: The self-fulfilling prophecy in ghetto education. *Harvard Educational Review, 40*, 411–451.

Rist, R. (1987, December). Do teachers count in the lives of children? *Educational Researcher, 16*, 41–42.

Rokeach, M. (1960). *The open and closed mind.* New York: Basic Books.

Rosenthal, R. (1973). The mediation of Pygmalion effects: A four factor "theory." *Papua New Guinea Journal of Education, 9*, 1–12.

Rosenthal, R. (1985). From unconscious experimenter bias to teacher expectancy effects. In J. Dusek (Ed.), *Teacher expectancies* (pp. 37–65). Hillsdale, NJ: Erlbaum.

Rosenthal, R. (1989). *The affect/effort theory of the mediation of interpersonal expectation effects.* Donald T. Campbell Award Address, Annual convention of the American Psychological Association, New Orleans.

Rosenthal, R., & Babad, E. (1985). Pygmalion in the gymnasium. *Educational Leadership* (September), 36–39.

Rosenthal, R., & Jacobson, L. (1968). *Pygmalion in the classroom.* New York: Holt, Rinehart and Winston.

Rosenthal, R., & Rubin, D. (1978). Interpersonal expectancy effects: The first 345 studies. *Behavioral and Brain Sciences, 3*, 377–415.

Rosenthal, R., & Rubin, D. (1982). A simple general purpose display of magnitude of experimental effect. *Journal of Educational Psychology, 74*, 166–169.

Rubovits, P., & Maehr, M. (1973). Pygmalion black and white. *Journal of Personality and Social Psychology, 25,* 210–218.

Salomon, G. (1981) Self-fulfilling and self-maintaining prophecies and behaviors that realize them. *American Psychologist, 36,* 1452–1453.

Smith, F., & Luginbuhl, J. (1976). Inspecting expectancy: Some laboratory results of relevance for teacher training. *Journal of Educational Psychology, 68,* 265–272.

Smith, M. (1980). Teacher expectations. *Evaluation in Education, 4,* 53–55.

Snyder, M. (1984). When belief creates reality. In L. Berkowitz (Ed.), *Advances in experimental social psychology* (Vol. 18, pp. 247–305). New York: Academic Press.

Soule, C. (1988). *Collaborative intervention research: An array of findings.* Paper presented at the annual meeting of the American Educational Research Association, New Orleans.

Tal, Z., & Babad, E. (1989). The "teacher's pet" phenomenon as viewed by Israeli teachers and students. *Elementary School Journal, 90,* 99–110.

Tal, Z., & Babad, E. (1990). The teacher's pet phenomenon: Rate of occurrence, correlates, and psychological costs. *Journal of Educational Psychology, 82,* 637–645.

Terry, J. (1980). *Student performance and school related attitudes as a function of teacher expectation and behavior.* Unpublished manuscript, MIT, Division for Study and Research in Education.

Thorndike, R. (1968). Review of *Pygmalion in the classroom. American Educational Research Journal, 5,* 708–711.

Tom, D., & Cooper, H. (1983). Teacher cognitive style, expectations, and attributions for student performance. In J. Staussner (Chair), *Adult cognitive functioning and the expectancy phenomenon.* Symposium presented at the Meeting of the American Psychological Association, Anaheim, CA.

Tom, D., Cooper, H., & McGraw, M. (1984). Influences of student background and teacher authoritarianism on teacher expectations. *Journal of Educational Psychology, 76,* 259–265.

Weinstein, R. (1985). Student mediation of classroom expectancy effects. In J. Dusek (Ed.), *Teacher expectancies* (pp. 329–350). Hillsdale, N.J.: Erlbaum.

Weinstein, R. (1988). An expectancy model for improving the motivational climate of classroom and schools. In T. Good (Chair), *Expectations and high school change: Teacher-researcher collaboration in preventing school failure.* Symposium presented at the meeting of the American Educational Research Association, New Orleans.

Weinstein, R. (1989). Perceptions of classroom processes and student motivation: Children's views of self-fulfilling prophecies. In C. Ames & R. Ames (Eds.), *Research on motivation in education. Vol. 3. Goals and cognitions* (pp. 187–221). New York: Academic Press.

Wineburg, S. (1987, December). The self-fulfillment of the self-fulfilling prophecy. *Educational Researcher, 16,* 28–44.

7. Interpersonal expectations in organizations

DOV EDEN

From laboratory to classroom to factory

Summarizing a dozen or so studies of the experimenter effect in the *American Scientist*, Rosenthal (1963) wondered in print whether similar expectancy effects might occur among physicians, psychotherapists, employers, and teachers. He soon accepted Jacobson's challenge to conduct a teacher-expectation experiment in her school. Thus was launched the famous experiment that led to the publication of *Pygmalion in the Classroom*. Given what we have since learned about interpersonal expectancy effects in organizations, there can be no doubt that, had an industrial psychologist invited Rosenthal to his plant to replicate the experimenter effect in the real world of the shop floor, the landmark report would have been titled *Pygmalion in the Factory*. The Pygmalion effect would be widely known today as a management phenomenon, and organizational psychologists and consultants would be seeking ways to improve job performance by creating interpersonal expectancy effects. For subsequent research in organizations has abundantly confirmed Rosenthal's early hunch: Expectancy effects occur among adults in the workplace. This chapter presents a review of research on interpersonal expectancy effects in nonschool organizations and some ideas for practical applications designed to improve organizational effectiveness. Many of these proposals are relevant for schools, which are also organizations that employ adults. Generalizing interpersonal expectancy effects from teacher–pupil relations to principal–teacher interaction has not been duly considered by education experts.

Expectations in management

The notion that performance expectations play an important role in determining managerial effectiveness is not new, nor did it enter the management literature via the Pygmalion research. Organizational scholars and practitioners have long known that managers who expect more get more (e.g., Likert, 1961, 1967; McGregor, 1960). In parallel, work motivation theorists have long postulated the central role of expectancy in motivating the exertion of effort in job performance and in determining productivity (e.g., Atkinson, 1957; McClelland, Atkinson, Clark, & Lowell, 1953; Vroom, 1964; Zuroff & Rotter, 1985). There is a consensus among scholars that expectations and motivation are positively associated. However, none of these theoreticians has proposed utilization of this relationship by purposely raising worker expectations in order to boost work motivation. Moreover, theory and research have largely ignored the interface between the manager's expectations of the subordinate and the subordinate's self-expectations. The manager-as-Pygmalion model is unique in focusing on the interlinking expectations of managers and subordinates as a key to understanding – and enhancing – the motivational power of effective leadership. The proactive approach to interpersonal expectations in organizations, not only as a subject worthy of discourse and research but also as an object of action designed to produce valued outcomes, is a uniquely Pygmalion-inspired innovation.

Preexperimental Pygmalion in management

Fresh in the wake of *Pygmalion in the Classroom*, Livingston (1969) argued cogently for the relevance of the Pygmalion concept to management. He wrote that subordinates' job performance and careers are determined largely by what their managers expect of them. The best managers create high performance expectations that subordinates fulfill. Livingston realized that expectations can be created and transmitted in many ways, and that managers' belief in their own capacity to lead subordinates to outstanding performance determines how they play Pygmalion's role. Livingston discussed the negative impact of low expectations, invoked the theory of achievement motivation to explain expectation effects, and spoke of self-esteem as mediating the relationship between expectations and performance. Livingston's only evidence for most of his propositions was from case material. However, in this early article he raised many of the issues that were subsequently investigated experimentally.

In a retrospective commentary 20 years later, Livingston (1988) wrote that the counterproductive self-fulfilling prophecy (SFP) engendered by low manager expectations was much more widespread in American industry than positive Pygmalion effects. Babad, Inbar, and Rosenthal (1982) have dubbed the negative impact of low expectations on achievement the *Golem effect*. SFP research and applications in education have the remedial purpose of undoing the wrongs endured by victims of the Golem effect. A balanced approach to application would involve a combination of both uprooting low expectations to eradicate negative Golem effects and implanting high expectations to create positive Pygmalion effects.

The first interpersonal expectancy experiments in industry

Disadvantaged trainees

King (1971) replicated the Pygmalion effect in an industrial training program for disadvantaged persons using the experimental approach pioneered by Rosenthal and Jacobson. He randomly designated four pressers, five welders, and five mechanics as high-aptitude personnel (HAPs), leading the instructors to expect superior performance from these individuals. The designations produced the hypothesized effect. The HAPs obtained higher test scores, higher supervisor and peer ratings, and shorter learning times and had lower dropout rates, evidencing the Pygmalion effect.

Organizationwide expectancy effects

King (1974) next focused on expectancy effects at the organizational level. He suspected that managers' expectations regarding the outcomes of organizational innovations produce effects on those outcomes that are distinguishable from the effects of the innovations themselves. He was concerned that uncontrolled expectancy effects confound evaluation research on the impact of various interventions in organizations. His aim was to tease out the effects of an innovation from the effects of the expectations that it would succeed using a 2×2 experimental design among machine operators in four similar industrial plants. He introduced the same changes differently in each plant. Job enlargement was the innovation installed in two plants and withheld from two enlargement-control plants, which got job rotation as a sham innovation. The second independent variable was management's productivity expectations, which were manipulated to be high in one enlargement plant and in one rotation plant, and unmanipulated and therefore at control levels in the two remaining plants. Thus, four comparable plants got different treatment combinations: a high-expectation enlargement plant, a high-expectation rotation plant, a control-expectation enlargement plant, and a control-expectation rotation plant.

Productivity over 12 months showed that enlargement had no effect but that expectations did. Both high-expectation plants increased their output by similar amounts, irrespective of whether they had gotten enlargement or rotation, whereas output in both control-expectation plants was unchanged. That is, if manager expectations were raised, productivity improved, regardless of which intervention was introduced. If expectations were not raised, productivity remained constant, regardless of which innovation was installed. Thus, manager expectations concerning performance due to the innovations had produced an SFP effect. King pointed out the methodological implications of his findings for evaluation research in organizations. However, beyond methodology, producing so-called organizationwide SFP (Eden, 1990d) has profound practical implications for management and consulting. People who expect more from a program are likely to benefit more from it. This implies that one way to increase the success of organizational changes of all sorts is to create expectancy effects by getting people to expect them to work.

Organizationwide SFP is not a Pygmalion effect, for it is not an *interpersonal* expectancy effect. These different varieties of SFP are distinguishable in terms of how the newly acquired high expectations are anchored. To produce a Pygmalion effect, one must get a manager to expect more of a subordinate on the basis of some characteristic of the subordinate. In contrast, in creating organizationwide SFP, King took advantage of his expert role to anchor high manager expectations in properties of the new *program* to be implemented. This can be an alternative way to create a productive SFP when managers know, or think they know, their subordinates' limitations well. Firmly crystallized expectations are hard to change, rendering those who hold them resistant to Pygmalion effects.

King's rotation plants got what in medical science would be called a *placebo*, and the high-expectation rotation plant showed a placebo effect. (See Friedman, this volume.) Job design research has shown job rotation to be an ineffective way to improve productivity (e.g., Hackman & Oldham, 1980). That is why King used rotation in his control-innovation condition. Boosting productivity by combining expectations for improved productivity with an otherwise unproductive change in work procedures is akin to producing the placebo effect in medicine. Even King's inert "sugar capsule" (i.e., rotation) proved to be an efficacious remedy for problems in productivity if (and only if) the "patients" (i.e., plant personnel) believed it could improve productivity. A menace to valid inference, placebo effects must be controlled in research evaluating treatment effectiveness (Critelli & Neumann, 1984). However, practice is not research. We should harshly judge the clinician who abstains from using the placebo effect as an aid to treatment. If smiling, nodding reassuringly, and saying to a patient "I'm sure the medication I've prescribed will help you feel better" can augment the drug in promoting healing, then physicians should add these placebo interventions to their treatment repertoire. Refraining from creating physician expectation effects on methodological grounds would be wrong both practically and ethically. The same reasoning applies to willful creation of manager expectation effects. If "merely" raising performance expectations can boost productivity, then raise them we should!

The particular type of expectation effect dubbed *organizationwide SFP* earlier is not to be confused with the famous Hawthorne effect (Roethlisberger & Dickson, 1939). Elsewhere (Eden, 1986) I have discussed the distinction between the two effects. The causal agent to which the Hawthorne effect is most frequently attributed is supervisor attention, not supervisor expectations. On the contrary, if the two effects are related, it is likely that the Hawthorne experimenters actually inadvertently produced a Pygmalion effect, unknown at the time. In Roethlisberger and Dickson's (1939) detailed written account of the Hawthorne experiments, there are numerous explicit expressions of high expectations on the part of both management and the experimenters in presenting the experimental changes to the workers and in answering their queries about the research. Thus, the Hawthorne effect may be just another expectation effect.

Pygmalion goes to boot camp: The IDF combat training experiment

The next three field experiments using variations on the classical Pygmalion research design were carried out by my students and me in the Israel Defense Forces (IDF). The first (Eden & Shani, 1982) replicated the basic Pygmalion paradigm in a culture and an age group different from those of previous experiments. An additional aim was to render the mediating variables revealed in classroom research applicable to management. Rosenthal (1973) had summarized several dozen class-room studies and identified four clusters of teacher behaviors that me-diate the teacher expectation effect: climate, feedback, input, and out-put. (See part II, this volume, and Harris, this volume. See also Harris & Rosenthal, 1985.) *Socioemotional climate* results from nonverbal, and mostly subconscious, teacher behaviors that convey positive or negative feelings toward pupils. Teachers have been found to smile more at pupils of whom they expect a lot, to maintain eye contact with them more frequently and for longer duration, to get physically closer to them, and to convey greater warmth, acceptance, and approval to them via various forms of posture and body language, such as touching and nodding approvingly. Teachers give more *feedback* and more varied feedback to pupils of whom they expect more (see Babad, this volume). *Input*, in the form of teaching more material and harder material, is provided more to those expected to do well. This communicates high expectations to these pupils, challenges them, and spurs them on to greater achievement. *Output* is defined as producing a learning result, as in answering a question in class. Teachers give pupils opportunities to produce output by assigning them challenging projects or by calling upon them to do something extra, beyond the minimal requirements. Research has revealed a tendency for teachers to provide greater output opportunities for pupils expected to achieve more, and to withhold such opportunities from pupils deemed unlikely to deliver.

The combination of all four factors points to a straightforward expla-nation of the Pygmalion effect: High expectations work their "magic" by making teachers more effective instructors for those whom they expect to do well. The four mediating factors comprise good teaching behavior. The SFP process appears deceptively simple: Teachers expect some pupils to perform well, treat those pupils to the best teaching behaviors they can muster, and consequently those pupils do well.

On the face of it, the same four factors operate also in manager–subordinate relations. It is more than mere coincidence that most models of managerial leadership define four similar factors, or styles. We rea-soned that Rosenthal's factors should be detectable using a managerial leadership questionnaire. We therefore hypothesized that the man-ager's leadership behavior mediates the Pygmalion effect in organiza-tions.

The first IDF experiment was conducted in a combat command course. We induced differential expectations in the four instructors by telling them that we had compiled information on the trainees including test scores, sociometric evaluations, grades in previous courses, and ratings by previous commanders; that based on these data we had predicted the command potential (CP) of each soldier; that experience had shown that course grades predict CP in 95% of the cases; that based on CP scores, we had designated each trainee as having either high, regular, or unknown CP, the last due to incomplete records; and that soldiers of all three CP levels had been divided equally among the four training classes. Each instructor then got a list of his trainees, in which about a third were designated high CP, a third were unmarked to indicate regular CP, and a third were marked with a question mark, indicating that they were unclassifiable. Unknown to the instructors, the assignments to the four training groups and to the three CP conditions were random. The manipulation check verified that we had influenced instructor expectations as intended. One week after the course had begun, the instructors expected significantly better performance of trainees designated as having high CP, indicating that the experimental manipulation "took."

Analysis of achievement confirmed the SFP hypothesis. Those designated as high in CP significantly outperformed their classmates in four objectively graded subjects. The differences evidenced a substantial Pygmalion effect – about 15 points on a conventional 100-point grade scale. Analysis of the overall Performance Index showed that the experimentally induced expectations accounted for nearly three-quarters of the variance in performance. Each trainee also filled out a self-report questionnaire. Trainees in the high-expectation condition expressed more favorable attitudes toward the course on each item and also obtained a higher mean on the Attitude Index, instructor expectations accounting for two-thirds of the variance.

We measured leadership as a potential mediator of expectation effects. Each trainee described his instructor's leadership on items from the Survey of Organizations (Taylor & Bowers, 1972). These items operationalize the four factors of leadership (support, interaction facilitation, goal emphasis, and work facilitation) conceptualized by Bowers and Seashore (1966). Trainees designated as having high CP rated their instructors' leadership significantly higher, induced expectations accounting for 28% of the variance. This is evidence that leadership mediates the Pygmalion effect. Raising manager expectations improves leadership, which in turn promotes subordinate performance. Supervisory leadership is composed of behaviors that are very similar to Rosenthal's four factors of teacher mediating behavior. Both Bowers and

Seashore's four factors and Rosenthal's four factors boost subordinate performance. These leadership findings help to demythologize the Pygmalion effect. Prophecies are not mysteriously *self*-fulfilling. Rather, manager expectations work their "magic" on subordinates by inducing managers to provide better leadership to subordinates of whom they expect good performance. Better leadership promotes greater achievement. Leadership is thus a means by which both managers and classroom teachers fulfill their prophecies. Evidently, *high expectations bring out the best leadership in a manager.* We concluded that the sarcastic adage that "managers get the subordinates they deserve" should be replaced with one that expresses what we know about expectation effects: *Managers get the subordinates they expect.*

Pygmalion and Galatea: The IDF adjutancy experiment

We wanted to extend our understanding of *intra*trainee factors in the Pygmalion effect. One possibility was that when a manager communicates high expectations to a subordinate, the latter raises his or her *own* performance expectations. This reasoning integrates the manager expectation effect and the expectancy theory of work motivation (Lawler, 1973; Vroom, 1964), which postulates that the more an individual expects to succeed in performing a task, the greater the effort he or she exerts in performing it. We invoked expectancy theory and hypothesized that self-expectations mediate the Pygmalion effect. We tested this hypothesis by comparing trainees' self-expectations before and after inducing high expectations in their instructors.

On further reflection, it seemed that if the subordinate's own self-expectations were the intrapsychic key to the Pygmalion effect, the manager may be tangential to the core motivational process. It should be possible to short-circuit the SFP process and enhance performance by directly raising the subordinate's self-expectations, bypassing the supervisor. We dub this the *Galatea effect*, after the mythical Pygmalion's sculpture, as it involves working directly on the statue, so to speak. Therefore, we hypothesized that directly raising subordinates' self-expectations enhances their performance.

We (Eden & Ravid, 1982) conducted the second IDF experiment in two adjutancy courses. The trainees were divided at random into five training groups. The procedure was similar to that of the combat course, except that there were four conditions instead of three. About 25% of the trainees were described to the instructors as having high potential

(Pygmalion condition) and 25% were designated regular (Pygmalion-control condition); 50% were described to the instructors as having unknown potential due to incomplete information. The instructors were told the same background story as in the combat experiment, and their expectations were raised in the same manner. The unclassified 50% were further split into two trainee-expectation conditions, Galatea and Galatea-control, each comprising 25% of the trainees. All these assignments were random. The Galatea trainees were given a 5-minute personal interview by a military psychologist, at the end of which he said: "To conclude, I wanted to tell you that, in light of information we've gathered about trainees, you have high potential for success." The Galatea-control trainees were similarly interviewed, except that they were told at the end, "You have regular potential for success." The interviews with the trainees in the Pygmalion conditions ended without the last sentence.

We measured trainees' self-expectations thrice: on the day they arrived on base, in the fourth week, and in the final week of the course. Mean preinduction self-expectation scores in the four conditions were very similar, reflecting random assignment. Analysis revealed substantially rising self-expectations throughout the course among trainees in both the Pygmalion and the Galatea conditions, in contrast to relatively stable or slightly declining expectations among the controls. The increase in self-expectations among the Pygmalion trainees confirmed the hypothesis that raising manager expectations of certain subordinates causes those subordinates to expect more of themselves. This is the expectation link we sought. For the Galatea trainees, the rise in self-expectations could not have resulted from raising the instructors' expectations, as trainees in both the Galatea and the Galatea-control conditions had been designated as unclassifiable. Rather, this served as a manipulation check. The 5-minute interviews did raise self-expectations as intended.

Analysis of weekly examination scores and instructor ratings revealed that raising instructor expectations and raising trainee self-expectations boosted performance. Between a quarter and a third of the variance in performance was attributable to expectations. Although both the Pygmalion effect and the Galatea effect were significant, they did not differ significantly from each other. More research is needed to determine whether these effects are equally potent in general, as in this experiment.

Self-sustaining prophecy. One of the adjutancy courses was particularly interesting due to the unscheduled replacement of the instructors after the third week, when the original instructors were reassigned elsewhere on very short notice. This created a natural experiment. The weekly performance ratings by the original instructors and by the relief instructors changed little in any of the four conditions when the instructor substitution occurred. The effects of the initial expectancy induction spilled over to the relief instructors, whose expectations had not been manipulated. This underscores the potency of interpersonal expectancy effects in organizations and shows that expectations can produce self-*sustaining*, as well as self-fulfilling, prophecies (Salomon, 1981). The manner in which the spillover occurred seems obvious. Expectation effects are contagious. There was a period of several hours during which each instructor transferred his affairs to his replacement. In these discussions the instructors probably passed along the expectations we had created 3 weeks earlier. Expectations must have been passed on from instructor to instructor, as they evidently are passed from instructor to trainee. This would be a case of one instructor passing a Pygmalion effect on to another instructor. Similar transfer of information about pupils takes place in teachers' rooms and about employees in "bull sessions" among managers. This "second-generation" Pygmalion effect may also be sustained beyond the course. The near-disruption of the adjutancy experiment due to personnel exigencies is typical of field experiments and simulates organizational reality. There is little doubt that the spillover of expectancy effects also simulates everyday management actualities.

This spillover interpretation, being based on the transfer of experimentally induced *instructor* expectations, cannot explain the stability of the Galatea effect because the Galatea trainees had been described to their original instructors as unclassifiable. Consequently, the instructor replacement could not have had any differential impact on these trainees. Therefore, an additional explanation for maintenance of the effect over time is necessary. It is likely that both the Pygmalion and Galatea effects are self-sustaining due to *intratrainee* factors. Once aroused to high performance expectations by a manager or by a psychologist, a subordinate may persist in high performance under subsequent supervisors, regardless of the latters' initial expectations. The subordinate's subsequent high performance may be sustained by the high *self*-expectations that he has internalized, and not by the expectations of the new supervisor. This interpretation focuses on the subordinate as the prophet who fulfills his or her own expectations after initial exposure to a manager with high expectations.

Conclusions. Subordinate self-expectations are a key in the SFP process. They mediate the manager expectation effect, and they can be raised directly to produce similar performance gains in the Galatea effect. The common denominator of these two SFP effects is the subordinate's self-expectations. Credible high expectations communicated by an authority figure, whether experimenter, instructor, manager, psychologist, or consultant, lead individuals to expect more of themselves and to perform better.

However, Galatea is not Pygmalion. In the Pygmalion condition, the supervisor *unwittingly* treated subordinates differently in accordance with his expectations. In contrast, in the Galatea experiment, the psychologist imparted his "expectations" to the trainees *knowingly*. After the interviews, the psychologist had no further contact with the trainees. Therefore, he could not have fulfilled his prophecy by means of his own behavior. Calling the psychologist a prophet in this situation misses the point. The Galatea effect, as organizationwide SFP, is not an *inter-personal* expectation effect. Raising self-expectations relies on the subordinate's capacity to mobilize his or her *own* resources to perform better. In the Galatea effect, the *subordinate* is the one who functions as a prophet and fulfills his or her own expectations.

Whole-group Pygmalion: The IDF squad leaders experiment

The classical Pygmalion research design does not control contrast effects. Since Rosenthal's earliest work on the experimenter effect, with few exceptions the standard procedure has been to designate some members of a group as worthy of high performance expectations. The remaining individuals in the same group are in a control condition for the sake of comparison. However, this may induce leaders to treat different members differently, not necessarily in response to differential expectations. Though the researcher says nothing to deprecate the control subjects, perhaps conveying information about the high potential of their experimental peers implies that they are of lower potential. Thus, it is possible that raising expectations toward some is tantamount to unintended lowering of expectations toward others. It may be the *difference* in what managers expect of subordinates, rather than high expectations per se, that creates the performance differences that constitute the Pygmalion effect.

Uncontrolled interpersonal contrast effects raise three concerns. First, can the Pygmalion effect be produced without control subjects? The contrast between subjects assigned to experimental and control conditions, which has characterized most Pygmalion experiments, may be an indispensable ingredient in the Pygmalion potion. It had to be shown that producing positive SFP effects for some does not require *not* raising expectations toward others. Otherwise, generalization to situations in which there are no control subjects in the leader's group would be unwarranted. If Pygmalion were to boil down to a mere unintended contrast effect, rather than a positive expectancy effect, SFP would not seem applicable to management.

The second issue is productivity. Does the Pygmalion effect represent a real net performance gain for the organization? If creating the effect requires control subjects who do not gain, application would be impractical. Our efforts would better be spent seeking management innovations that raise the productivity of *all* workers, rather than only some. Classical comparative analysis contrasts experimental and control subjects in the same natural groups to reveal treatment-caused differences; however, the frequently used *after-only* design cannot disentangle gains among experimental subjects from losses among control subjects. Therefore, the differences found in many past Pygmalion experiments could have resulted from elevated achievement among high-expectancy subjects, depressed achievement among control subjects, or both. This ambiguity derives from the potential confounding of expectancy effects with contrast effects and the lack of a performance pretest. Moreover, if experimental subjects gained at the expense of their control counterparts, we could not justify creating Pygmalion effects for the sake of organizational effectiveness. Managerial action that makes some individuals more productive and others less so is equivalent to the proverbial "Robbing Peter to pay Paul" (see Rosenthal & Jacobson, 1968, pp. 156–159); the organization gains nothing in aggregate. However, some individuals would be aggrieved.

This grievance is the third, but not least important, concern raised by contrast effects. If Pygmalion effects could be created only at the expense of individuals assigned randomly to the control condition, it would be unfair to them. Even if being in the control condition did not degrade their performance, being outperformed by peers chosen by chance for the high-expectancy treatment may create relative deprivation. This ethical dilemma is discussed in the American Psychological Association's (1982) *Ethical Principles in the Conduct of Research with Human Participants* under the heading "Withholding Potential Benefits from Control Participants."

Besides ethical ambiguities in research, it would be difficult or impossible to apply Pygmalion in management (or in the classroom) if it were dependent upon contrast effects. Establishing its feasibility must go beyond showing that control subjects are not actually harmed. If creating the effect required discrimination of any sort, it would be unacceptable to researchers and practitioners alike.

The way to eliminate contrast effects in a Pygmalion experiment is to assign *whole groups* and their leaders to conditions at random. Raising expectations toward subordinates as a group produces no interpersonal contrast effects because it makes no distinction among individuals within groups. This randomized whole-groups design was used in the next Pygmalion experiment (Eden, 1990c), conducted among 10 companies brought to the IDF School for Squad Leaders for combat and command training. Each company was composed of three platoons; each platoon was trained by its own platoon leader. The platoon is the natural training group in the school. The platoon was therefore adopted as the unit of analysis. One platoon in each company was chosen at random for the Pygmalion condition, and the other two platoons served as controls. Once a platoon was assigned to a condition, all of its members were assigned with it. One company had only two platoons, which were assigned to conditions at random. Therefore, we had 10 experimental platoons and 19 control platoons. One day before each company arrived to begin its course, the school's organizational psychologist met individually with the leader of the experimental platoon and told him, as in the previous experiments, that we could predict the CP of the soldiers. However, this time the psychologist added the statement that "Comparing the mean CP of your platoon with other groups, it is evident that the average CP of your trainees is appreciably higher than usual. Therefore, you can expect unusual achievements from the trainees in this platoon." The psychologist also met with the leader of each control platoon and described the study similarly, except that nothing was said about the CP of their men. The random assignment and conversations with the psychologist thus created two groups of platoons comparable in everything except the CP information provided to the leaders. This procedure created an experimental group of 10 Pygmalion platoons and a control group of 19 platoons whose leaders' expectations were not manipulated.

As a manipulation check, all 29 leaders were asked to rate their soldiers' CP three times. The leaders of the Pygmalion platoons rated their trainees significantly and consistently higher than did the control leaders, indicating that the conversations succeeded in raising expectations, as intended. Analysis of scores in objectively assessed performance areas revealed that the Pygmalion leaders led their men to greater achievement than comparable leaders of comparable subordinates. This shows that the Pygmalion effect is not a contrast effect, a mere methodological artifact. Leaders do not create SFP for the benefit of a favored few at the expense of the rest. Rather, raising leaders' expectations toward their subordinates as a group boosts those subordinates' average performance. These results open the way for whole-group SFP applications.

All of the IDF Pygmalion experiments involved individuals of average or above-average aptitude. They created positive Pygmalion effects, not nullification of Golem effects. SFP is a double-edged sword; so are the actions it inspires.

Even Pygmalion does not work every time

When supervisors have prior personal knowledge of subordinates' competence, their expectations become resistant to change and require information that is especially convincing. Sutton and Woodman (1989) reported an unsuccessful attempt to produce a Pygmalion effect among retail sales personnel. Considering Sutton and Woodman's procedure in detail (Eden, 1988a, 1990d), it is doubtful that they actually raised their managers' expectations. If expectations were not raised, the Pygmalion hypothesis was not tested. This highlights some potential pitfalls in willfully creating interpersonal expectation effects. Given the circumstances in which Sutton and Woodman tried to produce the SFP, especially considering that the supervisors knew their subordinates before getting information intended to raise their expectations, it would have been preferable to attempt an organizationwide SFP rather than a Pygmalion effect based on new information about the subordinates.

Self-efficacy: A mediator of expectancy effects

Possunt, quia posse videntur.

Virgil's *Aeneid*, Book V
(Fairclough, 1967, p. 461)

In these marvelous words describing the surging motivation of men
nearing the glory of victory in a contest at sea, Virgil concisely conveyed
the concept of self-efficacy: "They can because they think they can." A
key to the willingness to commit oneself to a highly demanding undertaking is one's belief in one's capacity to mobilize the physical, intellectual, and emotional resources needed to succeed, that is, self-efficacy
(Bandura, 1986). Self-efficacy is emerging as an important determinant
of work motivation (Eden, 1984, 1988b; Locke & Latham, 1990). Self-
efficacy may also be the crux of SFP at work. Managers influence their
subordinates' self-efficacy, often unwittingly. Expecting much of subordinates and conveying high performance expectations to them via myr-
iad channels, the manager-as-Pygmalion acts in ways that boost their
sense of self-efficacy. Higher self-efficacy, in turn, raises their performance expectations. Then, according to the expectancy theory of work
motivation, expecting to do well motivates greater effort and culminates
in improved performance. The reverse is true for low self-efficacy,
which brings on Golem effects. Thus, subordinate self-efficacy is pos-
ited to be a crucial intrapsychic mediator of expectation effects. The
mediating effect of self-efficacy can also explain the second-generation
SFP found among subordinates whose leaders were replaced in the
adjutancy experiment. Traitlike self-efficacy serves as a firm mooring to
preserve an individual's high self-expectations during and after manager transition.

Bandura (1986) has summarized four sources of information (enactive
attainment, vicarious experience, verbal persuasion, and physiological
state) from which people derive their notions about their self-efficacy.
Recently, self-efficacy has become a focus for organizational psychologists seeking to improve training effectiveness and to effect a variety of
productive behaviors (Caplan, Vinokur, Price, & van Ryn, 1989; Frayne
& Latham, 1987; Gist, Schwoerer, & Rosen, 1989). In the SFP context,
raising subordinates' self-efficacy gets them to expect more of themselves; they then act as prophets, exerting the effort and emitting the
behaviors required to effect the expected performance. Experimentation
on practical ways of boosting self-efficacy in work-relevant contexts has
begun.

Boosting self-efficacy to speed reemployment

We (Eden & Aviram, in press) conducted a randomized field experiment to evaluate training designed to increase the self-efficacy of unemployed persons. Copious research has documented the severe blow to self-efficacy caused by job loss, and the vicious circle of despair and diminishing job-seeking behavior due to ebbing self-efficacy. We aimed to reverse this downward spiral by boosting self-efficacy. The workshop was based on behavioral modeling and targeted enactive attainment, vicarious experience, and verbal persuasion as channels for getting across to the trainees that they could effect the requisite behaviors to land a job. We predicted that strengthening their belief in their capacity to perform job-seeking behaviors would motivate them to engage more in the kinds of activities that would increase their likelihood of finding work and speed their reemployment. The manipulation check showed that the workshop training did succeed in raising self-efficacy. Furthermore, compared to the control group, workshop participants appreciably intensified their job-seeking activities. Finally, among persons initially low in self-efficacy, a higher proportion of those trained in the workshops gained reemployment than of those in the control condition. As these participants found their own jobs, the treatment helped them to help themselves. Instead of letting them degenerate into impotent Golems, the self-efficacy training turned them into Galateas. Having their self-efficacy boosted culminated in their effectuating the quintessential organizational behavior – being there to do a job at all.

Boosting self-efficacy to increase volunteering for special forces

Taking a different tack, we (Eden & Kinnar, 1991) joined in the efforts of the IDF to increase the volunteer rate among service candidates qualified for special forces duty. Prescreened youths on the threshold of conscription, who have obtained sufficiently high scores on preliminary aptitude tests, are invited to attend an informative program designed to increase their volunteering for special forces. Those who decline are "lost" to the special forces. Unduly low self-efficacy stifles the willingness to test one's mettle, reduces volunteering, and removes one from the arena where success is attainable. We tested the effectiveness of a modified information program based on modeling and persuasion that was aimed at augmenting the candidates' self-efficacy for special forces. The SFP prediction was that, feeling more efficacious and expecting to succeed, more experimental candidates would "go for it," putting eventual success within their reach. Candidates randomly assigned to the experimental program scored higher in self-efficacy, expressed greater willingness to volunteer for special forces, and actually did volunteer more. Losses of qualified candidates due to nonvolunteering were reduced by a third in comparison both to their peers exposed to the conventional program and to all candidates during the preceding year. Their self-efficacy appreciably enhanced, the experimental candidates were more willing to undertake the challenge of demanding service.

Again, the behavior effected was crucial to the organization's existence; the dependent variable was not level of performance once there, but being there to perform at all. Such is the power of self-efficacy that it determines such primordial dichotomies as being unemployed or reemployed and volunteering or refraining from doing so. Together with convergent findings from other organizational experiments, the results show that it is within our power to create productive Galatea effects by augmenting self-efficacy.

Pygmalion at sea

An earlier study of expectation training was the U.S. Navy's Pygmalion at Sea project. Crawford, Thomas, and Fink (1980) targeted chronically low-performing sailors on a combatant ship for remedial treatment designed to improve their motivation and performance. Supervisory personnel were given a workshop designed to change their negative expectations toward the problem sailors. The high supervisor expectations thus aroused were buttressed by teaching principles of behavior modification and brainstorming actions that the low performers would perceive as positive reinforcers. Second, 15 additional senior enlisted supervisors selected to serve as mentors for the low performers were given a workshop in counseling and guidance skills. Finally, 12 low performers participated in a personal growth workshop. The communication and cultivation of high performance expectations – among both the supervisors and the subordinates – were the hallmark of this intervention.

The low performers on the experimental ship were compared to some of their shipmates and to comparable low performers on similar ships. There were significant improvements in the experimental sailors in overall performance as rated by their supervisors. The authors concluded that the program succeeded in engendering SFP in the sailors and their supervisors. Crawford et al. pioneered the practical application of manager expectation effects. Their example is worthy of emulation.

Self-efficacy training is emerging as a practical tool to aid individuals in mustering the wherewithal to tackle challenges in the workplace. We know that when an experimenter pinpoints self-efficacy for special treatment, it can increase desirable behavior, with profitable outcomes. The next step is to train managers to do what experimenters and trainers have done in past research, for managers' ongoing efforts to boost their subordinates' self-efficacy ought to have even more powerful effects.

Though managers' interpersonal style often is a source of subordinates' high (or low) self-efficacy and expectations, there are other sources. The individual's personal history of success and failure is one. The organization's culture is another important source of expectations regarding success and failure, one that managers can be trained to do something about. An achievement-oriented, optimistic culture of success nourishes all players with high expectations and increases the likelihood that productive SFP will augment the organization's accomplishments. Conversely, a cynical culture supporting images of impotence and prophecies of doom can drag an organization from one disaster to the next in a downward spiral in which its true productive potential is underutilized. Organizationwide Golem effects result. The emerging literature on culture change and management makes this a prime content area for expectancy training (e.g., Boje, Fedor, & Rowland, 1982; Deal & Kennedy, 1982; Morgan, 1986; Peters, 1978; Schein, 1985).

The Messiah effect

The phenomenal success of leading management consultants may be in part a consequence of their ability to inspire high self-expectations and self-efficacy in their clients (Eden, 1986, 1990a). Some consultants are aware of this and use expectation raising deliberately as a "secret weapon" whose power would be diluted by disclosure. In the case of famous consultants of high repute, their very arrival on the scene is sufficient to raise the expectations of key individuals in the organization that "things will certainly improve now." The resulting optimism causes these clients to redouble their efforts in getting on with what must be done to revitalize the organization. This mobilization of client energy and the subsequent SFP brought about by the very arrival of a renowned consultant is the Messiah effect. The "Messiah's" power to help clients is derived from their own positive expectations, sparked by the would-be redeemer's coming, and fueled by their eagerness to cooperate in fulfilling their own newly acquired expectations. Effecting change of transformational proportions requires the creation of new sources of human energy (Ackerman, 1984; Bradley, 1986). The arrival of a Messiah expands the amount of human energy available in an organization due to the high expectations aroused.

The future of expectancy effects in organizations

Pygmalion is alive and well in organizations. Empirical studies, literature reviews, and theoretical models of expectancy effects in management have appeared in leading academic journals and practitioner-oriented periodicals. The latest expositions of charismatic and transformational leadership have cited the Pygmalion effect as a manifestation of the kind of effective management that organizations need to be competitive in today's turbulent environment (e.g., Bass, 1985; Bennis & Nanus, 1985; House, Howell, Shamir, Smith, & Spangler, 1990). Producing expectancy effects in order to enhance work motivation is no longer an outlandish idea. The ability of the Pygmalion model to integrate concepts so diverse, yet so indispensable for organizational effectiveness, as leadership, expectancy, motivation, attribution, and performance, strengthens its usefulness. Moreover, the fact that expectancy effects have been produced in organizations using rigorous field experimental methods lends it an enviable degree of internal and external validity that cannot be ignored.

Unfortunately, the amount of research published on expectancy effects in organizations has not been overwhelming; virtually all of it was reviewed earlier in this chapter. However, the huge accumulation of findings from school-based Pygmalion research serves as a solid foundation for generalization to nonclassroom settings. After all, schools are organizations, too, and the school and nonschool studies are mutually confirmatory. Nevertheless, judging from the one-sided cross-referencing in the school and nonschool literatures, it is apparent that the manager expectancy effects research has yet to enrich classroom investigators. If educators have not made the connection between teacher and manager expectancy effects, then perhaps Pygmalion will find his way into educational leadership via the management and organizational literatures. It is a debt waiting to be repaid.

Thus, the future for Pygmalion research in organizations looks promising. However, it should not consist of repeated replications of the basic manager expectancy effect using the worn deceptive manipulation. We now need to test SFP applications in which the participants are active partners, not passive dupes. Merton's (1948) analysis of the operation of the Federal Deposit Insurance Corporation (FDIC) exemplifies an innovative means of eradicating destructive SFP. The FDIC has largely protected the banks (and their clients) from bankruptcy due to precipitous withdrawals by hordes of panicky depositors who, acting on (often unfounded) rumors of pending disaster, unwittingly fulfill their own prophecy of doom. The FDIC was a brilliant social invention that has reduced this tragic SFP by minimizing depositor anticipation of personal financial loss in the event of bank failure. Imagine the bedlam that the current multi-billion-dollar crisis in the U.S. savings and loan associations would have revisited upon depositors and financial markets were it not for similar federal insurance protection. We are benefiting today from lessons learned half a century ago about the deliberate blockage of destructive SFP. However, practical utilization of SFP theory depends on our ability to develop new organizational inventions to provide FDIC-like blocks to negative SFP, as well as innovative means to facilitate positive SFP. Ideas for practical application have been proposed (Eden, 1984, 1986, 1988a, 1988b, 1990a, 1990d). These include creating Pygmalion and Galatea effects and eliminating Golem effects (see Blanck, this volume); immunizing potential victims against the Golem effect; fighting negative stereotypes (see Taylor, this volume); setting challenging goals and objectives (see Babad, volume); clearing employees' records of stigmatizing evidence of past failure to prevent recurring Golem effects every time someone peruses the file; piggybacking on changes in organizational structure, personnel assignments, product lines, work methods, and operating procedures as opportunities for raising expectations; and fostering a high-expectation culture. The most promising avenue for dissemination of applicable knowledge about leader-inspired expectancy effects is manager training. Therefore, such training is now a prime research target.

Pygmalion Leadership Style training

The Pygmalion Leadership Style (PLS) is composed of the manager behaviors that facilitate productive SFP effects in organizations (Eden,

1990d). My students and I have begun experimentation on PLS workshop training in army companies, industrial plants, bank branches, and summer camps. We teach participants about SFP and expectancy effects and challenge them to acquire the requisite skills to enact the Pygmalion role. The program uses none of the deception inherent in basic Pygmalion research. Rather, the true aims of the training are stated at the outset. These include understanding SFP at work, raising participants' leadership self-efficacy and their expectations concerning what subordinates are capable of accomplishing, and mastering the behavioral skills required to be an effective Pygmalion. The workshop techniques include (1) lecturettes and brief written material about expectancy effects, (2) small-group exercises that demonstrate the power of interpersonal expectations, (3) introspective work followed by small-group discussion in which participants clarify for themselves what they truly expect of each of their current subordinates and how these expectations manifest themselves in their treatment of each, (4) behavioral modeling in which participants view someone similar to themselves enacting effective Pygmalion behaviors, (5) role playing in which participants rehearse giving self-efficacy-enhancing feedback to others in the wake of success and failure, stressing the relevant principles of attribution theory (see Eden, 1990d), (6) brainstorming ways of creating Galatea effects, and (7) organizational culture analysis geared to facilitating positive organizationwide SFP. Culture analysis entails compiling stories and myths prevalent in the organization and extracting the expectancy effects – positive and negative – that they engender.

Training effectiveness is to be evaluated in terms of the subsequent performance of the participants' subordinates. Though Pygmalion-inspired concepts have found their way into many varieties of executive training, no research on the effectiveness of dedicated Pygmalion management training has yet been reported. As most past Pygmalion-at-work research has been done in military settings, replication and application in civilian organizations are overdue. Although Pygmalion-inspired teacher training has been undertaken (Banuazizi, 1981; Greenfield, Banuazizi, & Ganon, 1979; Kerman, 1979; Nicholsen, 1982; Terry, 1985), the focus of teacher training has been somewhat different from that proposed here for managers. The teacher programs seem aimed more at increasing equality among pupils in the classroom and at decreasing Golem effects, whereas the manager training emphasizes more the creation of positive expectancy effects to boost productivity, though increased inequality may result. This difference reflects the different goals, philosophies, and social functions of educational and production-oriented organizations.

To date, the invisible but nearly impermeable boundary that segregates the educational and organizational literatures has limited cross-referencing and mutual enrichment of the separate but parallel research and applied efforts in these two crucial spheres of human endeavor. The school and the workplace, teaching and managing, learning and producing, have much more in common than most of us realized. Hopefully, the publication of this chapter in a book destined to be read by a new generation of interpersonal expectancy researchers will bridge this pointless abyss and contribute to demolishing one more divisive wall in our generation.

SFP is not an overpowering fact of life that we must regard with awe and accommodate, for better or for worse. Rather, it is a social process that savvy leaders can manage, at least partially, for the benefit of organizations, their members, and others whom they serve. If we keep our expectations high but realistic, we shall certainly succeed with this agenda.

References

Ackerman, L. S. (1984). The flow state: A new view of organizing and managing. In J. D. Adams (Ed.), *Transforming work* (pp. 113–137). Alexandria, VA: Miles River Press.

American Psychological Association. (1982). *Ethical principles in the conduct of research with human participants.* Washington, DC.

Atkinson, J. W. (1957). Motivational determinants of risk-taking behavior. *Psychological Review, 10*, 209–232.

Babad, E. Y., Inbar, J., & Rosenthal, R. (1982). Pygmalion, Galatea, and the Golem: Investigations of biased and unbiased teachers. *Journal of Educational Psychology, 74*, 459–474.

Bandura, A. (1986). *Social foundations of thought and action: A social-cognitive view.* Englewood Cliffs, NJ: Prentice-Hall.

Banuazizi, A. (1981). *An evaluation of the first year's activities of the National Demonstration Title II Project (Basic Skills Improvement Program) in selected elementary grades of Cambridge public schools.* Unpublished manuscript, Boston College.

Bass, B. M. (1985). *Leadership and performance beyond expectations.* New York: Free Press.

Bennis, W. G., & Nanus, B. (1985). *Leaders: The strategies for taking charge.* New York: Harper & Row.

Boje, D. M., Fedor, D. B., & Rowland, K. M. (1982). Myth making: A qualitative step in OD interventions. *Journal of Applied Behavioral Science, 18*, 17–28.

Bowers, D. G., & Seashore, S. E. (1966). Predicting organizational effectiveness with a four-factor theory of leadership. *Administrative Science Quarterly, 11*, 238–263.

Bradley, R. T. (1986). *Transforming order: A study of charisma, power, and communion*. New York: Paragon House.

Caplan, R. D., Vinokur, A. D., Price, R. H., & van Ryn, M. (1989). Job seeking, reemployment, and mental health: A randomized field experiment in coping with job loss. *Journal of Applied Psychology, 74*, 759–769.

Crawford, K. S., Thomas, E. D., & Fink, J. J. (1980). Pygmalion at sea: Improving the work of effectiveness of low performers. *Journal of Applied Behavioral Science, 16*, 482–505.

Critelli, J. W., & Neumann, K. F. (1984). The placebo: Conceptual analysis of a construct in transition. *American Psychologist, 39*, 32–39.

Deal, T. E., & Kennedy, A. A. (1982). *Corporate cultures: The rites and rituals of corporate life*. Reading, MA: Addison-Wesley.

Eden, D. (1984). Self-fulfilling prophecy as a management tool: Harnessing Pygmalion. *Academy of Management Review, 9*, 64–73.

Eden, D. (1986). OD and self-fulfilling prophecy: Boosting productivity by raising expectations. *Journal of Applied Behavioral Science, 22*, 1–13.

Eden, D. (1988a). Creating expectation effects in OD: Applying self-fulfilling prophecy. *Research in Organizational Change and Development, 2*, 235–267.

Eden, D. (1988b). Pygmalion, goal setting, and expectancy: Compatible ways to raise productivity. *Academy of Management Review, 13*, 639–652.

Eden, D. (1990a). Consultant as Messiah: Applying expectation effects in managerial consultation. *Consultation, 9*, 37–50.

Eden, D. (1990b). Industrialization as a self-fulfilling prophecy: The role of expectations in development. *International Journal of Psychology, 25*, 871–886.

Eden, D. (1990c). Pygmalion controlling interpersonal contrast effects: Whole groups gain from raising expectations. *Journal of Applied Psychology, 75*, 394–398.

Eden, D. (1990d). *Pygmalion in management: Productivity as a self-fulfilling prophecy*. Lexington, MA: Lexington Books.

Eden, D., & Aviram, A. (in press). Self-efficacy training to speed reemployment. *Journal of Applied Psychology*.

Eden, D., & Kinnar, J. (1991). Modeling Galatea: Boosting self-efficacy to increase volunteering. *Journal of Applied Psychology, 76*, 770–780.

Eden, D., & Ravid, G. (1982). Pygmalion vs. self-expectancy: Effects of instructor- and self-expectancy on trainee performance. *Organizational Behavior and Human Performance, 30*, 351–364.

Eden, D., & Shani, A. B. (1982). Pygmalion goes to boot camp: Expectancy, leadership, and trainee performance. *Journal of Applied Psychology, 67*, 194–199.

Fairclough, H. R. (1967). *Virgil*. Cambridge, MA: Harvard University Press.

Frayne, C., & Latham, G. P. (1987). Application of social learning theory to employee self-management of attendance. *Journal of Applied Psychology, 72*, 387–392.

Gist, M. E., Schwoerer, C., & Rosen, B. (1989). Effects of alternative training methods on self-efficacy and performance in computer software training. *Journal of Applied Psychology, 74*, 884–891.

Greenfield, D., Banuazizi, A., & Ganon, J. (1979). *Project STILE: An evaluation of the second year*. Unpublished manuscript, Boston College.

Hackman, J. R., & Oldham, G. R. (1980). *Work redesign*. Reading, MA: Addison-Wesley.

Harris, M. J., & Rosenthal, R. (1985). Mediation of interpersonal expectancy effects: 31 meta-analyses. *Psychological Bulletin, 97*, 363–386.

House, R. J., Howell, J., Shamir, B., Smith, B., & Spangler, D. (1990). *Charismatic leadership: A 1990 theory and four empirical tests.* Working paper, Department of Management, The Wharton School of Management, University of Pennsylvania.

Kerman, S. (1979). Teacher expectations and students' achievement. *Phi Delta Kappan, 60,* 716–718.

King, A. S. (1971). Self-fulfilling prophecies in training the hard-core: Supervisors' expectations and the underprivileged workers' performance. *Social Science Quarterly, 52,* 369–378.

King, A. S. (1974). Expectation effects in organization change. *Administrative Science Quarterly, 19,* 221–230.

Lawler, E. E., III. (1973). *Motivation in work organizations.* Monterey, CA: Brooks/Cole.

Likert, R. (1961). *New patterns of management.* New York: McGraw-Hill.

Likert, R. (1967). *The human organization: Its management and value.* New York: McGraw-Hill.

Livingston, J. S. (1969). Pygmalion in management. *Harvard Business Review, 47*(4), 81–89.

Livingston, J. S. (1988, September–October). Retrospective commentary. *Harvard Business Review, 66*(5), 125.

Locke, E. A., & Latham, G. P. (1990). *A theory of goal setting and task performance.* Englewood Cliffs, NJ: Prentice-Hall.

McClelland, D. C., Atkinson, J. W., Clark, R. A., & Lowell, E. L. (1953). *The achievement motive.* New York: Appleton-Century-Crofts.

McGregor, D. (1960). *The human side of enterprise.* New York: McGraw-Hill.

Merton, R. K. (1948). The self-fulfilling prophecy. *Antioch Review, 8,* 193–210.

Morgan, G. (1986). *Images of organization.* Beverly Hills, CA: Sage.

Nicholsen, S. (1982). *Report on fieldwork: An evaluation of Project STILE on participants in the Cambridge public schools.* Cambridge, MA: Harvard University Graduate School of Education.

Peters, T. J. (1978). Symbols, patterns, and settings: An optimistic case for getting things done. *Organizational Dynamics, 7,* 3–23.

Roethlisberger, F. J., & Dickson, W. V. (1939). *Management and the worker.* Cambridge, MA: Harvard University Press.

Rosenthal, R. (1963). On the social psychology of the psychological experiment: The experimenter's hypothesis as unintended determinant of experimental results. *American Scientist, 51,* 268–283.

Rosenthal, R. (1973). *On the social psychology of the self-fulfilling prophecy: Further evidence for Pygmalion effects and their mediating mechanisms* (Module 53). New York: MSS Modular Publications.

Rosenthal, R., & Jacobson, L. (1968). *Pygmalion in the classroom: Teacher expectation and pupils' intellectual development.* New York: Holt, Rinehart and Winston.

Salomon, G. (1981). Self-fulfilling and self-sustaining prophecies and the behaviors that realize them. *American Psychologist, 36,* 1452–1453.

Schein, E. H. (1985). *Organizational culture and leadership.* San Francisco: Jossey-Bass.

Sutton, C. D., & Woodman, R. W. (1989). Pygmalion goes to work: The effects of supervisor expectations in a retail setting. *Journal of Applied Psychology, 74,* 943–950.

Taylor, J. C., & Bowers, D. G. (1972). *The survey of organizations: A machine scored standardized questionnaire instrument.* Ann Arbor, MI: Institute for Social Research.

Terry, J. P. (1985, February). *Student performance and school related attitudes as a function of teacher expectations and behavior.* Unpublished manuscript, MIT, Program for Science, Technology and Society.

Vroom, V. H. (1964). *Work and motivation.* New York: Wiley.

Zuroff, D. C., & Rotter, J. B. (1985). A history of the expectancy construct in psychology. In J. B. Dusek, V. C. Hall, & W. J. Meyer (Eds.), *Teacher expectations* (pp. 9–36). Hillsdale, NJ: Erlbaum.

8. Interpersonal expectations and the maintenance of health

HOWARD S. FRIEDMAN

It is a wise experimenter who knows his artifact from his main
effect; and wiser still is the researcher who realizes that today's
artifact may be tomorrow's independent variable.
(McGuire, 1969, p. 13)

Faith healing, self-healing, and related phenomena of the mind's effects
on the body present some of the most fascinating puzzles of philosophy, psychology, and medicine. The role of healer or doctor is one of
the oldest and noblest, appearing prominently in civilizations throughout recorded history. Yet speculation about the distinction (or lack
thereof) between healer and quack has an equally prominent history. It
is only during the past century that physicians have had available some
scientifically proven treatments for some specific diseases. Most healing
in the past relied on successful social influence, quacks and health fraud
notwithstanding. And, I will argue, so does much healing today.

A physician who "cures" three very ill patients of the flu by prescrib-
ing a new drug is almost sure to believe in the drug's efficacy. The
physician thus makes two major errors of inference. First, there is no
control group; there is no way to know whether the patients would
have recovered without treatment by this drug. Second, the numbers
are probably too small to allow reliable inference; in a different set of
patients, different results might occur (Kahneman, Slovic, & Tversky,
1982). In brief, this is the problem of distinguishing the artifact from the
main effect. Although it appears obvious when presented to experienced scientists, it will trip up more than half a class of medical or
psychology students. It will also often trap the individual practitioner.
The faulty inference results in the use of many worthless drugs and
procedures for many years.

The new flu drug (though biochemically worthless) may, however, have a real effect due to the beliefs of the patient. Effects of faith on health, generally called *placebos*, are notoriously difficult (even for experienced clinicians) to distinguish from pharmaceutical treatment effects. Placebos are often disparaged and sometimes even defined as *sugar pills*. This is a serious misconception. A sugar pill may act as a placebo, but so may any intervention that does not have a specific, predictable physiological effect on the body. But placebos, including sugar pills, can have major effects. This is where today's artifact may become tomorrow's independent variable. If the control group (placebo group) improves, perhaps improving even more than the treatment group, the control variable should become the next independent variable to be examined.

The work of Robert Rosenthal brilliantly turned these subtle artifacts into independent variables worthy of systematic study. By drawing attention to the interpersonal expectancy effects that others ignored, denied, or disparaged as error, he opened up whole new fields of study. In his early work, Rosenthal was inspired by Shapiro (1960), who urged, "You should treat as many patients as possible with the new drugs while they still have the power to heal" (p. 114). Rosenthal saw the clinician's faith being beneficially transmitted to the patient. (This is in contrast to the situations in which the transmission usually involves teachers' negative expectancies or experimenters' biasing hypotheses.) He asserted, "The clinician's expectancy about the efficacy of a treatment procedure is no doubt subtly communicated to the patient with a resulting effect on his psychobiological functioning" (Rosenthal, 1966, p. 134). This flat, bald assertion, perhaps influenced by the author's youth, is the subject of this chapter. Do people's expectations about their health, derived from others, have a meaningful effect on their psychobiological functioning? Substantial evidence for an affirmative answer has accumulated during the past quarter century, including evidence about mediating mechanisms.

The self-healing personality

In many well-designed medical studies, the control group does improve, even though it might not improve as much as the experimental group. This improvement is regarded as error variance, since the study is designed (rightfully) to ascertain the independent effect of the experimental treatment. Relatedly, studies of medical utilization find that most patients feel better after visiting the doctor (or psychotherapist), even if the doctor's specific medical expertise was not employed in treatment. Doctors also often report giving patients drugs, regimens, or referrals that may not be absolutely necessary, because the patient really seems to want such treatment. Such uses of the medical care system are condemned by utilization experts as a waste of expensive resources.

It is not just what the patient believes, but also how those beliefs affect the patient's behavior, that is important. Many medical problems are ones that could have been prevented with proper behaviors on the part of the individual. Smoking, drug and alcohol use, poor nutrition, unprotected sexual relations, lack of exercise, and other behaviors account for a significant proportion of present-day morbidity and premature mortality. Is it up to the physician to change these behaviors? Most physicians have not the training, ability, or inclination to intervene significantly in these matters.

In short, there is a major conflict between the psychosocial factors (placebo and behavioral) that seem to promote health and the usual treatment approach based on biomedical science. This problem is fundamental and can be traced to the traditional medical model of illness, which by its very nature cannot fully integrate psychosocial influences on health (Friedman & DiMatteo, 1989). Surgeons can set or repair a broken part or valve, much as can an auto mechanic. Internists can prescribe drugs that kill microscopic invaders or fool a body system into reacting in a helpful way. But patients are not machines; people think about and respond actively to the world around them. Automobiles don't mind if they have a dented body, but people do mind, and react, and respond.

The health psychologist Suzanne Ouellette Kobasa (1990), emphasizing the depth and complexity of these biopsychosocial issues, recently drew attention to a story by Gordon Allport that bears repeating. Allport's true story concerns a gravely ill man: "The medical staff had told him frankly that they could not diagnose his disease, but that if they knew the diagnosis they could probably cure him. . . . Within a few days the [famous] diagnostician arrived and proceeded to make the rounds. Coming to this man's bed, he merely glanced at the patient, murmured 'Moribundus,' and went on. Some years later, the patient called on the diagnostician and said, 'I've been wanting to thank you for your diagnosis. They told me that if you could diagnose me I'd get well, and so the minute you said 'moribundus' I knew I'd recover' " (Allport, 1964, p. 7).

A complementary true story is told by Dr. Bernard Lown, the world-famous Harvard cardiologist and a great believer in psychosocial effects on health. When Dr. Lown was a postdoctoral fellow, he was assisting a Dr. Levine in treating a woman who had a narrowing in her tricuspid heart valve. She had remained in moderately good health for a decade. But one day, Dr. Levine examined this woman, said that she had "TS," and walked out of the room. Dr. Lown was left with a woman who immediately began hyperventilating, since she believed "TS" meant "terminal situation." Dr. Lown reports, "I was initially amused at this misinterpretation of the medical acronym for 'tricuspid stenosis.' My amusement, however, rapidly yielded to apprehension, as my words failed to reassure and as her [lung] congestion continued to worsen. . . . Later that same day she died from intractable heart failure" (Lown, 1983, p. 14).

Several years ago, an interesting report appeared about Felipe Garza. Felipe, a 15-year-old boy living in California, fell in love with a 14-year-old girl. Soon after, it was discovered that the girl was dying of heart disease. Felipe, who seemed in fine health himself, told his mother that when he died, he wanted Donna to have his heart. Less than a month later, Felipe suffered a cerebral hemorrhage and died. As he had requested, his heart was transplanted to his girlfriend by surgeons in San Francisco. Except for some investigation of voodoo death, no one has much studied the idea of a *will to die*. It is not apparent how a teenager could will himself a stroke. Puzzling cases like Felipe Garza's are useful in stretching our thinking. In short, it is plausible that we are *underestimating* the powers of self-healing and self-destruction.

I have presented an extensive analysis of why some people achieve health, whereas seemingly similar people succumb to illness (Friedman, 1991). I have tried to go beyond vague notions like *will to live* and evaluate the scientific evidence for self-healing. For example, the effects of self-healing should be apparent in observable emotional/motivational styles, and indeed they are (Booth-Kewley & Friedman, 1987; Friedman & Booth-Kewley, 1987a, 1987b). Briefly stated, I believe that the best way to characterize the self-healing personality is in terms of *enthusiasm*. The word *enthusiasm* literally means "having a godly spirit within." *Cheerfulness* is another good emotional term. It is derived from the word for *face*, and cheerful people express good spirits through their faces. Enthusiastic people are alert, responsive, and energetic, although they may also be calm and self-assured. They are curious, secure, and constructive. These emotional aspects of their personality are apparent to the trained observer.

There are several good clues that indicate emotional balance and an inherent resilience. Enthusiastic, sanguine people tend to infect others with their exuberance. They are not ecstatic but rather are generally responsive and content. They are people one likes to be around. Cheerful people look you in the eye during greetings and a substantial portion of the time while talking and listening. They are not downcast or shifty-eyed. They also smile naturally. The eyes, eyebrows, and mouth are synchronized and unforced; there is usually no holding back of expression of pleasant feelings. Such enthusiastic people have smooth gestures that tend to move away from the body. (That is, they are less likely to pick, scratch, and touch their bodies.) They are unlikely to fidget, and their legs are often uncrossed and open rather than tight and defensive. They are not apt to make aggressive gestures with their hands. Emotionally balanced individuals not only walk smoothly, they talk smoothly. They are inclined to show fewer speech disturbances such as saying "ah," and their speech is modulated rather than full of sudden loud words. Their voices are less likely to change in tone under stress. Obviously, there are exceptions to these rules. A single nonverbal gesture does not tell us much. Still, it is remarkable how much valid information we can gather about a person's healthy emotional style from just a few episodes of social interaction.

A sense of continual growth and resilience is also relevant. Dr. Walter Cannon (1939), who developed the ideas of homeostasis on which modern notions of self-healing are based, emphasized that the body has developed a margin of safety. By this Cannon meant that the body is not built with "niggardly economy," but rather makes allowance for contingencies, which we may count on in times of stress. The lungs, the blood, and the muscles have much greater capacity than is ordinarily needed. The liver, pancreas, stomach, and other digestive and metabolic centers can be seriously damaged and yet still sustain life. And so on. In other words, the body naturally prepares itself for the rare extra challenge, and self-healing people do what they can to increase these margins of safety. William James, who anticipated much of our modern scientific understanding of emotional responses, summed up this idea succinctly when he advised, "Keep the faculty of effort alive in you by a little gratuitous exercise every day. That is, be systematically ascetic or heroic in little unnecessary points, do every day or two something for no other reason than that you would rather not do it, so that when the hour of dire need draws nigh, it may find you not unnerved and untrained to stand the test" (James 1890, ch. 4, p. 126).

What about the personality characteristics of such self-healing people? As psychologist Abraham Maslow (1970) pointed out, healthy people first need to achieve balance in their basic biological needs; then they need to obtain affection and self-respect. But he emphasized what he called *self-actualization* – the realization of personal growth and fulfillment. People with this growth orientation are spontaneous and creative, are good problem solvers, have close relationships with others, and have a playful sense of humor. As people become more self-actualized, they become more concerned with issues of beauty, justice, and understanding. They develop a sense of humor that is philosophical rather than hostile. They become more independent and march to the beat of a different drummer. They become more ethical and more concerned with harmony among members of the human race. These characteristics of the self-healing personality are not merely the opposite of such disease-prone characteristics as suspiciousness, bitter cynicism, despair and depression, or repressed conflicts. Rather, they are positive, meaningful motives, behaviors, and goals in their own right.

Viktor Frankl (1962), the existential philosopher and therapist, developed his theories of a healing personality as an inmate in a Nazi concentration camp. Although most inmates died, the quickest to go were those who had their sense of identity and purpose taken away from them. By contrast, survival was more likely for those who tried living in a meaningful way, even in dire straits. A person's sense of dignity has more than psychological and ethical importance. It is also an aspect of health. Lack of attention to this crucial factor during medical treatment seems to be what angers cancer patients the most. Much more distressing than the cancer itself is the sense of being a "cancer," a "tumor," a "disease." Literally hundreds of writers with cancer, representing millions and millions of cancer victims, have pleaded and pleaded, "Don't talk to my spouse about me as if I'm not here"; "Don't pretend that everything is okay"; "Don't be afraid to look at me and touch me"; "Treat me as a person, not as a disease." Once a sense of dignity and meaning is gone, the will to live disappears as well.

An attempt at integration has been put forward by the medical sociologist Aaron Antonovsky (1990). He has proposed a general theory of *salutogenesis* – a theory of how people stay healthy. Central to health is a sense of coherence – the belief that the world is understandable, manageable, and meaningful. According to this approach, the world must not necessarily be controllable, but rather controlled or ordered in the grand scheme of things. For example, someone with a strong perception that she was carrying out God's orders might have a high sense of coherence. Further, a relaxed, optimistic style is not necessarily healthy. Although much has been said about the importance of a sense of control and a sense of optimism to health, neither is necessary. Instead, a sense of meaningful challenge and a sense of peace is often the key. For example, Mahatma Gandhi had much challenge and often little control over external events. What defined Gandhi's life was a commitment to principle. As he aged, he grew more and more content with his life but remained humble. He certainly was not blindly optimistic, carefree, or lackadaisical. Various sorts of research indicate that alienation is unhealthy, but obligation and dedication are healthy (Friedman, 1990, 1991, 1992). Boredom too is a warning sign that health problems may be on the way. The German philosopher Arthur Schopenhauer said that the two foes of human happiness are pain and boredom.

"Is your health good or poor?"

If people's expectations and orientations affect their future health, then it should be the case that those who report higher expectations can be shown subsequently to have better health and longer lives. Although the hypothesis is sensible when stated this way, the answer is not so obvious if we phrase it as the question "Can people predict how long they are likely to live (beyond the short term)?"

This broad question has been addressed in a series of intriguing studies by Idler and her colleagues (Idler & Angel, 1990; Idler & Kasl, 1991; Idler, Kasl, & Lemke, 1990). The research has found that people's self-evaluations of their health are indeed a significant predictor of mortality, even after controlling for physical health at baseline and other risk factors. (Interestingly, physicians' exams were found to be much poorer at predicting long-term health.) For example, in one study of samples from New Haven, Connecticut, and Iowa and Washington counties, Iowa, a steep gradient was found: As self-reported health decreased, risk of mortality dramatically increased, even after adjusting for various relevant health risk and sample factors (Idler et al., 1990). There are various possible explanations for why self-reported health predicts longevity, but it seems clear that pessimism about one's health is a risk factor for mortality in middle-aged adults.

It is important not to reduce these findings to the conclusion that optimism promotes health. As noted previously, it is not at all clear that optimism itself is a causal factor; optimism may well be a sometime correlate of a more basic healthy lifestyle or social pattern. Further, there are undoubtedly times when it is not beneficial to be blindly optimistic – especially in the face of real threats that need immediate action. Finally, there is good evidence for the belief that self-reported optimism is a marker for a lack of neuroticism and depression. It is likely that it is these negative emotional patterns that are unhealthy, not necessarily anything about optimistic or pessimistic thoughts per se (Hardy & Smith, 1988; Smith, Sanders, & Alexander, 1990).

In the cases just described, the expectations (for good or poor health outcomes) are presumably in the person's awareness, since the poor outlook can be reported. There is reason to suspect, however, that there are also many cases in which an expectation of tragedy or incoherence exists at an unconscious level. These notions have their roots in psychoanalytic theorizing but have recently been subjected to more rigorous experimental analysis (e.g., Pennebaker 1990, 1992; Weinberger & Schwartz, 1990). Actively or unconsciously holding back distressing thoughts and feelings seems itself to be a type of stress that can take its toll on health, just as can externally induced stress. In brief, psychological traumas that have not been resolved, and the basic worries and uncertainties about the future that they generate, also point toward a relationship between expectations and health.

Finally, if interpersonal expectations, not just individual expectations, affect health, then we should expect to find direct effects of others. One of the best-established findings in social epidemiology is that people who are well integrated into their family and community are likely to live longer. For example, evidence from the prospective Alameda County Study continues to show links between poor social ties and mortality (Seeman, Kaplan, Knudsen, Cohen, & Guralnik, 1987). People who are married, have close friends, and have community involvement are less likely to die of all causes. This phenomenon is usually termed *social support* (Cohen & Wills, 1985; House, Landis, & Umberson, 1988), but it is not yet clear precisely what it is about social integration that is healthy. Major social institutions (such as churches and community groups) do, however, tend to promote a forward-looking, coherent, and sensible lifestyle.

Is there experimental evidence for these epidemiological findings? Dramatic confirmation of a salutary effect of positive group support comes from an intervention with metastatic breast cancer conducted at Stanford University. Women receiving routine oncological care were randomly assigned to support groups or not (Spiegel, 1991; Spiegel, Bloom, Kraemer, & Gottheil, 1989). In these groups, the women discussed their deepest fears and learned to deal with their distress. The initial goal was to evaluate the effects of support on emotional well-being, but the dramatic result was that these women lived longer. By 48 months after entry into the study, all of the control patients had died but a third of those in the support groups were still alive. It is not yet known precisely why some of the women in these support groups were better able to fight their cancer, and indeed, I think it unlikely that any single study will uncover the whole answer. But such studies should not prove as shocking to the scientific community as they usually do appear. They are simply another piece in a long series of studies linking psychosocial factors to physical health.

I do not try, in this chapter, to lay out in detail the various pathways and mechanisms through which expectations are related to health. Tracing such pathways is extremely important since they are as close as we are likely to come to proof of causal links. (Random assignment of people to negative health expectancies is not likely.) There is, however, ample reason to believe in the existence of several important mechanisms (Friedman, 1990, 1991, 1992).

The nature of the links

There are three major types of causal links between people's expectations and their health outcomes. There is evidence for all three kinds of effects. There is also evidence for noncausal (artifactual) links between expectations and health, so every study should be carefully examined for bias.

The first kind of link involves behavior. Just as students with positive expectations may try harder and do more homework, people with positive expectations about their health will sometimes eat more nutritiously, exercise, and use a series of prophylactic measures ranging from seat belts to condoms. They may also be more likely to cooperate with their medical regimens, such as taking medications properly and returning for medical follow-ups. Surprisingly (to me at least), there is little solid, systematic evidence about the extent to which people with positive expectations engage in a range of healthy behaviors in a variety of situations and thus improve their health and longevity (see, e.g.,

Ratliff-Crain & Baum, 1990; Scherwitz & Rugulies, 1992). This is certainly an area deserving of future research.

The second type of causal link between expectations and health outcomes is an indirect one, involving underlying third variables. These underlying variables may be mostly biological (temperamental) or mostly interpersonal (socialization). For example, tendencies to be cheerful and agreeable, with positive expectations (or moody and pessimistic, with negative expectations), may be partly biologically based, and these same biological influences may be related to health (e.g., Eysenck, 1991). Alternatively, some children might be socialized to think positively and to take good physical care of themselves. In the case of such a link, of course, the proper intervention to improve health would be to improve socialization practices rather than to focus on positive thinking.

The third kind of link between people's expectations and their health involves psychophysiological mediating mechanisms. For example, psychosocial stress (such as witnessing a terrible event) may trigger excessive activation of the sympathetic nervous system and thereby bring on a heart attack. These types of links are what people usually mean when they speak of *psychosomatic* effects. Although most researchers in the area of psychosomatics preface their reports with qualifiers like "There is some evidence to suggest that . . .", I believe that the overall evidence is quite strong for these types of effects (Friedman, 1991). There is good evidence that major external challenges, chronic negative emotions, and poor coping can upset internal bodily equilibrium and increase the likelihood that illness will develop or progress (Antonovsky, 1990; Cohen & Williamson, 1991; Kamarck & Jennings, 1991; Williams & Barefoot, 1988). More specifically, there is increasing evidence that excessive sympathetic nervous system activation and hormonal influences on immune function are two important physiological mechanisms for psychosomatic effects.

The problem is that simple and direct effects are relatively rare and unreliable. Most people who witness a terrible event will not have a heart attack. Although a number of methodological points are undoubtedly relevant here, there is also a biological fact: Most illnesses are complexly caused (multiply determined) and so are not easily explained. Just as many people exposed to the flu virus do not catch the flu, many people facing psychosocial stressors do not become ill. Illness is often an interaction of biological predisposition, biological invasion, improper nutrition, stress, and other factors affecting homeostatic processes. Although usually ignored by the biomedical community, psychosomatic effects are probably as important as most other major risk factors (such as diet or exercise) for many major diseases.

The strength of the effects

Medical practitioners who acknowledge the importance of a patient's expectations often view them as minor. Sure, it's better if the patient has a good outlook, but the prescription drug is the real thing. In many cases, this belief is accurate. For a strep throat or Lyme disease, prompt antibiotic treatment will usually (but not always) effect a swift cure. It probably does not matter much if the patient is a self-healing guru or a pessimistic old scrooge (as long as he takes his pills).

But for most of today's serious, chronic diseases, cures are simply not available. A cancerous tumor begins growing, or the human immunodeficiency virus begins replicating, or arteries begin narrowing, or the body's immune system begins attacking the body's own organs, and the body must attempt to restore homeostasis. The struggle can continue in many ways for many years, and a convergence of helpful or harmful factors can tip the balance.

To my knowledge, there is no comprehensive and systematic comparison of the sizes of psychosocial effects on health with those of drug and surgical treatments of chronic diseases. My own exploratory attempts in this area suggest that many psychosocial interventions are as effective as many biomedical interventions trumpeted in the news media: a relative risk in the range of 1.5 to 2 or a correlation (r) of approximately .10.

Further, not only are effect sizes of many standard treatments (such as antihypertensive medication effects on longevity) quite small, but their side effects are not thoroughly evaluated. Let us use the term *side effects* quite broadly, because much biomedical research uses it too narrowly. A new cancer treatment might be deemed successful if a larger percentage of treated patients do not have a recurrence within 5 years; but what about the quality of life, the economic and social costs of the treatment, and the occurrence of other health problems? For example, consider the case of cholesterol-lowering drug treatment widely hailed in certain parts of the medical community for preventing death from cardiovascular disease. First of all, such treatment is very expensive, thus diverting funds from other, more cost-effective treatments and preventive efforts. Even more shocking, however, is a series of findings that patients treated with cholesterol-lowering drugs do have fewer cardiovascular attacks but do not live any longer; they die of other causes (Kaplan, Manuck, & Shumaker, 1992). Only with attention to the size and the full meaning of successful treatment effects can we sensibly judge their value.

Conclusion

The evidence for interpersonal effects on healing is stronger than many skeptical scientists imagine but probably weaker than many health gurus proclaim. When the evidence is carefully evaluated, the phenomenon is seen to have moved from artifact to main effect. Or, more precisely, to main effects and interaction effects, as the complexity of the issue has now been delineated. The body is a homeostatic system, and so feedback loops, interactions, and changes across time need to be carefully considered.

Since everyone will die, there comes a point at which even the most positive expectation for a recovery must fail. In many cases, it is known that one's condition is terminal, that the end is near. Blind optimism may prove counterproductive in such instances, as realistic preparations may be advisable. More generally, there are vast individual differences in the willingness to hope for the best or go the extra mile. It is often not sensible to deny the sad facts. But even in such cases, it appears that serenity is better than panic or depression.

Although not a miracle cure, so-called placebo effects are likely to be just as effective as many expensive, painful, and dangerous interventions currently employed as accepted medical practice. Physicians in the mainstream medical establishment teach the importance of doctors' expectations and patients' expectations to the patients' physical health. Yet this teaching is mostly preaching; it turns out to be only lip service, as the practice of medicine mostly ignores psychosocial influences on health. Those practitioners who do try to broaden significantly the narrow biomedical emphasis are viewed as (and sometimes are) unscientific hucksters working at the fringes. Yet the narrow traditionalists are also unscientific – ignoring the vast scientific literature on the relevance of interpersonal influences on health. The challenge of integrating notions of expectations into the health care system is as great as or greater than the difficulties faced in the classroom, the courtroom, and other social institutions.

Note

This research is supported by Grant No. AG08825 from the National Institute on Aging (NIA). Howard S. Friedman, principal investigator. The views expressed here are those of the author and are not necessarily those of the NIA.

I would like to thank Professor Robert Rosenthal for laying the intellectual groundwork for this chapter and for the continuing inspiration he provides.

References

Allport, G. W. (1964). Mental health: A generic attitude. *Journal of Religion and Health, 4*, 7–21.

Antonovsky, A. (1990). Personality and health: Testing the sense of coherence model. In H. S. Friedman (Ed.), *Personality and disease* (pp. 155–177). New York: Wiley.

Booth-Kewley, S., & Friedman, H. S. (1987). Psychological predictors of heart disease: A quantitative review. *Psychological Bulletin, 101*(3), 343–362.

Cannon, W. B. (1939). *The wisdom of the body.* New York: Norton.

Cohen, S., & Williamson, G. M. (1991). Stress and infectious disease in humans. *Psychological Bulletin, 109*(1), 5–24.

Cohen, S., & Wills, T. (1985). Stress, social support, and the buffering hypothesis. *Psychological Bulletin, 98*, 310–357.

Eysenck, H. J. (1991). *Smoking, personality, and stress: Psychosocial factors in the prevention of cancer and coronary heart disease.* New York: Springer-Verlag.

Frankl, V. E. (1962). *Man's search for meaning: An introduction to Logotherapy.* Revised and enlarged ed. of *From death-camp to existentialism* (I. Lasch, Trans.). New York: Simon & Schuster.

Friedman, H. S. (Ed.). (1990). *Personality and disease.* New York: Wiley.

Friedman, H. S. (1991). *The self-healing personality: Why some people achieve health and others succumb to illness.* New York: Henry Holt.

Friedman, H. S. (Ed.). (1992). *Hostility, coping, and health.* Washington, DC: American Psychological Association.

Friedman, H. S., & Booth-Kewley, S. (1987a). Personality, type A behavior, and coronary heart disease: The role of emotional expression. *Journal of Personality and Social Psychology, 53*(4), 783–792.

Friedman, H. S., & Booth-Kewley, S. (1987b). The "disease-prone personality." A meta-analytic view of the construct. *American Psychologist, 42*(6), 539–555.

Friedman, H. S., & DiMatteo, M. R. (1989). *Health psychology.* Englewood Cliffs, NJ: Prentice-Hall.

Hardy, J. D., & Smith, T. W. (1988). Cynical hostility and vulnerability to disease: Social support, life stress, and physiological response to conflict. *Health Psychology, 7*(5), 447–459.

House, J. S., Landis, K. R., & Umberson, D. (1988). Social relationships and health. *Science, 241*(4865), 540–545.

Idler, E. L., & Angel, R. J. (1990). Self-rated health and mortality in the NHANES-I Epidemiologic Follow-up Study. *American Journal of Public Health, 80*(4), 446–452.

Idler, E. L., & Kasl, S. (1991). Health perceptions and survival: Do global evaluations of health status really predict mortality? *Journal of Gerontology, 46*(2), S55–S65.

Idler, E. L., Kasl, S. V., & Lemke, J. H. (1990). Self-evaluated health and mortality among the elderly in New Haven, Connecticut, and Iowa and Washington counties, Iowa, 1982–1986. *American Journal of Epidemiology, 131*(1), 91–103.

James, W. (1890). *The principles of psychology*. London: Macmillan.

Kamarck, T., & Jennings, J. R. (1991). Biobehavioral factors in sudden cardiac death. *Psychological Bulletin, 109*(1), 42–75.

Kahneman, D., Slovic, P., Tversky, A. (Eds.). (1982). *Judgment under uncertainty: Heuristics and biases*. New York: Cambridge University Press.

Kaplan, R. M., Manuck, S., & Shumaker, S. (1992). Cholesterol lowering and depression, suicide and accidents. In H. S. Friedman (Ed.), *Hostility, coping, and health* (pp. 117–123). Washington, DC: American Psychological Association.

Kobasa, S. O. (1990). Lessons from history: How to find the person in health psychology. In H. S. Friedman (Ed.), *Personality and disease* (pp. 14–37). New York: Wiley.

Lown, B. (1983). Introduction. In N. Cousins (Ed.), *The healing heart* (Foreword). New York: Norton.

McGuire, W. J. (1969). Suspiciousness of experimenters' intent. In R. Rosenthal and R. L. Rosnow (Eds.), *Artifact in behavioral research* (pp. 13–57). New York: Academic Press.

Maslow, A. H. (1970). *Motivation and personality* (2nd ed.). New York: Harper & Row.

Pennebaker, J. W. (1990). *Opening up: The healing power of confiding in others*. New York: Morrow.

Pennebaker, J. W. (1992). Inhibition as the linchpin of health. In H. S. Friedman (Ed.), *Hostility, coping, and health* (pp. 127–140). Washington, DC: American Psychological Association.

Ratliff-Crain, J., & Baum, A. (1990). Individual differences and health: Gender, coping and stress. In H. S. Friedman (Ed.), *Personality and disease* (pp. 226–253). New York: Wiley.

Rosenthal, R. (1966). *Experimenter effects in behavioral research*. New York: Appleton-Century-Crofts.

Scherwitz, L., & Rugulies, R. (1992). Lifestyle and hostility. In H. S. Friedman (Ed.), *Hostility, coping, and health* (pp. 77–98). Washington, DC: American Psychological Association.

Seeman, T. E., Kaplan, G. A., Knudsen, L., Cohen, R., & Guralnik, J. (1987). Social network ties and mortality among the elderly in the Alameda County Study. *American Journal of Epidemiology, 126*(4), 714–723.

Shapiro, A. K. (1960). A contribution to a history of the placebo effect. *Behavioral Sciences, 5*, 109–135.

Smith, T. W., Sanders, J. D., & Alexander, J. F. (1990). What does the Cook and Medley hostility scale measure? Affect, behavior, and attributions in the marital context. *Journal of Personality and Social Psychology, 58*(4), 699–708.

Spiegel, D. (1991). Mind matters: Effects of group support on cancer patients. *The Journal of NIH Research, 3*, 61–63.

Spiegel, D., Bloom, J. R., Kraemer, H. C., & Gottheil, E. (1989). Effect of psychosocial treatment on survival of patients with metastatic breast cancer. *Lancet, 2*(8668):888–891.

Weinberger, D. A., & Schwartz, G. E. (1990). Distress and restraint as superordinate dimensions of self-reported adjustment: A typological perspective. *Journal of Personality, 58*(2), 381–417.

Williams, R. B., Jr., & Barefoot, J. C. (1988). Coronary-prone behavior: The emerging role of the hostility complex. In B. K. Houston & C. Snyder (Eds.), *Type A behavior pattern: Research, theory and intervention* (pp. 189–211). New York: Wiley.

9. Precursors of interpersonal expectations: The vocal and physical attractiveness stereotypes

MIRON ZUCKERMAN, HOLLEY S. HODGINS, AND KUNITATE MIYAKE

Introduction

Interpersonal expectations are often based on initial impressions of a target person. Initial impressions, in turn, depend in part on the target's appearance, including his or her level of physical attractiveness. Since the early work of Dion, Berscheid, and Walster (1972) on the "What is beautiful is good" phenomenon, numerous studies have shown that individuals high in physical attractiveness elicit more favorable impressions than individuals low in physical attractiveness (for reviews, see Berscheid & Walster, 1974; Hatfield & Sprecher, 1986; Sorrel & Nowack, 1981). There is, in fact, some indication that the physical attractiveness stereotype may act as a self-fulfilling prophecy. Snyder, Tanke, and Berscheid (1977) showed that male perceivers who interacted over the phone with women they believed (as a result of experimental manipulation) to be physically attractive behaved in a manner that was more sociable, independent, sexually warm, and so on, than perceivers who believed the women to be unattractive. More important, female targets who were perceived to be physically attractive behaved in a manner that was more friendly, likeable, and so on, than female targets who were perceived to be unattractive. Evidently, the physical attractiveness stereotype channeled the interaction so as to influence social reality.

Can physical attractiveness also act as a self-fulfilling prophecy in real life? There are reasons to believe that the answer is yes. After all, real life provides a more continuous differential treatment of attractive and unattractive targets than does a single experiment. For example, attractive people are more likely to be helped (Benson, Karabenick, & Lerner, 1976), more likely to be sought out as dates (Krebs & Adinolphi, 1975; Walster, Aronson, Abrahams, & Rottman, 1966), and, as early as nursery school age, more likely to be selected in sociometric choices (Dion & Berscheid, 1974; Kleck, Richardson, & Ronald, 1974).

On the other hand, there is no strong evidence that physically attractive people actually possess the positive traits that are attributed to them. Stated differently, the self-fulfilling prophecy that Snyder et al. (1977) identified in the laboratory does not seem to generalize to real life. The question of whether attractiveness can elicit a self-fulfilling process will be discussed again at the end of the chapter. First, however, we would like to propose that this question is relevant not only to a person's physical appearance but also to his or her voice.

The vocal attractiveness stereotype: Rationale and evidence

The physical attractiveness stereotype represents the influence of the visual portion of appearance. However, appearance also includes an auditory component – the person's voice. It is possible, therefore, that interpersonal impressions vary as a function of not only physical but also vocal attractiveness. To establish the existence of a vocal attractiveness stereotype, it is necessary to show that people agree on judgments of vocal attractiveness and that such judgments are related to impressions of personality. There is evidence for both of these conditions.

First, observers tend to agree on a variety of judgments about vocal cues: They agree on personality traits inferred from the voice (e.g., Addington, 1968; Allport & Cantril, 1934; Scherer, 1972; for reviews, see Kramer, 1964; Scherer, 1979, 1986); they agree on emotions inferred from the voice (Scherer, 1974a; Scherer & Oshinsky, 1977); and they agree on the acoustic characteristics associated with various voices (Scherer, 1974b). To the extent that people agree on various judgments about the voice, they are likely to agree on judgments of vocal attractiveness.

Second, the voice affects a variety of personality judgments. Researchers have examined the relation between observers' impressions of personality and various vocal parameters (e.g., Aronovitch, 1976); alternatively, they have examined observers' impressions as a function of systematic variations in the voice (e.g., Addington, 1968). This latter technique was particularly popular in studies of speakers' credibility, with credibility operationalized as ratings of competence and dominance, on the one hand, and likability and benevolence, on the other hand. The results tend to show that a faster speech rate (e.g., Smith,

Brown, Strong, & Rencher, 1975), fewer pauses and repetitions (e.g., Miller & Hewgill, 1964; Sereno & Hawkins, 1967), and dynamic delivery (e.g., Pearce & Conklin, 1971) produced higher ratings on competence and dominance; effects for likability and benevolence were weaker and less consistent. To the extent that impressions vary as a function of vocal characteristics, they are likely to be influenced by vocal attractiveness.

The question of whether observers agree on targets' vocal attractiveness was examined by Zuckerman and Driver (1989; Study 1 and Study 2) and by Zuckerman, Hodgins, and Miyake (1990). In each of the three studies, subject-targets ($n = 200$, 200, and 106, respectively) were videotaped as they read a statement that was neutral in content. The text was standard content in two studies (Zuckerman & Driver, 1989, Study 1; Zuckerman et al., 1990) and randomly selected from different novels in the third study (Zuckerman & Driver, 1989, Study 2). Judges rated the senders' vocal attractiveness from the auditory portion of the tape and their physical attractiveness from the visual portion. No training was given before the rating task. It was found that judges were able to agree on the attractiveness of targets' voices (mean interrater reliability across the three studies was .85); agreement on senders' physical attractiveness was somewhat more pronounced (mean interrater reliability was .92). Clearly, there is an attractiveness quality in human voices that people can agree on.

The studies by Zuckerman and Driver (1989) and Zuckerman et al. (1990) also addressed the question of whether targets high in vocal attractiveness elicit more favorable impressions than targets low in physical attractiveness. In each study, judges rated the targets' personality on various adjectives on the basis of their voice (auditory condition), face (visual condition), or face plus voice (visual-auditory condition). In all three studies, the personality-rating task and the attractiveness-rating task were performed by different judges.

In each study, the ratings were averaged across judges and adjectives, yielding a global impression score for each target. These scores were regressed on targets' sex and their vocal attractiveness in the auditory condition, targets' sex and their physical attractiveness in the visual condition, and targets' sex and their vocal and physical attractiveness in the visual-auditory condition. Table 9.1 presents the results for each study by experimental condition. In each case, the table shows the partial r between the predictor (attractiveness) and the dependent vari-

Table 9.1. *Vocal and physical attractiveness effects by study and experimental condition*

	Vocal attractiveness effects					
	Auditory condition			Visual-auditory condition		
Study	df	F	r	df	F	r
Zuckerman and Driver (1989, Study 1)	197	134.94	.64	197	78.80	.54
Zuckerman and Driver (1989, Study 2)	197	73.12	.52	197	34.90	.41
Zuckerman et al. (1990)	103	37.28	.52	102	19.00	.40
	Physical attractiveness effects					
	Visual condition			Visual-auditory condition		
Study	df	F	r	df	F	r
Zuckerman and Driver (1989, Study 1)	197	84.96	.55	197	23.39	.33
Zuckerman and Driver (1989, Study 2)	197	43.92	.43	197	8.95	.21
Zuckerman et al. (1990)	103	32.20	.49	102	1.89	.13

able (global personality impression) with the effect of sex removed; the F test of the partial r is also presented. In the visual-auditory condition, the partial r for each type of attractiveness was obtained after both sex and the other type of attractiveness were controlled for. However, because vocal and physical attractiveness were only minimally related (mean r across the three studies $= .12$; Zuckerman & Driver, 1989; Zuckerman et al., 1990), the effect of one type of attractiveness changed very little when the other type of attractiveness was held constant.

The top section of Table 9.1 provides strong support for the existence of a vocal attractiveness stereotype. In each of the studies presented, higher levels of vocal attractiveness were associated with more favorable ratings. The combined effect, aggregated across all three studies, was significant in both the auditory condition (combined $z = 13.64$, $p < .001$, mean $r = .56$), and the visual-auditory condition (combined $z = 10.36$, $p = < .001$, mean $r = .45$). The lower section of Table 9.1 provides strong support for the physical attractiveness stereotype. The

198   Miron Zuckerman, Holley S. Hodgins, and Kunitate Miyake

combined effect, aggregated across all studies, was significant in both the visual condition (combined $z = 11.52$, $p < .001$, mean $r = .49$) and the visual-auditory condition (combined $z = 5.21$, $p < .001$, mean $r = .22$).

The effects described document the influence of vocal and physical attractiveness on global impressions. That is, the dependent variable in all analyses was the average of judges' ratings on all the adjective scales that were used. It is possible, however, that the dimensions that are most influenced by vocal attractiveness differ from those most influenced by physical attractiveness.

In Zuckerman and Driver's (1989) two studies, the judges rated the targets on nine adjectives, which were divided into three subscales: dominance, achievement, and likability. The results did not show consistent differences between the effects of vocal and physical attractiveness on the three domains. Such differences were found, however, in studies by Zuckerman et al. (1990) and Miyake and Zuckerman (1991). In the Zuckerman et al. (1990) study, judges rated the senders on 10 adjectives that were divided into five subscales; each subscale represented one of the five factors from the NEO Personality Inventory (PI) (Costa & McCrae, 1985). These factors were neuroticism, extraversion, openness to new experience, agreeableness, and conscientiousness. The five factors have emerged in a large number of studies, using a variety of instruments including both peer and self-ratings (Costa & McCrae, 1980, 1988; McCrae, 1982; McCrae & Costa, 1983, 1985a, 1985b, 1987; Norman, 1963; Tupes & Christal, 1961). In the Miyake and Zuckerman (1991) study, judges rated targets high and low in vocal and physical attractiveness on five adjectives, each representing one of the five NEO PI factors. In both of these studies, the dimension most influenced by physical attractiveness was extraversion and the dimension least influenced by physical attractiveness was conscientiousness. In fact, targets high in physical attractiveness were perceived as less conscientious than targets low in physical attractiveness. Interestingly, conscientiousness was the dimension most influenced by vocal attractiveness in the Miyake and Zuckerman (1991) study (in the Zuckerman et al. 1990 study, conscientiousness was third among the five factors in terms of the size of the vocal attractiveness effect). Finally, both studies showed that the effect of vocal attractiveness on impressions of agreeableness was relatively small. Thus, there is some evidence that whereas physical and vocal attractiveness both influence global personality impressions, their effects on specific personality dimensions differ. The strong effect of physical attractiveness on extraversion is consistent with findings reported by other researchers (Kenny, Horner, Kashy, & Chu, 1992). The difference between the effects of physical and vocal attractiveness on conscientiousness is of particular interest, suggesting that for some dimensions the two stereotypes work in opposite directions. Clearly, attractiveness effects depend to some degree on the particular combination of attractiveness channel (auditory/visual) and the personality dimension that is being examined.

Beyond personality impressions

So far we have described the effects of vocal and physical attractiveness in terms of their influence on personality impressions. It is of interest, however, to consider the attractiveness phenomenon in a broader context. Attractiveness may influence a range of attitudes, behavioral choices, and preferences that go beyond mere personality impressions. Accordingly, Miyake and Zuckerman (in press) examined the effects of attractiveness on variables related to the theme of perceived similarity between the self and other people. These variables included false consensus, choice of comparison other, affiliation, and assumed and perceived similarity.

The term *false consensus* was introduced by Ross, Greene, and House (1977) to describe the tendency of most people to see their beliefs and behaviors as relatively similar to those of others. Numerous investigations have provided strong support for this phenomenon (for reviews, see Marks & Miller, 1987; Mullen et al., 1985). Several studies have shown, however, that people see themselves as more similar to physically attractive others than to unattractive others (Marks & Miller, 1982; Marks, Miller, & Maruyama, 1981; Mashman, 1978). The perception of similarity between the self and attractive targets may enhance self-value, validate one's opinions and behaviors, and maintain cognitive balance between self-view and the view of the favorable other. Because similarity is related to liking (Byrne, 1971), the perceived similarity between self and attractive targets may create a preference for affiliation with these targets. Affiliation goes hand in hand with a desire for information about and comparison with others (Rofe, 1984; Suls, 1977). Under threat, however, these two activities may diverge, with affiliation sought from those who do well (upward contact) and self-evaluation made against those who do not do well (downward comparison; Taylor & Lobel, 1989). Because the comparison in the Miyake and Zuckerman (in press) study was considered nonthreatening, it was predicted that both comparison and affiliation would be directed upward, toward the more attractive targets. Of course, it is possible to argue that the more attractive others are seen as more similar and that a preference for comparisons with attractive targets reflects a preference for comparison with similar others (Festinger, 1954; Goethals & Darley, 1977).

Earlier we proposed that there are two types of attractiveness, physical and vocal, and that effects previously linked to physical attractiveness may also be obtained for vocal attractiveness. Accordingly, the first purpose of the Miyake and Zuckerman (in press) study was to examine how physical and vocal attractiveness influence false consensus, comparison, affiliation, and perceived similarity. The second purpose of this study was to examine the interaction between the two stereotypes in relation to the new dependent variables.

The three studies reviewed previously (Zuckerman & Driver, 1989; Zuckerman et al., 1990) showed an interaction between physical and vocal attractiveness in relation to personality impressions; the combined interaction effect, aggregated across the three studies, was significant ($z = 2.70$, $p < .005$, mean $r = .12$). The direction of this effect was such that the influence of each type of attractiveness was more pronounced at higher levels of the other type of attractiveness. When the interaction effects were added to the main effects of vocal and physical attractiveness, the joint effect of the two stereotypes suggested a synergistic pattern. Specifically, personality impressions were relatively positive when the targets were high on both vocal and physical attractiveness and relatively negative when the targets were low on one or both types of attractiveness. The Miyake and Zuckerman (in press) study examined whether the Vocal Attractiveness × Physical Attractiveness interaction and the synergistic pattern of their joint effect would be obtained for variables other than personality impressions.

Subjects in the current study ($n = 76$) viewed the videotapes of 32 targets who were selected from among participants in the earlier studies (Zuckerman & Driver, 1989; Zuckerman et al., 1990). The targets were individuals with the highest and lowest vocal and physical attractiveness scores. The crossing of the two attractiveness dimensions yielded four cells (high/high, high/low, low/high, and low/low), each composed of four male and four female targets. Mean physical attractiveness ratings of the high and low physical attractiveness targets were 4.49 and 2.17, respectively [$F(1,24) = 197.52$, $p < .001$, $r = .94$]; mean vocal attractiveness ratings of the high and low vocal attractiveness targets were 4.75 and 2.23, respectively [$F(1,24) = 189.09$, $p < .001$, $r = .94$].

For each target person, subjects predicted the target's yes–no behavioral choices in four hypothetical situations. Earlier, subjects indicated their own choices in these same situations, yielding a false consensus variable that ranged from 0 (no agreement between subjects' own behavioral choices and those predicted for the target) to 4 (full agreement between subjects' own behavioral choices and those predicted for the target). Subjects also rated on a 7-point scale how strongly they wanted to examine information regarding each target's academic record and success after college (targets were described as recent alumni who participated in a study on success in life). Subjects also rated on a 7-point scale desire for association with and degree of similarity to each target. This latter scale served as a measure of perceived similarity. Finally, subjects rated themselves and each target on five adjective scales, with each adjective representing one of the five NEO PI factors (Costa & McCrae, 1985). Absolute differences between self- and target ratings served as a measure of assumed similarity (correlations between self- and target ratings were also calculated but did not show any effect of targets' attractiveness). All together, there were five dependent variables.

Mean target ratings across the five adjectives served as a manipulation check. It was found that targets high in vocal attractiveness were rated more positively ($M = 5.65$) than targets low in vocal attractiveness [$M = 5.24$, $F(1,74) = 47.63$, $p < .001$, $r = .63$] and that targets high in physical attractiveness were rated more positively ($M = 5.77$) than targets low in physical attractiveness [$M = 5.11$, $F(1,74) = 134.42$, $p < .001$, $r = .80$]. As expected, a Vocal Attractiveness × Physical Attractiveness interaction was also obtained [$F(1,74) = 125.03$, $p < .001$, $r = .79$], indicating that the effect of one type of attractiveness was more pronounced at higher levels of the other type of attractiveness. The mean ratings for the four attractiveness cells formed a synergistic pattern. The mean rating in the high physical/high vocal attractiveness cell ($M = 6.21$) was higher than the mean rating in the high physical/low vocal ($M = 5.33$), low physical/high vocal ($M = 5.09$), and low physical/low vocal ($M = 5.14$) cells; the latter three means showed minimal variation.

Table 9.2 presents the results of the study for all five dependent variables. The upper part of the table presents the mean scores and the lower part presents the results of the statistical analyses. It can be seen that all main effects and interactions were significant. Thus, higher physical attractiveness and higher vocal attractiveness each elicited (1) greater false consensus, (2) greater desire for social comparison, (3)

Table 9.2. *Vocal and physical attractiveness effects on five dependent variables*

	Mean scores of dependent variables by target attractiveness[a]			
Dependent variable	High phys./ high vocal	High phys./ low vocal	Low phys./ high vocal	Low phys./ low vocal
False censensus	2.49	2.11	2.14	2.13
Social comparison	4.20	3.42	3.24	3.33
Affiliation	4.40	3.50	2.88	2.73
Perceived similarity	3.58	2.92	2.47	2.32
Assumed similarity	1.95	2.24	2.38	2.35

	Significance and size of attractiveness effects[b]							
	Physical attract.		Vocal attract.		Physical × vocal attract.		Synergistic contrast	
Dependent variable	F	r	F	r	F	r	F	r
False consensus	6.99	.29	14.40	.40	13.75	.40	32.79	.55
Social comparison	40.96	.60	34.38	.56	54.44	.65	124.05	.79
Affiliation	203.12	.86	56.92	.66	57.17	.66	303.35	.90
Perceived similarity	125.43	.79	31.41	.55	25.11	.50	168.01	.83
Assumed similarity	29.25	.53	12.17	.38	10.54	.35	50.48	.64

[a] High scores indicate more of the quality represented by the variable.
[b] For analyses presented in the three left-hand columns, $df=1,74$ and $p<.05$ when $F \geq 4.00$; for analyses in the right-hand column (the synergistic contrast), $df=1,222$ and $p<.05$ when $F \geq 3.90$.

greater desire for affiliation, (4) greater perceived similarity, and (5) greater assumed similarity. The significant interactions indicated that for all five variables, the effect of one type of attractiveness was more pronounced for higher levels of the other type of attractiveness. Finally, the mean scores of all dependent variables show a synergistic pattern, with the high/high cell either higher or lower than the other three cells and the latter three cells showing minimal variation. The right-hand column in the lower portion of the table shows that the synergistic contrast (with a +3 weight assigned to the high/high cell and −1 weights assigned to each of the remaining cells) was significant for all five dependent variables.

For exploratory purposes, subjects' physical and vocal attractiveness were also measured. In addition, the subjects filled out Snyder's (1974,

1979) Self-Monitoring (SM) scale. The question of interest was whether any of these variables moderated the effects of targets' attractiveness on the dependent variables. It was found that subjects' vocal attractiveness did not influence any of the effects of targets' vocal attractiveness (F's < 1.41). On the other hand, the effects of targets' physical attractiveness on false consensus and perceived similarity were more pronounced for more physically attractive subjects (p's $< .05$); a similar moderator effect for affiliation approached significance ($p < .10$). The existence of a moderator effect for targets' physical attractiveness but not for their vocal attractiveness is consistent with the finding that people are differentially aware of the visual and auditory channels. For example, Driver (1987) showed that people know how physically attractive they are but not how vocally attractive. There is also evidence that facial displays of emotions are more controllable than vocal cues (Zuckerman, Larrance, Spiegel, & Klorman, 1981). If vocally attractive people are not aware of their own vocal attractiveness, they also may not be sensitive to others' vocal attractiveness. In contrast, people high in physical attractiveness are aware of their attractiveness and, hence, may become sensitive to that of others.

Self-monitoring had only minimal influence on the effects of vocal attractiveness, physical attractiveness, or vocal–physical attractiveness interaction. Of 15 analyses (vocal/physical/vocal–physical interaction $\times$ five dependent variables), only 2 produced significant SM moderator effects. A more dramatic picture emerged, however, when SM was examined in relation to the synergistic contrast. For three of the five dependent variables (false consensus and social comparison were the exceptions), the effect of the synergistic contrast was more pronounced for high self-monitors (p's $< .05$); the same pattern emerged for social comparison, but the interaction only approached significance ($p < .11$). Thus, high self-monitors (relative to low self-monitors) were more likely to distinguish between targets high on both physical and vocal attractiveness and all other targets. It appears that the former group represented desirable traits and behaviors, which elicited from high self-monitors greater perceived and assumed similarity, greater desire for affiliation, and somewhat greater desire for social comparison.

Overall, the results of the Miyake and Zuckerman (in press) study support and extend the concept of the vocal attractiveness stereotype. It was found that subjects saw themselves as particularly similar to vocally attractive targets in terms of three measures – false consensus, perceived similarity, and assumed similarity. Subjects were also more likely to choose vocally attractive targets as comparison others and to express greater desire to associate with them. Physical attractiveness had the same effects on these variables, indicating a parallel between the two stereotypes.

The combined effects of physical and vocal attractiveness supported a synergistic model. Apparently, subjects tended to combine visual and auditory information into a unitary all-or-nothing concept of attractiveness. Targets were viewed as attractive (and, hence, as more similar, better to affiliate with, etc.) if they were high on both physical and vocal attractiveness; targets were viewed as unattractive if they were low on either physical or vocal attractiveness. The fact that the synergistic effect was moderated by self-monitoring lends additional support to this view of attractiveness. High self-monitors are known to seek cues of appropriate behavior and to model their behavior after that of attractive people (Snyder, Berscheid, & Glick, 1985). If high self-monitors distinguish between different levels of attractiveness on a synergistic basis, both physical and vocal attractiveness must be essential for an overall assessment of general attractiveness.

All of these effects were obtained for college-age subjects. An important question is whether they can be obtained for younger age groups or whether they are the end result of various developmental changes. This issue is examined in the next section.

Developmental changes in attractiveness effects

There is evidence that the effect of physical attractiveness can be obtained at an early age. Several studies have shown that infants ranging from 3 to 6 months old look longer at attractive than at unattractive faces (Langlois, Ritter, Roggman, & Vaughn, 1991; Langlois, Roggman, Casey, Ritter, Rieser-Danner, & Jenkins, 1987; Samuels & Ewy, 1985; Shapiro, Hazan, & Haith, 1984). The stimuli in these studies were both adult and infant faces, and attractiveness was determined by adult judges. Clearly, these findings contradict the assumption that standards of attractiveness are learned through gradual exposure to cultural norms. Langlois et al. (1991) offered two explanations for infants' preferences for attractive faces. One was that attractive faces are the "average" or prototypical representation of the category of faces, and that infants as well as adults show a preference for prototypical stimuli. The other was that evolutionary pressures favor the average value of the population, inducing a preference for faces closer to the population mean.

Table 9.3. *Personality ratings for four age levels by targets' physical attractiveness and vocal attractiveness*

Age level	Physical attractiveness			Vocal attractiveness		
	High	Low	Difference	High	Low	Difference
1	3.40	2.59	.81	3.10	2.89	.21
2	3.47	2.83	.64	3.33	2.96	.37
3	3.38	2.81	.57	3.30	2.90	.40
4	3.33	2.98	.35	3.34	2.96	.38
Mean	3.39	2.80	.59	3.27	2.93	.34

Note: Higher scores indicate more positive ratings.

Given the early onset of the physical attractiveness stereotype, it is of interest to examine whether and how it changes as children grow older. Of equal interest is the developmental pattern of the vocal attractiveness stereotype and of the interaction between physical and vocal attractiveness. These issues were addressed in a study by Zuckerman and Hodgins (1991).

Subjects watched the 32-target videotape that was used by Miyake and Zuckerman (in press). They were asked to rate each target on five 5-point adjective scales. The adjectives loosely represented the five NEO PI factors (Costa & McCrae (1985). More exact representation was not possible because of the need to use wording that would be understood by young children. For all subjects, the adjectives and the factors they represented were as follows: upset–not upset (Neuroticism); not fun–fun (Extraversion); does not have good ideas–has good ideas (Openness); not friendly–friendly (Agreeableness); and not smart–smart (Conscientiousness). A single average score across the five adjectives served as the dependent variable (Cronbach alphas ranged from .65 to .80).

The subjects were 192 students from elementary school, high school, and college. Because the number was too small to allow the use of each grade as a separate category in the analysis, the subjects were divided into four levels: Level 1 – grades 2–4 (38 females, 29 males); Level 2 – grades 5–8 (21 females, 26 males); Level 3 – grades 9–12 (17 females, 23 males); Level 4 – college (17 females, 23 males).

Table 9.3 presents mean ratings for targets high and low in physical attractiveness (left section) and for targets high and low in vocal attractiveness (right section). Targets high in physical attractiveness elicited more positive ratings [$F(1,184) = 398.95$, $p < .001$ $r = 83$], an effect that was less pronounced for higher age levels [Physical Attractiveness × Age linear contrast $F(1,184) = 33.79$, $p < .001$, $r = .39$]. Targets high in vocal attractiveness also elicited more positive ratings [$F(1,184) = 308.78$, $p < .001$, $r = .79$], but this effect increased from Level to Level 2 and then remained constant [Vocal Attractiveness × Age linear contrast $F(1,184) = 12.72$, $p < .001$, $r = .25$]. It was also found that the decline in the effect of physical attractiveness with age was more pronounced for female targets ($p < .05$); in contrast, the increase in the effect of vocal attractiveness with age was more pronounced for male targets ($p < .05$).

The decline in the effect of physical attractiveness indicates that children learn from their own experience that physical appearance is not a good predictor of personality. In fact, Zuckerman et al. (1990) have shown that impressions of college students familiar with the target are not influenced by the target's attractiveness. If people can learn to distinguish between the stereotype and reality, the effect of the stereotype should decline with age. Because physical attractiveness is more strongly related to the feminine sex role, people may learn to discount it even more in relation to female targets.

Unlike the effect of physical attractiveness, that of vocal attractiveness first increased and then remained steady. This pattern is consistent with the previous suggestion that people are less aware of the effects of vocal than of facial attractiveness. If people are not aware of the effect of vocal attractiveness, they will not attempt to suppress its influence. Because the voice exerts strong influence on judgments of dominance (DePaulo, Rosenthal, Eisenstat, Rogers, & Finkelstein, 1978; Rosenthal, Hall, DiMatteo, Rogers, & Archer, 1979), it is not surprising that vocal attractiveness becomes a more important source of information about male targets than about female targets.

Turning to the question of how age affects the joint influence of vocal and physical attractiveness, Table 9.4 presents mean personality ratings for the cells created by the crossing of the two channels. Overall, the effect of one type of attractiveness was more pronounced for higher levels of the other type of attractiveness [Physical Attractiveness × Vocal Attractiveness $F(1,184) = 120.09$, $p < .001$, $r = .63$], an effect that was more pronounced at later ages [Physical Attractiveness × Vocal Attractiveness × Age linear contrast $F(1,184) = 17.11$, $p < .001$, $r < .29$]. This latter three-way interaction was more pronounced for female subjects ($p < .001$).

Table 9.4. *Personality ratings for four age levels by targets' physical and vocal attractiveness*

Age level	High phys./ high vocal attract.	High phys./ low vocal attract.	Low phys./ high vocal attract.	Low phys./ low vocal attract.
1	3.54	3.27	2.66	2.52
2	3.78	3.15	2.89	2.77
3	3.74	3.03	2.85	2.78
4	3.65	3.00	3.03	2.93
Mean	3.68	3.11	2.86	2.75

Note: Higher scores indicate more positive ratings.

Because the interaction between the two stereotypes was more pronounced for older children, it is possible that their joint effect reflects an additive model at early ages and a synergistic model at later ages. In an additive model, the combined vocal and physical effect is the simple sum of their independent contributions. In a synergistic model, the effect emerges only when the target is high on both types of attractiveness. Accordingly, the data at each age level were examined in a synergistic contrast (+3 weight assigned to the high/high cell and −1 weight assigned to each of the remaining cells) and in an additive contrast (+2 weight assigned to the high/high cell, 0 weight assigned to the high/low and low/high cells, and −2 weight assigned to the low/low cell). For each contrast, we calculated the level of significance (F test) as well as the effect size (partial r). The results showed that both the synergistic and additive contrasts were significant at each age level. This finding should not be surprising in view of the fact that the correlation between the synergistic and additive contrast weights is .82. Partial r values for the additive contrast in Levels 1, 2, 3, and 4 were .85, .89, .93, and .91, respectively; the corresponding partial r values for the synergistic contrasts were .81, .88, .94, and .94. We also examined a contrast that tested the difference between the synergistic and additive contrasts. The partial r values for this contrast were −.44 for Level 1, −.09 for Level 2, .37 for Level 3, and .51 for Level 4. The linear contrast of the four difference coefficients was highly significant ($z = 5.35$, $p < .001$). It thus appears that the additive contrast accounts for more variance at lower age levels, whereas the synergistic contrast accounts for more variance at higher age levels. Perhaps older children tend to combine physical and vocal attractiveness into a more unitary concept of attractiveness. The end result is that older children react more positively only to targets that are high on all dimensions of attractiveness.

It should be recalled that the Vocal Attractiveness × Physical Attractiveness × Age linear contrast (which gives rise to the development of the synergistic pattern) was more pronounced for female than for male targets. In Western culture, the concept of attractiveness is more relevant to the feminine sex role. Thus, it seems appropriate that perceivers are more likely to develop a unitary concept of attractiveness in relation to females than in relation to males. After all, it is in relation to females that one most utilizes such a concept.

In summary, the Zuckerman and Hodgins (1991) study identified developmental patterns of the physical and vocal attractiveness stereotypes. The effect of physical attractiveness declined with age, particularly for female targets; the effect of vocal attractiveness initially increased and then stabilized, particularly for male targets; a synergistic pattern of vocal plus physical attractiveness effect also developed with age, particularly for female targets.

Cross-channel effects of vocal and physical attractiveness

If both vocal and physical attractiveness affect personality impressions, they may also affect impressions of the person's attractiveness in the cross channel. That is, targets' physical attractiveness may affect impressions of their vocal attractiveness and targets' vocal attractiveness may affect impressions of their physical attractiveness. This hypothesis was examined in a study by Zuckerman, Miyake, and Hodgins (1991).

Target persons in the investigation were the 400 videotaped subjects from the two studies completed by Zuckerman and Driver (1989). These targets were rated by new groups of judges on three measures: mixed attractiveness, mixed attractiveness with warning, and general attractiveness. For the mixed attractiveness measure, judges observed each target in a visual-auditory condition and rated either the target's physical attractiveness or the target's vocal attractiveness. The term *mixed attractiveness* was used to distinguish these ratings from ratings of physical and vocal attractiveness on the basis of face only or voice only. These latter ratings (which were obtained in the Zuckerman and Driver study and reused in the present investigation) were now termed *pure attractiveness*. The prediction was that in a visual-auditory situation, inferences of one type of attractiveness (either vocal or physical) would be based in part on attractiveness in the cross channel. Specifically, inferences of mixed vocal attractiveness would be influenced by inferences of pure physical attractiveness, and inferences of mixed physical attractiveness would be influenced by inferences of pure vocal attractiveness.

For the mixed attractiveness with warning ratings, judges followed the same procedure used to obtain the mixed attractiveness ratings, except that, in addition, they were warned not to pay attention to the inappropriate channel. Specifically, judges rating physical attractiveness in the visual-auditory condition were told to ignore targets' voices completely and to base their ratings only on physical appearance, and judges rating vocal attractiveness were told to ignore targets' physical appearance completely and to base their ratings only on the targets' voices. Of interest was the question of whether the warning would eliminate the cross-channel effects.

For the general attractiveness measure, the instructions required judges to rate the targets' attractiveness without mentioning either vocal or physical attractiveness. Of interest was the question of whether impressions of targets' general attractiveness would be influenced by both physical and vocal attractiveness or by physical attractiveness alone.

For all analyses, judges' ratings were averaged, yielding the following attractiveness scores for each target: mixed vocal attractiveness, mixed vocal attractiveness with warning, mixed physical attractiveness, mixed physical attractiveness with warning, and general attractiveness. As previously mentioned, pure vocal and pure physical attractiveness scores for each target were available from the Zuckerman and Driver (1989) study.

To determine cross-channel effects, mixed vocal attractiveness scores were regressed on sex, pure vocal attractiveness, and pure physical attractiveness; mixed physical attractiveness scores were regressed on sex, pure physical attractiveness scores, and pure vocal attractiveness scores. Similar analyses were conducted for the mixed attractiveness with warning scores. Targets served as the units of analysis.

To determine the contributions of physical and vocal attractiveness to prediction of general attractiveness, the latter was regressed on sex followed by pure vocal plus pure physical attractiveness (the contribution of each type of pure attractiveness was thus determined after the other type of pure attractiveness was controlled for). Targets again served as the units of analysis.

Table 9.5. *Contribution of pure attractiveness from the cross-channel to explained variance of three variables: Mixed attractiveness, mixed attractiveness with warning, and general attractiveness*

	Study 1		Study 2	
Dependent variable	F^a	Partial r^b	F^a	Partial r^b
	Predictor: Pure vocal attractiveness (sex and pure physical attractiveness are partialed out)			
Mixed physical attractiveness	12.31**	.24	20.77**	.31
Mixed physical attractiveness with warning	13.24**	.25	4.64*	.15
General attractiveness	66.36**	.50	22.37**	.32
	Predictor: Pure physical attractiveness (sex and pure vocal attractiveness are partialed out)			
Mixed vocal attractiveness	19.45**	.30	19.76**	.30
Mixed vocal attractiveness with warning	19.30**	.30	6.56*	.18
General attractiveness	181.20**	.64	289.05**	.77

[a] F test of the increment in variance accounted for. The df values vary from (1,198) to (1,196), depending on the number of variables in the equation.
[b] Partial correlations between predictor and dependent variable.
*$p < .05$.
**$p < .001$.

The results (see Table 9.5) show significant cross-channel effects for both physical and vocal attractiveness. Specifically, when that portion of the variance in mixed attractiveness that is due to actual (i.e., pure) attractiveness of the same channel was partialed out, a significant portion of the remaining variance was accounted for by the actual (i.e., pure) attractiveness of the cross channel. For example, a portion of the variance of mixed physical attractiveness was accounted for by pure vocal attractiveness after sex and pure physical attractiveness were partialed out; for Study 1, $F(1,197) = 12.31$, $p < .001$, $r = .24$; for Study 2, $F(1,197) = 20.77$, $p < .001$, $r = .31$ (see the first row in Table 9.5). The warning failed to eliminate cross-channel effects, although it did reduce their magnitude in Study 2. Finally, both physical and vocal attractiveness contributed to impressions of general attractiveness, although the contribution of physical attractiveness seemed somewhat greater than that of vocal attractiveness.

The existence of cross-channel effects gives rise to two predictions concerning the effects of attractiveness on interpersonal impressions. Because impressions of mixed attractiveness are influenced by pure attractiveness of the cross channel, they must differ from impressions of pure attractiveness of the same channel. Specifically, impressions of mixed vocal attractiveness are not the same as impressions of pure vocal attractiveness, and impressions of mixed physical attractiveness are not the same as impressions of pure physical attractiveness. If pure and mixed attractiveness differ, pure attractiveness should exert stronger influence on personality impressions in the single channel (where personality impressions are derived from pure attractiveness) than on personality impressions in the visual-auditory channel (where personality impressions are derived from mixed attractiveness). This prediction received strong support by the findings reported in Table 9.1. In every instance, the effect of pure attractiveness on personality impressions in the single channel (auditory condition or visual condition) was stronger than the corresponding effect in the visual-auditory condition.

The complementary prediction is that personality impressions in the visual-auditory condition will be more influenced by mixed vocal and mixed physical attractiveness (from which they are derived) than by pure vocal and pure physical attractiveness. To examine this prediction, it was necessary to conduct two analyses. In the first analysis, mean personality ratings obtained in Study 1 and Study 2 by Zuckerman and Driver (1989) were regressed on sex and then on pure vocal attractiveness and pure physical attractiveness (the latter two predictors were entered together in the second step). The results showed that the contributions of pure vocal plus pure physical attractiveness to the proportion of variance accounted for (squared semipartial correlations) were .37 in Study 1 and .18 in Study 2 (p's $< .001$). In the second analysis, the same mean personality ratings were regressed on sex and then on mixed vocal attractiveness and mixed physical attractiveness (the latter two predictors were entered together in the second step). The results showed that the contributions of mixed vocal plus mixed physical attractiveness to the proportion of variance accounted for were .52 in Study 1 and .30 in Study 2 (p's $< .001$). Clearly, in a visual-auditory condition, the mixed attractiveness measures did a better job than the pure attractiveness measures.

It can be concluded that the optimal predictor of personality impressions is the type of attractiveness from which these impressions are derived. Accordingly, pure attractiveness is a better predictor of personality impressions in single-channel conditions than in the visual-auditory situation; and in a visual-auditory situation, mixed attractiveness is a better predictor of personality impressions than is pure attractiveness.

One or two stereotypes

The studies reviewed suggest that attractiveness is not only a property of the face but also a feature of the voice. People distinguish reliably between attractive and unattractive voices. Furthermore, variables affected by physical attractiveness (e.g., personality impressions, perceived similarity, affiliation, and social comparison) are similarly influenced by vocal attractiveness. Finally, in a visual-auditory situation the perception of vocal attractiveness is influenced by the target's physical attractiveness, the perception of physical attractiveness is influenced by the target's vocal attractiveness, and the perception of general attractiveness is influenced by both physical and vocal attractiveness. Clearly, a vocal attractiveness stereotype exists alongside a physical attractiveness stereotype.

It is more difficult to determine whether the two stereotypes are two aspects of the same phenomenon or two separate constructs. In support of the former view, the two stereotypes seem to operate in a synergistic fashion. Specifically, the joint effect of vocal and physical attractiveness was such that perceivers distinguished between targets high on both vocal and physical attractiveness and all other targets. For example, in the Miyake and Zuckerman (in press) study, targets were rated more positively only if they were high on both vocal and physical attractiveness. Targets high on one of the two attractiveness types were not rated more positively than targets who were low on both. In addition, the Zuckerman and Hodgins (1991) study showed that the synergistic pattern is acquired; attractiveness effects in early ages seem to follow an additive pattern.

The synergistic pattern implies that for observers attractiveness is a unitary concept. Stated differently, observers tend to combine vocal and physical attractiveness into a single entity. They see a target as attractive when he or she is high on both attractiveness channels; they see a target as unattractive when he or she is low on one or both attractiveness channels.

There is also support, however, for the view that vocal and physical attractiveness operate separately. First, different personality dimensions were influenced by each type of attractiveness. The effect of physical attractiveness was high for extraversion and low for conscientiousness; the effect of vocal attractiveness was high for conscientiousness and low for agreeableness. Furthermore, the two stereotypes follow different developmental trends. The effect of physical attractiveness declines with age, whereas the effect of vocal attractiveness first increases and then stabilizes. Clearly, then, vocal and physical attractiveness are neither components of a single entity nor completely independent. Early in life they function as two separate attributes. Later, people learn to combine their effects synergistically, but they apparently retain a degree of independence: Related yet separate may be the best way to describe these two stereotypes.

On the self-fulfilling prophecy of attractiveness

Earlier we noted that physical attractiveness may elicit self-fulfilling effects in the laboratory but not in real life. Such findings are consistent with our previous suggestion that people are aware of their own level of attractiveness, as well as of the effects of attractiveness on interpersonal impressions. Awareness that personality impressions are based on attractiveness may lead people to discount them. Indeed, the age-related reduction in the effects of physical attractiveness seems to indicate that the older the perceiver, the greater the discounting. If adult perceivers minimize the value of attractiveness-based impressions, so can the targets of the impressions. Sigall and Michela (1976) and Major, Carrington, and Carnevale (1984) showed that female targets discounted praise when they had reason to believe that its source saw them as physically attractive (see also Crocker & Major, 1989). It is plausible that in real life attractiveness-based impressions would appear suspect and, hence, fail to elicit a self-fulfilling process. The latter can occur in the laboratory (Snyder et al., 1977) because there attractiveness is experimentally manipulated. Stated differently, the targets in the Snyder et al. study had no reason to believe that the treatment they received was due to their level of attractiveness. Thus, those targets who were treated in a more friendly manner had no reason to discount the perceiver's friendliness and, therefore, responded in kind.

Earlier we suggested that people are not aware of their own level of vocal attractiveness and of the effects of vocal attractiveness on interpersonal impressions. If targets are not aware that the treatment they receive is due to vocal attractiveness, they will be less likely to discount it. Clearly, the next topic of research should be the self-fulfilling prophecy of both the physical and vocal attractiveness stereotypes. When examined separately, each type of attractiveness may exercise a self-fulfilling effect in the laboratory, but only vocal attractiveness may exercise such an effect in real life. Once again, however, it is not entirely clear that the two stereotypes work separately. Perhaps research on the self-fulfilling effect may again produce a synergistic pattern. That is, only those with attractive faces *and* attractive voices receive special treatment and stand to benefit from it.

Note

The research reported in this chapter was supported in part by National Institute of Mental Health Grant RO1 MH40498.

References

Addington, D. W. (1968). The relationship of selected vocal characteristics to personality perception. *Speech Monographs, 35,* 492–503.

Allport, G. W., & Cantril, H. (1934). Judging personality from voice. *Journal of Social Psychology, 5,* 37–54.

Aronovitch, C. D. (1976). The voice of personality: Stereotyped judgments and their relation to voice quality and sex of speaker. *The Journal of Social Psychology, 99,* 202–207.

Benson, P. L., Karabenick, S. A., & Lerner, R. M. (1976). Pretty please: The effects of physical attractiveness, race, and sex on receiving help. *Journal of Experimental Social Psychology, 12,* 409–415.

Berscheid, E., & Walster, E. (1974). Physical attractiveness. In L. Berkowitz (Ed.), *Advances in experimental social psychology* (Vol. 7, pp. 158–215). New York: Academic Press.

Byrne, D. (1971). *The attraction paradigm.* New York: Academic Press.

Costa, P. T., Jr., & McCrae, R. R. (1980). Still stable after all these years: Personality as a key to some issues in adulthood and old age. In P. B. Baltes & O. G. Brim, Jr. (Eds.), *Life span development and behavior* (Vol. 3, pp. 65–102). New York: Academic Press.

Costa, P. T., Jr., & McCrae, R. R. (1985). *The NEO Personality Inventory manual.* Odessa, FL: Psychological Assessment Resources.

Costa, P. T., Jr., & McCrae, R. R. (1988). From catalog to classification: Murray's needs and the five-factor model. *Journal of Personality and Social Psychology, 55,* 258–265.

Crocker, J., & Major, B. (1989). Social stigma and self-esteem: The self-protective properties of stigma. *Psychological Review, 96,* 608–630.

DePaulo, B. M., Rosenthal, R., Eisenstat, R. A., Rogers, P. L., & Finkelstein, S. (1978). Decoding discrepant nonverbal cues. *Journal of Personality and Social Psychology, 36,* 313–323.

Dion, K. K., & Berscheid, E. (1974). Physical attractiveness and peer perception among children. *Sociometry, 37*, 1–12.

Dion, K., Berscheid, E., & Walster, E. (1972). What is beautiful is good. *Journal of Personality and Social Psychology, 245*, 285–290.

Driver, R. (1987). *The voice in person perception: An investigation of the vocal attractiveness stereotype.* Unpublished doctoral dissertation, University of Rochester.

Festinger, L. (1954). A theory of social comparison processes. *Human Relations, 7*, 117–140.

Goethals, G., & Darley, J. (1977). Social comparison theory: An attributional approach. In J. M. Suls & R. L. Miller (Eds.), *Social comparison processes: Theoretical and empirical perspectives* (pp. 259–278). New York: Halsted.

Hatfield, E., & Sprecher, S. (1986). *Mirror, mirror . . . the importance of looks in everyday life.* Albany: State University of New York Press.

Kenny, D. A., Horner, C., Kashy, D. A., & Chu, L. (1992). Consensus at zero acquaintance: Replication, behavioral cues, and stability. *Journal of Personality and Social Psychology, 62*, 88–97.

Kleck, R. E., Richardson, S. A., & Ronald, L. (1974). Physical appearance cues and interpersonal attraction in children. *Child Development, 45*, 305–310.

Kramer, E. (1964). Personality stereotypes in voice: A reconsideration of the data. *The Journal of Social Psychology, 62*, 247–251.

Krebs, D., & Adinolphi, A. A. (1975). Physical attractiveness, social relations, and personality style. *Journal of Personality and Social Psychology, 31*, 245–253.

Langlois, J. H., Ritter, J. M., Roggman, L. A., & Vaughn, L. S. (1991). Facial diversity and infant preferences for attractive faces. *Developmental Psychology, 27*, 79–84.

Langlois, J. H., Roggman, L. A., Casey, R. J., Ritter, J. M., Rieser-Danner, L. A., & Jenkins, V. Y. (1987). Infant preferences for attractive faces: Rudiments of a stereotype? *Developmental Psychology, 23*, 363–369.

McCrae, R. R. (1982). Consensual validation of personality traits: Evidence from self-reports and ratings. *Journal of Personality and Social Psychology, 43*, 293–303.

McCrae, R. R., & Costa, P. T., Jr. (1983). Joint factors in self-reports and ratings: Neuroticism, extraversion, and openness to experience. *Personality and Individual Differences, 4*, 245–255.

McCrae, R. R., & Costa, P. T., Jr. (1985a). Openness to experience. In R. Hogan & W. H. Jones (Eds.), *Perspectives in personality: Theory, measurement, and interpersonal dynamics* (Vol. 1, pp. 145–172). Greenwich, CT: JAI Press.

McCrae, R. R., & Costa, P. T., Jr. (1985b). Updating Norman's "adequate taxonomy": Intelligence and personality dimensions in natural language and in questionnaires. *Journal of Personality and Social Psychology, 49*, 710–721.

McCrae, R. R., & Costa, P. T., Jr. (1987). Validation of the five-factor model of personality across instruments and observers. *Journal of Personality and Social Psychology, 52*, 81–90.

Major, B., Carrington, P. I., & Carnevale, P. (1984). Physical attractiveness and self-esteem: Attributions to praise from an other-sex evaluator. *Personality and Social Psychology Bulletin, 10*, 43–50.

Marks, G., & Miller, N. (1982). Target attractiveness as a mediator of assumed attitude similarity. *Personality and Social Psychology Bulletin, 8*, 728–735.

Marks, G., & Miller, N. (1987). Ten years of research on the false consensus effect: An empirical and theoretical review. *Journal of Personality and Social Psychology, 102,* 72–90.

Marks, G., Miller, N., & Maruyama, G. (1981). Effect of targets' physical attractiveness on assumptions of similarity. *Journal of Personality and Social Psychology, 41,* 1986206.

Mashman, R. C. (1978). The effect of physical attractiveness on perception of attitude similarity. *Journal of Social Psychology, 106,* 103–110.

Miller, G. R., & Hewgill, M. A. (1964). The effect of variations in nonfluency on audience ratings of source credibility. *Quarterly Journal of Speech, 50,* 36–44.

Miyake, K., & Zuckerman, M. (in press). Beyond personality impressions: Effects of physical and vocal attractiveness on false consensus, social comparison, affiliation, and assumed and perceived similarity. *Journal of Personality.*

Mullen, B., Atkins, J., Champion, D. S., Edwards, C., Hardy, D., Story, J. E., & Vanderblok, M. (1985). The false consensus effect: A meta-analysis of 115 hypothesis tests. *Journal of Experimental Social Psychology, 21,* 262–283.

Norman, W. T. (1963). Toward an adequate taxonomy of personality attributes: Replicated factor structure in peer nomination personality ratings. *Journal of Abnormal and Social Psychology, 66,* 574–583.

Pearce, W. B., & Conklin, F. (1971). Nonverbal vocalic communication and perceptions of a speaker. *Speech Monographs, 38,* 235–241.

Rofe, Y. (1984). Stress affiliation: A utility theory. *Psychological Review, 91,* 235–250.

Rosenthal, R., Hall, J. A., DiMatteo, M. R., Rogers, P. L., & Archer, D. (1979). *Sensitivity to nonverbal communication: The PONS test.* Baltimore: Johns Hopkins University Press.

Ross, L., Greene, D., & House, P. (1977). The "false consensus effect": An egocentric bias in social perception and attribution. *Journal of Experimental Social Psychology, 13,* 279–301.

Samuels, C. A., & Ewy, R. (1985). Aesthetic perception of faces during infancy. *British Journal of Developmental Psychology, 3,* 221–228.

Scherer, K. R. (1972). Judging personality from voice: A cross-cultural approach to an old issue in inter-personal perception. *Journal of Personality, 40,* 191–210.

Scherer, K. R. (1974a). Acoustic concomitants of emotional dimensions: Judging affect from synthesized tone sequences. In S. Weitz (Ed.), *Nonverbal communication* (pp. 249–253). New York: Oxford University Press.

Scherer, K. R. (1974b). Voice quality analysis of American and German speakers. *Journal of Psycholinguistic Research, 3,* 281–297.

Scherer, K. R. (1979). Voice and speech correlates of perceived social influence. In H. Giles & R. N. St. Clair (Eds.), *Language and social psychology* (pp. 88–120). London: Arnold.

Scherer, K. R. (1986). Vocal affect expression: A review and a model for future research. *Psychological Bulletin, 99,* 143–165.

Scherer, K. R., & Oshinsky, J. (1977). Cue utilization in emotion attribution from auditory stimuli. *Motivation and Emotion, 1,* 331–346.

Sereno, K. K., & Hawkins, G. J. (1967). The effects of variations in speakers' nonfluency upon audience ratings of attitude toward the speech topic and speaker's credibility. *Speech Monographs, 34,* 58–64.

Shapiro, B. A., Hazan, C., & Haith, M. (1984, March). *Do infants differentiate attractiveness and expressiveness in faces?* Paper presented at the meeting of the Southwestern Society for Research in Human Development, Denver, CO.

Sigall, H., & Michela, J. (1976). I'll bet you say this to all the girls: Physical attractiveness and reactions to praise. *Journal of Personality, 44,* 611–626.

Smith, B. L., Brown, B. L., Strong, W. J., & Rencher, A. C. (1975). Effects of speech rate on personality perception. *Language and Speech, 18,* 145–152.

Snyder, M. (1974). Self-monitoring of expressive behavior. *Journal of Personality and Social Psychology, 30,* 526–537.

Snyder, M. (1979). Self-monitoring processes. In L. Berkowitz (Ed.), *Advances in experimental social psychology* (Vol. 12, pp. 85–128). New York: Academic Press.

Snyder, M., Berscheid, E., & Glick, P. (1985). Focusing on the exterior and the interior: Two investigations of the initiation of personality relationships. *Journal of Personality and Social Psychology, 48,* 1427–1439.

Snyder, M., Tanke, E., & Berscheid, E. (1977). Social perception and interpersonal behavior. On the self-fulfilling nature of social stereotypes. *Journal of Personality and Social Psychology, 35,* 58–64.

Sorell, G. T., & Nowak, C. A. (1981). The role of physical attractiveness as a contributor of individual development. In R. M. Lerner & N. A. Busch-Rossnagel (Eds.), *Individuals as producers of their development: A life-span perspective* (pp. 389–446). New York: Academic Press.

Suls, J. M. (1977). Social comparison theory and research: An overview from 1954. In J. M. Suls & R. L. Miller (Eds.), *Social comparison processes: Theoretical and empirical perspectives* (pp. 3–19). New York: Halsted.

Taylor, S. E., & Lobel, M. (1989). Social comparison activity under threat. *Psychological Review, 96,* 569–575.

Tupes, E. C., & Christal, R. E. (1961). Recurrent personality factors based on trait ratings. *USAF ASD Technical Report* (No. 61-97).

Walster, E., Aronson, V., Abrahams, D., & Rottman, L. (1966). Importance of physical attractiveness in dating behavior. *Journal of Personality and Social Psychology, 4,* 508–516.

Zuckerman, M., & Driver, R. (1989). What sounds beautiful is good: The vocal attractiveness stereotype. *Journal of Nonverbal Behavior, 13,* 67–82.

Zuckerman, M., & Hodgins, H. S. (1991). *Developmental changes in the effects of the physical and vocal attractiveness stereotypes.* Unpublished manuscript, University of Rochester.

Zuckerman, M., Hodgins, H. S., & Miyake, K. (1990). The vocal attractiveness stereotype: Replication and elaboration. *Journal of Nonverbal Behavior, 14,* 97–112.

Zuckerman, M., Larrance, D. T., Spiegel, N. H., & Klorman, R. (1981). Controlling nonverbal displays: Facial expressions and tone of voice. *Journal of Experimental Social Psychology, 17,* 506–524.

Zuckerman, M., Miyake, K., & Hodgins, H. S. (1991). Cross-channel effects of vocal and physical attractiveness and their implications for interpersonal perception. *Journal of Personality and Social Psychology, 60,* 545–554.

10. In search of a social fact: A commentary on the study of interpersonal expectations

HARRIS COOPER

The expectations of one person influence the behavior of another, typically in a confirming direction. I would like to make three points about this statement. First, I argue that no other single hypothesis better captures the essence and spirit of social psychology. Second, I consider reasons why the expectation hypothesis has generated such an enormous amount of research across seemingly diverse fields. Third, I contend that the expectancy hypothesis is not a hypothesis at all but is rather a social fact, and a scientifically proven one at that.

The quintessential social hypothesis

According to Gordon Allport (1985), social psychology is the study of "how the thought, feeling, and behavior of individuals are influenced by the actual, imagined, or implied presence of others" (p. 3). One would be hard pressed to find a topic more archetypal of social psychology than interpersonal expectancy effects. Mind is the instigator of the expectancy process, yet the phenomenon itself involves some *transfer* between persons. Anyone who has struggled to define the proper unit for the statistical analysis of an expectancy study has grappled with the true heart of social psychology ("Is the teacher my unit of analysis, or the teacher–student dyad? Perhaps it is the number of classrooms that dictates my degrees of freedom?").

In addition, Kurt Lewin, a central influence on the development of social psychology, wrote:

> [Close cooperation between theoretical and applied psychology] can be accomplished . . . if the theorist does not look toward applied problems with highbrow aversion or with a fear of social problems and if the applied psychologist realizes that there is nothing as practical as a good theory. (Lewin, 1951, p. 169)

218

Few groups of social psychologists can claim to have taken Lewin's admonition to heart as have interpersonal expectations researchers. In the preceding pages we have seen how theory and practice can interact in the courtroom, classroom, workplace, and doctor's office, and between the races and genders.

The pervasiveness of expectation research

Why have expectancy phenomena generated interest across so many fields? Four features of expectations and the expectation hypothesis initially come to mind.

First, the concept of *expectation* is drawn from everyday language. Many social psychological concepts meet this criteria (*attitude, attraction*) whereas many others do not. Certainly, those concepts that are in the first instance part of everyday speech rather than the jargon of a discipline, and therefore are understood without specialized training, are easiest for researchers in other disciplines to evaluate for relevance to the particular circumstance of interest to them.

Conversely, the term *self-fulfilling prophecy* (having been coined by Robert Merton, 1948) was not part of everyday language initially but it made its way into common usage because of its utility (*cognitive dissonance* is another bit of social psychological jargon that has accomplished this feat, but certainly not to the extent of Merton's term). Numerous related concepts did exist in everyday language, including for example, as Friedman (this volume) points out, "faith-healing" in health. Also, the phenomena had been observed in many applied contexts but had not yet found a label, including for example, as Blanck (this volume) points out, the courtroom (*State v. Wheat*, 1930). Rosenthal (1985) identified discussion of experimenter expectancy phenomena dating back to 1885. Twenty years before Merton coined the term self-fulfilling prophecy, Thomas and Thomas (1928) wrote that if men define situations as real, then they are real in their consequences.

A second reason for the scope of interest in the expectation hypothesis is that it is simple, yet abstract. With the expectation hypothesis as the main premise, specific predictions are easy to make. Predictions also come, at least initially, as main effects. More important, the expectation hypothesis is conceptual, that is, it is not tied to any particular time or space. Its relevance can be seen whenever two people meet, regardless of their roles or surroundings. Much like the idea of *gravity* in physics, the expectation hypothesis focuses the intellect on a common element in what on the surface seem to be disparate phenomena (falling apples, planetary motions in physics; doctors and patients, African-Americans and whites in social psychology).

Of course, it can be argued that many social hypotheses meet this criteria. Therefore, I would suggest these are necessary but not sufficient criteria for a hypothesis to generate hundreds of studies across numerous disciplines. A third ingredient called for is controversy. Controversy generates attention and the expectation hypothesis generated more than its share of controversy. It is indeed rare for social psychological studies to receive coverage on the front page of the *New York Times*, as did the Rosenthal and Jacobson (1968) *Pygmalion in the Classroom* study (August 8, 1967).

Although the methodological controversy that surrounded *Pygmalion* added to its visibility, I think the contention it engendered stemmed from something much more fundamental. In essence, *Pygmalion* revealed that a cultural icon of fairness and equity, namely, the American classroom, might be flawed. (Experimenter expectancy research had observed this earlier within the small scientific public.) *Pygmalion* suggested that school performance and grades, and even something so seemingly immutable as intelligence, might not be the sole product of a student's ability and effort, but might also be the product of the teacher's predilections and, yes, prejudices. Given the cultural upheaval of the late 1960s, the appearance of *Pygmalion* could not have occurred at a more propitious time. Its exportation to analogous contexts, where the meritocracy hinged at some level on interpersonal judgment, was assured, and almost immediate.

Anyone who has approached a school principal or factory manager and asked their permission to perform an expectancy study in their workplace has sensed the implied threat the hypothesis holds for the subjects of study. It is often necessary to reassure potential site managers that expectation effects are not unique to their building or profession; expectation effects are part of the human condition. Assuring anonymity helps as well.

Today, the imperfect nature of American meritocracies is less controversial (though no teacher, judge, or manager wants to be the next object lesson) and expectation research is more often cast in the role of productivity-enhancer. "If we can only teach people about the effects of interpersonal expectations," it is argued, "then we can harness the power of expectations to help each student or worker fulfill their potential." Yet, Babad (this volume) outlines several good reasons why interventions in the expectation process have lagged behind demonstrations of the phenomena and its mediating mechanisms. I would add to his list the lack of controversy in performing such interventions. More attention goes to those who show a problem exists and why it exists, as opposed to those who attempt to solve it.

The fourth ingredient contributing to the widespread, sustained interest in interpersonal expectations research involves the attributes of its central figure, Robert Rosenthal. Not only has he personally contributed to the research base for three decades, but he has also advanced the field theoretically, trained and inspired numerous young researchers to pursue expectancy topics, and acted as a conduit of information open to any individual interested in the area. Further, he has done so with grace, openness, high professional standards, and a smile.

Is the self-fulfilling prophecy a social fact?

I have argued elsewhere that the interpersonal expectancy effect could be elevated from the status of a hypothesis to that of a social fact (Cooper, 1984). My argument was based on the distinction between method and theory. I contended that most of the prescriptions found in social research methods texts are based on principles of logic, casual ordering, and statistical assumption. The experimenter expectancy effect, in contrast, appears in methods texts because of its repeated observation in so many different experimental contexts. It is as if the scientific community had agreed that evidence for the expectancy effect was so strong and its influence so pervasive that researchers needed to take special precautions *not* to have them obfuscate the study of other things. I wrote, "what is uncertain is theory and uncollected data, what is 'proven' becomes methodology" (Cooper, 1984, p. 64).

Is the expectation hypothesis accepted by all? Although many remain skeptical (and that is good) one would be hard pressed to find a scholar who answers this question flatly "no." Theodore X. Barber, perhaps the most visible critic of the experimenter expectancy literature, wrote, "At times, but much less often than implied . . . , experimenters unwittingly transmit their expectancies and desires to their subjects, influencing them so as to confirm their expectancies" (Barber, 1978, p. 389).

Likewise, most critics of the teacher expectation literature do not take issue with the viability of the proposition but rather with the adequacy of the research available to support it. The best known of these critiques are summarized by Rosenthal (1985). Since the publication of Rosenthal and Rubin's (1978) meta-analysis of 345 interpersonal expectancy studies, the "existence" dispute has abated. The attention of researchers has shifted to examinations of how expectancy effects operate (a common progression of research in all scientific domains).

Thus, the debate seemed to be not so much over the *existence* of expectancy effects but rather over their *generality* and the *quality* of our evidence for them. Of course, I do not mean to imply that even critics implicitly accept the extreme position that the expectation hypothesis qualifies as a social fact. However, the parameters of the debate are perhaps narrower than the scholar with casual interest in the field might first assume.

Still, the question of generality must be addressed if a good case is to be made for the proposition that the expectancy phenomena is a law of human behavior. Evidence for *situational* generality is provided by the preceding chapters. *Cultural* generality is attested to by the diverse countries in which expectancy phenomena have been demonstrated, including the United States, Canada, England, Northern Ireland, Australia, Israel, the Netherlands, the former Soviet Union, the West Indies, Pakistan, and India (R. Rosenthal, personal communication, January 14, 1992). Finally, *temporal* generality is attested to by the ancient myths that have given expectation effects their name. *Pygmalion* derives from Greek mythology; *Golem* derives from Jewish mythology (Babad, Inbar, & Rosenthal, 1982). Clearly, the idea has been with us for some time.

Finally, the progression of topics examined in expectancy effect research seems prototypical of the pattern followed by most programs of study in the physical, life, and social sciences. Initial interest springs from a simple observation, and often a fortuitous one. Rosenthal (1985) relates that his curiosity about the experimenter expectancy effect arose when he "did a statistical analysis that was quite extraneous to the main purpose" of his dissertation (p. 39). Systematic study of the phenomenon then occurs, involving controlled experimentation in particular. After the existence of the phenomena has been established, scientists undertake an appraisal of its generality. These steps are well documented in the preceding chapters. Next, the *micromediating* processes that intervene between the independent and dependent variables become the focus of study (Cook & Campbell, 1979). Typically, this involves the placement of numerous steps into a temporal sequence and a reduction in the size of units of analysis. For example, the observation that "heat causes wood to flame" becomes "heat causes a chemical reaction between oxygen and carbon, the creation of carbon dioxide releases energy that causes flame." In expectancy research, we find "expectancies cause certain expecter behaviors and these behaviors cause changes in expectees." The introduction of Rosenthal's four factor model is an example of this process. Not only does behavior mediate the expectancy communication process but the units of behavior studied have also grown smaller as the theory has grown more sophisticated. Thus, Zuckerman, Hodgins, and Miyake (this volume) examined fine-grained vocal characteristics for their ability to communicate expectancies.

Conclusion

I have tried to make the case that the study of interpersonal expectation effects exemplifies the best that social psychology has to offer. It is clearly both social and psychological in nature, it is relevant to many circumstances, it has captured the public imagination, and it approaches the status of a social scientific law. In making my case, I admit to some hyperbole. Still, it seems we (social scientists) often sell ourselves short. No need. There is great value and scientific rigor in what we do. Take, for example, the study of interpersonal expectancy effects.

References

Allport, G. W. (1985). The historical background of social psychology. In G. Lindsey & E. Aronson (Eds.), *The handbook of social psychology* (3rd ed.). New York: Random House.

Babad, E. Y., Inbar, J., & Rosenthal, R. (1982). Pygmalion, Galatea, and the Golem: Investigations of biased and unbiased teachers. *Journal of Educational Psychology, 74,* 459–474.

Barber, T. X. (1978). Expecting expectancy effects: Biased data analysis and failure to exclude alternative interpretations in experimenter expectancy research. *The Behavioral and Brain Sciences, 3,* 388–390.

Cook, T. D., & Campbell, D. T. (1979). *Quasi-experimentation: Design and analysis issues for field settings.* Chicago: Rand McNally.

Cooper, H. M. (1984). Methodology as the depository of social facts. *Contemporary Social Psychology, 10,* 63–64.

Lewin, K. (1951). *Field theory in social science.* Chicago: University of Chicago Press.

Merton, R. K. (1948). The self-fulfilling prophecy. *Antioch Review, 8,* 193–210.

Rosenthal, R. (1985). From unconscious experimenter bias to teacher expectancy effects. In J. B. Dusek (Ed.), *Teacher expectations.* Hillsdale, NJ: Erlbaum.

Rosenthal, R., & Jacobson, E. (1968). *Pygmalion in the classroom.* New York: Holt, Rinehart & Winston.

Rosenthal, R., & Rubin, D. B. (1978). Interpersonal expectancy effects: The first 345 studies. *The Behavioral and Brain Sciences, 3*, 377–386.

State v. Wheat. 131 Kan. 562, 569, 292 P. 793 797 (1930).

Thomas, W., & Thomas, D. (1928). *The child in America*. New York: Knopf.

Research on the mediation of interpersonal expectations through nonverbal behavior

11. The spontaneous communication of interpersonal expectations

ROSS BUCK

To a graduate student in a program of experimental social psychology in the 1960s, few studies were more significant than Robert Rosenthal's (1966, 1967) analysis of the effects of experimenter expectations in psychological research. It was a revelation: The responses of subjects to carefully defined and manipulated variables could be affected by mysterious forces of *covert communication* set into motion by subtle and poorly understood *expectations*. Even in such apparently simple and straightforward experiments as obtaining judgments of photographs of faces and running rats in a maze, the expectations of experimenters were somehow inadvertently leading their subjects to show the responses expected.

Later came another revelation: that such expectations not only affected behavior in the laboratory but also had powerful and significant effects in real life: The Rosenthal and Jacobson (1968) demonstration of the power of teachers' expectations in creating self-fulfilling prophecies affecting the achievement and even perhaps the apparent intelligence of their students remains one of the major contributions of the social sciences to our culture, even though our culture, and indeed the social sciences, have yet to respond adequately to its implications. The Rosenthal and Jacobson result created controversy (Jensen, 1969; Thorndike, 1968), but subsequent studies replicated their findings beyond a reasonable doubt (Harris & Rosenthal, 1985; Babad, this volume). Moreover, other studies demonstrated the power of the covert communication process in socially relevant settings: in the vocal patterns of a physician referring patients for further treatment, for example (Milmoe, Rosenthal, Blane, Chafetz, & Wolf, 1967), or in the nonverbal behavior of a judge during a criminal jury trial (Blanck, Rosenthal, & Cordell, 1985; Blanck, this volume).

The response to the evidence of socially relevant self-fulfilling prophecies being created in a mysterious covert communication process by such insubstantial things as expectations has been curious. Among experimental social psychologists, perhaps the dominant response was to scramble for ways to control the demand characteristics in their experiments by presenting instructions via tape recording, minimizing face-to-face contact between experimenter and subject, and in general making many experimental situations better controlled but also perhaps more artificial and contrived than they had been before. This allowed experimenters to continue to study phenomena that had always been of interest – social influence, causal attribution, person perception, social cognition, and the like – from the point of view of familiar, cognitively based approaches. The basic assumptions underlying these approaches, which arguably were called into question by the very mystery of the power exerted by expectations in the covert communication process, went unexamined.

Another, less common, response was to ask how expectations came to have such power; to inquire into the mystery of their effects. Robert Rosenthal from the beginning recognized that these effects were exerted primarily via nonverbal communication: by vocal intonations, facial expressions, and bodily movements that are largely involuntary and unintended. Moreover, he was one of the first to find ways to measure the covert communication process: both the nonverbal behaviors by which the covert messages are sent and the patterns of sensitivity to such cues on the part of the receiver. There resulted some of the most theoretically significant, and at the same time most socially relevant, findings in psychology.

Part II of this volume collects some of the most recent efforts to analyze how interpersonal expectations are mediated by nonverbal behavior. Dane Archer, Robin Akert, and Mark Costanzo examine the process of interpersonal perception from this point of view, and Bella DePaulo takes up the issue of whether we can communicate high expectations nonverbally if we try to do so. Judith Hall and Nancy Briton examine the issue of gender differences in the operation of expectations via nonverbal behavior, and M. Robin DiMatteo discusses the role of nonverbally communicated expectations in the physician–patient relationship.

My goal in this introduction is not to summarize or review these individual contributions; instead, I examine the nature of the covert communication process itself. My thesis is that the covert communication process identified by Robert Rosenthal is in fact a biologically based process involving the spontaneous communication of motivational/ emotional states: desires (or expectations) and feelings. I define and discuss spontaneous communication and then go on to point out several relevant areas of research – particularly in the neurosciences – that speak to the nature of this process. These include studies of the initial response to events, of perceptual preattunements, of the brain mechanisms underlying vocalization in monkeys, and of the emotional communication mechanisms of the right cerebral hemisphere.

The communication of motivation/emotion

The nature of emotion

Cognitive and physiological factors in emotion. One of the most influential theories of emotion in the social sciences is the self-attribution theory of Schachter and Singer (1962), which views emotion as the product of an interaction between physiological arousal and cognitive explanations for that arousal. Schachter and Singer argued that a state of arousal induced by an injection of epinephrine (adrenalin) could be manipulated into anger or euphoria by cognitive factors. This basic idea had been presented earlier by Gustave Maranon (1924) and Bertrand Russell (1927/1961). Thus, in 1927, Russell reflected on his experience with an injection of epinephrine during a dental procedure: He felt the same bodily reactions he felt when experiencing a strong emotion, but he did not really experience an emotion. He concluded that there are two determinants of emotion: physiological changes and appropriate cognition: "In normal life . . . there is always a cognitive element present . . . But when [epinephrine] is artificially administered, this cognitive element is absent, and the emotion in its entirety fails to arise" (Russell, 1927/1961, p. 227).

It is often assumed that the experiential qualities that differentiate emotions are based upon cognitive factors: that anger and euphoria, for example, are similar physiologically and that their differences are based upon cognitive factors. However, there has always been a recognition that there are limits to the extent to which cognition can influence experience: Schachter (1964), for example, acknowledged that "it is unlikely that anyone with undiagnosed peritonitis could ever be convinced that he is euphoric, high, or anything but deathly ill" (p. 79). Russell (1927/1961) went further: "There are, however, other emotions, such as melancholy, which do not demand an object. These, presum-

ably, can be caused in their entirety by administering the proper secre-
tions" (p. 227).

Emotion as cognition. Recent research on the physiological bases of
emotion makes it clear that specifiable neurochemical systems are involved in different emotions, and that the body in fact contributes not
only undifferentiated arousal but structured information to the organism. Indeed, specific neuropeptides have been linked directly with the
experiences of at least euphoria, pain, fear/anger, and hunger. The
subjective experiences associated with emotion contribute a kind of
cognition – a kind of knowledge – to the organism.

It is this sort of emotional cognition, I suggest, that mediates the
effects of interpersonal expectations. Motivational/emotional systems
exist as neurochemical systems that are preattuned to respond to the
nuances of expressive behavior – the tone of voice, the momentary
facial expression, the flash of an eye – and to alter behavioral tendencies
accordingly. These responses are carried by the covert communication
process recognized by Rosenthal, which I have defined formally as
spontaneous communication (Buck, 1984; Buck & Duffy, 1980).

Spontaneous communication

Communication is usually defined as involving a sender encoding
meaning into symbols that are sent along a channel to a receiver, who
decodes the symbols and extracts the meaning. The elements of this
process are symbols, which bear arbitrary relationships with their referents (e.g., the relationship between the English word *tree* and the object
is arbitrary). This *symbolic* communication is based upon learning: Both
sender and receiver must have learned the meaning of the symbols for
communication to occur. Also, it is assumed that the encoding is intentional at some level on the part of the sender. Such communication is
propositional in the sense that a proposition is a statement capable of
logical analysis (Russell, 1903). The simplest sort of logical analysis is
the test for truth or falsity, so a proposition is a statement that can be,
in principle, false.

Symbolic communication is an overt process involving an intended
message. It is accompanied by a covert communication process that
carries the unintended effects of expectations. The latter is spontaneous
communication, and it differs from symbolic communication in the
following respects. First, the elements of spontaneous communication

are biologically structured intention movements or displays reflecting motivational/emotional states. These are not symbols but rather *signs* that bear natural relationships with such states. They are socially accessible aspects of the motivational/emotional states, just as the darkness of clouds is an externally accessible aspect of their moisture content in the statement "Dark clouds are a sign of rain." Second, because signs are aspects of their referents, they cannot exist if the referent is absent, so that by definition they cannot be false. Thus, spontaneous communication is nonpropositional. Third, spontaneous communication is unintended: The tendency to display is phylogenetically determined. Fourth, the spontaneous communication process is biologically based in both its sending and receiving aspects: The meaning of the intention movement or display is determined by evolution and is known directly by the receiver as a kind of inherited knowledge. In this sense, spontaneous communication is *direct*, involving no intentional encoding or decoding process.

Spontaneous communication is a species-specific communication system characteristic of human beings that includes expressive displays constituting social affordances that, given attention, activate emotional preattunements and are directly perceived by the receiver. The meaning of these displays is known directly by the receiver, just as, given attention, the feel of one's shoe on one's foot is known directly. This spontaneous motivational/emotional communication system constitutes, as it were, a *conversation between limbic systems* that occurs simultaneously and interactively with both verbal and nonverbal symbolic communication. The displays and preattunements on which spontaneous emotional communication is based have evolved as phylogenetic adaptations. This biologically based communication system involves human beings *directly* with one another: The individuals in spontaneous communication constitute literally a biological unit (Buck & Ginsburg, 1991). It might be noted that spontaneous communication does not function at the level of reflexes and instincts, as some have averred. Although it is in itself a "special-purpose system" that is based upon phylogenetic adaptation, it functions at a level in the hierarchy of control systems in the brain where there is considerable interaction with "general-purpose systems" involving conditioning, learning, and higher-order cognition, and consequently great flexibility of functioning (see Buck, 1985, 1988a).

This interaction with general-purpose systems ensures that spontaneous communication does not function reflexively, as it does, for example, in the social insects. Rather, human beings can inhibit and control intention movements and displays in many ways, including the voluntary expression initiation system considered later, in which we can voluntarily "put on" or pose the same "hard-wired" displays that are characteristic of emotion. Thus, we and other complex social animals are designed with the ability to lie emotionally with great effect: to look happy when we are seething with anger or sad when we are secretly pleased. As George Burns said, "The secret to being a good actor is honesty. If you can fake *that*, you've got it made." But as the effects of expectations demonstrate, our true feelings and desires can and do *leak* in many subtle and unintended ways.

The argument that the unintended effects of interpersonal expectations are mediated by a process of spontaneous communication can be illustrated and supported by recent work on the biological bases of emotional expression, perception, and communication. The following paragraphs review briefly several lines of research that are particularly relevant.

The initial processing of events

One of the major areas of controversy in contemporary theories of emotion concerns whether affect or cognition is primary in the organism's response to events. Zajonc (1980, 1984) argued for the primacy of affect, whereas Lazarus (1984) argued for cognition. The resolution of this controversy depends in great part on how one defines *cognition*: whether cognition can involve immediate perceptual knowledge (knowledge by acquaintance), or whether it requires more complex information processing (knowledge by description: Buck, 1988a, 1990). Recently, Lazarus (1991) has acknowledged the need to distinguish knowledge by acquaintance versus description. This largely defuses the controversy, for although it is clear that *some* sort of basic sensory or bodily information is necessary for the stimulation of motivational/emotional systems, it is also clear that affective processing may precede higher-level information processing.

The evidence for an affective "shortcut" in the initial processing of sensory events comes from the work of Joseph LeDoux and his colleagues on the neural pathways that signal the emotional significance of auditory stimuli (LeDoux, 1991). The classical auditory pathway proceeds from the cochlea, to auditory nuclei in the brainstem, to the inferior colliculus, to the medial geniculate body near the thalamus, and thence to the auditory cortex. LeDoux found that a parallel pathway, running from the thalamus to the amygdala, is responsible for the expression of emotional responses (freeze behavior and blood pressure increases) that have been conditioned to auditory stimulation. LeDoux (1991) argues that, in general, emotional responses can be initiated by the amygdala based upon primitive sensory representations derived relatively quickly from the thalamus, higher-order information derived more slowly from the cortex, or both.

It thus appears that there is an initial rapid response to emotional stimuli that can influence higher-order processing. The adaptive value of such a system is clear: "[E]motional processing systems . . . tend to use the minimal stimulus representation possible to activate emotional response control systems. . . . Emotional reactions . . . need to be executed with speed, and the use of a higher level of stimulus processing is maladaptive when a lower level will do. . . . The emotional system does not need to know everything about a stimulus before starting the emotional reaction" (LeDoux, 1991, p. 50). The implication for the communication of interpersonal expectations is that such expectations may derive their influence by affecting emotional processing systems with relatively little input from higher-order cortical systems. Instead, the effects of expectations in the receiver are initiated directly from the displays of the sender via perceptual preattunements.

Perceptual preattunements

An implication of the notion of spontaneous communication is that the process of receiving as well as of sending is based upon innate factors: Biologically based displays would be useless without corresponding preattunements to those displays on the part of receivers. This is consistent with the preceding evidence that emotional processing systems are sensitive to certain basic stimulus characteristics. Specifically, one might expect that displays embody the sorts of basic stimulus information needed to activate appropriate emotional responses: Thus a threatening, submissive, or courting display might be expected to be "picked up" by perceptual preattunements that activate appropriate sorts of emotional responses. Indeed, there is considerable evidence from a variety of sources of the reality of such preattunements.

One source of information comes from animal studies: It is clear that some stimuli (releasers) acquired significance during evolution and that the ability to respond appropriately to them involves a kind of innate knowledge. Thus it is the case that infant rhesus monkeys isolated from other monkeys since birth show appropriate fearful behavior when confronted with a photograph of an adult male monkey making a threat display (Sackett, 1966) and that a "hard stare" directed at a monkey will excite a response in the temporal lobe that is reduced if the stare is directed a few degrees away (Perrett, Rolls, & Caan, 1982). The extent to which the subcortical emotional response systems are independently involved in such responses is unclear: LeDoux (1991) argues that facial perception requires the involvement of the cortex. Certainly, the exploration of the brain mechanisms involved in the preattunements to emotional displays is a topic of great interest.

Studies of social perception in human beings have also found persuasive evidence for preattunements. For example, the feature of cardioidal strain has been identified as a sign of age: As the face matures, it is geometrically transformed in a way that preserves its structural invariants (Todd, Mark, Shaw, & Pittenger, 1980). This *slow event* provides the perceptual support for the identification of age (Shaw & Pittenger, 1977). Moreover, older persons who are "baby-faced" – whose facial appearance includes the large round eyes, high eyebrows, and small chin that are characteristic of infants – are perceived to be naive, honest, kind, and warm (Berry & McArthur, 1985, 1986, 1988). Similarly, persons with childlike voices are perceived to be weak, less competent, and warm; and those with youthful gaits to be more powerful and happy (Montepare & Zebrowitz-McArthur, 1987, 1988).

Whereas the evidence of the response to baby-facedness relates to the slow event of craniofacial change, there is also evidence of preattunements to the faster events involved in emotional displays. One of the simplest and most persuasive examples is that threatening faces "pop out" of crowds: When presented with photographs of persons showing characteristic facial displays, one picks out an angry face from a sea of happy or neutral faces much faster than one picks out a happy face from a sea of angry or neutral faces (Hansen & Hansen, 1988).

This evidence is consistent with a Gibsonian or ecological view of social perception in which the characteristics of people – their feelings and desires, traits, and relationships – are revealed in visual and auditory information that is directly perceived (Berry, 1990; Buck, 1984, 1988a; McArthur & Baron, 1983). The responses to such *social affordances* are not necessarily correct; the response to baby-facedness may be overgeneralized in that it inaccurately ascribes the characteristics of infants to adults – but they nevertheless exert powerful influences upon behavior. Such a conception of social perception is quite consistent with the power demonstrated by interpersonal expectations, which arguably are likewise based upon relatively direct responses to visual and auditory cues.

Neural mechanisms of vocalization

The studies we have considered on the process of spontaneous communication, the initial response to events, and perceptual preattunements have hopefully shed some light on the covert communication process underlying the effects of expectations. However, the objection is often heard that the process of spontaneous communication seems to imply veridicality, and that it is all too obvious that in fact emotional communication is often quite inaccurate. We have touched upon some of the reasons for inaccuracy: the suppression and control of displays on the part of senders and overgeneralizing responses to displays on the part of receivers. What may be less apparent is the fact that the sender's control is not due only to the capacity of logic and reason on the part of human beings, but that there are specific brain mechanisms devoted to the control of the display.

This conclusion is based upon studies of the neurological control of spontaneous vocalization conducted by Detlev Ploog, Uwe Jurgens, and their colleagues (Jurgens & Ploog, 1981). Extensive studies of nonhuman primates indicate that this control is organized in a hierarchical manner. The motor coordination of specific behaviors necessary for phonation involves mechanisms in the brainstem at the level of the pons and medulla, including nuclei responsible for facial movement and respiratory control. The second hierarchical level is in the midbrain region, specifically the caudal periaqueductal gray and laterally adjacent tegmentum between the inferior colliculus and the brachium conjunctivum. Ploog suggests that this area may be "the neural substrate of the vocal innate releasing mechanism" (1990, p. 386). This midbrain vocalization-eliciting area is associated with call production in birds, reptiles, amphibians, and even fish, despite the differences in sound production in these different vertebrate classes (Jurgens, 1979). It is, in fact, the "phylogenetically oldest structure for the generation of species-specific calls" (Ploog, 1990, p. 367).

The third level of the hierarchy involves the areas of the brain that simultaneously elicit both vocalizations and motivational/emotional responses: for example, parts of the limbic system including the amygdalae. This is "the neuroanatomical substrate of emotion, involved in emotional experience as well as emotional expression" (Ploog, 1988, p. 229). These areas project into the midbrain, and Jurgens and Ploog (1981) suggest that vocal patterns are selected and triggered by the latter area according to influences from the motivational/emotional systems. Thus, it appears to be this midbrain area, under the influence of motivational/emotional systems, that is responsible for the spontaneous "readout" of the display.

It is possible, however, for a virtually *identical* vocalization pattern to be elicited voluntarily: a process termed *voluntary expression initiation*. This is associated with the anterior limbic cortex of the squirrel monkey and the supplemental motor cortex and anterior cingulate cortex of human beings. This area controls vocalizations independently of motivational/emotional states, apparently by influencing the midbrain mechanism. In other words, displays hard-wired in the midbrain are initiated voluntarily in the absence of active motivational/emotional states. As a result, the individual is able to initiate affectively significant calls voluntarily and, in effect, possesses a built-in ability to lie emotionally: intentionally to look happy when we are angry, sad when we are secretly pleased, and so on. Such an ability is arguably crucial for complex social regulation.

An additional level of the control of vocalization exists only in human beings. This is a direct pathway from the primary motor cortex to laryngeal motoneurons in the medulla, which bypasses the midbrain vocalization mechanism. Ploog (1990, p. 373) states that "this serves as the neuronal basis for the voluntary control of the vocal folds" in human beings that is necessary for speech. In contrast to the voluntary expression initiation mechanism, this constitutes a mechanism of voluntary expression *formation*, in which the expression is formed by higher-order structures in the brain as opposed to being hard-wired in the midbrain.

Brain mechanisms of emotional expression and perception

The preceding paragraphs concern one of the fundamental dimensions of brain functioning: the vertical dimension in which the phylogenetically more ancient parts of the brain are involved in more hard-wired automatic functions, whereas more recently evolved portions serve more complex learned and voluntary functions. Two other fundamental dimensions of brain functioning have been suggested: an anterior-posterior dimension in which the posterior portions are involved in sensory functions and the anterior portions in motor functions, and a left-right dimension in which the right side of the brain is associated with holistic, synthetic cognitive functioning (syncretic cognition) and the left side with analytic, sequential cognitive functioning (analytic cognition: Tucker, 1981, 1986). For example, damage confined to the anterior portions of the left hemisphere is typically associated with expressive or motor aphasia (Broca's aphasia) in which the ability to speak is affected but the comprehension of speech is retained; damage confined to the posterior portions of the left hemisphere is typically associated with receptive or sensory aphasia (Wernicke's aphasia) in which speech expression is retained but comprehension lost.

Whereas left hemisphere damage typically results in language deficits, and more generally in deficits in symbolic communication (since such nonverbal abilities as signing, finger spelling, and pantomime are lost as well), damage to the right hemisphere has been associated with deficits in spontaneous communication. Buck and Duffy (1980) found right hemisphere-damaged patients to be less facially/gesturally expressive in response to color slides. This finding was replicated by Borod, Koff, Perlman, and Nicholas (1985) among patients with anterior right hemisphere damage.

Elliott Ross (1981; Gorelick & Ross, 1987) has suggested that damage to the anterior and posterior portions of the right hemisphere is associated, respectively, with deficits in the expression and comprehension of the emotional aspects of speech, which he terms *expressive* and *receptive aprosodia*. He has designed bedside tests analogous to those used with aphasic patients to test aprosodia: To test expression, he asks the patient to say a standard sentence expressing different emotions; to test comprehension, he asks the patient to identify the emotions being expressed. He has found evidence of expressive aprosodia in patients with damage in the right hemisphere analogous to those that would cause Broca's aphasia in the left hemisphere; conversely, damage in the right hemisphere equivalent of Wernicke's area is associated with symptoms of receptive aprosodia (Ross, 1981, in press). Studies using the Wada test, in which the right hemisphere is temporarily inactivated by intracarotid injections of sodium amytal, have supported this analysis. In several cases, a person relating an extremely traumatic personal experience manifests less emotion, but gives a more objective and detailed account, when the right hemisphere is inactivated (Ross & Homan, 1986).

Conclusions

This introduction has considered the process of covert communication identified by Rosenthal in his initial studies of the effects of interpersonal expectation. It seems clear that such a covert communication process is real, although its existence and importance continue to be denied, ignored, or at best controlled for by many social scientists who emphasize cognitive approaches to the study of behavior. This is unfortunate, for as the work of Robert Rosenthal and his students and associates has made abundantly clear, the covert communication process is not of merely theoretical interest. Its effects are manifested in every interpersonal encounter, including those where rational objectivity is particularly vital: those between teacher and student, doctor and patient, judge and jury. The influence of the covert communication process is not, however, confined to interpersonal situations, as the displays that carry them are effective when transmitted via mass media as well (Buck, 1988b). As a result, the politician who is a charismatic "great communicator" is the one who is an effective covert communicator, and the importance of reasoned and objective political platforms and programs accordingly has declined.

The full recognition of the existence and importance of the covert, spontaneous communication process by the social sciences has yet to occur. When it does, the result will be revolutionary, not only affording greater understanding of such phenomena as interpersonal relationships, persuasion, and social influence, but also allowing new bridges to be built between social and biological approaches to the study of behavior.

References

Berry, D. S. (1990). What can a moving face tell us? *Journal of Personality and Social Psychology, 48,* 1004–1014.

Berry, D. S., & McArthur, L. Z. (1985). Some components and consequences of a babyface. *Journal of Personality and Social Psychology, 48,* 312–323.

Berry, D. S., & McArthur, L. Z. (1986). Perceiving character in faces: The impact of age-related craniofacial changes on social perception. *Psychological Bulletin, 100,* 3–18.

Berry, D. S., & McArthur, L. Z. (1988). The impact of age-related craniofacial changes on social perception. In T. R. Alley (Ed.), *Social and applied aspects of perceiving faces* (pp. 63–87). Hillsdale, NJ: Erlbaum.

Blanck, P. D., Rosenthal, R., & Cordell, L. H. (1985). The appearance of justice: Judges' verbal and nonverbal behavior in criminal jury trials. *Stanford Law Review, 38,* 89–136, 157–158.

Borod, J. C., Koff, E., Perlman, M., & Nicholas, M. (1985). Channels of emotional expression in patients with internal brain damage. *Archives of Neurology, 42,* 345–348.

Buck, R. (1984). *The communication of emotion.* New York: Guilford Press.

Buck, R. (1985). Prime theory: An integrated view of motivation and emotion. *Psychological Review, 92,* 389–413.

Buck, R. (1988a). *Human motivation and emotion* (2nd ed.). New York: Wiley.

Buck, R. (1988b). Emotional education and mass media: A new view of the global village. In R. Hawkins, J. Weimann, & S. Pingree (Eds.), *Advancing communication science: Merging mass and interpersonal processes* (Vol. 16, Sage Annual Review of Communication Research). Beverly Hills, CA: Sage.

Buck, R. (1990). William James, the nature of knowledge, and current issues in emotion, cognition, and communication. *Personality and Social Psychology Bulletin, 16,* 612–625.

Buck, R., & Duffy, R. (1980). Nonverbal communication of affect in brain-damaged patients. *Cortex, 16,* 351–362.

Buck, R., & Ginsburg, B. (1991). Emotional communication and altruism: The communicative gene hypothesis. In M. Clark (Ed.), *Altruism. Review of personality and social psychology* (Vol. 11, pp. 149–175). Newbury Park, CA: Sage.

Gorelick, P. B., & Ross, E. D. (1987). The aprosodias: Further functional-anatomic evidence for the organization of affective language in the right hemisphere. *Journal of Neurology, Neurosurgery, and Psychiatry, 50,* 553–560.

Hansen, C. H., & Hansen, R. D. (1988) Finding the face in the crowd: An anger superiority effect. *Journal of Personality and Social Psychology, 54*(6), 917–924.

Harris, M. J., & Rosenthal, R. (1985). Mediation of interpersonal expectancy effects: 31 meta-analyses. *Psychological Bulletin, 97,* 363–386.

Jensen, A. R. (1969). How much can we boost IQ and scholastic achievement? *Harvard Education Review, 39,* 1–123.

Jurgens, U. (1979). Neural control of vocalization in nonhuman primates. In H. D. Steklis & M. J. Raleigh (Eds.), *Neurobiology of social communication in primates* (pp. 11–44). New York: Academic Press.

Jurgens, U., & Ploog, D. (1981). On the vocal control of mammalian vocalization. *Trends in Neuroscience, 4,* 135–137.

Lazarus, R. S. (1984). On the primacy of cognition. *American Psychologist, 39,* 124–129.

Lazarus, R. S. (1991). Cognition and motivation in emotion. *American Psychologist, 46*(4), 352–367.

LeDoux, J. (1991). Emotion and the brain. *The Journal of NIH Research, 3*(11), 49–51.

McArthur, L. Z., & Baron, R. M. (1983). Toward an ecological theory of social perception. *Psychological Review, 90,* 215–238.

Maranon, G. (1924). Contribution à l'étude de l'action emotive de l'adrenaline. *Revue Francaise d'endocrinologie, 2,* 301–325.

Milmoe, S., Rosenthal, R., Blane, H. T., Chafetz, M. E., and Wolf, I. (1967). The doctor's voice: Postdictor of successful referral of alcoholic patients. *Journal of Abnormal Psychology, 72,* 78–84.

Montepare, J. M., & Zebrowitz-McArthur, L. (1987). Perceptions of adults with childlike voices in two cultures. *Journal of Experimental Social Psychology, 23,* 331–349.

Montepare, J. M., & Zebrowitz-McArthur, L. (1988). Impressions of people created by age-related qualities of their gaits. *Journal of Personality and Social Psychology, 55,* 547–556.

Perrett, D. I., Rolls, E. T., & Caan, W. (1982). Visual neurons responsive to faces in the monkey temporal cortex. *Experimental Brain Research, 47,* 329–342.

Ploog, D. (1988). Neurobiology and pathology of subhuman vocal communication and human speech. In D. Todt, P. F. D. Goedeking, & F. Symmes (Eds.), *Primate vocal communication* (pp. 195–212). Berlin, Heidelberg, and New York: Springer-Verlag.

Ploog, D. (1990). Neuroethological foundations of human speech. In L. Deecke, J. C. Eccles, & V. B. Mountcastle (Eds.), *From neuro to action: An appraisal of fundamental and clinical research* (pp. 365–374). Berlin and Heidelberg: Springer-Verlag.

Rosenthal, R. (1966). *Experimenter effects in behavioral research.* New York: Appleton-Century-Crofts.

Rosenthal, R. (1967). Covert communication in the psychological experiment. *Psychological Bulletin, 67,* 356–367.

Rosenthal, R., & Jacobson, L. (1968). *Pygmalion in the classroom.* New York: Holt, Rinehart, and Winston.

Ross, E. D. (1981). The aprosodias: Functional-anatomic organization of the affective components of language in the right hemisphere. *Archives of Neurology, 37,* 561–569.

Ross, E. D. (in press). Right hemisphere's role in language, affective behaviors, and emotions: Implications for diagnosing depression in brain injured persons. In W. G. Gordon (Ed.), *Advances in stroke rehabilitation.* New York: Andover.

Ross, E. D., & Homan, R. W. (1986) Evidence for differential hemispheric storage of affective and factual memories for an emotionally laden life event in patients undergoing right-sided Wada test. *Neurology* (Supplement 1) 36, 168.

Russell, B. (1903). *The principles of mathematics.* London: Allen and Unwin.

Russell, B. (1961). *An outline of philosophy.* Cleveland: World. (Original work published 1927)

Sackett, G. P. (1966). Monkeys reared in isolation with pictures as visual input: Evidence for an innate releasing mechanism. *Science, 154,* 1468–1473.

Schachter, S. (1964). The interaction of cognitive and physiological determinants of emotion state. In L. Berkowitz (Ed.), *Advances in experimental social psychology* (Vol. 1, pp. 49–80). New York: Academic Press.

Schachter, S., & Singer, J. E. (1962). Cognitive, social, and physiological determinants of emotional state. *Psychological Review, 69,* 379–399.

Shaw, R. E., & Pittenger, J. (1977). Perceiving the face of change in changing faces: Implications for a theory of object perception. In R. E. Shaw & J. Bransford (Eds.), *Perceiving, acting and knowing* (pp. 103–132). Hillsdale, NJ: Erlbaum.

Thorndike, R. L. (1968). Review of *Pygmalion in the Classroom. American Educational Research Journal, 5,* 708–711.

Todd, J. T., Mark, L. S., Shaw, R. E., & Pittenger, J. B. (1980). The perception of human growth. *Scientific American, 242,* 106–114.

Tucker, D. M. (1981). Lateral brain function, emotion, and conceptualization. *Psychological Bulletin, 89,* 19–46.

Tucker, D. M. (1986). Neural control of emotional communication. In P. D. Blanck, R. Buck, & R. Rosenthal (Eds.), *Nonverbal communication in the clinical context* (pp. 258–307). University Park, PA: Pennsylvania State University Press.

Zajonc, R. B. (1980). Feeling and thinking: Preferences need no inferences. *American Psychologist, 35,* 151–175.

Zajonc, R. B. (1984). On the primacy of affect. *American Psychologist, 39,* 117–123.

12. The accurate perception of nonverbal behavior: Questions of theory and research design

DANE ARCHER, ROBIN AKERT, AND MARK COSTANZO

Introduction

The publication in 1968 of Rosenthal and Jacobson's *Pygmalion in the Classroom* catalyzed phenomenal interest in the apparent power of interpersonal expectations but also in the possible *communication processes* that might be responsible. The question seemed to be how such expectations could be "sent" by a teacher (or experimenter, coach, therapist, etc.) and also "received" by a pupil (or research subject, student, patient, etc.). Although verbal cues could not be ignored, attention quickly focused on nonverbal communication as the most promising vehicle for the unintentional, implicit transfer of interpersonal expectations.

The nonverbal channels thought most likely to play a role included tone of voice, facial expressions, eye contact, hesitations, gestures, touch, and proxemics. One reason the nonverbal channels were quickly implicated in the expectancy process was that, 5 years prior to the publication of *Pygmalion*, a landmark experiment showed that expectation could be communicated between people and rats (Rosenthal & Fode, 1963). Even with the human-to-human communication of expectation in *Pygmalion* – and in the hundreds of replications that followed (Rosenthal & Harris, 1985; Rosenthal & Rubin, 1980) – subtle nonverbal channels seemed to offer more promising explanations than explicit verbal cues. Just as it seemed unlikely that experimenters could affect the behavior of rats by *telling* them they were "maze dull," it seemed improbable that therapists would tell some patients that they were unlikely to respond to treatment, that coaches would tell certain campers they were unlikely to learn to swim, and so on. The transmission of expectations seemed certain to occur via nonverbal communication.

Whereas systematic research on nonverbal communication dates at least to Darwin's *The Expression of the Emotions in Man and the Animals*, in 1872, it is only in the last 25 years that research on nonverbal behavior has begun to capture some of the subtlety, realism, and complexity of real nonverbal behavior. In large part, breakthroughs in this area have rested on the maturation and increasing availability of visual and auditory media for recording behavior. Just as the invention of photography and the movie camera made it possible to learn whether running horses lift all four feet off the ground at the same time (they do; Muybridge, 1902), the availability of film, audiotape, and particularly videotape made it possible to capture and edit complex samples of nonverbal behavior.

The history of early and recent research with samples of nonverbal behavior is reviewed in some detail elsewhere (Archer & Akert, in preparation). A watershed effort,and one of the most ambitious of these studies, was a multichannel paradigm designed for the study of individual differences in the ability to decode nonverbal behavior (Rosenthal, Hall, DiMatteo, Rogers, & Archer, 1979). The basic paradigm involved videotaping a woman with three cameras, one focused on her face (Face Channel), a second on her from the neck down (Body Channel), and a third on both (Figure – i.e., Face + Body Channel). These three visual channels were combined with two methods designed to filter out content from audio recordings on speech. One method removed from taped voices the higher frequencies containing the consonant sounds that make words recognizable (Content Filtered Speech Channel), and a second edited together fragmentary audiotape segments in a scrambled order (Randomized Spliced Channel). These two methods preserved qualities like emotion but made it impossible to recognize the original words.

The 3 visual channels (plus a fourth option of no video) were combined with the 2 audio channels (plus a third option of no audio) to create a total of 11 additive channels of nonverbal communication, such as Face + No Audio, Face + Content Filtered Speech, and Body + No Audio; Body + Content Filtered Speech. The project used this multichannel system to record one woman performing 20 different scenes intended to tap a range of interpersonal interactions and affects, such as admiring nature, talking about one's divorce, helping a customer, leaving on a trip, and asking for forgiveness. She appeared alone on camera but directed herself to another person standing off camera.

The resulting instrument became known as the *Profile of Nonverbal Sensitivity* (*PONS*). It was originally made as a videotape. A 16mm film version was also made, and both were in black and white. Since there were 11 additive channels and 20 interpersonal scenes, this yielded a total of 220 stimuli. For each one, a viewer/listener was asked to choose from among two alternatives the correct nature of the original sequence – for example, (1) talking about one's divorce or (2) asking for forgiveness. Although the researchers originally planned to use relatively long sequences of behavior, it was discovered that accuracy rates were unacceptably high if the stimuli were longer than 2 seconds in length. There were intervals and identifying numbers separating the 220 stimuli, and the overall length of the PONS film was roughly 45 minutes.

The PONS film made possible an energetic agenda of data collection and hypothesis testing and led to a rich array of provocative findings (Rosenthal et al., 1979). These include the now familiar finding that women are in general more accurate than men at reading nonverbal cues; the discovery that people could read nonverbal stimuli such as facial expressions at speeds as low as $1/24$th of a second; establishing that the ability to read nonverbal cues is unrelated to conventional measures of intelligence; the finding that parents of prelanguage infants appear to be unusually acute at reading nonverbal communication; identification of groups (such as actors, artists, and clinicians) unusually skilled at decoding nonverbal cues; and cross-cultural research suggesting that people in cultures relatively similar to the culture of the woman in the PONS film were better able to interpret her nonverbal behavior accurately than people from dissimilar cultures.

Theoretical approaches and design alternatives

In research on nonverbal communication, there are a variety of theoretical approaches, and these have significant consequences for how one proceeds. The PONS film was the first work in the paradigm of studying individual differences in the ability to decode samples of nonverbal behavior. The film that resulted was extremely well suited for this purpose. At the same time, any single approach forces a researcher to make methodological decisions that have theoretical consequences. Whether these decisions are made consciously or not, they influence (1) the rationale for studying nonverbal behaviors and the types of inferences one wishes to draw, (2) whether the researcher samples posed or natural nonverbal behaviors, (3) which types of context are stripped from (or preserved with) the nonverbal behaviors studied, and (4) the very notion of accuracy itself. These four design decisions are now described briefly, and their theoretical consequences are indicated.

Nonverbal behaviors: Rationale and inferences

The research literature includes both nomothetic and idiographic approaches to the study of nonverbal communication. The former refers to studies that seek to describe functional and systematic aspects of nonverbal communication. *Nomothetic* studies of nonverbal behavior tend to focus on a specific channel of nonverbal behavior. For example, a book by Morris, Collett, Marsh, and O'Shaughnessy (1979) describes the distribution of hand gestures across Europe; Archer (1992a, 1992b) has produced a video on the nature, function, and meaning of gestures in different cultures. Other examples are the works of Hall (1969) and Sommer (1969) on the functions of personal space; the work of Goffman (1979) on gender differences in body posture; the work of Ekman and Friesen (1975) on facial expressions of emotion; and the work of Scherer (1986) on perceived qualities of vocal paralanguage. What these works have in common is that they aspire to inform us about the *generic* nature and function of nonverbal behaviors – that is, patterns and general properties.

By contrast, the *idiographic* approach focuses on individual differences in how nonverbal behavior is either encoded or decoded. The idiographic approach develops out of the measurement, personality, and testing traditions in psychology. The focus is on the performance of the individual in comparison to other individuals. This approach sometimes considers the performance of groups (e.g., women vs. men, medical doctors vs. therapists) rather than just individuals, but the focus continues to be on accurate performance on a standardized task.

The two approaches are easily contrasted. Given any particular area of nonverbal behavior, one could conceivably choose either approach. Consider the study of lying as an example. The nomothetic approach asks questions such as the following: Can lying be detected? What happens to the face when a person is lying? Are there vocal changes during a lie? By contrast, the idiographic approach tends to ask: Are some people better liars than others? Are some people better at detecting lying than others? Are women better at detecting lies? The point is that these two approaches are pursuing radically different research paradigms and, as a result, they tend to serve very different theoretical traditions.

In the study of accurate decoding, both approaches have been pursued. Examples of the nomothetic approach are Ekman and Friesen's (1975) work on how to decode specific aspects of facial expression, and

Archer's (1980) work on social intelligence and how the interpretation of specific interactions is possible. Both of these efforts used nonverbal stimuli and studied decoding accuracy, but the focus is more on the general *process* of interpretation (e.g., What does the upper face look like when the person is surprised? How do people recognize the nature of the relationship between two people when looking at a photograph?) and less on individual differences in accuracy.

On the other hand, the PONS film (Rosenthal et al., 1979) clearly pioneered the idiographic approach in the study of nonverbal communication. There are other individual difference instruments as well, and these are described later in this chapter. They include the Social Interpretations Task (SIT) by Archer and Akert and the Interpersonal Perception Task (IPT). The ways in which the SIT and IPT differ from the PONS, both theoretically and methodologically, are discussed below.

Nonverbal behaviors: Posed versus natural

Systematic research on nonverbal behavior obviously requires that some of these behaviors be obtained. Although many strategies are theoretically possible, almost all research on nonverbal communication has used one of three sampling procedures: (1) *posed behavior* – individuals are asked to act *as if* they are feeling anger, surprise, embarrassment, fear, disgust, and so on; (2) *induced behavior* – a laboratory manipulation *produces* anger, surprise, embarrassment, fear, disgust, and so on; (3) *naturalistic behavior* – the researcher records ongoing interactions without trying to induce particular expressions or asking individuals to pose certain affects.

All three approaches have merit, but they also impose unique methodological and theoretical costs. Posed behavior allows the researcher maximum control over the "menu" of situations and emotions to be captured, since these are performed on command. On the other hand, researchers using posed behaviors are forced to assume (or, more rarely, to investigate whether) such posed behaviors resemble real, unposed behaviors. Use of induced behavior has potential ethical costs (e.g., Knapp & Hall, 1992, p. 275); there is also the problem that what one records may be in fact the emotions one hoped to induce, or only the person's efforts to mask them within the public world of the research lab. Finally, naturalistic behavior has the exceptional advantage that the researcher captures unposed, authentic nonverbal behavior. On the other hand, the naturalistic approach restricts what can be studied, since situations involving rage, grief, remorse, and so on are unlikely to occur while the camera is rolling.

The PONS film clearly falls within the posed tradition, since the young woman in the film pretended to experience a range of affects. The SIT and IPT videos, on the other hand, both sampled naturalistic behavior. The viewer is shown two people who have just played a basketball game; two people who are brother and sister; two men, one of whom is the father of the little girl shown in the sequence; a man and a woman who say they are in love; two people, one of whom is the supervisor of the other; and others. Although it is not possible to argue that one sampling procedure is superior to others, it is important to recognize the theoretical strengths and costs of each. The use of posed behavior maximizes experimental control, whereas the use of naturalistic behavior maximizes external validity.

Nonverbal behaviors: Seven context types

In real social interaction, we interpret nonverbal behavior in context. It is rare (although not unknown) for us to have to interpret a single "slice" of nonverbal behavior, absent words or other nonverbal cues, from a person we see only for an instant. In real interaction, nonverbal acts occur in context, and researchers – knowingly or not – preserve or destroy context when they sample nonverbal acts. Although the word *context* obviously implies a variety of qualities, we believe that seven *context types* are relevant to research on nonverbal communication:

1. *Multichannel nonverbal behavior.* In ongoing social interaction, we are confronted with a virtual symphony of communication from different nonverbal channels – facial expressions, tones of voice, gestures, proxemics, and so on. Each nonverbal act therefore occurs in context with other nonverbal acts, and the meaning of one act is presumably influenced by others. For example, sarcasm may involve an exaggerated facial expression plus a vocal stress on key words. Research designs that isolate one nonverbal channel (e.g., only still photographs or only audio recordings) obviously cannot replicate the multichannel context of real nonverbal behavior.

2. *Joint presence of verbal and nonverbal information.* Although some nonverbal behaviors occur in pure form, most nonverbal communication is in fact *coverbal*, that is, it occurs with words. In perceiving communication, we may focus both on what is said (the verbal channel) and on how it is performed (the nonverbal channels). This natural

"ecology" of communication is obviously compromised if a researcher removes words from stimuli, uses silent videotapes, and so on. In other words, although technology makes it methodologically possible to present "purified" nonverbal behavior stripped of the verbal channel, this is not how in vivo nonverbal communication occurs; therefore, it is not clear that purified stimuli are *theoretically* desirable.

3. *Prior experience with the encoder.* One type of context absent from virtually all research using nonverbal stimuli involves prior experience with the encoder. Although it is true that we sometimes try to decode the behaviors of strangers, the decoding of individuals familiar to us involves a much more subtle process. We may contrast present levels of facial expression, vocal affect, gestural animation, and other factors with the historic levels of these behaviors for this particular person. This allows us to know that this person is *unusually* upset, happy, depressed, and so on. Our history with an encoder provides a contextual baseline, something systemized collections of nonverbal stimuli cannot include.

4. *Continuous behavior streams.* A specific gesture, facial expression, or tone of voice is always embedded in a continuous, flowing context that we need to "read" to determine the meaning of behavior. Real nonverbal acts arrive at our senses in the hundreds, enabling us to contrast each act with those that preceded it and forcing us to sift through hundreds of nonverbal acts before attaching importance to a small number of them. Obviously, still photographs and excerpted audio fragments prevent this stream from flowing, simplifying our decoding task but in artificial ways.

5. *Real-time exposure lengths.* Unlike most laboratory stimuli, in vivo nonverbal acts are ephemeral. They occur in real time, race by us, and are gone as soon as they occur. One form of natural context therefore involves time; real interpersonal perception can succeed only if it can operate at breathtaking speed. Studies using still photographs obviously operate in unreal time, allowing decoders to examine at length fragments that are extremely fleeting in actual interaction. One of the most extraordinary aspects of the interpretation of behavior, our ability to attach meaning to the most transitory of nonverbal acts, is lost unless real-time exposure lengths are used.

6. *Situational antecedents.* Most nonverbal acts are embedded in an interactional context. If a person looks sad, for example, we are likely to know from the situational context whether this emotion results from a lost basketball game or a failed marriage. The situational context

provides an interpretive frame within which we attach meaning to the nonverbal acts we observe. Situational antecedents include the number of persons in an interaction, their relative status, the presence of interpersonal bonds like kinship or marriage, the past history of the interactants, the immediate history of the interaction, and the physical setting in which an interaction takes place. A smile in response to one's playing 2-year-old presumably differs from a smile in response to a joke told by one's employer. The situational context helps us endow nonverbal acts with qualitative meaning, and the absence of such a context forces us to read "unframed" nonverbal fragments in vitro rather than in naturalistic form.

7. *Recognition versus interpretation.* Much research has studied whether judges can decode behaviors (e.g., emotions) that the encoder makes no effort to disguise. In real social interaction, we often need to interpret overt and covert cues, conflicted messages, the symptoms of ambivalence, and others. For example, is a person's hearty congratulation of another genuine, or does it conceal resentment or bitter disappointment – and how do we tell the difference? This illustrates the difference between *recognition* (the perception of simple, unconflicted, isolated stimuli such as happy faces) and *interpretation* (inferences drawn by contrasting, combining, and weighing cues available in many different channels). Interpretation rests on subtle, multifaceted, and often ambiguous data from verbal and many nonverbal channels. This complexity is generally impossible in studies using excerpted nonverbal stimuli.

Nonverbal behaviors: Different notions of accuracy

A final issue affecting both theory and research design concerns the question of accuracy itself: When a decoder tries to decode a sample of nonverbal behavior, what is the correct answer? At first glance, this seems self-evident and a simple matter. Surely, one might think, the correct answer is that a given photograph shows a happy face, a given tape sample contains anger, or a given video sequence shows surprise. In fact, this question is not even addressed in most studies, where the right answer is simply assumed to be what the encoder intended to portray or, alternately, whatever the researcher (or other expert) believes was in fact captured.

Upon closer examination of many research paradigms, it becomes clear that the theoretical basis for determining the right answer is often quite problematic. This issue is generally referred to as the *criterion* problem (Archer & Akert, 1984). It becomes particularly worrisome in studies involving emotion, and indeed, emotions have traditionally held center stage in research on nonverbal behavior.

The problem is easily illustrated. Suppose that we present a decoder with a photograph (video, audio segment, etc.) and ask the decoder to guess whether it illustrates (1) happiness or (2) regret. It may be worth asking what we (the researchers) *actually mean* by our question. Do we mean that the encoder was *in fact* feeling either happiness or regret? Probably not, particularly if the sample was derived from posed behavior – in which case we can be positive that the encoder was in fact feeling neither of these two affects. On the other hand, more epistemologically accurate formulations are awkward and imply validity problems – for example, "Was the person in this photograph pretending to be happy or pretending to be regretful?" or "Which of these two photographs looks more like an ideal or stereotypic version of happiness?"

Clearly, the criterion problem can be far thornier than is first thought. It would be unthinkable to create and score an algebra examination without first being certain about what the right answers are to the questions, and yet something very much like this occurs routinely in research on nonverbal behavior. There are three major strategies for solving the criterion problem, and the first two are the most conventional: (1) *face validity or encoder's intent* – this approach uses as the correct answer whatever the encoder was told to portray or whatever the researcher thinks has been captured; (2) *expert opinion or ratings* – this approach asks a panel of judges to determine what the sampled behavior shows, and the pooled ratings are accepted as the right answer; and (3) *objective or biographic information* – this approach uses as the correct information factual data about the encoders or the sampled interaction.

Examples of an objective criterion are to ask decoders to guess something factual about encoders or an interaction – for example, "Is this person telling a lie?" or "Which of these two people won their racquetball game?" or "Which of these two women is the mother of the young boy?" or "Are these two people brother and sister, or strangers who have just met?" The third approach has been described as the "ideal" criterion (Cook, 1971), although it has been used far less often than the other two. In part, this may reflect the field's interest in emotion, which many see as difficult or even impossible to verify objectively.

We believe that an objective criterion is possible, even in studies of emotion, if the criterion is not the emotion per se. For example, one cannot use an objective criterion when asking whether one person loves another. But one can ask whether A is the mother of B; whether A and B are a married couple or brother and sister; whether A and B have been dating for 1 month or 1 year; and so on. All of these questions invite the decoder to use a variety of possible cues (including, but not limited to, perceptions about the encoders' emotions), but emotions are not per se the point of the question. In this way, researchers can include the emotions in research using nonverbal behavior and still incorporate an ideal, objective criterion of accuracy.

New methods and measures: The IPT

Within the framework of the theoretical issues and design alternatives discussed previously, it is clear that research based on the landmark PONS film (1) was idiographic (rather than nomothetic); (2) used posed (rather than induced or naturalistic) behavior; (3) arguably possessed *Context Types* 1, 4, and 5 (but not Types 2, 3, 6, and 7); and (4) based the criterion for accurate answers on face validity (rather than expert opinion or objective information). As noted earlier, researchers are forced to make these design choices, whether consciously or not, and each choice contains unique advantages but also theoretical constraints.

In this last section, we briefly describe an approach to studying nonverbal behavior that, although strongly influenced by the PONS film, clearly makes different design choices. This approach has produced two instruments, the *Social Interpretations Task* (*SIT*) by Archer and Akert (1977, 1980, 1984, 1990, in preparation) and the *Interpersonal Perception Task* (*IPT*) (Archer & Costanzo, 1986, 1989; Costanzo & Archer, 1989, 1991; Smith, Archer, & Costanzo, 1991). The SIT was the earlier of the two and strongly influenced the design of the IPT, but because the IPT is a professional-quality, full-color video, most of our discussion addresses this instrument.

The IPT is about both nonverbal communication and social perception. In terms of the four design and theoretical issues discussed in this chapter, the IPT (1) is generally idiographic (but also nomothetic in the sense that one can use it to generalize about lying and other emotions); (2) uses naturalistic (rather than posed or induced) behavior; (3) arguably possesses Context Types 1, 2, 4, 5, 6, and 7 (but not Type 3); and (4) uses as the criterion for accuracy objective information (rather than face validity or expert opinion).

The IPT contains 30 brief scenes, each 30 to 60 seconds in length.

Each scene is paired with a question that has two or three possible answers; this gives the viewer a chance to decode something important about the people he or she has just seen. For example, the viewer may see a woman talking on the telephone; the viewer is asked whether the woman is talking to her mother, a close female friend, or her boyfriend. In another scene, the viewer sees two men who have just played basketball; the viewer is asked which man won the game. In a third scene, a woman presents two very different versions of her childhood; the viewer tries to identify which version is a lie. In each scene of the IPT, there is an *objectively correct* answer to the question. In the examples just mentioned, the woman on the phone *is* talking to one of those three people; one of the two men *did* win the basketball game; and one of the woman's two versions of her childhood *is* in fact a lie.

The IPT challenges the viewer to identify the right answer to each question by using *verbal* clues and also different types of *nonverbal communication* present in each scene – facial expressions, tones of voice, hesitations, eye movements, gestures, personal space, posture, and touching behavior. These different channels of nonverbal communication occur simultaneously in the IPT scenes, just as they do in everyday life. All of the IPT scenes contain spontaneous, naturalistic interaction, and a total of 54 people (28 women and 26 men) are shown. The 30 scenes include six examples of each of five different *Scene Types:* Status, Intimacy, Kinship, Competition, and Deception.

The basic method in creating the IPT uses spontaneous and naturalistic behavior, full-channel communications (verbal and nonverbal), many different encoders, and inferences of different types. The scenes in the IPT show unrehearsed, spontaneous behavior. Genuine relationships and experiences are used to maximize the naturalism of the captured behavior. Brief segments of much longer interactions were selected to produce the 30 IPT scenes. The IPT pairs these 30 scenes with multiple-choice questions. In each case, the questions were constructed to have unambiguously correct answers. For example, rather than ask which of two men in one of the scenes is happy (an obviously subjective state), we asked which of the two men had just won the basketball game they played (an objective question).

The multiple-choice format of the IPT makes it possible to determine whether viewers are more accurate than chance alone would predict. For example, in the case of a scene with two possible answers, 50% of the viewers should get the right answer by chance alone – that is, even if they are merely guessing. Similarly, for a scene with three possible

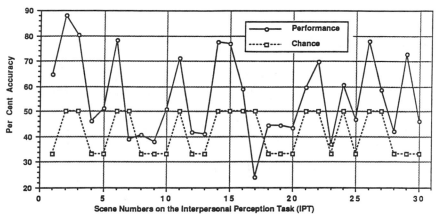

Figure 12.1. Performance on the IPT: norm group (*n* = 438) versus chance level of accuracy.

answers, 33% of the viewers would be expected to get the right answer to the question merely by guessing. If viewers of an IPT scene perform above this chance level of accuracy, it indicates that they are able to use the verbal and nonverbal clues in the scene to solve the problem and reach the correct answer. For example, if 72% of viewers get the right answer on an IPT scene with two alternative answers, they are performing above the chance level, and we can conclude that useful, interpretable clues are present in this scene. We can also use this information to identify IPT scenes that are relatively easy or hard.

Who does well on the IPT?

Research with the IPT indicates that people score well above chance levels of accuracy. The performance of a norm group of 438 university students on the IPT is indicated in Figure 12.1. The solid line in the graph indicates the percentage accuracy of the sample on each of the 30 IPT scenes; for example, 64.5% of the sample answered the question for Scene 1 correctly, 88.1% answered the one for Scene 2 correctly, and so on. The broken line in the graph indicates the chance level of accuracy (50% for scenes with two possible answers; 33% for scenes with three possible answers) for each IPT scene.

The distance between the solid line and the dotted line indicates how people in the norm group performed *compared* to chance levels of accuracy; for example, the sample was roughly 30 points above chance on

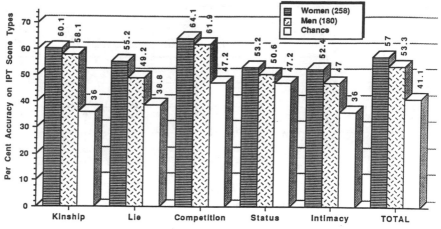

Figure 12.2. Gender differences in performance on the IPT.

Scene 1, roughly 38 points above chance on Scene 2, and so on. In interpreting the *relative* difficulty of different IPT scenes, the dotted line in the graph needs to be kept in mind, since IPT scenes with two answers have a chance accuracy level of 50%, whereas scenes with three answers have a chance accuracy level of 33%. The smaller the gap between the solid and dotted lines, the more difficult the IPT scene.

Performance levels on the IPT are significantly above chance ($p < .001$) for both men and women. For 28 of the 30 IPT scenes (all but Scenes 7 and 17), the performance exceeded chance levels. The poor performance on these two scenes suggests that some of the clues in the scenes systematically mislead, that is, influence viewers to choose the wrong answer. In general, however, the data in this graph indicate that the IPT scenes contain important, useful, interpretable nonverbal behavior that enables viewers to reach the correct answers. In other words, people are systematically choosing the correct answers, and not merely guessing, when they answer the IPT questions.

Social scientists have become interested in what kinds of people are good readers of nonverbal communication. For example, Rosenthal and his colleagues (Rosenthal, Archer, DiMatteo, Koivumaki, & Rogers, 1974; Rosenthal, et al., 1979) were among the first to report that women were somewhat more accurate than men at decoding nonverbal behavior. This conclusion has now been supported by a wide body of research (e.g., Hall, 1985). Research with the IPT supports this conclusion, as Figure 12.2 indicates. This bar graph compares overall (TOTAL) performance of women and men, and also performance on the five IPT Scene Types: Kinship, Lie, Competition, Status, and Intimacy. Each of these five Scene Type scores consists of six individual IPT scenes; for example, the "Lie" Scene Type score consists of IPT scenes 5, 9, 15, 19, 24, and 30. "Kinship" consists of scenes 1, 4, 10, 14, 18, and 29. "Competition" includes scenes 6, 11, 16, 21, 23, and 26. "Status" consists of scenes 3, 7, 12, 17, 22, and 27. "Intimacy" includes scenes 2, 8, 13, 20, 25, and 28.

As this graph shows, gender differences were consistent; women were slightly more accurate (with a difference of roughly 3.6 percentage points) than men on all five of the IPT Scene Types. Overall, women had a mean of 17.1 correct answers (out of 30), whereas men had a mean of 16.0 correct answers ($t = 3.26$, $df = 434$, $p < .001$). These results indicate that women are slightly more accurate on the IPT – either because they detect more nonverbal clues or, perhaps, because they interpret what they detect differently.

Reliability and validity of the IPT

The stability or retest reliability of the IPT was assessed in a study of 46 U.S. college students given the IPT twice with a test-retest interval of 5 weeks. In this study, the retest reliability coefficient was .70, comparable to retest values found in earlier person perception tasks (e.g., Rosenthal et al., 1979, p. 76). In an analysis of internal consistency, using IPT data from 438 individuals, the obtained value of KR-20 was .52, perhaps reflecting both the diversity of the IPT items and the fact that the IPT has only 30 items; the *effective reliability* is influenced by the number of items in an instrument (Rosenthal et al., 1979, p. 74).[1]

Costanzo and Archer (1989) examined different aspects of the validity of the IPT. In one study, 18 female university students living on the same floor of a university dormitory completed peer ratings regarding one another. Each person rated all the others on four dimensions of perceived interpersonal sensitivity – "Is able to correctly interpret the nonverbal behavior of others"; "Is sensitive to the feelings of others"; "Is responsive to the feelings of others"; and "Is good at dealing with other people."

These four sensitivity items were all highly related (with a mean interitem correlation of .78), and all four were combined into a single "Interpersonal Sensitivity" score. The 18 women were given the IPT, and scores on the IPT were significantly correlated with the Interpersonal Sensitivity ratings the women received from their peers ($r = .48$, $df = 16$, $p < .05$). This suggests that individuals judged by peers as more sensitive to other people tend to have higher accuracy scores on the IPT; that is, this performance on the IPT is related to social skills important in everyday life.

There is also some evidence for the convergent validity of the IPT. Specifically, research indicates that the IPT is positively related to an earlier black-and-white videotape designed for research on the interpretation of behavior, SIT. Costanzo and Archer (1989) found that the IPT was significantly related to this earlier interpersonal sensitivity task ($r = .31$, $n = 65$, $p < .01$) and was more strongly related to the SIT items that involved types of interaction similar to those on the IPT ($r = .39$, $p < .001$).

Finally, Costanzo and Archer (1989) conducted a study of the content validity of the IPT. A series of codes were developed to reflect findings from the research literature regarding the five different Scene Types in the IPT. For example, research on interaction between status unequals has found that the lower-status person tends to assume a more formal or rigid posture; to display a more constricted range of movement; to be more visually attentive to the higher-status person than vice versa; and so on (e.g., Henley, 1977; Knapp, 1978). These findings were used to create simple codes, and three coders (who were blind not only to the IPT answers but to the IPT questions as well) independently coded the behaviors of the participants in 26 of the IPT scenes. Four scenes could not be coded due to lack of relevant previous research (e.g., those scenes showing a single person engaged in a telephone conversation).

For each coded scene, the number of coding judgments was equal to the number of coders (three) times the number of behaviors the literature predicts should be present in an interaction. For example, a total of seven behaviors were predicted to be present in status-unequal interactions, and the number of coding judgments for each status scene on the IPT was therefore 21 (three coders × seven predicted behaviors). The number of coding judgments was different for each of the five Scene Types in the IPT, depending on the number of predicted behaviors that could be identified from previous research. Interjudge reliability was high (roughly .81), and the median agreement (between the behaviors predicted by the literature and the behaviors actually coded from the IPT videotape) was 83.3%. This suggests that even though the behavior in the IPT was unscripted and spontaneous, nearly all the IPT scenes do provide valid samples of the behaviors found in previous research to characterize the types of interactions in the IPT.

Example of one IPT scene

Here is an example of the *verbal* content from one IPT scene. The following transcript, of course, includes none of the nonverbal behavior in the video. In the purely verbal channel reproduced here, the scene is quite difficult to interpret. When shown to decoders in the full (verbal + nonverbal) format of the IPT video, however, 88.1% of the decoders answer the question correctly.

> SCENE 2. What is the relationship between the man and the woman?
> a. They are lovers who have been together for about 10 months.
> b. They are lovers who have been together for about 3 years.
>
> | *Left* | *Right* |
> |---|---|
> | Person 1 | Person 2 |
> | (woman) | (man) |
>
> 1 (woman): I think maybe one child's nicer to have from the parent's point of view. . . . Less work. Um. But as one of three, I felt a lot different. I grew up sharing a room with my sister, as you know.
> 2 (man): Right.
> 1 (woman): And that way, sharing a room in college with a roommate was a lot easier. And didn't fight over things . . . and then there were a lot of times where I think I would have been really lonely, if I didn't have her, and also a little brother. I grew up where there weren't very many kids my age, and we had each other. We wouldn't have had each other.
> 2 (man): Uh huh.
> 1 (woman): If they weren't there. I mean I can see your point, about –
> 2 (man): I don't know, I just . . .
> 1 (woman): I guess all the advantages, but I think there's other advantages too, not just advantages of all the attention
> 2 (man): Uh huh.
> 1 (woman): But advantages of having playmates, um, peers.
> 2 (man): Yeah, I just remember how I felt when I had a step – I have a stepbrother and a stepsister, and when they'd come for the summer, and I always felt, when I was a little kid, I always felt like . . . my turf was being invaded on just a little bit.

It is also possible to use the IPT to examine some of the cues decoders report as significant (Archer & Costanzo, 1989). One can ask decoders not only what the answer to an IPT question is but also for detailed explanations of *why* they chose this particular answer. Concerning Scene 2, the transcript of which appears here, commentary focuses on both verbal and nonverbal channels. Viewers who correctly guess that these two people have been a couple for only 10 months comment that the relationship seems new and tentative. As one viewer remarked, "These two people are still getting to know each other; they are careful about what they say to each other, and are still explaining themselves to one another." Another viewer said, "There is an element of formality, still, in how they interact; their postures and eye contact indicate that they know each other, but not yet perfectly."

Future research on nonverbal communication and interpersonal behavior

As this chapter indicates, there are four important dimensions according to which studies using nonverbal behavior can be classified: (1) the types of inferences one wishes to draw (nomothetic or idiographic); (2) whether the researcher samples natural (vs. posed or induced) behavior; (3) which of seven different "Context Types" are preserved or lost in the design; and (4) whether accurate judgments are determined using objective information (vs. face validity or expert opinion).

In this chapter, we have discussed the PONS film and two subsequent instruments – the SIT and the more recent IPT – influenced by, but quite different from, the PONS film. These instruments are contrasted according to the theoretical consequences of the four design issues described in the chapter. Although it is difficult to argue that any one design choice on these four dimensions is *inherently* and in all cases superior to the others, it is clear that these choices do have *theoretical* consequences in terms of our ability to generalize about the role of nonverbal behavior in naturalistic social interaction. If nothing else, the discussion in this chapter alerts researchers to the variety and consequences of design decisions that are *inherent*, whether recognized or not, in research on nonverbal communication.

Note

1. For example, Rosenthal et al. found an overall KR-20 value of .86 working with an instrument 220 items in length. The much shorter 20-item subscales, however, had a median KR-20 value of roughly .35 before adjustment using the Spearman-Brown prophecy formula.

References

Archer, D. (1980). *Social intelligence.* New York: Evans.
Archer, D. (1992a). *A world of gestures: Culture and nonverbal communication* [Videotape]. Berkeley, CA: UC Extension Media Center.

Archer, D. (1992b). *A world of gestures: Culture and nonverbal communication – A guide for instructors and researchers*. Berkeley, CA: UC Extension Media Center.

Archer, D. & Akert, R. M. (1977). Words and everything else: Verbal and nonverbal cues in social interpretation. *Journal of Personality and Social Psychology, 35*, 443–449.

Archer, D., & Akert, R. M. (1980). The encoding of meaning: A test of three theories of social interaction. In D. H. Zimmerman & C. West (Eds.), *Language and Social Interaction*, a special issue of *Sociological Inquiry, 50*, 393–419.

Archer, D., & Akert, R. M. (1984). Problems of context and criterion in nonverbal communication: A new look at the accuracy issue. In M. Cook (Ed.), *Issues in person perception* (pp. 114–144). New York and London: Methuen.

Archer, D., & Akert, R. (1990). How well do you read body language? In Paul Chance & T. George Harris (Eds.), *The best of Psychology Today* (pp. 210–216). New York: McGraw-Hill.

Archer, D., & Akert, R. M. (In prep.). *The interpretation of behavior: Verbal and nonverbal factors in person perception*. New York: Cambridge University Press.

Archer, D., & Costanzo, M. (1986). *The Interpersonal Perception Task (IPT)* [Videotape]. Berkeley, CA: UC Extension Media Center.

Archer, D., & Costanzo, M. (1989). *A Guide to the Interpersonal Perception Task (IPT) for instructors and researchers*. Berkeley, CA: UC Extension Media Center.

Cook, M. (1971). *Interpersonal perception*. Baltimore: Penguin Books.

Costanzo, M., & Archer, D. (1989). Interpreting the expressive behavior of others: The Interpersonal Perception Task. *Journal of Nonverbal Behavior, 13*, 225–245.

Costanzo, M., & Archer, D. (1991). A method of teaching about verbal and nonverbal communication. *Teaching of Psychology, 18*, 223–226.

Ekman, P., & Friesen, W. V. (1975). *Unmasking the face*. Englewood Cliffs, NJ: Prentice-Hall.

Goffman, E. (1979). *Gender advertisements*. New York: Harper & Row.

Hall, E. T. (1969). *The hidden dimension*. Garden City, NY: Doubleday.

Hall, J. A. (1985). *Nonverbal sex differences: Communication accuracy and expressive style*. Baltimore: Johns Hopkins University Press.

Henley, N. (1977). *Body politics: Power, sex, and nonverbal communication*. Englewood Cliffs, NJ: Prentice-Hall.

Knapp, M. L. (1978). *Nonverbal communication in human interaction*. New York: Holt, Rinehart, and Winston.

Knapp, M. L., & Hall, J. A. (1992). *Nonverbal communication in human interaction*. Fort Worth, TX: Harcourt, Brace, Jovanovich.

Morris, D., Collett, P., Marsh, P., & O'Shaughnessy, M. (1979). *Gestures: Their origins and distribution*. London: Jonathan Cape.

Muybridge, E. (1902). *Animals in motion: An Electro-photographic investigation of consecutive phases of animal progressive movements*. London: Chapman & Hall.

Rosenthal, R., Archer, D., DiMatteo, M. R., Koivumaki, J. H., & Rogers, P. (1974). The language without words. *Psychology Today, 8*, 44–50.

Rosenthal, R., & Fode, K. L. (1963). The effect of experimenter bias on the performance of the albino rat. *Behavioral Science, 8*, 183–189.

Rosenthal, R., Hall, J. A., DiMatteo, M. R., Rogers, P., & Archer, D. (1979). *Sensitivity to nonverbal communication: A profile approach to the measurement of differential abilities*. Baltimore: Johns Hopkins University Press.

Rosenthal, R., & Harris, M. J. (1985). The mediation of interpersonal expectancy effects: 31 meta-analyses. *Psychological Bulletin, 97*, 363–386.

Rosenthal, R., & Jacobson, L. (1968). *Pygmalion in the classroom: Teacher expectation and pupil intellectual development.* New York: Holt, Rinehart and Winston.

Rosenthal, R., & Rubin, D. B. (1980). Summarizing 345 studies of interpersonal expectancy effects. In R. Rosenthal (Ed.), *New directions for methodology of social and behavioral science: Quantitative assessment of research domains* (pp. 79–85). San Francisco: Jossey-Bass.

Scherer, K. R. (1986). Vocal affect expression: A review and a model for future research. *Psychological Bulletin, 99*, 143–165.

Smith, H., Archer, D., & Costanzo, M. (1991). "Just a hunch": Accuracy and awareness in person perception. *Journal of Nonverbal Behavior, 15*, 3–18.

Sommer, R. (1969). *Personal space: The behavioral basis of design.* Englewood Cliffs, NJ: Prentice-Hall.

13. Nonverbal communication of expectancy effects: Can we communicate high expectations if only we try?

BELLA M. DePAULO

To most mortals, publishing one comprehensive and exhaustive meta-analysis would be cause enough to swing triumphantly from the chandeliers. But Monica Harris is, after all, a Bob Rosenthal student, and so she and Bob published 31 meta-analyses in a single paper (Harris & Rosenthal, 1985). From this monumental effort, we now know, with no small measure of confidence, how people act differently when they expect the best from others (compared to when their expectations are less sanguine), and we also know whether these different ways of treating others seem to be associated with good or bad things happening to them. Some ways of behaving seem doubly possessed of these seemingly magical qualities – they are associated with both fond expectations and enviable outcomes. For example, teachers who expect their students to do well (compared to those who are not so optimistic) are more likely to smile at their students; look into their eyes; encourage and praise them; ask them more questions; teach them more material; interact with them more often, more closely, and for longer periods of time; and generally treat them in ways that seem affectionate and hopeful. As Bob Rosenthal has been heard to say, they "warm at" them. Further, students who have been warmed at in these ways seem to reciprocate by living up to their teachers' fond expectations; they do better work than students who are treated more coolly.

It would be oh so easy to slip from these empirical descriptions into prescriptions for all of our educational maladies. Students are not up to snuff? Train their teachers to smile at them and praise them and look into their eyes. Although the kindly intent of this prescription would be in keeping with the Rosenthalian legacy, the medicine is not (yet) what Dr. Rosenthal would order. For as he and Monica Harris duly noted, the methodological underpinnings of these conclusions are, at this point, too perilous. Too many of the studies that contributed to these empirical

261

generalizations were correlational, and as all good Rosenthalians know well, experiments are the best medicine.

Still, I suspect that there will be many tender-hearted souls out there who will say, in less than tender tones, "Screw the methodology." Despite Harris and Rosenthal's most solemn words of caution, they will want to take these findings and use them to make the world better. This chapter is dedicated to these warm-hearted (but soft-minded) do-gooders.

But not only to them. The issue I discuss is whether people can, if only they try, behave in all these warm ways that seem so promising and reap heartening outcomes as a consequence. The issue is more than methodological. In fact, I say no more about the dangers of according correlational data the respect due only to true experiments. Instead, I take on the theoretical challenge of whether we can, simply and straightforwardly, perform these warming behaviors at will. An impressive number of these behaviors are nonverbal ones, such as smiling and gazing. But even those behaviors that seem to be verbal ones, such as praising and encouraging, are almost always performed nonverbally; for example, they might be conveyed with a bouncy tone of voice and a perky face. When teachers feel genuinely warm and optimistic about their students, I think it is almost entirely nonproblematic for them to act that way. The theoretically more provocative instances are those in which they do not feel so warmly.

Teachers' expectations

Not warm, but not cold either

Some teachers, at some points, have rather undistinguished expectations about their students. Perhaps they have not met them yet or heard much about them, and so do not know what to expect. Or maybe what they do know has led them to expect bland academic performances – not particularly impressive and not particularly unimpressive. Let us suppose further that these teachers have decided to try to act as if they have high expectations for these students. They have read Harris and Rosenthal and have vowed to create for these students a warm climate filled with smiling and gazing, encouragement and praise, and close interactions. Is there any reason why these attempts at nonverbal warming might not be entirely successful? Actually, I think there are quite a few reasons (see also DePaulo, 1992).

Spontaneity and genuineness. If teachers are trying to convey warmth that they do not really feel, it is possible that their manner will appear to lack spontaneity and genuineness. Perhaps the students will notice that their teachers are trying to be warm, but also that their attempts seem forced. Warmth that seems to be an effort may not be very warming in its effects.

Can students and other perceivers distinguish genuinely spontaneous nonverbal behaviors from behaviors that were not produced spontaneously? My students and I are currently working on just this problem (DePaulo, Bell, & Klaaren, in preparation). The answer is important, because it indicates whether attempts at deliberate regulation of nonverbal behaviors can be recognized. Expressive behaviors are likely to be interpreted quite differently if they are seen as deliberate rather than spontaneous.

Personal style. Some teachers are simply not very warm people. That is not their personal style. Gordon Allport maintained that "Style . . . develops gradually from within; it cannot for long be stimulated or feigned" (1937, p. 493). If Allport is right (as well as Abraham Maslow [1949], who seemed to share much the same belief), then teachers who have not developed personal warmth from within may not be able to convey warmth convincingly to students for whom they do not have particularly high expectations.

Again, though, the question is empirical, and we do not know whether people can or cannot simulate a style that is not their own over extended interactions, such as those that teachers have day after day with the students in their classes. We *do* know, however, that they can do so over the course of rather brief interactions (e.g., DePaulo, Blank, Swaim, & Hairfield, 1992; Lippa, 1976; Toris & DePaulo, 1984).

Expressive characteristics. Teachers' attempts to convey warmth that they do not feel can be constrained not only by their personal style (which refers to all of their expressive behaviors and mannerisms considered together), but also by their specific expressive characteristics. Some of these characteristics that could be important are permanent physical features. For example, people who have voices that characteristically sound gruff or stern, or who have faces with features that seem harsh or hardened, may find it much more difficult to convey warmth compellingly than those who are endowed with voices or faces that seem softer or kinder.

The empirical question of whether physical features relevant to expressiveness can be constraining has been addressed in a variety of ways. For example, the voluminous literature on physical attractiveness is pertinent in that it suggests that people who are not very pretty are less often ascribed laudatory characteristics such as warmth, creativity, and brilliance than their more glamorous peers (Hatfield & Sprecher, 1986). Therefore, in attempting to convey warmth to their students, attractive teachers may at the outset have this attributional edge over their co-workers whose looks are at best only ordinary. Adults who have babyish faces and voices have a similar attributional advantage; people see them as warmer and kinder than those whose features are less childlike (Berry & McArthur, 1985, 1986; Montepare & Zebrowitz-McArthur, 1987).

There is also evidence for what I would call *angel faces*. Some people have honest-looking faces, and these people seem to be telling the truth whether they are or not (Zuckerman, DeFrank, Hall, Larrance, & Rosenthal, 1979). There are *angel voices*, too, whose owners always sound sincere (Zuckerman, Larrance, Spiegel, & Klorman, 1981). Pleasantness, too, seems to run in faces and voices; some people typically look or sound pleasant and sweet whether they feel that way or not (Zuckerman et al., 1979, 1981). These characteristic ways people have of looking or sounding have been dubbed *demeanor biases*. They are constraining to those who are not on the side of the angels or the sweethearts because it is more difficult for them to convey warmth and genuineness.

Dynamic cues. There are certain specific nonverbal behaviors that people either cannot control at will or rarely think to do so. For example, Ekman and his colleagues (e.g., Ekman, 1985; Ekman, Davidson, & Friesen, 1990; Ekman, Friesen, & O'Sullivan, 1988) have suggested that smiles of genuine enjoyment differ from other kinds of smiles in that they involve movements of particular facial muscles (the zygomatic major, which pulls up the corners of the lips, and the outer strands of the orbicularis oculi, which causes the crinkling around the eyes). Typically, people who are faking enjoyment do not make these facial movements. The differences between smiles of genuine enjoyment and other kinds of smiles can be subtle, though. So if teachers are trying to fake warmth, their students may not notice the ways in which their smiles are not genuine. It is possible, however, that they can sniff out a vague scent of insincerity. This possibility should be tracked down with data.

Expressiveness and expressive control. Some people are characteristically more spontaneously expressive than others. Their feelings and emotions are apparent in their faces and voices even when they are making no attempt to make them so. People who so readily show what they are feeling seem in many ways to lead charmed lives (DePaulo, 1992). They are liked better than less expressive types, they often appear more attractive, and they also influence others more successfully. The advantage of expressiveness is especially striking in the teaching profession. Expressive teachers are evaluated much more glowingly by their students than are more subdued ones (e.g., Abrami, Leventhal, & Perry, 1982; Basow & Distenfeld, 1985). When trying to convey warmth and optimism, expressive teachers, by their very expressiveness, may manage a warmer warmth and a more exuberant and convincing optimism; those who lack such animation, in contrast, may find it more difficult to sing praises in tones that ring clear and true.

Spontaneous expressiveness seems to be a natural quality. It is different from another expressive quality that is also of great significance – expressive control. Expressive control is a matter of deliberate regulation. For people who have such control, it is often the case that their wishes are their nonverbal behaviors' command. If they want to put on a happy face, for example, they can do so. Teachers who can deliberately manage their nonverbal behaviors should, theoretically, be successful at conveying warmth or enthusiasm or virtually any quality that can be simulated with a meaningful expression, gesture, or tone.

It may be possible, though, to "overcontrol" one's nonverbal behaviors. And it may be just those people who are inclined to control their expressive behaviors and skilled at doing so, such as high self-monitors (Snyder, 1987), who may be especially susceptible to overcontrolling their behaviors. Relevant data come from a study designed to test the hypothesis that the expectations of expressive teachers will be communicated more clearly than the expectations of unexpressive teachers (Sullins, Friedman, & Harris, 1985). Results supported the hypothesis only for teachers who were not only high in expressiveness but also low in expressive control (self-monitoring). Teachers who were high in both expressiveness and expressive control actually appeared to be conveying expectations that were different from the ones they really held. It appeared that while teaching the students for whom they had low expectations, they tried so intently not to convey any negativity that they seemed to be acting even more positively toward them than toward the students for whom their positive regard was genuine.

Awareness. There is a very interesting reason why people cannot always convey exactly what they would like to convey: Nonverbally, people simply may not know themselves very well. When interacting with others, people cannot see their own faces. In this sense, they literally do not know what they look like to others. Intuitively, it may seem that they at least know what they sound like, but even this is not true. Because the sound of their voices travels in different ways to get to their own ears than to other people's, they do not even hear their voices in the same ways that others do. If people do not know how they look or sound to others, it may be difficult for them to adjust their nonverbal behavior so that it conveys just the right impression. They just do not know how their nonverbal behavior appears in the first place, nor how it appears after the adjustments.

Feedback and attentiveness. Of course, there are many ways for people to learn something about how they appear to others short of seeing or hearing themselves exactly as others do. Most important, perhaps, is the fact that they can get feedback from others. "You seem to be in a good mood today," "You look great," and "You sound happy" are the kinds of comments others might make that provide clues to people about how they appear to others. There are many limitations to this sort of feedback, though.

First, these kinds of comments indicate only indirectly what people's nonverbal behaviors actually look or sound like. They are comments on the impressions conveyed by those behaviors and not on the behaviors themselves. Moreover, behaviors other than expressive ones contribute to such impressions. For example, people's eagerness to joke and tease may contribute as much as their smiling eyes to the impression that they are in a good mood.

Second is the obvious point that others sometimes say not what they really mean but what they think they should say. Those who are known to be seriously ill, for example, may well be among the most popular recipients of endless comments about how good they look. There is a clear (and empirically documented) bias in what people do convey to others and it is, indeed, mostly only the good stuff (e.g., Blumberg, 1972; Felson, 1980; Tesser & Rosen, 1975).

The moral of this story for the teachers who are trying to convey impressions of warmth and optimism to students toward whom they do not feel particularly warmly or optimistically is that they may not appear, nonverbally, the way they think they do, and they are probably not going to learn that from others. For teachers in particular, and for anyone else who is in a position of power with regard to the targets of their behaviors, the likelihood of hearing negative feedback is especially slim. Students and other underlings are not often heard to tell their superiors how phony they seem.

Students can, though, convey their impressions of their teachers in more subtle ways, such as with their own nonverbal behaviors. But that sort of feedback may go unnoticed. Dave Kenny and I have been studying people's awareness of the impressions they make on others. We have done a few of our own studies (DePaulo, Kenny, Hoover, Webb, & Oliver, 1987; Kenny & DePaulo, 1991) and reviewed numerous others (Kenny & DePaulo, 1992). We have been consistently underwhelmed by people's attentiveness to any feedback that might be available to them about how they are coming across to others. When we ask people to tell us how they think others viewed them during a particular interaction, they tell us about the same thing as when we ask them how they viewed themselves during the interaction. They seem to be looking mostly only at their own behavior, or perhaps only at their own theories about themselves, rather than at the reactions of other people. Further, people in more powerful roles, such as teachers, may be even less aware of the impression they are making on others than are people in less powerful roles, such as students (Snodgrass, 1985, 1992).

Cold

The teachers discussed previously who do not feel particularly warmly toward their students and who face all of the obstacles just described are the lucky ones. Maybe they are not the luckiest ones of all. (Those would be the teachers who want to convey high expectations to their students and who really do have high expectations for those students.) But they are far better off than the next category of teachers I describe – those who also would like to communicate positive expectations to their students but whose actual expectations are decidedly negative. Teachers who feel negatively but want to act positively face every one of the constraints described previously as pertaining to teachers who feel neutrally. But in addition, they face several more.

Emotional "leakage." Emotions seem to have lives of their own. When they are elicited, they seem to rush to make themselves known by trying to appear instantly on their owners' faces and in their voices and gestures. Strong emotions seem especially intent on exposing themselves. This spells trouble for the teachers who harbor cold or despairing feelings toward their students but who are trying to act warmly. For in addition to trying to simulate warmth, they must also try to stifle or bat away any signs of their negativity lest these "leak" through their expressive displays. Some people characteristically experience emotions more deeply than do others (e.g., Goldsmith et al., 1987; Larsen & Diener, 1987); teachers who are among these *affectively intense* individuals may have an even harder time than their more affectively moderate friends in keeping their negativity in check.

Motivational undercutting. Perhaps teachers can overcome all of these obstacles and more if only they try hard enough. Qualities like motivation and effort are so often what teachers try to instill in their students that it would be only fair for them to be well served by such qualities in themselves. Often, though, they are not. I have conducted study after study in which people try to convey a false impression under conditions in which they really care about doing so successfully (and presumably are trying especially hard) and conditions in which they do not care so much. And always, the results are the same. People's faked communications (compared to their genuine ones) are less likely to be believed, the more they want them to be believed (DePaulo & Kirkendol, 1989; DePaulo, Kirkendol, Tang, & O'Brien, 1988; DePaulo, Lanier, & Davis, 1983; DePaulo, Stone, & Lassiter, 1985a, 1985b). People's concern, their motivation, and their efforts seem to undercut their effectiveness. The implications for teachers are clear. Teachers can try too hard to convey warmth to students toward whom they feel anything but warmly. And that can show.

Clarion call

This might seem to be the time in this chapter for me to issue the mandatory clarion call for further research. I might propose, for example, that what we need is an experiment in which teachers teach a lesson and administer a test to students who perform either outstandingly or dreadfully while trying always to praise the student, regardless of the quality of the student's performance. I might also suggest that it would be worthwhile to manipulate experimentally the teacher's liking for the student, perhaps through some clever ruse. Then the question would be whether the teacher's nonverbal behavior would conceal or reveal that the student (in some conditions) in fact was *not* performing well, the teacher's praise notwithstanding, or that the teacher in fact did *not* like the student. Fortunately, I can dispense with such sage advice, for this study has already been done. Bob Feldman published it almost two decades ago (Feldman, 1976).

In Feldman's study, observers who watched tapes of the teachers indicated how pleased the teachers seemed to be with their students. In a sense, the teachers were quite successful at conveying the impression that they felt positively toward their students, for in all conditions, the observers thought that they were in fact pleased. (That is, the observers' ratings were substantially above the midpoint.) This is a finding we have seen time and again in the literature on deception. People generally believe each other's intended impressions, even when they are false (e.g., DePaulo et al., 1985a). Bob Rosenthal and I found this in the first deception study we conducted together, in which people talked about people they knew both honestly and deceptively (DePaulo & Rosenthal, 1979). When people were pretending to like people they actually despised, others thought they really did like those people; and when they were pretending to dislike people they really liked, others believed that there really were hard feelings.

Yet, in the person description study and in most other deception studies, others are not totally taken in by faked performances. Though they might believe, for example, that someone claiming falsely to like another person really does feel fondly toward that person, they sense that the fondness is a bit less intense than it is for people who are professing their genuine liking for another. They also think it seems a little less sincere. And of course, they will be right about this (e.g., DePaulo et al., 1985a). Sometimes it is mostly a vague sense of something being awry that seems to guide people in their judgments. For example, they notice a bigger difference between genuine expressions of liking and faked ones if they are asked how internally discrepant the communications seem or how ambivalent or indifferent the speakers seem than if they are asked directly whether the speakers are lying (DePaulo, Rosenthal, Green, & Rosenkrantz, 1982).

The observers in the Feldman (1976) study were no exception. Even though they thought that the teachers were basically pleased with their students in all conditions, they noticed accurately that some teachers were more pleased than others. When the student performed poorly, they could tell that the teacher was less pleased than when the student performed well, even though the teacher always dutifully praised each student for every response. Similarly, when the teacher was led to dislike the student (by "accidentally" overhearing the student make an unflattering comment about the teacher), she appeared to the observers to be less pleased with the student than when she was led to like the student (by overhearing a kind comment), even though, once again, the teacher always praised every response from every student.

To the question of whether teachers can communicate high expectations if only they try, the Feldman (1976) study, as well as the body of literature on the communication of deception, suggests the answer "sort of." Teachers who try to convey high expectations will probably appear to have such expectations. However, they will be a tad (but a significant tad) less convincing than teachers whose expectations really are high.

The other lesson provided by these teachers and researchers is that the leakage of genuinely negative feelings through a warm facade may be quite subtle. An intriguing finding that could be an example of this comes from a study of Marylee Taylor's (1979) in which teachers instructed white or black students. Teachers instructing blacks said that they expected their students to do better than did the teachers instructing whites. However, when their students came up with the right answer, they were more likely to move on with the lesson without praising them. They were also less likely to "slip" and tell their black student a helpful hint by mistake.

Students' sensitivity, awareness, and self-perceptions

The other answer to the question of whether we can communicate high expectations if only we try is "it depends." Predictably, it will depend on many things. But among the most important of these may be the characteristics of the person who is the target of our expectations.

When teachers try to convey warmth that they do not feel, their success will depend in part on the degree to which their students go along with their performances. Our inclination to take each other's self-presentations at face value and to assume that a kind word betokens a kind heart at times seems virtually irrepressible (e.g., Goffman, 1959; Jones, 1979, 1990). But of course, it is not. We can be alerted by a variety of contextual hints that all may not be as it appears. Further, there are systematic individual differences in the tendency to take people at their word (or smile).

Bob Rosenthal and I discovered this in a series of studies we conducted on sex differences in understanding nonverbal cues. We did not set out to study sex differences because I thought that would be boring and trite. (Those were the androgyny days.) But the sex differences popped out of all of our computer printouts, and they did not put either of us to sleep. The initial studies were ones in which we had tested people for their sensitivity to various nonverbal cues that differed in their overtness or controllability. Facial expressions, for example, are very overt cues that are relatively easy for people to regulate and control; tone of voice cues, in contrast, are more difficult to manage. Sometimes when people try to convey one impression (especially a false one), tone of voice cues will leak a different one. In some studies we had as many as five kinds of cues arranged along our continuum of overtness or controllability. When we looked at sex differences in understanding such cues (which we did at first, simply out of diligence), we found that women were generally better than men at understanding these nonverbal cues, which by then was news to no one (Hall, 1978). But what *was* news was that they were clearly better only at reading the most overt and controllable nonverbal cues. As cues became more covert and uncontrollable, women systematically lost their advantage over men (Rosenthal & DePaulo, 1979a, 1979b). It was as if women were politely refraining from reading just those cues that others might prefer that they ignore. But they were great at reading those cues that others presumably wanted them to read.

When we added back the words and used a whole different paradigm, the story line was still the same. The words we used were from the person description study in which people were describing others honestly or dishonestly (DePaulo & Rosenthal, 1979). When women listened to people pretending to like someone they disliked, or pretending to dislike someone they liked, they, even more than the men, believed the faked feeling (Rosenthal & DePaulo, 1979a, 1979b). Since the women in that study, more than the men, believed that feigned expressions of liking conveyed truly warm sentiments, it is likely that the same might happen in a classroom. When teachers try to convey positive expectations that they do not necessarily harbor, it may be their female students, more than the males, who are warmed by them.

Intuitively, it may seem that young children, compared to older children and adults, are especially likely to believe what they hear. But this is not necessarily so. In a developmental study of deception-detection, my students and I played the person description tapes to listeners ranging from sixth graders to college students (DePaulo, Jordan, Irvine, & Laser, 1982). We asked them to tell us, for each description, how honest the speaker seemed. Unsurprisingly, the younger listeners were less adept than the older ones at distinguishing the honest descriptions from the dishonest ones. However, their perceptions of honesty were hardly random. Rather than varying with the actual honesty of the descriptions, though, they varied systematically with the degree of positivity or negativity that was expressed. When the speakers said kind things about the people they were describing, either because they really liked them or because they were pretending to like them, the younger listeners were especially likely to think that they were telling the truth, and when they said unkind words, the younger listeners were especially likely to think that they were lying. The older listeners showed a more cynical bias, rating the nastier descriptions as relatively more truthful than the kinder ones.

For the many teachers of grade school children, the documented age effects could be good news. The results suggest that young children are unlikely to be able to distinguish genuinely warm expressions from faked ones, and that they may be especially inclined to equate kindliness with truthfulness. Perhaps, then, teachers' purposeful attempts to convey positive expectations to them will be rewarded with equally positive student performances.

Other kinds of students who may be especially vulnerable to their teachers' expectations for them may be those who are uncertain of themselves on competence-relevant dimensions (e.g., Swann, 1987; Swann & Ely, 1984), as well as those who deeply value their teachers' opinions (e.g., Jussim, 1986).

The focus of this analysis has been on the purposeful communication of positive expectations because I suspect that few teachers are so perverse as to try deliberately to convey expectations that are more negative than those that they actually hold (and even fewer would recognize it or admit to it even if they did). But of course, genuinely negative impressions do get formed and communicated, even if unintentionally. Further, evidence of negative expectations can leak, or sometimes even pour out, even when teachers are trying to squelch such evidence. Students, though, will not necessarily be washed away by their teachers' negativity. If they become aware of their teachers' negative perceptions of them, they can work to try to dissuade the teachers of those views, and they may even succeed (e.g., Hilton & Darley, 1985).

The more serious (though perhaps infrequent) threat to the students' achievement could occur if, for some reason, despite the teacher's best intentions (and expectations), the students become convinced that the teacher does not like them or does not think they are smart. When this happens, there may be little the teacher can do that will not be interpreted by the students as supporting their "poor me" theory (Kleck & Strenta, 1980).

The Pygmalion study of several decades ago (Rosenthal & Jacobson, 1968) captured the imagination of many a teacher, student, layperson, and scholar from the moment it became known. Maybe it was the spell cast by such a provocative piece of science that led so many subsequent expectancy researchers to do their work in the classroom. The smell of chalk dust wafts through this literature, and so I have written this chapter on a blackboard. But the hypotheses and conclusions I have drawn may well apply to expectancy processes in virtually all domains. The relevant research will probably be done, and as Bob Rosenthal has often noted, it will surely be fun.

References

Abrami, P. C., Leventhal, L., & Perry, R. P. (1982). Educational seduction. *Review of Educational Research, 52,* 446–464.

Allport, G. W. (1937). *Personality.* New York: Holt.

Basow, S. A., & Distenfeld, M. S. (1985). Teacher expressiveness: More important for male teachers than female teachers? *Journal of Educational Psychology, 77,* 45–52.

Berry, D. S., & McArthur L. Z. (1985). Some components and consequences of a babyface. *Journal of Personality and Social Psychology, 48,* 312–323.

Berry, D. S., & McArthur, L. Z. (1986). Perceiving character in faces: The impact of age-related craniofacial changes on social perception. *Psychological Bulletin, 100,* 3–18.

Blumberg, H. H. (1972). Communication of interpersonal evaluations. *Journal of Personality and Social Psychology, 23,* 157–162.

DePaulo, B. M. (1992). Nonverbal behavior and self-presentation. *Psychological Bulletin, 111,* 203–243.

DePaulo, B. M., Bell, K. L., & Klaaren, K. (1991). *Genuine and faked spontaneity.* In preparation.

DePaulo, B. M., Blank, A. L., Swaim, G. W., & Hairfield, J. G. (1992). Expressiveness and expressive control. *Personality and Social Psychology Bulletin.*

DePaulo, B. M., Jordan, A., Irvine, A., & Laser, P. S. (1982). Age changes in the detection of deception. *Child Development, 53,* 701–709.

DePaulo, B. M., Kenny, D. A., Hoover, C., Webb, W., & Oliver, P. (1987). Accuracy of person perception: Do people know what kinds of impressions they convey? *Journal of Personality and Social Psychology, 52,* 303–315.

274   Bella M. DePaulo

DePaulo, B. M., & Kirkendol, S. E. (1989). The motivational impairment effect in the communication of deception. In J. Yuille (Ed.), *Credibility assessment* (pp. 51–70). Belgium: Kluwer.

DePaulo, B. M., Kirkendol, S. E., Tang, J., & O'Brien, T. (1988). The motivational impairment effect in the communication of deception: Replications and extensions. *Journal of Nonverbal Behavior, 12,* 177–202.

DePaulo, B. M., Lanier, K., & Davis, T. (1983). Detecting the deceit of the motivated liar. *Journal of Personality and Social Psychology, 45,* 1096–1103.

DePaulo, B. M., & Rosenthal, R. (1979). Telling lies. *Journal of Personality and Social Psychology, 37,* 1713–1722.

DePaulo, B. M., Rosenthal, R., Green, C. R., & Rosenkrantz, J. (1982). Diagnosing deceptive and mixed messages from verbal and nonverbal cues. *Journal of Experimental Social Psychology, 18,* 433–446.

DePaulo, B. M., Stone, J. I., & Lassiter, G. D. (1985a). Deceiving and detecting deceit. In B. R. Schlenker (Ed.), *The self and social life* (pp. 323–370). New York: McGraw-Hill.

DePaulo, B. M., Stone, J. I., & Lassiter, G. D. (1985b). Telling ingratiating lies: Effects of target sex and target attractiveness on verbal and nonverbal deceptive success. *Journal of Personality and Social Psychology, 48,* 1191–1203.

Ekman, P. (1985). *Telling lies.* New York: Norton.

Ekman, P., Davidson, R., & Friesen, W. V. (1990). Duchenne's smile: Emotional expression and brain physiology II. *Journal of Personality and Social Psychology, 58,* 342–353.

Ekman, P., Friesen, W. V., & O'Sullivan M. (1988). Smiles when lying. *Journal of Personality and Social Psychology, 54,* 414–420.

Feldman, R. S. (1976). Nonverbal disclosure of teacher deception and interpersonal affect. *Journal of Educational Psychology, 68,* 807–816.

Felson, R. B. (1980). Communication barriers and the reflected appraisal process. *Social Psychology Quarterly, 43,* 223–233.

Goffman, E. (1959). *The presentation of self in everyday life.* Garden City, NY: Doubleday, Anchor Books.

Goldsmith, H. H., Buss, A. H., Plomin, R., Rothbart, M. K., Thomas, A., Chess, S., Hinde, R. A., & McCall, R. B. (1987). Roundtable: What is temperament? Four approaches. *Child Development, 58,* 505–529.

Harris, M. J., & Rosenthal, R. (1985). Mediation of interpersonal expectancy effects: 31 meta-analyses. *Psychological Bulletin, 97,* 363–386.

Hatfield, E., & Sprecher, S. (1986). *Mirror, mirror.* Albany: State University of New York Press.

Hilton, J. L., & Darley, J. D. (1985). Constructing other persons: A limit on the effect. *Journal of Experimental Social Psychology, 21,* 1–18.

Hall, J. A. (1978). Gender effects in decoding nonverbal cues. *Psychological Bulletin, 85,* 845–857.

Jones, E. E. (1979). The rocky road from acts to dispositions. *American Psychologist, 34,* 104–117.

Jones, E. E. (1990). *Interpersonal perception.* New York: Freeman.

Jussim, L. (1986). Self-fulfilling prophecies: A theoretical and integrative review. *Psychological Review, 93,* 429–445.

Kenny, D. A., & DePaulo, B. M. (1991). *Accuracy of meta-perceptions.* Unpublished data, University of Connecticut.

Kenny, D. A., & DePaulo, B. M. (1992). *Do we know how others view us? An empirical and theoretical account.* Manuscript submitted for review.

Kleck, R. F., & Strenta, A. (1980). Perceptions of the impact of negatively valued physical characteristics on social interactions. *Journal of Personality and Social Psychology, 39,* 861–873.

Larsen, R. J., & Diener, E. (1987). Affect intensity as an individual difference characteristic: A review. *Journal of Research in Personality, 21,* 1–39.

Lippa, R. (1976). Expressive control and the leakage of dispositional introversion-extraversion during role-playing teaching. *Journal of Personality, 44,* 541–559.

Maslow, A. H. (1949). The expressive component of behavior. *Psychological Review, 56,* 261–272.

Montepare, J. M., & Zebrowitz-McArthur, L. (1987). Perceptions of adults with childlike voices in two cultures. *Journal of Experimental Social Psychology, 23,* 331–349.

Rosenthal, R., & DePaulo, B. M. (1979a). Sex differences in accommodation in nonverbal communication. In R. Rosenthal (Ed.), *Skill in nonverbal communication* (pp. 68–103). Cambridge, MA: Oelgeschlager, Gunn, & Hain.

Rosenthal, R., & DePaulo, B. M. (1979b). Sex differences in eavesdropping on nonverbal cues. *Journal of Personality and Social Psychology, 37,* 273–285.

Rosenthal, R., & Jacobson, L. (1968). *Pygmalion in the classroom: Teacher expectation and pupils' intellectual development.* New York: Holt, Rinehart and Winston.

Snodgrass, S. E. (1985). Women's intuition: The effect of subordinate role upon interpersonal sensitivity. *Journal of Personality and Social Psychology, 49,* 146–155.

Snodgrass, S. E. (1992). Further effects of role versus gender on interpersonal sensitivity. *Journal of Personality and Social Psychology, 62,* 154–158.

Snyder, M. (1987). *Public appearances, private realities: The psychology of self-monitoring.* New York: Freeman.

Sullins, E. S., Friedman, H. S., & Harris, M. J. (1985). Individual differences in expressive style as a mediator of expectancy communication. *Journal of Nonverbal Behavior, 9,* 229–238.

Swann, W. B., Jr. (1987). Identity negotiation: Where two roads meet. *Journal of Personality and Social Psychology, 53,* 1038–1051.

Swann, W. B., Jr., & Ely, R. J. (1984). A battle of wills: Self-verification versus behavioral confirmation. *Journal of Personality and Social Psychology, 46,* 1287–1302.

Taylor, M. C. (1979). Race, sex, and the expression of self-fulfilling prophecies in a laboratory teaching situation. *Journal of Personality and Social Psychology, 37,* 897–912.

Tesser, A., & Rosen, S. (1975). The reluctance to transmit bad news. In L. Berkowitz (Ed.), *Advances in experimental social psychology* (Vol. 8, pp. 194–232). Orlando, FL: Academic Press.

Toris, C., & DePaulo, B. M. (1984). Effects of actual deception and suspiciousness of deception on interpersonal perceptions. *Journal of Personality and Social Psychology, 47,* 1063–1073.

Zuckerman, M., DeFrank R. S., Hall, J. A., Larrance, D. T., & Rosenthal, T. (1979). Facial and vocal cues of deception and honesty. *Journal of Experimental Social Psychology, 15,* 378–396.

Zuckerman, M., Larrance, D. T., Spiegel, N. H., & Klorman, R. (1981). Controlling nonverbal displays: Facial expressions and tone of voice. *Journal of Experimental Social Psychology, 17,* 506–524.

14. Gender, nonverbal behavior, and expectations

JUDITH A. HALL AND NANCY J. BRITON

People have a persistent desire to understand where their patterns of social behavior come from, and this is never more evident than in the search for the sources of gender differences. Explanations for gender differences have pointed to genes, hormones, hemispheric specialization, modeling, identity and conformity processes, social status, social and occupational roles, self-expectations, and social expectations. Obviously, these are not mutually exclusive, as they represent explanations at different levels of analysis or different positions in a causal stream. As far as we know, no one has the correct recipe for combining different proximal and distal causes to produce the final gender-difference soup. And, just as a recipe varies with the kind of soup one wants, so is it likely that the determinants of a gender difference vary with the behavior one wishes to explain.

Such uncertainty over the sources of a gender difference is clearly evident in the case of nonverbal communication (Hall, 1984, 1987). In contrast to the ease with which differences can be found between males and females in nonverbal skills and behavior, there is no consensus on where the differences come from. Commonly cited is the possibility that status or dominance differences between men and women shape their nonverbal repertoires (Henley, 1977). However, it has not been articulated at what point these differences have their effect. Women's oppression could be a distal, historical cause, shaping society's roles and expectations, or a proximal, here-and-now cause (e.g., a woman needs to smile in order to appear nonthreatening).

The hypothesis that oppression produces nonverbal gender differences has had mixed support (see Hall, 1984, and Vrugt & Kerkstra, 1984, for reviews). Perhaps this is inevitable, considering that nonverbal behavior is often ambiguous and heavily context dependent in meaning. Thus, a smile may mean appeasement but it may also mean friendliness, joy, reassurance, embarrassment, anxiety, lechery, or even threat, depending on contextual factors and other associated nonverbal behaviors. The fact that nonverbal behaviors do not have unique social meanings complicates the search for reasons why men and women differ in their use.

Regardless of one's theoretical preference, however, there can be no doubt that society has strong expectations for male and female behavior styles, which are embodied in gender stereotypes. In the first half of this chapter, we document these stereotypes in the realm of nonverbal communication, and we show that there is good correspondence between these expectations and actual gender differences. We then discuss possible causal connections between these expectations and actual male–female differences in nonverbal communication, with emphasis on the interpersonal expectancy effect or self-fulfilling prophecy.

In the second half of the chapter, we apply a different framework for understanding the relations among gender, nonverbal behavior, and expectations. Here our concern is also with interpersonal expectancy effects; however, the question we ask is not how gender differences come about, but rather what the role of gender is in determining the magnitudes of expectancy effects in randomized experiments. Though it has long been hypothesized that individual differences play a role in interpersonal expectancy effects, the role of gender as a moderator has not been systematically examined since 1969, when Robert Rosenthal addressed this issue in the context of photo-rating studies (Rosenthal, 1969).

Expectations for male and female behavior

Stereotypes contribute significantly to expectations for male and female behavior. Studies of college students, parents, and teachers show that the behavior of children and adults is perceived to differ by gender, both in the United States and cross-culturally (Antill, 1987; Bem, 1974; Dusek & Joseph, 1983; Spence, Helmreich, & Stapp, 1975; Williams & Bennett, 1975; Williams & Best, 1982). As an illustration, Antill (1987) gathered free responses from parents in Australia and found that they considered boys to be more aggressive, dominant, rough, strong, noisy and loud-mouthed, outgoing, friendly, cheeky, and mischievous. They considered girls to be more temperamental, emotional, devious, cunning, gentle, sensitive to others, neat, and responsible. When children are respondents, gender stereotypes are also evident, both within the

Table 14.1. *Representative gender-stereotypic adjectives*

Gender	Descriptor
Male	aggressive, dominant, rough, loud-mouthed, active, lazy, clever, adventurous, self-confident, strong, rational, independent, enterprising, boastful, coarse, ambitious, analytical, competitive, worldly, not timid, makes decisions easily, feels superior
Female	emotional, gentle, sensitive, neat, patient, vain, weak, helpful, affectionate, charming, excitable, sentimental, understanding, warm, loyal, gullible, flatterable, frivolous, compassionate, considerate, kind

United States and cross-culturally (Payne, 1981; Zammuner, 1987). Zammuner's Italian and Dutch children applied to females the adjectives *patient, shy, sensitive, chatterbox, gossipy, vain,* and *weak* and the verbs *comfort, cure, spend, cry, be curious, serve,* and *obey.* To males they applied the adjectives *lazy, superficial, clever, absentminded, loud, violent,* and *strong* and the verbs *yell, protect, make jokes, construct, repair, break,* and *punish.*

Often, subjects in studies apply more favorable adjectives to males, though a recent study found the reverse among American college students (Eagly & Mladinic, 1989). Table 14.1 presents a representative list of gender-stereotypic adjectives and phrases from various instruments (Archer & Lloyd, 1985). In general, "masculine" and "feminine" traits fall into two categories: agentic or instrumental for the masculine and expressive or communal for the feminine (Bem, 1974; Spence et al., 1975).

Self-descriptions tend to fall in line with the stereotypes. Most adjective-rating studies employ instruments containing mainly positive adjectives such as the Bem Sex-Role Inventory (Bem, 1974) and the Personal Attributes Questionnaire (Spence et al., 1975). For these studies, gender differences are sometimes smaller for masculine items than for feminine items, perhaps because it is more acceptable in our society for females to admit to having positive male traits such as independence and self-confidence than for males to claim they have positive female traits such as sensitivity and gentleness (Hall & Halberstadt, 1980). For an instrument containing only negative masculine and feminine traits, self-reports also converge with the stereotypes (Spence, Helmreich, & Holahan, 1979).

Self-descriptions may be biased by the respondents' knowledge of stereotypes, and may therefore show gender differences that are larger than the ones that occur in daily life. It is therefore important to look for behavioral validation of self-reported gender differences. In the following pages we summarize the relevant validation data for nonverbal gender differences.

Social sensitivity

Popular stereotypes depict women as more sensitive, more understanding, more aware of others' feelings, and generally more socially sensitive than men. This stereotype is reflected in femininity scales, fictional writing, ratings and free-response descriptions collected from undergraduates (Briton & Hall, 1992a), and self-reports using psychometric instruments (Zuckerman & Larrance, 1979). The last study asked subjects to respond in detail about their nonverbal decoding and encoding skills, and found sex differences surprisingly similar in magnitude to those documented in objective decoding tests. Interestingly, however, the correlations between actual skills and self-perceived skills were small, indicating that subjects are aware of the stereotype but are poor judges of their own nonverbal skill levels. Briton and Hall (1992a) also asked students to rate men and women on their ability to decode nonverbal cues, as well as their ability to recognize faces. Subjects perceived women to excel in both.

Empirical research on nonverbal communication skills finds that girls and women are in fact more accurate at decoding nonverbal cues of emotion, especially facial expressions (Hall, 1978; Rosenthal & DePaulo, 1979; Rosenthal, Hall, DiMatteo, Rogers, & Archer, 1979). This finding holds up across cultures and over many different kinds of measuring instruments, including, most recently, the Interpersonal Perception Task (Costanzo & Archer, 1989), a test requiring judgments of kinship, status, relational intimacy, and deception rather than specific affects.

Recent evidence suggests that there may be an exception to women's superior decoding skills where expressions of anger are concerned; here, women appear to read facial cues less accurately than men do, especially when the encoder is a man (Rotter & Rotter, 1988; Wagner, MacDonald, & Manstead, 1986).

Females were found to be more accurate in facial recognition in one review (Hall, 1984), though another review concluded that there was no gender difference (Shapiro & Penrod, 1986).

Expression skills and expressiveness

According to the stereotype, women are more expressive and do not hide their emotions. This stereotype has been documented in femininity scales, in self-reports (Zuckerman & Larrance, 1979), in research specifically on stereotypes of male and female emotional expressiveness and expression skills (Briton & Hall, 1992a; Fabes & Martin, 1991), and in students' free responses (Briton & Hall, 1992a). Research that assesses actual differences related to this stereotype finds that females have more expressive faces, bodies, and voices and are more accurate at sending spontaneous and intentional nonverbal cues of emotion, especially via the face (Hall, 1984; Wagner et al., 1986). For the voice, in fact, little overall evidence of a gender difference in posed encoding skill has emerged (Hall, 1984).

Cheer, warmth

According to the popular stereotype, women are more cheerful, warm, and affectionate than men. Affiliation and warmth are often expressed through nonverbal cues (Andersen, 1985). Examples of these nonverbal *immediacy* cues are closer distance, more direct body orientation, more forward lean, more touching, more nodding, more gazing, and more smiling. In light of this finding, it is consistent with the stereotype that in surveys, college students indicated a belief that women engage in more smiling and gazing than men (Briton & Hall, 1992a).

Research on males' and females' actual nonverbal behavior finds that female behavior is more warm, immediate, and direct in terms of smiling, gazing, interpersonal distance, angle of body orientation, and touch (Hall, 1984, 1987). A qualification to this generalization is probably in order, however; typically, research is done in friendly, nonthreatening situations (Hall & Halberstadt, 1986). When the situation is threatening or involves total strangers, females may be as defensive, or more so, than males are (Fisher & Byrne, 1975; Meisels & Guardo, 1969).

Observer bias

In sum, research has provided an impressive degree of validation for stereotypes of male and female nonverbal skills and behavior. However, an important caveat should be issued because many studies that have the capacity to validate self-reported gender differences in behavior use *observers* as data gatherers, and observers probably hold stereo-types about male and female nonverbal behavior. A reasonable hypoth-esis, therefore, is that observers' knowledge of the stereotypes biases their observations of the sexes (Hall, 1984).

Several studies in which infants and children were observed by adults suggest that gender-stereotypic observational bias may be a problem (Culp, Cook, & Housley, 1983; Lyons & Serbin, 1986; Meyer & Sobi-eszek, 1972; Rubin, Provenzano, & Luria, 1974). Rubin et al. (1974) interviewed new parents of a first-born child, asking them to describe their day-old infants. Daughters were described by both parents as softer, smaller, weaker, and more inattentive. Sons were described as larger, firmer, better coordinated, more alert, and stronger. Fathers were more extreme than mothers in providing stereotyped descriptions. The children did not actually differ by gender in birth weight, length, or other physiological measures.

Meyer and Sobieszek (1972) asked adults to observe a videotape of two children, alternately described as a boy or a girl. They found that men, especially those with little experience interacting with children, tended to describe the "boy" and "girl" using sex-role stereotyped adjectives. In the Culp et al. (1983) study, adults, who had children of their own, played with a child (not their own), who was sometimes described as a boy and sometimes as a girl. The adults acted differently toward the 'boy" and the "girl." Both men and women spoke more to the child if it was a "girl" but smiled more at the "boy." A feminine or neutral toy was selected for the "girl," especially by the women. Al-though all the parents treated the child differently according to its perceived gender, all reported that there is no difference in the way they treat their own male and female children. Nearly all the adults reported that there should be no difference in the kinds of toys that boys and girls play with at that age. All were unaware that they had treated the child differently.

Studies that have not specifically focused on bias due to gender stereotypes also indicate that expectations can produce bias when be-havior is observed (e.g., Binning, Zaba, & Whattam, 1986; Langlois & Prestholdt, 1977). Therefore, it is important to ascertain whether observ-ers' preexisting beliefs about nonverbal gender differences influence the gender differences that they describe. In our laboratory, we have exam-ined this, using the nonverbal behavior of smiling (Briton & Hall, 1992b). We examined the relationship between observers' preexisting belief in smiling sex differences and how much of a sex difference in smiling they recorded when observing a videotaped person's behavior. We were surprised to find no significant differences in scoring between observers who believed that women smile more than men and those who believed that there is no sex difference in smiling. We also induced an expectation in some of our observers. We told these observers to expect to see women smile more than men or to expect to see no sex difference in smiling. Again, we found no significant difference in the amount of smiling observed by participants in either expectancy condition. In other words, we obtained null results for expectancy, whether the expectancy was a preexisting belief held by the observer or an expectancy induced by an experimenter.

Why did we obtain these null results? First, it is possible that the nonverbal behavior of smiling may be a very straightforward behavior for an observer to score. Smiling may not be as susceptible to bias as other nonverbal behaviors, or as human traits like aggressiveness and softness, which are judged by a combination of behaviors. Second, results obtained in such a laboratory condition may not be generalizable to behavior that occurs in everyday conditions. Our laboratory observers may have been very vigilant in their observation, careful to score the smiles correctly. Participants in everyday interactions may be less careful and may think they see behaviors from others that do not exist, or they may exaggerate real differences that are consistent with the stereotype.

Processes linking expectations to gender differences

If nonverbal gender differences do exist, then stereotypes (expectations) may simply reflect society's acknowledgment of these differences. However, it seems far more likely that causation goes both ways – from expectations to behavior and back.

One way that expectations based on stereotypes may shape nonverbal gender differences is through self-socialization (Maccoby & Jacklin, 1974). In this process, a person internalizes a concept of maleness or femaleness and then conforms to his or her notions of what this entails. Liberal parents who are dismayed at a toddler daughter's insistence on wearing pastel colors and frilly socks and playing with fluffy toys will surely recognize this process at work. Society offers no dearth of clues as to what is appropriately male and female, starting with choices for infant room decor, toys, and clothes and progressing through children's literature, advertising, and media depictions. Pomerleau, Bolduc, Malcuit, and Cossette (1990) compared the toys, clothing, and accessories of 120 first-born boys and girls, aged 3 to 25 months, and found obvious evidence of gender-role stereotyping. The parents had provided dolls, kitchen and household appliances and furniture, telephones, and type-writers as toys for their daughters; sons had more tools, sports equipment, medical kits, and vehicles. More girls than boys were dressed in pink and had jewelry; more boys wore blue and had blue bedding and curtains.

A second process whereby expectations shape gender differences involves conforming, more or less deliberately, to others' real or imagined expectations. Such normative conformity processes rest on the need for approval. Zanna and Pack (1975) demonstrated that college women presented themselves as more stereotypically feminine and performed worse on an anagrams task when they anticipated meeting an attractive young man with traditional gender-role values than when their anticipated interactant had nontraditional values. In a follow up study, von Baeyer, Sherk, and Zanna (1981) found that women believing that an interviewer had more traditional gender-role attitudes wore more makeup and accessories, gazed less while speaking, and spoke less than females believing that their interviewer had more progressive attitudes. Such strategic shaping of oneself for public consumption is a common experience. Most of the time, it does not feel disingenuous because what we choose to emphasize in self-presentation often falls within the range of our usual or possible behavior. Thus, a wide range of behavior can feel authentic or natural to us.

Pressure to conform to gender stereotypes can be great. Men who are gesturally or facially expressive, for example, may be stigmatized as being weak or feminine, and women who do not smile much may be perceived as hostile or may be told to "cheer up" or "gimme a smile." What transpired in the minds of the subjects of Zanna and Pack and of von Baeyer et al. is unknown, but over time, the repeated experience of selectively presenting oneself to different audiences could produce real changes in self-image and associated behaviors (Bem, 1972). Thus, one's expectations for what others expect, in conjunction with actual rewards and punishments, produce gender-stereotypic behavior.

A third process whereby stereotypes translate into gender differences is through interpersonal expectations, or the self-fulfilling prophecy – a process in which targets respond (often unconsciously) to unintentional behavioral cues emitted by perceivers. Though the bulk of research on expectancy effects has been done to assess the impact of experimenters' and teachers' expectations, common sense as well as empirical research tell us that interpersonal self-fulfilling prophecies occur often in daily life, in routine social interactions such as meeting, greeting, working together, and living in a family. Thus, Snyder, Tanke, and Berscheid (1977) demonstrated that the expectation that another is physically attractive will make that person behave attractively (on the telephone). Jones and Panitch (1971) found that the belief that one is liked by another person produces changes in actual returned liking, as well as more cooperative responses in a competitive game (at least for males).

It is reasonable to assume that self-fulfilling prophecies may shape nonverbal gender differences, just as they shape other gender-related behaviors (Eccles, Jacobs, & Harold, 1990; Skrypnek & Snyder, 1982; Towson, Zanna, & MacDonald, 1984–1985). Deaux and Major (1987) and Hamilton, Sherman, and Ruvolo (1990) describe some of the ways in which stereotype-based expectancies can affect the behavior of perceivers and targets.

In everyday social situations where gender-difference expectations would typically have an effect, the mediating mechanism is likely to be reciprocity, or the return of a similar behavior. Thus, in Snyder et al. (1977), the perceivers' belief that the target was physically attractive led the perceivers to act more warm, humorous, outgoing, and socially adept – a pattern of behavior to which targets responded in kind. Thus, the interpersonal *climate,* shown to be an important mediator of teacher expectations (Harris & Rosenthal, 1985), is probably key in producing gender-stereotypic nonverbal behavior. Climate includes verbal behavior and nonverbal warmth, smiles, gazing, forward lean, head nods, touch, and interpersonal distance. As examples of how such mediation could occur in the production of nonverbal gender differences, a person who expects a man to be relatively distant emotionally might avoid extended gazes and initiatives on intimate topics, and a person who expects a woman to be receptive and warm might smile at her a lot, stand close, and engage in interpersonal touch. Recipients of such behaviors are likely to respond with similar behaviors, or with different behaviors that are similarly valenced in terms of immediacy (e.g., repaying a smile with closer distance). Smiling, one of the preeminent nonverbal gender differences, is extremely likely to produce reciprocal smiling in another (Cappella, 1981; Hinsz & Tomhave, 1991; Jorgensen, 1978).

However, it must be noted that in the nonverbal literature there are many demonstrations of compensation as opposed to reciprocation (i.e., engaging in opposite or offsetting behavior rather than reciprocal behavior), and some studies of self-fulfilling prophecies find that people behave in the opposite manner to what is expected of them (Hilton & Darley, 1984; Jussim, 1990). Clearly, people sometimes react against the expectations that society and other individuals communicate to them. Determining when this happens and with what effect, with respect to the development of nonverbal gender differences, would be an important topic of study.

Gender as a moderator in interpersonal expectancy effects

So far, we have concentrated on ways in which expectations might produce nonverbal gender differences and vice versa. But we can also approach the relation of gender to expectations by asking whether interpersonal expectancy effects are moderated (affected) by the gender of the people involved. Here we shall summarize preliminary results of a meta-analysis conducted to answer this question (Briton & Hall, 1992c).

Let us begin by considering what kinds of moderating effects might occur and why. Several authors have suggested that the combination of male perceivers and female targets would produce the greatest expectancy effects (Compton, 1970; Wessler & Strauss, 1968). One theoretical foundation for predicting the largest expectancy effect in male perceiver–female target dyads would be that men's communications are more closely monitored than women's by virtue of men's higher status in society. Thus, any cues sent by men may be influential, and if those cues happen to be biasing cues, then men will bias the responses of targets more than women will. Conversely, targets may view female perceivers (usually experimenters or teachers in the literature) as less important, may care less about making a good impression, and may be less influenced by female-sent cues. As for target gender, the stereotype that women are submissive, passive, and generally eager to please (perhaps especially eager to please men) would lead one to predict that, as targets, women would be most vulnerable to bias cues – for in responding in line with expectations, one is behaving as the other hopes one will behave.

Another pattern of predictions rests on gender differences in nonverbal communication. Because women are more spontaneously expressive through nonverbal cues, one might predict that as perceivers they would be more likely to "leak" biasing cues. By the same token, females' superior decoding skill might make them more likely to notice biasing cues, and therefore (assuming that they are motivated to comply), women might be more likely to be biased by the expectations of others. These predictions, then, are that females are both more biasing as perceivers and more susceptible to bias as targets.

The hypothesis that better encoding skill in perceivers and better decoding skill in targets would produce stronger expectancy effects has been around for some years, and indeed to test it was one purpose behind the development of the Profile of Nonverbal Sensitivity (PONS) test of nonverbal decoding ability (Rosenthal, Hall, DiMatteo, Rogers, & Archer, 1979). The hypothesis has received support, but not extremely strong support. In an experiment, Zuckerman, Hall, DeFrank, and Rosenthal (1978) found joint moderating effects of experimenters' encoding skill and subjects' decoding skill, such that high-encoding experimenters paired with high-decoding subjects experienced the greatest expectancy effect. However, Hazelrigg, Cooper, and Strathman (1991), using a photo-rating task, found no significant influence of experimenters' and subjects' encoding and decoding skills, respectively, on the magnitude of expectancy effects.

In a meta-analysis of personality moderators of expectancy effects, Cooper and Hazelrigg (1988) did conclude that subjects' decoding skill significantly predicted the magnitude of expectancy effects, in a positive direction – that is, better decoding skill in the target was associated with greater expectancy effects.

These results are consistent with our earlier hypothesis that women would be more biasing as perceivers and more vulnerable to bias as targets. However, a different set of predictions can also follow from the same gender differences in nonverbal communication. Women's greater skill in controlling their facial expressions and other nonverbal behaviors could result in less, not more, leakage of expectancy cues compared to men. Similarly, women's greater skill in decoding nonverbal cues might make them not only more able to notice biasing cues, but also better able to discount them if they are so inclined. Superior decoding skill could thus serve a protective function such that women are less easy to bias with expectancy cues. Hence, alternate predictions are that women are less biasing as perceivers and less vulnerable to bias as targets.

Other personality predictors of expectancy effects may also suggest hypotheses for gender differences. In their meta-analysis, Cooper and Hazelrigg (1988) found that the perceiver's "need for social influence" was associated with more bias. Moreover, in the Hazelrigg et al. (1991)

experiment described previously, done subsequent to their meta-analysis, the trait "desire for control" was a significant moderator such that high desire-for-control experimenters obtained the largest expectancy effects. If one is willing to argue that men are higher on this trait, then a reasonable hypothesis would be that male perceivers in general would bias their targets more. However, the Cooper and Hazelrigg (1988) meta-analysis also found that the perceiver's expressiveness and likeability (including the traits pleasant, friendly, encouraging, and personal) had marginally significant positive relations to expectancy bias; in light of this, *women* might be predicted to be more biasing as perceivers.

On the target side, Cooper and Hazelrigg (1988) found, as mentioned earlier, that greater nonverbal decoding skill was associated with more bias, as was "influenceability" (a cluster including low dominance and social evaluation orientation). In their more recent experiment (Hazelrigg et al., 1991), targets' need for social approval was also a significant predictor of the expectancy effect. From this, one might predict that females would be more biased by perceivers' expectations.

Clearly, previous research lends little firm guidance on what to anticipate for the moderating effect of gender: Different findings lead to contradictory predictions.

In the only attempt to address these questions in a systematic way, Rosenthal (1969) tabulated the results of studies that used the paradigmatic photo-rating task. Limiting his analysis to studies showing a difference of $p < .20$ (two-tail), Rosenthal concluded (tentatively, because few studies were available) that male experimenters (perceivers) bias their subjects (targets) more than female experimenters do. Results for male versus female subjects (targets) were inconclusive.

The meta-analysis

In our meta-analysis, studies were accumulated using computer searches of the PsychLit and ERIC databases for the years 1972 to 1991, as well as manual searches of key journals and cross-referencing of bibliographies. For inclusion, a study had to be published in English, be conducted on normal (e.g., not mentally retarded) populations, induce expectations experimentally, measure perceivers' behavior or targets' responses, and indicate the genders of the perceiver or the target subjects. Here we summarize only effects pertaining to the responses of targets.

The moderating effect of gender (either perceiver's or target's) was examined in two ways. In what we call the *Interaction Analysis*, we looked for reports of perceiver's or target's Gender × Expectancy Condition interactions. These effects would indicate whether the predicted expectancy effect was relatively greater for males or females, either as perceivers or targets. Unfortunately, it was not common for investigators to conduct such analyses (and indeed, such an interaction could not be calculated when perceivers or targets were of only one gender). Therefore, a more inclusive method was added, which we call the *Main Effects Analysis*. Here we tabulated the magnitudes of expectancy effects separately for male and female perceivers, and for male and female targets, and then compared the average magnitudes to see if one gender was more likely to bias with expectations or to be biased by expectations. This method permitted the inclusion of single-gender studies. The Main Effects Analysis, in summary, tested for a gender-moderating effect on a between-studies basis, whereas the Interaction Analysis did so on a within-studies basis.

In this chapter we present data on effect size, expressed as the product-moment correlation r. For the Interaction Analysis, this effect size index was based on the 1-df interaction of gender of perceiver (or target) and expectancy condition (always two categories). These effect sizes were given a positive sign if female perceivers (or targets) showed greater expectancy effects in the predicted direction than did male perceivers and a negative sign if the reverse was the case. For the Main Effects Analysis, a positive sign indicated an expectancy effect in the predicted direction, and a negative sign indicated an expectancy effect in the nonpredicted direction. Only one effect size was included in either the perceiver or target analysis for a given group of subjects. Calculation of average effect sizes across studies was done using known effect sizes only (unweighted and weighted by sample size) and using all studies coding unknown effect sizes as zero (unweighted only). The tasks for which expectations were induced included photo ratings, psychomotor tasks, other laboratory tasks, learning and academic performance, and everyday social behaviors.

The Interaction Analysis showed little evidence of a moderating effect of perceivers' gender (unweighted average $r = .14$, based on three known effect sizes; unweighted average $r = .04$, based on three known and seven unknown effect sizes, with the unknowns included as zero; weighted average $r = .08$, based on three known effect sizes). With the signs changing from one summary statistic to the next, it is fair to

Table 14.2. *Gender as a moderator of expectancy effects: Summary of Main Effects Analysis*

Gender of target	Gender of perceiver			
	Male	Female	Both/unknown	Average
Male	−.12 (1)	.37 (3)	.39 (4)	.32 (8)
	−.03 (4)	—	.24 (7)	.19 (14)
	−.12 (1)	.21 (3)	.22 (4)	.19 (8)
Female	.00 (6)	.22 (5)	.20 (5)	.13 (16)
	.00 (9)	.11 (10)	.11 (9)	.08 (28)
	.02 (6)	.08 (5)	.00 (5)	.03 (16)
Both/unknown	.55 (5)	.17 (9)		
	.32 (9)	.13 (12)		
	.27 (5)	.07 (9)		
Average	.24 (12)	.22 (17)		
	.13 (22)	.15 (25)		
	.08 (12)	.09 (17)		

Note: The first line in a cell is the unweighted average r based on known effect sizes. The second line is the unweighted average r based on all effect sizes, counting unknown ones as zero. If there were no unknown effect sizes, the second line is left blank. The third line is the average of the known effect sizes, weighting by sample size. The number of studies is given in parentheses.

conclude that this analysis suggests no overall difference. However, because only three effect sizes were available for this analysis, any conclusion is tentative at best.

Similarly, the Interaction Analysis suggested no moderation by target gender (unweighted average $r = .08$, based on 8 known effect sizes; unweighted average $r = .03$, based on 8 known and 15 unknown effect sizes, with unknowns included as zero; weighted average $r = .01$, based on 8 known effect sizes).

Table 14.2 presents a summary of the Main Effects Analysis. The three lines within each cell represent average effect sizes calculated in the same three ways just presented (unweighted, known effects only; unweighted, all effects; weighted, known effects only). The rows and columns of the table represent different gender combinations of perceivers and targets; as perceivers or targets, a study could have employed males, females, or both/unknown. The last row and last column represent averages over the preceding three cells and represent the comparisons of interest: male versus female targets and male versus female perceivers. For target gender, we found that larger expectancy effects

Table 14.3. *Perceiver gender and target gender main effects, for adult targets*

Role	Males		Females	
	Unweighted	Weighted	Unweighted	Weighted
Perceiver	.28 (11)	.10 (11)	.05 (3)	.13 (3)
Target	.67 (2)	.81 (2)	.15 (10)	.10 (10)

Note: The number of studies is given in parentheses.

were associated with male targets; this contrast was significant ($Z = 2.60$, $p < .009$ two-tail). On the other hand, a contrast on perceiver gender was far from significant ($Z = .26$).

Separate analyses of Main Effects were conducted for studies using children/adolescents versus adults as targets. These revealed that neither the perceiver nor the target gender difference in magnitude of expectancy effect was significant for children, $Z = .09$ (15 studies) and .48 (13 studies), respectively. However, for adult targets, the situation was different. For male versus female perceivers, the contrast Z was 1.52, $p < .13$, two-tail (14 studies), indicating that male perceivers tended to produce more biased responses from targets than female perceivers did. The Z for the target gender contrast was 4.48, $p < .0001$ (12 studies), indicating that male targets were more influenced by expectations than female targets were. Table 14.3 summarizes these two comparisons, showing unweighted and weighted average effect sizes based on known effect sizes. Additional comment is called for regarding the target gender contrast, however, owing to the fact that there were only two studies of male adult targets, one of which (Eden & Shani, 1982) had an unusually large effect size ($r = .89$) and used an atypical sample and task (male Israeli Army trainees learning military skills). Because there was no remotely comparable population or task represented among studies using female targets, we must be very cautious about interpreting the significant contrast. When this study is removed, the contrast for adult targets is far from significant ($Z = .17$), although here too caution is in order, since there was only 1 study of male targets remaining in the analysis (compared to 10 using female targets).

Altogether, our analyses suggest no strong evidence that male and female perceivers differ in their tendencies to bias their targets by means of expectations. Similarly, the most conservative interpretation of the target-gender analysis is that male and female targets are equally biased by expectations. However, the analysis of target gender was seriously compromised by the small number of studies of adult male targets. Clearly, further research on these questions is warranted.

Conclusions

This chapter has looked at the manner in which expectations might be related to gender differences, especially in nonverbal communication. We have presented evidence that gender stereotypes affect our expectations of our own and others' behavior. We have noted that the process of self-socialization provides a link between culturally held stereotypes and self-expectations, where conforming to stereotyped expectations may produce real or imagined rewards. Both societal and individual expectations may thus work on individuals to produce actual gender differences that are consistent with stereotypes.

Several possibilities were presented regarding gender as a moderator variable in interpersonal expectancy effects, based on past research and speculation. We performed a meta-analysis that found little support for any of the predictions. Our results definitely did not confirm the hypothesis that a combination of male perceivers and female targets would produce the largest effects, as the combination of male perceiver and female target produced the *smallest* average effect sizes of any cell (see Table 14.2).

These meta-analytic results are preliminary and are based only on effect sizes. Results of combining probabilities will add additional insight. Also, as suggested by Rosenthal (1969), moderating effects of gender may not be uniform across different tasks and settings. In our present analysis, we pool results across different tasks such as academic performance, photo ratings, and other experimental tests. Separate examination of different domains of research may prove informative, though the small number of studies of any one kind is a limiting factor. Finally, as was made evident by the Eden and Shani (1982) study, our Main Effects Analysis is compromised by the problem of noncomparability of tasks and settings when results for men and women are compared. The Interaction Analysis, which equates tasks by examining gender on a within-studies basis, provides much stronger inference in principle. These effects suggested little in the way of gender differences, but again the number of studies was small.

References

Andersen, P. A. (1985). Nonverbal immediacy in interpersonal communication. In A. W. Siegman & S. Feldstein (Eds.), *Multichannel integrations of nonverbal behavior* (pp. 1–36). Hillsdale, NJ: Erlbaum.

Antill, J. K. (1987). Parents' beliefs and values about sex roles, sex differences, and sexuality: Their sources and implications. *Review of Personality and Social Psychology, 7*, 294–328.

Archer, J., & Lloyd, B. (1985). *Sex and gender.* New York: Cambridge University Press.

Badini, A. A., & Rosenthal, R. (1989). Visual cues, student sex, material taught, and the magnitude of teacher expectancy effects. *Communication Education, 38*, 162–166.

Bem, D. J. (1972). Self-perception theory. In L. Berkowitz (Ed.), *Advances in experimental social psychology* (Vol. 6, pp. 1–62). New York: Academic Press.

Bem, S. L. (1974). The measurement of psychological androgyny. *Journal of Consulting and Clinical Psychology, 42*, 155–162.

Binning, J., Zaba, A., & Whattam, J. (1986). Explaining the biasing effects of performance cues in terms of cognitive categorization. *Academy of Management Journal, 29*, 521–535.

Briton, N. J., & Hall, J. A. (1992a). *Perceived gender differences in nonverbal communication.* Manuscript submitted for publication.

Briton, N. J., & Hall, J. A. (1992b, July). *The effects of pre-existing belief and induced expectancy on scoring gender differences in smiling.* Paper presented at the XXVth International Congress of Psychology, Brussels.

Briton, N. J., & Hall, J. A. (1992c). [Gender as a moderating factor in interpersonal expectancy effects: A meta-analysis.] Unpublished raw data.

Cappella, J. N. (1981). Mutual influence in expressive behavior: Adult–adult and infant–adult dyadic interaction. *Psychological Bulletin, 89*, 101–132.

Compton, J. W. (1970). Experimenter bias: Reaction time and types of expectancy information. *Perceptual and Motor Skills, 31*, 159–168.

Cooper, H. M., & Hazelrigg, P. (1988). Personality moderators of interpersonal expectancy effects: An integrative research review. *Journal of Personality and Social Psychology, 55*, 937–949.

Costanzo, M., & Archer, D. (1989). Interpreting the expressive behavior of others: The Interpersonal Perception Task (IPT). *Journal of Nonverbal Behavior, 13*, 225–245.

Culp, R. E., Cook, A. S., & Housley, P. C. (1983). A comparison of observed and reported adult–infant interactions: Effects of perceived sex. *Sex Roles, 9*, 475–479.

Deaux, K., & Major, B. (1987). Putting gender into context: An interactive model of gender-related behavior. *Psychological Review, 94*, 369–389.

Dusek, J., & Joseph, G. (1983). The bases of teacher expectancies: A meta-analysis. *Journal of Educational Psychology, 75*, 327–346.

Eagly, A. H., & Mladinic, A. (1989). Gender stereotypes and attitudes toward women and men. *Personality and Social Psychology Bulletin, 15*, 543–558.

Eccles, J. S., Jacobs, J. E., & Harold, R. D. (1990). Gender role stereotypes, expectancy effects, and parents' socialization of gender differences. *Journal of Social Issues, 46*(2), 183–201.

Eden, D., & Shani, A. B. (1982). Pygmalion goes to boot camp: Expectancy, leadership, and trainee performance. *Journal of Applied Psychology, 67*, 194–199.

Fabes, R. A., & Martin, C. L. (1991). Gender and age stereotypes of emotionality. *Personality and Social Psychology Bulletin, 17,* 532–540.

Fisher, J. D., & Byrne, D. (1975). Too close for comfort: Sex differences in response to invasions of personal space. *Journal of Personality and Social Psychology, 32,* 15–21.

Hall, J. A. (1978). Gender effects in decoding nonverbal cues. *Psychological Bulletin, 85,* 845–857.

Hall, J. A. (1980). Voice tone and persuasion. *Journal of Personality and Social Psychology, 38,* 924–934.

Hall, J. A. (1984). *Nonverbal sex differences: Communication accuracy and expressive style.* Baltimore: Johns Hopkins University Press.

Hall, J. A. (1987). On explaining gender differences: The case of nonverbal communication. *Review of Personality and Social Psychology, 6,* 177–200.

Hall, J. A., & Halberstadt, A. G. (1980). Masculinity and femininity in children: Development of the Children's Personal Attributes Questionnaire. *Developmental Psychology, 16,* 270–280.

Hall, J. A., & Halberstadt, A. G. (1986). Smiling and gazing. In J. S. Hyde & M. C. Linn (Eds.), *The psychology of gender: Advances through meta-analysis* (pp. 136–158). Baltimore: Johns Hopkins University Press.

Hamilton, D. L., Sherman, S. J., & Ruvolo, C. M. (1990). Stereotype-based expectancies: Effects on information processing and social behavior. *Journal of Social Issues, 46*(2), 35–60.

Harris, M. J., & Rosenthal, R. (1985). Mediation of interpersonal expectancy effects: 31 meta-analyses. *Psychological Bulletin, 97,* 363–386.

Hazelrigg, P. J., Cooper, H., & Strathman, A. J. (1991). Personality moderators of the experimenter expectancy effect: A reexamination of five hypotheses. *Personality and Social Psychology Bulletin, 17,* 569–579.

Henley, N. M. (1977). *Body politics: Power, sex, and nonverbal communication.* Englewood Cliffs, NJ: Prentice-Hall.

Hilton, J. L., & Darley, J. M. (1985). Constructing other persons: A limit on the effect. *Journal of Experimental Social Psychology, 21,* 1–18.

Hinsz, V. B., & Tomhave, J. A. (1991). Smile and (half) the world smiles with you, frown and you frown alone. *Personality and Social Psychology Bulletin, 17,* 586–592.

Jones, S. C., & Panitch, D. (1971). The self-fulfilling prophecy and interpersonal attraction. *Journal of Experimental Social Psychology, 7,* 356–366.

Jorgenson, D. O. (1978). Nonverbal assessment of attitudinal affect with the smile-return technique. *Journal of Social Psychology, 106,* 173–179.

Jussim, L. (1990). Social reality and social problems: The role of expectancies. *Journal of Social Issues, 46*(2), 9–34.

Langlois, J., & Prestholdt, P. (1977). Information: A control for observer bias. *Journal of Social Psychology, 102,* 133–141.

Lyons, J., & Serbin, L. (1986). Observer bias in scoring boys' and girls' aggression. *Sex Roles, 14,* 301–313.

Maccoby, E. E., & Jacklin, C. N. (1974). *The psychology of sex differences.* Stanford, CA: Stanford University Press.

Meisels, M., & Guardo, C. J. (1969). Development of personal space schemata. *Child Development, 40,* 1167–1178.

Meyer, J. W., & Sobieszek, B. I. (1972). Effect of a child's sex on adult interpretations of its behavior. *Developmental Psychology, 6,* 42–48.

Payne, B. D. (1981). Sex and age differences in the sex-role stereotyping of third- and fifth-grade children. *Sex Roles, 7,* 135–143.

294   Judith A. Hall and Nancy J. Briton

Pomerleau, A., Bolduc, D., Malcuit, G., & Cossette, L. (1990). Pink or blue: Environmental gender stereotypes in the first two years of life. *Sex Roles, 22,* 359–367.

Rosenthal, R. (1969). Interpersonal expectations: Effects of the experimenter's hypothesis. In R. Rosenthal and R. L. Rosnow (Eds.), *Artifact in behavioral research* (pp. 181–277). New York: Academic Press.

Rosenthal, R., & DePaulo, B. M. (1979). Sex differences in accommodation in nonverbal communication. In R. Rosenthal (Ed.), *Skill in nonverbal communication: Individual differences* (pp. 68–103). Cambridge, MA: Oelgeschlager, Gunn & Hain.

Rosenthal, R., Hall, J. A., DiMatteo, M. R., Rogers, P. L., & Archer, D. (1979). *Sensitivity to nonverbal communication: The PONS test.* Baltimore: Johns Hopkins University Press.

Rotter, N. G., & Rotter, G. S. (1988). Sex differences in the encoding and decoding of negative facial emotions. *Journal of Nonverbal Behavior, 12,* 139–148.

Rubin, J. Z., Provenzano, F. J., & Luria, Z. (1974). The eye of the beholder: Parents' views on sex of newborns. *American Journal of Orthopsychiatry, 44,* 512–519.

Shapiro, P. N., & Penrod, S. (1986). Meta-analysis of facial identification studies. *Psychological Bulletin, 100,* 139–156.

Skrypnek, B. J., & Snyder, M. (1982). On the self-perpetuating nature of stereotypes about women and men. *Journal of Experimental Social Psychology, 18,* 277–291.

Snyder, M., Tanke, E. D., & Berscheid, E. (1977). Social perception and interpersonal behavior: On the self-fulfilling nature of social stereotypes. *Journal of Personality and Social Psychology, 35,* 656–666.

Spence, J. T., Helmreich, R., & Holahan, C. K. (1979). Negative and positive components of psychological masculinity and femininity and their relationships to self-reports of neurotic and acting out behaviors. *Journal of Personality and Social Psychology, 37,* 1673–1682.

Spence, J. T., Helmreich, R., & Stapp, J. (1975). Ratings of self and peers on sex role atributes and their relation to self-esteem and conceptions of masculinity and femininity. *Journal of Personality and Social Psychology, 32,* 29–39.

Towson, S. M. J., Zanna, M. P., & MacDonald, G. (1984–1985). Self-fulfilling prophecy: Sex role stereotypes as expectations for behavior. *Imagination, Cognition and Personality, 4,* 149–160.

von Baeyer, C. L., Sherk, D. L., & Zanna, M. P. (1981). Impression management in the job interview: When the female applicant meets the male (chauvinist) interviewer. *Personality and Social Psychology Bulletin, 7,* 45–51.

Vrugt, A., & Kerkstra, A. (1984). Sex differences in nonverbal communication. *Semiotica, 50,* 1–41.

Wagner, H. L., MacDonald, C. J., & Manstead, A. S. R. (1986). Communication of individual emotions by spontaneous facial expressions. *Journal of Personality and Social Psychology, 50,* 737–743.

Wessler, R. L., & Strauss, M. E. (1968). Experimenter expectancy: A failure to replicate. *Psychological Reports, 22,* 687–688.

Williams, J. E., & Bennett, S. M. (1975). The definition of sex stereotypes via the adjective check list. *Sex Roles, 1,* 327–37.

Williams, J. E., & Best, D. L. (1982). *Measuring sex stereotypes: A thirty nation study.* Beverly Hills, CA: Sage.

Zammuner, V. L. (1987). Children's sex-role stereotypes. *Review of Personality and Social Psychology, 7,* 272–293.

Zanna, M. P., & Pack, S. J. (1975). On the self-fulfilling nature of apparent sex differences in behavior. *Journal of Experimental Social Psychology, 11,* 583–591.

Zuckerman, M., DeFrank, R. S., Hall, J. A., & Rosenthal, R. (1978). Accuracy of nonverbal communication as determinant of interpersonal expectancy effects. *Environmental Psychology and Nonverbal Behavior, 2,* 206–214.

Zuckerman, M., & Larrance, D. T. (1979). Individual differences in perceived encoding and decoding abilities. In R. Rosenthal (Ed.), *Skill in nonverbal communication: Individual differences* (pp. 171–203). Cambridge, MA: Oelgeschlager, Gunn & Hain.

15. Expectations in the physician–patient relationship: Implications for patient adherence to medical treatment recommendations

M. ROBIN DiMATTEO

Prior to the mid-twentieth century, the important effects of physicians' expectations for their patients were recognized and accepted, and seemed to require little empirical study. As early as the fourth century B.C., Hippocrates noted: "The patient, though conscious that his condition is perilous, may recover his health simply through his contentment with the goodness of the physician" (Hippocrates, fourth century B.C., 1923 translation). The proliferation of modern medical techniques in the past five decades, however, has been so impressive that demonstration of the contribution of interpersonal factors in medical care has become imperative.

Milmoe, Rosenthal, Blane, Chafety, and Wolf (1967) demonstrated that despite modern medicine (in this case, an effective method for treating alcoholism), a patient's willingness to take advantage of the opportunity to control the disease depended, in large part, upon the emotional expressions of the doctor. Their study found that the degree of hostility expressed by a doctor's voice tone while talking about alcoholic patients was highly correlated with the doctor's failure to get patients into treatment. This demonstration of the role of affect in the physician–patient relationship and Bob Rosenthal's enthusiasm for quantitatively analyzing therapeutic communication have inspired decades of research on physician–patient relationships and communication.

The two physician–patient interactions that follow may help to illustrate how a physician's interpersonal behavior toward and expectations for a patient can be communicated. These powerful messages can affect patients' understanding of what they must do to care for themselves, as well as their willingness and sense of competence to take positive health actions.

296

Harold Greene tried to pay close attention to what his doctor was saying. "I'm noting some hypertension, Harold. We'd better treat you for it." Harold felt surprised and a little confused. Was the doctor saying that something was wrong with his health? Harold didn't really know the meaning of *hypertension*. Harold didn't ask because Dr. Harrison had begun writing rather rapidly in the chart, and Harold did not want to disturb him.

"Take two of these pills a day," said the doctor as he was writing out the prescription. "Get some exercise and try to lose a little weight." Doctor Harrison tore the prescription from its pad and handed it to Harold. As Harold reached to take it, he felt dizzy and emotionally a bit numb. But the doctor was clearly impatient and ready to move on. As Dr. Harrison stood up, he looked toward the door and his entire body seemed to orient in its direction. Then, with his hand on the doorknob, he frowned slightly. "Do you have any questions, Harold?" Harold breathed deeply, but before he could answer, the doctor interrupted. "The treatment's pretty straightforward, Harold. Just do what I said, and you'll be fine. Try to relax, and I'll see you in about a month to check how things are going. Bye now."

The doctor was gone before Harold had a chance to collect his thoughts. Harold was first aware that his heart was beating very fast, his hands were clenched, and the muscles in his neck and shoulders were very tight. Harold felt afraid. He was aware that something was wrong with his health, but he had no idea whether hypertension was serious or not.

Harold began to relax as he tried to make some sense of the previous 5 minutes. Dr. Harrison had said something about diet and exercise. But Harold figured that the doctor said that to everybody but didn't really expect much of a change. After all, Harold had cut back on cigarettes recently, but Dr. Harrison merely mumbled "Good" when he told him. Dr. Harrison didn't push for any kind of commitment from Harold for diet and exercise, so these did not seem to be all that important.

The medication was a little trickier, in Harold's opinion. Did hypertension mean that he was highly tense? If so, was the prescription something to calm him down? Harold thought to himself, I certainly can't take medication that makes me sleepy. I have to function at work. Harold felt a pang of anger, too, as if someone had tried to exert control over him. The more he thought about it, the more he felt that he would have to make some of his own decisions about treatment.

Karen Carlson, MD, sat down to explain the test results. "The tests show that you have a mild case of diabetes, Mrs. Smith," she said to her patient gently. "That means that your body has some difficulty metabolizing, or using the sugars and starches that you eat. Fortunately, your diabetes is mild, and that means that you can keep it very much under control. You can stay healthy with medication that helps to take care of the sugars and starches, as well as by controlling your diet and exercising. How are you feeling about what I just said?"

"Well," said her patient, "I was hoping there was nothing wrong with me. I'm a little frightened about having a disease."

Karen Carlson spent a few moments helping her patient talk about her fears of the future and giving her encouragement. Mrs. Smith finally expressed relief that the condition could be controlled. "You have a lot to say about how healthy you will be," Dr. Carlson told her patient. "I really believe that with some help from our medical staff, you will be able to incorporate the best methods for diabetes control into your everyday life." Dr. Carlson maintained eye contact with her patient and explained the need to walk at least four times a week. She watched her patient for signs of resistance or confusion. She asked her for feedback about what was being discussed. She encouraged Mrs. Smith to join a weight loss group that incorporated education with social support for maximum success at permanent, lifelong weight control.

Sitting opposite her patient, leaning forward, maintaining eye contact with her, and expressing positivity and warmth, the doctor listened to her patient's fears and concerns and helped her formulate a plan for taking her medications several times a day and for following the exercise and weight loss regimen. She emphasized her patient's responsibility for her own care and validated her patient's concerns.

Patient adherence to medical treatment

Although medical diagnosis and the planning of effective treatments can be costly enterprises, they have the potential to improve vastly the health and well-being of patients. Despite the tremendous costs in time, money, and expertise associated with medical visits, however, somewhere between 15% and 93% of patients leave their doctors' offices and fail to follow the advice they were given (Kaplan & Simon, 1990).

Patient nonadherence to medical recommendations is one of the major unsolved problems in medicine today. Fewer than four out of five patients who receive a prescription for a symptomatic, short-term, acute condition (like a throat infection) manage to take their medication as prescribed. Patients with chronic conditions such as hypertension and diabetes may be required to take medication every day throughout their lives, and upward of 50% of these patients fail to take their medications correctly (Kruse & Weber, 1990; Luscher & Vetter, 1990). When lifestyle changes are involved, more than 70% of patients fail to do the things necessary to promote their own well-being, but instead continue in habits that jeopardize their health (Brownell, Marlatt, Lichtenstein, & Wilson, 1986; U.S. Preventive Services Task Force, 1989). In this age of skyrocketing health care costs, totaling over $600 billion per year and constituting over 12% of the gross national product, such a waste of resources can hardly be afforded by individuals or by society as a whole (Savitz, 1991; Todd, Seekins, Krichbaum, & Harvey, 1991).

The cost in human terms of nonadherence (or *noncompliance,* as it is also called in the copious literature on this topic) may be considerable (DiMatteo, 1991). Patients who fail to follow treatment recommendations may lose confidence in themselves and even the power of their bodies to heal (Epstein, 1984; Friedman, this volume). They may become passive recipients of a powerful but potentially hazardous medical technology (Roter, 1977). Alternatively, they may lose confidence in their medical professionals and in the value of medicine in general, failing to rely on it when medical care might be extremely helpful in saving their lives or in promoting their future well-being (Cassileth, Lusk, Strouse, & Bodenheimer, 1984).

The benefits of adhering to medical treatment recommendations are being identified. Kravitz, Hays, Sherbourne, DiMatteo, Greenfield, Ordway, and Rogers (1992) recently demonstrated that among patients participating in the Medical Outcomes Study (Tarlov et al., 1989), those who adhered to treatment had better physiological outcomes than those who did not. Considerable research compiled by the U.S. Preventive Services Task Force (1989) demonstrates that when patients adhere to treatments for hypertension, their blood pressure does indeed go down, and that patients who adhere to diabetes and heart disease treatment regimens remain healthier than those who do not. Such findings are not very surprising and may even serve only to give us some reassurance of the efficacy of the more commonly prescribed medical treatments. What is fascinating from the point of view of social psychologists interested in expectations, however, is that compliance with medical treatment *in itself* appears to result in more positive health outcomes. In reviewing the literature, Epstein (1984) found five studies that had used both a treatment and a placebo and reported patients' adherence under both conditions. All five studies found that subjects who were more compliant had better health outcomes (greater weight loss, greater reduction in fever and infection in cancer patients, and even fewer deaths among coronary patients). These better health outcomes were obtained *regardless of whether subjects complied with a real treatment or a placebo.* This finding may have several possible explanations. Patients who adhered to treatment recommendations may have had more positive expectations for their own health outcomes, and these expectations may have served a self-fulfilling prophecy. On the other hand, the act of adhering may have generated new habits and cognitive patterns that brought about improvement and even more self-confidence, resulting in the enactment of still more health-related behaviors. It appears that, assuming that a recommendation is not intrinsically harmful, adhering to treatment can lead to better patient health.

The determinants of patient adherence

A great deal of research has been conducted to try to determine what contributes to patient adherence to medical treatment and what impedes it (Becker & Rosenstock, 1984; DiMatteo & DiNicola, 1982a; Haynes, Taylor, & Sackett, 1979; Meichenbaum & Turk, 1987). Using both uni-variate approaches and multivariate models, researchers have attempted to sort out the factors that contribute to patients' following of medical recommendations. In the earliest days of this research, the focus was on patients' beliefs (Becker, 1974; Rosenstock, 1966). It was hypothesized that patients fail to follow treatment recommendations because of their own inaccurate cognitions about what caused their illnesses and what could be done to treat them successfully. Research-ers had hypothesized that what mattered were patients' concerns about their susceptibility to serious illness if they failed to cooperate with medical recommendations. What researchers found consistently, how-ever, was that the best cognitive predictor of the patient's willingness to adhere to treatment was whether the patient believed that the treat-ment was valuable and potentially effective (DiMatteo et al., in press; Ronis & Harel, 1989; Sutton & Eiser, 1990). Furthermore, although cognitive factors have quite nicely predicted patients' willingness and *good intentions* to adhere to medical recommendations, whether or not patients are actually able to adhere depends a great deal more upon the practical difficulties that patients encounter (Champion, 1984; DiMatteo et al., in press; Janz & Becker, 1984; Jones, Jones, & Katz, 1988). Medical recommendations typically fall by the wayside when patients face too many barriers to and not enough support for their adherence. Thus, patient adherence to treatment is heavily influenced by what goes on in patients' minds, as well as by the practical assistance available to pa-tients to deal with the barriers that they face.

Although cognitive issues and practical factors weigh heavily in the adherence equation, they do not fully capture the determinants of pa-tient cooperation with medical treatment. From the time of Hippocrates (4th century B.C., 1923 translation), the physician–patient relationship has been recognized to figure prominently in patients' responses to medical recommendations (DiMatteo, 1991; DiMatteo & DiNicola, 1982b). The interpersonal communication between physician and patient can affect how well patients understand what they are supposed to do to take care of themselves, as well as their motivation to adhere to the recommendations made to them (Hall, Roter, & Katz, 1988). Probably through the mediating factor of adherence, though quite possibly in a direct effect, the physician–patient relationship can even influence the outcomes of medical care (Ben-Sira, 1980; Egbert, Battit, Welch, & Bartlett, 1964; Langer, Janis, & Wolfer, 1975).

Why do the character and quality of the physician–patient relationship affect patient adherence to treatment recommendations? One possible reason is that, as demonstrated in the preceding vignettes, medical care does not involve simply the straightforward application of technology by one person to another. Rather, medical care is an *interpersonal process*. Patients and physicians deal with each other in an interpersonal exchange *out of which* emerge the technical phenomena of diagnosis and treatment (DiMatteo, 1979; see also Zuckerman, Hodgins, & Miyake, this volume). As Cassell (1985) has noted, "all medical care flows through the relationship between the physician and patient" (p. 1). The complexities of the therapeutic relationship, including the shared communications and interpersonal expectations, are crucial elements in determining patients' willingness and ability to follow treatment advice and to engage in challenging but necessary behaviors for promoting their health and well-being.

Communication, interpersonal expectations, and patient adherence

The interpersonal interactions that form the basis for the medical care exchange are extremely complex. Physicians and patients often have different agendas and expect different things from their interchange. For example, a physician may wish to ask the patient about the severity of his or her pain only because pain is one of many symptoms to consider in formulating a diagnosis. The patient, on the other hand, may wish to expound on the severity of the pain in order to ensure its immediate relief (DiMatteo, 1991). Physicians usually need only information in order to solve the puzzle of diagnosis, but patients usually need (in addition to information) emotional support and reassurance. Sometimes, patients and physicians operate on the basis of different premises (Cassell, 1985). For example, a patient may be worried about the cosmetic consequences of a growth, believing that in the absence of pain and other symptoms such a growth is of little concern. The physician, on the other hand, may be very distressed about the possibility of malignancy. Finally, physicians and patients are usually in very different emotional states during the treatment process. The process of med-

ical care, including the sounds and smells of hospitals and office treatment rooms, are routine for physicians. For patients, however, the
entire medical environment is frightening, and patient anxiety wreaks
havoc on the accuracy of the information that patients provide and on
patients' recollection of information they are given in the medical care
exchange (Barnlund, 1976; see also Hall & Briton, this volume, for a
discussion of gender factors that are relevant to expectations).

The complexities of physician–patient interaction demand effective
communication so that different agendas can be reconciled, opposing
premises understood, and problematic emotional states dealt with.
However, although there is a tremendous amount to do in the medical
care exchange, there is often very limited time in which to do it (Beisecker & Beisecker, 1990). Furthermore, some aspects of communication
are so problematic that it is often a wonder that physicians and patients
ever understand each other at all.

Research literature abounds on the subject of problems in medical
communication. As this literature is reviewed in the following sections,
it is important to keep in mind that the problems examined are two-
sided and that blame is not being assigned. Although the various studies cited have focused on either physicians' or patients' behaviors,
physicians and patients affect each other reciprocally. Each problematic
behavior tends to play out in the interactive system, leading to a problematic response. For example, one interactant's propensity to talk a lot
allows the other interactant, in a limited time frame for the medical
visit, to talk only minimally (Bain, 1976; Davis, 1971; Freemon, Negrete,
Davis, & Korsch, 1971; Roter, 1984). Furthermore, for every practitioner
who fails to provide critical information to enhance adherence, there is
a patient who has failed to ask for it. For every patient who walks away
confused about the regimen, there is a physician who has failed to
check whether it was understood. So we examine the medical care
exchange as an *interaction* and recognize that even the most technical of
medical events is a reciprocal social exchange.

Medical jargon

As noted earlier, communication between medical professionals and
patients is the essence of medical care, and words (including how those
words are spoken) are extremely powerful entities. Patients can become
confused and terrified when they misunderstand their medical professional's words (Cassell, 1985). Yet, confusion and misunderstanding

happen regularly because patients typically do not understand medical jargon. "Doctor talk" is used by physicians, though it can be completely mystifying to their patients. The use of medical jargon is even a source of considerable patient dissatisfaction with medical care (Barnlund, 1976). Medical practitioners typically talk with one another using complex and high-sounding medical terms, and may do so with considerable efficiency. However, the result for patients is usually confusion. Interestingly, doctor talk does convey an interpersonal meaning that may explain the lack of direct patient protest about its use. Doctor talk sounds impressive to some patients, who tend to take the fact that the physician has used medical jargon with them as a compliment to their intelligence (Korsch, Gozzi, & Francis, 1968). Patients are nonetheless confused, and they often miss crucial pieces of information that they need in order to adhere to their treatment regimens (Samora, Saunders, & Larson, 1961; Segall & Roberts, 1980).

Listening to patients

In the process of medical care, listening to the patient is essential. The famous medical educator Sir William Osler (1899) told medical students that they should listen to the patient because the patient will tell them the diagnosis. Modern physicians who are sensitive to patients' unique perspectives on their illnesses recognize that patients can provide valuable information. Patients are often correct in their guesses about what is wrong with them (Cassell, 1985). At the very least, listening closely to patients prevents physicians from prematurely deciding upon diagnoses. Listening also conveys respect to patients (Stone, 1979). Unfortunately, in practice, listening appears to be difficult for physicians to do effectively. Several major empirical studies have tape-recorded and carefully analyzed physician–patient encounters and have found that physicians themselves tend to spend so much time talking that they leave little time for their patients to talk (Bain, 1976; Davis, 1971; Freemon et al., 1971; Stiles, Putnam, Wolf, & James, 1979; Waitzkin & Stoeckle, 1976). Despite the varied settings in which these studies took place, physicians spent much more time talking to their patients than listening to them. Physicians' self-reports of their own behavior were greatly in error, however, for most believed that they spent much more time listening, and that their patients did more talking than they actually did.

Educating patients

Despite the fact that physicians have the floor more often than not, they do not tend to use this time to provide critical education to foster their patients' adherence. Research suggests that physicians spend less than 10% of their interaction time with patients giving them any information or educating them about their conditions (Bain, 1976; Davis, 1971; Freemon et al., 1971; Stiles et al., 1979; Waitzkin, 1984, 1985). In one study, it was found that during medical visits that lasted, on the average, 20 minutes, physicians spent an average of less than 1 minute communicating information to patients (Waitzkin & Stoeckle, 1976). Those same physicians estimated that they spent between 10 and 15 minutes (that is, between 50% and 75% of their interaction time) educating patients. In another study, out of an average interaction time of 16.5 minutes, physicians spent an average of 1.3 minutes giving information to their patients (Waitzkin, 1985). When asked to estimate how much time they did spend, however, their average guess was 8.9 minutes. These findings suggest that feedback of how time is actually used in the medical interaction may be essential if physicians' communication behavior is to be improved.

The small amount of time that is spent giving information to patients is sometimes not used adequately to instruct them in what they need to do to adhere to recommendations. In one study, physician–patient interactions were observed and coded by a researcher (Svarstad, 1976). Instruction about how to take medications was found to be minimal. Of the 347 drugs prescribed, 60 were never even discussed with patients, and in 90% of the incidents in which drugs were prescribed, the physician gave no specific advice to the patient on how to use the medication (e.g., to take three pills a day or to take the medication on an empty stomach). Further, several studies found that because many physicians expect their patients to need prolonged explanations or to be unable to understand medical information altogether, they avoid providing any (Kane & Deuschle, 1967; Waitzkin, 1985). Physicians tend, however, to underestimate how much information their patients can understand, as well as how much information they desire to have (Waitzkin, 1985).

Patients' passivity

Perhaps because of expectations for the *good patient* role (Taylor, 1979), patients tend to avoid asking physicians questions. The studies cited previously that analyzed the interactions between physicians and patients found that patients asked questions of their physicians during less than 7% of the interaction time. Most patients did not offer correct information when their physicians apparently misunderstood something about them or their care. Patients did not request further clarification of confusing things that were said to them. In general, patients have been found to convey complete acceptance of what their physicians tell them, perhaps because they are reluctant to betray their ignorance or to suggest that they mistrust their physicians (Matthews, 1983). Patient passivity likely supports physicians' expectations that patients do not want to know very much.

Unfortunately, patients also tend to forget a great deal of the little they are told during medical visits. One study found that shortly after their medical visits, clinic outpatients forgot about one-third of what was told to them during the physician–patient interaction, and they forgot 56% of the instructions and 48% of the statements made to them about treatment (Ley & Spelman, 1965).

Models of therapeutic interaction

How can expectations for the physician–patient relationship help both physicians and patients to assume mutual responsibility for patient care? The character of the relationship that the physician and patient develop depends partly upon the circumstances of their association and partly upon the conscious and unconscious choices they make regarding the responsibilities they will assume. Szasz and Hollender (1956) outlined three models of the physician–patient relationship, and argued that adherence and the success of long-term care depend upon establishing and sustaining the third.

The first model, the *active-passive model*, occurs when the patient is unable to participate in his or her own care and cannot make decisions. Although such a situation actually occurs relatively infrequently and is characterized by emergency conditions in which the patient is usually unconscious, patient passivity and physician action tend to be played out in more than emergency circumstances and often characterize the care of many acutely ill patients. Patient passivity is evident in the second model as well, the most common type of physician–patient relationship, and one clearly illustrated by the findings detailed earlier: *the guidance-cooperation model*. The underlying contract in this second model involves the physician taking responsibility for deciding on the diagnosis and treatment and then pronouncing such to the patient, from whom flawless cooperation is expected. Of course, it is quite common for patients who have had no input into their initial treatment decisions to have considerable difficulty implementing them. Because of the communication problems identified earlier, patients may even have failed to understand what their treatments involve. *The mutual-participation model* is hailed as representing the most effective physician–patient relationship (Stone, 1979). Questions and concerns are aired freely, and with clear and effective communication, physician and patient each apply their own expertise to the task of achieving the patient's health.

Although the mutual participation model is hardly widespread in current physician–patient interaction, in recent years patients have become more involved than in previous decades in the decision making involved in their own medical care. *Active patienthood* is a behavioral style characterized by a patient's active participation in the health care process, and the assumption of shared responsibility between physician and patient for both the medical outcome and the psychological well-being of the patient (Dye & DiMatteo, in press). Congruent with *negotiated patienthood* (Lazare, Eisenthal, Frank, & Stoeckle, 1978), *patient involvement* (Greenfield, Kaplan, & Ware, 1985), and *patient participation* (Speedling & Rose, 1985), active patienthood involves both physician and patient having a high degree of control and responsibility in the medical interaction. Participation and involvement in decision making on the part of the patient tend to have an important positive effect on patient satisfaction with care (although, unfortunately, not on clinician satisfaction with the medical care visit) (Eisenthal, Koopman, & Lazare, 1983). Active patienthood has been demonstrated to influence patients' medical outcomes, including improvement of symptoms (Henbest & Stewart, 1989; Lerman et al., 1990), adherence to treatment and to appointments (Roter, 1977; Schulman, 1979; Swain & Steckel, 1981), and the management of chronic conditions (Greenfield, Kaplan, Ware, Yano, & Frank, 1988; Uhlmann, Inui, Pecoraro, & Carter, 1988). When patients engage in strategies designed to avoid their health concerns, they have considerably more difficulty with adherence to medical treatment than when they are actively engaged in coping (Sherbourne, Hays, Ordway, DiMatteo, & Kravitz, 1992). Researchers, clinicians, and patients themselves are recognizing the key role played by patients' self-determination in their health and well-being, and research is focusing on the role of expectations in promoting patients' involvement in their own care.

Physicians' expectations and rapport with patients

Physicians' positive expectations for their patients and for themselves are of critical importance to patient involvement, and hence to patient adherence and the outcomes of treatment. Certainly, if physicians expect their patients to be incompetent, unaware, and irresponsible, they are unlikely to share responsibility with them. Research suggests that medical decisions are affected by such expectations (Eisenberg, 1979; Franks, Culpepper, & Dickinson, 1982; Johnson, Kurtz, Tomlinson, & Howe, 1986).

A physician's ability to establish rapport with patients and to understand and support patients' emotional needs, particularly in the midst of pain and illness, is an essential element of care. Bedside manner, the instillation of trust, and responsiveness to patients' needs involve at least politeness (Mayerson, 1976), and at most a full understanding of patients' psychosocial needs and empathy for the role of pain and illness in patients' lives (Kleinman, 1988). Research suggests that the essential elements of this rapport and physicians' expectations for patients may be transmitted by means of nonverbal cues (Harrigan, Oxman, & Rosenthal, 1985).

There is evidence that physicians' interpersonal behavior toward their patients can have observable effects on patients' physiological conditions. A physician's manner in dealing with patients can affect patients' reactions to prescribed medications (Uhlenhuth, Canter, Neustadt, & Payson, 1959), as well as such physiological indicators as blood pressure (Pickering et al., 1988). A significant increase in the sudden deaths of cardiac patients during or shortly after formal ward rounds has been noted, and the formality and lack of supportive emotional care have been cited as possible causes (Jarvinen, 1955; Lynch, Thomas, Mills, Malinow, & Katcher, 1974).

Physicians' expectations for *themselves* appear to be very important to their behavior with patients. Many physicians avoid encouraging their patients to make lifestyle changes for health promotion and disease prevention because the physicians have poor expectations for their *own* abilities to inspire behavioral change in their patients (Demak & Becker, 1987; Mandel, Franks, & Dickinson, 1985). How physicians feel about their work also affects their patients. Physicians' satisfaction with the quality of care they deliver has been found to be significantly related to their own patients' satisfaction with medical treatment (McGlynn, 1988). Further, in the longitudinal Medical Outcomes Study, physicians' over-all job satisfaction positively predicted their patients' adherence to treatment for chronic disease over a 2-year period (DiMatteo et al., in press).

It is important to note that two components are essential in bringing about active patienthood and a mutual participation model of physician–patient interaction. Physician and patient must have both the commitment and the skill to deal with one another effectively in the communication-based social exchange of the physician–patient relationship. What happens in the interaction between physicians and patients depends upon what each party is capable of doing and what each party holds to be true about the therapeutic relationship (i.e., their beliefs, viewpoints, philosophies, and expectations) (DiMatteo, 1979). These phenomena can be interrelated, of course, because people may fail to develop the communication skills they do not value and may devalue the things that they cannot do. In order to achieve a mutually responsible relationship, however, physician and patient must both value and develop the communication skills necessary for mutual participation.

Time

A limiting factor in this entire picture of physician–patient interaction is time. Time is an extremely important issue in the medical visit. Physicians don't have enough of it, and patients usually want more. Physicians who don't spend enough time with their patients risk losing them to other practitioners, for patients cite lack of time from the physician as their reason for changing doctors (DiMatteo & DiNicola, 1982a). Time has a paradoxical effect on physicians' income, however, because other research suggests that the more time physicians spend with their patients, the less money they earn (Waitzkin, 1985). The objective amount of time that a physician spends with a patient influences how much information seeking can take place (Beisecker & Beisecker, 1990), but patient satisfaction with the medical visit depends more upon the patient's *subjective* feeling that enough time was spent to meet the needs of communication (DiMatteo & Hays, 1980). Surveys show that the average medical visit with an internist in the United States is about 18 minutes, and with a specialist it is about 15 minutes (Feller, 1979). For full patient participation, information seeking, and question asking to take place, research has estimated that at least 19 minutes is essential (Beisecker & Beisecker, 1990). Thus, it may be expected that the trend toward briefer and briefer medical visits, such as in health maintenance organizations, would reduce both the accuracy and the interpersonal quality of physician–patient communication. Such a prediction may be somewhat premature, however, because of the complexity of the issue. McGlynn (1988), for example, found that patient satisfaction with medical visits was affected not only by the length of time a patient spent with his or her physician but also by the physician's *own satisfaction* with the quality of care provided. Physicians who were highly satisfied with the quality of care they delivered, but who had shorter average visit lengths, actually had higher average patient satisfaction scores than did physicians whose ratings of satisfaction with the quality of care they delivered were low but who had longer average visit lengths.

An advantage of effective nonverbal communication in the physician–patient exchange is, of course, that nonverbal messages can occur simultaneously with verbal messages, taking no extra time and communicating a wealth of support and caring (DiMatteo & DiNicola, 1982b). Physicians' smiles and head nods can communicate supportiveness and help to reduce patient anxiety; bodily orientation toward the patient can communicate interest in what the patient has to say and encourage the patient to provide necessary information (DiMatteo, 1991). Even when interaction time is brief, unhurried concern can be expressed with nonverbal cues.

Conclusions

This chapter ends, as have many like it in the past, with a call for more research on the physician–patient relationship. The situation is unlike that of 20 years ago, however, when researchers were just beginning to understand the social psychology of this important dyad. Now research questions are considerably more specific, and the need for programmatic research on the therapeutic relationship has become apparent.

One important issue that deserves further exploration involves the precise manner in which physicians' expectations about their patients are formed. What is the role of initial impressions (see Zuckerman, Hodgins, & Miyake, this volume), and how important are both physicians' and patients' stereotypes based on gender (see Hall and Briton, this volume)? What cues, verbal and nonverbal, do physicians use to convey their expectations to patients, and what cues do patients use to convey their own interest, competence, and self-efficacy? How do the expectations of physicians and patients directly and indirectly affect treatment outcomes? Precisely what kinds of outcomes (e.g., physical functioning, emotional adjustment, commitment to health behaviors) are most susceptible to these expectations and why?

A second important topic for future research involves the effects of these expectations on the process of medical care. How do both physicians' and patients' expectations affect clinical decision making? What kinds of assumptions do physicians make about their patients' values when they consider possible treatments? What factors affect whether patients are included in or excluded from decisions about their own care, and in what ways do physicians' expectations influence the process of informed consent?

The research necessary to answer these and related questions must take account of many aspects of an enormously complicated clinical setting. Many relevant medical and psychosocial variables must be assessed or controlled, because any picture of the physician–patient relationship is set amid the details of a complex medical care system. Despite the difficulties of studying real, and not simulated, medical care interactions, future research needs to focus on detailed examination of the social psychology of actual doctor–patient interactions. Only then can the contribution of interpersonal factors to the improvement of medical care be clearly documented and understood.

Note

Recently, my research on adherence to medical treatment has been supported by grants from the Agency for Health Care Policy and Research (No. HS 06171; Ron Hays, P.I.) and the Research Network on Health and Behavior of the John D. and Catherine T. MacArthur Foundation, and by Intramural and Intercampus Research Grants from the University of California, Riverside.

I would like to express my gratitude to Bob Rosenthal for encouraging me 20 years ago to pursue my interest in physician–patient communication even though, then, it was on the fringes of social psychology.

References

Bain, D. J. G. (1976). Doctor–patient communication in general practice consultations. *Medical Education, 10,* 125–131.

Barnlund, D. C. (1976). The mystification of meaning: Doctor–patient encounters. *Journal of Medical Education, 51,* 716–725.

Becker, M. H. (1974). The health belief model and sick role behavior. *Health Education Monograph, 2,* 409–419.

Becker, M. H., & Rosenstock, I. M. (1984). Compliance with medical advice. In

A. Steptoe & A. Mathews (Eds.), *Health care and human behavior* (pp. 175–208). London: Academic Press.

Beisecker, A. E., & Beisecker, T. D. (1990). Patient information-seeking behaviors when communicating with doctors. *Medical Care, 28*(1), 19–28.

Ben-Sira, Z. (1980). Affective and instrumental components of the physician–patient relationship: An additional dimension of interaction theory. *Journal of Health and Social Behavior, 17,* 3–11.

Brownell, K. D., Marlatt, G. A., Lichtenstein, E., & Wilson, G. T. (1986). Understanding and preventing relapse. *American Psychologist, 41,* 765–782.

Cassell, E. J. (1985). *Talking with patients.* Vol. 1: *The theory of doctor–patient communication.* Cambridge, MA: MIT Press.

Cassileth, B. R., Lusk, E. J., Strouse, T. B., & Bodenheimer, B. J. (1984). Contemporary unorthodox treatments in cancer medicine: A study of patients, treatments, and practitioners. *Annals of Internal Medicine, 101,* 105–112.

Champion, V. L. (1984). Instrument development for health belief model constructs. *Advances in Nursing Science, 6,* 73–85.

Davis, M. S. (1971). Variations in patients' compliance with doctors' orders. Medical practice and doctor–patient interaction. *Psychiatry in Medicine, 2,* 31–54.

Demak, M. M., & Becker, M. H. (1987). The doctor–patient relationship and counseling for preventive care. *Patient Education and Counseling, 9,* 5–24.

DiMatteo, M. R. (1979). A social-psychological analysis of physician–patient rapport: Toward a science of the art of medicine. *Journal of Social Issues, 35,* 12–33.

DiMatteo, M. R. (1991). *The psychology of health, illness, and medical care: An individual perspective.* Pacific Grove, CA: Brooks/Cole.

DiMatteo, M. R., & DiNicola, D. D. (1982a). *Achieving patient compliance: The psychology of the medical practitioner's role.* New York: Pergamon Press.

DiMatteo, M. R., & DiNicola, D. D. (1982b). Social science and the art of medicine: From Hippocrates to holism. In H. S. Friedman & M. R. DiMatteo (Eds.), *Interpersonal issues in health care* (pp. 9–31). New York: Academic Press.

DiMatteo, M. R., & Hays, R. (1980). The significance of patients' perceptions of physician conduct: A study of patient satisfaction in a family practice center. *Journal of Community Health, 6*(1), 18–34.

DiMatteo, M. R., Hays, R. D., Gritz, E. R., Bastani, R., Crane, L., Elashoff, R., Ganz, P., Heber, D., McCarthy, W., & Marcus, A. (in press). Factors affecting patient adherence to cancer control regimens: Development and validation of a multivariate assessment instrument. *Psychological Assessment.*

DiMatteo, M. R., Sherbourne, C. D., Ordway, L., Hays, R. D., Kravitz, R., McGlynn, E., & Rogers, W. (1991). Physicians' characteristics influence patients' adherence to medical treatment: Results from the Medical Outcomes Study. *Health Psychology.*

Dye, N. E., & DiMatteo, M. R. (in press). Empowerment in the medical encounter: The theory of active patienthood. In J. Vogt (Ed.), *Empowerment: Cases in context.* San Francisco: Jossey-Bass.

Egbert, L. D., Battit, G. E., Welch, C. E., & Bartlett, M. K. (1964). Reduction of post-operative pain by encouragement and instruction of patients: A study of doctor–patient rapport. *New England Journal of Medicine, 270,* 825–827.

Eisenberg, J. M. (1979). Sociological influences on decision-making by clinicians. *Annals of Internal Medicine, 90,* 957–964.

Eisenthal, S., Koopman, C., & Lazare, A. (1983). Process analysis of two dimensions of the negotiated approach in relation to satisfaction in the initial interview. *Journal of Nervous and Mental Diseases, 171*(1), 49–54.

Epstein, L. H. (1984). The direct effects of compliance on health outcomes. *Health Psychology, 3*(4), 385–393.

Feller, B. A. (1979). *Characteristics of general internists and the content of care of their patients* (HRA-79-652). Washington, DC: U.S. Department of Health, Education and Welfare.

Franks, P., Culpepper, L., & Dickinson, J. (1982). Psychosocial bias in the diagnosis of obesity. *Journal of Family Practice, 14*, 745–750.

Freemon, B., Negrete, V. F., Davis, M., & Korsch, B. M. (1971). Gaps in doctor–patient communication: Doctor–patient interaction analysis. *Pediatric Research, 5*, 298–311.

Greenfield, S., Kaplan, S. H., & Ware, J. E., Jr. (1985). Expanding patient involvement in care: Effects on patient outcomes. *Annals of Internal Medicine, 102*(4), 520–528.

Greenfield, S., Kaplan, S. H., Ware, J. E., Jr., Yano, E. M., & Frank, H. J. L. (1988). Patients' participation in medical care: Effects on blood sugar control and quality of life in diabetes. *General Internal Medicine, 3*, 448–457.

Hall, J. A., Roter, D. L., & Katz, W. R. (1988). Meta analyses of correlates of provider behavior in medical encounters. *Medical Care, 26*, 1–19.

Harrigan, J., Oxman, T., & Rosenthal, R. (1985). Rapport expressed through nonverbal behavior. *Journal of Nonverbal Behavior, 9*, 95–110.

Haynes, R. B., Taylor, D. W., & Sackett, D. L. (Eds.). (1979). *Compliance in health care*. Baltimore: Johns Hopkins University Press.

Henbest, R. J., & Stewart, M. A. (1989). Patient centeredness in the consultation: A method for measurement. *Family Practice, 6*, 249–254.

Hippocrates. (4th century b.c./1923 Translation). *On decorum and the physician*, Vol. EE (W. H. S. Jones, Trans.). London: Heinemann.

Janz, N. K., & Becker, M. H. (1984). The health belief model: A decade later. *Health Education Quarterly, 11*(1), 1–47.

Jarvinen, K. A. (1955). Can ward rounds be a danger to patients with myocardial infarction? *British Medical Journal, 1*, 318–320.

Johnson, S. M., Kurtz, M. E., Tomlinson, T., & Howe, K. R. (1986). Students' stereotypes of patients as barriers to clinical decision-making. *Journal of Medical Education, 61*, 727–735.

Jones, P. K., Jones, S. L., & Katz, J. (1988). Health belief model intervention to increase compliance with emergency department patients. *Medical Care, 26*(12), 1172–1185.

Kane, R. L., & Deuschle, K. W. (1967). Problems in doctor–patient communications. *Medical Care, 5*(4), 260–271.

Kaplan, R. M., & Simon, H. J. (1990). Compliance in medical care: Reconsideration of self-predictions. *Annals of Behavioral Medicine, 12*(2), 66–71.

Kleinman, A. (1988). *The illness narratives: Suffering, healing, and the human condition*. New York: Basic Books.

Korsch, B. M., Gozzi, E. K., & Francis, V. (1968). Gaps in doctor–patient communication. I. Doctor–patient interaction and patient satisfaction. *Pediatrics, 42*, 855–871.

Kravitz, R., Hays, R. D., Sherbourne, C. D., DiMatteo, M. R., Greenfield, S., Ordway, L., & Rogers, W. (1992). *Receipt of recommendations and adherence to advice among patients with chronic medical conditions: Results of the Medical Outcomes Study*. Manuscript submitted for publication.

Kruse, W., & Weber, E. (1990). Dynamics of drug-regimen compliance – its assessment by microprocessor-based monitoring. *European Journal of Clinical Pharmacology, 38,* 561–565.

Langer, E. J., Janis, I. L., & Wolfer, J. A. (1975). Reduction of psychological stress in surgical patients. *Journal of Experimental Social Psychology, 11,* 155–165.

Lazare, A., Eisenthal, S., Frank, A., & Stoeckle, J. (1978). Studies on a negotiated approach to patienthood. In E. Gallagher (Ed.), *The doctor–patient relationships in the changing health scene* (pp. 119–140). DHEW Publication No. (NIH) 78-183. Washington, DC: U.S. Department of Health, Education, and Welfare.

Lerman, C. E., Brody, D. S., Caputo, G. C., Smith, D. G., Lazaro, C. G., & Wolfson, H. G. (1990). Patients' perceived involvement in care scale: Relationship to attitudes about illness and medical care. *Journal of General Internal Medicine, 5*(1), 29–33.

Ley, P., & Spelman, M. S. (1965). Communication in an outpatient setting. *British Journal of Social and Clinical Psychology, 4,* 114–116.

Luscher, T. F., & Vetter, W. (1990). Adherence to medication. *Journal of Human Hypertension, 4*(Suppl 1), 43–46.

Lynch, J. J., Thomas, S. A., Mills, M. E., Malinow, K., & Katcher, A. H. (1974). The effects of human contact on cardiac arrhythmia in coronary care patients. *Journal of Nervous and Mental Disease, 158,* 88–99.

McGlynn, E. (1988). Physician job satisfaction: Its measurement and use as an indication of system performance. Santa Monica, CA: RAND Graduate School doctoral dissertation.

Mandel, I., Franks, P., & Dickinson, J. (1985). Improving physician compliance with preventive medicine guidelines. *Journal of Family Practice, 21,* 223–224.

Matthews, J. J. (1983). The communication process in clinical settings. *Social Science and Medicine, 17,* 1371–1378.

Mayerson, E. W. (1976). *Putting the ill at ease.* New York: Harper & Row.

Meichenbaum, D., & Turk, D. C. (1987). *Facilitating treatment adherence: A practitioner's guidebook.* New York: Plenum Press.

Milmoe, S., Rosenthal, R., Blane, H. T., Chafetz, M. L., & Wolf, I. (1967). The doctor's voice: Postdictor of successful referral of alcoholic patients. *Journal of Abnormal Psychology, 72,* 78–84.

Osler, Sir William. (1899). Lecture to medical students. *Albany Medical Annals, 20,* 307.

Pickering, T. G., James, G. D., Boddie, C., Harshfield, G. A., Blank, S., & Laragh, J. H. (1988). How common is white coat hypertension? *Journal of the American Medical Association, 259*(2), 225–228.

Ronis, D. L., & Harel, Y. (1989). Health benefits and breast examination behaviors: Analyses of linear structural relations. *Psychology and Health, 3,* 259–285.

Rosenstock, I. M. (1966). Why people use health services. *Millbank Memorial Fund Quarterly, 44,* 94–127.

Roter, D. L. (1977). Patient participation in the patient–provider interaction: The effects of patient question-asking on the quality of interaction, satisfaction and compliance. *Health Education Monographs, 5,* 281–308.

Roter, D. L. (1984). Patient question asking in physician–patient interaction. *Health Psychology, 3*(5), 395–410.

Samora, J., Saunders, L., & Larson, R. F. (1961). Medical vocabulary knowledge among hospital patients. *Journal of Health and Human Behavior, 2,* 83–89.

Savitz, E. J. (1991). No miracle cure. *Barrons, 71*(31), 8–23.

Schulman, B. A. (1979). Active patient orientation and outcomes in hypertensive treatment: Application of a socio-organizational perspective. *Medical Care, 17*(3), 267–280.

Segall, A., & Roberts, L. W. (1980). A comparative analysis of physician estimates and levels of medical knowledge among patients. *Sociology of Health and Illness, 2*(3), 317–334.

Sherbourne, C. D., Hays, R. D., Ordway, L., DiMatteo, M. R., & Kravitz, R. L. (1992). Antecedents of adherence to medical recommendations: Results from the Medical Outcomes Study. *Journal of Behavioral Medicine, 15*(5), 1–22.

Speedling, E. J., & Rose, D. N. (1985). Building an effective doctor–patient relationship: From patient satisfaction to patient participation. *Social Science and Medicine, 21*(2), 115–120.

Stiles, W. B., Putnam, S. M., Wolf, M. H., & James, S. A. (1979). Interaction exchange structure and patient satisfaction with medical interviews. *Medical Care, 17*, 667–681.

Stone, G. C. (1979). Patient compliance and the role of the expert. *Journal of Social Issues, 35*, 34–59.

Sutton, S. R., & Eiser, J. R. (1990). The decision to wear a seat belt: The role of cognitive factors, fear, and prior behaviour. *Psychology and Health, 4*, 111–123.

Svarstad, B. (1976). Physician–patient communication and patient conformity with medical advice. In D. Mechanic (Ed.), *The growth of bureaucratic medicine* (pp. 220–238). New York: Wiley.

Swain, M. A., & Steckel, S. B. (1981). Influencing adherence among hypertensives. *Research on Nursing and Health, 4*, 213–222.

Szasz, T. S., & Hollender, M. H. (1956). A contribution to the philosophy of medicine. The basic models of the doctor–patient relationship. *Archives of Internal Medicine, 97*, 585–592.

Tarlov, A. R., Ware, T. E., Greenfield, S., Nelson, E. C., Perrin, E., & Zubkoff, M. (1989). Medical Outcomes Study: An application of methods for evaluating the results of medical care. *Journal of the American Medical Association, 262*, 907–913.

Taylor, S. E. (1979). Hospital patient behavior: Reactance, helplessness, or control. *Journal of Social Issues, 35*(1), 156–184.

Todd, J. S., Seekins, S. V., Krichbaum, J. A., & Harvey, L. K. (1991). Health access American – Strengthening the U.S. health care system. *Journal of the American Medical Association, 265*(19), 2503–2506.

Uhlenhuth, E. H., Canter, A., Neustadt, J. O., & Payson, H. E. (1959). The symptomatic relief of anxiety with neprobamate, phenobarbital, and placebo. *American Journal of Psychiatry, 115*, 905–910.

Uhlmann, R. F., Inui, T. S., Pecoraro, R. E., & Carter, W. B. (1988). Relationship of patient request fulfillment to compliance glycemic control, and other health care outcomes in insulin-dependent diabetes. *Journal of General Internal Medicine, 3*, 458–463.

U.S. Preventive Services Task Force. (1989). *Guide to clinical preventive services.* Baltimore: Williams & Wilkins.

Waitzkin, H. (1984). Doctor–patient communication: Clinical implications of social scientific research. *Journal of the American Medical Association, 252*, 2441–2446.

Waitzkin, H. (1985). Information giving in medical care. *Journal of Health and Social Behavior, 26*(2), 81–101.

Waitzkin, H., & Stoeckle, J. D. (1976). Information control and the micropolitics of health care: Summary of an ongoing research project. *Social Science and Medicine, 10,* 263–276.

16. Comment: Interpersonal expectations, social influence, and emotion transfer

KLAUS R. SCHERER

The need for theory-driven research on real phenomena

I was recently given the assignment of preparing a state-of-the-art report for social psychology, with the request to focus on the advances and key developments in the field, as well as on promising research perspectives for the next decade (Scherer, 1992). In trying to go beyond my personal prejudices, I informally polled a number of colleagues in Europe and the United States with respect to their opinions on key developments and shortcomings in our discipline, and looked at the evolution of different content areas in major social psychology journals and textbooks (assuming that it is here that a discipline tries to put its best foot forward). I concluded that in spite of the explosion of research and publication activity in the field, real advances in knowledge that could figure prominently in our textbooks have been few and far between in the past two decades. Although there has been much progress in our understanding of human social cognition and interaction, our ability to explain some of the central social psychological phenomena (such as person perception, group dynamics, or the effects of culture on behavior) and to unravel the processes involved leaves much to be desired.

In attempting to analyze the causal factors responsible for this situation, I became convinced that social psychologists might lean too much toward paradigm-driven rather than phenomenon-driven research. This has resulted in an impressive number of elegant and methodologically sophisticated studies on ever more complex paradigms that, however, may not always contribute to the understanding of real-life phenomena. To give but one example, one that is close to my heart: The large majority of publications in the area of person perception and impression formation has been concerned with the paradigm of studying the cog-

316

nitive processing of verbal trait labels rather than studying the phenomenon of the *person perception process* (involving the utilization of appearance and behavior cues in inferring traits and states) as it occurs in ongoing social interaction (see Bruner & Tagiuri, 1954; Schneider, Hastorf, & Ellsworth, 1979).

In evaluating possible orientations of future social psychological research, I strongly advocate phenomenon-driven research. Furthermore, I promote applied research, interdisciplinary approaches, and cross-cultural comparison as safeguards against losing the phenomenon and drifting toward the perpetuation of paradigms that may have been very fruitful at the outset of a research tradition but that threaten to become an end in themselves. Research efforts concerned with real-world problems may help to alleviate this danger, since the potential users of the applied research work are likely to keep reminding us of the real phenomenon and of their concrete needs. To avoid the pitfalls of blind action orientation and to ensure progress in basic research, it is essential to adopt a *scientifically minded* (as opposed to a *utilitarian*) approach to applied research. The natural sciences are replete with examples demonstrating that such an approach is eminently realistic. Interdisciplinarity will keep us focused on a phenomenon, since the pet paradigms tend to vary among the different disciplines concerned; thus, due to a system of mutual checks and balances, a phenomenon is likely to remain at the center of attention. Finally, cross-cultural comparison is useful, since it forces us to define the phenomenon in a general fashion, independent of cultural preferences and fashions.

George Miller (1986), in a state-of-the-art report on cognitive psychology, suggested that psychology is prone to succumb habitually to a state of "analytic pathology." He argued that the field has been repeatedly snatched from the brink of futility by a new application, or by a new integrative theory providing synthetic insights, or both. Since paradigm-driven research is unlikely to make much use of integrative theory, social psychology may be in danger of succumbing to the ills that George Miller painted on the wall. In consequence, I argue for a more important role of integrated middle-range theories and theory-driven research in social psychology (Scherer, 1992).

If this state-of-the-art report had left me slightly depressed, the content of the present volume has done much to improve my spirits. The research reported here clearly demonstrates that interpersonal expectations and their effects are a real and powerful phenomenon (backed up by some of the most advanced meta-analyses available; see Rubin and

Harris, this volume; Rosenthal, 1991). Furthermore, there is no dearth of applied research or of interdisciplinarity in this area: The phenomenon has been studied in many different domains of application, ranging from the classroom to the doctor's office to the courtroom and even the boardroom (see the research reviews in this volume). Many of the studies have been done outside the United States, and although there have been only a few attempts at direct cross-cultural comparison, we can be reassured not only about the existence but also about the universality of the phenomenon.

How does the field of interpersonal expectation research fare with respect to explanatory theory, particularly of an integrative nature? Although the concept of a *self-fulfilling prophecy* occupies a central position and describes both process and effect, it does not quite merit the status of a theory. The major purpose of such a theory would be to specify the conditions and the context in which, and the mechanism whereby, interpersonal expectations produce their effects. This is no easy matter since cognition, motivation, and behavior are complexly intermeshed and are mediated through communication processes. An integrative theory should allow us to interrelate the different domains and to specify the contingencies and causal effects.

I will mention two promising approaches to the development of such a theory: Rosenthal's model, highlighting the process and the factors involved in the mediation of interpersonal expectancy effects, and social psychological attempts to anchor these effects in social interaction models (as exemplified by the work of Darley and Snyder and their respective collaborators).

Rosenthal (1981, 1991) has suggested a *10-arrow model* to conceptualize the effects of independent predictor variables (like moderator and expectancy variables for the expecter) on mediating process variables (expecter behavior) and the direct and indirect effects of these on dependent (outcome) variables such as immediate and long-term expectancy confirmation effects. So far, this model has been used primarily for the systematic description of effects revealed in meta-analyses of expectancy studies (Harris & Rosenthal, 1985). However, it would seem that this model lends itself perfectly well to further development into a full-fledged theoretical model, one that would be ideally suited for path analyses and structural modeling.

The nature of the variables in the different classes of the model and their causal interconnections are in part derived from a number of empirical studies conducted in this area. Focusing on the mediation of teacher expectancies, Rosenthal and Harris (Rosenthal, 1973; Harris &

Rosenthal, 1986) have proposed and tested a four-factor theory, comprising affective climate (warmth), teaching inputs, responding to opportunities for students (outputs), and differentiated feedback. There has also been some attempt to specify the communication channels involved in the mediation of these factors. Rosenthal (1989) has suggested an *affect-effort* approach, arguing that the affective factor (e.g., warmth) is mainly communicated via nonverbal behavior, whereas effort, reflecting time, energy, and cognitive resources, is more likely to be transmitted in the verbal channel.

The motivational underpinnings of expectation confirmatory behavior are obviously central to a theory of interpersonal expectation effects. In the introduction to the classic study *Pygmalion in the Classroom,* Rosenthal and Jacobson (1968) suggested that the ability to predict events and outcomes is a selective advantage in phylogenetic adaptation, arguing that humans try to avoid surprises as much as possible (to the point of preferring predictable negative outcomes to unpredictable positive ones). This need for cognitive order and stability has been one of the major topics of research in cognitive social psychology. It is not surprising, then, as the review by Darley and Oleson (this volume) shows, that social psychological research (much of it based on attribution theory) has greatly contributed to the identification of pertinent variables and their causal interactions. The development of theoretical models in the area of interpersonal expectation can also greatly benefit from the work on self-fulfilling prophecies in interaction process theory. Darley and Oleson (this volume) summarize studies that have investigated moderator and mediating variables such as bystander effects and the role of awareness. In particular, they stress the importance of sender and target interaction goals as powerful determinants of expectancy confirmation.

In this chapter, I complicate the issue still further in insisting on an important role for emotion in this context. This role transcends the affective factor of interaction climate or warmth that has been highlighted by Rosenthal and his collaborators for the case of teacher expectations. As I try to show, it is strongly linked to the issue of sender and target values, needs, and interaction goals, as highlighted by interaction process theorists.

The role of emotion in interpersonal expectation

The mediation of interpersonal expectancy effects via nonverbal behavior is the central process in the phenomenon. I vividly remember the sense of excitement when, as a graduate student, I started to work with Robert Rosenthal on the role of vocal cues in the mediation of experimenter expectancy effects (Scherer, Uno, & Rosenthal, 1972). In my favorite study in this series, we differentially manipulated the speech intensity level of different parts of an experimenter's instruction (accenting the description of the positive or the negative end of a judgment scale). This simple manipulation of the recording level of the message did, in fact, significantly influence the subjects' ratings (Scherer, Rosenthal, & Koivumaki, 1972). At the time, I was absolutely thrilled by the possibility of surreptitiously changing people's attitudes by subtle manipulations of a persuasive message. Having become older (and maybe somewhat wiser), I am a bit more skeptical with respect to what it takes to bring about social influence (in the form of expectancy effects or otherwise).

I tend to think that subtle cues, such as differential loudness of different parts of an instruction or other nonverbal aspects of persuasive messages, may well influence the responses of subjects in domains that are not very close to their heart or where they have little prior knowledge or conviction. To choose an analogy from nature: The slightest breeze may blow away a dry leaf on the ground, but it takes something close to a storm to tear off a leaf that is still firmly attached to its branch. In the absence of strong anchoring of attitudes or behavior, any differential experimental cue may have significant effects on those attitudes and behaviors. Examples abound in the social psychological literature. This is not to say that we need very potent and/or obvious cues to bring about attitudinal or behavioral change. Let us assume that subjects in an experiment have a heartfelt desire, of which they may not even be aware, to please the experimenter and to confirm his or her expectations. In this case, even very subtle cues communicating such expectations are likely to have a powerful effect.

What I am arguing, then, is that one of the most important issues in the confirmation of interpersonal expectancies is the target's (conscious or nonconscious) evaluation of the sender's expectancy-mediating behavior *with respect to his or her own needs, goals, and values.* If the sender as a person and the content of the expectancy are highly pertinent to the target, high ego involvement, and in consequence some form of emotional response, are likely to occur as the result of this automatic appraisal process. For example, the teacher is obviously a highly pertinent person for a student. Similarly, one's own capacities and the teacher's (professional) evaluation of them are of high relevance for one's self-concept or self-esteem, as well as for the goal of succeeding in school. In consequence, teacher expectations will provoke high, emotionally toned ego involvement. I believe that it is this emotional factor that determines the role and efficacy of a sender's expectancy-mediating behaviors with respect to the target's attention to, interest in, and tendency to conform to the expectation. An integrative theory of interpersonal expectancy effects will need to specify these relationships further and to anchor them in a process-oriented perspective linking cognition, motivation, emotion, and behavior.

The effect of emotional expression on social influence

Since I consider myself an outsider to the field of interpersonal expectation, I will not be so bold as to attempt to contribute to the development of such an integrated theory of interpersonal expectation. Rather, in what follows I will briefly discuss the potential role of emotion, and particularly the expression of emotion, in the process of social influence, of which interpersonal expectation effects can be considered a special case.

Much of my work, starting with early collaborative studies with Robert Rosenthal and Judy Hall (e.g., Scherer, Koivumaki, & Rosenthal, 1972), has focused on the vocal expression of emotion (see Scherer, 1985, 1986, for reviews). This has, in due course, gotten me into the quagmires of emotion theory (see Scherer, 1984, 1988, for reviews). More recently, I have applied some of these interests to a phenomenon that has fascinated me ever since my early dissertation plans – persuasion, particularly the role of the vocal expression of emotion in the persuasion process (Scherer, 1979). Motivated by an invited lecture,[1] I proposed a psychobiological explanation for the role of pathos in persuasion. In thinking about interpersonal expectancy effects and reading some of the drafts of chapters for this part of the volume, I was struck by some of the parallels and was encouraged to make a – rather speculative – attempt to apply the argument to the expectancy domain. I first outline a dual-path model of the role of emotional expression in persuasive social influence.[2]

My interest in the role of emotional expression in persuasion was triggered by two observations: (1) concluding from an extensive review of the literature on propaganda campaigns directed to better acceptance of minorities (including the mentally ill) that pure information (i.e., cognition-directed influence) does not seem to have any effect at all on

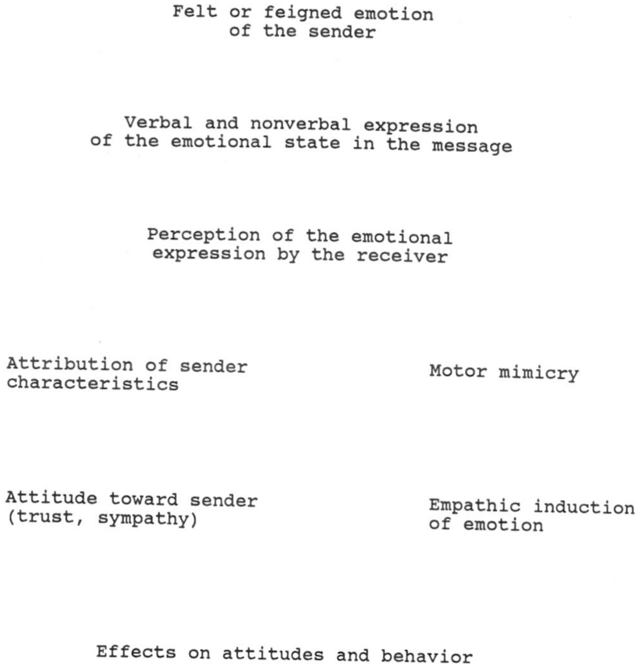

```
Felt or feigned emotion
     of the sender



 Verbal and nonverbal expression
of the emotional state in the message



   Perception of the emotional
   expression by the receiver



Attribution of sender              Motor mimicry
characteristics



Attitude toward sender             Empathic induction
(trust, sympathy)                  of emotion



   Effects on attitudes and behavior
```

Figure 16.1. Dual-path model of the role of emotion in persuasion.

changes in behavior toward minority group members (Scherer, 1975); (2) rediscovering writers in the Greek and Roman rhetorical tradition who insist on authentic emotional expression of the persuader as the most important element of an effective persuasion process (e.g., Cicero's *De Oratore* or Quintilian's *Institutio Oratoria*).[3]

Figure 16.1 shows the dual-path model that I propose to account for the effectiveness of emotional expression by a social influence agent. The first path accentuates credibility and the persuadee's attribution of persuader states and traits. The argument basically stems from Aristotle, who in his *Nicomachean Ethics* underlined the important role of anger expression as an essential element of social competence. He pointed out that the person who is not able to get angry in the right way, about the right things, at the right time will be seen as a fool (see Aristotle, 1941, p. 996). Obviously, then, a speaker who wants to persuade an audience to take action against an unjust state of affairs needs to show an appropriate amount of indignation in order to be credible. The important role of emotional expression in social interaction has also been pointed out by Darwin (1872/1965), who argued that emotional expression endows speech with force and vividness. He specifically stated that nonverbal expression in the voice and the face can be trusted to a higher degree than words, which are all too easily manipulated (p. 364).

Emotions reflect the evaluation of situations and events with respect to important goals and needs of an organism. They focus the attention of the organism on the emotion-eliciting object or event, and provide drive and direction for appropriate coping reactions. Most important, they allow the communication of reactions and behavioral intentions to the social environment. Thus, when we see the expression of someone's emotion, we are informed about his or her evaluation of an important event, the reaction to it, and the behavioral intention designed to cope with it. In consequence, anyone wanting to advocate a change of attitude or behavior concerning an important issue in an audience needs to demonstrate, via the expression of personal emotion, that he or she is evaluating the situation in the appropriate way and is prepared to take appropriate action. The effect of emotional expression in lending authenticity and credibility to the communication of behavioral reactions and intentions is probably phylogenetically continuous. Even if it were possible, an alarm call of a macaque monkey would probably not be taken seriously if it was produced "cold," without the appropriate display of emotionality. In fact, the acoustic characteristics of primate alarm calls are in themselves iconic signs of emotional arousal, with emotional-motivational significance and symbolic representation inextricably linked (Jürgens, 1979; Marler, 1984; Scherer, 1985).

The first path of the model postulates, then, that a communicator displaying appropriate emotional expressions will be more effective because the audience will attribute credibility to him or her and consequently will be more prone to be influenced in the direction of the persuasive argument, since an attitude of trust or sympathy has been developed toward the sender. The mechanism described by this path basically consists of the attribution of states and traits to the sender, which involves cognitive processing (without necessarily being conscious). Although knowledge of these processes dates back to antiquity, and although there has been much concern with communicator credibility in the early social psychological studies on attitude change and persuasion (McGuire, 1969), there has been little focused research on this phenomenon in recent years. Much of the newer work on the role of affect in persuasion is directed at affective message cues or the mood state of the receiver (see the chapters in Part 3 of Forgas, 1991). Although it deals with only one aspect of the process, the research on the persuasive effect of the sender's speech style and delivery (e.g., Miller, Maruyama, Beaber, & Valone, 1976) is pertinent. As Banse (1987) has shown for speech rate in persuasion, situational factors have important mediating effects. This is probably generally true for inferences of the sender's characteristics based on emotional expression. In consequence, empirical research is needed to elucidate the exact nature of the first path in the model outlined here.

The second path is entirely affective in nature and involves the transfer of emotion from the persuader to the persuadee. This is admittedly much more speculative than the first path, since it relies on a phenomenon that is far from being generally accepted: the process of *Einfühlung*, as suggested by Theodor Lipps (1909, pp. 228–231). In English, this term might be best rendered as "empathy via motor mimicry." This notion, after having fallen into disrepute for quite a number of years, seems to be slowly becoming rehabilitated (Hoffman, 1984; Wispé, 1987). I felt sufficiently encouraged by this renewed interest and by some promising empirical data (see Bavelas, Black, Lemery, & Mullett, 1987; Bernal & Berger, 1976; Dimberg, 1982; Eisenberg & Strayer, 1987; Vaughan & Lanzetta, 1980) to give the mechanism a try in the model.

Lipps suggested that the mere fact of observing someone's motor expression of emotion triggers a tendency to reproduce, if only in a very rudimentary fashion, the same motor movements oneself. This rudimentary motor mimicry of the expressive aspects of the other's emotion reproduces, again usually in much weaker form, the same emotion in the observer, who is thus able to "understand" the other's emotion. This chapter is not the place to discuss the well-foundedness and empirical justification of such a process of emotion communication via transfer or contagion in detail. However, the important role of emotional expression for social interaction and coordination in all socially living species (see Buck, 1984), as well as the importance of social sharing of emotion in humans (Rimé, Mesquita, Philippot, & Boca, 1991) – which is likely to be strongly linked to empathic phenomena like pity – provide sufficient grounds for examining the emotion transfer mechanism more seriously than has been done so far.

A series of studies conducted by McHugo, Lanzetta, and their collaborators has investigated the claim for emotion transfer via mass media presentation of a persuader's message – in this case, political leaders. McHugo, Lanzetta, Sullivan, Masters, and Englis (1985) showed videotaped excerpts of happiness/reassurance, anger/threat, and fear/evasion expressive displays by President Reagan to their subjects. They found specific responses in facial muscle innervation, skin resistance, and heart rate to the different displays (which, contrary to self-reports of emotional state, did not depend on prior attitude toward Reagan). In a follow-up study, McHugo, Lanzetta, and Bush (1991) were able to replicate one of the major findings: specific facial muscle reactions to expressive displays of two political leaders (videotaped excerpts shown without sound). As expected on the basis of the motor mimicry hypothesis, positive expressions (happiness/reassurance) produced significantly greater zygomatic activity, whereas negative expressions (anger/threat) produced greater corrugator activity. Consistent with the notion that such motor mimicry effects might produce empathic emotion induction, the authors found, despite large differences among subjects in attitudinal predisposition, a fair amount of correspondence between differential facial muscle activity and reported subjective feeling (although there were large individual differences in the degree of correspondence). Contrary to the earlier study, however, prior attitude of the subjects did interact with the type of expressive display in determining the facial reactions, as measured by facial electromyography, demonstrating the complexity of the processes involved. Clearly, effects of prior attitude, situation, and other context variables are likely to mediate strongly the emotion transfer process.

However, if indeed emotions can be transferred from persuader to persuadee by such a process of motor mimicry and empathy, the effects on persuasion are obvious even if the effect is relatively subtle. To begin with, feeling the same emotion toward an object, event, or state of affairs implies taking the same stance toward it and evaluating it in the same way. This may obviously bring about a change of attitude and evaluative frame in the direction of what the persuader is trying to achieve. In addition, we can expect at least some of the following effects on the cognitive processes: direction of attention to the emotional message of the communicator, production of cognitive arousal, narrowing of the field of attention, modification of the information processing capacity (especially of the critical, rational thought processes), and activation of unconscious automatic schemata. Furthermore, judgment processes may change; for example, risk is accepted more readily, the potential for engaging in action is augmented, and the inhibition threshold for the triggering of emotion-congruent behavior may be lowered.

To summarize: It is argued that appropriate emotional expression by a persuader will tend to increase the effectiveness of the persuasive message because of (1) the attribution of greater credibility and trustworthiness and (2) the production of appropriate emotions in the audience, which may induce the desired attitudes or behaviors or make the cognitive processing more amenable to accepting the message emitted by the persuader.[4]

It is interesting to ask whether the persuader really has to feel the emotion he or she expresses or whether it can be fabricated for the occasion. The classic rhetoricians were convinced that the orator needs to work up the emotion, to actually experience it, and that it is not sufficient to just fake the respective emotional expression. Clearly, if the audience discovers the lack of authenticity of the underlying emotion, the attribution processes described by the first path might actually produce a boomerang effect in terms of a devaluation of credibility and trustworthiness. Also, emotion transfer may not take place unless all appropriate muscular structures are in action (for an interesting example, see the distinction between a social smile and a real smile, with the orbicularis oculi muscle as a critical element, in Ekman, Friesen, & O'Sullivan, 1988).

So far, I have argued that the credibility effect and the emotion transfer due to a persuader's (authentic) emotional expression are likely to further the effects of social influence attempts. How does this fit in with my earlier insistence on the role of ego involvement in social influence? Again, I assume that the effects described so far might well be sufficient to change attitudes or behaviors that are not firmly rooted in a person's need or value system. However, I do not think that they are sufficient to change strongly anchored beliefs, attitudes, or behaviors. It might be helpful to use the tripartite classification of influence effects suggested by Kelman (1958) in the present context. *Emotional compliance* would be present only as long as the immediate emotion transfer from the persuader is actually impinging on the target. *Emotional identification* might have effects even when the persuader's emotion is no longer perceived, but the empathy with the person continues. Only *emotional internalization*, however, would seem to have long-lasting effects, independent of the specific empathic relationship with a person. Emotional internalization, I would argue, is restricted to cases where the persuader has succeeded in affecting the target's needs, values, and situational appraisal patterns in such a way that specific events will automatically produce the kind of emotion originally suggested by the persuader. For example, emotional internalization of a persuader's emotional message concerning the disappearance of the rain forests would occur when a target (who did not care about rain forests before being exposed to this issue by an emotionally expressive communicator) actually feels strong anger (or sadness) in seeing footage of burning stretches of the Amazon forest, independent of the presence of an emotionally expressive influence agent (like the one who originally expressed overt anger or sadness in the message and thus produced the internalized affective reaction in the receiver). Most of the previous discussion deals with the prerequisites for emotional compliance. It would take a separate chapter and many additional assumptions to deal with the conditions for emotional identification or internalization.

Interpersonal expectation effects as a form of social influence

How is all this related to the topic of the present volume, interpersonal expectations, and to the specific section, the mediation of the expectancy effects? My central point is that most of the settings in which interpersonal expectancy effects have been studied so far, and which are described in this volume, are social influence settings. In other words, most of the expecters, whose interpersonal expectations have been shown to have an effect on the expectees, can be considered to be social change agents or professional persuaders. Clearly, teachers, doctors, lawyers, and managers constantly attempt to influence their clientele and to get them to change their attitudes and behavior. In this sense, the situation of an orator attempting to persuade an audience might be comparable to the situation in which interpersonal expectations produce their effects. Obviously, there are many differences. Expecters generally are not conscious of their persuasive efforts, at least not as far as their interpersonal expectations are concerned. Their interest in and insistence upon achieving the desired outcome of their influence efforts are probably less strong than in the case of a professional propagandist. Furthermore, in terms of the social definition of the situation, the settings of a doctor's office or a classroom are not generally considered to be oriented toward propaganda. Yet, if one considers the difficult tasks doctors face in trying to change their patients' behavior in the direction of compliance with the prescribed medical regimen, the parallels with other attitude or behavior change situations become quite pronounced (see DiMatteo, this volume). With respect to the boardroom, or particularly the courtroom, the analogy does not seem farfetched at all; persuasion in court has been one of the most important examples of classic rhetoric.

If this analysis is correct, the dual-path model might be applicable to the communication of interpersonal expectations and their effects on the expectees. There are a number of assumptions that need to be made, however. The first one is that the interpersonal expectation entails an emotional component. Obviously, the emotion involved could be quite different from the violent emotion that an orator who engages in diatribes against an unjust situation would need to feel and/or display. It might not be a full-blown emotion at all, but rather a specific emotional coloring of the cognitive content of the expectation. This does not seem unreasonable. For example, one could assume that a teacher would feel more positive, including elements of contentedness, joy, pride, optimism, and other positive emotions, if he or she expects a student to succeed. On the other hand, a more negative affective tone should accompany expectations of failure (including possibly worry, sadness, pessimism, disappointment, hopelessness, etc.). If this is the case, these affective feelings are likely to be mobilized in an interaction with the expectee and should (if one assumes a component process model of emotion, involving all of the organism's subsystems; see Scherer, 1984) affect the expressive motor system. Obviously, the outward expression of such affectively toned expectations would be much more subtle than the full-blown emotional expressions that are generally discussed in the psychology of emotion literature. Still, contrary to more general affective phenomena, such as positive mood or warmth, one would assume differential effects of the specific underlying emotions. Much of the work reported in this volume (by Archer, DePaulo, Hall, DiMatteo, and Zuckerman and their colleagues) shows how effectively even very subtle expressive cues can be used by an observer.

Another assumption is that the Lippsian process of motor mimicry and empathy will lead to some affect transfer even in these situations of relatively subdued emotions, and that this information will be sufficient for the credibility attributions postulated in the first path of the model. If the expecter is credited with greater credibility and trustworthiness, the expectee might be more prone to search for cues relevant to interpersonal expectations. Furthermore, the emotion transferred through the affective expression of the expecter may have a direct effect with respect to the self-fulfilling prophecy: If the gloomy emotionality accompanying negative expectations is communicated to the expectee, he or she is likely to feel equally gloomy, a mood that does not exactly generate the optimism and enthusiasm that are often seen as required for success.

As in the case of persuasion, one might ask whether it is possible to feign positive affect while having negative expectations. The chapters by Bella DePaulo and Miron Zuckerman and colleagues (this volume) provide important empirical evidence with respect to this question. It may be necessary, as suggested by the rhetoricians, to actually work up the real emotion, possibly using Stanislavski's techniques, in order to communicate affect authentically.

The affective climate or warmth factor, as identified by Rosenthal and his colleagues (see the earlier discussion) is obviously pertinent to the emotional effects discussed here. It would be interesting to study whether specific emotions have differential effects over and above a rather general positive tone. For example, is there a difference in expectancy confirmation when the emotion of pride (in one's own students' expected achievements) is added to general positive affect? This might be related to the issue of emotional compliance, identification, and internalization discussed earlier. It is possible that general positive affect, or warmth, is sufficient to produce compliance effects but that more differentiated, and consequently more informative, emotional messages are necessary to produce identification or internalization. For example, the expression of pride (or even admiration) in the context of expectancy-mediating behavior should give rise to very different attribution processes than would interpersonal warmth alone.

Conclusion

I have been arguing that the blooming field of interpersonal expectation research, which with respect to its phenomenality, applicability, interdisciplinarity, and even cross-culturality, encourages us to have very high hopes for real advancement in this area, may benefit from greater efforts to develop integrative theories. I have argued for the need to view the communication of interpersonal expectation as a social influence situation and to give more attention to the role of emotion in this process. I am conscious of the fact that the rash transfer of a model for standard persuasion situations that has not yet been worked out in all details to the communication of interpersonal expectation is a somewhat dubious enterprise. Clearly, the implications for the different settings as described in this volume need to be developed in much more detail. Also, the rather speculative vein in much of the foregoing discussion may not meet with the approval of sober empiricists. I did feel, though, that with all the hard data represented in this volume, a little speculation could not hurt. In any case, in my role as a persuader, intent upon demonstrating the need to better understand the emotional processes underlying our behavior, I would be happy to have sparked some interest in linking the work on interpersonal expectation to research on emotion and social influence.

Notes

This chapter is dedicated – with deeply felt gratitude – to Robert Rosenthal, whose immensely positive interpersonal expectations for his students have been a steady source of warmth, intellectual input, opportunity for output, and differentiated feedback throughout our careers. It might almost be immodest to hope for expectancy confirmation.
I gratefully acknowledge helpful advice in the preparation of this manuscript from Rainer Banse, Ursula Scherer, and Robert Rosenthal.

1.   I am indebted to the Siemens-Stiftung, Munich, for an invitation (March 1988) that was instrumental in rediscovering my interest in persuasion and in Theodor Lipps. The talk has not been published. A "popular" version appeared in the *Neue Zürcher Zeitung* (Scherer, 1989), where some further detail of the argument can be found.
2.   After having been informally suggested in an invited talk (see note 1), the model has not yet been properly worked out. Nor has all the relevant literature been reviewed and integrated. In spite of this unsatisfactory state of affairs, an outline of the model is described here to illustrate the link between the study of emotional expression in social influence and in interpersonal expectation. Given this intent, readers are asked to excuse the blatant lack of scholarly referencing of pertinent literature in the field of social influence.
3.   I am strongly indebted to Rainer Banse for having collected a number of the major classical writings on this topic.
4.   It should be noted that both of the paths I am positing would seem to be considered as part of the "peripheral route" in the model of persuasion suggested by Petty and Cacioppo (1986; see also Eagly & Chaiken, 1984; Petty, Gleicher, & Baker, 1991). I tend to disagree with these authors about the relative importance of such affective as compared to cognitive routes to attitude and behavior change. However, this chapter is not the place for a systematic discussion of this dissension.

References

Aristotle (1941). *Ethica Nicomachea*. In R. McKeon (Ed.), *The basic works of Aristotle* (pp. 935–1126). New York: Random House.
Banse, R. (1987). *Der Einfluss der Sprechgeschwindigkeit auf Sprecherevaluation und Einstellungsänderung in Abhängigkeit vom situativen Kontext*. Unpublished diploma thesis, University of Giessen, Germany.
Bavelas, J. B., Black, A., Lemery, C. R., & Mullett, J. (1987). Motor mimicry as primitive empathy. In N. Eisenberg & J. Strayer (Eds.), *Empathy and its development* (pp. 317–338). Cambridge and New York: Cambridge University Press.

Bernal, G., & Berger, S. U. (1976). Vicarious eyelid conditioning. *Journal of Personality and Social Psychology, 34,* 62–68.

Bruner, J., & Tagiuri, R. (1954). The perception of people. In G. Lindzey & E. Aronson (Eds.), *Handbook of social psychology* (Vol. 2, pp. 634–654). Reading, MA: Addison-Wesley.

Buck, R. (1984). *The communication of emotion.* New York: Guilford Press.

Darwin, C. (1872). *The expression of the emotions in man and animals.* London: Murray. (Reprinted Chicago: University of Chicago Press, 1965)

Dimberg, U. (1982). Facial reactions to facial expressions. *Psychophysiology, 19,* 643–647.

Eagly, A. H., & Chaiken, S. (1984). Cognitive theories of persuasion. In L. Berkowitz (Ed.), *Advances in experimental social psychology* (Vol. 17, pp. 268–361). Orlando, FL: Academic Press.

Eisenberg, N., & Strayer, J. (Eds.). (1987). *Empathy and its development.* Cambridge and New York: Cambridge University Press.

Ekman, P., Friesen, W. V., & O'Sullivan, M. (1988). Smiles when lying. *Journal of Personality and Social Psychology, 54,* 414–420.

Forgas, J. P. (Ed.). (1991). *Emotion and social judgment.* Oxford: Pergamon.

Harris, M. J., & Rosenthal, R. (1985). Mediation of interpersonal expectancy effects: 31 meta-analyses. *Psychological Bulletin, 97,* 363–386.

Harris, M. J., & Rosenthal, R. (1986). Four factors in the mediation of teacher expectancy effects. In R. S. Feldman (Ed.), *The social psychology of education* (pp. 91–114). Cambridge and New York: Cambridge University Press.

Hoffman, M. L. (1984). Interaction of affect and cognition in empathy. In C. E. Izard, J. Kagan, & R. B. Zajonc (Eds.), *Emotion, cognition, and behavior* (pp. 103–131). New York: Cambridge University Press.

Jürgens, U. (1979). Vocalization as an emotional indicator: A neuroethological study in the squirrel monkey. *Behaviour, 69,* 88–117.

Kelman, H. C. (1958). Compliance, identification, and internalization: Three processes of attitude change. *Journal of Conflict Resolution, 2,* 51–60.

Lipps, Th. (1909). *Leitfaden der Psychologie.* Leipzig: Engelmann.

McGuire, W. J. (1969). The nature of attitudes and attitude change. In G. Lindzey & E. Aronson (Eds.), *Handbook of social psychology* (2nd ed.) (Vol. 3, pp. 136–314). Reading, MA: Addison-Wesley.

McHugo, G. J., Lanzetta, J. T., & Bush, L. K. (1991). The effect of attitudes on emotional reactions to expressive displays of political leaders. *Journal of Nonverbal Behavior, 15,* 19–41.

McHugo, G. J., Lanzetta, J. T., Sullivan, D. G., Masters, R. D., & Englis, B. G. (1985). Emotional reactions to a political leader's expressive displays. *Journal of Personality and Social Psychology, 49,* 1513–1529.

Marler, P. (1984). Animal communication: Affect or cognition? In K. R. Scherer & P. Ekman (Eds.), *Approaches to emotion* (pp. 345–368). Hillsdale, NJ: Erlbaum.

Miller, G. A. (1986). Dismembering cognition. In S. H. Hulse & B. F. Green, Jr. (Eds.), *One hundred years of psychological research in America: G. Stanley Hall and the Johns Hopkins tradition* (pp. 277–298). Baltimore: Johns Hopkins University Press.

Miller, N., Maruyama, G., Beaber, R. J., & Valone, K. (1976). Speed of speech and persuasion. *Journal of Personality and Social Psychology, 34,* 615–624.

Petty, R. E., & Cacioppo, J. T. (1986). *Communication and persuasion: Central and peripheral routes to attitude change.* New York: Springer.

Petty, R. E., Gleicher, F., & Baker, S. M. (1991). Multiple roles for affect in persuasion. In J. P. Forgas (Ed.), *Emotion and social judgment* (pp. 181–200). Oxford: Pergamon.

Rimé, B., Mesquita, B., Philippot, P., & Boca, S. (1991). Beyond the emotional event: Six studies on the social sharing of emotion. *Cognition and Emotion, 5*, 435–466.

Rosenthal, R. (1973). The mediation of Pygmalion effects: A four factor "theory." *Papua New Guinea Journal of Education, 9*, 1–12.

Rosenthal, R. (1981). Pavlov's mice, Pfungst's horse, and Pygmalion's PONS: Some models for the study of interpersonal expectancy effects. In T. A. Sebeok & R. Rosenthal (Eds.), *The Clever Hans phenomenon* (pp. 182–198). Annals of the New York Academy of Sciences, No. 364.

Rosenthal, R. (1989). *Experimenter expectancy, covert communication, and meta-analytic methods.* Invited address at the annual meeting of the American Psychological Association, New Orleans.

Rosenthal, R. (1991). Teacher expectancy effects: A brief update 25 years after the Pygmalion experiment. *Journal of Research in Education, 1*, 3–12.

Rosenthal, R., & Jacobson, L. (1968). *Pygmalion in the classroom.* New York: Holt, Rinehart, and Winston.

Scherer, K. R. (1975). Gutachten zum Abbau von Vorurteilen gegenüber psychisch Kranken und Behinderten – aus sozialpsychologischer Sicht. In *Bericht über die Lage der Psychiatrie in der Bundesrepublik Deutschland.* Bonn: Drucksache 7/4201 des Deutschen Bundestages (pp. 1140–1160).

Scherer, K. R. (1979). Voice and speech correlates of perceived social influence. In H. Giles & R. St. Clair (Eds.), *The social psychology of language* (pp. 88–120). London: Blackwell.

Scherer, K. R. (1984). On the nature and function of emotion: A component process approach. In K. R. Scherer & P. Ekman (Eds.), *Approaches to emotion* (pp. 293–317). Hillsdale, NJ: Erlbaum.

Scherer, K. R. (1985). Vocal affect signalling: A comparative approach. In J. Rosenblatt, C. Beer, M.-C. Busnel, & P. J. B. Slater (Eds.), *Advances in the study of behavior* (Vol. 15, pp. 189–244). New York: Academic Press.

Scherer, K. R. (1986). Vocal affect expression: A review and a model for future research. *Psychological Bulletin, 99*, 143–165.

Scherer, K. R. (1988). Criteria for emotion-antecedent appraisal: A review. In V. Hamilton, G. H. Bower, & N. H. Frijda (Eds.), *Cognitive perspectives on emotion and motivation* (pp. 89–126). Dordrecht: Nijhoff.

Scherer, K. R. (1989). Emotion und Propaganda: Zur Psychobiologie des Pathos. *Neue Zürcher Zeitung, 227*, 30.9/1.10.

Scherer, K. R. (1992). Social psychology evolving. A progress report. In M. Dierkes & B. Biervert (Eds.), *European social science in transition: An assesment and outlook* (pp. 178–243). Frankfurt and Boulder, CO: Westview.

Scherer, K. R., Koivumaki, J., & Rosenthal, R. (1972). Minimal cues in the vocal communication of affect: Judging emotions from content-masked speech. *Journal of Psycholinguistic Research, 1*, 269–285.

Scherer, K. R., Rosenthal, R., & Koivumaki, J. (1972). Mediating interpersonal expectancies via vocal cues: Differential speech intensity as a means of social influence. *European Journal of Social Psychology, 2*, 163–176.

Scherer, K. R., Uno, H., & Rosenthal, R. (1972). A cross-cultural analysis of vocal behavior as a determinant of experimenter expectancy effects: A Japanese case. *International Journal of Psychology, 7*, 109–117.

Schneider, D. J., Hastorf, A. H., & Ellsworth, P. C. (1979). *Person perception* (2nd ed.). Reading, MA: Addison-Wesley.

Vaughan, K. B., & Lanzetta, J. T. (1980). Vicarious instigation and conditioning of facial expressive and autonomic responses to a model's expressive display of pain. *Journal of Personality and Social Psychology, 38*, 909–923.

Wispé, L. (1987). History of the concept of empathy. In N. Eisenberg & J. Strayer (Eds.), *Empathy and its development* (pp. 17–37). Cambridge and New York: Cambridge University Press.

PART III

The study of interpersonal expectations

17. The methodological imagination: Insoluble problems or investigable questions?

DANE ARCHER

Introduction

The relationship between social scientists and the research methods they use is often curious. Although much is published about the substance of research, methodological dilemmas, debates, and dead ends are rarely reported. Because of an emphasis on results and findings, scholarly books and journal articles rarely provide more than a list of the techniques used to generate the final version of a study. One seldom encounters reflective commentary about how researchers weighed alternative methods or conquered unanticipated obstacles. Finally, except by chance, one almost never reads of projects abandoned or analyses not attempted because of methodological constraints or prohibitions.

There appears to be increasing interest in such questions. There are a few works that provide provocative "backstage" accounts of the methodological conflicts, dilemmas, and debates scholars encounter (e.g., Berger, 1990; Glazer, 1972; and Golden, 1976). There are also autobiographical works that become central to raging controversies about research methods, sometimes decades after the original scholarship appeared (e.g., Freeman, 1983; Malinowski, 1989; and Mead, 1972, 1977). There are even fascinating inquiries into whether or not scholarship is being as well protected as many have believed by revered practices such as *peer review* (Broad, 1980), *replication* (Mulkay & Gilbert, 1986), and, of course, *fraud detection* (Broad & Wade, 1982; Colt, 1983; Fletcher, 1991; Kohn, 1987).

A different and somewhat more subtle question involves how researchers are affected by recognized or emerging methodological problems. For example, when confronted with an apparently devastating design problem, does a researcher dejectedly abandon a method or line of inquiry, or is a more creative response identified? The outcome may depend on a researcher's *epistemological* bent, that is, his or her theoretical orientation to the origin, nature, methods, and limits of knowledge. Researchers with a *rote* or "cookbook" epistemology are likely to regard methodological rules as absolute and design problems as insoluble. Researchers with a more *imaginative* epistemology may scrutinize critical issues to understand their precise empirical implications; they tend to regard design problems as investigable questions, not as reasons not to investigate.

Rote versus imaginative epistemology

The difference between rote and imaginative epistemologies can be illustrated easily. For example, social scientists have long been interested in using records from other societies to examine patterns and correlates of child-rearing and other variables (e.g., Whiting & Child, 1953; Whiting & Whiting, 1975). When one assembles a large number of records drawn from different societies, however, there is inevitably the problem of differential data quality. In the ethnographic record, accounts of non-Western societies vary in quality. Some were assembled by trained ethnographers; others derive from explorers, merchants, or missionaries. Similarly, even ethnographic accounts vary in terms of the length of an ethnographer's length of stay, immersion in the culture, linguistic fluency, and other factors.

This variation is sometimes called the *data quality* problem, and it clearly poses a threat to simple research designs that treat all data as equally reliable. To researchers with a rote epistemology, the data quality problem may seem fatal, leading to an abandonment of large-sample, cross-cultural data bases. To researchers with a more imaginative epistemology, the problem itself becomes a challenge. To the imaginative epistemologist, the question is whether the data quality problem can be incorporated into the research design, so that its impact can be assessed or at least controlled.

In this instance, an imaginative anthropologist named Raoul Naroll was able to envision just such a solution, called *data quality control* (Naroll, 1962; Naroll, Michik, & Naroll, 1980). The solution is elegantly simple. Rather than analyze some bivariate relationship (e.g., parenting style with subsequent adult behavior) across all cases in a cross-cultural sample, the data quality control method calls for the relationship to be assessed *within each level of the known variation in data quality*. The correlation is first examined using only the best data sets, then examined within the next best data sets, and so on. In this way, the variation in data quality (although never eliminated) is built into the research design and controlled. In this illustration, conclusions about the correlation between parenting style and subsequent adult behavior cannot be contaminated by variation in data quality.

The brilliance of this solution is that *the research design is strengthened by sophisticated incorporation of the known methodological problem rather than prevented by it.* This is the essence of imaginative epistemology. In this instance, Naroll was able to identify and then operationalize an *implicit* empirical question: Given that different data sets vary in reliability, can this difference be controlled to prevent spurious results? Where most people saw only an important methodological dilemma, Naroll was able to peer far enough inside the dilemma to construct a research design adapted to its precise empirical implications. Whereas a rote view of a methodological problem can paralyze a research project, Naroll's imaginative response liberates us from the confines of the problem.

There are also applications of data quality control outside anthropology. For example, researchers using international data on homicide rates in 110 nations wanted to determine whether wars are followed by postwar increases in homicide rates, that is, whether the model of state violence somehow increases the probability of private acts of violence. In this case, the data quality problem was the presence of different indicators for homicide in the cross-national data set. Some countries record offenses known (considered the best crime indicator); others record arrests, convictions, or even incarcerations. The researchers used the data quality control method to test for the effect of wars while controlling for data quality. The effect of wars was assessed separately for nations using the best indicators for homicide rates and then for nations using less reliable indicators. In this instance, postwar increases in homicide rates were found no matter what indicator was used (Archer & Gartner, 1984).

There are other examples of imaginative epistemology. One of the best known involves *unobtrusive measures* (Webb, Campbell, Schwartz, Sechrest, & Grove, 1981). This work was catalyzed by mounting concerns about *reactivity*, the tendency of individuals to give inaccurate reports about attitudes and behavior when asked questions dealing with sensitive or value-laden subjects. A rote epistemological response to this problem might have been to recommend that sensitive and value-laden research topics be abandoned.

But Webb and his colleagues instead demonstrated imaginative epistemology in identifying clever *nonreactive* measures that could provide accurate traces of emotions, attitudes, and behaviors free of reactive distortion. These included analyzing floor wear to determine the interests of museum patrons, recording garbage contents to estimate alcohol consumption, and using automobile radio settings to determine music preferences. This work demonstrated that indirect measures could be as useful as (and perhaps even more valid than) direct inquiry, thereby giving researchers a previously unrecognized alternative to conventional methodology. This imaginative approach to archival data even makes viable research that would be impossible using any other means, for example, using decades'-old records on gun purchases to reconstruct a community's fearful response to extraordinary violence (Archer & Erlich-Erfer, 1991).

The importance of imaginative epistemology

In what we have described as rote epistemology, social research is seen as a mystified body of fixed rules, constraints, and methodological "thou shall nots." In all too many cases, this seems to be an unintentional lesson of courses in research methods and statistics: The emphasis lies on what cannot be done. Given the need to cover a great deal of ground, the *theoretical* reasons behind rules and prohibitions may not be understood by students or even explained by the instructor. If the theoretical basis for methodological problems is not understood, informed *empirical* assessments of these problems are unlikely. The legacy of this approach, rote epistemology, involves an intellectual Procrustean bed – a truncated view of the problems that can be studied and of the techniques that can be used to study them. The result leaves important problems unexamined, potentially revealing analyses never performed, and potentially valuable designs prematurely abandoned.

Robert Rosenthal and imaginative epistemology

The social and behavioral sciences are fortunate in having some rare individuals who, not content with inherited wisdom about methodology, are able to transform passive methodological problems into imaginative empirical questions. In the process, such individuals contribute not only findings about concrete substantive questions, but also original methodological additions to the repertoire of the social sciences.

In the five examples to be presented, all derived from the research of social psychologist Robert Rosenthal and his colleagues, the emphasis is on the difference between rote and imaginative research design decisions. In some cases, the imaginative response is elegantly simple; in others, the solution is more elaborate. Some of these examples involve research design, whereas others concern statistical procedures. In all five cases, however, the use of an imaginative epistemology has not only made possible a specific study but has also enriched our understanding of what is possible in the future.

Experimenter expectancy and the double-blind design

When the first publications on experimenter effects appeared (e.g., Rosenthal, 1963; Rosenthal & Fode, 1963), the work was widely misperceived as a sweeping and potentially fatal assault on experimental psychology. Presenting evidence that main effects could be an unwitting artifact of experimenter bias, expectancy research was seen by some as threatening the entire enterprise of laboratory experimentation in psychology. Such pessimism could, indeed, result from a rote reading of the work by Rosenthal and his colleagues.

In fact, nothing could be further from the intent of these researchers or from the net effect of this work. Because the underlying orientation reflected a highly imaginative epistemology, the authors were able to accomplish two distinct objectives: (1) to demonstrate convincingly that experimental bias and expectancy were problematic, but also (2) that these powerful forces could be controlled in experimental research by using *double-blind* research designs in which data collectors and subjects alike are uninformed about each subject's experimental condition. The net effect was therefore enormously constructive. Rosenthal and his colleagues produced evidence of an important validity problem but also made possible its solution, thereby paving the way for more valid laboratory experiments in the future.

Errors of use and nonuse in statistics

Few researchers go beyond a rote understanding and use of statistics. For most, statistics are a collection of techniques and prohibitions, imperfectly understood even if well memorized. When doing some research on individual differences in the accurate perception of nonverbal stimuli, Rosenthal, Hall, DiMatteo, Rogers, and Archer (1979) developed a factorial design (e.g., Subject Gender × Communication Channel × Emotional Scene) that lent itself to the analysis of variance (ANOVA) as the preferred analytic model. The problem was that the dependent variable was logically a dichotomy: Did the subject get the correct answer (1) or not (0)? A rote understanding of ANOVA traditionally proscribes dichotomous dependent variables, and most researchers might have abandoned the most elegant design for one that would fit traditional statistical assumptions.

Rosenthal recognized, however, that the key question was whether alpha values are distorted when ANOVAs are applied to dichotomous data: That is, the issue is best seen as an empirical question, not an unexamined taboo. Fortunately, this issue appears to have been resolved in a little-known Monte Carlo study using dichotomous data (Lunney, 1970). This empirical study showed that significant alpha values were in the correct range (5% or less), using randomly sampled dichotomous data as the dependent variable. This finding made it possible for Rosenthal et al. to use ANOVA in their research design, and indeed so enables future users of dichotomous data. From the point of view of imaginative epistemology, the point is that researchers are often ill served by doctrinal notions of what cannot be done. Many methodological rules have eminently empirical implications, and rigorous empirical research – not traditional belief – needs to govern the use and nonuse of statistical procedures.

The science of male sophomore volunteers?

External validity – the ability to generalize from laboratory experiments to the real world – has long been a methodological concern in the behavioral sciences. Pundits hostile to laboratory experiments have found amusement in the tired witticism that "Psychology is the science of male college sophomore volunteers." The implicit critique is, of course, that generalization from laboratory findings to nonresearch settings may be unwarranted. At first glance, this seems an intuitively reasonable argument, given that all of these adjectives (*volunteer*, etc.) might well undermine the external validity of laboratory research. From the perspective of rote epistemology, this critique seems to threaten our confidence in the laboratory paradigm as a whole.

Seen from the vantage point of imaginative epistemology, however, this critique again contains a series of empirical propositions. As a single example, the critique includes the eminently testable hypothesis that volunteers are detectably different from nonvolunteers. In a series of intriguing studies, Rosenthal and his colleagues (Rosenthal & Rosnow, 1975) assembled data bearing on this hypothesis. This literature indeed shows areas of difference, with volunteers being better educated, more intelligent, lower in authoritarianism, more sociable, more often firstborn, and perhaps even more likely to provide data that support the investigator's hypothesis. At the same time, this careful research program cautions against other sweeping generalizations about volunteers. For example, women were more likely to volunteer than men in general, but the reverse was true for unusual tasks: The variable of gender interacts with the type of task for which volunteers are sought. This research enlarges our understanding of the ways in which research populations have special characteristics, and the findings move us from simple speculation about volunteers to precise characterization. Again, the beneficiaries of this imaginative approach include future laboratory researchers.

Small correlations and not so small effects

Empirical social science would be impossible without statistics, and training in most of the social sciences features at least some exposure to descriptive and inferential statistics. Again, however, a difference exists between the rote and imaginative epistemological understandings. The rote approach involves mastery of the purpose and technique of statistical procedures, but also more or less cookbook understandings of what is important.

Although some indices of importance are explicitly taught (e.g., .05 alpha levels in inferential statistics), others are more abstract or vague. An example concerns how large a correlation (r or r-*squared*) needs to be before it is judged important. As an illustration, with a sample of 40, an r of .32 is statistically significant, but widespread conventions in the social sciences would regard this as a barely "medium" effect, far from the r of .50 widely regarded as necessary to justify the label "large" (e.g., Cohen, 1977). A social scientist with a rote epistemological bent would regard such a .32 correlation as only marginally important, perhaps not worth discussing in detail or even reporting.

A more imaginative epistemological question, however, might concern what conventional notions of small, medium, and large effects might mean in real terms, using benchmarks less likely to mystify users and consumers of statistics. Rosenthal and his colleagues have asked precisely this question, with surprising results (Rosenthal, 1991b; Rosenthal & Rubin, 1982). For example, returning to our barely medium correlation of .32, one needs to ask how important this relationship would be, say, in an experimental test of a new drug with seriously ill patients. It turns out that our "barely medium" r of .32 corresponds to the difference between a survival rate of 66% in the experimental condition but only 34% in the control condition! Having escaped the dry world of rote statistical conventions, who would not label such a difference as not only "large" but "important"?

Rosenthal and his colleagues argue that there is a widespread tendency in the social (and biomedical) sciences to underestimate the importance of small and medium correlations precisely because these are arithmetic abstracts in a continuum for which most people lack any intuitive understanding. Rosenthal and his colleagues present a *binomial effect size display* (BESD) that in tabular form shows that correlations of various sizes correspond to dichotomous *success rate* outcomes – an r of .10 reflects a success rate difference of 10%, an r of .30 reflects a success rate difference of 30%, an r of .50 reflects a success rate difference of 50%, and so on. In readily understandable form, Rosenthal and his colleagues have provided a reinterpretation of two of the statistical measures thought to be most familiar in the social and physical sciences, r and r-*squared*. The imaginative genius of this approach is that it provides lucid empirical evidence that conclusions about "unimportant" correlations may have been premature. Again, this research enlarges our understanding both about a methodological issue (what is a small correlation?) and about the potential importance of future research findings.

Resolving controversial results

In the natural sciences, replications are supposed to resolve controversies. When one lab reports a result other labs cannot replicate, a problem exists – an error, an artifact, or another nonreproducible factor. In some of the natural sciences, the resolution of controversies is aided by the speed of replication; some lab experiments in molecular biology can be repeated in a matter of hours. By contrast, some of the social sciences proceed at a glacial pace. In anthropology, this helps to explain controversies that persist, defying simple resolution through replication (e.g., Freeman, 1983). Traditional norms for ethnographic field work called for 2 years in the field – an effective deterrent for most would-be replicators.

Psychology is less demanding in this respect than ethnography, but perhaps also more demanding than most of the natural sciences. The timetable for most behavioral science research requires months of work, more if longitudinal data are involved. At the same time, as the behavioral sciences mature, it becomes increasingly clear that issues cannot be decided by single studies. Individual studies are inherently idiosyncratic – the population sampled, the individual investigator, the measures selected, the time period in which the study was performed, and so on. The critical questions involve the *theoretical significance of the hypothesis investigated,* not the specific methodological tools used. It therefore becomes important to frame an appropriate response to debates that center on specific research procedures.

An illustration is in order. The Rosenthal and Jacobson (1968) study that found that teacher expectations could have a positive impact on pupil performance is arguably the most famous experiment ever conducted in a school setting. The study garnered not only acclaim, but also controversy. Some of the controversy was produced by those who admired the study and called for an end to IQ testing, curricular ability tracking, and other educational practices likely to produce high or low teacher expectations. Other controversies focused on methodological details such as the validity of the IQ test used, the age level of the greatest impact, and so on. The debate was occasionally fierce, and spilled over into newspaper headlines and editorials.

How best to respond to such controversy? The most obvious response is to enter into a discussion of the piecemeal elements of a critique. This involves a detailed treatment of the methodological issues raised, and this is what Rosenthal and his colleagues did in several discussions (e.g., Rosenthal, 1972; Rosenthal & Rubin, 1971). Although indispensable to scholarly debate, the shortcomings of such a response are that the exchange necessarily centers on technical issues such as measurement, effect sizes, design decisions, and so on. The audience for such debate is often understandably smaller than the audience interested in the original question. In addition, most readers are ill prepared to judge the merits of sophisticated debates about statistics and procedures. Finally, some of the issues under debate may involve preferences rather than facts; for example, some critics may prefer a different IQ test, others would have liked to see a different manipulation used, and so on. The net effect of this exchange is that many in the audience for behavioral science findings are left unable to follow the debate and unprepared to weigh the arguments.

A rote response to such debate might be to allow it to simmer once the response to the original critique was given. Indeed, simmering seems to be the modal response of the behavioral sciences. This is regrettable, since it leaves many important studies tainted with controversy and mired in a legacy of doubt over the appropriateness of a given test, whether a one-tailed test should have been used, and so on. A much more imaginative epistemological response is to focus future research on the question that really matters: *Does subsequent research – using a variety of settings, methods, procedures, and statistical tests – lead us to believe that the original theoretical proposition has empirical support in a series of replications?* In other words, to use lay terminology, is the finding generally true?

In this regard, behavioral scientists are indeed beneficiaries of the imaginative epistemology of Robert Rosenthal. The legacy of this work includes one of the largest bodies of systematically replicated work in all the social sciences, including a summary of 345 studies of interpersonal expectancy (Rosenthal & Rubin, 1980). The effort also produced a methodological interest in *how* to summarize large bodies of replicated work. This yielded 31 meta-analyses of the research literature on expectancy effects (Harris & Rosenthal, 1985), as well as methodological tools for performing meta-analysis in future social science research (Rosenthal, 1991a).

This awesome scholarship has done what no debate, no matter how provocative or entertaining, could ever do. The monumental task of assembling and summarizing hundreds of replications has affirmed the existence, power, and theoretical importance of expectancy effects. Such effects exist across research designs, across measures, across investigators, and across time periods. In assembling this body of work, Rosenthal and his colleagues have not only pioneered new meta-analytic procedures for summarizing replications but have also provided a model for how scholarly debates can best be resolved. What matters, we learn from this body of work, is not the merits and defects of specific research tools, but the momentum that transcends individual studies. In this body of work, the social sciences are presented with a model for their own coming of age.

The legacy of imaginative epistemology

In the five examples of imaginative epistemology reviewed here, we discern models for research progress in the social and behavioral sciences. This approach, as reflected in the work of Rosenthal and his colleagues, provides a model of research effectiveness. To paraphrase the cliché, imaginative epistemology can transform problems into opportunities. Research problems can become investigable empirical questions rather than dispirited dead ends for lines of inquiry. In the preceding examples, we can see that imaginative epistemology makes for more valid research, because the impact of methodological problems in this perspective is either controlled, mitigated, or assessed.

Imaginative epistemology calls for a change in our traditional relationship to research methodology. Rather than act as passive consumers of an accepted technology that is imperfectly understood, researchers need to (1) extend their knowledge of the implicit empirical consequences (i.e., hypothesized effects) of methodological problems; (2) actively construct empirical assessments to test for the presence of such consequences; and (3) if such consequences are found, envision design procedures that mitigate or control for them. In this way, rather than merely prevent investigable problems, methodological issues *become* investigable problems.

As the chapters in this part make clear, there are also benefits in addition to the enabling of more valid individual substantive studies. One of these is a more sophisticated approach to how new knowledge is produced and how such knowledge should be evaluated. Along the road to a more imaginative epistemology, Rosenthal and his colleagues have increased the repertoire of the social and behavioral sciences. These imaginative epistemologists have invented powerful new procedures, methods, and statistical tools. For scholars of this and later generations, this legacy opens wider the door to future discovery in the social and behavioral sciences.

References

Archer, D., & Erlich-Erfer, L. (1991). Fear and loading: Archival traces of the response to extraordinary violence. *Social Psychology Quarterly, 54,* 343–352.
Archer, D., & Gartner, R. (1984). *Violence and crime in cross-national perspective.* New Haven, CT: Yale University Press.
Berger, B. (Ed.). (1990). *Authors of their own lives: Intellectual autobiographies by twenty American sociologists.* Berkeley: University of California Press.

Broad, W. J. (1980). Would-be academician pirates papers. *Science, 208,* 1438–1440.

Broad, W. J., & Wade, N. (1982). *Betrayers of the truth.* New York: Simon and Schuster.

Cohen, J. (1977). *Statistical power analysis for the behavioral sciences* (2nd ed.). New York: Academic Press.

Colt, G. H. (1983, July–August). Too good to be true. *Harvard Magazine,* 22–28, 54.

Fletcher, R. (1991). *Science, ideology, and the media: The Cyril Burt scandal.* New Brunswick, NJ: Transaction.

Freeman, D. (1983). *Margaret Mead and Samoa: The making and unmaking of an anthropological myth.* Cambridge, MA: Harvard University Press.

Glazer, M. (1972). *The research adventure.* New York: Random House.

Golden, M. P. (1976). *The research experience.* Itasca, IL: Peacock.

Harris, M. J., & Rosenthal, R. (1985). The mediation of interpersonal expectancy effects: 31 meta-analyses. *Psychological Bulletin, 97,* 363–386.

Kohn, A. (1987). *False prophets.* New York: Basil Blackwell.

Lunney, G. H. (1970). Using analysis of variance with a dichotomous dependent variable: An empirical study. *Journal of Educational Measurement, 7,* 263–269.

Malinowski, B. (1989). *A diary in the strict sense of the term.* Stanford, CA: Stanford University Press.

Mead, M. (1972). *Blackberry winter; My earlier years.* New York: Morrow.

Mead, M. (1977). *Letters from the field, 1925–1975.* New York: Harper & Row.

Mulkay, M., & Gilbert, G. N. (1986). Replication and mere replication. *Philosophy of the Social Sciences, 16,* 21–37.

Naroll, R. (1962). *Data quality control: A new research technique.* New York: Free Press.

Naroll, R., Michik, G. L., & Naroll, F. (1980). Holocultural research methods. In H. C. Triandis & J. W. Berry (Eds.), *Handbook of cross-cultural psychology: Vol. 2, Methodology* (pp. 479–521). Boston: Allyn and Bacon.

Rosenthal, R. (1963). On the social psychology of the psychological experiment: The experimenter's hypothesis as unintended determinant of experimental results. *American Scientist, 51,* 268–283.

Rosenthal, R. (1972). Pygmalion revisited, revisited: On a loud and careless call for caution. *Interchange, 3,* 86–91.

Rosenthal, R. (1991a). *Meta-analytic procedures for social research* (rev. ed.). Newbury Park, CA: Sage.

Rosenthal, R. (1991b). Effect sizes: Pearson's correlation, its display via the BESD, and alternative indices. *American Psychologist, 46,* 1086–1087.

Rosenthal, R., & Fode, K. L. (1963). The effect of experimenter bias on the performance of the albino rat. *Behavioral Science, 8,* 183–189.

Rosenthal, R., Hall, J. A., DiMatteo, M. R., Rogers, P., & Archer, D. (1979). *Sensitivity to nonverbal communication: A profile approach to the measurement of differential abilities.* Baltimore: Johns Hopkins University Press.

Rosenthal, R., & Jacobson, L. (1968). *Pygmalion in the classroom: Teacher expectation and pupil's intellectual development.* New York: Holt, Rinehart and Winston.

Rosenthal, R., & Rosnow, R. (1975). *The volunteer subject.* New York: Wiley-Interscience.

Rosenthal, R., & Rubin, D. B. (1971). Pygmalion reaffirmed. In J. D. Elashoff &

R. E. Snow (Eds.), *Pygmalion reconsidered* (pp. 139–155). Worthington, OH: C. A. Jones.

Rosenthal, R., & Rubin, D. B. (1980). Summarizing 345 studies of interpersonal expectancy effects. In R. Rosenthal (Ed.), *New directions for methodology of social and behavioral science: Quantitative assessment of research domains* (pp. 79–95). San Francisco: Jossey-Bass.

Rosenthal, R., & Rubin, D. B. (1982). A simple, general purpose display of magnitude of experimental effect. *Journal of Educational Psychology, 74,* 166–169.

Webb, E. J., Campbell, D. T., Schwartz, R. D., Sechrest, L., & Grove, J. B. (1981). *Nonreactive measures in the social sciences* (2nd ed). Boston: Houghton-Mifflin.

Whiting, B. B., & Whiting, J. W. M. (1975). *Children of six cultures.* Cambridge, MA: Harvard University Press.

Whiting, J. W. M., & Child, I. (1953). *Child training and personality.* New Haven, CT: Yale University Press, 1953.

18. Issues in studying the mediation of expectancy effects: A taxonomy of expectancy situations

MONICA J. HARRIS

The expectations we hold of other people can act as self-fulfilling prophecies. A major component of research on interpersonal expectancy effects addresses the behavioral processes underlying this phenomenon. How are perceivers' expectations communicated to targets so as to create a self-fulfilling prophecy? Oddly, although expectancy mediation has been such a major question in this area of research, it remains the most glaring gap in our knowledge, especially at the theoretical level.

The problem is not that data on expectancy mediation do not exist; most studies in this area address mediation to some extent. Rather, as Bob Rosenthal and I noted in our meta-analysis of the mediation literature, the great weakness was the lack of a coherent, theoretically meaningful organization of the mediating behaviors that had been studied, as well as a lack of understanding of how the mediators fit into the wider expectancy process (Harris & Rosenthal, 1985). With the exception of Rosenthal's (1989) affect-effort theory of expectancy mediation, practically nothing had been done since 1985 to remedy these weaknesses.

The major obstacle to developing a comprehensive theory of expectancy mediation is that the behaviors exhibited by perceivers will necessarily depend on the situational context and the nature of the expectancy manipulation. The mediation of teacher expectancy effects will be different from the mediation of expectancy effects in a getting-acquainted situation, because the role demands and situational constraints for the two contexts differ. Thus, an adequate theory of expectancy mediation will inevitably require two components: (1) a taxonomy of situations where expectancy effects are likely to occur and (2) a listing of behaviors for each situation that are associated with differential perceiver expectations.

Cast in these terms, it is not surprising that a sophisticated theory of expectancy mediation does not exist because, as Magnusson (1981) notes, we have not yet managed to come up with a good psychology of situations. I will not be so foolhardy as to try to do so myself. Rather, my more limited goal for this chapter is to present an initial effort at developing a taxonomy of expectancy situations. The result should be a step forward in our understanding of the processes underlying expectancy effects, as well as some methodological guidance for how to choose mediating behaviors to examine in expectancy research. Before presenting this taxonomy, however, I will review briefly the current state of mediation research.

Current state of expectancy mediation research

Over the years, a number of models of expectancy effects have been proposed (Darley & Fazio, 1980; Jussim, 1986), with most of them proposing a similar sequence of steps: (1) the perceiver forms an expectancy about the target; (2) the perceiver behaves toward the target in accordance with the expectancy; and (3) the target responds to the perceiver's behavior. The models vary, however, with respect to how detailed they are in specifying what is involved when the perceiver behaves in accordance with the expectancy.

Perhaps the most useful theoretical treatment of expectancy mediation to appear recently is Rosenthal's (1989) affect-effort theory. Building on previous work on the four-factor theory of teacher expectancy mediation (Rosenthal, 1973), Rosenthal (1989) argues that differential expectations lead to changes in perceiver behavior along the relatively orthogonal dimensions of affect and effort. According to this analysis, affect is communicated primarily, although not exclusively, through nonverbal channels, and effort (amount of material taught, etc.) is conveyed largely through verbal channels. Although the affect-effort theory was developed to explain teacher expectancy effects, it can easily be generalized to other domains.

What is known empirically about the mediation of expectancy effects? DePaulo (this volume) provides a good overview of the literature. In 1985, Harris and Rosenthal conducted a meta-analysis of the expectancy mediation literature. Our review identified 31 behaviors that had been examined in four or more studies, and the meta-analysis suggested support for 16 of them in the mediation process. The meta-analysis, however, revealed several limitations in the literature: (1) as mentioned previously, there was no framework organizing the 31 behaviors; (2)

empirical evidence for many of the behaviors was scanty, as only 6 behaviors had been examined in more than 20 studies; and (3) the great majority of the studies (over 75%) involved a teaching context, so that little is known about the mediation of expectancies in other situations. The framework presented in this chapter can do nothing for problem 2, but it should help somewhat with problems 1 and 3.

A taxonomy of expectancy situations

Focus of analysis

The first decision to be made in generating a taxonomy of expectancy situations is whether to take an *interaction-centered* approach or an *expectancy-centered* approach. In other words, all expectancy situations consist of two components: the content of the expectancy itself and the context of the interaction between the perceiver and the target. Thus, a prototypical expectancy study has a teacher holding differential expectancies for his or her students' ability within a classroom context. However, it is certainly feasible to manipulate teachers' expectancies about their students' *personalities* in a classroom, just as one could manipulate perceivers' expectancies about their partners' IQ during a getting-acquainted conversation.

Although an argument could be made for basing the taxonomy on the content of the expectancy, I have chosen to focus instead on categorizing the interaction contexts. I did this for several reasons. First, context, more often than not, is consonant with expectancy. This is particularly true with respect to laboratory studies where the expectancy is experimentally manipulated; researchers tend, logically enough, to pick an experimental context that is compatible with the expectancy manipulation.

The second, more compelling reason for creating a taxonomy on the basis of the interaction context is that the nature of the interaction, more than the expectancy, will constrain the range of exhibited behaviors. In other words, situational tasks may very well dictate the range of possible behaviors to a greater extent than do the cognitions people hold while undertaking the tasks. For example, a teacher who holds positive expectancies about the ability levels of certain students will teach those students more difficult material in the classroom. However, a teacher who holds exactly the same expectancies, yet is told merely to get acquainted with the students, most likely will not deliver willy-nilly a lecture full of difficult material.

A further argument in favor of categorizing by context is based on the suspicion that, in many cases, variations in types of expectancies may prove to be of little importance in determining the types of mediating behaviors that are displayed. Rather, it may be merely the valence of the expectancy that drives the choice of perceiver behavior. For example, in a getting-acquainted context, we would probably behave similarly toward someone whom we were told had a great sense of humor versus someone we believed to be physically attractive (both positive expectancies), and we would probably display many of the same avoidant behaviors toward someone whom we were told had been convicted for rape versus someone with acquired immunodeficiency syndrome (AIDS) (both negative expectancies). The specific nature of the beliefs accompanying the positive or negative affect may just not matter that much, although, of course, that is an empirical question.

Should this hunch be correct, a methodological implication is that a good strategy for designing measures of expectancy mediation and outcomes is to tailor them to features of the situation more than to the manipulation itself. In the next section, I analyze a set of expectancy situations with respect to six important situational features. This analysis should therefore aid in identifying key features for which measures should be developed.

Taxonomy structure

Table 18.1 lists the expectancy situations addressed in this chapter. Situations were chosen for inclusion either because they had been employed in past research on interpersonal expectancy effects or because they were common contexts for which expectancy effects were deemed likely to occur. In Table 18.1, each of the situations is evaluated with respect to six features: power relations, formality of interaction, task orientation, intensity of interaction, intimacy of interaction, and degree of structure. It should be readily apparent that these six features are not orthogonal; for example, an intense interaction is often highly intimate as well, but it may be instructive to look at those cases where the two do not correspond.

Power relations

The second column of Table 18.1 lists the roles taken by the parties in a given situation, and the third column contains my judgment as to whether the power relations are equal or not equal. An important

Table 18.1. *Features of expectancy situations*

Situation	Roles of interactants	Power relations	Formality of interaction	Task orientation	Intensity of interaction	Intimacy of interaction	Degree of structure
Getting acquainted	Peers	Equal	Low	Very low	Low	Low to moderate	Very low
Dating	Peers	Equal	Low	Low	Moderate	Varies	Low to moderate
Home life	Spouses, roommates	Equal	Very low	Very low	Varies	Moderate to very high	Very low
Child care	Caregiver/child	Not equal	Very low	Low	Typically low	Moderate	Low
Workplace (a)	Co-workers	Equal	Low	Varies	Low	Low to moderate	Moderate
Workplace (b)	Employer/employee	Not equal	Typically high	Very high	Moderate	Low	Moderate to very high
Consumer exchange	Sales clerk/customer	Varies	Moderate	High	Low	Low	High
Medical settings	Health professional/patient	Not equal	Very high	Moderate to very high	Moderate to high	Moderate	Very high
Psychotherapy	Therapist/client	Not equal	Varies	Moderate to very high	Moderate to very high	High to very high	Moderate to high
Institutional (e.g., nursing home)	Caregiver/patient	Not equal	Moderate	Low to moderate	Low	Moderate	High
Classroom	Teacher/student	Not equal	Moderate to high	High to very high	Moderate	Low	Moderate to very high
Courtroom	Judge, lawyer/defendant	Not equal	Very high	Very high	High	Low	Very high
Behavioral research	Experimenter/subject	Not equal	High	Very high	Low	Low	Very high

caveat applying to these ratings, as well as to all the ratings for the other situational features in Table 18.1, is that they are meant to be of the prototypical case of the given situation. There are certainly idiosyncratic exceptions in each case that would render the ratings inaccurate. For example, I have rated the power relations among spouses in the home life situation as being equal, though I am well aware that there are many households where one spouse is definitely the dominant partner and wields all the power in the relationship. The only reason I did not include hedges such as "usually" or "often" to all the table entries is that it would make an unreadable mess; readers should take care to supply such hedges themselves.

The most striking characteristic pertaining to power relations and expectancy effects is that a substantial majority of the expectancy situations listed involve unequal power relations. The research emphasis on asymmetrical power relations is more striking when it is considered that two of the situations with equal power relations (dating and home life) that were included in the table have been examined in few, if any, studies of expectancy effects.

Moreover, studies of expectancy effects have almost always been designed such that the person with the higher power is the perceiver and the person with lower power is the target. (One rare exception is the Feldman & Prohaska, 1979, study where students' expectancies that their teachers were especially good were manipulated.) The habit of studying expectancy effects in contexts where perceivers are the high-power interactant undoubtedly stems historically from the two situations (laboratory and classroom) where research on expectancy effects had its roots.

Intentional or not, one methodological implication of designating the high-power source as the perceiver is likely an increased frequency of significant expectancy effects. Early reviews of the expectancy literature have suggested that stronger expectancy effects are obtained when the perceiver is of higher status (Rosenthal, 1969). Although this hypothesis has not been rigorously or recently addressed empirically, there is a compelling theoretical reason why higher-power perceivers (and, correspondingly, lower-power targets) are more likely to obtain an expectancy effect: People with higher power more often control the interaction to a greater degree, thus facilitating the expression of behaviors reflecting the perceiver's expectancy. Moreover, targets with less power may not be willing to challenge a higher-power perceiver's erroneous expectations, which also should increase the likelihood that expectancy effects occur.

Formality of interaction

Formality here refers to social formality in the sense of adhering to explicit and fixed customs or social rules. It is related to one of the other dimensions considered here, *degree of structure*, but the two are not completely redundant. Most highly formal situations are also highly structured, but it is possible to have structured situations (e.g., playing Trivial Pursuit) that are not at all formal. Highly formal situations are easier to code because individuals have less freedom to act as they wish, and therefore there is less variability in the behaviors that are expressed.

Formality probably affects the expectancy process by dictating what is considered appropriate behavior in a given situation. A reasonable hypothesis, though untested, is that negative expectancies would have less influence in highly formal situations, as etiquette constrains the expression of negative affect more in formal situations than in informal situations. For example, one cannot ignore one's neighbor at a dinner table in a formal setting, but one easily can and does avoid one's enemies at a casual party.

Task orientation

The situations listed here vary with respect to how much the interaction focuses on a specific goal or task to be completed. The greater the degree of task orientation, the easier it is for the researcher to identify mediating behaviors and the narrower the spectrum can be of behaviors that are assessed. But does task orientation facilitate or inhibit the occurrence of interpersonal expectancy effects? Although (once again) the data are lacking on this question, a reasonable prediction is that task orientation would facilitate expectancy effects when the manipulation concerns a task-related characteristic but would inhibit them when the manipulation is not related to the task. If I am told that my partner is physically unattractive, presumably that information would not affect my behavior very much if we were then induced to concentrate on solving brain teasers; my strategy in approaching the task, though, might be radically altered if I were told that my partner was below normal in intelligence.

Intensity of interaction

The ramifications of the emotional intensity of an interaction for the expectancy process are less easy to predict. With greater intensity, the interpersonal stakes are higher, and one could plausibly predict that expectations will matter more. Similarly, greater intensity should lead to greater sensitivity on the part of the targets to the cues given by the perceiver, thus potentially magnifying their effect. But one could just as plausibly predict that perceivers may be even more motivated to act preventively in the case of negative expectancies, leading to compensatory behavior that might result in a self-defeating prophecy.

Intimacy of interaction

Intimacy, as defined here, refers to self-disclosure and emotional closeness, and as such it is obviously positively related to intensity. However, again, it is possible to think of highly intimate conversations – such as those occurring between spouses – that are not high in intensity, just as it is possible to imagine a high-intensity interaction (e.g., a civil court trial) that is quite low in intimacy.

In highly intimate situations, I suspect that the affect dimension assumes primary importance in the communication of expectancies, with cues such as tone of voice, smiles, interpersonal distance, and so forth probably attended to more and given greater weight by the targets.

Degree of structure

Structure refers to how well scripted the interaction is, that is, the extent to which the roles are highly specified and articulated. As noted earlier, this is related to the formality of the situation, though it is more accurate to say that formal situations are a subset of structured situations.

The degree of structure influences the study of expectancies in two ways. First, the greater the structure, the easier it is to identify potential mediators of expectancy effects. Second, as was postulated in the case of task orientation, highly structured situations probably restrict the range of expectancies that are likely to be influential. Expectancies involving characteristics of the target that are wildly irrelevant to the context may have little impact. An exception to this would be in the case of extremely negative expectancies (e.g., this person has AIDS or this person is a child molester) that carry overriding salience. In addition, increased structure may reduce behavioral variability, leading to smaller magnitudes of expectancy effects. Indirect support for this notion is seen in two studies with children that my colleagues and I have conducted. In both studies we obtained fewer effects of expectancies in the more structured task (a talk-show role playing and a coloring-by-numbers contest) than we obtained in the less structured Lego block design game (Harris, Milich, Corbitt, Hoover, & Brady, 1992).

There are two important ways in which structure can be considered in the present analysis. The first way is to compare the various situations with respect to their typical degree of structure. This is what is shown in Table 18.1 and what has just been discussed. The second important sense of structure is to consider it as a dimension *within* situations. Obviously, a situation that is highly structured in a certain manner will constrain how expectancies are communicated. For example, if you are examining the effects of expectancies on a getting-acquainted conversation where the interactants talk on the telephone (e.g., Snyder, Tanke, & Berscheid, 1977), expectancies simply cannot be communicated through the visual channel; you must focus on tone of voice and verbal content as mediators.

Researchers designing expectancy studies therefore often structure the situation highly so as to enhance the likelihood that the expectancies will be expressed in similar, previously identified ways. A good example of this is the work by Snyder and Swann (1978a), where perceivers' beliefs about the targets' hostility were manipulated, and then they were asked to engage in a laboratory game where blasts from a "noise weapon" could be exchanged. In the real world, our expectancies about another's hostility are rarely vented through the use of noise weapons (except on the California freeways!), but in the laboratory this structure had the advantage of allowing a precise specification of the processes underlying the self-fulfilling prophecy in this particular example.

In sum, the disadvantage of incorporating high degrees of structure in an experimental design is that the ecological validity and generalizability of the findings are weakened. The advantages, however, are that it facilitates the identification and coding of mediating behaviors, and it yields a clear and unambiguous understanding of the behavioral processes underlying the interactions. In the discussion of the expectancy situations to follow, I describe potential mediators for circumstances assuming low degrees of imposed structure. Depending on the nature and extent of constraints imposed in a given study, some or most of the mediators listed here thus may not be applicable.

Mediation of expectancies in different situations

The remainder of this chapter will be devoted to a closer look at each of the expectancy situations listed in Table 18.1. My goal is to identify for each situation a number of verbal and nonverbal behaviors that are likely to be important in the mediation of interpersonal expectancy effects; I conclude with a section containing general methodological suggestions for studying expectancy mediation. A few general comments are needed before discussing the individual situations. First is the obvious caveat that these lists of mediators are by no stretch of the imagination exhaustive. My approach was to select the most immediately obvious behaviors and those that had garnered the greatest research support. A related point harks back to the previous discussion, namely, that these lists apply best to prototypes of the situations, and they necessarily omit mediators relevant to idiosyncratic features of a given situation. Yet these more idiosyncratic mediators may in some cases be the most important behaviors in the expectancy process, for example, the Snyder and Swann (1978a) noise weapon example. The bottom line is that each researcher will need to supplement this taxonomy with specific behaviors tied directly to the tasks or setting employed. A third point is that empirical evidence for much of what I am presenting is lacking. As noted earlier, the majority of mediation research has focused on teacher expectancies, and many of the situations listed here haven't been examined in great detail.

Getting-acquainted situations

The getting-acquainted session is a perennial favorite of experimental social psychologists. In many respects it is the ideal setting for studying expectancy effects: It avoids the complications and causal ambiguities encountered when using subjects who know each other; it makes it much easier to deliver a plausible expectancy manipulation; and it entails an ecologically valid experimental task with which subjects are familiar and comfortable.

A list of behaviors mediating expectancy effects in the getting-acquainted context is shown in Figure 18.1. I suspect that the two most important classes of variables here are the affect variables, namely, tone of voice and eye contact, and the conversation variables, such as choice of topic and number and type of questions asked. This latter variable, perhaps, has garnered the most attention, with several researchers documenting that individuals display a preference for expectancy-confirming questions (Darley, Fleming, Hilton, & Swann, 1988; Snyder & Swann, 1978b; Swann & Giuliano, 1987; though see Trope & Bassok, 1983, for a dissenting view).

Another critical variable is the "avoids interaction" variable. Darley

Nonverbal warmth
Eye contact
Smiles/Laughter
Tone of voice
Interpersonal distance
Forward lean
Touch
Verbal support/Praise
Frequency and duration of interaction
Choice of conversation topic
Number of questions asked
Type of questions asked
Avoids interaction

Figure 18.1. Getting-acquainted situations.

and Fazio (1980) wrote of *terminated sequences* where negative expectancies may lead the perceiver to avoid interacting with the target completely, and therefore the negative expectancy would never be disconfirmed. Terminated sequences are rarely studied in the laboratory, as we usually design our studies deliberately to force interactions among our subjects. Yet terminated sequences undoubtedly play major roles in real-world interactions, especially in cases of outgroups such as minorities or homosexuals. If targets are never given the opportunity to correct erroneous expectancies held by the perceiver, at best a stalemate can occur where the prophecy is neither behaviorally confirmed nor disconfirmed.

Dating relationships

Dating relationships are a specialized and advanced form of the getting-acquainted situation, but they are such a ubiquitous and distinct part of modern culture they merit their own category. Figure 18.2 lists the hypothesized mediators, and as can be seen, most of the behaviors from the getting-acquainted situation are relevant here as well. However, additional behaviors stemming from dating norms are also applicable.

Obviously, the choice of activities, setting, dress, and so forth communicate the expectations your date holds of you and the future of the relationship. Being asked out for Kentucky Fried Chicken and an evening of bowling says something very different than being asked out to

> **Nonverbal warmth**
> **Smiles/Laughter**
> **Tone of voice**
> **Interpersonal distance**
> **Forward lean**
> **Touch**
> **Physical affection (kissing, hugging, etc.)**
> **Initiating interactions (calling partner,**
>   **asking out on dates)**
> **Frequency and duration of interactions**
> **Choice of activity, restaurant**
> **Style of dress**
> **Avoids interaction**

Figure 18.2. Dating relationships.

dinner at a French restaurant and the opera. More important, your behavior at a bowling alley versus that at the opera will be constrained in very different ways, and you will come across to your date as different personalities in such situations.

In the dating realm, pessimistic expectations are particularly self-fulfilling. A man who is convinced that the attractive woman he met the other evening at a party would not accept a date will not risk asking her out. As another example, I once had the unfortunate experience on a blind date where the first words the gentleman uttered, after "hello," were "So, do you think I am too overweight?" The evening was doomed, not because of his appearance (which was actually fine), but because his apparent belief that I would not find him attractive made our interaction uncomfortable.

Home life

Although this may seem like a nebulous situation to include, the people who share our households (romantic partner, family members, room-mates) comprise our most important social relationships, and as such, it would seem useful to consider how expectancies may influence interactions with them. Having said that, though, I will predict that interpersonal expectancy effects happen less often in the home setting than in the other situations discussed here because of the heightened familiarity among people who share living quarters. This suspicion draws support from Jussim's reflection-construction model, which contends that in

```
Nonverbal warmth
Smiles
Eye contact
Tone of voice
Praise/Criticism
Sarcasm
Displays of anger
Frequency and duration of interactions
Avoids interaction
```

Figure 18.3. Home life.

naturalistic settings, the perceiver's *accuracy* in judging characteristics of the target is more strongly related to outcomes than is the perceiver's expectancies (Jussim, 1989, 1991). Further support is seen in Raudenbush's (1984) meta-analysis showing a negative correlation between the length of acquaintanceship prior to the induction of expectancies and the subsequent magnitude of expectancy effects.

In short, members of a family or people who share living quarters may get to know one another so well that erroneous expectancies are less likely to be formed and therefore less likely to operate as self-fulfilling prophecies. However, expectancy effects are still possible in such settings, especially when a household is first set up and members gradually establish routines and get to know each other better. Family systems theorists, in discussing the phenomenon of *scapegoating* or the *identified patient*, have also noted the role played by family members' beliefs and expectancies about other members in establishing and maintaining maladaptive behavior patterns (Satir, 1968).

To the extent that expectancy effects exist in such situations, how might they be mediated? Figure 18.3 lists the hypothesized behaviors. Given the typically high levels of intimacy exhibited in these situations, it is predicted that the affect dimension will be of greatest importance in expectancy mediation, with cues such as smiles, eye contact, and nonverbal warmth playing vital roles in communicating expectancies. This is not to say that the effort dimension is unimportant, as the amount of time spent talking with the other person is ordinarily a very good indicator of how the relationship is going.

Nonverbal warmth
Smiles
Touch
Tone of voice
Encouragement
Praise/Criticism
Verbalization of rules/standards
Displays of anger
Physical punishment
Goal setting
Leisure activities provided (e.g., choice of
**   games, sports, movies)**
Educational activities provided (e.g., books,
**   music lessons, visits to museums)**
Parents' own behavior with respect to
**   moral/legal standards**
Frequency and duration of interactions
Avoids interaction

Figure 18.4. Child care.

Child care

Although interactions between teachers and children have attracted the most attention in research on expectancy effects, interactions between children and the most important adults in their lives – their parents – have been curiously neglected. Yet on an intuitive level, most of us would agree that our parents' expectations for the kinds of persons we would be exerted an enormous effect on our lives. Figure 18.4 lists ways in which parents' expectations may be communicated. These behaviors include many of the mediators of teacher expectancies (discussed later), but there are additional behaviors due to parents' special access to and greater control over their children's lives. These additional behaviors nearly all involve the way parents structure their children's time, for example, choice of leisure activities and educational opportunities. A parent who stresses involvement in sports activities and rewards primarily sports successes more often than not will produce a child with different priorities than one reared by parents who stress academic achievements. Similarly, parents with traditional sex role stereotypes will be less likely to produce extremely career-oriented daughters.

Despite the importance of parental expectancies in child development, research on this issue will probably always be greatly constrained by pragmatic and ethical considerations. There are ethical concerns with

> **Nonverbal warmth**
> **Tone of voice**
> **Praise/Criticism**
> **Encouragement**
> **Sarcasm**
> **Frequency and duration of interactions**
> **Extent of direct supervision**
> **Responsibilities given to employee**
> **Duties given to employee**
> **Skills training opportunities**
> **Official workplace policies**
> **Official performance standards (quotas, etc.)**
> **Promotions/demotions/raises**
> **Unofficial performance norms**

Figure 18.5. Workplace relationships.

manipulating expectancies, even positive ones, in parents about their children, and the manipulations may not be believed by parents who have an intimate acquaintance with their children's traits and abilities. Yet studying naturally occurring expectancies would require fairly long-term longitudinal designs and thus may be equally difficult.

Workplace

There are two important determinants of an employee's behavior and productivity: (1) the expectations and demands communicated by the supervisor or employer and (2) workplace norms developed through interactions with co-workers. Figure 18.5 lists the behaviors associated with both of these influences.

Despite the fact that expectancy effects in the workplace could potentially translate into the loss (or gain) of enormous amounts of money due to decreases (or increases) in worker productivity, they have received surprisingly little research attention. Eden's chapter in this volume is an excellent summary of the empirical studies to date on expectancy effects in organizations. An example of field studies in this area is the work by King (1970, 1971). Subjects were welders, pressers, mechanics, nurses' aides, assemblers, and their supervisors. King (1970) reports that "[those employees] from whom exceptional performance was expected were given closer, more favorable, and special attention by their supervisors" (p. 290).

Affect variables such as those described by King may also play a large role in employee theft or misbehavior. Employees who feel trusted and liked by their employers may be less likely to goof off or use workplace resources in an unauthorized manner. In his book on self-fulfilling prophecies, Russ Jones (1977) gives the poignant example of Liebow's (1967) description of a man who justified giving an otherwise competent employee subpar wages with the argument that he "knew" all his employees stole regularly and thus reduced their wages accordingly. Yet the below-subsistence-level salary, as well as the lack of trust and hostility underlying the salary, can only increase the likelihood that an employee will steal to survive.

Employers' allocations of duties and standards for performance are the other vital class of mediating mechanisms. Anybody who has worked in sales understands the motivating effects of operating under quotas that must be reached before commissions can be earned. A good supervisor sets such quotas at levels that are continually demanding but not impossible. Employers also have at their disposal more formalized channels of communicating expectancies (e.g., job description codes, written procedures for promotion and raises) and systematic sanctions (including termination) for suboptimal performance.

The expectations of one's co-workers can also be important in determining worker productivity, particularly if the workplace setting has relatively less direct supervision by the superiors. The power of worker norms to influence productivity was first documented in the Hawthorne studies, where it was found that workers who produced at levels either well above or below the norm were subjected to subtle and blatant pressure on the part of their colleagues to change their pace to adhere to workplace norms (Roethlisberger & Dickson, 1939).

We should try harder to harness the power of positive expectancies in the workplace. The potential payoffs in terms of worker satisfaction and productivity are enormous, and the costs are few. Research in applied social psychology and industrial/organizational psychology would thus be well directed toward studying the effects of employer and employee expectations and designing interventions for inducing positive expectancies.

Consumer exchange/service relationships

Outside of our family members and co-workers, many of our other social interactions involve a category of situations I call *consumer exchange*. This category includes exchanges with all types of merchants, as

> **Selective demonstration of features or products**
> **Initial asking price/ counter-offers**
> **Frequency and duration of interactions**
> **Ignores customer**
> **Nonverbal warmth**
> **Smiles**
> **Tone of voice**
> **Eye contact**
> **Hand shaking**
> **Ingratiation (e.g. use of customer first name)**

Figure 18.6. Consumer exchange/service relationships.

well as representatives from the service professions (e.g., sales clerks, repair personnel, bank tellers). The majority of these exchanges are governed fairly strictly by role requirements. Expectancies do not often play a big role, for example, in our dealings with the person standing behind the counter at McDonald's.

However, there are some cases where our interactions with service personnel are extended or repeated enough such that expectancies may enter into the process. Indeed, expectancies may play a large role in the case of major purchases (e.g., automobiles, houses) or transactions (e.g., obtaining a loan). Figure 18.6 lists the ways in which sellers or service people communicate their expectancies about their customers.

Perhaps the biggest way in which expectancies influence the consumer exchange process is through variations in service quality and the differential presentation of products or features based on the seller's expectations regarding the customer's socioeconomic status. With respect to the former, most of us have had the experience of finding it more difficult to attract attention or service from salespeople when we are sloppily dressed compared to when we are attired in a suit. A coin and jewel dealer of my acquaintance once explained to me that he will spend less time showing products to women wearing costume jewelry, a deliberate strategy, though he acknowledged he might be losing out on some sales that way.

Another prime example of the differential selling process can be found in Jessica Mitford's fascinating exposé of the American funeral industry (Mitford, 1978). She describes how funeral directors will ask seemingly innocent questions ("What was the occupation of the deceased?" or "Should we bill the insurance company directly?") in order

Nonverbal warmth
Tone of voice
Eye contact
Verbal and nonverbal confidence
Body orientation
Treatment regimen prescribed
Physical format of placebo
  --pills vs. injections
  --size of pill
  --use of complicated equipment

Figure 18.7. Medical settings.

to gauge how much money the family will have available for the funeral and thus what to charge for identical services. She quotes one funeral director as saying "If a person drives a Cadillac, why should he have a Pontiac funeral?" and another who refused to sell his lowest-priced funeral to families who obviously have means (Mitford, 1978, p. 37).

Medical settings

It has been said that the history of medicine up to the 19th century has been the history of the placebo effect (Shapiro, 1960). Most of the accepted medical practices of historical times had no physiological basis for efficacy, yet patients improved, presumably as a result of the psychological effects associated with the knowledge that they were being treated for their problems and the expectations that the treatment would help. Today the power of placebos is well documented, with studies showing that, on average, placebos are effective in one-third of patients for treating a wide variety of medical problems such as headaches, rheumatoid arthritis, hay fever, warts, and bleeding ulcers (Kirsch, 1990). Success rates of over 75% using placebos have been reported (Kirsch, 1990).

One important component of placebo effects is the patients' own self-expectancies about the course of their illness and the treatment; the second important component is the communication of the health professionals' expectations. Figure 18.7 shows the mediators associated with both of these components. With respect to self-expectancies, the form of the placebo has great impact. For example, placebo morphine is more effective than placebo Darvon, which is more effective than placebo aspirin (Evans, 1974). Subjects being treated with placebos for arthritis also reported greater relief if they were given injections rather than pills and if the injections were administered closer to the problematic joints (Kirsch, 1990).

With respect to the health professional's expectancies, affect variables are undoubtedly the most important. A physician's confidence, as communicated through tone of voice, gaze, posture, and utterances, can work wonders for patients. Physicians' nonverbal skills have further been shown to be related to rapport and patient satisfaction with treatment (DiMatteo, this volume; Friedman, this volume; Harrigan & Rosenthal, 1986). Conversely, negative emotions communicated through the same channels can have adverse effects; for example, Milmoe, Rosenthal, Blane, Chafetz, and Wolf (1967) found that doctors whose voice tone was rated as more hostile were less effective at referring their patients for alcoholism counseling.

The treatment regimen the physician chooses to prescribe obviously will also greatly influence patient outcomes. A physician family member once told me that he will not prescribe certain regimens involving major lifestyle changes unless he is convinced that the patient will and can make those changes. This is an example where a negative expectancy on the part of the physician ("This patient will not stick to a low-sodium diet, so I won't bother telling him about it") is truly self-fulfilling.

The role of physician behavior in pleasing and curing patients has been well documented. However, only recently has attention been paid to the "art of medicine" (i.e., the socioemotional aspect of patient care) in medical school curricula. As in the case of employee productivity, this relative neglect is puzzling considering the very large potential payoffs in terms of human comfort.

Psychotherapy

The psychotherapeutic setting obviously has a lot of overlap with the medical setting, but it has been studied widely in the expectancy realm as a distinct situation and so merits separate attention. Figure 18.8 describes how therapists may act in ways to elicit self-fulfilling prophecies. One of the first ways this can happen is in the diagnosis stage. The hypothesis-confirming biases discussed in the earlier section on getting-acquainted processes are again relevant here. There is an extensive clinical literature on biases in the diagnostic process and how these biases can lead to flawed information-gathering strategies that are self-fulfilling (e.g., Turk & Salovey, 1988). For example, studies have shown

Selective questions about client history
Nature of interpretations offered
Nonverbal warmth
Tone of voice
Eye contact
Smiles
Facial expressions
Nods
Touch
Interpersonal distance

Figure 18.8. Psychotherapy.

that clinicians often form working diagnoses literally within 60 seconds of speaking with a new client (Gauron & Dickinson, 1969). These diagnoses will shape the way the clinician obtains a history from the client and will constrain the questions asked by the clinician (Snyder & Thomsen, 1988). For example, if a therapist believes that a client's current problems are related to her conflicted relationship with her father, the therapist may devote considerable time to asking about negative experiences with the father. None of us has perfect parents, and if prodded, we could all generate incidents in which our fathers were either angry or absent. As more and more such examples are generated, the therapist may become more convinced of the correctness of the hypothesis, and the client herself may grow to believe that conflicted paternal interactions are at the root of her present difficulties.

I have emphasized the hypotheses-confirming biases in the diagnostic process because it is unique to the clinical context, but it should be clear that other behaviors, particularly nonverbal cues such as smiles, gaze, and touch, all serve to communicate therapists' expectancies and may be instrumental in producing expectancy effects. The intensity of a therapy session is almost always extraordinarily high. Clients are hypervigilant to nuances in therapists' verbal and nonverbal behavior (which is why Freud advocated the use of the couch), and even barely perceptible changes in the therapist's voice tone, for example, may be interpreted heavily by the client.

Institutional care

This class of situations includes settings such as nursing homes, mental hospitals, and rehabilitation hospitals, that is, long-term facilities for

```
Nonverbal warmth
Nonverbal condescension
Eye contact
Touch
Baby talk
  --higher pitch
  --greater variability in pitch
  --limited vocabulary
  --repetition
  --clarifying devices
Control over activities
Restrictions on timing of activities
  (e.g., sleeping, eating)
Type of entertainment provided (e.g. TV)
Performing basic bodily and hygienic
  functions (e.g. eating, grooming)
```

Figure 18.9. Institutional care.

the care of people who suffer from physical or psychological problems. Assuming the most common case where the care provider is the perceiver, Figure 18.9 lists the variables hypothesized to be important mediators of expectancy effects in these settings. The variables can be categorized into two major classes: (1) nonverbal behaviors serving to infantilize the target and (2) behaviors stemming from care providers' efforts to exert control over the patients' actions.

Within the first category, a series of studies by Caporael and her colleagues has demonstrated that baby talk is a significant component of caregivers' speech toward the institutionalized elderly and is associated with lower expectations for the functional abilities of the residents (Caporael, 1981; Caporael, Lukaszewski, & Culbertson, 1983). Similarly, DePaulo and Coleman's (1986) study of speech directed toward various groups showed that adults talking to retarded individuals used significantly more clarifying devices (paraphrases and repetitions), more pronouns (a measure of simplification), and fewer pauses than when talking to normal adults.

The category of control-related variables may also be of major importance. Most long-term care institutions are understaffed, and the amount of care required by patients is large, meaning that care providers are motivated to control the situation so as to minimize disruptions and to have things run as smoothly as possible. This goal is typically accomplished by instituting a relatively strict schedule of eating, entertainment, and treatment, and the options provided within each area are generally extremely limited.

What are the implications of these considerations for the expectancy process? From an applied perspective, the most problematic case is one in which caretakers hold overly negative expectations about the capabilities of their patients. This can then lead them to engage in more of the controlling behaviors listed in Figure 18.9 and to do more things for the patient (e.g., grooming) because they believe the patient cannot handle the tasks personally. The consequence can be what Ellen Langer termed *self-induced dependence* (Langer & Benevento, 1978), which occurs when people who are induced to adopt a subordinate role on a task subsequently become less able to carry out the task. Similarly, Rodin and Langer (1980) reviewed research documenting that subjects who suffer loss of control over their activities may experience detrimental effects to their psychological and physical health.

The preceding discussion applies to the transmission of negative expectancies. In the cheerier case of positive expectancies, one would expect perceivers to display the opposite pattern of behaviors: for example, not using baby talk, giving more opportunities for activities and greater choice of activities, spending more time with them. In addition, affect variables such as smiles and eye contact may play a larger role. In the case of institutions that include an educational component (e.g., homes for the mentally retarded), the behaviors listed in the following section would also be relevant.

Classroom situations

As noted earlier, more is known about the mediation of teacher expectancy effects than about any of the other situations discussed here. Because there already exists a large literature on this topic (see Brophy, 1983; Harris & Rosenthal, 1985; Jussim, 1986, for reviews), I will be brief here. Figure 18.10 lists the behaviors associated with teacher expectancies. Essentially they can all be reduced to Rosenthal's (1989) affect-effort theory: Teachers are friendlier to high-expectancy students and spend more time teaching them. Both dimensions are critical: Teachers' affect is instrumental in motivating students, but in the final analysis, students learn only as much as they are taught. Indeed, in the Harris and Rosenthal (1985) meta-analysis, the climate and input factors yielded nearly equivalent effect sizes, $r = .27$ and $.29$, respectively.

Frequency and duration of interactions
Number of questions asked
Amount of material taught
Type of assignments given
Difficulty level of material taught
Task-related contacts
Encourages
Praise/Criticism
Wait time for responses
Corrective feedback
Nonverbal warmth
Eye contact
Smiles
Interpersonal distance
Nods

Figure 18.10. Teaching.

Courtroom

The courtroom is a setting that most of us encounter at some point in our lives despite our preference to avoid it. It is also a setting where expectancies may play a vital role: It brings together people who for the most part are unacquainted with each other, it usually entails a highly motivated person perception process, and the stakes on the outcome of this process can be exceedingly high. Judges, counsel, and jurors rapidly form expectations about the defendants and plaintiffs; expectations about the jurors and their probable verdict are also formed.

Thus it is reasonable to ask about the extent to which expectancy effects happen in the courtroom (see Blanck, this volume, for an extended discussion of this topic). There is reason to believe that expectancy effects may be *less* likely to occur in this context than in others. Neuberg (1989) shows that expectancy effects are attenuated when perceivers are given instructions to be accurate in the impressions they form of the targets. No other setting in the world stresses accuracy and the need to find out the truth as much as the courtroom, so it may well be that erroneous expectations do not often result in self-fulfilling effects.

Empirical data on this question are sorely lacking. Obviously, expectations cannot be ethically manipulated in the courtroom, and mock jury research has not, to my knowledge, looked at this topic. There is, however, an important field study that examined the impact of judges'

Nonverbal warmth
Nonverbal competence and professionalism
Facial expressions
Tone of voice
Disparaging remarks or gestures
Bias in rulings on objections
Comments on evidence
Failing to control misconduct of counsel
Type of questions asked of witnesses
Differential vocal emphasis
   (e.g. "guilty" or "innocent")
Plea-bargain offers and counter-offers
Sentencing recommendations

Figure 18.11. Courtroom/legal settings.

naturally occurring expectations regarding defendants' guilt (Blanck, Rosenthal, & Cordell, 1985). In this study, five judges were videotaped while delivering final instructions to the jury in 34 trials; they also completed a questionnaire asking their opinion of whether the defendant was truly guilty and would be found guilty by the jury. Results showed that judges who expected a guilty verdict were significantly less warm, competent, and wise and were more anxious in giving the instructions (Blanck et al., 1985). However, judges' expectancies were *not* significantly related to actual trial verdicts, although the sample of judges and trials was so small that power was a significant problem.

In short, expectancies influence judges' behavior, though it is not clear yet that these changes influence the juries. A speculative list of ways in which judges and counsel can influence each other and the jury is shown in Figure 18.11. These behaviors are taken primarily from those examined or mentioned in Blanck et al. (1985). Given the potentially major consequences that could occur if expectancy effects happen regularly in the courtroom, it is clear that this is an area in great need of further research.

Behavioral research

The first research done on interpersonal expectancy effects was in the behavioral research context when Robert Rosenthal and his colleagues conducted a series of experiments in the 1960s documenting that experimenters might unintentionally elicit the behavior they expected from

> **Variations in instructions (when possible)**
> **Deviations from standardization**
> **Differential vocal emphasis**
> **Unintentional verbal reinforcement**
>   **('uh-huhs,' "good," etc.)**
> **Nonverbal warmth**
> **Smiles**
> **Nods**
> **Gaze**
> **Forward leans**

Figure 18.12. Behavioral research.

their subjects (Rosenthal, 1969). The role of nonverbal behavior in the expectancy process was quickly highlighted, as expectancy effects were shown to occur even when experimenters were employing standard-ized scripts.

Figure 18.12 shows the behaviors that have been implicated in com-municating experimenter expectancies. Foremost among these are dif-ferential vocal emphasis and unintentional reinforcement of subjects' responses. The vocal emphasis cue was studied extensively using the standard photo rating paradigm, and it is clear that experimenters who are led to expect high success ratings from their subjects emphasize success-related words and rating anchors when describing the task to the subjects; this emphasis has, in turn, been shown to influence the ratings given by naive subjects (Adair & Epstein, 1968).

Unintentional reinforcement is also likely to occur, as it is difficult for experimenters to monitor their own nonverbal behavior sufficiently to prevent slight head nods, smiles, or verbal encouragement in response to their subjects' behavior. These seemingly minor behaviors can greatly influence subjects' responses, particularly because most subjects in ex-periments are apprehensive. They want to give "good" data, so they may be especially sensitive to any cues the experimenter may be giving off about their performance.

Concluding comments

My goals for this chapter were to describe situations where expectancy effects are likely to occur, to compare those situations on a number of theoretically meaningful dimensions, and to offer a compilation of behaviors that can be predicted to mediate expectancy effects within the various situations. In a pragmatic sense, this taxonomy should be helpful for researchers when they are designing their studies and choosing behaviors to code. A useful strategy to follow is to select a small number of global variables reflecting the affect and effort dimensions (two good variables are ratings of nonverbal friendliness and talking time) and an additional small number of variables more specific to the task or situation at hand.

I emphasize the words *small number.* It is easy to get swept up in the excitement and generate a long list of possible verbal and nonverbal behaviors to code. There are a couple of problems with this. First, the job of coding quickly becomes unmanageable. Given a decent N and interactions lasting beyond a few minutes, it can take literally months to code a large number of variables. Second, these variables are probably highly interrelated and may not be very meaningful considered separately. For example, how would one want to interpret a finding that positive expectancies are related to an increased frequency of foot jiggling? Global judgments of dimensions such as warmth, anxiety, dominance, and competence are not only easier to obtain but also may reflect more accurately the psychological meaning derived by the targets of the perceivers' behavior. Lastly, Cohen (1990) makes a wonderfully compelling case that "less is more" and that a small number of key dependent variables results in greater statistical and conceptual clarity.

I hope further that this chapter provides encouragement and impetus to pay greater attention to expectancy mediation. Much of the recent work on expectancy effects has focused on moderators of expectancy effects. This is important work, but we need to understand the underlying process, too.

On a broader level, a major goal of the chapter was to draw attention to the situational half of the behavior equation. Definitions of social psychology stress, explicitly or implicitly, the impact of the situation on individual behavior. Yet a frequent refrain in the literature is that very little is known about the psychological effects of situational variables (Magnusson, 1981). Too often our experimental methods are a consequence of what is easy to do or what has worked before; too often we restrict a phenomenon to a given paradigm and do not adequately test how it might be altered in other situations. Research on interpersonal expectancy effects would thus benefit from greater attention to situational influences. I hope this chapter can and will be a step in that direction.

376   Monica J. Harris

References

Adair, J. G., & Epstein, J. S. (1968). Verbal cues in the mediation of experimenter bias. *Psychological Reports, 22,* 1045–1053.
Blanck, P. D., Rosenthal, R., & Cordell, L. H. (1985). The appearance of justice: Judges' verbal and nonverbal behavior in criminal jury trials. *Stanford Law Review, 38,* 89–151.
Brophy, J. (1983). Research on the self-fulfilling prophecy and teacher expectations. *Journal of Educational Psychology, 75,* 631–661.
Caporael, L. R. (1981). The paralanguage of caregiving: Baby talk to the institutionalized aged. *Journal of Personality and Social Psychology, 40,* 876–884.
Caporael, L. R., Lukaszewski, M. P., & Culbertson, G. H. (1983). Secondary baby talk: Judgments by institutionalized elderly and their caregivers. *Journal of Personality and Social Psychology, 44,* 746–754.
Cohen, J. (1990). Things I have learned so far. *American Psychologist, 45,* 1304–1312.
Darley, J. M., & Fazio, R. (1980). Expectancy confirmation processes arising in the social interaction sequence. *American Psychologist, 35,* 867–881.
Darley, J. M., Fleming, J. H., Hilton, J. L., & Swann, W. B., Jr. (1988). Dispelling negative expectancies: The impact of interaction goals and target characteristics on the expectancy confirmation process. *Journal of Experimental Social Psychology, 24,* 19–36.
DePaulo, B. M., & Coleman, L. M. (1986). Talking to children, foreigners, and retarded adults. *Journal of Personality and Social Psychology, 51,* 945–959.
DiMatteo, M. R. (1979). A social psychological analysis of physician–patient rapport: Toward a science of the art of medicine. *Journal of Social Issues, 35,* 12–33.
Evans, F. J. (1974). The placebo response in pain reduction. *Advances in Neurology, 4,* 289–296.
Feldman, R. S., & Prohaska, T. (1979). The student as Pygmalion: Effect of student expectation on the teacher. *Journal of Educational Psychology, 71,* 485–493.
Gauron, E. F., & Dickinson, J. K. (1969). The influence of seeing the patient first on diagnostic decision-making in psychiatry. *American Journal of Psychiatry, 126,* 199–205.
Harrigan, J. A., & Rosenthal, R. (1986). Nonverbal aspects of empathy and rapport in physician-patient interaction. In P. D. Blanck, R. Buck, & R. Rosenthal (Eds.), *Nonverbal communication in the clinical context* (pp. 36–73). University Park, PA: Pennsylvania State University Press.
Harris, M. J., Milich, R., Corbitt, E. M., Hoover, D. W., & Brady, M. (1992). Self-fulfilling effects of stigmatizing information on children's social interactions. *Journal of Personality and Social Psychology, 63,* 41–50.
Harris, M. J., & Rosenthal, R. (1985). Mediation of interpersonal expectancy effects: 31 meta-analyses. *Psychological Bulletin, 97,* 363–386.
Jones, R. A. (1977). *Self-fulfilling prophecies: Social, psychological, and physiological effects of expectancies.* Hillsdale, NJ: Erlbaum.
Jussim, L. (1986). Self-fulfilling prophecies: A theoretical and integrative review. *Psychological Review, 93,* 429–445.
Jussim, L. (1989). Teacher expectations: Self-fulfilling prophecies, perceptual biases, and accuracy. *Journal of Personality and Social Psychology, 57,* 469–480.
Jussim, L. (1991). Social perception and social reality: A reflection-construction model. *Psychological Review, 98,* 54–73.

King, A. S. (1970). *Managerial relations with disadvantaged work groups: Supervisory expectations of the underprivileged worker.* Unpublished doctoral dissertation, Texas Tech University.

King, A. S. (1971). Self-fulfilling prophecies in training the hard-core: Supervisors' expectations and the underprivileged workers' performance. *Social Science Quarterly, 52,* 369–378.

Kirsch, I. (1990). *Changing expectations: A key to effective psychotherapy.* Pacific Grove, CA: Brooks/Cole.

Langer, E., & Benevento, A. (1978). Self-induced dependence. *Journal of Personality and Social Psychology, 36,* 886–893.

Liebow, E. (1967). *Tally's corner: A study of Negro streetcorner men.* Boston: Little, Brown.

Magnusson, D. (Ed.). (1981). *Toward a psychology of situations: An interactional perspective.* Hillsdale, NJ: Erlbaum.

Milmoe, S., Rosenthal, R., Blane, H. T., Chafetz, M. E., & Wolf, I. (1967). The doctor's voice: Postdictor of successful referral of alcoholic patients. *Journal of Abnormal Psychology, 72,* 78–84.

Mitford, J. (1978). *The American way of death.* New York: Simon and Schuster.

Neuberg, S. L. (1989). The goal of forming accurate impressions during social interactions: Attenuating the impact of negative expectancies. *Journal of Personality and Social Psychology, 56,* 374–386.

Raudenbush, S. W. (1984). Magnitude of teacher expectancy effects on pupil IQ as a function of the credibility of expectancy induction: A synthesis of findings from 18 experiments. *Journal of Educational Psychology, 76,* 85–97.

Rodin, J., & Langer, E. (1980). Aging labels: The decline of control and the fall of self-esteem. *Journal of Social Issues, 36,* 12–29.

Roethlisberger, F. J., & Dickson, W. J. (1939). *Management and the worker.* Cambridge, MA: Harvard University Press.

Rosenthal, R. (1969). Interpersonal expectations: Effects of the experimenter's hypothesis. In R. Rosenthal & R. L. Rosnow (Eds.), *Artifact in behavioral research.* New York: Academic Press.

Rosenthal, R. (1973). The mediation of Pygmalion effects: A four-factor "theory." *Papua New Guinea Journal of Education, 9,* 1–12.

Rosenthal, R. (1989). *Experimenter expectancy, covert communication, and meta-analytic methods.* Invited address at the annual meeting of the American Psychological Association, New Orleans.

Satir, V. (1968). *Conjoint family therapy* (rev. ed.). Palo Alto, CA: Science and Behavior Books.

Shapiro, A. K. (1960). A contribution to a history of the placebo effect. *Behavioral Science, 5,* 109–135.

Snyder, M., & Swann, W. B., Jr. (1978a). Behavioral confirmation in social interaction: From social perception to social reality. *Journal of Experimental Social Psychology, 14,* 148–162.

Snyder, M., & Swann, W. B., Jr. (1978b). Hypothesis-testing processes in social interaction. *Journal of Personality and Social Psychology, 36,* 1202–1212.

Snyder, M., Tanke, E. D., & Berscheid, E. (1977). Social perception and interpersonal behavior: On the self-fulfilling nature of stereotypes. *Journal of Personality and Social Psychology, 35,* 656–666.

Snyder, M., & Thomsen, C. J. (1988). Interactions between therapists and clients: Hypothesis testing and behavioral confirmation. In D. C. Turk & P. Salovey (Eds.), *Reasoning, inference, and judgment in clinical psychology* (pp. 124–152). New York: Free Press.

Swann, W. B., Jr., & Giuliano, T. (1987). Confirmatory search strategies in social interaction: How, when, why and with what consequences. *Journal of Social and Clinical Psychology, 5,* 511–524.

Trope, Y., & Bassok, M. (1983). Information-gathering strategies in hypothesis-testing. *Journal of Experimental Social Psychology, 19,* 560–576.

Turk, D. C., & Salovey, P. (Eds.). (1988). *Reasoning, inference, and judgment in clinical psychology.* New York: Free Press.

19. Analysis of variance in the study of interpersonal expectations: Theory testing, interaction effects, and effect sizes

FRANK J. BERNIERI

The analysis of variance is only the first step in studying the results.
(Snedecor & Cochran, 1980, p. 224)

The analysis of variance (ANOVA) is the most common analysis strategy in social psychology. In a survey of three major social psychology journals in 1978, 84% of the articles used ANOVA at least some of their results (Kenny, 1985). Given this pervasiveness, one might expect ANOVA to be a robust, efficient, and powerful analytic tool. In terms of fulfilling its scientific potential, however, ANOVA has shown itself to be a disappointing underachiever. The amount of scientific knowledge that has been gained from it falls far short of the knowledge that could have (and should have) been attained.

In this chapter, several issues regarding the optimal application of ANOVA will be discussed as they pertain to social psychological research in general and interpersonal expectation research in particular. A hypothetical study involving expectation effects and interaction outcome on interpersonal attraction will be presented and analyzed. The experimental design chosen is typical. Although the data were contrived to demonstrate important points clearly, care was taken to make them representative of what might actually occur in a genuine study. The objective of this chapter is to demonstrate that the full potential of ANOVA is realized only when it performed in an active, mindful, and precise manner.

A "failed" study

An unanticipated and surprising finding to come out of the Pygmalion study (Rosenthal & Jacobson, 1966) was that the more the control group children gained in IQ, the more they were regarded as less well adjusted, less interesting, and less affectionate by their teachers, who did not expect such improvement (Rosenthal, 1974, 1985). Related effects reported by others suggested that teachers may have reacted negatively to the unexpected intellectual growth in students (Leacock, 1969; Shore, 1969).

People who behave in a manner consistent with expectations are predictable and are probably regarded as appearing more familiar. Familiarity has been shown to correlate positively with the positive evaluation of objects (Zajonc, 1968) and people (Swap, 1977). Swann (1984) has argued that people are attracted to and seek out those who are predictable to them. Thus, an *Expectancy Confirmation* theory of interpersonal attraction may be worth exploring. Simply stated, individuals who confirm initial expectations may be evaluated relatively more positively than those who do not confirm initial expectations. Consider the following hypothetical scenario.

A researcher wanted to investigate the social consequences of expectancy confirmation. A simplified version of the theory states that the behavior of others is perceived more positively to the degree that it confirms prior expectations, or alternatively, the behavior of others is perceived relatively negatively to the degree that it disconfirms initial expectations.

A controlled study was designed wherein teachers' expectations of students' performance was experimentally manipulated, as was students' apparent performance. Teachers and students were college undergraduates, and the roles of teacher and student were determined at random. The teachers' tasks were to explain the rules and objectives of a new video game to the student and then to coach the student by teaching various winning strategies. Teachers trained extensively with the game before the experimental session. Students were naive subjects who had some, but not much, experience with video games in general and no experience at all with the experimental video game. The teaching session ended after pupils were able to score a specified number of points in a single trial.

Teacher expectation was manipulated immediately prior to the teaching session. Teachers were told that their student scored either high, low, or average on "a validated and firmly established test of hand–eye coordination and tactical strategy designed by the United States Army." It was explained that the test measured aptitude for, among other

Table 19.1. *Teachers' general attitude toward their pupils: Reported by teachers' initial expectation and pupils' apparent performance*

Apparent performance	Expected performance			Mean
	Low	Medium	High	
Poor	36	27	18	27
Average	36	45	36	39
Good	36	45	54	45
Mean	36	39	36	37

Note: General attitude is a composite variable consisting of several items regarding the teachers' impression of the pupil (e.g., interesting, likes pupil, well adjusted).

things, video game performance. Bogus performance feedback was given to the teacher immediately after the teaching session. Performance was evaluated in terms of the amount of time it took for the pupils to reach their goal (i.e., point total). One of three levels of bogus performance feedback was provided at random to the teacher: good time, average time, or poor time.

Teachers were asked to report their reactions to the study in general, the video game, and their pupil. Likert Scale ratings such as "Finds pupil interesting," "Likes pupil," and "Pupil is well adjusted" were given to assess teachers' general attitude toward their pupil. A general attitude composite variable was formed by taking the sum of all related items scored in the appropriate direction. The grand mean of this favorability attitude scale over all 99 teachers was 37.

Summarizing, teachers' attitude toward pupils was the dependent variable measured under one of nine experimental conditions defined by the crossing of teacher expectation (high, medium, low) with pupil performance (good, average, poor), both of which were experimentally manipulated. Eleven teacher–student dyads were run under each of the nine conditions, for a total of 99 dyads. The table of means for teachers' general attitude toward their pupils appears in Table 19.1. The higher the mean, the more favorable the attitude.

A 3×3 (Expectancy $\times$ Performance) ANOVA was performed on the data, the results of which appear in Table 19.2. None of the effects listed reach the $p < .05$ level of significance, although pupil performance showed a nearly significant effect. On the basis of these results, the researcher

Table 19.2. *Default summary table generated from the 3×3 ANOVA of teacher's attitude*

Source of variance	SS	df	MS	F	p	eta
Between	9,702	8	1,213	1.35	>.20	.33
Teacher's expectancy (E)	198	2	99	0.11	>.20	.05
Student's performance (P)	5,544	2	2,772	3.08	.06	.25
(E × P) interaction	3,960	4	990	1.10	>.20	.22
Ts within groups	80,910	90	899	—	—	—
Total	90,612	98	—	—	—	—

might have concluded that the experiment, and perhaps the theory as well, was a failure (i.e., the Expectancy Confirmation theory of interpersonal attraction was not supported by the data).

Had this investigator chosen to exile these data to her file drawer of failed studies, the field of interpersonal expectations would have lost a priceless set of empirical evidence directly pertinent to the validation of the Expectancy Confirmation theory. Had this investigator succeeded in publishing this research as a null finding, further research in this area may have been halted. It is even conceivable that the publication of these findings may have set back the science surrounding this theory several years!

It is difficult to judge how likely such a scenario is, but even a superficial examination of a sample of journals should clearly demonstrate that such analysis strategies and conclusions are not rare. The problem with the preceding analysis is not that it was done incorrectly. The problem is that it was incomplete, and therefore largely uninformative with respect to the theoretical objectives the study was designed to meet. Researchers need to be aware that an ANOVA is incomplete until the pattern of differences between group means is examined and their sizes are quantified (Snedecor & Cochran, 1980, p. 224; later, Kenny, 1985; Rosenthal & Rosnow, 1991).

Increasing the utility of ANOVA

Several issues are involved in the inappropriate application of ANOVA. These include (1) the testing of effects that correspond *directly* to theoretically derived hypotheses (see, e.g., Rosenthal & Rosnow, 1985; Rosenthal & Rosnow, 1991, chap. 21), (2) the appropriate display and interpretation of interaction effects (Rosenthal & Rosnow, 1991, chap. 17; Rosnow & Rosenthal, 1989a), and (3) the complete reporting of results necessary for the proper documentation of research (Kenny, 1985; Rosenthal 1984).

Theory testing in ANOVA

The key to using ANOVA effectively involves an understanding of the null hypothesis that a given F-statistic tests and how single degree-of-freedom F tests can be constructed by the researcher to test whether a given set of data is consistent with a theoretically derived prediction.

Null hypotheses of F tests. Experiments in psychology are typically performed in order to determine how consistent a specific theoretical model is with the data (Kenny, 1985). Researchers involved in theory corroboration therefore are concerned with data *patterns* and their similarity to predicted models. The null hypothesis that an F tests is that the population means of all groups are identical (i.e., $\mu_1 = \mu_2 \ldots = \mu_i$). When more than two groups are under consideration, this particular null hypothesis is seldom useful for a researcher because rejecting it does not necessarily justify the advancement of any other precisely formulated alternative hypothesis or model.

For example, our hypothetical researcher expected pupil performance to affect teachers' attitudes for at least two reasons. In general, people tend to evaluate successful others more favorably due to halo effects (see, e.g., Rosenthal & Rosnow, 1991, pp. 175–176). Also, teachers of pupils who performed well may attribute their pupils' success in part to their own teaching ability, and thus may experience an overall positive shift in self-esteem and mood that may generalize to the more positive perception of others. For these reasons, our researcher anticipated that pupil performance would be related positively to teachers' attitude toward them.

Table 19.3 presents eight data patterns that are consistent with the rejection of the null hypothesis that $\mu_1 = \mu_2 = \mu_3$. Of the patterns listed, the researcher would like most to advance H_1, which specifies a linear trend. H_2 and H_3 are similar to H_1 but are not preferred. The data patterns displayed in H_4 to H_8 are inconsistent with our researcher's hypothesis. All eight alternative hypotheses, however, would be consistent with an F test that rejected the null. In other words, although the *null* hypothesis (H_0) was precisely formulated within our previous

Table 19.3. *Possible effects of pupil performance*

Pupil performance	Hypotheses consistent with researcher's theory			Hypotheses inconsistent with researcher's theory					The null
	H_1	H_2	H_3	H_4	H_5	H_6	H_7	H_8	H_0
Poor	−1	−1	−2	+1	+2	+1	+1	−1	0
Average	0	−1	+1	0	−1	+1	−2	+2	0
Good	+1	+2	+1	−1	−1	−2	+1	−1	0

Note: Values in the table represent relative levels of teachers' attitudes.

example, the *alternative* hypothesis (H_1), which is the one our researcher is interested in testing, was not. Therefore, the Type I error rate (p value) associated with the F testing the effect of performance appearing in Table 19.2 is *not* the Type I error rate associated with any theoretical model at all. As such, this F test and all other omnibus F tests (i.e., those having two or more df in the numerator) are greatly limited in scientific utility because of their ineffectiveness in advancing specific alternative hypotheses.

The null hypothesis that the F of an interaction effect tests is even less informative because the number of different alternative hypotheses is often greater. An interaction null hypothesis compares the data *patterns* caused by one factor (A) as they occur within different levels of another factor (B) ($pattern_1 = pattern_2 . . = pattern_i$). A data pattern in this case is a relative ordering of group means. Graphically, the null hypothesis defines the situations where the data patterns within each level of a given factor are parallel (Tukey, 1977).

In our hypothetical scenario, the rejection of the interaction null hypothesis signifies only that the relative ordering of means within a given level of, say, teacher expectation across the three levels of performance is not exactly identical to the relative ordering found within the other two levels of teacher expectation. Table 19.3 presents the patterns possible within any one level of teacher expectation. Each of the other two levels can show any of these nine patterns as well. Therefore, the number of pattern combinations possible across the three levels of teacher expectation is $9^3 = 729$. Of these, only nine are defined by the interaction null hypothesis. Therefore, when the interaction null is rejected, any one of 720 alternative hypotheses or models is plausible. The significance of the interaction F in Table 19.2 merely quantifies the Type I error rate of rejecting a paltry 1.2% (9 out of 729) of the possible competing theoretical models. If our researcher wanted empirical support to advance one particular interaction model, there would be 719 remaining models in our simple 3×3 factorial design left to reject!

A quick glance at the table of means may reveal to a perceptive data analyst that hundreds of the remaining 720 models do not fit the data. However, the Type I error rate found in an omnibus interaction F test is unrelated to this type of intuitive speculation and is inappropriate to cite as evidence for the advancement of a favored alternative hypothesis. In terms of probability theory, to do so would be nearly the conceptual equivalent to saying that the last three digits of someone's social security number are probably 7-3-3 because there is a greater than 95% probability that the person's number is not 0-0-1 through 0-0-9.

Unlike the Type I error rate associated with an omnibus F test, the Type I error of a 1 *df* F test (or t test) relates directly to an explicit alternative hypothesis (i.e., a specific pattern of results). Therefore, in order to advance any specific theory involving more than two sample means, a researcher must construct within the ANOVA a customized 1 *df* F test of his or her specific hypothesis.

Focused hypothesis testing: Contrast analysis in ANOVA. As stated earlier, our hypothetical researcher was interested in testing two theoretically derived hypotheses: (H_1) attitudes toward pupils become more favorable with increasing student performance, and (H_2) attitudes toward pupils become more favorable as student performance matches initial expectations.

Let's consider first the hypothesis predicting a positive relationship between teachers' attitudes and pupil performance. Figure 19.1 plots pupil performance against the group means of teachers' attitudes. Clearly, the data appear to fit the hypothesis well. The Pearson r between the group means of teachers' attitudes and the three levels of student performance is $r = .98$. One way to interpret this is that 96% ($.98^2$) of the between-group variance associated with pupil performance is explained by an increasing linear trend pattern (H_1).

The next step requires the construction of a focused significance test that generates a Type I error rate that is associated with the acceptance of this precise pattern of results (i.e., an increasing linear trend). What follows is a conceptual discussion of focused hypothesis testing involv-

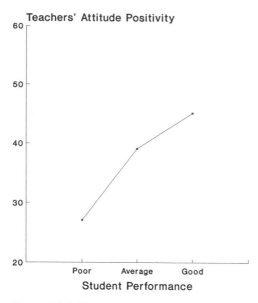

Figure 19.1. Teacher attitude and student performance.

ing the comparison of group means containing equal n values. Detailed procedures for the treatment of special cases, unequal n values, and repeated measures can be found elsewhere (Rosenthal & Rosnow, 1985, 1991; Snedecor & Cochran, 1980).

Conceptually, a focused comparison of means, called a *contrast analysis*, determines whether a linear combination of means (L) differs significantly from zero. A given predicted pattern of means or hypothesis generates a series of weights by which each of the means is multiplied before they are combined. Thus, if a linear combination of means with respect to H_1 in Table 19.3 is desired,

$$L_{\text{combination } H_1} = (-1)(27) + (0)(39) + (+01)(45) = 18$$

or more generally,

$$L = \lambda_1 \bar{X}_1 + \lambda_2 \bar{X}_2 + \ldots + \lambda_K \bar{X}_K \quad \text{(Snedecor \& Cochran, 1980, eq. 12.8.2)}$$

where the λs are weights generated by a specific hypothesis and $\bar{X}_K$ stands for the relevant group means. There also exists a computational requirement that $\Sigma \lambda_i = 0$.

The value of L increases to the extent that the pattern of group means matches the hypothesized pattern expressed in terms of the λ weights.

L can be interpreted as being directly related to the amount of variance explainable by any given theory or set of predicted values. When $L=0$, which is the null hypothesis for a focused test, it signifies that none of the variation between group means is attributable to the alternative hypothesis expressed in the pattern of λ weights.

When L is significantly greater than zero, it indicates that the set of predicted values accounts for a significant proportion of the between-group variance, providing direct support for the theory or model being tested. The value L is tested against zero, just as any other sample mean might be tested, by calculating its standard error and determining whether or not the value 0 lies within its 95% (or higher) confidence limits. In the preceding example, the test of our researcher's theory that attitudes will be positively related to student performance is the test of whether or not the sample value $L=18$ is significantly greater than zero.

It is important to note that L can be significantly *less* than zero as well. When this happens, the null hypothesis is rejected because the pattern of the tested theory is correct but its direction is opposite to what was predicted. In other words, if our researcher had predicted a negative association between attitudes and performance rather than a positive association, the value L would equal -18 and our researcher would have been exactly wrong. For this reason, focused comparisons require the data analyst to specify and identify the direction of the effect.

Within ANOVA, L is used to calculate an SS contrast term and a corresponding 1-df MS contrast term that is tested against the MS error in the model. The SS contrast can be interpreted as the variance attributable to the predicted pattern of means. Therefore the $F_{(1/df)}$ ratio (MS contrast/MS error) defines the precise test of whether or not a significant proportion of variance in a data set is attributable to the theoretical hypothesis (e.g., teachers' attitudes correlate positively with student performance).

In the simplified case of a between-group contrast with equal n values in each group,

$$MS \text{ contrast} = SS \text{ contrast} = \frac{(nL)^2}{n\Sigma(\lambda_i^2)}$$

where the sum of the λ weights equals zero. In the present example, n equals 33 and $\Sigma(\lambda_i^2)$ equals 2. Thus,

$$MS \text{ contrast} = SS \text{ contrast} = \frac{(33 \times 18)^2}{33(2)} = \frac{352,836}{66 = 5,346}$$

Employing the MS error from Table 19.2, the F testing the significance of our researcher's hypothesized linear effect of performance on teachers' attitudes is

$$\frac{MS\text{ contrast}}{MS\text{ error}} = \frac{5,346}{899} = 5.95 = F_{(1/90)}$$

and is significant at the $p < .02$ level.

In contrast to the common but relatively mindless, reflexively performed, and minimally informative ANOVA whose results appear in Table 19.2, our researcher's theoretically driven hypothesis has now been tested thoughtfully, actively, and unambiguously.

A wonderfully simple and robust alternative to computing the SS contrast has been outlined by Rosenthal and Rosnow (1985). To illustrate this approach consider Figure 19.1, which displays the means associated with the main effect of performance. Earlier it was stated that 96% of the variance among the means displayed in Figure 19.1 was attributable to our researcher's hypothesis involving a linear trend. This was derived from the fact that the correlation between the three means and the three λs was $r = .98$. In Table 19.2, the SS for performance lists the total variation due this effect. Accordingly, 96% of this variation is due to a linear trend in performance. Thus,

$$SS\text{ linear trend} = .96(5,544) = 5,346$$

More generally,

$$SS\text{ contrast} = r^2(SS\text{ means})$$

where r is the correlation between a set of means and the theoretically generated λs and SS means are those associated with the means used in the computation of r. In the present instance, SS performance was employed as the SS means because r was based on the three values that defined the main effect of pupil performance.

Alternatively, one could have computed a correlation between all nine original cell means with a set of nine λs that express the same linear trend of pupil performance. Employing all nine means the correlation between the data and the theoretically driven λs is $r = .74$. In this instance, the SS means = SS Between Total = 9,702 because the variance in question involves all nine means. Therefore, when computed across all nine means,

$$SS\text{ linear trend} = .74^2(9,702) = 5,346$$

Table 19.4. *Expectancy confirmation hypothesis*

Pupil performance	Expected performance			Mean
	Low	Medium	High	
Poor	+1	0	−1	0
Average	0	+1	0	+3/9
Good	−1	0	+1	0
Mean	0	+3/9	0	+1/9
Pupil performance	Expected performance			Mean
	Low	Medium	High	
Poor	+9	0	−9	0
Average	0	+9	0	+3
Good	−9	0	+9	0
Mean	0	+3	0	+1

Note: Values in the table represent relative levels of teachers' attitudes.

and is identical to what is found when the computations are performed on the marginal means,

$$SS \text{ linear trend} = .98^2(5{,}544) = 5{,}346$$

which, of course, is identical to what is found when one employs L,

$$SS \text{ linear trend} = \frac{(nL)^2}{n\Sigma(\lambda_i^2)} = \frac{(33 \times 18)^2}{33(2)} = 5{,}346$$

The correlational technique of computing SS contrast has the advantage of being computationally simple and is subject to less computation errors in more complex applications than is the L approach (Rosenthal & Rosnow, 1985).

And what of our researcher's second hypothesis? When performance either matches the expectation exactly or is highly discrepant from the expectation, there should be a corresponding effect on the teacher's attitude. In other words, a teacher's attitude is expected to become relatively more positive when there is a perfect match between performance and expectation and to become relatively more negative when there is an extreme discrepancy between performance and expectation. Table 19.4 displays the Expectancy Confirmation theory of interpersonal attraction as our researcher conceptualized it across the nine groups in our experimental design. The bottom half of Table 19.4 has been multi-

Table 19.5. *Contrast weights associated with the expectancy confirmation hypothesis*

Pupil performance	Expected performance			Mean
	Low	Medium	High	
Poor	+8	−1	−10	−1
Average	−1	+8	−1	+2
Good	−10	−1	+8	−1
Mean	−1	+2	−1	0

Note: Values in the table represent relative levels of teachers' attitudes. Values inside the marginals are a composite of two main effects (shown in the marginals) and one interaction effect (not shown).

plied by a factor of 9 in order to present the values to the nearest integer.

Although the values presented in Table 19.4 clearly and adequately describe and communicate our researcher's second theoretical hypothesis, they are not appropriate values to use in our contrast analysis because they do not sum to zero. Fortunately, any set of values can be transformed such that they sum to zero by simply subtracting from each their grand mean. Table 19.5 presents the de-meaned values that can now serve as λ weights in the computation of the *MS* contrast that corresponds to the Expectancy Confirmation hypothesis.

Inspection of Table 19.5 reveals that our researcher's theory is actually a composite of three distinct and identifiable orthogonal effects. First, the contrast weights shows a slight main effect of both expectation and performance. Both main effects are in the form of a quadratic pattern of means such that the middle level of both factors is predicted to generate relatively more positive values of teachers' attitudes. The final component (not displayed in Table 19.5) is an interaction component involving all nine cells. Figure 19.2 displays graphically the pattern of results defined by this interaction component.

The decomposition of a composite effect into its components allows one to check the orthogonality of the hypothesized effect against the other effects specified in the researcher's model. Effects are considered orthogonal when they are uncorrelated or independent. Mathematically, two effects are orthogonal when their cross-products sum to zero. For example, consider the linear and quadratic effects indicated by their λs:

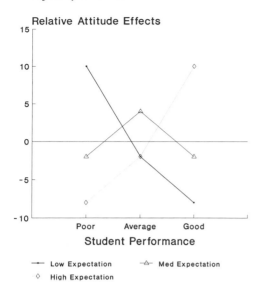

Figure 19.2. Relative attitude and student performance.

	A	B	C	Σ
Linear	−1	0	+1	0
Quadratic	−1	+2	−1	0
Linear × Quadratic	+1	0	−1	0

This shows that a linear trend and a quadratic trend are orthogonal effects.

The two hypotheses proposed by our investigator are orthogonal as well. The Expectancy Confirmation effect does not involve the linear trend in pupil performance. Multiplying the λ weights in Table 19.5 by the λ weights associated with a linear trend in performance confirms the mathematical independence of these effects:

	Cell no.									
	1	2	3	4	5	6	7	8	9	Σ
Expectancy Confirmation effect	+8	−1	−10	−1	+8	−1	−10	−1	+8	0
Performance linear trend effect	−1	−1	−1	0	0	0	+1	+1	+1	0
EC × Plt	$(-8)+(1)+(10)+0+0+0+(-10)+(-1)+(8)=0$									

The correlation between the weights displayed in Table 19.5 and the actual group means displayed in Table 19.1 is $(r = .67)$. The SS between

Table 19.6. *Theoretically driven ANOVA summary table*

Source of variance	SS	df	MS	F	p	r
Between	9,702	8	1,213	1.35	>.20	—
Linear contrast of student's performance (Plc)	5,346	1	5,346	5.94	.02	.25
Expectancy Confirmation theory–driven contrast (ECs)	4,356	1	4,356	4.85	.04	.23
Residual between-group variance	0	6	0	0	—	.00
Ts within groups	90,612	90	899	—	—	—
Total	89,892	98	—	—	—	—

is employed for the calculation of *MS* contrast because all nine group means are involved in the comparison between data and model. Thus,

$$MS \text{ confirmation hypothesis} = SS = .67^2(9,702) = 4,356$$

Employing the *MS* error from Table 19.2, the *F* testing the significance of the consistency between the observed data and the Behavioral Confirmation theory is

$$F_{(1/90)} = \left(\frac{MS \text{ confirmation hypothesis}}{MS \text{ error}}\right) = \frac{4,356}{899} = 4.85$$

and is significant at the $p < .04$ level.

This is remarkable news for our researcher because this result provides direct and unambiguous confirmation of her Expectancy Confirmation theory of interpersonal attraction.

Table 19.6 displays the ANOVA summary table that corresponds to the analysis just completed. The between and within sources of variance are identical to those found in Table 19.2. The difference is that the between-group variance has been divided into a different set of orthogonal components of variance. Table 19.2 shows the between-group variance divided into three orthogonal but theoretically uninteresting multi *df* sources, whereas Table 19.6 shows the between-group variance decomposed into only two theoretically meaningful single *df* sources plus one residual variance term (i.e., between-group variance left over after accounting for the two theoretical effects). In the example described here, all of the between-group variance was accounted for by a linear trend in performance and an Expectancy Confirmation effect. In other words, our hypothetical researcher managed to account for 100%

of the between-group variance in the data with her two theoretically derived hypotheses!

The data presented in Table 19.1, when subjected to direct tests of theoretical hypotheses, provided clear evidence that our researcher's predictions were correct. Far from being inconclusive, marginally successful, or even a failure, our researcher's experiment has to be considered an unqualified success. The difference between success and failure in this example turned on whether the investigator was willing to actively analyze the data herself by employing contrast analyses to test precisely defined alternative hypotheses or passively accept the analysis that her desktop computer so deftly, accurately, and thoughtlessly computed for her.

Our attention now turns to two remaining issues regarding the utility of ANOVA in research: the interaction term and effect size.

The interaction term

Displaying effects. A representative sample of 191 empirical articles employing ANOVA were surveyed from American Psychological Association journals published in 1985 (Rosnow & Rosenthal, 1989a). Rosnow and Rosenthal reported a distressing summary of their findings:

> 34% [of the 191 articles] reported nonsignificance or reported significance but did not proceed further because the observed interaction was stated to be irrelevant. Another 28% interpreted observed interactions but did not specify whether the interpretation was based on inspecting the residuals or on simple effects comparisons; in only 1% of these cases did the authors clearly specify that their interpretation was based on evaluating the residuals for the interaction that was present. In the remaining 37% of the cases, there were clear-cut indications that demonstrated confusion in thinking about interactions; that is, observed interactions were followed only by simple effects comparisons (e.g., contrasts computed on original cell or condition means), or they were followed by referring the reader to a table of original cell or condition means. None of the journals surveyed was immune from this kind of error in reporting the pattern of an observed interaction. (p. 143)

An interaction effect is defined by the cell means corrected for main effects. Therefore, it is always inappropriate and potentially misleading to interpret an interaction by referring to a pattern of raw cell means. An interaction effect should be treated, displayed, and interpreted in exactly the same manner in which main effects are treated, displayed,

Table 19.7. *Main effect of pupil performance displayed across all nine experimental groups*

Pupil performance	Expected performance			Mean
	Low	Medium	High	
Poor	27	27	27	27
Average	39	39	39	39
Good	45	45	45	45
Mean	37	37	37	37

and interpreted: by first correcting the means for all other orthogonal effects.

When row or column means are used to display and interpret a main effect in a two-way ANOVA, they are, in effect, a shorthand summary of the full table of residualized or corrected cell means. The procedure of collapsing (i.e., averaging) cell means over rows performs a mathematical operation that removes the main effect due to columns and removes the interaction of rows and columns. For example, the main effect of performance, as tested by the omnibus F found in Table 19.2, is interpreted appropriately by referring to the marginal means $\bar{X}_{poor}=27$, $\bar{X}_{average}=39$, $\bar{X}_{good}=45$ appearing in Table 19.1. Table 19.7 displays what these shorthand values actually represent. Note that the corrected cell means in Table 19.7 are devoid of the main effect of teacher expectation as well as the interaction effect.

The display and treatment of all effects within ANOVA, including those associated with focused hypothesis testing, are essentially identical. For our hypothetical study, a new table of residualized means needs to be constructed to display the two effects tested by the theoretical model employed, in this case the linear trend in pupil performance and the Expectancy Confirmation effect. Table 19.8 displays the residualized means, with and without the grand mean, associated with these two effects.

The values outside of the parentheses contain the grand mean, whereas the values inside the parentheses have the grand mean removed. Notice that the raw cell means are recovered completely by adding the residualized effects in parentheses to the grand mean, further evidence that the total between-cell variance has been accounted for by these two

Table 19.8. *Corrected cell means displaying the two focused theoretical effects tested*

Pupil performance	Expected performance			Linear effect
	Low	Medium	High	
Poor	45 (+8)	36 (−1)	27 (−10)	27 (−9)
Average	36 (−1)	45 (+8)	36 (−1)	36 (0)
Good	27 (−10)	36 (−1)	45 (+8)	45 (+9)
Grand mean				37 (0)

Note: The Expectancy Confirmation effect is displayed within the nine experimental cells. The linear effect of performance is displayed in the margin. The values in parentheses have had the grand mean removed.

effects (i.e., the pattern of cell means observed exactly matches the theoretical model).

The utility of hard-wired main effects and interactions. The preceding discussion should lead one to reexamine their loyalty to, and faith in, the factorial design model. The experimental design for the study we have discussed in this chapter seemed straightforward: a 3×3 fully crossed and balanced factorial design with two 2-*df* main effects and one 4-*df* interaction term. It should be obvious to the reader at this point that none of these effects were theoretically relevant or potentially very informative. Therefore, the calculation and presentation of these effects should never have been the main objective of the data analysis because their outcomes were only indirectly related to the effects of interest.

In other words, there is nothing sacred in the factorial design when it comes to hypothesis testing. The factorial design has a number of built-in, or hard-wired, tests of significance that are faithful to the experimental design employed, but these might be irrelevant to the theoretical models an investigator wishes to test. Researchers may assume that a 3×3 factorial design experiment tests only three effects (i.e., two main effects and one interaction effect), but in reality, this design is capable of testing hundreds of definable effects and theoretical models. It is the sole responsibility of the researcher to define the theoretical model under consideration and to *create* within the ANOVA the appropriate focused test with which it can be examined. In short, in order to maximize the theoretical utility of a particular ANOVA, a researcher must question whether or not a main effect and interaction need be tested and interpreted in the first place.

Reporting results

The point of publishing. The whole point of publishing is to disseminate knowledge or ideas to others so as to increase the cumulative process of science. It is far more efficient to read about a discovery or proof than it is to discover or prove. Therefore, when publishing the results of an empirical investigation, two principles should be followed. First, data should be reported in sufficient detail to justify the conclusions logically (American Psychological Association, 1983, p. 27). This was essentially the motivation behind the discussion of focused hypothesis testing and interaction effects presented earlier. And second, the degree of justification is quantifiable, and this quantity should be communicated via two distinct but related dimensions: probability and size.

The statistical validity of a theoretical conclusion is quantified by its associated Type I error rate (i.e., the probability that one's conclusion, which is often the rejection of the null hypothesis, is false). The determination of this Type I error rate is the primary objective of all significant tests (e.g., t, F, chi square, Mann-Whitney U). Important as this probability is, the Type I error rate communicates nothing that would indicate the *impact, explanatory power,* or scientific *utility* that a particular conclusion might have. Within the social sciences, the mere existence of an effect or phenomenon becomes important only when its *size* is large enough to make it consequential or noteworthy.

For example, the social significance and value of knowing that teachers' expectations affect students' subsequent gains in IQ would be reduced to trivia if the actual effect was less than 1/1,000th of a standard deviation. The effect just wouldn't make any difference! In the reporting and interpretation of results, therefore, researchers must be as concerned with the size of an effect as they are with the probability of its existence because the scientific value of knowing only one of these quantities is virtually nil without knowledge of the other.

Effect sizes in ANOVA. Within ANOVA F, the most generally useful effect-size estimate is probably eta (Rosenthal & Rosnow, 1991). It is defined as

$$\text{eta} = \sqrt{\left| \frac{SS \text{ between}}{SS \text{ between} + SS \text{ within}} \right.}$$

and can be computed directly from F:

$$\text{eta} = \sqrt{\left| \frac{F(df \text{ between})}{F(df \text{ between}) + df \text{ within}} \right.}$$

Eta^2 is interpreted as a proportion of variance accounted for. When F is based on only a single df, then eta and eta^2 are the conceptual and mathematical equivalents of r and r^2 and can be interpreted as indices of linear relationships (Rosenthal & Rosnow, 1991).

For example, the effect size associated with the Expectancy Confirmation effect observed in our hypothetical study is

$$\text{eta} = r = \sqrt{\frac{(4.85)1}{(4.85)1 + 90}} = .23$$

This correlation of $r = .23$ actually exists within the data set and refers to the association between teachers' attitudes and the λ weight associated with a particular experimental manipulation, as provided by the Expectancy Confirmation hypothesis. In other words, the correlation between the actual data and the λ weights displayed in Table 19.5 is what the formula for eta and r calculates given the single df significance test (i.e., F) for that hypothesis.

Effect sizes for all of the effects computed for this hypothetical study can be found in the summary tables reported in Tables 19.2 and 19.6. Again, note that the effect sizes reported in Table 19.6 are more informative than those reported in Table 19.2 because they are indices of linear relationships. The etas reported in Table 19.2 are effect size magnitudes with no reference point or direction. One knows from an eta the extent to which the data are affected by given effect, but an eta indicates nothing about exactly *how* the data are affected.

Another important reason to calculate and report effect sizes is that they are more stable and generalizable estimates of effects than are significance tests. Unlike significance tests, effect sizes are not affected by fluctuations in sample size. For example, if the same correlation between the raw data and the predicted values generated by the Expectancy Confirmation hypothesis displayed in Table 19.5 replicated exactly in another study with half as many subjects, the significance test in the replication study would fail to reach significance at the $p < .05$ level. Under these circumstances, a researcher obsessed with F tests may conclude that the data failed to replicate when in fact the replication was perfect. The results and explanatory power of the theory in both studies under these conditions would be identical (for discussions of effect sizes and significance tests, see Bernieri, 1991; Chow, 1991; Rosnow & Rosenthal, 1989b; Schmidt, 1992).

As demonstrated in other chapters (by Harris and Rubin) involving meta-analysis, it is the effect size and not the significance test that is the preferred medium of information exchange within the social sciences.

Concluding comment

ANOVA, when reflexively performed and incompletely reported, can impede theoretical advances in interpersonal expectation research, as well as in the social sciences in general. However, when theoretically driven and completely performed and reported, ANOVA is a powerful and efficient analytical tool.

Just as the scarecrow in *The Wizard of Oz* discovered that he, in fact, had a brain all along, our hypothetical researcher has discovered that she too had been correct all along.

Note

The ideas presented in this chapter were inspired by the writings and teachings of Bob Rosenthal. I wish to thank Peter Blanck, Bob Rosenthal, and Don Rubin for their comments on an earlier draft of this chapter while assuming full responsibility for any shortcomings that remain in spite of the excellent advice.

References

American Psychological Association (1983). *Publication manual of the American Psychological Association* (3rd ed.). Washington, DC: American Psychological Association.

Bernieri, F. (1991). Rigor is rigor: But rigor is not necessarily science. *Theory and Psychology, 1,* 369–373.

Chow, S. L. (1991). Conceptual rigor versus practical impact. *Theory and Psychology, 1,* 337–360.

Kenny, D. A. (1985). Quantitative methods for social psychology. In G. L. Lindzey & E. Aronson (Eds.), *Handbook of social psychology* (3rd ed.) (pp. 487–508). Hillsdale, NJ: Random House.

Leacock, E. B. (1969). *Teaching and learning in city schools: A comparative study.* New York: Basic Books.

Rosenthal, R. (1974). *On the social psychology of the self-fulfilling prophecy: Further evidence for Pygmalion effects and their mediating mechanisms* (Module 53, pp. 1–28). New York: MSS Modular Publications.

Rosenthal, R. (1984). *Meta-analytic procedures for social research.* Beverly Hills, CA: Sage.

Rosenthal, R. (1985). From unconscious experimenter bias to teacher expectancy effects. In J. B. Dusek, V. C. Hall, & W. J. Meyer (Eds.), *Teacher expectations* (pp. 37–65). Hillsdale, NJ: Erlbaum.

Rosenthal, R., & Jacobson L. (1966). Teachers' expectancies: Determinants of pupils' IQ gains. *Psychological Reports, 19,* 115–118.

Rosenthal, R., & Jacobson L. (1968). *Pygmalion in the classroom.* New York: Holt, Rinehart, and Winston.

Rosenthal, R., & Rosnow, R. L. (1985). *Contrast analysis: Focused comparisons in the analysis of variance.* Cambridge: Cambridge University Press.

Rosenthal, R., & Rosnow, R. L. (1991). *Essentials of behavioral research: Methods and data analysis* (2nd ed.). New York: McGraw-Hill.

Rosnow, R. L., & Rosenthal, R. (1989a). Definition and interpretation of interaction effects. *Psychological Bulletin, 105,* 143–146.

Rosnow, R. L., & Rosenthal, R. (1989b). Statistical procedures and justification of knowledge in psychological science. *American Psychologist, 44,* 1276–1284.

Schmidt, F. L. (1992). What do data really mean?: Research findings, meta-analysis, and cumulative knowledge in psychology. *American Psychologist, 47,* 1173–1181.

Shore, A. L. (1969). Confirmation of expectancy and changes in teachers' evaluations of student behaviors. *Dissertation Abstracts, 30,* 1878–1879.

Snedecor, G. W., & Cochran, W. C. (1980). *Statistical methods* (7th ed.). Ames: Iowa University Press.

Swann, W. B. (1984). Quest for accuracy in person perception: A matter of pragmatics. *Psychological Review, 91,* 457–477.

Swap, W. C. (1977). Interpersonal attraction and repeated exposure to rewarders and punishers. *Personality and Social Psychology Bulletin, 3,* 248–251.

Tukey, J. W. (1977). *Exploratory data analysis.* Reading, MA: Addison-Wesley.

Zajonc, R. B. (1968). Attitudinal effects of mere exposure. *Journal of Personality and Social Psychology, 9,* Monograph Supplement No. 2, part 2.

20. Statistical tools for meta-analysis: From straightforward to esoteric

DONALD B. RUBIN

Introduction

A traditional meta-analysis is an analytical synthesis of the literature on a research topic, which leads to summary judgments about the overall significance and typical sizes of effects reported in that research domain. A more idealized conceptualization of meta-analysis views the objective to be the estimation of an effect-size surface, which gives the expected effect sizes in the research area as a function of scientifically relevant factors. The effect-size surface perspective is more difficult to implement successfully in a data analysis than the literature-synthesis perspective because the effect-size surface can be estimated only by extrapolating a response surface estimated from observed studies to an idealized region of perfect studies.

Simple and direct statistical tools are particularly valuable for straightforward analyses supporting the literature-synthesis perspective. Technically complicated statistical tools that attempt to adjust for selection bias in the published versus unpublished studies in a literature synthesis are not really appropriate because the conceptualization of a population of studies from which existing studies are drawn is scientifically of little relevance. In contrast, the estimands of the effect-size surface perspective are scientifically relevant, and therefore it is appropriate to develop and use whatever tools are needed to draw inferences for these estimands. Continued work is needed on both fronts: straightforward statistical tools that can be used in literature synthesis and appropriate statistical tools for effect-size surface estimation, even if esoteric.

This chapter explains and advances this thesis by reviewing, first, the traditional view of meta-analysis and indicating, by illustration, the continuing need for the development of direct statistical tools for literature synthesis; and, second, by criticizing this perspective as valuable but scientifically limited, and proposing and arguing for the superiority of the effect-size surface perspective. Various parts of this discussion have been presented previously (Rosenthal & Rubin, 1988; Rubin, 1988, 1990, 1992), but I believe that the basic issues are important enough to support recasting, expansion, integration, and further dissemination, especially to the audience of this volume in tribute to Robert Rosenthal, a towering contributor to the field of meta-analysis.

The traditional view of meta-analysis

The term *meta-analysis*, at least as used commonly in the social and medical sciences, refers to an analysis of the final results of studies themselves rather than an analysis of the basic data collected by the studies (e.g., Glass, 1976). That is, the units of analysis in a meta-analysis are a collection of studies with their effect sizes and standard errors rather than of the individuals whose responses comprised the data in the studies. Examples of relatively early meta-analyses include Smith and Glass's seminal (1977) investigation of the efficacy of psychotherapy and Rosenthal and Rubin's (1978) investigation of expectancy effects. In both of these meta-analyses and in many others, studies were stratified by research area and quality, and the authors were conscientious about recovering as many studies as possible. Traditionally, the objective of a meta-analysis is to report average effects, often within strata or weighted by perceived quality, as well as to provide global indications of significance for the existence of the effects. These average effects are the *estimands* (the objects of estimation) in a traditional meta-analysis.

Issues arising due to the units being studies

Because the units of analysis in meta-analyses are the summary analyses from studies rather than raw data, two statistical issues arise. First, sometimes the results are reported simply as p values (significance levels) under a null hypothesis (or, even worse, simply as significant or not). Second, even if summary statistics such as means and variances are available, the specific outcome variables being studied typically change from study to study, even in the same research area.

The first problem can be partially addressed by using techniques designed for the analysis of a random variable with a uniform distribution under the null hypothesis; a standard approach is to first transform

p values to Z statistics and then to proceed with normal-based proce-dures (e.g., Rosenthal & Rubin, 1979). Even though such techniques work in the sense that the answers are valid under the null hypothesis, generally they do not yield effect estimates; in general, there is no fully satisfactory solution when the individual studies do not provide ade-quate summary data. Consequently, because the focus of this chapter is on statistical tools appropriate for meta-analysis, not on the limitations of data summarized from studies, the remainder of this chapter as-sumes access to adequate data from each study – in particular, an effect-size estimate accompanied by its standard error – as well as descriptors of the study such as sample sizes, indicators for whether the study was randomized or not, and so on.

Size-of-effect measures

The second problem, that of different outcome variables in the collec-tion of studies to be addressed by the meta-analysis, cannot be assumed away because it is nearly always present and, at least in the social sciences, is an aspect of the science. For example, in studies of expec-tancy effects, outcomes might include scores on a variety of achieve-ment tests and different attitude scales. A common metric is needed to combine the sizes of the effects in the studies; associated standard errors for the estimated effect sizes on this common metric are also needed for statistical inference.

For outcomes that are to be treated as normally distributed, the num-ber of standard deviations from a null value is a useful and common measure of effect size. For example, in the standard case of two groups, experimental and control, an obvious effect-size measure is the number of standard deviations between the means in the two groups, where there are various choices for how to calculate the standard deviation (e.g., pooled across both groups, the control group alone). Distribution theory for such effect-size estimators appears in many places, for ex-ample, in Hedges (1981). Alternative effect-size measures with two groups include the correlation coefficient and the binomial effect-size display (BESD; Rosenthal & Rubin, 1982), which summarizes the effect as a comparison of success rates in two groups centered at 50%, for example, 67% in the treated group versus 33% in the control group. It may seem surprising, but work is still needed to define effect-size measures.

When there are more than two groups, the use of simple and sensible single degree-of-freedom contrasts needs greater exposure, as the chapter in this volume by Bernieri suggests. In this case, the definition of sensible effect-size summaries may not always be obvious; consider measuring a specific type of deviation from the linear trend (or interaction) across studies with varying numbers of groups and varying levels for those groups. Alternative suggestions can be found in Cohen's (1977) classic text on power analysis and in recent texts focused on meta-analysis such as Cooper (1984); Glass, McGaw, and Smith (1981); Hedges and Olkin (1985); Hunter, Schmidt, and Jackson (1982); Light and Pillemer (1984); Rosenthal (1984); and Wolf (1986).

To illustrate that work may still be needed to define sensible effect-size measures, two recent contributions to the literature will be briefly discussed. Also, to indicate that work may still be needed to obtain useful expressions for standard errors for simple effect-size measures, a third recent contribution will be quickly reviewed.

An effect-size measure for multiple-choice situations

The topic of defining useful measures of effect size is not fully closed even for studies with only one group; for example, consider a collection of ganzfeld experiments for extrasensory perception (ESP). In each study the receiver of an ESP message is supposed to choose which of K pictures (objects) the sender is using; this study is repeated for n trials, with K new pictures at each trial. Under the null hypothesis of no ESP effect, the receiver guesses the correct picture at each trial with probability $1/K$, but if there is a positive effect, the probability of choosing the correct picture at each trial is greater than $1/K$. If all studies used the same number K, the obvious effect-size measure for each study would be the proportion correct, say p, but in fact, different studies use different values of K, typically between 2 and 10.

Different choices have been proposed for effect-size measures in this case, such as arcsin $\sqrt{p}$, but these have been based on considerations that do not seem to have much merit for this problem (e.g., variance stabilization). A new effect-size measure suggested by Rosenthal and Rubin (1989) is

$$\pi = \frac{p(K-1)}{1+p(K-2)},$$

which estimates the proportion correct had only two choices been offered (i.e., if K were 2) under the assumption that if there is an effect, it is additive on the logit scale. In other words, the ESP effect for a subject is assumed to modify the null odds against obtaining a correct response (i.e., $K-1$ to 1) by the same percentage, no matter what K is being used; equivalently, the ratio of a subject's odds of a correct response to the null odds of a correct response are assumed to be the same for all K. The standard error to associate with π is

$$\frac{1}{\sqrt{n}} \frac{\pi(1-\pi)}{\sqrt{p(1-p)}}.$$

The use of π is simple, intuitive, and rather obvious, yet seems to have been proposed only very recently. Once proposed, alternatives can be suggested (Schafer, 1991), although in cases with modest K, they appear to be practically the same as π (Rosenthal & Rubin, 1991).

An effect-size measure for evaluating predictions for categorical outcomes

To indicate that there are presumably many other situations for which appropriate effect sizes may still be needed, consider the following situation from Rubin and Stern (1992). Two distinctly different but equivalently complicated (in terms of the number of parameters) models are being used to predict a categorical ordered outcome variable (e.g., a latent class model and a linear regression model). How good are the models, and which appears to be better?

Let $k=1, \ldots, K$ index the number of distinct values of the predictor variables, where n_k is the number of subjects with that value. Also, let n_{ik} be the number of subjects at the Kth value of the predictor with outcome in the ith category, $i=1, \ldots, I$; the corresponding proportions are $p_{ik}=n_{ik}/n_k$. The null model's prediction for the ith outcome category is the same for all values of the predictor and is given by the marginal distribution of the outcome:

$$p_i = \sum_{k=1}^{K} n_{ik} \bigg/ \sum_{k=1}^{K} n_k = \sum_{k=1}^{K} n_k p_{ik} \bigg/ \sum_{k=1}^{K} n_k.$$

Suppose that the model's predictions are p^*_{ik}; then the corresponding effect size for the model indicating how much of the way it has moved from the null model (p_i) to the perfect model (p_{ik}) is

$$q^* = \frac{\sum_{k=1}^{k} n_k \left[\sum_{i=1}^{I} p_{ik} \ell np_{ik}^* \right] - \sum_{k=1}^{K} n_k \left[\sum_{i=1}^{I} p_{ik} \ell np_i \right]}{\sum_{k=1}^{K} n_k \left[\sum_{i=1}^{I} p_{ik} \ell np_i \right] - \sum_{k=1}^{K} n_k \left[\sum_{i=1}^{I} p_{ik} \ell np_i \right]}.$$

Rubin and Stern (1992) considered two parallel data sets and evaluated the effect size q_* for a latent class model and for a regression model with essentially the same number of parameters. The results gave values of q_* for the regression and latent class models of 23% and 39%, respectively, for the first data set and 28% and 42%, respectively, for the second data set. These results clearly suggest the superiority of the latent class model, which is far more attractive theoretically, and also indicates the variability of the effect sizes across replications. The effect-size measure q^* is essentially the same as an index proposed by Haberman (1982) and is clearly superior to the naive hit-rate index, based on the proportion of correct predictions, as discussed by Rubin and Stern (1992).

Simple standard error expressions for effect-size

In some cases, an effect-size measure can be useful without an associated standard error, but more typically, standard errors are needed to calibrate results. Even relatively standard and simple effect sizes can have cumbersome formulas for standard errors that inhibit their use. For example, when comparing two or more correlations based on the same sample, the standard error (even in large samples) involves unpleasant matrix expressions with many nuisance parameters. Meng, Rosenthal, and Rubin (1992), however, show that this standard error can be relatively easily approximated. In particular, suppose that Z_{r_1} and Z_{r_2} are the Fisher Z values for correlations r_1 and r_2 between two predictors and the same outcome, where the two predictors have correlation r_x. Then the standard error for $Z_{r_1} - Z_{r_2}$ is well approximated by

$$\sqrt{\frac{2(1-r_x)h}{N-3}}$$

where

$$h = 1 + \frac{\bar{r^2}}{1 - \bar{r^2}} \left[1 - \frac{1 - r_x}{2(1 - \bar{r^2})} \right];$$

$\bar{r^2}$ is the average squared r_i^2, $\frac{1}{2}(r_1^2 + r_2^2)$. Meng et al. (1992) show how extensions of this expression can also be used for handling sets of correlations. An even simpler expression, developed by Raghunathan, Rosenthal, and Rubin (1992), has broader applicability and appears to work nearly as well in many practical cases.

Statistical analysis of results treating the collected studies as a sample from a target population of studies

Once effect-size measures and associated standard errors have been defined for each study, the traditional view of meta-analysis is that the task is to analyze the collection of studies at hand as a sample from a target population of studies in order to estimate the average effect, possibly within strata or weighted, in that population. Assuming that the sample is representative of the population, the statistical effort needed here is quite direct, the main subtleties arising from concerns about the effects of small sample sizes on the nonnull distributions of effect sizes (e.g., dealing with noncentral t distributions rather than normals). The statistical research work involved in implementing this approach, although often useful, is typically really a matter of translating much older established results in mathematical statistics – for instance, those on noncentral t distributions – into the new jargon and describing them carefully to a less statistically sophisticated audience. The recent texts mentioned earlier all tend to accept this perspective, and range from those written for less statistically sophisticated audiences (e.g., Light & Pillemer, 1984) to those designed for more statistically sophisticated ones (e.g., Hedges & Olkin, 1985).

Two conceptual problems immediately arise in this traditional perspective, however. The first is one of sampling bias: The observed collection may not represent fairly all studies done, since there is arguably a tendency for studies with insignificant results not to be published relative to those with significant results. The second problem is, I believe, truly major: What is this target population, and even if we could conceptualize it, why should we care about average effects in it? Work from the literature-synthesis perspective of meta-analysis has addressed the first problem using both straightforward and sophisticated statistical tools, but it has not adequately addressed the second problem.

The file-drawer problem and its extensions

The problem of unretrieved studies in a meta-analysis has been aptly called the *file-drawer problem* by Rosenthal (1979), and he has provided a simple method for calculating the number n of null-result studies that need to be buried in file drawers before the results of the current meta-analysis of k studies, when coupled with these unretrieved studies, suggest no effect at the α level. Specifically, the number of such studies is

$$n = \left(\frac{k}{z_\alpha}\right)[k\bar{z}^2 - z_\alpha^2],$$

where z_α is the α percent point of the normal ($z_{.05} = 1.645$) and $\bar{z}$ is the average deviate across the k studies (i.e., $\bar{z} = \sum_1^k z_i$, where $z_i = 1.645$ if the p value from study i is .05). This file-drawer answer is a simple and direct statistical tool, which is useful in assessing a literature synthesis.

The problem of unobserved studies, however, can be viewed as a special case of missing data for which there now exists a vast arsenal of special statistical tools (e.g., see Little & Rubin, 1987), much of it centered on the *EM* algorithm (Dempster, Laird, & Rubin, 1977) and some on multiple imputation for nonresponse in surveys (Rubin, 1987). Newer work on iterative algorithms supplements *EM* techniques (*SEM* and *ECM*; Meng & Rubin, 1991, 1992), and even more exotic simulation-based tools exist, which can be thought of as combining and extending *EM* and multiple imputation. Rubin (1991) provides an introduction to these newer methods for a psychometrically oriented audience.

There now exist useful descriptions of how to implement some of these more sophisticated techniques (e.g., Hedges, 1984; Iyengar & Greenhouse, 1988), which are nice additions to general statistical methodology. However, when this work is applied to meta-analysis, it involves technically complicated methods, which need a computer to implement, are less transparent to the typical user than simple file-drawer calculations, and are often based on relatively complex and untestable special assumptions. Moreover, I believe that these fancy techniques generally represent no scientific advance over file-drawer calculations for the real issue of an ideal meta-analysis, which I do not believe is an inference for a hypothetical population of studies or even for the population of all studies actually done. That is, the foundations

of the literature-synthesis perspective are not strong enough to legitimately support analyses whose complexity goes beyond simple and
straightforward statistical techniques involving appropriate effect-size
estimates and associated standard errors, supplemented with simple
indications of potential effects of biased retrieval.

A new perspective on meta-analysis

Although I advocate, contribute to, and use the simple techniques
indicated in the previous section, especially the efforts directed at defining useful general measures of effect size with associated standard
errors, I do not subscribe to the view that fancier and fancier statistical
techniques should be used to try to estimate typical effects in some
target population from which existing studies are conceptualized as a
sample. I want to emphasize that I do not object to doing a literature
synthesis, as is done in a straightforward meta-analysis of published
articles, or of articles stratified by characteristics such as published,
unpublished, and so on. What I do object to is going beyond such
descriptive and inferentially relatively vague exercises, supplemented
by simple tools such as file-drawer calculations, to statistical procedures
for hypothetical estimands that are of no scientific relevance but have
the false glow of precision because of the substantial mathematical and
computational efforts behind them. Literature synthesis is fine, but
before scientifically valid statistical inference (e.g., estimation) can take
place, scientifically relevant quantities – estimands – must be defined,
and the population estimands in the traditional view are of limited
scientific interest, at best. The scientifically most interesting estimands
are defined by the hypothetical results of technically perfect studies,
not by the average of results from some population of fallible studies.

The response surface giving expected effect size as a function of scientific factors and design factors

Suppose that a meta-analysis has defined the effect-size measure τ (e.g.,
the number of standard deviations between the treated and control
groups), so that each study in the meta-analysis has an estimated τ, as
well as an associated standard error for this estimate. Also associated
with each study (each effect size) is a set of factors X of true scientific
interest (e.g., gender and age of subjects, classroom sizes) and a set of
design variables Z of incidental interest (e.g., sample sizes, types of

controls used, standard errors, randomized vs. nonrandomized indicators, laboratory indicators). The distinction between scientific factors X and design factors Z is not always precise, but the basic point is that X defines characteristics of scientific interest that can affect the effect size τ, whereas Z defines characteristics of studies that are more related to design compromises due to cost, experience, or skill considerations.

The size of effect τ can vary as a function of both X and Z, and of other variables as well. Nevertheless, we can conceptualize a response surface $f(X,Z)$ that gives the expected effect size as a function of X,Z,

$$E(\tau|X,Z) = f(X,Z),$$

which is a scalar function of both multivariate X and multivariate Z and so is a highly multidimensional surface.

The current collection of studies provides data but does not define the estimand

The current collection of studies is represented by particular choices of (X,Z) values. Good studies have statistically better values of Z (e.g., better control, larger sample sizes), and poorer studies have statistically worse values of Z. There may even be studies that are so poor that most meta-analysts might not want to call them studies (e.g., introspective studies), but in this perspective their failings can be represented using Z values. The literature-synthesis perspective attempts to retrieve all of these studies with their (X,Z) values and to summarize the typical effect size, perhaps stratified or weighted by (X,Z) characteristics. The fancier statistical techniques try to adjust such summaries for studies that have not been retrieved, using assumptions about differences between the (X,Z) values for retrieved and unretrieved studies or assumptions about the distribution of effect sizes τ in the population of all studies.

Of critical importance is that certain regions of this response surface are of no intrinsic scientific interest; that is, the function $f(X,Z)$ is of no scientific interest for values of Z that are associated with very poorly controlled studies. In fact, none of the studies itself is of direct scientific interest; the studies are of interest only as they tell us about the relationship of τ to X.

The scientific estimand is the effect-size surface

The true relationship of effect size τ to scientific factors X is what we would observe in infinitely large, perfectly controlled studies, and the reason for performing fallible studies and for summarizing their results as an ensemble is to learn about this scientific relationship. Specifically, let Z_0 be the values of the design factors representing the perfect study. Then what we really want to estimate is

$$E(\tau|X,Z=Z_0)=f(X,Z_0)$$

or in a more compact notation,

$$E(\tau|X,Z=Z_0)=f_0(X).$$

The *effect-size surface* $f_0(X)$ gives the expected effect as a function of scientific factors X, and so it too is a multivariate surface, but it is one that we can estimate only through extrapolation. That is, all studies we see have finite sample sizes and imperfect control, and so to estimate $f_0(X)$, we must first estimate $f(X,Z)$ and then extrapolate it to $Z=Z_0$.

As with any extrapolation, we will find greater uncertainty of estimation of the function $f(X,Z)$ at the extreme value $Z=Z_0$ than at commonly occurring values of Z. Thus the effect-size surface $f_0(X)$ may be poorly estimated, especially if better studies do not obtain consistent answers, but then that will be the honest answer. In contrast, we may find that as the studies improve, their estimated effects tend to stabilize with few important interactions, and then we may be able to estimate with some confidence the estimands of true scientific interest. In this regard, note the response to Rubin's (1988) comment on Begg and Berlin (1988, p. 462): "a casual glance at the data gives the impression that increased sample size leads inexorably to a mean effect size of zero, a rather pessimistic commentary on the current state of cancer research."

Averaging the effect-size surface

The effect-size surface is not a simple average effect but rather a function $f_0(X)$ giving the expected effect size as a function of all of the scientific factors X. Nevertheless, in many cases it will be desirable to obtain less conditional answers, that is, answers that do not condition on all of X. For example, if it is of interest to estimate the average effect size for a group such as female students attending college, the answer is obtained by averaging $f_0(X)$ over the conditional distribution of all X factors other than gender and college attendance status, with these fixed at "female, attending college."

An average estimand like this is of scientific interest in that its value is not affected by design factors Z, and so is not affected by the particular choice of studies being analyzed. The *estimate* of the estimand will, of course, be affected by the fallible studies we have, but the estimand itself is of direct scientific interest and free of dependence on Z.

The statistical effort needed to estimate the effect-size surface

Building a response surface model for $f(X,Z)$ is a standard, though not necessarily easy, statistical task (e.g., see Box, Hunter, & Hunter, 1981). Usually such models are used for interpolation rather than extrapolation, however, so some special features arise in our context. In particular, the functional form being used for $f(X,Z)$ must be such that letting Z tend to Z_0 leads to sensible results, which means, for instance, that parameterization in terms of inverse sample size makes more sense than parameterization in terms of sample size. Generally, nonlinear relationships with their implied asymptotes at Z_0 will be of continual concern, as will be interactions among (X,Z) factors and the need to consider them in the modeling. Another feature of this problem not always present in response surface models concerns the residual sampling variability of estimated effects from studies, which will most likely vary substantially with Z; for example, smaller, less well-blocked studies will presumably have larger variabilities about $f(X,Z)$, and as Z tends to Z_0, variability in estimated effect sizes from individual studies should decrease. Finally, because of the high dimensionality of the response surface and the possibility of interactions and curvilinear relationships, modern hierarchical and hyperparameter models will no doubt be highly useful, if not absolutely necessary (e.g., see Efron & Morris, 1977, and Rubin, 1989, for two accessible references).

A relatively massive statistical effort in the context of real examples will be needed to develop appropriate statistical tools, and the resulting tools might be rather complex. But because the estimands of the effect-size surface are of scientific interest, the complexity of the tools can be justified.

Comparing the literature-synthesis and effect-size surface perspectives

There are many points of comparison between the literature-synthesis and effect-size surface perspectives to meta-analysis, all of which I believe favor the effect-size surface approach. Some of these points of comparison are now listed, labeled by the positive attribute for the effect-size surface perspective.

There exists a precise conceptual definition of the estimand. The estimand of the meta-analysis is scientifically precise in the effect-size surface formulation but is often conceptually fuzzy in the literature synthesis perspective. What is the population of studies that is to be summarized? Does it include all studies, even very poor ones? Should studies be weighted by quality, and if so, how?

The estimand does not vary with attempts to measure it. In the effect-size surface formulation, the estimand remains the same as more and more studies are done, since it is the conditional distribution of effect size given scientific factors. In contrast, even accepting some definition for the population of studies, the estimand in the literature-synthesis approach, being an average of the response surface over the idiosyncratic choices of scientific and design factors used by current investigators, depends on these choices of X and Z.

Average effect sizes are of scientific interest. In the effect-size surface formulation, averaging may be of interest, but it is over specific distributional choices for the scientific factors alone, with the design factors Z set to the ideal study. Consequently, estimands that are average effects are defined without reference to the design choices made by current and past investigators. Average effects estimated from the literature-synthesis perspective can be deceptive. For example, suppose that in a particular domain of study, better-designed investigations use college students, whereas inferior ones use adults, and better studies show smaller effects. Then an analysis from the literature synthesis perspective might falsely conclude that effect sizes are larger for adults than for college students.

Representativeness of studies in the meta-analysis is not crucial. In the literature-synthesis approach, the sampling representativeness of the studies from the target population is critical for valid inference, and if it is in doubt, special missing-data procedures must be employed for full statistical inference. In the effect-size surface formulation, the only representativeness that is required is conditionally given (X,Z), so that bias can only arise due to selection or discarding of studies using some component of an unobserved factor that is independent of (X,Z) but is related to effect size. Lack of representatives of this type is probably of little concern, especially since, even if plausible, it is more likely for the more poorly controlled, difficult-to-retrieve studies, which will contribute relatively little to the estimation of the effect-size surface.

Any and all studies can be included. In the literature-synthesis approach, the issue of which studies to include in the meta-analysis is important, for it defines the estimand and creates possible biases because of non-representativeness of the sample. In the effect-size surface approach, all studies should be included, since they all help to estimate the response surface; proper modeling will automatically down-weight poorer studies when extrapolating to obtain the effect-size surface.

Nonindependence of studies is not crucial. Nonindependence of studies, due to multiple outcomes in one inclusive study or overlaps in members of investigative teams, can play a major role in literature synthesis, since these factors help to define the structure of the population of studies. But in the effect-size surface approach, one simply includes indicators in Z showing relationships among estimated effect sizes such as multiple outcomes, because the required independence is simply conditional independence given (X,Z) and is used in the estimation, but not to define the estimands.

New studies should be designed to increase our knowledge of the effect-size surface. The effect-size surface approach suggests a different focus when thinking about new studies, either in the sense of not yet collected for the meta-analysis or not yet conducted. For either, the effect-size surface perspective suggests that new studies should be chosen by experimental design considerations to increase maximally the precision of estimation of the effect-size surface $f_0(X)$. In contrast, the literature-synthesis perspective suggests that new studies should be added to make the current collection of studies more representative of the target population of studies, so that if the current meta-analysis focused on too many well-done studies, perhaps the supplemented meta-analysis should try to gather additional poorly done studies; clearly, this is a somewhat strange objective, plausible under the literature-synthesis approach but incorrect under the effect-size surface approach. In fact, if the target population for the meta-analysis is simply the existing collection of current studies, the literature-synthesis approach offers no guidance whatsoever on what kinds of studies to do next.

The effect-size surface estimand provides policy-relevant information. In policy-relevant contexts, the objective of a meta-analysis is typically to help make better decisions regarding policies – treatments – to be implemented. The implicit estimand is the average effect size for the distribution of X anticipated to exist in the population of individuals to be affected by the new policy. That is, the policy-relevant estimands describe what is expected to happen if the policies are implemented, and these are the effect-size surface estimands and not the literature-synthesis estimands.

Conclusion and the role of statistical techniques

I proposed the effect-size surface perspective at a presentation in Hedgesville, West Virginia, in 1987 (Rubin, 1990) as a device to stimulate discussion by disagreeing with the general flow of the evolving statistical technology for meta-analysis, which at that time seemed to me too uniform in some ways, yet lacking coherence. Despite its relatively ornery etiology, I believe that the new perspective brings a conceptual clarity that is extremely rewarding, and that it is far more cogent and lucid than the literature-synthesis approach.

It appears that some established researchers in meta-analysis agree with this view. Bob Rosenthal and I included it in one of our discussions (Rosenthal & Rubin, 1988). Also, Gene Glass (1991, p. 1141), when reviewing the Hedgesville Conference book for a statistical audience, wrote:

> But the chapter that truly speaks to the future of MA [meta-analysis] and not to its distant and recent past, is the chapter by Donald B. Rubin entitled "A New Perspective." . . . Platonism aside, his is an eminently sensible, indeed altogether wholesome, conceptualization of what research synthesis should be.

In addition, recently it was considered an appropriate perspective for some technical work at the European Institute of Business Administration in France (Vanhonacker & Price, 1992). Moreover, the new perspective seems to have been influential in helping formulate advice from the U.S. General Accounting Office on evaluating medical effectiveness research (U.S. General Accounting Office, 1992).

Nevertheless, others, including some experienced researchers in meta-analysis, have eschewed the effect-size surface perspective despite being exposed to it; for example, it remained recondite in a recent organized collection of articles on meta-analysis (Dean & Begg, 1992; Hedges, 1992; Mosteller & Chalmers, 1992; Olkin, 1992). This situation indicates a disparate variety of views on the importance of the new perspective, and justifies further proselytizing by those of us who feel it is useful.

I hope that many of you reading these chapters in tribute to Bob Rosenthal find the new perspective intellectually appealing, and further hope that, even if you do not attempt an active data analysis from the effect-size surface perspective, you find its conceptualization helpful both for evaluating meta-analyses and for judging when to use straightforward statistical tools and when to use sophisticated ones.

Note

I wish to thank the National Science Foundation for partial support for the preparation of this manuscript through grants SES 88-05433 and SES 92-07456.

References

Begg, C. B., & Berlin, J. A. (1988). Publication bias: A problem in interpreting medical data. *Journal of the Royal Statistical Society, Series A, 158,* 419–463.

Box, G. E. P., Hunter, W. G., & Hunter, J. S. (1981). *Statistics for experimenters: An introduction to design, data analysis, and model building.* New York: Wiley.

Cohen, J. (1977). *Statistical power analysis for the behavioral sciences.* Orlando, FL: Academic Press.

Cooper, H. M. (1984). *The integrative research review: A systematic approach.* Beverly Hills, CA: Sage.

Dean, K. B., & Begg, C. B. (1992). An approach for assessing publication bias prior to performing a meta-analysis. *Statistical Science, 7,* 237–245.

Dempster, A. P., Laird, N., & Rubin, D. B. (1977). Maximum likelihood estimation from incomplete data via the EM algorithm. *Journal of the Royal Statistical Society, Series B, 39,* 1–38.

Efron, B., & Morris, C. (1977). Stein's paradox in statistics. *Scientific American, 236,* 119–127.

Glass, G. V. (1976). Primary, secondary, and meta-analysis of research. *Educational Researcher 5,* 3–8.

Glass, G. V. (1991). Book review of *The Future of Meta-Analysis. Journal of the American Statistical Association, 86,* 1141–1142.

Glass, G. V., McGaw, B., & Smith, M. L. (1981). *Meta-analysis in social research.* Beverly Hill, CA: Sage.

Haberman, S. J. (1982). Analysis of dispersion of multivariate responses. *Journal of the American Statistical Association, 77,* 568–580.

Hedges, L. V. (1981). Distribution theory for Glass's estimator of effect size and related estimators. *Journal of Educational Statistics, 6,* 107–119.

Hedges, L. V. (1984). Estimation of effect size under nonrandom sampling: The effects of censoring studies yielding statistically insignificant mean differences. *Journal of Educational Statistics, 9,* 61–85.

Hedges, L. V. (1992). Modeling publication selection effects in meta-analysis. *Statistical Science, 7,* 246–255.

Hedges, L. V., & Olkin, I. (1985). *Statistical methods for meta-analysis.* Orlando, FL: Academic Press.

Hunter, J. E., Schmidt, F. L., & Jackson, G. B. (1982). *Meta-analysis: Cumulating research findings across studies.* Beverly Hills, CA: Sage.

Iyengar, S., & Greenhouse, J. B. (1988). Selection models and the file-drawer problem. *Statistical Science, 3,* 109–155.

Light, R. J., & Pillemer, D. B. (1984). *Summing up: The science of reviewing research.* Cambridge, MA: Harvard University Press.

Little, R. J. A., & Rubin, D. B. (1987). *Statistical analysis with missing data.* New York: Wiley.

Meng, X. L., Rosenthal, R., & Rubin, D. B. (1992). Comparing correlated correlation coefficients. *Psychological Bulletin, 111,* 172–175.

Meng, X. L., & Rubin, D. B. (1991). Using EM to obtain asymptotic variance-covariance matrices: The SEM algorithm. *Journal of the American Statistical Association, 86,* 899–909.

Meng, X. L., & Rubin, D. B. (1992). Recent extensions to the EM algorithm. In J. M. Bernardo, J. O. Berger, A. P. Dawid, & A. F. M. Smith (Eds.), *Bayesian Statistics IV* (pp. 307–320). Oxford: Oxford University Press.

Mosteller, F., & Chalmers, T. C. (1992). Some progress and problems in meta-analysis of clinical trials. *Statistical Science, 7,* 227–236.

Olkin, I. (1992). Meta-analysis: Methods for combining independent studies. *Statistical Science, 7,* 226.

Raghunathan, T. E., Rosenthal, R., & Rubin, D. B. (1992). Simple and accurate methods for comparing cross-lagged and related correlations. Unpublished manuscript, Harvard University.

Rosenthal, R. (1979). The "file drawer problem" and tolerance for null results. *Psychological Bulletin, 86,* 638–641.

Rosenthal, R. (1984). *Meta-analytic procedures for social research.* Beverly Hills, CA: Sage.

Rosenthal, R., & Rubin, D. B. (1978). Interpersonal expectancy effects: The first 345 studies. *The Behavioral and Brain Sciences, 3,* 377–386.

Rosenthal, R., & Rubin, D. B. (1979). Comparing significance levels of independent studies. *Psychological Bulletin, 86,* 1165–1168.

Rosenthal, R., & Rubin, D. B. (1982). A simple, general purpose display of magnitude of experimental effect. *Journal of Educational Psychology, 74,* 166–169.

Rosenthal, R., & Rubin, D. B. (1988). Assumptions and procedures in the file drawer problem. *Statistical Science, 3,* 120–125.

Rosenthal, R., & Rubin, D. B. (1989). Effect-size estimation for one-sample multiple-choice-type data: Design, analysis, and meta-analysis. *Psychological Bulletin, 106,* 332–337.

Rosenthal, R., & Rubin, D. B. (1991). Further issues in effect size estimation for one-sample multiple-choice-type data. *Psychological Bulletin, 109,* 351–352.

Rubin, D. B. (1987). *Multiple imputation for nonresponse in sample surveys.* New York: Wiley.

Rubin, D. B. (1988). Discussion of Begg and Berlin (1988). *Journal of the Royal Statistical Society Series A, 157,* 457–458.

Rubin, D. B. (1989). Some applications of multilevel models to educational data. In R. D. Bock (Ed.), *Multilevel analysis of educational data* (pp. 1–17). New York: Academic Press.

Rubin, D. B. (1990). A new perspective on meta-analysis. In K. W. Wachter & M. L. Straf (Eds.), *The future of meta-analysis* (pp. 155–165). New York: Russell Sage.

Rubin, D. B. (1992). Meta-analysis: Literature-synthesis or effect-size surface estimation? *Journal of Educational Statistics, 17,* 363–374.

Rubin, D. B., & Stern, H. (1992). An effect-size measure for discrete data. Unpublished manuscript, Harvard University.

Schafer, J. P. (1991). Comment on "Effect-size estimation for one-sample multiple-choice-type data: Design, analysis and meta-analysis." *Psychological Bulletin, 109,* 348–350.

Smith, M. L., & Glass, G. V. (1977). Meta-analysis of psychotherapy outcome studies. *American Psychologist, 32,* 752–760.

U.S. General Accounting Office (1992). *Cross design synthesis: A new strategy for medical effectiveness research*. (GAO/PEMD-92-18). Washington, DC: U.S. General Accounting Office.

Vanhonacker, W. R., & Price, L. J. (1992). Using meta-analysis results in Bayesian updating: The empty-cell problem. *Journal of Business and Economic Statistics, 10,* 427–435.

Wolf, F. M. (1986). *Meta-analysis: Quantitative methods for research synthesis*. Beverly Hills, CA: Sage.

21. The volunteer problem revisited

RALPH L. ROSNOW

This chapter is a retrospective look at an early aspect of Bob Rosenthal's work and its implications for present-day research. The theme of this particular work was the characteristics of subjects who volunteer for research participation and the effects associated with their perception of the experimenter's expectations. For a number of years, Bob and I collaborated in research and reviews on this topic. Our initial aim was to discover in what ways volunteers were not representative of the population under investigation. We also sought to discover whether subjects who volunteered were more likely to acquiesce to cues they perceived as reflecting the experimenter's expectancies. Our investigation of these problems began in the 1960s (e.g., Rosenthal, 1965; Rosnow & Rosenthal, 1966) and culminated in the following decade with several syntheses (e.g., Rosnow & Rosenthal, 1976), including our monograph entitled *The Volunteer Subject* (Rosenthal & Rosnow, 1975).

I begin by focusing on the significance of the topic. I then summarize what we learned about the characteristics of volunteer subjects and turn to a sample of studies (by ourselves and others) in order to show the way in which volunteer status affected a variety of experimental outcomes. Next, I summarize our recommendations for lessening volunteer bias by increasing subject participation. In reviewing the characteristics of volunteers and the factors that stimulate participation, I also mention the degree of confidence that we believed was warranted by each set of conclusions. Finally, I allude to the delicate balance that exists between artifacts and ethics, a topic that has more recently occupied our attention (Rosenthal & Rosnow, 1984b, 1991; Rosnow, 1990; Suls & Rosnow, 1981).

Why study the volunteer subject?

One of our interests when we began this work was to develop a clearer understanding of the nature of subject and experimenter artifacts that might be operating in the data collection situation. Referring to the experimenter–subject interaction specifically, Bob has wisely stated, "We can no more hope to acquire accurate information for our disciplines without an understanding of the data collection situation than astronomers and zoologists could hope to acquire accurate information for their disciplines without their understanding the effects of their telescopes and microscopes" (Rosenthal, 1977, pp. 253–254). The idea of an *artifact,* as defined in this work, refers generally to research findings resulting from factors other than the one intended by the investigator (e.g., Rosenthal & Rosnow, 1969a; 1984a; 1991; Rosnow, 1971, 1977). However, the term *artifact* does not refer simply to serendipitous findings, but also to scientific observations resulting from unsuspected or unrecognized factors that might jeopardize the tenability of the investigator's conclusions about what went on in the study.

For example, inferring broad conclusions from limited subject samples (such as volunteer subjects) might be conceptualized as a threat to external validity. Actually, this problem had been of concern to leading mathematical statisticians and social scientists long before it attracted our attention. They had devoted considerable effort to documenting the effects of *nonresponse bias* on the accuracy of estimates of various population values (e.g., Cochran, 1963; Cochran, Mosteller, & Tukey, 1953; Deming, 1944; Hansen & Hurwitz, 1946). Table 21.1 illustrates this type of artifact in quantitative terms; the basic analysis was first presented by William G. Cochran (1963).

Three waves of questionnaires were mailed out to fruit growers, and the number of respondents and nonrespondents to each wave was recorded. One of the questions dealt with the number of fruit trees owned, and data were available for the entire population of growers for just this question. Because of this fortunate circumstance, it was possible to compute the amount of bias attributable to nonresponse (or nonvolunteering) present after each wave of questionnaires. The top portion of Table 21.1 presents the basic data; the bottom portion gives the cumulative results and computes the amount of bias. Turning to the cumulative results, the first row indicates the mean number of trees owned by the average respondent ($\bar{X}$iYR) and the next row reports

Table 21.1. *Example of bias in survey sampling*

	First wave	Second wave	Third wave	Non-respon-dents	Total population
Basic data					
Number of respondents	300	543	434	1,839	3,116
Percent of population	10	17	14	59	100
Mean trees per respondent	456	382	340	290	329
Cumulative data					
Mean trees per respondent $(\bar{X}_R)$	456	408	385		
Mean trees per nonrespondent $(\bar{X}_{NR})$	315	300	290		
$D = \bar{X}_R - \bar{X}_{NR}$	141	108	95		
Percent of nonrespondents (P)	90	73	59		
Bias $= D \times P$	127	79	56		

Source: William G. Cochran, *Sampling Techniques* (3rd ed.), copyright © by John Wiley & Sons, Inc., 1977, page 360, reproduced by permission of John Wiley & Sons, Inc.

similar information for the nonrespondents $(\bar{X}_{NR})$. The difference between these two values within each wave of questionnaires is denoted as D in the next row, below which is shown the percentage of nonrespondents (P). Multiplying $D \times P$ gives the amount of bias remaining after each wave of questionnaires.

The results in the bottom row – which are fairly typical of studies of this kind – show that increasing the effort to recruit the nonvolunteer reduces bias in the sample estimates. In most circumstances of survey research, however, even though the investigators can compute the percentage of nonrespondents (P) and the statistic of interest for the respondents $(\bar{X}_R)$, they cannot usually compute the statistic of interest for those who do not respond $(\bar{X}_{NR})$. In other words, survey researchers are often in a position to suspect bias, but they may be unable to give an estimate of its magnitude. Cochran, and later others (including Bob), provided advice on how to minimize bias, given the greater cost of trying to recruit a second- or third-wave respondent compared to the cost of recruiting a first-wave respondent.

A second interest of ours grew out of Martin Orne's influential work in the social psychology of the psychological experiment. In a classic paper (Orne, 1962), he described some fascinating findings showing that many college students were more than willing to cooperate in psychology experiments. At one point in his hypnosis research, he had tried to devise a set of dull, meaningless tasks that nonhypnotized persons would either refuse to do or would try for only a short time. One task called for each subject to add thousands of rows of two-digit numbers. Five and a half hours after the subjects began, the experimenter gave up. When the subjects were told to tear each worksheet into a minimum of 32 pieces before going on to the next, they *still* persisted.

Orne believed the subjects were so compliant because they attributed meaning to a meaningless chore. Perhaps they thought that no matter how trivial and inane the task was made to seem, the experimenter had an important scientific purpose that justified their work. Feeling that they had a stake in the outcome of the study, the students may have reasoned that they were making a useful contribution to science by going along with what they perceived to be the experimenter's hypothesis. This motive, Orne believed, was not uncommon among research subjects. The typical participant, he argued, is an active, aware individual who is likely to be quite interested in what he or she sees as the experimenter's expectancy.

Characterizing the typical participants in psychological experiments as *good subjects*, Orne maintained that such subjects will try to comply with what they see as the experimenter's desires or expectations. The good subject's creed, according to this view, might be a paraphrase of the old song about Lola – "Whatever experimenters want, experimenters get" (Rosnow, 1970). Presumably the subjects evaluate interpersonal cues in the context of the instructions, the setting, rumors about the purpose of the experiment (see Rosnow, 1991), and their impressions of the experimenter. As a consequence, the good subject's ideas are a mixture of various hints in the experimental procedure. Orne called such hints the *demand characteristics* of the experimental situation – which he derived from Kurt Lewin's concept of *Aufforderungscharakter* (Orne, 1970). Of interest to us was both the mechanism by which the processing of demand cues might be operating (see Rosnow & Aiken, 1973; Rosnow & Davis, 1977) and the fact that Orne spoke of using only *volunteer* subjects in his studies.

A third reason for our interest developed as a consequence of new federal and professional directives that called for the use of informed subjects. There was an unprecedented amount of soul searching by psychologists and others, with the result that ethical questions of humans' rights to privacy and to informed consent became more salient than ever before (Rosnow, 1981). It seemed that the psychological science of the future could, because of both internally and externally imposed constraints, have less control than ever before over the kinds of human subjects who were used in research. One possible outcome was that the psychological science of the future might be based upon propositions whose tenability would come only from volunteer subjects who had been made fully aware of the responses of interest to the investigator. However, even without this extreme consequence of the ethical crisis, it remained essential that we discover the variables determining what makes an individual a subject and what prevents another individual from becoming one.

Before reviewing this work, it may be of interest to describe the way it was possible to identify the personal characteristics of someone who refuses to participate in research. One widely used technique consisted of recruiting research volunteers from a population for which archival data were available on all potential recruits. It was then a simple matter to correlate the subjects' volunteer or nonvolunteer status with such characteristics. Another illustrative technique involved soliciting volunteers from some sampling frame or list (reminiscent of Cochran's strategy in Table 21.1). After a suitable interval, another request for volunteers was made of those who were identified originally as nonvolunteers, and this process of repeated requesting was then employed several more times. The characteristics of persons responding at each request were plotted as data points, from which a tentative extrapolation was made to the characteristics of those who never responded.

Characteristics of subjects who volunteer

A basic question – also later raised in a critique of our work by Arie Kruglanski (1973; see Rosnow & Rosenthal, 1974) – was whether the willingness to participate in research was sufficiently reliable to expect any stable relationships between volunteering and various personal characteristics. The empirical evidence when we last addressed this question almost 20 years ago (Rosenthal & Rosnow, 1975) was generally consistent with psychometric expectations, with a median test-retest reliability for the act of volunteering of .52 and a range going from .22 to .97. As a standard against which to compare such results, the range of subtest correlations for the Wechsler Adult Intelligence Scale (WAIS) was reported by Wechsler (1958) to go from .08 to 85, with a median of .52. Consistent with our intuitive expectations, the median reliability for studies requesting volunteers for the same task was much higher ($r = .80$) than the corresponding value for studies requesting volunteers for different tasks ($r = .42$); both values were significantly different from zero.

On the assumption that the act of volunteering for research participation was sufficiently stable to expect reliable relationships with various characteristics of persons who are willing or unwilling to say they will be subjects (Table 21.2) illustrates one of Bob's meta-analytic strategies for carving out such relationships. Based on John W. Tukey's stem-and-leaf procedure, the table shows differences in volunteering rates between females and males for physically or psychologically stressful studies (e.g., electric shock, high temperature, sensory deprivation, sex behavior) and for more general types of studies. For each study, the percentage of males volunteering was subtracted from the percentage of females volunteering to give the values shown in this table. For instance, the "5" after the "+3" in the "General Studies" plot indicates that in one study 35% more females than males volunteered for research participation. A negative value tells us that more men than women agreed to participate in the type of study indicated. These graphs clearly reveal that females volunteered more than males for studies in general, whereas males volunteered more than females for studies involving stress.

Bob's detective work in turning up unpublished studies, and his meticulous probing and synthesizing of published and unpublished results, uncovered a number of relationships between the act of volunteering and various personal characteristics of willing and unwilling (or less willing) participants. Several groups of characteristics were discriminable, and within each group the characteristics could be ranked in approximately descending order of the degree of confidence that we can have in the relationship between volunteering and the underscored characteristics. The definition of degree of confidence involved an arbitrary, multiple cutoff procedure in which a conclusion was felt to be more warranted when (1) it was based on a larger number of studies, (2) a larger percentage of the total number of relevant studies significantly favored the conclusion, and (3) a larger percentage of just those studies showing a significant relationship favored the conclusion drawn.

In general, the results made clear that some people volunteer reliably

Table 21.2. *Stem-and-leaf plots of differences in volunteering rates between females and males*

	General studies ($N=51$)	Stress studies ($N=12$)
+3	5	
+3		
+2	5 9	
+2	0 1 1 1 2 2 2 4	
+1	6 6 7 8 8 8	
+1	0 1 1 1 2 2 2 3 3 3 4	
+0	5 5 5 6 8 8 9	9
+0	1 1 1 2 3 4 4	
0	0	
−0	2 4	1 2
−0		6 8
−1	1 3	0 4
−1		6
−2	0 3	0
−2	6	5 8
−3		
−3		
−4		
−4		6
−5		
Maximum	+35	+ 9
Quartile$_3$	+18	− 4
Median	+11	−12
Quartile$_1$	+ 3	−22
Minimum	−26	−46
$Q_3 - Q_1$	+15	+18
σ	11	14
S	12.6	14.6
Mean	+ 9.4	−13.9

Source: Rosenthal and Rosnow (1975, p. 23).

more than others for a variety of tasks, and these reliable differences can be further stabilized when the particular task for which volunteering was requested is specifically considered. To illustrate, the following five characteristics qualified for "maximum confidence" on the basis of at least 19 studies, of which at least 86% of significant studies favored the hypothesized relationship:

1. Volunteers tend to be better educated than nonvolunteers, especially in studies in which personal contact between investigator and respondent is not required.

2. Volunteers tend to have higher social class status than nonvolunteers, especially when social class is defined by respondents' own status rather than by parental status.
3. Volunteers tend to be more intelligent than nonvolunteers when volunteering is for research in general, but not when volunteering is for somewhat less typical types of research (such as hypnosis, sensory isolation, sex research, and small-group and personality research).
4. Volunteers tend to have a higher need for social approval than nonvolunteers.
5. Volunteers tend to be more sociable than nonvolunteers.

To qualify for "considerable confidence," the following six characteristics had to be based on at least 17 studies, of which at least 73% of significant studies favored the hypothesized relationship:

6. Volunteers tend to be more arousal-seeking than nonvolunteers, especially when volunteering is for studies of stress, sensory isolation, and hypnosis.
7. Volunteers tend to be more unconventional than nonvolunteers, especially when volunteering is for studies of sexual behavior.
8. Females are more likely than males to volunteer for research in general, but less likely than males to volunteer for physically and emotionally stressful research (e.g., electric shock, high temperature, sensory deprivation, interviews about sexual behavior).
9. Volunteers tend to be less authoritarian than nonvolunteers.
10. Jews are more likely to volunteer than Protestants, and Protestants are more likely to volunteer than Catholics.
11. Volunteers tend to be less conforming than nonvolunteers when volunteering is for research in general, but not when subjects are females and the task is relatively "clinical" (e.g., hypnosis, sleep, or counseling research).

The major difference between the categories of "considerable" and "some" confidence was in the number of studies available on which to base a conclusion, although some characteristics that often had been investigated were placed into the "some" category when the fraction of significant studies favoring the conclusion fell to below two-thirds. To qualify for this category, then, the following six characteristics had to be based either (1) on three studies, all of which were in support of the hypothesized relationship, or (2) on nine studies, most of which were in support of the relationship, with none showing a significant reversal:

12. Volunteers tend to be from smaller towns than nonvolunteers, especially when volunteering is for questionnaire studies.
13. Volunteers tend to be more interested in religion than nonvolunteers, especially when volunteering is for questionnaire studies.
14. Volunteers tend to be more altruistic than nonvolunteers.
15. Volunteers tend to be more self-disclosing than nonvolunteers.
16. Volunteers tend to be more maladjusted than nonvolunteers, especially when volunteering is for potentially unusual situations (e.g., drugs, hypnosis, high temperature, or vaguely described experiments) or for medical research employing clinical (rather than psychometric) definitions of psychopathology.
17. Volunteers tend to be younger than nonvolunteers, especially when volunteering is for laboratory research and when the subjects are females.

These 17 characteristics implied more clearly the potential threat to validity of the subjects' volunteer status. For example, imagine that a researcher used volunteer subjects to develop population norms in a test standardization study. A fundamental assumption is that the resulting values are actually representative of the specified population. However, if the researcher relied solely on people who volunteered to be tested, the population estimates could be seriously biased. The basis of our suspicion is the third conclusion, which implies that standardizing an intelligence test on volunteer subjects is likely to produce inflated norms. A similar hypothesis is implied for standardizing tests of the need for social approval (conclusion 4) and self-disclosure (conclusion 15).

Effects of volunteer status on experimental outcomes

Insofar as they may not be representative of the target population, it was of interest to ask whether the use of volunteers might also bias the outcome of an experimental investigation. In a series of studies, we matched the reactions of subjects who had volunteered for a psychology experiment with those of a comparable group of nonvolunteer subjects in experimental tasks in which they were all captive participants (e.g., Goldstein, Rosnow, Goodstadt, & Suls, 1972; Rosnow & Rosenthal, 1966; Rosnow, Rosenthal, McConochie, & Arms, 1969; Rosnow & Suls, 1970). Consistent with our hypothesis, volunteer subjects were more apt to play the good subject role – they were more sensitive and accommodating to demand cues than nonvolunteers were. To be sure, Bob has cautioned about relying only on studies by investigators who are "precorrelated" by virtue of their common background (Rosenthal, 1990). Thus it is of interest to note that results similar to, as well as extending, ours have been reported by independent replicators.

An early case was a study performed by Irwin Horowitz (1969), who examined a question that had been debated for several years in social psychology. It concerned whether a person's vulnerability to persuasion increases or decreases according to the amount of fear aroused by emotional statements. Horowitz noticed that results supporting the view that heightened fear increases influenceability seemed to be based on responses of volunteer samples. By contrast, studies supporting the opposite view seemed to be based on responses of captive samples (i.e., subject samples consisting of both volunteers and nonvolunteers). Following this lead, he then examined more directly the differences in persuasibility of volunteer and nonvolunteer subjects.

The subjects in Horowitz's experiment were students assigned randomly to two groups – one in which a high level of fear was aroused and one in which there was a low level of fear. The high-fear group read pamphlets on the abuse and effects of drugs, and watched two Public Health Service films on the hazards of LSD and other hallucinogens and the dangerous effects of amphetamines and barbiturates. The low-fear group did not see the films; they read pamphlets on the hazards of drug abuse, but the vivid verbal descriptions of death and disability were omitted. As Horowitz suspected, volunteer subjects in the high-fear group were more easily persuaded than those in the low-fear group, whereas nonvolunteers in the low-fear group were more easily persuaded than were those in the high-fear group. Horowitz theorized that the volunteers acquiesced more to increasingly heightened demand cues, whereas the nonvolunteers (because of their lower approval need) acquiesced less as demand cues intensified.

Other relevant studies have been reported in experimental psychology as well as other areas. For example, Kotses, Glaus, and Fisher (1974) compared the autonomic reactions of volunteers and nonvolunteers to random bursts of white noise. The subjects were introductory psychology students who either (1) volunteered without any inducement, (2) volunteered with the promise of being paid a nominal sum, (3) were in a pool in which the inducement was course credit rather than cash, or (4) were a coerced group that received no reward but was penalized for not participating. On one dependent measure, basal skin conductance, the changes were noticeably greater in the two volunteer groups; the coercion and pay groups were at opposite ends of the response continuum. On another dependent measure, basal heart rate, the coercion and pay groups were much more alike, with the coerced subjects now showing the strongest responses.

Another pertinent case in experimental psychology involved a perceptual motor skills study performed by Black, Schumpert, and Welch (1972). The subjects had to track a target circle on a pursuit rotor. They were assigned to groups having a predetermined level of feedback on their performance and were told that they could drop out of the study any time they felt bored. Reminiscent of Orne's earlier observation, the volunteers seemingly enacted the good subject role intuitively expected of them by showing considerably more staying power than did the nonvolunteers. That is to say, the more feedback given the subjects, the more the volunteers persisted in the experimental task.

Volunteer bias has also been explored in areas of clinical and counseling research. For example, Strohmetz, Alterman, and Walter (1990) examined baseline differences in alcoholism problem severity among alcoholics who did and did not volunteer to participate in a treatment effectiveness study. The level of the patient's volunteer status (i.e., willingness to participate in the treatment intervention) was positively correlated with the severity of alcoholism problems reported during the pretreatment period. Although such results can be interpreted in different ways, a plausible implication is that volunteer bias could seriously jeopardize the validity of intervention experiments because patients who agree to randomization may be different from the population of interest. King and King (1991) raised a similar concern regarding intervention research on Vietnam veteran adjustment.

The 17 differentiating characteristics allow us to predict the possibility of false positive and false negative conclusions as a consequence of the interaction of volunteer status with experimental variables. Imagine an experiment to test the effect of some given manipulation on the dependent variable of gregariousness. If a sample of highly sociable volunteers (conclusion 5) were drawn, any manipulation designed to increase gregariousness should be too harshly judged as ineffective because the untreated control group will already be unusually high on this factor (i.e., a false negative conclusion). The same manipulation should, however, prove effective in increasing the gregariousness of the experimental group relative to that of the control group if the total subject sample is characterized by a less restricted range of sociability.

To illustrate false positive conclusions, imagine that an investigator is interested in finding out how persuasive an advertising appeal is before recommending its use. She finds it convenient to use volunteer subjects, and her research design involves assigning them at random to a message treatment or a control group. Because subjects who volunteer are likely to be higher in social desirability than nonvolunteer subjects (conclusion 4), and insofar as people higher in this trait are more readily influenced by persuasive communications (e.g., Buckhout, 1965), it follows that the general effectiveness of the appeal should be overestimated when the total subject sample consists of first-wave volunteers.

So far, I have summarized our conclusions about the characteristics of those people who are likely to find their way into the role of data contributor in behavioral research. I have also mentioned how the use of volunteer subjects can increase the likelihood of false positive or false negative conclusions about causal relationships. The act of volunteering can be viewed as a nonrandom event, determined in part by specific attributes of the person asked to participate as a subject in behavioral research but also by more general situational conditions. It is these latter conditions to which I now turn, because they provide guidance for investigators wishing to minimize volunteer bias by drawing second- and third-wave respondents into the initial subject sample.

Situational characteristics of volunteering

Just as Bob meta-analyzed the research literature dealing with attributes of the volunteer subject, he did the same thing for the situational determinants of volunteering in order to develop a number of tentative suggestions for drawing more representative subject samples. The evidence was not as plentiful or as direct as it was for the relationship between volunteering and more or less stable characteristics of the potential participant in behavioral research. Nevertheless, there was sufficient evidence to permit a tentative rank ordering of the situational determinants of volunteering by the degree of confidence we can have in each relationship. The definition of confidence was again based on the number of studies relevant to the relationship under consideration and the proportion of such studies whose results supported the directional hypothesis.

Thus, the following two conclusions, in order to qualify for "maximum confidence," had to be based on at least 20 studies, and at least 6 out of 7 significant studies had to be in support of the hypothesized relationship:

1. Persons more interested in the topic under investigation are more likely to volunteer. It follows that by making the appeal as interesting as possible (keeping in mind the nature of the target population), it should be possible to create a more representative subject sample.
2. Persons with expectations of being favorably evaluated by the investigator are more likely to volunteer. Thus, by making the appeal as nonthreatening as possible (so that potential subjects will not be put off by unwarranted fears of an unfavorable evaluation), it should also be possible to stimulate participation.

Other situational characteristics suggested additional steps that can be expected to induce more people to enter the subject pool. The following three recommendations were based on characteristics that warranted "considerable confidence," because they, in turn, were based on at least 10 studies and at least two-thirds of significant studies supported the hypothesized relationship:

3. Emphasize the theoretical and practical importance of the research for which participation is requested, because studies show that persons perceiving the investigation as more important are more likely to enter the subject pool.
4. State in what way the target population is particularly relevant to the research being conducted, and underscore the responsibility of potential subjects to participate in studies that have potential for benefiting others. Here, the research showed that persons' feeling states at the time of the request for participants are likely to affect the probability of participating.
5. When possible, potential subjects should be offered not only pay for participation, but small courtesy gifts simply for taking time to consider whether they will want to participate. This recommendation was derived from results of studies showing that persons offered material incentives are more likely to participate, especially if the incentives are advance gifts and are not contingent on the decision to participate.

Finally, three additional recommendations qualified on the basis of conclusions that warranted "some confidence" – because they were based either (1) on three studies that were completely consistent or (2) on nine studies, most of which were in support of the hypothesized relationship, with none showing a significant reversal of the relationship:

6. Have the request for participation made by a person of perceived status as high as possible and preferably by a female. The reason was that recruiters higher in status or prestige were found to obtain higher rates of volunteering, as were female recruiters. This latter relationship, however, was especially moderated by the sex of the subject and the nature of the research.

7. When possible, avoid research tasks that may be psychologically or biologically stressful. There are good ethical reasons to accept this recommendation, but it is also supported by studies showing that persons are less likely to volunteer for tasks perceived as aversive (in the sense of being painful, stressful, or seemingly dangerous).

8. When possible, communicate the normative nature of the volunteering response. Persons are more likely to agree to participate when volunteering is presented as the normative, expected, appropriate thing to do.

A hasty reading of these eight recommendations might give the impression that they were designed only to lessen volunteer bias by increasing rates of participation. However, as Bob observed, a more deliberate reading will reveal that the recommendations may have other beneficial effects as well (Rosenthal & Rosnow, 1975). In particular, they should make us more careful and thoughtful not only in how we make our appeals for volunteers but also in our planning of the research. For example, if we tell our subjects as much as possible about the significance of our research – as though they were a granting agency, which in fact they are, granting us time instead of money – then we will have to make sure that our research is substantive and not trivial.

When artifacts and ethics collide

By the late 1970s, we had turned our attention away from the volunteer problem and toward other topics and research questions. Although there were still pockets of resistance to the artifact assault of the 1960s and 1970s, there was also relatively widespread acceptance of the view that certain previously overlooked factors were potentially damaging sources of bias. Propositions that a few years earlier had seemed only tentative were now treated in many textbooks almost as axiomatic. In social psychology at least, there were also procedural modifications that resulted from the artifact work (Suls & Gastorf, 1980). These developments were also well known outside of the United States (e.g., Gniech,

1976; Schuler, 1980), and the *Rosenthal effect* had become a scientific truism in many areas.

Ethical issues were now pointed out and discussed as a consequence of the implementation of various directives calling for informed consent on the part of research participants. However, it had become evident that compliance with human subjects regulations could present dilemmas for psychological researchers who were concerned about minimizing artifacts (Suls & Rosnow, 1981). To tell potential subjects what they were getting into when they were asked to participate could affect their subsequent reactions and, in turn, jeopardize the tenability of certain causal inferences (e.g., Gardner, 1978; Resnick & Schwartz, 1973). It was apparent that a compromise had to be struck between the aims of experimenters and the final decisions of review panels.

More recently, we have discussed the insufficiency of the decision model that evolved as the basis of cost-benefit analyses by institutional review boards. The model emphasizes the costs and benefits of *doing* research but ignores the costs of *not doing* certain research. The costs of doing might include possible harm to subjects, time, and expenditures of money, and the benefits of doing might include gains to science, to subjects, to other people at other times and places, and to the investigator. The insufficiency of the model is that it fails to consider what is lost by *not* permitting certain studies to be performed, which is also an ethical issue that needs to be pointed out and discussed. That is, seldom is due consideration given to the ethical implications of the *failure* to approve or conduct ethically ambiguous studies that might reduce violence, prejudice, mental illness, and so forth, but would involve deception, invasion of privacy, and other factors. As a consequence, we have proposed a new synthesis based on a more complete analysis of the costs and benefits of doing and not doing a study (e.g., Rosenthal & Rosnow, 1984b; 1991; Rosnow, 1990).

Edward C. Tolman once stated that "since all the sciences, and especially psychology, are still immersed in such tremendous realms of the uncertain and the unknown, the best that any individual scientist, especially any psychologist, can do seems to be to follow his own gleam and his own bent, however inadequate they may be" (1959, p. 152). Tolman's advice is also prudent when artifacts and ethics collide, as we confront the basic challenge of our technical and ethical responsibilities as scientists. On the one hand, we must protect the integrity of our research in order to ensure that it measures up to the standards of good scientific practice. On the other hand, we must respect the dignity of

Figure 21.1. Photograph taken during Eastern Psychological Association meeting in Atlantic City, New Jersey, in the early 1960s. Left front to rear: Ralph Rosnow, Robert Rosenthal, Duane Schultz, Sydney Schultz, Leslie Frankfurt, Robert Commack; right front to rear: Frederick Pauling, Gordon Russell, Robert Lana, Sara Tannenbaum, Joseph Tannenbaum, unknown.

those we study and the values that allow the pursuit of scientific knowledge. When artifacts and ethics collide, this confrontation of the technical with the moral may provide us with great problems, but it can also provide us with great opportunities. We must strive to develop scientific and analytical insights that will increase the morality of our research *and* its technical merit. This, surely, is the élan vital of Bob Rosenthal's numerous seminal contributions to behavioral science.

Note

More than 25 years ago, I had the very good fortune to be introduced to Bob Rosenthal at an Eastern Psychological Association (EPA) meeting at the Jersey shore. The colleague who introduced us, Gordon Russell (now at Lethbridge University in Canada), saved the vintage photograph shown as Figure 21.1. It shows a group of recently minted psychologists seated in a precasino Atlantic City restaurant sometime during that EPA meeting. Although Bob and I have since collaborated on additional projects, this chapter describes our earliest joint venture.

The work summarized here draws on a number of our previously published articles, chapters, and books, but especially Rosenthal and Rosnow (1969b, 1975, 1984b, 1991) and Rosnow and Rosenthal (1970, 1976). This work was supported by funding and other assistance that I received from the National

Science Foundation (NSF), Boston University, Harvard University, the London School of Economics, and Temple University, and also grants and other assistance that Bob received from NSF, the Center for Advanced Study in the Behavioral Sciences, and the John D. and Catherine T. MacArthur Foundation. I wish to thank all of these institutions on behalf of both of us for their generous support.

References

Black, R. W., Schumpert, J., & Welch, F. A. (1972). A "partial reinforcement extinction effect" in perceptual-motor performance: Coerced versus volunteer subject populations. *Journal of Experimental Psychology, 92,* 143–145.

Buckhout, R. (1965). Need for approval and attitude change. *Journal of Psychology, 60,* 123–128.

Cochran, W. G. (1963). *Sampling techniques* (2nd ed.). New York: Wiley.

Cochran, W. G., Mosteller, F., & Tukey, J. W. (1953). Statistical problems of the Kinsey report. *Journal of the American Statistical Association, 48,* 673–716.

Deming, W. E. (1944). On errors in surveys. *American Sociological Review, 9,* 359–369.

Gardner, G. T. (1978). Effects of federal human subjects regulations on data obtained in environmental stressor research. *Journal of Personality and Social Psychology, 36,* 628–634.

Gniech, G. (1976). *Störeffekte in psychologischen Experimenten.* Stuttgart: Kohlhammer.

Goldstein, J. H., Rosnow, R. L., Goodstadt, B. E., & Suls, J. M. (1972). The "good subject" in verbal operant conditioning research. *Journal of Experimental Research in Personality, 6,* 29–33.

Hansen, M. H., & Hurwitz, W. N. (1946). The problem of non-response in sample surveys. *Journal of the American Statistical Association, 41,* 517–529.

Horowitz, I. A. (1969). Effects of volunteering, fear arousal, and number of communications on attitude change. *Journal of Personality and Social Psychology, 11,* 34–37.

King, D. W., & King, L. A. (1991). Validity issues in research on Vietnam veteran adjustment. *Psychological Bulletin, 109,* 107–124.

Kotses, H., Glaus, K. D., & Fisher, L. E. (1974). Effects of subject recruitment procedure on heart rate and skin conductance measures. *Biological Psychology, 2,* 59–66.

Kruglanski, A. W. (1973). Much ado about the "volunteer artifacts." *Journal of Personality and Social Psychology, 28,* 348–354.

Orne, M. T. (1962). On the social psychology of the psychological experiment: With particular reference to demand characteristics and their implications. *American Psychologist, 17,* 776–783.

Orne, M. T. (1970). Hypnosis, motivation, and the ecological validity of the psychological experiment. In W. J. Arnold & M. M. Page (Eds.), *Nebraska symposium on motivation* (pp. 187–265). Lincoln: University of Nebraska Press.

Resnick, J. H., & Schwartz, T. (1973). Ethical standards as an independent variable in psychological research. *American Psychologist, 28,* 134–139.

Rosenthal, R. (1963). On the social psychology of the psychological experiment: The experimenter's hypothesis as unintended determinant of experimental results. *American Scientist, 51,* 268–283.

Rosenthal, R. (1965). The volunteer subject. *Human Relations, 18,* 389–406.

Rosenthal, R. (1977). Biasing effects of experimenters. *Et Cetera: A Review of General Semantics, 34,* 253–264.

Rosenthal, R. (1990). Replication in behavioral research. *Journal of Social Behavior and Personality, 5,* 1–30.

Rosenthal, R., & Rosnow, R. L. (Eds.) (1969a). *Artifact in behavioral research.* New York: Academic Press.

Rosenthal, R., & Rosnow, R. L. (1969b). The volunteer subject. In R. Rosenthal & R. L. Rosnow (Eds.), *Artifact in behavioral research* (pp. 59–118). New York: Academic Press.

Rosenthal, R., & Rosnow, R. L. (1975). *The volunteer subject.* New York: Wiley.

Rosenthal, R., & Rosnow, R. L. (1984a). *Essentials of behavioral research: Methods and data analysis.* New York: McGraw-Hill.

Rosenthal, R., & Rosnow, R. L. (1984b). Applying Hamlet's question to the ethical conduct of research: A conceptual addendum. *American Psychologist, 39,* 561–563.

Rosenthal, R., & Rosnow, R. L. (1991). *Essentials of behavioral research: Methods and data analysis* (2nd ed.). New York: McGraw-Hill.

Rosnow, R. L. (1968). A "spread of effect" in attitude formation. In A. G. Greenwald, T. C. Brock, & T. M. Ostrom (Eds.), *Psychological foundations of attitudes* (pp. 89–107). New York: Academic Press.

Rosnow, R. L. (1970, June). When he lends a helping hand, bite it. *Psychology Today, 4*(1), 26–30.

Rosnow, R. L. (1971). Experimental artifact. In L. Deighton (Ed.), *The encyclopedia of education* (Vol. 3, pp. 483–488). New York: Free Press and Macmillan.

Rosnow, R. L. (1977). Social research: Artifacts. In B. B. Wolman (Ed.), *International encyclopedia of psychiatry, psychology, psychoanalysis, and neurology* (Vol. 10, pp. 328–331). New York: Van Nostrand Reinhold.

Rosnow, R. L. (1981). *Paradigms in transition: The methodology of social inquiry.* New York: Oxford University Press.

Rosnow, R. L. (1990). Teaching research ethics through role-play and discussion. *Teaching of Psychology, 17,* 179–181.

Rosnow, R. L. (1991). Inside rumor: A personal journey. *American Psychologist, 46,* 484–496.

Rosnow, R. L., & Aiken, L. S. (1973). Mediation of artifacts in behavioral research. *Journal of Experimental Social Psychology, 9,* 181–201.

Rosnow, R. L., & Davis, D. J. (1977). Demand characteristics and the psychological experiment. *Et Cetera: A Review of General Semantics, 34,* 301–313.

Rosnow, R. L., & Rosenthal, R. (1966). Volunteer subjects and the results of opinion change studies. *Psychological Reports, 19,* 1183–1187.

Rosnow, R. L., & Rosenthal, R. (1970). Volunteer effects in behavioral research. In T. M. Newcomb (Ed.), *New directions in psychology* (Vol. 4, pp. 211–277). New York: Holt, Rinehart & Winston.

Rosnow, R. L., & Rosenthal, R. (1974). Taming of the volunteer problem: On coping with artifacts by benign neglect. *Journal of Personality and Social Psychology, 30,* 188–190.

Rosnow, R. L., & Rosenthal, R. (1976). The volunteer subject revisited. *Australian Journal of Psychology, 28,* 97–108.

Rosnow, R. L., Rosenthal, R., McConochie, R. M., & Arms, R. L. (1969). Volunteer effects on experimental outcomes. *Educational and Psychological Measurement, 29,* 825–846.

Rosnow, R. L., & Suls, J. M. (1970). Reactive effects of pretesting in attitude research. *Journal of Personality and Social Psychology, 15,* 338–343.

436   Ralph L. Rosnow

Schuler, H. (1980). *Ethische Probleme psychologischer Forschung.* Gottingen: Hogrefe.
Strohmetz, D. B., Alterman, A. I., & Walter, D. (1990). Subject selection bias in alcoholics volunteering for a treatment study. *Alcoholism: Clinical and Experimental Research, 14,* 736–738.
Suls, J. M., & Gastorf, J. (1980). Has the social psychology of the experiment influenced how research is conducted? *European Journal of Social Psychology, 10,* 291–294.
Suls, J. M., & Rosnow, R. L. (1981). The delicate balance between ethics and artifacts in behavioral research. In A. J. Kimmel (Ed.), *Ethics of human subject research* (pp. 55–67). San Francisco: Jossey-Bass.
Tolman, E. C. (1959). Principles of purposive behavior. In S. Koch (Ed.), *Psychology: A study of a science* (Vol. 2, pp. 92–157). New York: McGraw-Hill.
Wechsler, D. (1958). *The measurement and appraisal of adult intelligence* (4th ed.). Baltimore: Williams & Wilkins.

22. Assessment and prevention of expectancy effects in community mental health studies

MARY AMANDA DEW

"You still haven't evaluated your specific hypothesis because your F test has numerator df greater than 1."

"Examining only the overall cell means in your multifactorial AN-OVA will mislead you about the interpretation of interaction effects."

"I know that your test statistic was significant at $p < .05$. But what was the *size* of the effect?"

"If the project was worth doing, it's worth publishing."

At the risk of causing readers to wonder about the state of my mental health, I admit to hearing statements such as these knocking about in my head – statements gleaned from many interactions with Bob Rosenthal during my tenure as a graduate student at Harvard. I now make these comments, and similar others, to my own students and colleagues. Bob served as a mentor to me in the domain of quantitative methods, and I continue to be heavily influenced by his approach to research: by his delineation of the types of controls needed to reduce experimenter effects and other artifacts in behavioral research, by his zest for plunging into new areas of methodology and statistics, and by his concern for external as well as internal validity in empirical research.

In the present chapter, I would like to take up the issue of experimenter effects – and experimenter expectancies in particular – in the context of an applied area of research that heavily utilizes nonlaboratory, field interviewing. Specifically, I focus on the nature and manner by which researchers survey mental health in the community, and on difficulties and rewards encountered in such field interviewing when we attempt to limit the many ways in which researchers can inadvertently influence individuals' responses.

Twenty-five years ago, Bob began to write major treatises on such artifacts, primarily in the context of the social psychological laboratory (e.g., Rosenthal, 1966, 1969). What was unusual about his critique was that, perhaps reflecting his original training as a clinician, he prescribed a concrete "treatment plan" whereby investigators could reduce the influence of experimenter expectancies and other artifacts. Following his lead, then, this chapter is organized in true clinical fashion, with (1) a description of the presenting problem and why it warrants attention, (2) a brief history of developments leading up to the problem's current status, (3) a summary assessment of key areas of difficulty, and (4) application of Bob's treatment plan for the control of experimenter effects in research.

The problem: Why conduct psychiatric interviews in the community?

Mental disorders occur in every sociocultural group in the world. In the United States, an estimated 12% of children (Institute of Medicine, 1989) and 15% of adults (Regier et al., 1988) currently suffer from one or more disorders. Yet only a minority of mentally ill individuals, 30–40% (Dew, Bromet, Schulberg, Parkinson, & Curtis, 1991; Vernon & Roberts, 1982; Weissman, Myers, & Thompson, 1981), are identified by the health care system. It is this minority on which traditional research techniques of clinical observation and laboratory experimentation are typically based. Although this research has improved our understanding of factors associated with psychopathology, the relative role of such factors in the larger ill but untreated population remains less clear. By focusing on psychopathology under natural conditions in whole populations, researchers in the field known as *psychiatric epidemiology* provide an empirical base that complements and extends data gathered through traditional clinical and laboratory techniques.

Psychiatric epidemiology is the study of patterns of mental disorders in the population and of the risk factors that affect these patterns (Dew & Bromet, in press; Lilienfeld & Lilienfeld, 1980). The goal of the field is to provide data relevant for prevention and control of mental illness. In addition to requiring representative sampling from the community, a key requirement for research in this area is a *reliable and valid case definition.* Current diagnostic criteria, and interview schedules to implement them, were developed to allow for systematic psychiatric case identification in clinical and community settings. The importance of case identification through the field interview is best understood within a historical context.

A brief history

The development of systematic case identification techniques in psychiatric epidemiology has been described as evolving through three periods, or generations (Dohrenwend & Dohrenwend, 1982). First-generation studies, conducted prior to World War II, relied on key informants' reports and agency records for case ascertainment. The first field study of this sort was conducted in Massachusetts in 1854 by Edward Jarvis, who undertook a census on the "insane" by surveying general medical practitioners and other key informants, such as clergymen, and reviewing records of mental hospitals and other official agencies (Jarvis, 1971). He identified 2,632 "lunatics" and 1,087 "idiots" needing "the care and protection of their friends or of the public for their support, restoration or custody" (p. 17).

A classic first-generation study was conducted by Faris and Dunham (1939), who compared rates of mental illness across geographical areas. They reviewed medical records from four state hospitals serving the Chicago area between 1922 and 1934 in order to identify cases; they found that rates of mental illness, and schizophrenia in particular, decreased progressively as one moved away from the inner-city area.

As in most first-generation studies, Faris and Dunham relied on medical records rather than a community survey approach in order to identify cases. However, U.S. Army experiences during World War II, in which large numbers of presumably healthy recruits failed to pass a paper-and-pencil psychological symptom screen, suggested that treated cases represented only the tip of the iceberg. These Army findings prompted a series of community studies – second-generation studies – on the extent of psychiatric impairment in the general population. These studies were designed to use not only random sampling techniques, but also face-to-face interviews to collect data on respondents' psychological symptoms. The interviews focused on psychiatric "impairment" rather than specific diagnostic categories, which during the 1950s and 1960s could not be reliably operationalized. Most often, impairment was determined by asking whether respondents were experiencing any of a lengthy list of symptoms at the time of the interview. Whether or not a respondent was considered to be impaired was then often determined either by (1) a clinician's decision that the respondent represented a "case," based on a review of endorsed symptoms, or (2) whether the total number of symptoms a respondent endorsed exceeded an empirically derived cutting point applied to distinguish respondents with clinically significant impairment from the remaining community residents.

The hypothesis that treated cases represented a minority of all cases was strongly supported by the second-generation studies. Indeed, community sample impairment rates in studies such as the Midtown Manhattan Project (Srole et al., 1962) and the Nova Scotia study (Leighton, Harding, Macklin, Macmillan, & Leighton, 1963) were considerably higher than those found in first-generation pre–World War II research. Thus, whereas a median rate of 3.6% of the population were estimated to have mental disorders in first-generation studies (Dohrenwend & Dohrenwend, 1982), the median rate from second-generation studies was 20%.

How much of this difference in rates was attributable to improved case-finding techniques? Given their focus on symptom counts rather than formal diagnoses, how much were disorder rates in second-generation studies inflated by counting as "cases" those respondents who were symptomatic yet not so severely impaired that they would warrant a psychiatric diagnosis? How much of the rate difference was due to the interviewers' direct (probably unintended) influence on respondents' reports in second-generation studies? These are key issues for the current third generation of psychiatric epidemiologic studies, which rely on psychometric advances in the area of diagnosis accomplished in the 1970s. Thus, unlike their predecessors, many third-generation studies are characterized by their use of semistructured or fully structured diagnostic interview schedules – to be described – embodying the most recent psychiatric nomenclature.

Psychometric work leading to structured clinical interviewing was initially stimulated by Kramer's (1961) earlier observation that first-admission hospitalization rates for schizophrenia were higher in the United States, whereas those for depression were higher in England. He questioned whether these differences reflected true differences in morbidity or artifacts of diagnosis. This simple observation led to the first scientific study of the determinants of diagnosis, which demonstrated that the application of systematic interviewing techniques and comparable diagnostic criteria resulted in similar diagnostic distributions (Cooper, Kendell, Gurland, Sharpe, & Copeland, 1972). Several years later, the International Pilot Study of Schizophrenia demonstrated that patients could be reliably diagnosed in countries worldwide, including the United States, with structured diagnostic interview schedules (Sartorius et al., 1986; World Health Organization, 1975).

In the United States, the need to define homogeneous patient populations for clinical drug trials and multicenter collaborative research prompted further developments in structured interviewing techniques and reliable diagnostic criteria. Rejecting the use of general clinical descriptions to make diagnoses, Feighner, Robins, and Guze (1972) published the first set of specific research criteria that listed the symptoms and their duration required for each diagnosis. Six years later, the now widely used Research Diagnostic Criteria (RDC) (Spitzer, Endicott, & Robins, 1978) – which represent revisions of the Feighner et al. criteria – and an accompanying semistructured interview schedule were published. This interview, the Schedule for Affective Disorders and Schizophrenia (SADS) (Endicott & Spitzer, 1978), provides a set of questions (and possible probes) to ascertain each RDC symptom item. Weissman and Myers (1980) first applied the SADS to a community population and showed that diagnoses could be made systematically in the field.

Current diagnostic criteria, which represent revisions of the RDC, are now detailed in the *Diagnostic and Statistical Manual of Mental Disorders* (3rd ed., rev.) (DSM-III-R) (American Psychiatric Association, 1987). Spitzer, Williams, Gibbon, and First (1990) developed an accompanying Structured Clinical Interview for DSM-III-R (SCID) for use in treated patients samples, as well as general population samples. The SCID builds upon its predecessor, the SADS, and both require clinically experienced interviewers able to probe in order to determine whether each endorsed symptom is present at a clinically significant level.

Utilizing highly experienced clinicians can be costly; in epidemiologic studies of large community samples, training lay interviewers to conduct the field work may be more economical than hiring experienced mental health professionals. Thus, in the late 1970s, the National Institute of Mental Health (NIMH) decided to sponsor the development of a fully structured interview that could be administered by lay interviewers. Their ultimate goal was to estimate the rates of discrete psychiatric disorders in unbiased community populations. The new instrument was the Diagnostic Interview Schedule (DIS), a fully structured, DSM-III-based schedule (Robins, Helzer, Croughan, & Ratcliff, 1977). DIS questions, and patterns of probing for additional information, are entirely specified, so that lack of clinical training should not prevent interviewers from acquiring the necessary information (Robins, 1987). The DIS has been administered in several large-scale epidemiologic surveys, including most notably the Epidemiologic Catchment Area

Study (Regier et al., 1984). Reliability and validity studies have been carried out for the DIS, as well as for the semistructured interviews mentioned earlier.

Assessment of the potential impact of researcher expectancy effects on the field psychiatric interview

An appreciation of the nature of typical field interview questions in psychiatric epidemiologic studies is helpful for identifying avenues along which researcher behavior can be controlled or modulated. Consider, for example, the determination of whether respondents meet current (DSM-III-R) criteria for the diagnosis of major depression. Respondents meet the criteria if both (a) and (b) are true (American Psychiatric Association, 1987):

1. At least five of a total of nine symptoms have each been present at a clinically significant level during the same two-week (or longer) period, and represent a change from previous functioning.
2. At least one of the symptoms is either depressed mood or loss of interest or pleasure.

The critical judgments to be made concern whether each symptom has been present *at a clinically significant level* for *a long enough period*. To understand how an interviewer makes these decisions, study the first question in the semistructured SCID's Major Depression section. The interviewer asks:

	Rating		
	? 1	2	3

Have you ever had a period when you were feeling depressed or down most of the day nearly every day? (possible probes: What was that like? How long did it last? As long as two weeks?)
Respondent comments: _____

The interviewer records the respondent's description and continues to probe further, if necessary, in order to select one of four options regarding the presence of depressed mood: (1) ? = inadequate information to determine presence of symptom, (2) 1 = symptom absent or false, (3) 2 = subthreshold symptom, or (4) 3 = threshold or true symptom. Questions about other cardinal symptoms of major depression (e.g., appetite and/or weight change, sleep disturbance, difficulty concentrating) follow a similar pattern. The fully structured DIS utilizes similar questions, but the pattern and content of probing are fully specified, so that a respondent's simple yes–no answers to the probes determine whether a symptom is recorded as present at a clinically significant level.

To what extent are psychiatric epidemiologic data regarding community rates of psychiatric disorders, such as major depression, likely to be affected by researchers' unintended influence on respondents' reports during contemporary field interviews? Surprisingly, despite the extensive consideration of expectancy effects and other such artifacts in experimental social psychology, and in clinical psychiatry and psychology (e.g., Shapiro, 1959; Sullivan, 1936–1937), the analogous impact of the interviewer (and the potential impact of the researcher who supervises the interviewer) in field survey studies has been neglected of late, relative to other issues such as sampling and instrument design (Fowler, 1988). That expectancy effects have received short shrift in the context of field psychiatric interviewing, in particular, is disturbing, since interviewers continue to have at least some degree of clinical freedom when administering contemporary interview schedules. Even in fully structured schedules (e.g., the DIS), the opportunity for unintended communication of nonverbal cues remains present.

Perhaps there is some unique qualitative element of psychiatric interviewing that defies the study and potential elimination of expectancy effects and other artifacts. Indeed, even in nonpsychiatric field surveys, there remains the notion that, no matter how structured the interview, interviewing itself is a craft that is part art, part science (Judd, Smith, & Kidder, 1991; Lavrakas, 1987). In the psychiatric domain, the typical style of assessment interviewing has been described as

> a creative act. . . . The circumstances, the environment, and the people involved can never be duplicated. Even if the interviewer and interviewee wanted to replicate their own interaction, they could not; for with each sentence their relationship has subtly changed. (Shea, 1988, p. v)

The semistructured and fully structured research interviews conducted in the field tend to be less subtly changing than typically unstructured clinical assessments. However, as in clinical assessments, there is a heavy emphasis in structured field psychiatric research interviews on the interviewer's skill in establishing rapport. The critical question becomes, then, can we further standardize psychiatric interviewer behavior in these interviews, or is psychiatric research assessment so much an art that additional attempts to decompose, control, or guide it will result in diagnostic data that have no validity? Asked slightly differently, can we assemble and refine guidelines that will not eliminate the application of the psychiatric interviewer's clinical skills but will apply those skills more systematically?

Six points can be distinguished during the interview process (Fowler, 1988; Judd et al., 1991); interventions to reduce the potential for serious expectancy effects could be undertaken at any or all of these points: (1) the interviewer's presentation of the study and its specific tasks to the respondent, (2) the manner in which the questions are asked, (3) the manner in which inadequate answers are probed, (4) the way answers are recorded, (5) the manner in which interpersonal aspects of the interview are handled, and (6) the interactions between the interviewer and his or her supervisor (e.g., the project coordinator or principal investigator). Important elements in each of these areas are delineated prior to an application of Bob Rosenthal's treatment plan for the assessment and control of potential expectancy effects in this research domain.

Presenting the study and specific study tasks

The interviewer's initial concern is to present the study in a positive, succinct manner, and to do so consistently across all respondents. Each section of the interview must also be introduced with instructions detailed enough that respondents will understand their job during the interview. Interviewers often utilize a combination of oral and written instructions during the interview.

Asking the questions

The questions in structured psychiatric interviews are laid out in the order and wording in which they are to be asked. Depending on the degree of structure, interviewers may be allowed to provide explanations for questions that respondents do not understand.

Probing the respondent's answers

This is one of the most delicate and difficult aspects of the psychiatric research interview. Semistructured interviews provide examples of probes that may be used to clarify an answer or to determine the clinical significance of a response. Fully structured interviews specify the wording and precise ordering of probe questions, as well as the circumstances in which they are to be used.

Recording the answers

Most psychiatric interview schedules utilize a combination of closed- and open-ended questions. Closed-ended items require the interviewer to choose one category of response based on the respondent's comment (e.g., symptom absent; symptom present). Open-ended items require verbatim recording of responses.

Managing interpersonal relations with the respondent

Interviewer and respondent roles, and much of the nature of their interaction, resemble the roles and social situation created in the social psychological experiment. The interviewer's job is to motivate and enable the respondent to give a complete, accurate answer to each question. The social situation is a task-oriented one that is to be guided by the interviewer.

Interacting with the project supervisor

In psychiatric epidemiologic investigations, as in other areas of survey research, the principal investigator and project coordinator usually do not conduct the interviews. Instead, interviewers with clinical qualifications appropriate to the specific interview schedule are hired to complete the data collection. Interviewers are informed about the intent and goals of the study to the degree necessary to explain the study and individual question instructions to respondents. Interviewer activities are monitored throughout the data collection phase of the project.

A treatment plan for the control of expectancy effects

> Interviewers both explicitly and implicitly teach respondents what is expected and to varying degrees motivate them to strive for some goals, such as good, accurate reporting, and avoid others. . . . [This] is an often unappreciated but critical part of the interviewer's job. (Fowler, 1988, p. 109)

As Fowler implies, the goal in survey research is not to eliminate interviewer influence on respondents' reports. Rather, interviewers' expectations for good performance, and their ability to influence, should be channeled toward maximizing respondents' motivation to participate thoughtfully. It is *unintended* interviewer expectancies and associated

Table 22.1. *Primary, secondary, and tertiary efforts to prevent expectancy effects in field psychiatric research interviews*

Prevention level	Targeted area	Specific strategy[a]
Primary	Interviewer recruitment	**Recruit professional interviewers**
		Develop selection procedures
		Increase the number of interviewers
	Interviewer training	**Develop specific procedures**
		Maintain refresher training throughout the study
Secondary	Interviewer supervision	**Observe interviewers' behavior**
		Inspect each interview booklet at completion
	Interview procedures	**Maintain blind contact**
		Routinely assess interviewers' expectancies
		Minimize interviewer–respondent contact
Tertiary	Data management and analysis	**Analyze data and adjust for expectancy effects**
		Analyze data for order effects

[a]Strategies in boldface type were adapted from Rosenthal (1966).

cues, and their effects on responses, that are to be minimized and/or controlled.

As discussed earlier, there are several points in the interview process at which intervention efforts to prevent or reduce expectancy effects can be targeted. The majority of these interventions were originally specified 25 years ago in the context of experimental social psychological research (Rosenthal, 1966). As applied to the psychiatric epidemiologic research setting, Bob Rosenthal's treatment plan details the nature of these interventions, and – maintaining the analogy to a clinical case study introduced at the beginning of this chapter – these interventions can be organized in terms of whether they represent primary, secondary, or tertiary prevention efforts (Dew & Bromet, in press) (Table 22.1).

Primary prevention efforts are those that reduce the likelihood that a problem will arise and, in terms of expectancy effects, refer to actions the research team can take to preempt such effects. As outlined in Table 22.1, there are two areas on which primary prevention efforts can focus: interviewer recruitment strategies and interviewer training procedures.

With respect to the former, the importance of deciding to recruit professional interviewers, rather than relying on students or project coinvestigators, cannot be overestimated. It is critical because it helps to ensure that the persons who have direct contact with study respondents will be motivated by the desire to collect the most accurate data possible – after all, data collection is their profession – rather than being motivated by a desire to obtain data in support of preexisting expectations (Rosenthal, 1966). Fortunately, the size of psychiatric epidemiologic studies, and the frequent need to hire individuals with clinical expertise, generally necessitate the recruitment of professional, experienced interviewers rather than, say, the undergraduate assistants often employed in social psychological laboratory studies.

One result of the decision to hire professional interviewers is that additional explicit criteria can then be established in order to identify and select the best such personnel. In the case of psychiatric research interviewers, these criteria usually include a background of clinical training and experience, plus standard qualifications known to define more competent, accurate interviewing personnel, such as a relatively high level of education, better motivation, and so on (Rosenthal, 1966). Some of these desirable qualifications are themselves, however, related to interviewers' ability to influence respondents' reports. Thus, interviewers who are more self-confident, more professional and businesslike in manner, and more expressively voiced are more likely to obtain data consistent with their expectancies. To the extent that such interviewers can be *trained* to expect respondents to be interested in the interview, truthful, and complete, interviewers' propensity to apply expectancies may be transformed into a potential study strength.

Finally, increasing the total number of interviewers recruited (and randomly assigning them to respondents) has a number of salutary effects on the problem of potential expectancy confirmation by, for example, diluting the impact of any single interviewer's expectancy on the study data base and allowing each interviewer's accuracy, as well as bias and consistency, to be assessed (Rosenthal, 1966). The precision of survey estimates of the rates of psychiatric disorder in the sampled population will also increase as the number of interviewers increases (Fowler, 1988).

As already indicated, reduction of – or, at least, management of – potential expectancy effects can also be accomplished through interviewer training. Fortunately, it is standard practice in large-scale psychiatric epidemiologic investigations to include a period of extensive training in interview administration, as well as refresher training sessions after field work has begun. Much of the emphasis in typical training programs concerns ways to minimize random error, such as that arising from inadvertent omissions of items, miscoded responses, and so on. The power and pervasiveness of interviewer expectancies suggest that study trainers and investigators should carefully consider the nature and degree of the information provided to interviewers about the intent of the study and about specific hypotheses. The issue of blinding the interviewers will be addressed more fully later; it is noteworthy here that investigators must weigh interviewers' need to know about the study's intent in order, for example, to maintain their interest and reduce interviewer attrition, versus the investigators' need to collect unbiased data and their ability to pay to train new interviewers.

Turning to secondary prevention efforts, these traditionally refer to the early treatment of a problem in order to prevent recurrence or permanent impairment. In the context of expectancy effects, Bob Rosenthal's treatment plan prescribes several approaches for early detection and intervention to avert fatal flaws in the research project. There are two major categories of such activities: supervision of interviewers and establishment of interview procedures to identify and treat expectancy-related problems.

Supervision of interviewers' interactions with respondents can be achieved through activities such as sitting in on interviews or observing through a one-way window (Rosenthal, 1966), audio- and/or videotaping interviews to be studied later, or periodically role-playing the interview, with the supervisor taking the part of the respondent. Such supervision can identify problematic interviewer behavior, which can then be adjusted. It may also be the case that awareness of being observed by a supervisor may automatically inhibit an interviewer's unintentional communication of expectancies (Rosenthal, 1966).

An important additional element of supervision is the supervisor's careful review of interview booklets shortly after interview completion. Although structured psychiatric interviews include many closed-ended questions (and, in the case of the DIS, are exclusively closed-ended), interviewers are often required to provide qualitative summaries of their impressions of respondents. These summaries may reveal interviewer biases or assumptions that require modification.

In addition to ongoing supervision, a number of interview procedures can be implemented to control interviewer expectancy effects (Rosenthal, 1966). Most notably, maintaining "blind" contact with respondents – and continued supervision to identify and arrest breakdowns of this mechanism – are important. However, in contrast to experimental social psychological investigations, the notion of blind contact in the commonly *non*experimental field psychiatric research interview is sometimes difficult to define and implement. In studies designed to estimate rates of psychiatric disorders in the general population, interviewers may be kept blind about a number of characteristics of respondents, such as, for example, whether respondents have documented medical histories of certain types of disorders. (Such knowledge could bias interviewers toward eliciting enough symptoms to warrant a similar current diagnosis.) Or, in studies designed to compare rates of disorder in various groups of respondents, interviewers may be kept blind as to respondents' specific group membership. (Often, though, for ethical reasons, and to allow them to probe sensitively, interviewers are informed of the key group membership variables under investigation even though they are blind about specific respondents' status.) Thus, studies of psychiatric correlates of human immunodeficiency virus (HIV) infection, for example, may employ interviewers who are unaware of which respondents are infected with HIV and which are not (e.g., Dew, Ragni, & Nimorwicz, 1990). Frequently, however, respondents volunteer their group membership during the logical course of the interview. For example, when questioned about what triggered a major depressive episode, they may indicate that it was their discovery of their HIV infection. Collecting routine information from interviewers on the extent to which the blinding was broken, its impact on the interview, and any other general expectations and specific beliefs that interviewers held about respondents will at least allow the nature and degree of any resulting bias to be empirically examined, as will be discussed subsequently.

Another potentially useful procedural strategy is to build in mechanisms to minimize interviewer–respondent contact. The issue of contact in the psychiatric research interview is a delicate one, however. The researcher must weigh the critical need to establish rapport with respondents in order to elicit an accurate clinical history and minimize respondent attrition during follow-up assessments against the likelihood for data collection to be biased. One increasingly popular alternative for controlling contact is the use of telephone rather than face-to-face interviews (e.g., Dillman, 1978; Lavrakas, 1987). Despite constraints such as loss of some nonverbal data from the respondent, mounting evidence has shown that there are few differences in the quality of mental health data collected from telephone as opposed to face-to-face interviews, especially when interviewers are highly trained and closely supervised (e.g., Aneshensel, Frerichs, Clark, & Yokopenic, 1982). Indeed, the observation of interviewers is usually simpler to engineer in telephone than in face-to-face interviews (Lavrakas, 1987).

Finally, tertiary prevention efforts are designed to minimize long-term disability and handicap; in the context of controlling expectancy effects, data management and analysis efforts can be used to maximize the utility of an existing data base by (1) revealing how extensively such effects have occurred and (2) statistically adjusting for these effects when examining study outcomes. One approach possible when a relatively large number of interviewers have been employed, and their expectancies have been assessed, is to correlate their expectancies with the interview results they obtained (Rosenthal, 1966). A large correlation suggests that expectancy effects were operating, and it may be possible for subsequent analysis of key study relationships to be statistically adjusted to control for these effects.

Even when expectancy issues have been neglected during startup and field work phases of a psychiatric epidemiologic study, these issues can be broached in the analysis phase. Suppose, for example, that in a study examining the link between psychiatric distress and the presence of HIV infection, investigators were concerned that supposedly blind interviewers were nevertheless increasingly likely over the course of the study to expect HIV-infected respondents to be relatively highly distressed. One method to evaluate this possibility would be to partition and analyze study data according to whether they were collected earlier or later during the field phase. A breakdown of the blinding and the consequent operation of interviewer expectancy effects would be suggested if order effects were obtained, that is, if psychiatric distress levels differed between HIV-infected and -uninfected persons more during the later phase of the study than during the earlier phase. Systematic questioning of interviewers about their knowledge and hypotheses might be undertaken at this point to clarify further the nature and extent of interviewer biases.

Conclusions

As in the social psychological experiment, the data collector plays a central role in the survey interview, particularly when the survey focuses on mental health. Current psychiatric diagnostic formulations have allowed the development of increasingly structured psychiatric research interviews. The possibility remains, however, that interviewers' unintended communications – and those regarding their expectancies in particular – will influence significantly respondents' reports of their well-being. Prevention of expectancy effects remains an elusive goal in many applied research areas, and Bob Rosenthal is the first to acknowledge that the strategies he has offered for the control of such effects "will not, in all probability, solve the problem" (Rosenthal, 1966, p. x). Should we be discouraged? Bob won't allow it! Indeed, he has explicitly spurred the researcher on by repeated comments that "the outlook is anything but bleak" (1966, p. 401) and that "there is cause . . . to be optimistic" (pp. 403–404). It is his optimism and enthusiasm for what we have learned about human behavior *in spite of* experimenter (and interviewer) expectancy effects that encourage us to continue to toil in the "muddy vineyards" (Rosenthal, 1990) of the social and behavioral sciences.

In closing, returning momentarily to the psychiatric interview situation, I suggested earlier that it is neither necessary nor desirable to eliminate all expectancies held by the researcher-interviewer. Rather, the goals should be to retain the expectancies that produce more accurate, high-quality data and to eliminate or control those unintentional ones that may produce responses that are inaccurate and biased. The ability to create self-fulfilling prophecies is a valuable tool, provided that it is channeled appropriately. In effect, this is what Bob Rosenthal has done for his students: His unconditional positive regard and positive expectancies have brought out the best in those who have worked and trained with him. I am fortunate to have been one of those students.

Note

Preparation of this chapter was supported by grant MH45020 from the National Institute of Mental Health, Rockville, MD. I thank Ronna C. Harris, MPH, my projects' trainer and supervisor, for helping me to implement the "treatment plan" discussed in this chapter.

References

American Psychiatric Association. (1987). *Diagnostic and statistical manual of mental disorders* (3rd ed., rev.). Washington, DC: Author.
Aneshensel, C. S., Frerichs, R. R., Clark, V. A., & Yokopenic, P. A. (1982).

Measuring depression in the community: A comparison of telephone and personal interviews. *Public Opinion Quarterly, 46,* 110–121.

Cooper, J. E., Kendell, R. E., Gurland, B. J., Sharpe, L., & Copeland, J. R. M. (1972). *Psychiatric diagnosis in New York and London: A comparative study of mental hospital admissions.* London: Oxford University Press.

Dew, M. A., & Bromet, E. J. (in press). Epidemiology. In A. Bellack & M. Hersen (Eds.), *Psychopathology in adulthood: An advanced text.* New York: Pergamon Press.

Dew, M. A., Bromet, E. J., Schulberg, H. C., Parkinson, D. K., & Curtis, E. C. (1991). Factors affecting service utilization for depression in a white collar population. *Social Psychiatry and Psychiatric Epidemiology, 26,* 230–237.

Dew, M. A., Ragni, M. V., & Nimorwicz, P. (1990). Infection with human immunodeficiency virus and vulnerability to psychiatric distress. *Archives of General Psychiatry, 47,* 737–744.

Dillman, D. A. (1978). *Mail and telephone surveys.* New York: Wiley.

Dohrenwend, B. P., & Dohrenwend, B. S. (1982). ⊥erspectives on the past and future of psychiatric epidemiology: The 1981 Rema Lapouse Lecture. *American Journal of Public Health, 72,* 1271–1279.

Endicott, J., & Spitzer, R. (1978). A diagnostic interview: The Schedule for Affective Disorders and Schizophrenia. *Archives of General Psychiatry, 35,* 837–844.

Faris, R., & Dunham, H. (1939). *Mental disorders in urban areas: An ecological study of schizophrenia and other pyschoses.* New York: Hafner.

Feighner, J. P., Robins, E., & Guze, S. B. (1972). Diagnostic criteria for use in diagnostic research. *Archives of General Psychiatry, 26,* 57–63.

Fowler, F. J. (1988). *Survey research methods,* rev. ed. Newbury Park, CA: Sage.

Institute of Medicine (1989). *Research on children and adolescents with mental, behavioral, and developmental disorders: Mobilizing a national initiative.* Washington, DC: National Academy Press.

Jarvis, E. (1971). *Insanity and idiocy in Massachusetts: Report of the Commission on Lunacy, 1855.* Cambridge, MA: Harvard University Press.

Judd, C. M., Smith, E. R., & Kidder, L. H. (1991). *Research methods in social relations* (6th ed.). Fort Worth, TX: Holt, Rinehart, and Winston.

Kramer, M. (1961). Some problems for international research suggested by observations on differences in first admission rates to the mental hospitals of England and Wales and of the United States. *Proceedings of the Third World Congress of Psychiatry, Montreal* (Vol. 3, pp. 153–160). Toronto: University of Toronto Press.

Lavrakas, P. J. (1987). *Telephone survey methods: Sampling, selection, and supervision.* Newbury Park, CA: Sage.

Leighton, D. C., Harding, J. S., Macklin, D., Macmillan, A. M., & Leighton, A. H. (1963). *The character of danger.* Vol. III: *The Sterling County study of psychiatric disorder and socio-cultural environment.* New York: Basic Books.

Lilienfeld, A. M., & Lilienfeld, D. E. (1980). *Foundations of epidemiology* (2nd ed.). New York: Oxford University Press.

Regier, D. A., Boyd, J. H., Burke, J. D., Rae, D. S., Myers, J. K., Kramer, M., Robins, L. N., George, L. K., Karno, M., & Locke, B. Z. (1988). One-month prevalence of mental disorders in the United States based on five epidemiologic catchment area sites. *Archives of General Psychiatry, 45,* 977–986.

Regier, D. A., Myers, J. K., Kramer, M., Robins, L. N., Blazer, D. G., Hough, R. L., Eaton, W. W., & Locke, B. Z. (1984). The NIMH Epidemiologic

Catchment Area Program: Historical context, major objectives, and study population characteristics. *Archives of General Psychiatry, 41,* 934–941.

Robins, L. N. (1987). The assessment of psychiatric diagnosis in epidemiological studies. In R. E. Hales & A. J. Francis (Eds.), *Psychiatry update* (Vol. 6, pp. 589–609). Washington, DC: American Psychiatric Press.

Robins, L. N., Helzer, J. E., Croughan, J., & Ratcliff, K. S. (1977). National Institute of Mental Health Diagnostic Interview Schedule. *Archives of General Psychiatry, 34,* 129–133.

Rosenthal, R. (1966). *Experimenter effects in behavioral research.* New York: Appleton-Century-Crofts.

Rosenthal, R. (1969). Interpersonal expectations: Effects of the experimenter's hypothesis. In R. Rosenthal & R. L. Rosnow (Eds.), *Artifact in behavioral research* (pp. 181–277). New York: Academic Press.

Rosenthal, R. (1990). How are we doing in soft psychology? *American Psychologist, 45,* 775–777.

Sartorius, N., Jablensky, A., Korten, A., Ernberg, G., Anker, M., Cooper, J. E., & Day, R. (1986). Early manifestations and first-contact incidence of schizophrenia in different cultures: A preliminary report on the initial evaluation phase of the WHO Collaborative Study on Determinants of Outcome of Severe Mental Disorders. *Psychological Medicine, 16,* 909–928.

Shapiro, A. P. (1959). The investigator himself. In S. O. Waife & A. P. Shapiro (Eds.), *The clinical evaluation of new drugs* (pp. 110–119). New York: Hoeber-Harper.

Shea, S. C. (1988). *Psychiatric interviewing: The art of understanding.* Philadelphia: Saunders.

Spitzer, R., Endicott, J., & Robins, E. (1978). Research diagnostic criteria: Rationale and reliability. *Archives of General Psychiatry, 35,* 773–782.

Spitzer, R., Williams, J. B., Gibbon, M., & First, M. (1990). *Structured Clinical Interview for DSM-III-R (SCID, Version 1.0).* Washington, DC: American Psychiatric Press.

Srole, L., Langner, T. S., Michael, S. T., Kirkpatrick, P., Opler, M. K., & Rennie, T. A. C. (1962). *Mental health in the metropolis: The Midtown Manhattan Study.* New York: Harper & Row.

Sullivan, H. S. (1936–1937). A note on the implications of psychiatry, the study of interpersonal relations, for investigations in the social sciences. *American Journal of Sociology, 42,* 848–861.

Vernon, S. W., & Roberts, R. E. (1982). Prevalence of treated and untreated psychiatric disorder in three ethnic groups. *Social Science in Medicine, 16,* 1575–1582.

Weissman, M. M., & Myers, J. K. (1980). Psychiatric disorders in a U.S. community. The application of Research Diagnostic Criteria to a resurveyed community sample. *Acta Psychiatrica Scandinavica, 62,* 99–111.

Weissman, M. M., Myers, J. K., & Thompson, W. D. (1981). Depression and its treatment in a U.S. urban community, 1975–1976. *Archives of General Psychiatry, 38,* 417–421.

World Health Organization. (1975). *Schizophrenia: A multinational study.* Geneva: Author.

23. Comment: Never-ending nets of moderators and mediators

MARYLEE C. TAYLOR

Psychological social psychologists frequently discuss *moderators* and *mediators*, familiar concepts given systematic attention in Baron and Kenny's (1986) widely cited paper. Social psychologists linked to sociology, thinking of Morris Rosenberg's still useful 1968 book, are more likely to speak of *specifiers* or *conditional* variables than moderators, and to refer to mediators as *intervening* factors. Whether described as mediators and moderators or as conditional and intervening variables, these phenomena are the central concerns in the contributions to part III of this volume, and appropriately so, in view of the fact that they have occupied a substantial portion of Robert Rosenthal's scholarly attention.

Building on a review of selected points made by Baron and Kenny (1986) and by Rosenberg (1968), these concluding comments will consider ways in which the phenomena of moderation and mediation are represented in themes of the chapters that constitute part III. The exercise may suggest additional ways of thinking about the contributions to this part, generating along the way a few amendments to the Baron–Kenny and Rosenberg guidelines.

As noted in Baron and Kenny (1986), a *moderator* is a variable that interacts with the focal independent variable to influence the dependent variable. Within categories or across levels of a moderator, the strength and/or direction of the relationship between predictor and outcome vary. A moderator relationship is often represented in a path diagram with an arrow coming in perpendicular to the path linking the independent and dependent variables, as in Figure 23.1A. In contrast, a *mediator* is a variable that "represents the generative mechanism through which the focal independent variable . . . influence(s) the dependent variable" (Baron & Kenny, 1986, p. 1173). It is an effect of the independent variable that serves as a proximate cause of the dependent variable. A path diagram representation of mediation is represented in Figure 23.1B.

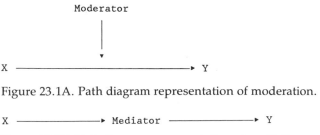

Figure 23.1A. Path diagram representation of moderation.

Figure 23.1B. Path diagram representation of mediation.

Though not offering a prescription, Baron and Kenny observe that a search for moderators is often spurred by an independent–dependent variable relationship that is surprisingly weak or changeable from study to study. In contrast, they note, mediational processes generally attract interest when the basic independent–dependent variable relationship is clearly established.

Baron and Kenny also observe that the interest in moderators is usually secondary to interest in the independent variable, whereas mediators may hold greater theoretical interest than the respective independent variables themselves. However, the limits of this generalization become evident as the analysts proceed to discuss the interplay of moderators and mediators, moderators sometimes "elucidating a mediator process" or evidence about mediation suggesting "moderator-type interventions" (Baron & Kenny, 1986, p. 1178). Baron and Kenny underline the potential intertwining of moderation and mediation through reference to the James and Brett (1984) illustration of *moderated mediation*. For James and Brett, moderated mediation occurs when the relationship between independent variable and mediator, or that between mediator and dependent variable and mediator, or that between mediator and dependent variable, or both, are moderated by some additional factor (1984, p. 314) (as in Figure 23.2A–C). Baron and Kenny apparently reserve the term *moderated mediation* for the moderation of a mediator–dependent variable relationship (as in Figure 23.2B); where the impact of the independent variable on the mediator is moderated by an additional factor (as in Figure 23.2A), Baron and Kenny speak of *mediated moderation* (1986, p. 1178).

Rosenberg's (1968) discussion of *conditional* and *intervening* variables rests on tabular analysis in the tradition of Lazarsfeld (e.g., Berelson, Lazarsfeld, & McPhee, 1954), a tradition that Alwin and Campbell (1987) suggest might be dominant today over the path analytic approaches

Figure 23.2A. Moderated mediation (James & Brett, 1984) or mediated moderation (Baron & Kenny, 1986).

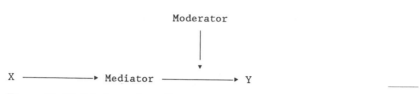

Figure 23.2B. Moderated mediation (Baron & Kenny, 1986; James & Brett, 1984).

Figure 23.2C. Moderated mediation (James & Brett, 1984).

featured in Baron and Kenny (1986), at least for survey data analysis, save for accidents of timing in the introduction of facilitating statistical techniques. The logic of Rosenberg's explanation and illustrations of conditional and intervening variables is entirely congruent with those of Baron and Kenny; only the names are changed.

Reflecting recent methodological emphases, particular features of their regression-based approach, and a focus on experimentation, Baron and Kenny raise topics not addressed in Rosenberg (1968), for example, the problems of measurement error and the potential relevance of experimental manipulation.

Conversely, Rosenberg's interest in survey research led him to some distinctive themes of his own. For example, Rosenberg insists that any single causal relationship be considered "an abstraction from a never-ending causal chain" (1968, p. 63). Thus readers are encouraged to envisage any independent–dependent variable pair as potential boundaries of some multistage causal process in which one or more intervening variables play a role. And the roles of particular variables in that chain are relative, changing with the analysts' focus: A variable that intervenes between some independent variable and its outcome can

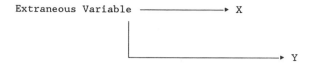

Figure 23.3A. *X-Y* relationship produced by an extraneous variable, inviting spurious interpretation, as described by Rosenberg (1968).

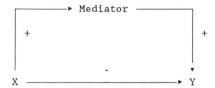

Figure 23.3B. A suppressor (if the indirect path equals the direct one) or distorter (if the indirect path is stronger), as described by Rosenberg (1968).

easily become the independent variable of focal interest, in which case Rosenberg would call the original independent variable *antecedent*. With the advent of graphically portrayed path models to accompany increasingly sophisticated techniques for structural equation modeling, today's researchers are more likely to think in terms of *nets* than *chains*. But Rosenberg's chain metaphor is a good starting point even now: Nets, after all, are merely intersecting segments of chain.

Like Baron and Kenny, Rosenberg talks about the heuristic value of linking the consideration of moderators and mediators. Acknowledging the rarity of direct evidence about intervening processes as one reality of survey research, Rosenberg notes that not only may observed conditional–moderator relationships suggest hypotheses about intervening–mediational processes; conditional relationships may also be systematically predicted and examined as one means of *testing* hypotheses about mediation.

Two other topics treated by Rosenberg will be touched on in the discussion to follow. Unable to rely on the security of experimental designs, survey researchers must worry about spurious interpretations, that is, about mistakenly concluding that one variable causes another when in fact the two are correlated because they are common effects of some third variable. In Rosenberg's language, the third variable serving as common cause to the two others is an *extraneous* factor (see Figure 23.3A). An important point is that extraneous and intervening third variables are *statistically indistinguishable*. Each must be related to the presumptive independent and dependent variables, and controlling on either will eliminate the relationship between the two focal variables. The crucial distinction is whether the third variable is an effect (and thus intervening) or a cause (and thus extraneous) of the focal independent variable, and the answer must come from independent evidence automatically available when the independent variable is experimentally manipulated but all too rarely available to the survey researcher. (Another possibility exists, namely, that no direct causal relationship in either direction exists between the third variable and the presumptive independent variable. Those two may themselves be related by virtue of being caused by some common antecedent. Such cases are often treated much like the extraneous variable instance.)

Second, Rosenberg introduces readers to the concept of *suppressor* and *distorter* variables. James and Brett (1984) discuss *incomplete mediation,* where the focal independent variable has impact through a mediator but also has some direct, unmediated impact; Baron and Kenny consider this situation as well. Noting that "direct" impact is probably most often not really direct, but rather mediated by some as yet unidentified and unmeasured third, fourth, fifth . . . variables, we can build on the incomplete mediation notion to understand what Rosenberg meant by suppression and distortion. To simplify and extrapolate a bit from Rosenberg's discussion, suppression exists when the focal independent variable has both mediated and unmediated impact (or impact with unspecified mediation) on the dependent variable *and the two causal dynamics run in opposite, countervailing directions* (see Figure 23.3B).

The possibility of *suppressor* dynamics suggests a qualifier to Baron and Kenny's earlier-noted statement that analysis for evidence of mediation "is best done in the case of a strong relation between the predictor and the criterion variable" (1986, p. 1178). Theoretically and pragmatically important patterns of mediation can exist, waiting for the analyst's discovery, even though the superimposition of a contrary unmediated impact suppresses evidence of their existence in the zero-order relationship between independent and dependent variables.

The *distorter* case is only slightly different: Here again, countervailing mediated and unmediated effects exist, but the mediated impact is stronger, swamping the other effect and determining the direction of the zero-order relationship. Controlling for the mediator's effect thus reverses the direction of the relationship. (Because extraneous variables are statistically indistinguishable from intervening variables, patterns of suppression and distortion can similarly be produced by the incomplete operation of extraneous variables. However, Rosenberg's examples focus on what James and Brett would call incomplete mediation.)

The background provided most recently by Baron and Kenny, and earlier by Rosenberg, furnishes tools for reflection on the operation of moderators and mediators, conditional and intervening variables, as represented in the contributions to part III of this collection.

Bernieri constructs a useful hypothetical example to demonstrate the desirability of using focused 1-*df* contrasts rather than omnibus *F* tests to examine specific predictions for main effects and interactions. Among other points, he emphasizes the efficiency of computing the sum of squares for the contrast from the correlation of the contrast weights with the corresponding means (Rosenthal & Rosnow, 1985).

The interaction effect predicted and found in Bernieri's hypothetical study represents an *expectancy confirmation* notion: Teachers' responses to pupils are in part a function of the congruence of pupil performance with teacher expectations. By implication, after main effects have been taken into account, pupils for whom teachers hold low expectations elicit the most positive teacher responses by performing poorly, just as high-expectation pupils evoke positive teacher responses by performing well.

Baron and Kenny correctly note that moderators may hold theoretical as well as pragmatic significance. Indeed, in Bernieri's hypothetical study, the moderator is of such great theoretical interest that it is not clear which of the two interacting variables, teacher expectations or pupil performance, should be labeled the moderator and which the independent variable. Not only are the two interacting predictors of equal scientific interest, but their interaction represents a meaningful construct in its own right – expectancy confirmation. A parallel exists in the research literature on psychological androgyny. Bem (1974) originally conceptualized androgyny as a balance between masculine and feminine dispositions, whether those levels be high or low. As pointed out in Taylor and Hall (1982), and later discussed in Hall and Taylor (1985) and Taylor (1983), "balance" of masculinity and femininity is appropriately operationalized as a straightforward linear interaction of the two components.

Baron and Kenny note that examination of the data for possible moderator effects is often prompted by an unexpectedly weak or inconsistent main effect. That statement may be descriptively accurate, but it should not be interpreted prescriptively. Just as a balance androgyny effect may exist and be of scientific interest, whether alone or accompanied by main effects of masculinity and femininity (Taylor & Hall, 1982), so also an expectancy confirmation effect may exist alone or, as in Bernieri's example, in the company of one or both main effects.

Had Bernieri's hypothetical example included a linear positive main effect of teacher expectations, as well the main effect of student performance he built into the data, the illustration would have closely resembled the *emergent properties* form of androgyny discussed by Hall and Taylor (1985): Outcomes are relatively uniform, save for the single circumstance in which levels of both predictor variables are high. In the context of Bernieri's hypothetical research question, teacher attitudes would show a noteworthy rise only when both teacher expectations and pupil performance were high. Where such a *multiple necessary causes* pattern appears, flawed interpretation of statistical results is common: The emergent property evidenced where high values of the two predictors coincide is often equated with interaction alone, rather than being accurately described as the superimposition of two main effects *and* an interaction.

Given that the emergent properties pattern is likely to receive substantive attention as a unitary phenomenon, would it be preferable to test for it statistically as a single pattern, to treat the crossed predictors as if they represented a single variable and assess the emergent properties pattern via a 1-*df* focused *t* test from a one-way analysis of variance (ANOVA)? Probably not. The literature on psychological androgyny offers ample illustrations of the danger in this strategy (Taylor & Hall, 1982). It is all too tempting to mistakenly take a simple, additive combination of two main effects as evidence of the emergent properties notion, unless the crossing of the two predictors is acknowledged in an analysis that separates main effects from interaction.

After tracing the history of psychiatric epidemiological research, Dew identifies points at which interviewer expectancy effects may enter, to the potential benefit or detriment of the research. Her suggested "treatment plans" include (1) encouraging interviewers to hold high expectations for respondents' interest and accuracy and (2) where possible, maintaining interviewer "blindness" about respondents' background characteristics that may evoke interviewer expectations for mental health outcomes.

As Dew considers ways to evoke respondents' full and accurate de-

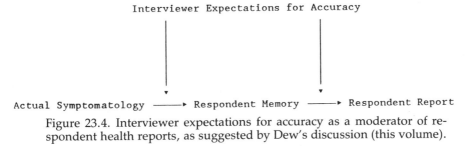

Figure 23.4. Interviewer expectations for accuracy as a moderator of re-spondent health reports, as suggested by Dew's discussion (this volume).

scriptions of symptoms, interviewers' expectations are projected to be potential moderators. In terms of causal chains, actual symptomatology can be seen as an independent variable, potentially producing memory-based respondent knowledge at the time of the interview (a mediator). Optimally, respondent knowledge then leads to reasonably veridical respondent reports (the dependent variable). The researcher hopes, of course, to maximize the strength of these causal relationships. The rarely if ever attainable ideal would be perfect relationships constituting the two links of the just described chain, leading to absolutely accurate reports of symptoms.

In suggesting that data quality can be improved by training interview-ers to hold high expectations for respondent accuracy, Dew points to the potential moderating role of those expectations. At each stage of the causal chain, interviewer expectations can affect the strength of the correspondence, first between actual symptomatology and remembered knowledge, second between that knowledge and the respondent re-ports (see Figure 23.4). (Of course, interviewer training and expertise may also moderate subsequent links in the causal chain, especially that between respondents' reports and interviewers' recorded versions of the data: Optimally trained interviewers record and code data so as to maximize correspondence of the final research record with raw inter-view content.)

Dew's chapter powerfully illustrates the point that similar or identical variables may serve either moderating or mediating functions, depend-ing on the context: After encouraging researchers to cultivate one kind of interviewer expectation as a potentially functional moderator, Dew warns that another form of interviewer expectation can serve as an unwanted mediator. By way of illustration, Dew notes that interviewers who cannot be kept blind to respondents' human immunodeficiency virus (HIV) status may produce reports that exaggerate the correlations of HIV status with depression. If a strong correlation exists, the presumptive causal path would be from HIV status (the independent variable) to actual depression (the mediator) to interviewer-recorded depression (the dependent variable). In other words, the correlation would ordinarily be interpreted as if the mediator linking HIV status to recorded depression is actual depression. Without interviewer blindness, however, there is a danger that the correlation of HIV status with depression may have been produced by an alternate mediator, interviewer expectations.

Rosenberg (1968) noted that it is a mistake to dismiss all correlations produced by extraneous variables as spurious, presenting as an illustration the substantively meaningful correlation Durkheim noted between the form of justice and egoism, produced by their common root in the societal division of labor. Dew's discussion can be used to make the converse of that point with respect to mediators: Understanding that researcher expectations mediate an independent–dependent variable relationship changes the meaning of that relationship altogether, in effect rendering the commonsense interpretation spurious.

Where interviewer expectations are not entirely responsible for an observed zero-order correlation but accentuate a direct effect that really does exist – that is, where there is incomplete mediation via interviewer expectations – the relationship itself is not spurious, though an exaggerated estimate of its strength is produced. Undoubtedly, there are also occasions when interviewer expectations run counter to actual effects, not magnifying them but suppressing or even distorting evidence of the direct effect in which the researcher is interested.

Dew's recommended treatment for the problematic mediational role of interviewer expectations is interviewer blindness. Degree of blindness, in other words, is recognized as a moderator of the contribution made by interviewer expectations to relationships between status characteristics (e.g., HIV status) and measured psychiatric outcomes (e.g., interviewer-recorded depression) (see Figure 23.5A). When blindness is not maintained, status characteristics can produce expectancies that lead to misleading reports of psychiatric symptoms. When blindness is maintained, the causal link from status characteristics to expectancies is broken, and expectancies cannot mediate the relationship between status and reported psychiatric symptoms. James and Brett (1984) would call this phenomenon one form of moderated mediation. For Baron and Kenny (1986) it is mediated moderation.

Dew suggests an alternate treatment for the dysfunctional operation

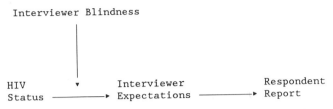

Figure 23.5A. Interviewer blindness as a moderator of interviewer expectancy effects, as suggested by Dew's discussion (Dew, this volume).

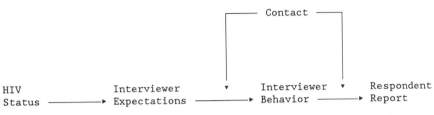

Figure 23.5B. Contact as a moderator of interviewer expectancy effects, as suggested by Dew's discussion (Dew, this volume).

of expectancies as mediators: reduction of contact between interviewer and respondent. We are reminded here that causal chains are "never-ending," in Rosenberg's (1968) words, because independent variables have antecedents and dependent variables consequences, but also because there are so often additional mediational links to be specified and *inserted* in a causal chain. Earlier, we considered HIV status as an independent variable, interviewer expectancy as a potential mediator, and reported psychiatric symptoms as the dependent variable. Dew's "reduction of contact" suggestion reminds us that interviewer expectancies would not operate directly on respondent reports of symptoms: That relationship must itself be mediated by various interviewer behaviors. Just as interviewer blindness would break the chain by destroying the relationship between HIV status and expectancies, reduction of contact could weaken the chain by diminishing or eliminating the sending and/or receiving of behavioral cues that potentially intervene between interviewer expectations and respondent reports. Thus degree of contact, like degree of blindness, serves as a moderator (see Figure 23.5B). Baron and Kenny (1986) would join James and Brett (1984) in calling this moderated mediation. But the plot has thickened: Now we are talking about *moderating the mediation of a mediator's impact* on the dependent variable.

Bravely pushing on, we recall that Dew rightly identified a trade-off

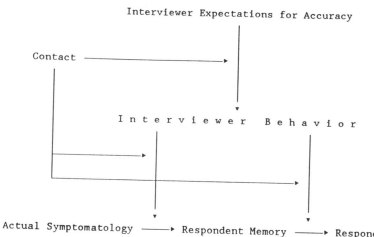

Figure 23.6. Contact as a moderator of the moderating impact of interviewer's expectations for accuracy, as suggested by Dew's discussion (Dew, this volume).

involving the degree of contact between interviewer and respondent. Minimizing contact would presumably hamper the potentially dysfunctional operation of substantive expectancies, but it would at the same time hamper the potentially facilitating operation of expectations for accuracy. After all, expectations for accuracy do not magically moderate the relationship between actual symptomatology and respondents' reports. Interviewer behaviors deriving from those expectancies undoubtedly serve as the proximal moderators. If degree of contact moderates the impact of interviewer expectancies for accuracy by influencing the sending and/or receiving of behavioral cues generated by interviewer expectancies, we presumably have one or more forms of moderated moderation: Contact may moderate the impact of the distal moderator on the proximal moderator, and/or contact may moderate the impact of the proximal moderator on either the independent variable or the mediator, or both (see Figure 23.6). The labeling possibilities are rapidly becoming frightening!

There may be a moral here. Mediation is ubiquitous. Any time we focus on some two variables in one of Rosenberg's never-ending causal chains, the specified or yet-to-be-specified variables lying between them are mediators. Moderation is similarly ubiquitous: For any link of the causal chain, there are undoubtedly one or more moderators. Finally, it will often be the case that an identified moderator is not itself the active agent, conditioning the relationship between some other two variables, but lies back a ways on its particular causal chain, serving as an antecedent or correlate of the actual proximal moderator. Given these circumstances, the possibilities for compounded moderation and mediation are virtually limitless. It is undoubtedly less productive to devise tongue-twisting labels for compound patterns than to have a very clear grasp of the building blocks, the straightforward processes of moderation and mediation, together with an understanding that we are always looking at segments of chain intersecting to form an intricate net. In this context, we can expect the processes of moderation and mediation to form an infinite variety of combinations, piquing our interest and taxing our ingenuity.

Experimenter expectancy effects, though not the primary focus of Rosnow's chapter, do make an appearance there – as Rosnow opens with a review of Orne's (1962) laboratory demonstrations of demand characteristics, noting that one characteristic of volunteer subjects may be their heightened sensitivity to experimenter expectations. In this fashion, Rosnow's discussion is linked to Dew's consideration of substantive expectancy effects that impede rather than facilitate survey research: *Experimenter* expectations potentially function in precisely the same fashion as interviewer expectations can work in nonexperimental research – as mediators that encourage incorrect conclusions about the impact of the focal independent variable, here the experimental manipulation.

   Rosnow's central purpose is to trace the collaborative research conducted by Robert Rosenthal and himself on the characteristics of those who volunteer to serve as research subjects. Translated into the vocabulary of this discussion, the interest in volunteer subject characteristics has been driven by the worry that variables influencing the decision to serve as research subjects, *or their correlates*, may moderate the relationship between the experimentally manipulated variable and their respective outcome measures.

   To explore the relevance of our moderator–mediator discussion to Rosnow's chapter, let us focus on one factor found to be associated with volunteering – gender. In general, women are more likely than men to volunteer for participation in scientific research.

   Gender and volunteering can be envisioned to constitute a rudimentary, single-link causal chain, with no ambiguity about the direction of causation. But the observed association of gender with volunteering will probably become more useful if we think about potential mediators

466   Marylee C. Taylor

Figure 23.7. Affiliative tendency as a mediator of the gender effect on volunteering, as suggested by the moderating impact of task type. Relevant to Rosnow's discussion (Rosnow, this volume).

of the relationship. After all, it is not plausible that something about biological sex itself promotes volunteering for social scientific research. Rather, biological sex presumably leads to certain psychological patterns (arguably socially rooted outcomes of sex-linked nurture) that are the actual, proximal causes of volunteering. Hypothetically, affiliative tendency may be one such proximal cause. Statistical analysis could reveal whether affiliative tendency completely mediates the relationship between gender and volunteering, or whether its mediation is incomplete, in which case other, yet-to-be-identified sex-linked psychological tendencies may prove to share the mediational role. As Baron and Kenny pointed out, clues about mediational processes are often provided by observed moderation. An observation that the gender difference in volunteering is particularly strong for group tasks, for example, might have suggested the hypothesis that affiliative tendency is a mediator of the gender effect (see Figure 23.7).

As noted earlier, attention to the gender difference in rates of volunteering is driven by concern about potential moderation of the impact of experimental manipulations. If an experimental manipulation were uniformly effective across the two genders, then subjects of either gender could teach us about the behavior of both, and gender differences in volunteering would be irrelevant. It is only if gender moderates the impact of the independent variable on the outcome measure that an imbalance of male and female subjects is a problem.

Again, however, it is unlikely to be gender per se that serves the moderating function for a given independent–dependent variable relationship. Rather, some psychological pattern or behavioral tendency associated with biological sex will presumably be the actual moderator. To understand fully the implications of that moderation, it would, of course, be useful to identify the sex-linked factor that serves as the actual, proximal moderator.

Is identification of a proximal, sex-linked moderator likely to suggest something useful about mediating processes that may intervene between the experimentally manipulated variable and the dependent measure? Yes, just as the hypothetical moderating influence of group versus individual task type points to the role of affiliative tendency in mediating the relationship between gender and volunteering. Is a variable demonstrated to mediate the relationship between sex and volunteering (affiliative tendency, in our hypothetical example) the major potential worry as a sex-linked proximal moderator of the relationship between a given experimental manipulation and an outcome measure? By no means! *Any* correlate of gender will predictably exist in unrepresentative proportions among experimental subjects. Thus the list of potential moderators that could interfere with the external validity of experimental results is probably very long indeed.

The preceding paragraph calls to mind again Rosenberg's never-ending causal chain, more completely described as a never-ending net of intersecting causal chains, and it underlines the breadth of the potential for volunteer subject effects to limit the external validity of experimental findings. This would be true even if our starting point were not a characteristic with as many recognized ramifications as gender. Let us suppose that all the hypothetical conditions described previously held, except that affiliative tendency rather than gender had been identified in the first instance as the worrisome antecedent of volunteering. This would not imply that a potential moderating effect of affiliative tendency on the impact of the experimental manipulation should be our only worry. Any correlates of affiliative tendency – in this example including gender and all associated variables – will predictably exist at unrepresentative levels among our subjects, and moderating influences by any of them could limit the external validity of our findings (see Figure 23.8).

Harris sets out to identify plausible expectancy effect mediators, which she reasonably suggests are linked to the situational context – classroom, courtroom, nursing home, and so on. Although such situations may each contain unique possibilities for the mediation of expectancy effects, Harris notes that at least some of the variability among situations can be understood in terms of their location on a set of dimensions: the relative power of perceiver and target, intensity of interaction, formality of interaction, degree of structure, and so on.

In identifying situational dimensions that may influence the form of

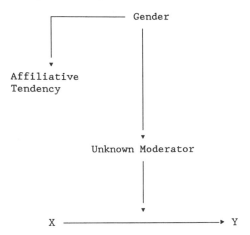

Figure 23.8. Sex-linked proximal moderator of the treatment effect, a threat to external validity if the sex-linked affiliative tendency encourages volunteering. Relevant to Rosnow's discussion (Rosnow, this volume).

mediation, Harris names moderators – moderators of the causal relationship between the perceiver's expectancy and mediating behavior (the link describing the *sending* process), or of the relationship between mediating behavior and target response (the *receiving* link), or both.

The James and Brett (1984) example of moderated mediation involved moderation by a single variable, self-esteem, at both stages of a two-link causal process. But Baron and Kenny's (1986) stressor illustration is a reminder that a moderating impact on the independent–dependent variable relationship can be produced by a variable that interacts with *either* the independent variable to affect the mediator *or* with the mediator to affect the dependent variable. In suggesting that a superior power position may give the perceiver control over mediating mechanisms, Harris focuses on the first, sending link: Power relations interact with perceiver expectancies, superior power by the perceiver increasing the impact of expectancies on mediating behaviors. Intensity of interaction, on the other hand, is suggested by Harris to come into play at the second, receiving stage of the causal chain, increasing the target's responsiveness to the perceiver behaviors that play the role of mediator (see Figure 23.9). If unequal power relations influence receiving as well as sending, as plausibly they might, then power relations would moderate the mediated transmission of expectancies in a manner that fully parallels the moderating function of self-esteem in the James and Brett

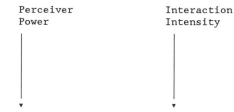

Figure 23.9. Potential moderators of expectancy effects, as suggested by Harris (Harris, this volume).

example, interacting with the first variable in the causal sequence to influence the second, and also with the second to influence the third.

Formality of interaction is suggested by Harris to be another dimension affecting expectancy transmission, plausibly interfering with behavioral communication of negative expectations. But just *how* would formality imply moderation of the impact of perceiver expectancy on mediating behavior or the impact of the mediator on target response? On the one hand, formality may mean that normatively prescribed behaviors substitute for volitionally based behaviors; in such cases, formality would represent a straightforward moderator, simply canceling the impact that expectations otherwise would have. On the other hand, it is not implausible that formality's impact comes as a main effect on certain mediating behaviors, shifting their distribution in a positive direction. In such cases, there is no reason to expect an automatic shift in the *strength of relationships* with those behaviors. For example, the mean level of vocal respect normative in a formal setting could be unusually high, whereas deviations from that mean nonetheless serve quite effectively to convey both low and high expectations (see Figure 23.10A).

There are circumstances, however, in which the independent variable has a main effect on the mediator, shifting its distribution upward (or downward), *and* moderation comes as part of the package. One such circumstance is when a ceiling (or floor) exists for the mediator. For example, if formality were to encourage such positive behavior that positive expectations basically had no room for expression, a moderating effect of formality would be entailed in what was fundamentally its main effect on the mediator. Schuman and Johnson call such a phenomenon, for which the "underlying theoretical model" is "additive" rather

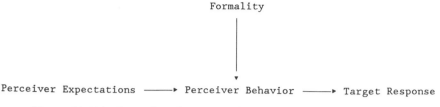

Figure 23.10A. Formality showing only a main effect on perceiver behavior (the mediator). Related to Harris's discussion (Harris, this volume).

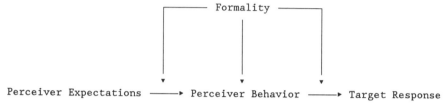

Figure 23.10B. Formality showing moderating effects as well as a main effect on perceiver behavior (the mediator). Related to Harris's discussion (Harris, this volume).

than "truly interactive," an *apparent interaction* (1976, p. 187). An intervention representing such a moderation-via-ceiling pattern would not just damp the impact of expectations on mediating behaviors; it would also shrink the relationship between mediating behaviors and the dependent variable by diminishing the variability of the mediators ("restricting their range") (see Figure 23.10B).

Alternately, a simple shift in the central tendency of the mediator could imply moderation of expectancy transmission if the relationship between the mediator and the dependent variable were nonlinear. For example, if receivers don't discriminate behaviorally among sender behaviors at the positive end of the scale in question, and if a situational factor like formality shifts the distribution of sender behaviors in the positive direction, the strength of the relationship between mediator and target response will be diminished.

This discussion opens the door to some elaboration of Baron and Kenny's claim that knowledge of mediation can suggest "moderator-type interventions" (1986, p. 1178). Understanding mediation can certainly point to interventions, but this does *not* imply that a successful intervention necessarily involves moderation. An intervention may often represent manipulation of an additional variable that has an independent, additive effect counteracting the undesirable impact of the original

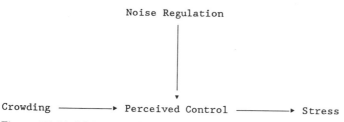

Figure 23.11. Noise regulation showing only a main effect on perceived control (the mediator). Related to Baron and Kenny (1986).

independent variable. To illustrate the function of intervention, Baron and Kenny consider the case of crowding and stress, an independent–dependent relationship presumed to be mediated by perceived loss of control. As they suggest, understanding of the mediating process might suggest an intervention to "increase the controllability of social encounters" (1986, p. 1178). For example, quiet hours might be imposed in crowded settings where perceived control would otherwise be especially low. However, the effectiveness of quiet hours in reducing stress in high-density situations by no means implies that quiet hours is necessarily a moderator of the relationship between crowding and stress. A highly plausible supposition is that noise regulation has a simple, additive main effect on perceived control (see Figure 23.11). The direction of this main effect, however, may be such that a quiet hours intervention would boost the mean level of perceived control among those whose crowded conditions would otherwise leave them feeling out of control and stressed.

Of course, an intervention such as quiet hours *can* represent a variable that is "truly interactive" (Schuman & Johnson, 1976, p. 187). Or, as suggested previously, such an intervention may fundamentally shift the distribution of the mediator, but with moderation coming as part of the package, because (1) there is a ceiling or floor in the variability of the mediator or (2) the main effect represented by the intervention capitalizes on a nonlinear relationship between the mediator and the dependent variable, so that the intervention pushes the distribution on the mediator to a level where its impact on the dependent variable shrinks (or expands).

Rubin's intriguing chapter begins by describing conventional meta-analytic techniques. Typically, potential moderators of the focal effect are identified, and effects are then summarized within categories of these moderators. Rubin draws a major distinction, however, between potential moderating variables "of scientific interest" and "design factors," dimensions such as randomization or completeness of controls that affect the credibility of results. Rubin notes that current practice may entail differentially weighting studies that vary on dimensions of design desirability, so as to give greatest influence to results from the most credible studies. His two-dimensional design surface would take this principle a quantum jump further: Information about the moderating effects of design factors would be used to extrapolate to the hypothetical study free of design imperfections. The goal, then, would be to estimate the focal effect within levels of moderators having scientific interest, assuming ideal designs rather than the flawed methodology social scientists have actually been able to produce.

From some perspectives, Rubin's argument is persuasive. Certainly it seems undesirable to devote great statistical effort to generating precise estimates of what would be found in a universe of identifiably flawed studies. But there is also cause for a qualm or two about Rubin's proposal. For one thing, there are research domains in which objections can legitimately be raised to conventional notions of what constitutes an ideal design. For example, Taylor (1988) and Pettigrew and Taylor (1992) argue that the selection of any given constellation of control variables for estimating race and sex discrimination is not a methodological issue, as generally presented, but represents the installation of one particular definition of social justice, a definition unlikely to receive the scrutiny it warrants when camouflaged as methodological necessity.

More broadly, the perspective of Baron and Kenny (1986) and Rosenberg (1968), reinforced by applications in the preceding pages, is that even moderators of little intrinsic interest may have great heuristic value, pointing to insights about the causal processes of focal interest. From this perspective, there may be some danger in Rubin's proposed dichotomization of moderators – those identified as scientifically interesting destined to be featured in reports of meta-analyses, those identified as design factors useful primarily as building blocks for estimating the projected yield from some hypothetical perfect study.

It is fitting that this discussion end by insisting on the liabilities of drawing a firm distinction between scientifically interesting variables and methodological imperfections to be adjusted for and erased from view. In his graceful introduction to part III, Archer contrasts *rote* and *imaginative* responses to methodological problems, correctly identifying imaginative responses as a hallmark of Bob Rosenthal's work. Rubin's contrast of *design factors* with *scientifically relevant variables* provides another vocabulary for making a related point. In substantial part, Robert Rosenthal's contributions to social science have grown from acknowledgment of certain moderating and mediating processes that complicate the interpretation of research findings, impeding our understanding of relationships among variables customarily seen as scientifically relevant. Refusing to treat them as mere nuisances, Rosenthal has transformed these pestiferous complications into scientifically relevant objects of analysis, interesting in their own right. Among the questions about moderation and mediation that have come to life under Bob Rosenthal's eye, some have been answered through his scholarship. Enthusiasm for the enterprise, generated by Bob in his students, colleagues, and readers, surely gives us a head start on addressing the rest.

References

Alwin, D. F., & Campbell, R. T. (1987). Continuity and change in methods of survey data analysis. *Public Opinion Quarterly, 51,* S139–S155.

Baron, R. M., & Kenny, D. A. (1986). The moderator–mediator variable distinction in social psychological research: Conceptual strategies and statistical considerations. *Journal of Personality and Social Psychology, 51,* 1173–1182.

Bem, S. L. (1974). The measurement of psychological androgyny. *Journal of Consulting and Clinical Psychology, 42,* 155–162.

Berelson, B. R., Lazarsfeld, P. F., & McPhee, W. M. (1954). *Voting: A study of opinion formation in a presidential campaign.* Chicago: University of Chicago Press.

Hall, J. A., & Taylor, M. C. (1985). Psychological androgyny and the masculinity by femininity interaction. *Journal of Personality and Social Psychology, 49,* 429–435.

James, L. R., & Brett, J. M. (1984). Mediators, moderators, and tests for mediation. *Journal of Applied Psychology, 69,* 307–321.

Orne, M. T. (1962). On the social psychology of the psychological experiment: With particular reference to demand characteristics and their implications. *American Psychologist, 17,* 776–783.

Pettigrew, T. F., & Taylor, M. C. (1992). Discrimination. In E. F. Borgatta & M. L. Borgatta (Eds.), *Encyclopedia of sociology* (pp. 498–503). New York: Macmillan.

Rosenberg, M. (1968). *The logic of survey analysis.* New York: Basic Books.

Rosenthal, R., & Rosnow, R. L. (1985). *Contrast analysis: Focused comparisons in the analysis of variance.* Cambridge: Cambridge University Press.

Schuman, H., & Johnson, M. P. (1976). Attitudes and behavior. *Annual Review of Sociology, 2,* 161–207.

Taylor, M. C. (1983). Masculinity, femininity, and androgyny: Another look at three androgyny scoring systems. *Psychological Reports, 53,* 1149–1150.

Taylor, M. C. (1988). *Estimating race and sex inequity in wages: Substantive implications of methodological choices.* Paper presented at the Research Conference of the Association of Public Policy and Management, Seattle, October 27–29.

Taylor, M. C., & Hall, J. A. (1982). Psychological androgyny: Theories, methods, and conclusions. *Psychological Bulletin, 92,* 347–366.

Author index

Subject index

achievement
  black students, 97
  and managerial expectations, 155–156
  organizationwide culture in, 171
active patienthood, 306
adaptation level, 34–35
affect / effort theory, 11, 51, 319
  and transfer of expectancy, 51–52, 351
affective behavior
  getting acquainted situations, 359–360
  interventions, 148–149
  in teacher expectancy, 136–138, 144, 148–149; students' perception, 139–140
affective climate, see socioemotional climate
affective processing of events, 232–233
affiliation tendency
  and attractiveness stereotypes, 199–204
  gender differences, 466–468
affirmative action
  effect on black beneficiaries, 111
  effect on white employees, 108–111
  public opinion, 107
  self-fulfilling prophecy dynamics, 109
  white reactions, 106–111
  and workplace expectations, 104
after-only design, 165
Alameda County Study, 186
The American Jury (Kalven and Zeisel), 78–79, 82–85
amygdala, and vocalization, 235–236

analysis of variance, 342, 379–398
  contrast analysis in, 385–393, 459
  and data patterns, 383–385
  effect size, 396–398, 459–460
  interaction term in, 393–396, 459
  theory testing in, 383–393
  weakness as method, 379–382
anchored attitudes
  and persuasion, 326
  resistance to expectancy, 320
androgyny studies, 459–460
angel faces/voices, 264
anger expression, 322
angry faces, 234, 279
animal studies, experimenter bias, 7
antecedent variables, 457
anterior cingulate cortex, 236
anterior limbic cortex, 236
anterior-posterior brain dimension, 236–237
antihypertensive medication, 189
apparent interactions, 471
aprosodia, 237
artifact problem
  ethical considerations, 431–433
  volunteer subjects, 419, 431–433
attitudes, and affirmative action, 108–111
attributional bias
  and affirmative action, 110
  and self-fulfilling prophecies, 48
attributional retraining, teachers, 146
authoritarian personality, 141
autistic perception, 36
average effect sizes, 412
awareness of expectancy, 54
  in teacher–student interactions, 270–273

Studies in Emotion and Social Interaction

Editors: Paul Ekman and Klaus R. Scherer